Lecture Notes in Computer Science 3147

Commenced Publication in 1973
Founding and Former Series Editors:
Gerhard Goos, Juris Hartmanis, and Jan van Leeuwen

Hartmut Ehrig   Werner Damm
Jörg Desel   Martin Große-Rhode
Wolfgang Reif   Eckehard Schnieder
Engelbert Westkämper (Eds.)

Integration of Software Specification Techniques for Applications in Engineering

Priority Program SoftSpez
of the German Research Foundation (DFG)
Final Report

 Springer

Volume Editors

Hartmut Ehrig
Technische Universität Berlin, Sekr. FR 6-1, Franklinstr. 28/29, 10587 Berlin
E-mail: ehrig@cs.tu-berlin.de

Werner Damm
Carl von Ossietzky Universität, PO Box 2503, 26111 Oldenburg, Germany
E-mail: damm@informatik.uni-oldenburg.de

Jörg Desel
Katholische Universität Eichstätt-Ingolstadt, Ostenstr. 14, 85072 Eichstätt, Germany
E-mail: joerg.desel@ku-eichstaett.de

Martin Große-Rhode
Fraunhofer ISST Berlin, Mollstr. 1, 10178 Berlin, Germany
E-mail: Martin.Große-Rhode@isst.fhg.de

Wolfgang Reif
Universität Ulm, Oberer Eselsberg, 89069 Ulm, Germany
E-mail: reif@informatik.uni-ulm.de

Eckehard Schnieder
Technische Universität Braunschweig
Langer Kamp 8, 38106 Braunschweig, Germany
E-mail: e.schnieder@tu-bs.de

Engelbert Westkämper
Institut für Industrielle Fertigung und Fabrikbetrieb (IFF)
Nobelstr. 12, 70569 Stuttgart, Germany
E-mail: Engelbert.Westkaemper@iff.uni-stuttgart.de

Library of Congress Control Number: 2004111959

CR Subject Classification (1998): D.2, D.3, F.3, J.2, J.6

ISBN 978-3-540-23135-6   ISBN 978-3-540-27863-4 (eBook)
DOI 10.1007/978-3-540-27863-4

Springer is a part of Springer Science+Business Media

springeronline.com

© Springer-Verlag Berlin Heidelberg 2004
Originally published by Springer-Verlag Berlin Heidelberg New York in 2004

Typesetting: Camera-ready by author, data conversion by PTP-Berlin, Protago-TeX-Production GmbH
Printed on acid-free paper   SPIN: 11323723   06/3142   5 4 3 2 1 0

Preface

This volume is a documentation of the main results in the research area "Integration of Software Specification Techniques for Applications in Engineering". On one hand it is based on the Priority Program "Integration von Techniken der Softwarespezifikation für ingenieurwissenschaftliche Anwendungen", short SoftSpez, of the German Research Council (DFG). On the other hand it contains new contributions of international experts in this research area, some of which were presented at the third international workshop INT 2004 on "Integration of Specification Techniques for Applications in Engineering". INT 2004 was launched as a satellite event of ETAPS in Barcelona, the "European Joint Conferences on Theory and Practice of Software".

The Priority Program SoftSpez was initiated by W. Brauer, M. Broy, H. Ehrig, H.J. Kreowski, H. Reichel, and H. Weber concerning different aspects from computer science, and by E. Schnieder and E. Westkämper concerning two main application areas in engineering, namely "Traffic Control Systems" and "Production Automation". After acceptance of SoftSpez by the German Research Council for the period of 1998–2004 a call for specific projects within this priority program was launched, where 11 projects from about 75 project proposals were accepted for a period of two years. Since 1998 each year the main research proposals and results of the projects have been presented at an annual colloquium of the priority program, and every two years the projects have been evaluated by an independent group of referees appointed by the German Research Council. At this point we would like to thank A. Engelke and G. Sonntag, the responsible officers from the DFG, the group of referees, with chairman W. Brauer, and our colleagues mentioned above for setting up the initial proposal for SoftSpez.

The cooperation between the projects was organized into different subject areas, with several meetings since 1999. In addition to the annual colloquia and the subject area meetings on a national level, also three international workshops were organized by SoftSpez. The workshops INT 2000, 2002, and 2004 were launched in cooperation with the ETAPS conferences in order to present the concepts and results of SoftSpez to the international scientific community and to get feedback from international experts.

The contributions in this volume are organized according to the six different subject areas of SoftSpez, where the coordinators for the subject areas are the coeditors for the corresponding parts of this volume. All papers were carefully reviewed by national and international experts.

In addition to a general introduction to the research area of this volume there are also introductions for each subject area. They present an overview and a short introduction into each paper of the corresponding subject area, including contributions from the projects of SoftSpez and papers from international (non-German) experts in this area.

The organization of the priority program SoftSpez and of the six subject areas was coordinated during the program and for this documentation by the editor and the coeditors of this volume, respectively. For great support we would like to thank the following researchers of the project: M. Bengel, A. Braatz, B. Braatz, R. Geisler, H.M. Hanisch, L. Jansen, G. Juhás, M. Klar, M. Klein, J. Klose, R. Lorenz, G. Saake, Ch. Schaeffer, G. Schellhorn, G. Schröter, R. Slovak, A. Thums, and B. Westphal.

Finally let us thank all national and international reviewers and authors of the papers in this volume and Springer for a smooth publication.

We hope that this volume offers new insights and suggests new research topics and applications in various related areas of computer science and engineering.

July 2004

Hartmut Ehrig
Werner Damm
Jörg Desel
Martin Große-Rhode
Wolfgang Reif
Eckehard Schnieder
Engelbert Westkämper

Table of Contents

Part I: Reference Case Study Production Automation

Part II: Reference Case Study Traffic Control Systems

Part III: Petri Nets and Related Approaches in Engineering

Coordinator: Jörg Desel

Part IV: Charts

Coordinator: Werner Damm

Part V: Verification

Coordinator: Wolfgang Reif

Part VI: Integration Modelling

Coordinator: Martin Große-Rhode

Integration of Software Specification Techniques for Applications in Engineering: Introduction and Overview of Results

Hartmut Ehrig

Institute for Software Engineering and Theoretical Computer Science
Technical University of Berlin, Germany
ehrig@cs.tu-berlin.de

Abstract. This contribution is a short introduction into the research area, which was subject of the priority program SoftSpez of the German Research Council (DFG) in the years 1998-2004. Starting with the aims of this priority program, we give an overview of the activities of SoftSpez and the related international workshops INT 2000-2004 and of the results in six different subject areas presented in this volume.

1 Aims of the Research Area

The research area "Integration of Software Specification Techniques for Applications in Engineering" has been established as a priority program of the German Research Council (DFG) for the period of 1998-2004 and was subject of the international workshops INT 2000, 2002, and 2004 as satellite events of the "European Joint Conferences on Theory and Practice of Software" (ETAPS). The aim of the priority program SoftSpez was to establish the integration of different specification and modeling techniques for the development of reliable safety and security related software systems for applications in engineering, especially in the areas of production automation and traffic control systems. The results of this research should lead to a theoretically well founded integration of mathematical and pragmatic techniques and tools for software specifications in different application areas. The research proposal of SoftSpez includes mainly the following four areas, which are presented in [1] in more detail.

1.1 Integration of Software Specification Techniques

In the 90s there has been already a large variety of software specification techniques which are suitable for specific aspects in the software development process. In most applications, however, it is not sufficient to use only one technique, but various techniques have to be used for different purposes. For data type aspects there are date type specification techniques, like algebraic specification, Z and B, while process techniques, like process algebras, Petri nets and statecharts, are used for dynamic aspects of systems. All these are formal specification techniques

H. Ehrig et al. (Eds.): INT 2004, LNCS 3147, pp. 1–8, 2004.

with a well-defined mathematical syntax and semantics. For object oriented software development the Unified Modeling Language UML provides a large variety of different diagram techniques for different purposes.

Most of the UML techniques are semiformal in the sense that there is a well-defined syntax, but in most cases there is only a textual description of the intended semantics. This leads to several integration tasks:

1. Integration of different formal techniques in order to have a united technique for different aspects, like data types and processes, including well-defined semantical foundations and verification techniques.
2. Integration of semiformal and formal techniques in order to apply formal semantics and verification techniques also to semiformal techniques.
3. Integration of methods and tools for different specification techniques in order to provide a suitable software development environment.

1.2 Integration of Techniques and Methodologies in Computer Science and Engineering

Based on techniques and methodologies in engineering on one hand and results concerning the integration of software specification techniques in computer science on the other hand it is necessary to integrate these techniques including the following tasks:

1. Compatibility of the specification for functions performed by physical components in engineering, especially sensor-actuator and other physical devices of embedded systems, with those of software components including real-time aspects.
2. Integration of established graphical means of description and visual modeling techniques which have been developed separately in both areas in order to support the intuitive understanding of physical systems as well as software systems.
3. Integration of views, aspects and related models in both areas in order to bridge the gap between different methodologies in computer science and engineering leading to reliable embedded systems in the application areas.

1.3 Meta Models for Integration

In areas 1.1. and 1.2 above it is intended to integrate specific specification techniques from computer science and engineering. It remains to study the general principles how to integrate specification techniques not only on the syntactical, but also on the semantical and the methodological level. The meta model for UML, which includes meta models for all the different UML diagrams, is a typical example for the syntactical integration of different modeling techniques. This concept, which can certainly be applied also to other visual modeling techniques, can be considered as a meta model for syntactical integration. In order to support correctness and verification of systems, however, it is even more important to develop a meta model for semantical integration which can be applied to different concrete specification techniques, especially to the UML diagram techniques.

1.4 Reference Case Studies in Production Automation and Traffic Control Systems

In order to support the cooperation between computer science and engineering one of the main aims of the priority program SoftSpez is not only the integration of software specification techniques but also the applications of these techniques to realistic problems in engineering.

For this purpose two experts from engineering, E. Westkämper and E. Schnieder, have been asked to join the group of initiators from computer science and to provide realistic reference case studies from different application areas in engineering:

1. The aim of the Reference Case Study Production Automation is to give a practical insight into future requirements of software specification on the example of material flow. The specific challenge is to develop agent-based software structures which help to increase the reliability of production systems via mechanisms of self-configuration, self-analysis and self-optimization.
2. In the area of Traffic Control Systems a typical example for a safety related case study is the level crossing with barriers. This second reference case study was developed with support of the Deutsche Bahn AG. Its challenges are radio based communication and dual hybrid dynamics with discrete events and continuous behavior.

2 Organization of the Priority Program SoftSpez

After acceptance of the priority program SoftSpez by the German Research Council (DFG) in 1997 a call for specific projects within this program was launched, where especially the cooperation between computer scientists and engineers within one project was required. From about 75 project proposals 11 projects were selected by an independent group of referees appointed by the DFG. In the first colloquium of the priority program end of 1998 it was decided to organize the work in seven different subject areas, where later two of these areas were joined leading to the following six areas:

1. Reference Case Study Production Automation
   (Coordinator: Engelbert Westkämper)
2. Reference Case Study Traffic Control Systems
   (Coordinator: Eckehard Schnieder)
3. Petri Nets and Related Approaches in Engineering (Coordinator: Jörg Desel)
4. Charts (Coordinator: Werner Damm)

5. Verification (Coordinator: Wolfgang Reif)
6. Integration Modeling (Coordinator: Martin Große-Rhode).

The subject areas 1 and 2 are the two parts of research area 4 (Reference Case Studies in Production Automation and Traffic Control Systems), subject area 6 corresponds to research area 3 (Meta Models for Integration), and the subject areas 3, 4 and 5 cover main parts of research areas 1 and 2 (Integration of Software Specification Techniques resp. Techniques and Methodologies in Computer Science and Engineering). Although there is in principle a large variety of specification techniques suitable for the SoftSpez proposal, it turned out that in the accepted projects different kinds of charts, closely related to corresponding UML techniques, as well as Petri nets and related approaches in engineering were dominant and that also verification techniques should be grouped together in a separate subject area. Altogether it turned out that each of the 11 accepted projects are strongly related to two or three subject areas, especially because each project was required to provide a solution to one of the reference case studies or closely related industrial problems.

Each of the six subject areas has organized a corresponding annual workshop, where not only the problems but also the solutions of the different projects for this subject area were discussed. The main results were presented on the annual symposium of SoftSpez.

In order to discuss the topics and results of SoftSpez also within the international community a first international workshop on "Integration of Software Specification Techniques with Applications in Engineering", short INT 2000, was organized as satellite events of the prestigious international ETPAS 2000 conference in Berlin. The forum of ETAPS (European Joint Conferences on Theory and Practice of Software) has allowed starting a discussion of the SoftSpez research area with leading international experts. Due to its success the INT workshop was repeated twice with INT 2002 and INT 2004 as satellite event of ETAPS 2002 in Grenoble and ETAPS 2004 in Barcelona. In each of these INT workshops the SoftSpez coordinator gave a short overview of the ongoing priority program in Germany, and for each of the subject areas one main contribution from one of the projects and also from an invited international speaker were presented. The workshops were organized by key members of SoftSpez in cooperation with international experts in the field. Some of these international speakers have been invited again for a contribution in this volume.

3   Overview of Results

In this section we give a short overview with selected, typical examples how the aims of the research areas 1.1-1.4 presented in section 1 have been realized within the priority program SoftSpez in the subject areas 1-6. For a mid-term report we refer to [2] and for more details to the introductions of the corresponding subject areas and to the papers in this volume.

3.1   Results in Research Area 1.1

The integration of software specification techniques was mainly studied in the subject areas 4 and 5 with focus on different kinds of charts and verification techniques. For the subject area "charts" main contributions have been provided by the projects USE, FORMOSA and SFC-Check and D. Harel as international expert. Charts comprise statecharts in the UML semantics and also the classical statemate semantics, Sequential Function Charts (SFC) and Live Sequence Charts (LSC). A prime topic of this subject area was the definition of a rigorous semantics of the considered charts languages, which is a prerequisite for formal correctness and verification. The important role of LSCs was pointed out by D. Harel in his invited lecture at INT 2004, concerning his novel approach to programming of reactive systems. In this approach - presented in his book [3] - inter-object scenario-based behavioral requirements are "played in" directly from the systems GUI (graphical user interface), and behavior can then be "played out" freely adhering to all the requirements. The language he used is an enriched version of the LSCs, that were originally developed by him and W. Damm [4]. A complete formal semantics of LSCs is one of the main aims of the project USE presented in this volume [5].

Verification - considered by the projects FORMOSA, ISILEIT, USE, SFC-Check and GRASP in subject area 5 - allows proving rigorously that a certain property holds for a formal system model. As discussed in the introduction to this subject area the verification task can be split into three parts. The first step is to build a formal model of the system using suitable specification techniques, e.g. those considered in subject area 4 or those presented by D. Bjørner as international expert in [6]. The second step is to identify important safety properties, where safety analysis techniques like FTA and FMEA from engineering can help to find them. Combining these safety analysis techniques with formal specification and verification techniques is the aim of the FORMOSA project presented in this volume [7], which has been applied to an important industrial case study, the "height control in the Elbtunnel" (see [8]). The third step is then the verification for the properties for a given system using well-known interactive verification or model checking techniques and tools.

3.2   Results in Research Area 1.2

The integration of techniques and methodologies in computer science and engineering was mainly studied in the subject areas 1-3, where areas 1-2 will be discussed in 3.4. The main aim of subject area 3 (Petri Nets and Related Approaches in Engineering) is to study the relationship of process specification methods and languages in the areas of computer science and engineering (see [9]). The contributions in this volume have been provided by the projects SPECIMEN, GRASP, KNOSSOS and DISPA, and the international experts L.M. Kristensen and K. Jensen. One typical example for this subject area is the well-known specification language MFERT for production automation systems studied in the GRASP project (see [10]). MFERT-models have many similarities with Petri nets, but MFERT has no formal semantics as basis for verification. For this reason MFERT models are translated to I/O Interval Structures, which allows using the model checker RAVEN to check real-time properties of the MFERT model. These properties are specified in RT-OCL, a real-time extension of the language OCL for the specification of constraints in UML. Among other examples is the synthesis of control in automation systems in the project SPECIMEN using signal nets, an extension of Petri nets by signal arcs (see [11]).

3.3   Results in Research Area 1.3

General concepts of integration, which can be applied to different specific specification techniques, have been studied in subject area 6 (Integration Modeling). According to [12] integration modeling includes methodological, ontological and formal semantics integration. One of the main results is the language- and method-independent model integration of the project IOSIP presented in the EATCS Monographs in TCS [13]. This semantical framework for model integration is based on a uniform concept of transformation systems, which allows the semantic integration of heterogeneous software specifications. The integration model has been adapted to object-oriented systems in [14], which allows studying semantical integration of object-oriented viewpoint specification techniques as considered in UML. The approach presented by the international expert F. Orejas [15] addresses the orthogonal issue of the integration of specification modules that are presented in different notations based on the categorical framework of institutions.

3.4   Results in Research Area 1.4

In the subject areas 1 and 2 different solutions have been presented for the reference case studies in production automation and traffic control systems respectively.

For the case study in production automation and a closely related flexible production system solutions are presented in this volume by the projects IOSIP, DISPA and ISILEIT based on UML, UML-PA and UML and SDL respectively (see [16]). UML-PA is a process automation extension of UML developed within the project DISPA. In cooperation between the GRASP and the IOSIP project a simulation tool has been developed, which allows illustrating the reference case study production automation. An important achievement for the application area of production automation is the development of the object-oriented specification method ODEMA (Object-oriented Method for Developing Technical Multi-Agent-System) based on UML (see [17]), which has been developed in the project IOSIP and applied to the reference case study.

The reference case study Traffic Control Systems was especially considered by the projects KNOSSOS, SafeRail, and HYBRIS, which are discussed by E. Schnieder in [18] in more detail. In order to demonstrate the corresponding specifications a scaled model of a level crossing and a train model were conceived, constructed and validated using simulations. This test environment was frequently used by the projects within this subject area. The results have been presented on an international level not only on the INT-workshops mentioned above, but also on the international conferences FORMS 1998-2000 and FORMS 2003 (Formal Methods for Railway Operation and Control Systems, see [19]).

3.5 Conclusion

As sketched above and shown in more detail in this volume the main aims of the research area Integration of Software Specification Techniques for Applications in Engineering have been achieved by the projects of the priority program SoftSpez. The corresponding results have been presented not only on national, but also on several international conferences and workshops. The feedback with international experts, especially with those presented in this volume, was important for a smooth development of the research area on a high international level. Moreover the cooperation between scientists from computer science and engineering was important to achieve results which are relevant for both communities. The techniques presented in this volume have been applied successfully not only to the reference case studies in production automation and traffic control systems, but also to several industrial projects.

References

1. Ehrig, H., Geisler, R., Klar, M.: DFG-Schwerpunktprogramm ab 1998. Integration von Techniken der Softwarespezifikation für ingenieurwissenschaftliche Anwendungen. Informatik Forschung und Entwicklung **13** (1998) 43–46
2. Ehrig, H., Große-Rhode, M.: Integration von Techniken der Softwarespezifikation für ingenieurwissenschaftliche Anwendungen. Informatik Forschung und Entwicklung **16** (2001) 110–117
3. Harel, D., Marelly, R.: Come, Let's Play: Scenario-Based LSCs and the Play-Engine. Springer (2003)
4. Damm, W., Harel, D.: LSCs: Breathing Life into Message Sequence Charts. Formal Methods in System Design **19** (2001) 45–80
5. Brill, M., Damm, W., Klose, J., Westphal, B., Wittke, H.: Live Sequence Charts. (In this volume)
6. Bjørner, D., George, C., Haxthausen, A., Madsen, C., Holmslykke, S., Pěnička, M.: "UML–ising" Formal Techniques. (In this volume)
7. Ortmeier, F., Thums, A., Schellhorn, G., Reif, W.: Combining Formal Methods and Safety Analysis - The For MosSA Approach. (In this volume)
8. Ortmeier, F., Reif, W., et al: Safety Analysis on the Height Control System for the Elbtunnel. Reliability Engineering and System Safety **81** (2003) 259–268
9. Desel, J.: Process Description Languages and Methods: Introduction to Subject Area Petri Nets and Related Approaches in Engineering. (In this volume)
10. Flake, S., Müller, W., Ruf, J., Pape, U.: Specification and Formal Verification of Temporal Properties of Production Automation Systems. (In this volume)
11. Desel, J., Hanisch, H., Juhás, G., Lorenz, R., Neumair, C.: Guide to Modelling and Control with modules of Signal Nets. (In this volume)
12. Große-Rhode, M.: On Model Integration and Integration Modelling. (In this volume)

13. Große-Rhode, M.: Semantic Integration of Heterogeneous Software Specifications. Monographs in Theoretical Computer Science. Springer (2004)
14. Braatz, B., Klein, M., Schröter, G.: Semantical Integration of Object-Oriented Viewpoint Specification Techniques. (In this volume)
15. Orejas, F., Pino, E.: On the Integration of Heterogeneous Specifications. (In this volume)
16. Westkämper, E., Bengel, M., Fischer, K.: Basic Principles for Software Specification. (In this volume)
17. Westkämper, E., Braatz, A.: Eine Methode zur objektorientierten Software-Spezifikation von dezentralen Automatisierungssystemen mit der Unified Modeling Language (UML). at – Automatisierungstechnik **5** (2001) 225–233
18. Schnieder, E.: Specification Methodology, Case Studies and Experiments - An Introduction to the Subject Area of Traffic Control Systems. (In this volume)
19. Tarnai, G., Schnieder, E., eds.: Formal Methods for Railway Operation and Control Systems (Forms 2003), L'Harmattan Budapest (2003)

Basic Principles for Software Specification

Introduction to Subject Area Reference Case Study Production Automation

Engelbert Westkämper[1], Matthias Bengel[1], and Katja Fischer[2]

[1] Institute of Industrial Manufacturing and Management (IFF), University of
Stuttgart, Nobelstrasse 12, D-70569 Stuttgart, Germany
{engelbert.westkaemper|matthias.bengel}@iff.uni-stuttgart.de
[2] Chair of Automation and Process Control Engineering (LFA), University of
Wuppertal, Rainer-Gruenter-Strasse 21, D-42119 Wuppertal, Germany
kfischer@uni-wuppertal.de

1 Introduction

The applicability of the integrated techniques and methods, which are developed
within the DFG priority program Software Specifications, is shown by means of
two reference case studies, that describe typical systems from engineering point
of view. One belongs to the area Production Automation. The characteristic
aspects of process automation and the realized systems are focused in the case
study, including open and closed loop control, real-time aspects as well as distribution of control functions.

As an introduction, the requirements of process automation and the case
study Production Automation itself are discussed. This is followed by three papers, which are developed from project partners in the DFG priority program
Software Specifications [1]. The fourth paper is a look into the future. It handles
the future requirements in software specification for manufacturing systems [2].

2 General Characteristic Aspects of Production Automation

Concerning the requirements of process automation the case study Production
Automation was chosen. The requirements of Production Automation can be
structured regarding different aspects like open and closed loop control, real-
time and distribution. In the following, some of these aspects are described.

Mostly, the technical process requires a temporally defined and cyclic machining. So it requires a deterministic behavior regarding real-time aspects of
the control algorithms. Processes and their controlling algorithms respond sen-
sitively to jitter in cycle times.

For processing of execution controls, the monitoring of limit values and of
asynchronous events' return values is extremely important. Some tasks have to
be executed at absolute times. These requirements cause complying with the

H. Ehrig et al. (Eds.): INT 2004, LNCS 3147, pp. 9–22, 2004.

real-time behaviour. The term real-time behavior includes requirements for simultaneity and timeliness within quasi parallel program execution. DIN 44300 [3] defines real-time as the deterministic behavior of a control system to be available for unexpected events within a given period of time. This functionality is supposed to be a standard for each real-time operating system. In practice, there is a differentiation between hard and soft real-time. Hard real-time considers the exceeding of a given period of time as a total failure of the whole system. Soft real-time still accepts this exceeding if the resulting damage is not too bad. DIN 44300 reduces real-time capability to maximal reaction times, i. e. bounded responses.

Manufacturing systems are often distributed systems with different targets connected via field bus. The sum of distribution aspects is listed in table 1. This table shows the first level of a morphologocal box for distributed systems. This morphological box [4] was developed on the basis of properties in automation literature [5, 6, 7] and heuristics. This box is an appliance for the morphological method, whereas a problem is split multidimensionally into single parts.

In the Reference Case Study Production Automation a special form of distributed systems is utilized. The so-called agents are explained in the following.

In general, an agent is someone acting on the order of someone else. A technical agent in the Production Automation can be described as follows. Regarding technical systems, agents are understood as autonomous, cooperating entities in distributed, decentral systems [9]. Basically, technical agents are to be distinguished from software agents. In contrast to technical agents, software agents are software entities. Based on the definition of Lüth, a technical agent can be seen as an autonomous, interactive entity with its goal to optimize and stabilize a process. Further on, the technical agent is equipped with intelligence, i. e. mainly the capability to learn, and the capabilities to cooperate and coordinate [10]. Autonomy is the agent's capability to take decisions on its own and to create plans depending on its role [11]. The agentification is the process of identification and modeling of technical processes and systems.

3   Characteristics of the Reference Case Study Production Automation

3.1   Introduction

The aim of the Reference Case Study Production Automation is to give a practical insight into future requirements of software specification on the example of material flow. Agent-based software structures will help to increase the reliability of production systems via mechanisms of self-configuration, self-analysis and self-optimization.

As physical manufacturing environment for the Reference Case Study a rather simple production system has been selected on the basis of a shop floor system for deburring of metal parts. Typical metal parts for deburring in this shop floor are: motor blocks, crank shafts, exhaust pipes etc. The shop floor

Table 1. Sum of distribution requirements.

Distribution aspect	Specificity	Description
Autonomy / self-government	− Independent / non-cooperating − Dependent-cooperating − Stand-alone functioning − Interacting	Dimension for independence of certain functions from regular influences.
Heterogeneity	− Homogeneous − Heterogeneous	Configuration description of several − maybe different − hardware and software modules.
Transparency	− Access − Concurrency − Parallelism − Degree − Failure − Location − Migration − Persistence − Relocation − Replication − Fragmentation − Name − Scalability	Hiding of distribution from users and applications. With a certain degree of transparency the impression of a single processor system could be given.
Modularity	− Openness − Flexibility − Scalability	The term modularity consists of these three items. If a system is open, then it is flexible and scalable as well.

Dependability	− Reliability
	  • Availability
	  • Certainty
	    ∗ Safety
	    ∗ Security
	− Fault tolerance
	− Fault processing
		These items are well discussed in conventional literature [5, 6, 7, 8].

Synchronization	− Asynchronous process − Synchronous process	Synchronization regarding the real-time ability of considered systems.
Performance	− User aspects − System aspects − Cost aspects	The performance regarding information technology.

consists of three different machining centers: a five-axes milling machine and a three-axes milling machine (machine tools), both for deburring, and a final washing machine. Input of parts in terms of material flow is an automatic shelf storage in which all parts that are waiting for deburring are stored. Output of all parts, after the process of deburring and washing is completed, is a second automatic shelf storage waiting for all finished parts to come in for further delivery to the next shop floor area.

The material flow system – while deciding on all transport tasks and assigning them – is fully responsible for the resulting throughput and production rates on the shop floor. In this case study three free-ranging Automatic Guided Vehicles (AGV) are in charge of performing all transport tasks. But in contrast to traditional AGV systems, in this case there is no central disposition dispatcher involved, assigning given tasks to AGVs. Therefore the three AGVs act completely on their own, independent of any central supervisor. They are autonomous, self-responsible, cooperative agents, that behave like little taxi drivers in a modern city, assigning themselves to individual transport tasks that are offered by a broadcasting system. Such an agent-oriented behavior in manufacturing is leading to a Holonic Manufacturing System (HMS) with holonic AGVs (H-AGVs) [12] which is considered as a special case of technical agents.

Taking into account the features explained in table 1, table 2 can be derived.

Table 2. Distribution aspects applied to the Reference Case Study Production Automation.

Distribution aspect	AGV	Machine tool
Autonomy	Dependent-cooperating	Stand-alone functioning
Heterogeneity	Homogeneous	Heterogeneous
Dependability	Only applicable in the extended version	Only applicable in the extended version
Synchronization	Asynchronous	Synchronous
Performance	System and cost aspects	System aspects

In figure 1 the Reference Case Study is modeled in a simulation program provided by the project GRASP [13]. On the right is a hall housing the AGVs when they are not used. On the lower side there are the two automatic shelf storages for input and output. On the left and on the top the two milling machines are located, and on the top right, there is the washing machine. Finally, on the free area in the middle, the three AGVs are handling transport tasks.

A specification of the Reference Case Study Production Automation was already prepared using the ODEMA method (Object-oriented Method for Developing Technical Multi-Agent-Systems) [14, 15].

The aim of this case study is to maximize performance of work pieces without losing the easy configurability. Therefore, the control systems for the AGVs, the machine tools and the storages have to be specified.

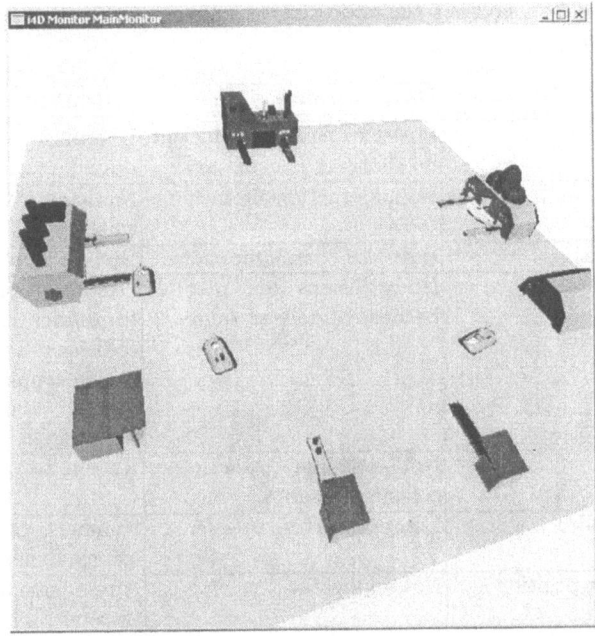

Fig. 1. Reference Case Study modeled in the GRASP simulation tool.

Extension of the Reference Case Study: The Reference Case Study consists of a basic version and an extended version. Basically, the extended version demands a more realistic model of the real world. In more detail, the resources have to be handled as well as malfunctions and failures. Another important detail is that there are less restrictions to the numbers of available subsystems.

All the differences between these two versions are shown in table 3.

3.2   Control Systems

Generally, the system decomposition of automation systems and their control systems respectively may be described by a model consisting of five levels which are characterized by their functions regarding the application processes [16, 17, 8, 18, 19]. This model is also known as the CIM pyramid (Computer Integrated Manufacturing). The lower three levels are depicted in figure 2.

In the factory management level, the Enterprise Resource Planning Systems (ERP) are located to handle the whole factory's logistics, e. g. gathering orders. In the second level, the production management level, Manufacturung Execution Systems (MES) are responsible for one production site, they create production orders etc. The process management level synchronizes various machines and offers user interaction, whereas the process control level consists of different functions with various time constraints:

Table 3. Differences between the basic version and the extended version of the Reference Case Study.

Property	Basic version	Extended version
Power supply	Power capacity is sufficient: no charging is necessary.	Charging station is required.
Machine tools' malfunctions	No malfunctions in machine tools.	Mechanical failures are possible.
Communication	Loss-free communication.	Disturbances are possible.
Collisions of AGVs	No collisions are possible because of defined routes.	Extension of layout leads to reserving routes to avoid collisions. This is supposed to be implemented by a Routes' Management System.
Deadlocks	Not possible because of collision-freedom.	Have to be avoided.
Number of AGVs	Limited to three AGVs.	Number of AGVs can change dynamically.
AGV's waiting position	Not applicable.	After having finished a transportation task, the AGV moves to a defined waiting position.

1. Axis Control
   Usually a closed loop system to control the axes' positions that is quasi-continuous.
2. Motion Control
   Mostly a closed loop system to handle the movements of axes, actuators and so on. This is as well quasi-continuous.
3. Logic Control
   A state-based discrete control of behavior.
4. Process Control
   Control of additional functions.
5. Man-Machine Control
   Event-discrete as a part of the Logic Control.

Finally, the Process Level houses sensors and actuators to establish the connection to the physical process.

This layer model acts on the assumption of a hierarchical approach, i. e. the higher levels use services and data from the lower ones. Therefore, the functions of application processes need certain properties offered by the hardware components. This means that by this layer model types of automation devices are defined as well. Components located near the process itself possess a real-time operating system leading to a deterministic behavior of application processes. Simple field devices (sensors, actuators) do not make use of control functions,

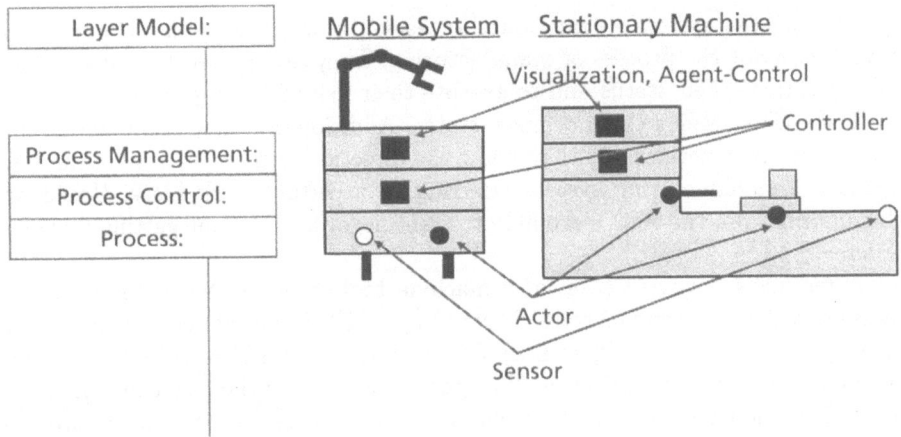

Fig. 2. Factory Layer Model.

but in fact they are the interface to the technical process. So-called intelligent field devices are components that link sensors or actuators to control functions.

As a matter of principle, control systems are seen as distributed systems. This means that the devices are linked by various communication systems, of which the properties are defined as well by the layer model. Typically, there is a difference between the field bus to transmit small amounts of data in hard real-time (cf. next section) and the factory bus to transmit larger data without any temporal restriction.

In the layer model above at least the lower two levels are distributed. The communication objects involved are mainly events, real-time process data, synchronization signals, alarm signals, status, and configuration values.

Configuration: Each system, i. e. machine tools, AGVs and shelf storages, has its own control system which is to be specified. Furthermore, there is a system technology consisting of sensors for navigation, obstacle avoidance etc. and actuators for driving, steering, and work piece handling.

The system technology is encapsulated and transparent with regard to the needs of designing the control systems. It can be considered as a black box, i. e. the layers of process control and process in the factory layer model (cf. figure 2) are not demanded by the Reference Case Study.

All the manufacturing system's subsystems synchronize themselves via a radio-based broadcast communication system. It ensures that every message is delivered to each connected system. The development of an architecture based on a broadcasting communication model is shown in [20].

It has to be pointed out that the AGVs' controls are the only ones being holonic, i. e. autonomous. The other ones' actions are dependent on the current system status.

To keep the system's configurability easy the machine tools do not know anything about the process of manufacturing. They are limited to transmitting (broadcasting) their status and to execute their manufacturing steps.

The AGVs receive the machines' states. Additionally, they know about the process of manufacturing as they know the direction and order of material flow inside the manufacturing system referring to a certain work piece. Based on this information, the AGVs are able to start negotiating about getting transfer orders.

A module's behavior (i. e. of a machine tool or an AGV) is described by message sequence charts or state charts. As an AGV is considered as a transport agent (cf. Agent-oriented Open Loop Control), the agent's head is responsible for the behavior and communication. The agent's body with the axis controllers for example are left out here. This correlates to the process control and the process itself in the factory layer model, as explained above.

Decentralization: The AGVs' control systems are holonic. A holon is a mixture of autonomy and ability of cooperation, i. e. it is ambitious to keep its autonomy as well as integrate itself into holarchies. In this context, a holarchie is a dynamic hierarchy of holons [21]. As holonic architectures cannot be implemented by conventional methods, other concepts have to be used. The concept of intelligent agents is suitable for holonic systems as there is as well a decentralized way of problem solving by autonomous and cooperative entities. If within one system multiple agents interact or cooperate, it is called a Multi-Agent-System (MAS).

Agent-Oriented Open Loop Control: The AGVs are identified as technical agents to form a transport MAS [22]. Braatz developed the UML-based method ODEMA (Object-oriented Method for Developing Technical Multi-Agent-Systems) to design technical agents [14, 15].

Conventional structuring methods for manufacturing are following two philosophies:

- Material flow: control is mainly determined by the transport system.
- Work flow: control is mainly determined by the manufacturing processes.

In conventional systems, the control hierarchy does not allow to optimize and adapt the ratio of material flow and work flow. Agent control fills in this gap.

The AGVs are the only agentified parts in the whole manufacturing system.

If a machine tool transmits its status, the AGVs extract a transfer order out of it if there is a workpiece to be moved. The first AGV to recognize the transfer order becomes a moderator and broadcasts a call for bids. The other AGVs receive this call and calculate their costs to move this workpiece, based on their distance to the workpiece and the difficulty to reach it. If its own bid is better than the other ones, it takes part in the bidding. After a certain amount of time the moderator finishes the bidding and accepts the best one. This procedure maximizes the system's load at the lowest costs.

Holonic Material Flow: In contrast to hierarchical systems, holonic systems are able to combine hierarchical and heterarchical properties. If a module of the whole system changes or fails, this can be compensated by adaptation of the whole system. Moreover, fixed hierarchies are said to doom in nature while dynamic holarchies assure stability and growth [23, 24].

Holonic manufacturing systems (HMS) are based on the approach that holons (agents) cooperate and act to increase common welfare (cf. Decentralization). The main goal of holonic manufacturing systems is that each holonic AGV (H-AGV) acts autonomously and cooperatively on its own. There is no central disposition system needed for job assignment. This goal is reached by several properties:

- *Autonomy and self-organization*
  Transport tasks are only negotiated if the H-AGV is not currently allocated by another task. The H-AGV plans its way to the goal individually and it takes care of the battery load status, i. e. the resource management, on its own.
- *Cooperativeness*
  Transport tasks are only negotiated if no other holon can perform it better. The H-AGV publishes all information on its status and decisions to others.
- *Self-optimization*
  The H-AGV takes the best way to the target, depending on the traffic situation. For reducing waste of energy, it tries to avoid traveling without load. In case of road obstacles it surrounds them or replans its way. To maximize the system performance, the most important task is handled first.
- *Intelligence*
  Transport tasks are only negotiated if they can be executed. The H-AGV checks for and avoids dead-lock situations on shop floor level.
- *Forecasting*
  If no transport tasks are active or pending, the H-AGV forecasts new tasks and already goes there.
- *Considerateness*
  If no transport tasks are active or pending, the H-AGV does not disturb the others.

It has to be mentioned that some of these items like intelligence, forecasting and considerateness are not required in any version of the Reference Case Study. The extended version demands for self-optimization in addition, which is not part of the basic version.

Components and Interfaces: The agent- and object-oriented specification method ODEMA was applied to this case study. By using system and software decomposition the system to be specified is described by UML function blocks, components and later on by classes and interfaces [25].

4   Application of the Reference Case Study Production Automation

In the topic area Reference Case Study Production Automation there are various projects dealing with this case study. A short overview about the results is following.

4.1   IOSIP

The function block-model as a notation is the most common approach for describing control applications in automation systems. For establishing UML-based methods in this area, it is required to map this domain-specific notation to design techniques of UML. Bearing in mind that the model of function blocks is established as a descriptive notation for distributed control systems in automation systems, the mapping to the UML harnessed a well-known tool in the world of software development to the engineering in automation. Further on, an approach is given to change methodically from system and control development to software development, like it is required in the ODEMA method's conception [14, 15].

Motivated by the wide acceptance of component-based technologies in software development it is shown by example, how to apply component concepts for software engineering to modeling in the field of production automation. The example of the modeling of a holonic transport system shows how function blocks in the sense of production automation can be understood as software engineering components. Thus, the advantages of component-based modeling with respect to structuring, exchange and reuse can be transferred to systems in production automation [25].

As a third part the semantical consistency of viewpoint-oriented modeling techniques in production automation is considered. The role of the viewpoint concept, known from software engineering, is of increasing importance for modeling in production automation. While most often only a syntactical consistency check is performed for viewpoint oriented modeling techniques, this work examines semantical consistency. Semantical modeling and model-based consistency checks are presented along an example of a machining tool robot [25].

4.2   DisPA

In the project DisPA a draft for an object oriented approach for the domain of automation and process control engineering is derived. This approach includes UML stereotypes for control (closed and open loop) and uses configuration of attributes and operations to achieve reusability of modules. Besides, constraints for real time applications are necessary. This developed UML subset is called UML-PA (PA – Process Automation) [26].

The case study Production Automation has been selected to serve as evaluation environment for the embedded software to be designed with UML-PA. The

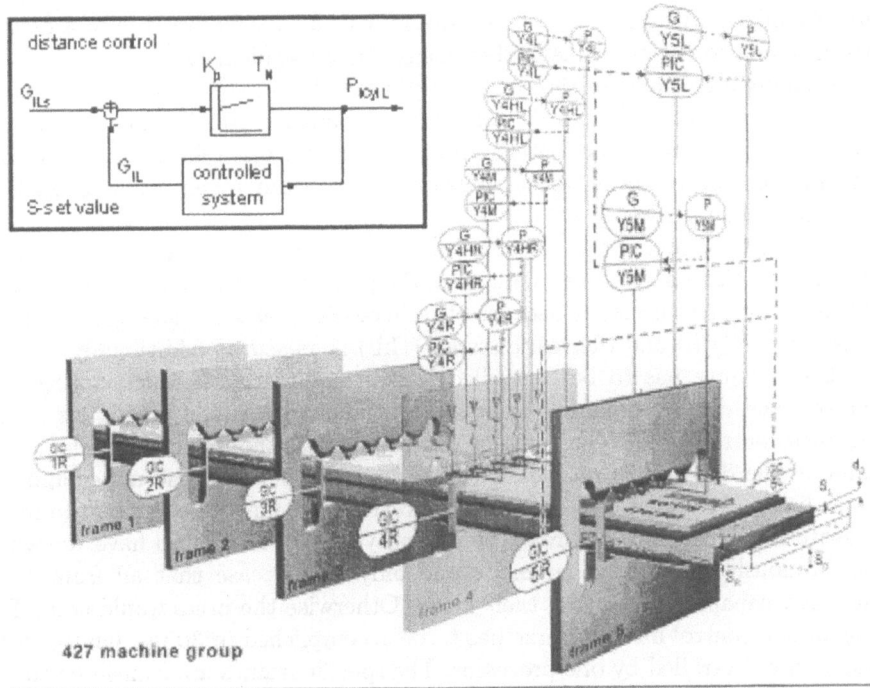

Fig. 3. Part of a continuous hydraulic press in Timber Industry with Block Diagram (block diagram for frame i, i= 1- 80, L - left system).

practicability of UML-PA as well as the code size and the required computational performance of the software will be evaluated. Therefore, the extended part of the Reference Case Study Production Automation is realized at the University of Wuppertal, LFA [27].

The demonstrator is built of several single board computers (SBC) with a real-time operating system (RTOS-UH) connected via CAN bus. The behavior of the continuous hydraulic press is realized via C code processing on SBCs. The implementation of the UML-PA model is realized semi manual.

The interfaces to the existing UML model from the project IOSIP [15, 25, 28] are concerned during the development of this demonstrator.

For realistic image the Reference Case Study is extended to evaluate the developed techniques and methods in the project DisPA [29]. To consider hard real-time aspects as well as automation control aspects, a further machining center is added. This machining center is a so-called continuous hydraulic press (figure 3). This is a part of a manufacturing plant from timber industry, which is the component with the most restrictive requirements. The whole plant mass-produces fibreboards. Time-critical closed loop control has to be combined with open loop control and switching to other control loops. For a better understanding one feature is explained simplified in the following. The material, which is already mixed with glue, has to be pressed with a specific pressure to a certain distance due to the set value of the finished board's thickness.

In figure 3 this part of the continuous hydraulic press is shown. Such a press could be composed of almost 80 frames. Every frame has two distance sensors and from two to five hydraulic systems, that consist of a valve for pressure increase and pressure decrease as well as a sensor. The distance control is realized by these hydraulic systems.

During the process the pressure has to be kept in a certain limit, but the thickness of the material (i.e. distance of the press gap, GiLs) should be reached. A maximum pressure is set because of technological reasons. The real hydraulic pressure (PICyiL) and the real distance (GiL) is measured additionally.

The pressure has to be controlled in two modes: the distance control and the pressure control mode. Usually the continuous hydraulic press runs in the distance control mode. The distance control mode is the mode in which the set value of the distance is reached with the pressure between the upper and the lower limit. If the distance could not be reached within these limits, the mode is switched to pressure control. The difficulty is that all frames have to switch synchronously into the other mode and only in the case that all frames are currently capaple of changing their mode. Otherwise the press would stop. The closed loop control of each frame has to be accomplished in 30 ms. Only several frames are controlled by one processor. The specific frames are connected to the processors and the specific processors among themselves via field bus.

4.3   GRASP

In the GRASP project the specification language MFERT and visual behavior descriptions are integrated by using formal methods of specification. The method to validate formal properties is using simulation techniques. Here, the simulation tool shown in figure 1 was developped in cooperation with the IOSIP project to illustrate the Reference Case Study Production Automation. As an extension of this simulation-based technique, local areas of the state space can be explored additionally. In this way, the validation of complex systems described in a highly detailed way becomes possible, whereas the validation was not possible so far because of complexity [13].

4.4   ISILEIT

The main goal of the ISILEIT project is to develop a methodology to integrate design, tool-supported analysis and validation of distributed manufacturing systems. Parts of the specification languages UML and SDL are used here. The integration of the models is performed by formally describing the operational semantics of the used specification techniques. In this way, the analysis and validation of the system models via model-checking and simulation becomes possible.

Within this project, a similar case study to the Reference Case Study is used. It is as well a flexible production system, containing several NC controlled processing machines and Scara robots. The material flow is realized by a rail-based system. In contrast to the Reference Case Study, the focus is not on holonic systems here, but on the integration of tools to create a tool chain. Thus the engineer is able to improve existing techniques with respect to formal analysis, simulation and automatic code generation [30].

References

1. N.N.: DFG Priority Program Software Specifications. http://tfs.cs.tu-berlin.de/projekte/indspec/SPP/index-eng.html (2004)
2. Valckenaers, P.: Challenges of Next Generation Manufacturing Systems. In: This Volume. (2004)
3. N.N.: DIN 4430: Informationsverarbeitung, Begriffe, Alphabetisches Gesamtverzeichnis. DIN Standard (1993)
4. Fischer, K., Katzke, U., Vogel-Heuser, B.: A Conceptual Design of an Engineering Model for Plant Automation based on an Application Oriented Requirements Analysis. In: SCI 2004, Orlando, Florida (2004) Accepted.
5. Tanenbaum, A.S., van Steen, M.: Distributed Systems. Prentice Hall (2002)
6. Coulouris, G., Dollimore, J., Kindberg, T.: Distributed Systems. Addison Wesley (2000)
7. Rembold, U., Levi, P.: Einführung in die Informatik. Hanser Verlag, München, Wien (1999)
8. Lauber, R., Göhner, P.: Prozessautomatisierung 2. Springer Verlag, Berlin (1999)
9. Ritter, A., Braatz, A., Winz, G.: Agentensysteme in der Produktion. In: Tagungsband SPS/IPC/DRIVES, Nürnberg, Hüthig (2000) 11. Fachmesse und Kongress.
10. Lüth, T.: Technische Multi-Agenten-Systeme: verteilte autonome Roboter- und Fertigungssysteme. Carl Hanser Verlag, München (1998)
11. Ritter, A.: Ein Multi-Agenten-System für mobile Einrichtungen in Produktionssystemen. PhD thesis, Universität Stuttgart, Stuttgart (2003)
12. Westkämper, E., et al.: Case Study Production Automation. In Ehrig, H., et al., eds.: INT 2000: Integration of Specification Techniques with Applications in Engineering, Berlin (2000) ISSN 1436-9915.
13. N.N.: DFG Priority Programme Software Specifications, Subproject GRASP. http://www.c-lab.de/grasp (2004)
14. Westkämper, E., Braatz, A.: Eine Methode zur objektorientierten Spezifikation von dezentralen Automatisierungssystemen mit der Unified Modelling Language (UML). at Automatisierungstechnik 49 (2001) 225–233
15. Braatz, A.: Entwicklung einer Methode zur objektorientierten Spezifikation von Steuerungen. Submitted, Universität Stuttgart (2004)
16. N.N.: Auswahl von Feldbussystemen durch Bewertung ihrer Leistungseigenschaften für industrielle Anwendungsbereiche. VDI-Richtlinie 3687. Beuth-Verlag, Berlin (1999)
17. N.N.: Lasten-/Pflichtenheft für den Einsatz von Automatisierungssystemen. VDI-Richtlinie 3694. Beuth-Verlag, Berlin (1991)
18. Scherff, B., et al.: Feldbussysteme in der Praxis – Ein Leitfaden für den Anwender. Springer Verlag, Heidelberg, Berlin (1999)

19. Hoang, S.H., Rieger, P.: Komponentenbasierte Automatisierungssoftware. Hanser Verlag, München, Wien (1999)
20. Krüger, I., Prenninger, W., Sandner, R., Broy, M.: Development of Hierarchical Broadcasting Software Using UML 2.0. In: This Volume. (2004)
21. Koestler, A.: The Ghost in the Machine. Arkana Books, London (1989)
22. Ritter, A., Baum, W., Höpf, M., Westkämper, E.: Agentification for Production Systems. In: INT 2002, Grenoble (2002)
23. Höpf, M., Schaeffer, C., Westkämper, E.: Holonic Manufacturing Systems. In: Entwicklung und Betrieb komplexer Automatisierungssysteme. Institut für Regelungs- und Automatisierungstechnik, Braunschweig (1997) 127–137
24. Struger, O.: Wir stecken in einer Innovationslawine – Tendenzen in der Automatisierungstechnik. Elektrotechnik für die Automatisierung **3** (1995) 18
25. Klein, M., Braatz, B., Schröter, G., Bengel, M.: A Formal Component Concept for the Specification of Industrial Control Systems. In: This Volume. (2004)
26. Fischer, K., Göhner, P., Gutbrodt, F., Vogel-Heuser, B.: Conceptual Design of an Engineering Model for Plant Automation. In: This Volume. (2004)
27. N.N.: Automation and Process Control Engineering (LFA), University of Wuppertal, Germany. http://www.lfa.uni-wuppertal.de (2004)
28. N.N.: DFG Priority Programme Software Specifications, Subproject IOSIP. http://tfs.cs.tu-berlin.de/projekte/indspec/SPP/iosip.html (2004)
29. N.N.: DFG Priority Programme Software Specifications, Subproject DisPA. http://www.lfa.uni-wuppertal.de/DisPA (2004)
30. Schäfer, W., Gausemeier, J., Wagner, R., Eckes, R.: An Engineer's Workstation to support Integrated Development of Flexible Production Control Systems. In: This Volume. (2004)

Challenges of Next Generation Manufacturing Systems

Paul Valckenaers

Department of Mechanical Engineering, Katholieke Universiteit Leuven,
Celestijnenlaan 300B, B3001 Leuven, Belgium
Paul.Valckenaers@mech.kuleuven.ac.be

1 Introduction

This chapter discusses a number of challenges to be fulfilled and considered
regarding software specification for industrial engineering and control software
within manufacturing systems. It does not provide an extensive list of detailed
functionalities, but rather discusses generic critical success factors. The common
thread is the complex interaction between software development and the techno-
socio-economic context in which this activity occurs. The software development
needs to produce much more sophisticated artefacts in the future, which requires
developers to account for factors that could be ignored in the past. In the future,
developers need to widen their view. This chapter describes in which ways they
need to enlarge their scope.

2 Software Implemenation Costs

A first important challenge is to *decrease the implementation costs of advanced
concepts*, like multi-agent or holonic manufacturing control [1, 2, 3, 4]. Today,
this cost generally is prohibitive. The main reason is that such software currently
is custom-developed for every single implementation. This means that costs can
be spread neither over multiple customers nor over time.

In the recent past, two types of effort can be distinguished in manufacturing control. First, there is the generative approach, in which a completely new
and unique multi-agent manufacturing control system is generated at each occasion. This research aims to automate and systematize the software generation
process as much as possible. The main motivation for this approach is that it
generates systems with a small footprint, imposing low requirements on computer and communication resources; such resources are relatively expensive in
manufacturing. This is however an artificial problem, mostly resulting from the
geographical dominance of hardware vendors across the world. In manufacturing, computer and communication hardware is lagging mainstream computing
significantly on cost-performance, but performance is nevertheless improving ex-
ponentially (given fixed cost). Therefore, emphasis on modest hardware requirements is an answer to a problem that will disappear eventually.

H. Ehrig et al. (Eds.): INT 2004, LNCS 3147, pp. 23–28, 2004.
© Springer-Verlag Berlin Heidelberg 2004

The second approach develops multi-agent manufacturing control systems that have as much software in common as technically feasible. This common part might be called a *manufacturing operating system* on which the customer-specific parts of the control systems are installed as applications. A first advantage of this approach is that multiple customers use this common software, which allows spreading development and maintenance costs. Hence, more economic effort can be spent on such common software parts than on specific implementations for a single factory. A second advantage is that the learning process for such software goes much faster. The software is used in more and more diverse situations, providing feedback to developers from their users. As a consequence, such reusable software matures much more rapidly. A third advantage is that such a manufacturing operating system necessarily possesses a wider operating range than a small-footprint specific control system. This means that it is more likely to cope with changing circumstances in the manufacturing system, probably benefiting from the experience in other places that came across similar situations already, without requiring any software maintenance.

The advantages of the second approach are self-reinforcing: if some software is better, it attracts more users, more economic resources and more information feedback, which makes it even better, and the self-reinforcing loop is closed. Such software is likely to dominate as soon as one such implementation succeeds in the market. Most importantly, only this type of software is able to mobilize the significant amount of economic resources needed to have successful sophisticated software systems in manufacturing. As long as each implementation has to bear its efforts in isolation, the software will remain costly and primitive. A larger hardware footprint is a small price to pay for these more powerful solutions when seen on a medium-range perspective.

In conclusion, the important future challenge for software specifications is to support carving out what is common, reusable and long-lived. The most important common parts should be specified explicitly to ensure that critical and sophisticated software only has to be implemented once and can be used in factories all over the world during extended periods of time.

3   Exception Handling

Exception handling must become exceptional. Software specifications must address non-nominal but common situations as normal. For instance, control software must not assume that configurations remain unchanged or that any change will be communicated in time. Instead, systems constantly will have to rediscover configurations and forget stale data collected in the past.

A valid exception is for instance a computer crash or a computer network malfunction. In contrast, examples of what often are considered exceptions today and should not be considered to be exceptions at all are:

– Late delivieries
– Equipment malfunctions and maintenance
– Test results indicating the need for repair

- Rush order entries
- Equipment replacement
- ...

In other words, changes and disturbances in the underlying manufacturing system must be business-as-usual to the software; the software must cope with any possible life cycle of the underlying system. Computer crashes or a faulty database, triggering system restore operations, are the real exceptions.

Software specification technology should encourage designers to consider more than the nominal trajectories, configurations etc. of the production systems as it operates today. This requires, among others, the emergence and dissemination of a number of design templates and guidelines that enable the development of such robust systems.

4 Reusable Software Components

Software specification needs to enclose and support design methodologies that create effective reusable software components. Software specification technology encourages, by its nature, which type of components will be developed/specified. Not all types are suitable for integration, especially in dynamic and demanding environments.

Consider traffic as analogy. Maps are highly reusable components when solving navigation problems. In contrast, route descriptions are very fragile components with limited application. Even worse would be traffic regulations for trucks as a separate component from traffic regulations for cars. Manufacturing control software devel-opment needs to catch up with modern software development technology. More than the specification language, the design approach needs to be addressed.

Modern software engineering no longer prescribes functional requirements as the main starting point for the development. In the initial phases, a business case describes why the envisaged software development makes sense. Next, a number of 'use cases' provide 'points solutions' in the continuum that the software needs to cover by design. Then, a rough outline of the system architecture provides a backbone to the software development activity. The first detailed development activities focus on the so-called 'essential model' [5]. This is our map in the navigation applications. An essential model reflects the relevant parts of the world for the software application and adds the functionality (sensors and actuators) to keep the essential model synchronized with the world. Finally, the user functionality is added incrementally.

Essential models and parts of essential models are very likely to be highly reusable. For instance, a model of a conveyor belt is reusable wherever such a conveyor belt is used and as long as these belts are used. Note that integration issues will be cosmetic (e.g. syntax issues) since the software components correspond to parts of a real world that actually fits together (think of maps of parts of the world). Functional components never achieve this level of reusability and integrate-ability.

Summarizing, software specification technology needs to adopt the proper methodologies, which emphasize essential modelling (sometimes called conceptual modelling) as the main activity in the initial phases. This is more important than adopting fancy modelling languages.

5   Make Use of Mainstream Development

Manufacturing software needs to ride on mainstream development waves. Manufacturing cannot afford the investments needed to reinvent mainstream IT. Mainstream IT reflects the highest level of sophistication that can be born by its extensive user community. Manufacturing, a much smaller community, cannot hope to match this on its own. When mainstream IT fails to deliver specific functionality, manufacturing must first look at solutions that add this functionality to mainstream IT, not solutions that require the reimplementation of mainstream IT.

Alternatively, the manufacturing community may proactively influence the mainstream community to provide the extra functionality that is vital for manufacturing applications. The challenge is to follow mainstream developments closely, identify what is missing, and find sufficient allies, which also benefit from the enhancements needed by manufacturing, to push the desired enhancements into the mainstream developments. Fortunately, manufacturing is finding more and more natural allies for this in the multimedia, high-quality communication and computer games communities.

Ethernet penetration, in its high-performance implementation, is an illustration of this phenomenon in the past. USB and FireWire are examples of mainstream competitors for Fieldbus technologies. Wireless communications is another domain in which mainstream developments are likely to dominate. Computer operating systems, web technologies, computer languages and multi-agent platforms [6] also are elements in the mainstream that impact on manufacturing software system developments.

Software specification technology must not expect every manufacturing user to enter the information about mainstream systems; important mainstream systems and standards should be supported within the software specification tool itself. Moreover, the mainstream has its own software specification technology. Manufacturing should not re-invent it, but add its specific functionality to it and influence the design of future versions of the mainstream software design technology.

6   Co-design of a Manufacturing System and Its Control System

In practice, the design and development of a manufacturing control system actually is a co-design of the manufacturing system and its control system. Consequently, a software specification environment must seamlessly integrate with a manufacturing system specification environment. Indeed, the control software being specified can only be properly defined in relation to the underlying production system(s).

In such a co-development exercise, most decisions, impacting economic performance, are taken before the production system is built or modified or the control system is deployed. Consequently, there is a need to elaborate the control system connected to an emulation of the underlying production system.

Moreover, this configuration must support experimentation campaigns that provide reliable information about the performance of such a system when actually deployed. Therefore, it needs to support the necessary functionality, some of which is not available in any commercial systems. An example is the combination of real-time emulation while the control is 'thinking' with event-based emulation when the control system is inactive. Another feature is support for dithering/jitter on timing of control action triggers in combination with executing sufficient replications such that the variation in behaviours of the deployed system is properly estimated. At lower levels of control, the emulation must even reflect the time-continuous behaviour of manufacturing processes. Overall, this is an area in which a significant amount of research and development is needed.

7   Conclusions

This chapter lists some important requirements concerning software specification for industrial engineering and control software within manufacturing systems. These requirements do not list specific functionalities that are needed in the future. The chapter addresses more generic aspects:

- Achieving large, long-lived and diverse user communities for the software to be able to create and maintain solutions exhibiting an unprecedented increase in so-phistication and user functionality.
- Handling disturbances and changes in the manufacturing environment as business as usual. Exception handling has to be restricted to malfunctions and failures related to the computer infrastructure, not the underlying industrial systems.
- The community needs to support state-of-the-art software engineering methods and more specifically essential models as reusable software components. It must develop reusable components that are for manufacturing control problems what maps are for navigation.
- The technology must facilitate to 'ride the mainstream wave.' Again, size and diversity of the user community is the key success factor.
- The software specification support needs to address the wider issue of software and manufacturing system co-design. This is the phase in which most of the investment decisions are made. Designing software as an afterthought and without a solid link to the related underlying manufacturing system is unworkable in the longer run.

Overall, software in industrial engineering and control within manufacturing systems is about to make a quantum leap in sophistication. The enabling information technologies exist and constantly penetrate the manufacturing world at increasing speed. The above addresses key success factors to make this happen.

Acknowledgement. This chapter was written in the framework of research sponsored by the Research Council of the K.U.Leuven.

References

1. Valckenaers, P., Van Brussel, H., Hadeli, Bochmann, O., Saint Germain, B., Zamfirescu, C.: On the Design of Emergent Systems: an Investigation of Integration and Interoperability Issues. In: Engineering Applications of Artificial Intelligence 16 (2003) 377-393.
2. Bussmann, S. and Schild K.: Self-Organizing Manufacturing Control: An Industrial Application of Agent Technology. Proc. 4th Int. Conf. on Multi-Agent Systems, pp.87-94 (2000), Boston, MA, USA.
3. Valckenaers, P., Van Brussel, H., Kollingbaum, M., Bochmann, O.: Multi-agent coordination and control using stigmergy applied to manufacturing control. In: Lecture Notes in Artificial Intelligence, Vol. 2086 (2001), Springer, Berlin, pp.317-334.
4. Parunak, H.V.D., Baker, A.D. and Clark, S.J.: The AARIA Agent Architecture: An Example of Requirements-Driven Agent-Based System Design. In: Proceedings of the First International Conference on Autonomous Agents (1997), pp.482-483 Marina del Rey, CA.
5. Cook, S., Daniels, J.: Designing Object Systems. Prentice-Hall, 1994, London.
6. The foundation for intelligent physical agents. http://www.fifa.org, April 2004.

Development of Hierarchical Broadcasting Software Architectures Using UML 2.0*,**

Ingolf Krüger[1], Wolfgang Prenninger[2], Robert Sandner[3], and Manfred Broy[2]

[1] Department of Computer Science & Engineering, University of California,
San Diego, La Jolla, CA, 92093-0114, USA, ikrueger@ucsd.edu
[2] Institut für Informatik, Technische Universität München,
D-80290 Munich, Germany, {prenning|broy}@in.tum.de
[3] BMW AG, D-80788 Munich, Germany
robert.sandner@bmw.de

Abstract. The definition of a transparent software architecture is one of the key issues in the early development phases for complex distributed and reactive software systems. We show how to derive an architecture systematically for systems with communication models based on broadcasting. Adequate graphical description techniques for capturing interaction requirements and logical component architectures for broadcasting systems are unavailable so far. We introduce an extension to UML's sequence diagrams to capture broadcasting scenarios. Furthermore, we present methodological steps for constructively deriving structural and behavioral aspects of the architecture under consideration from the captured scenarios.

1 Introduction

Broadcasting is the central communication paradigm in practical embedded system applications, as found in the automotive, avionics and wireless communications domains. The increasing complexity and interconnection of such systems calls for a careful identification and documentation of their logical software architecture. Adequate methodological support for architectural modeling is, however, limited to point-to-point (p2p) communication paradigms so far. In this paper we address this challenge by providing notational and methodological extensions to UML 2.0 [1], leading to an architecture-centric approach to the analysis & design of broadcasting-based embedded systems.

The Importance of Software Architecture. A decisive step in the development process for complex distributed and reactive systems is the identification of an adequate software architecture; this is especially important for long-living systems and products where adaptability to changing requirements, but also correctness and quality are major concerns.

A software architecture, in our view, comprises three central ingredients: the (hierarchical) decomposition of the system into components, the precise specification of

---

* Our research was supported by the Deutsche Forschungsgemeinschaft within the priority program "SoftSpez" (SPP 1064) under project name *InTime*.
** This paper is a revised version of [16].

H. Ehrig et al. (Eds.): INT 2004, LNCS 3147, pp. 29–47, 2004.

the roles and the relationships (often called interfaces) between these components, and the forces and constraints that govern the chosen decomposition and component relationships (cf., for instance, [4,5,10] for other definitions of this term). A key issue in creating a software architecture is, therefore, the decomposition of the system under consideration, and the definition of clear component interfaces.

The importance of system decomposition, as well as of structural and behavioral aspects of component interfaces induces challenges at our approach to system development: How to represent the structural and behavioral aspects of an architecture in a concise yet comprehensive way? Can we systematically turn captured requirements into an initial architecture? For a set of captured requirements, is there hope for automatic construction of components such that they fit into a given architecture? How to refine the components thus obtained without destroying the selected architecture?

In the remainder of this text we deal with these challenges especially in the domain of distributed, reactive systems whose components employ broadcast communication.

UML 2.0: Modeling Architectural Aspects. To represent the important architectural aspects outlined in the preceding subsubsections we employ the notation of UML 2.0 for modeling structures [3,1]. UML 2.0 adopted the concepts of mature modeling languages ROOM [19] (Real-Time Object-Oriented Modeling) and SDL [9] (Specification and Description Language) in order to support specifying components and system architectures of real-time applications.

For a thorough understanding of UML 2.0's recently added capabilities for modeling system architectures we refer the reader to the citations already given. Here it suffices to observe that UML 2.0 provides graphical description techniques for capturing hierarchical structural decomposition (via *structure diagrams* and *class diagrams*), asynchronous point-to-point (p2p) component interactions (via *sequence diagrams*), and individual component behavior (via state machines). These notational elements cover already most of what we have identified above as essential for representing architectures. In the following we assume familiarity with the UML's class diagram notation, and concentrate briefly on structure diagrams describing structured classes, and sequence diagrams; these are the major models we work with in subsequent sections.

We start with a brief overview of UML 2.0's component model. A structured class in UML 2.0 represents a potentially active component whose communication with its environment proceeds by means of asynchronous signal exchange via its ports. A port is an interface point between a class's internals and its environment through which messages are sent either into or out of the class. The outgoing and incoming messages of a port are specified by so called required and provided interfaces, respectively. A structured class can be hierarchically decomposed into parts. Each part represents the use of a class in the context of the containing class. The ports of the parts are wired by connectors that establish p2p communication links between different ports. In the context of structured classes an interface consists of a set of signals. Depending on the role required or provided in association with a port the interfaces defines the messages sent and received through a port. The ports are graphically represented by outlined squares. Optionally the provided and required interfaces of a port are graphically represented by "lollipop" and "socket" notation, respectively. Figure 1 shows an example of a structure diagram of a structured class; we explain the details of this diagram in Section 4.2.

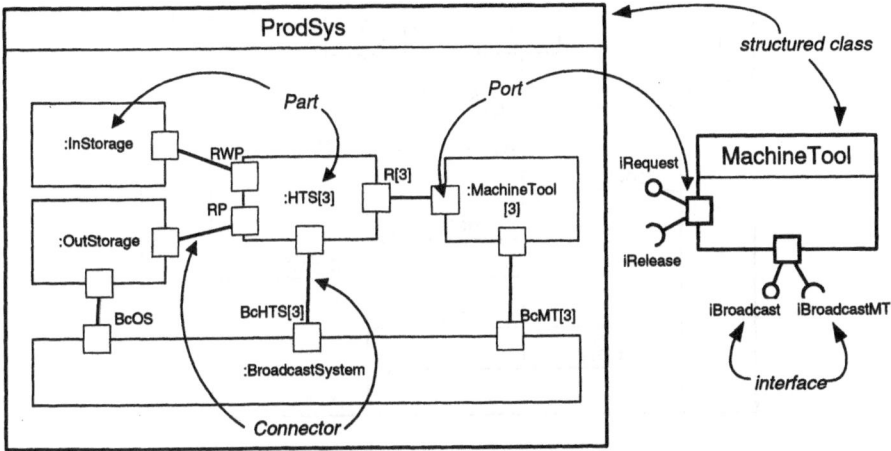

Fig. 1. Structured classes

Structured classes can nest hierarchically to arbitrary depth by means of decomposing their parts; an enclosing class communicates with its parts also via ports and connectors just as it does with its environment. There is no means for accessing the internals of a part directly from the environment of their container. The behavior of each structured class must, in particular, conform to the interfaces the class commits to via its port definitions.

UML 2.0 suggests the use of sequence diagrams (SDs, for short), a variant of Message Sequence Charts [8,11] (MSCs) for modeling interactions. Figure 2 shows an example of an SD. It depicts a certain section of the communication among the four components W, X, Y, and Z within an imaginary distributed system. In this figure, labeled axes represent components, whereas labeled directed arrows indicate message exchange from the source (at the arrow's tail) to the destination component (at the arrow's head). Time advances from the top to the bottom of the figure; this induces a temporal order on the depicted messages. Intuitively, Figure 2 captures a situation where Y and Z, in turn, send the message *subscribe* to X. Then, X receives message *update* from W. Subsequently, X sends message *notify* to Y and Z (in that order). Upon receipt of message *notify*, component Y sends message *request* to W, and receives message *reply* in return.

This simple example already allows us to illustrate one of the strengths of SDs. They contain information on the distribution structure, as well as on the interaction behavior of the system under consideration. This combination helps to make explicit the coordination aspect of system behavior, beyond the local scope of individual components. SDs, such as the one in Figure 2, show one particular interaction pattern (or *scenario*) among the depicted components; there are possibly several other such patterns differing from this particular one. In this sense, SDs complement other forms of specification that capture the *complete* behavior of individual components. Unless stated otherwise we view all SDs as scenarios in the remainder of this text; we refer the reader to [11,13] for other SD interpretations.

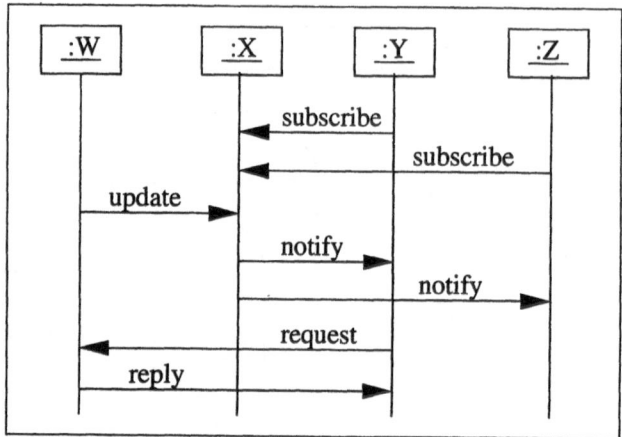

Fig. 2. Simple sequence diagram

Broadcasting vs. UML 2.0's Communication Model. From our brief presentation of the novel descriptions techniques in UML 2.0 in the preceding subsubsections it should be clear that UML 2.0 has strengthened in architectural modeling of systems based on p2p communication. Unfortunately, UML 2.0 has no adequate notational or methodological support for broadcasting. However, because broadcasting is so fundamental in many technical applications, description techniques and methodological steps for capturing architectural requirements concisely are particularly desirable for this application domain.

To reconcile the hierarchic, p2p-based communication model built into UML 2.0 with broadcasting – without drastic changes to UML's description techniques – we introduce a combination of three methodological tools in this paper. First, we suggest to integrate the notion of broadcasting into the system's architecture instead of dealing with it by resorting to special-purpose description techniques, such as the full statechart notation[1]. We define dedicated message mediators at appropriate places in the system's architecture; the purpose of these mediators is to distribute and filter the broadcast messages relevant for particular sub-trees in the component hierarchy. Second, we introduce a graphical description technique, a slight extension of the UML's SDs, for capturing broadcasting scenarios for the services provided by sets of components. Third, we provide transformation procedures for deriving component structure and behavior from the captured scenarios. This allows us to use the scenarios constructively in deriving the system's architecture at all levels of the structural hierarchy.

An Integrated, Architecture-Centric Development Process for Broadcasting in UML 2.0. From these methodological tools we obtain an integrated methodology for deriving interfaces for broadcasting systems using UML 2.0. The idealized development process we follow starts with the capturing of all relevant entities and their (structural)

---

[1] The statechart notation as introduced in [7] employs a broadcasting-based communication model.

relations in the system under consideration in a class diagram. We call the resulting model the system's *domain model*. Then we identify those entities in the domain model which are active components and capture their relevant interaction patterns using broadcast sequence diagrams. These interaction patterns cover architectural manifestations imposed by the requirements explicitly: components and the communication paradigms. This enables us to derive prototypical component structures and behaviors including interfaces for both p2p and broadcast communication within the system which can be refined in subsequent development steps. Following the architectural scheme of introducing dedicated message mediators on all levels of the component hierarchy enables uniform treatment of component refinement; this allows us to perform the development process described so far in a truly iterative, top-down fashion.

Overview. The remainder of this text is structured as follows. In Section 2 we describe the running example – an autonomous transport system – we use to illustrate our approach. The architectural pattern we use to handle broadcasting within the framework of UML 2.0 is the topic of Section 3. In Section 4 we describe our sequence diagram extensions for representing broadcast messages, as well as the constructive transition from scenarios to component structure and behavior. Section 5 contains our conclusions and an outlook.

2   A Running Example

In order to illustrate our methodology we use an early version of the DFG reference case study "Production Automation" [6] which is an autonomous transport system within a production plant. This system transfers workpieces from their present location to another one where the next production step is then carried out. In the beginning, fresh workpieces reside in an "in store". Workpieces whose processing is finished are transported to an "out store". Machine tools perform the actual processing of workpieces. Whenever a machine tool is free it requests to obtain a workpiece, which is then delivered by an autonomous vehicle (termed "holonic transport system", or "HTS" for short).

Machine tools and HTSs use broadcasting to negotiate the delivery of a workpiece: a machine tool broadcasts its requests to all HTSs; the HTSs, in turn, broadcast their offer (an estimate on how long it takes them to satisfy the request). Finally, the machine tool broadcasts which HTS has "won the deal".

The domain model of Figure 3 captures the mentioned entities, as well as a few additional ones, in the form of a UML 2.0 class diagram. The entire production is driven by a production plan, modeled by class `ProdProg`. This plan defines, among others, the required daily throughput of workpieces. The classes `Database` and `Status` model the storage of information about the HTSs' and machine tools' view of the current state of the production process. `Job` is the class for modeling the pick-up tasks negotiated between machine tools and HTSs. The destination of an HTS to pick up a workpiece is captured by the class `Location`. We take the class `BroadcastSystem` as the explicit architectural manifestation of the requirement to use broadcasting in the p2p communication model of UML 2.0. By means of this domain model we have covered the logical associations between the classes of the system under consideration. The corresponding

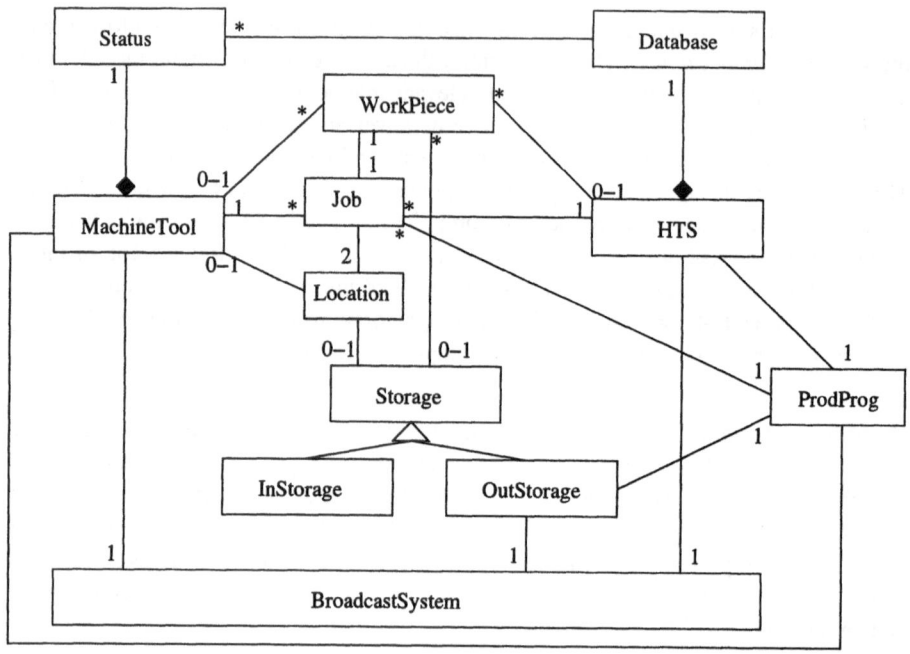

Fig. 3. Domain model

communication paths will be identified by developing interaction scenarios (cf. Section 4.1). Furthermore, the domain model is the starting point for deriving an initial architecture (cf. Section 4.2).

3   An Architectural Pattern for Broadcasting

We face different options in modeling a software architecture supporting broadcast communication. We could, for instance, select a broadcasting-based execution model as provided by standard statecharts [7], and avoid the p2p communication model used in UML 2.0's composite structures right away at the beginning of requirements analysis.

As a consequence we would, however, commit to a very design- and implementation-oriented description technique and an execution model at a very early stage in the development process; in particular, there would be no clear separation of structure and behavior in the system decomposition. In addition to inheriting all of the other problems statecharts bring along with respect to their semantics (cf. [2] for an overview), we would lose much potential for systematic abstraction and refinement of individual components; this is due to the lack of clear component interfaces in statecharts.

Another approach would be to introduce and abuse specialized ports in UML 2.0 like they are provided by ROOM as a connection between actor implementations and the runtime system they operate on. Relying on these service provision points (SPPs) and service access points (SAPs) yields an implicit, implementation-oriented solution

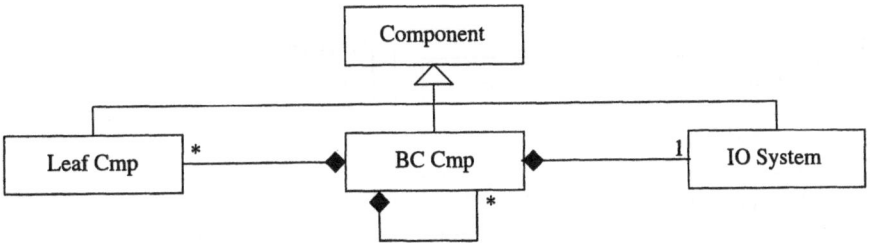

Fig. 4. Architectural pattern for broadcasting

for establishing broadcasting. However, we aim at a more general solution for the problem at the level of architecture (instead of implementation) which is also applicable beyond ROOM's or UML 2.0's tool support, respectively. In particular, more flexible communication regimes than pure broadcasting would lead to a proliferation of SPPs and SAPs; this, in turn, would contribute to obscuring as opposed to clarifying the system's architecture.

As we have outlined in Section 1, we aim at a clear notion of a component and its interfaces, as indispensable ingredients for defining and representing software architectures. Therefore, we stick with UML2.0's novel component, interface, and communication model, and integrate broadcasting into this model by means of explicit components within the software architecture we aim at.

The design we suggest is a variant of the recursive control and subsystem controller patterns described in [18] and [5], respectively. Consider Figure 4 for an overview of the basic structural decomposition we associate with components in our architecture. We distinguish three kinds of components:

- *leaf components*, which form the leafs of the component hierarchy,
- *broadcasting components*, which play the roles of containers for leaf components, nested broadcasting components, and an IO system,
- *IO system components*, which act as mediators for broadcasting messages received or generated by their container.

The idea is that every hierarchically decomposed component has an IO system, which handles the broadcasting of messages among the relevant subcomponents of the container, and between the container and its environment. Intuitively, to perform a broadcast, a component sends a message to the IO system of its container. This IO system is then responsible for distributing this message to all other relevant components within the container, as well as to the IO system of the container's parent in the component hierarchy. This ensures that all broadcast messages reach all components participating in the broadcast communication. In Section 4 we describe the concrete realization of this protocol scheme in more detail.

We note several benefits of this architectural pattern. First, the hierarchic structuring of broadcasting components enables direct application of classical techniques for top-down structural system design. From the viewpoint of broadcasting to refine a component structurally simply means adding a new IO system, and connecting it properly

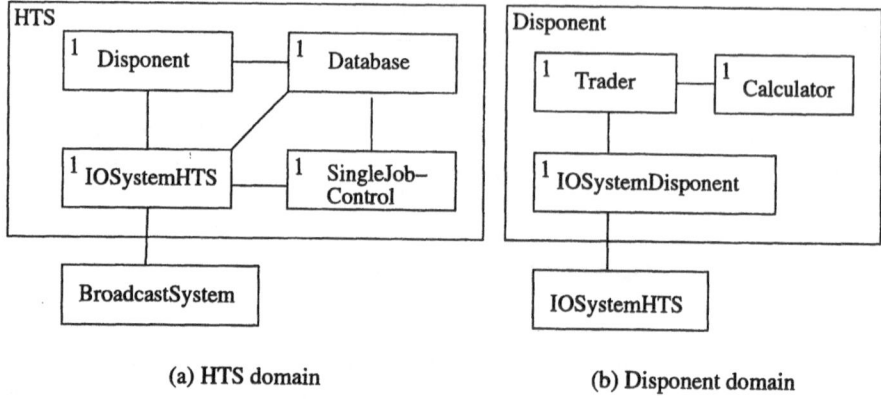

(a) HTS domain   (b) Disponent domain

Fig. 5. Decomposed domain models

to the refining sub-components, and to the container's environment. This is directly supported by UML 2.0's novel component and interface notion. Second, beyond their mere purpose of being mediators for broadcast messages the IO systems can also filter messages irrelevant for a particular subtree in the component hierarchy; this can lead to more efficient design and implementation strategies. Furthermore, components not participating in broadcasting need not to have connections to IO system components at all. Third, the switch from broadcasting to other communication paradigms is immediately possible by simple redefinition of the purpose of the IO systems. According to the architectural pattern above we determine sub-domains for the class HTS of the running example.

Example (continued). Figure 5(a) shows the internal structure of an HTS in more detail. The HTS is an example of a broadcasting component. In addition to Database the HTS contains the components here captured by the classes Disponent, SingleJobControl and IOSystemHTS. Following the pattern introduced above the IOSystemHTS corresponds to the IO system component and handles the communication between the BroadcastSystem and the other subcomponents. The responsibility of IOSystemHTS includes also message filtering, i.e. the IOSystemHTS forwards only broadcast messages to subcomponents which need this message. Disponent and SingleJobControl are responsible for the two main tasks of an HTS: negotiating jobs, and executing an acquired job, respectively.

The disponent is also a broadcasting component. Its refinement is depicted in Figure 5(b). The disponent contains the components IOSystemDisponent, Trader and Calculator. According to our pattern IOSystemDisponent is responsible for broadcast messages and connects the subcomponents of the disponent to the superior broadcasting component IOSystemHTS of the Disponent's environment. Trader and Calculator conduct the negotiation and the computation of a bid for an order, respectively.

4   From Broadcasting Scenarios to Component Interfaces

Now we link our guiding architectural pattern for dealing with broadcasting with methodological steps for constructing both the system's hierarchic decomposition, and prototypes for the behavior of its components, starting from interaction scenarios.

In Section 4.1 we introduce extensions to the UML's Sequence Diagrams (SDs) to capture scenarios for broadcasting interactions; we exploit the requirements captured by such scenarios to systematically construct important parts of the software architecture we target. Furthermore, we briefly discuss the notion of structural refinement which allows us to apply our methodological approach on all levels of structural abstraction. In Sections 4.2 and 4.3 we discuss the systematic derivation of component structure and behavior from captured broadcasting scenarios.

4.1   Sequence Diagrams for Broadcasting

As stated above, the precise description of component interaction is of particular importance in defining an adequate architecture. Modeling component interaction both covers important aspects of the requirements analysis and is a first design step since it identifies "active" components among the entities defined in the domain model (Fig. 3). The major modeling technique of the UML employed in this step are SDs (see Section 1). Yet, SDs provide no notational means for dealing with broadcast communication. Furthermore, there is no sufficient methodological integration with other UML diagrams, such as statecharts. In this section, we show how SDs can be extended easily to model broadcast communication in addition to p2p communication, and to express relations to behavior models. To discuss these extensions, let us consider an application scenario of the autonomous transport system. Figure 6 shows a scenario for the negotiation of a transport task.

Extending Sequence Diagrams for Broadcast Communication Patterns. Just as in classical SDs (as introduced in Section 1) labeled, vertical axes represent part of the behavior of the corresponding components in our extended SD notation. Labeled horizontal arrows indicate p2p communication. Broadcast communication is expressed by communication lines without arrow heads. An outlined circle marks the originator of the message and filled circles mark the receivers of the message. This allows us to model broadcast and even multicast communication succinctly. The semantics of the new communication construct is easily embedded into the semantics of "normal" SDs: Each broadcast line corresponds to a set of messages, each directed from the originator to one recipient. A formal semantics definition for broadcasting in the context of MSCs is defined in [15].

We use additional features of SDs for a succinct representation of interaction patterns like rectangular labeled boxes which denote local actions of a component, and states depicted by labeled boxes with rounded corners. States appear on axes in our SDs; they identify control states of the corresponding component. Using states we can combine SDs to more complex scenarios: Different SDs starting with the same state label express

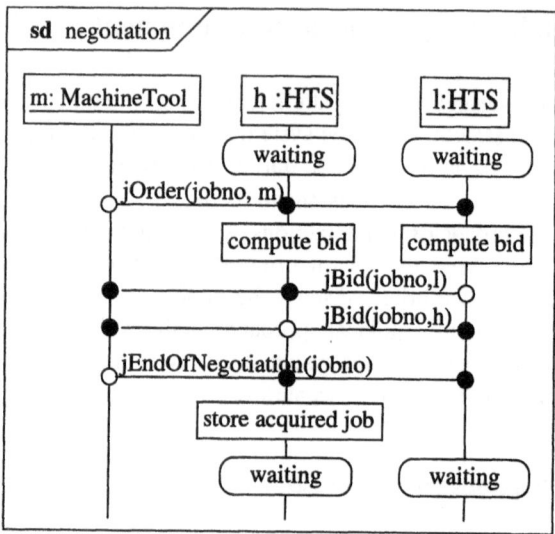

Fig. 6. Broadcast SD for scenario "order negotiation"

nondeterministic choice; SDs starting and ending with the same state label indicate repetition. Both simple and composite SDs should be understood as exemplary interaction patterns (scenarios) in the sense of [11,12], not as complete behavior specifications.

Example. In the example of Figure 6, a machine tool announces an order using broadcast communication. Each HTS calculates the time it needs to satisfy the request within the locally performed action compute bid. In this scenario, two HTSs announce a bid for the order and finally, after the machine tool ends the negotiation, the HTS denoted by h has won the deal. After the negotiation, the HTS components reside in the same state as they started. Figure 7 shows a combination of broadcast and p2p communication occurring during the execution of a transport: When the HTS arrives at a machine tool to pick up a workpiece, it sends a request to the machine tool which, in turn, responds by a release message. Finally, the HTS announces the picking up of the workpiece by means of a broadcast message.

Hierarchic Component Refinement: Integrating the Architectural Pattern with Systematic SD Usage. In Section 3 we have introduced an architectural pattern for dealing with broadcasting messages in a hierarchic decomposition of the system under consideration. We mimic this notion of decomposition by introducing a notion of structural refinement for axes within broadcasting SDs. Before performing a structural refinement we view the component corresponding to the axis under consideration as a "black box", and do not care about how this box internally handles the messages it receives. Afterwards the component has become a "glass box", i.e. we have additional knowledge about its internals that we can refer to in our specifications. Intuitively, a decomposed component relays all messages it receives from its environment (and does not want to react on itself)

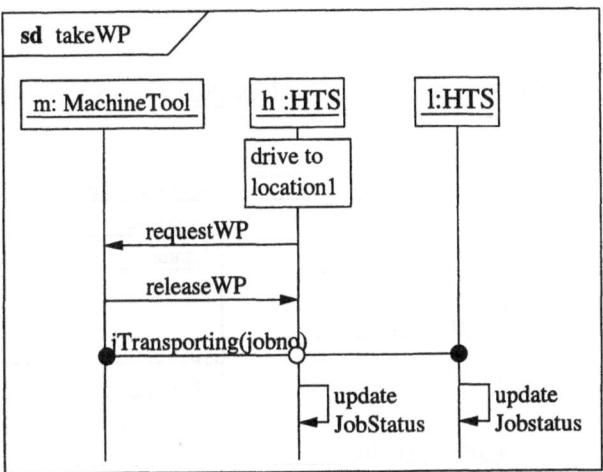

Fig. 7. Broadcast SD for scenario "picking up a workpiece"

to its subcomponents; similarly, it relays all messages received from its subcomponents via its own interfaces to the environment. We explain UML 2.0's notion of structural refinement, which directly corresponds to the idea outlined here, in Section 4.2.

For a structurally refined component within an SD we add further SDs representing the communication patterns within the refined architecture. These SDs capture the interactions among the refining components, as well as the relay of messages between the refined and the refining components. In the decomposition we respect the following important rule: the SDs of the decomposed view have to be consistent with SDs of the non-decomposed view. Messages arriving at the refined component in the abstract SD must also occur (as relayed messages) in the refining SD; similarly, messages emanating from the refined component in the abstract SD must also occur (as relayed messages) in the refining SD. We represent messages sent to or received from the environment of a refining SD by lines and arrows ending or originating at the bounding box of the SD, respectively. For a formal treatment of structural refinement within sequence diagrams see [11].

Example (continued). In the following we turn our attention to the running example again, and derive SDs for the different hierarchic levels for HTS and Disponent introduced in Section 3. Figures 6, 7, 8 and 9 depict a subset of the scenarios related to the top level domain (cf. Figure 3) and different decomposed levels (cf. Figure 5), respectively.

As an example for structural refinement we decompose the axis corresponding to component h: HTS in the scenario for order negotiation (cf. Figure 6). The decomposition of this axis is shown in Figure 8; it respects the architectural pattern introduced in Section 3 (cf. Figures 4 and 5(a)). The refined SD shows the internal interactions within the HTS, which are necessary to decide whether a bid is submitted for an order, and to check whether the negotiation has been successful. The messages exchanged between

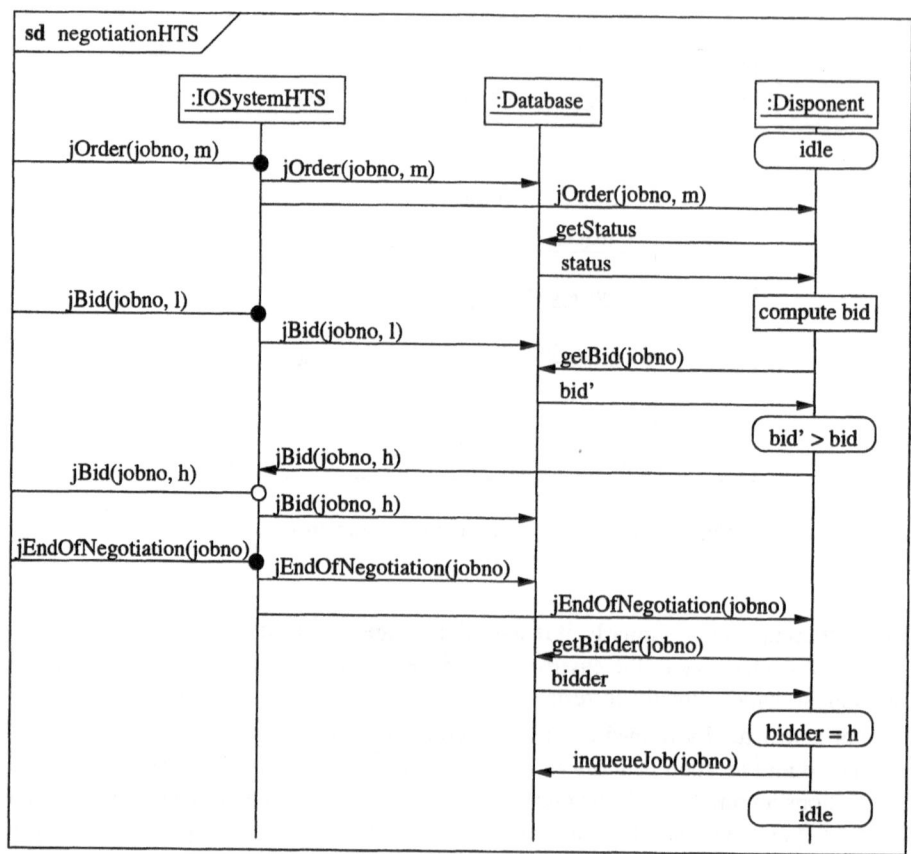

Fig. 8. Refined HTS axis

IOSystemHTS and the environment of HTS match with the messages associated with the h : HTS axis of Figure 6.

In Figure 9 we show the next hierarchical level according to the domain model of Figure 5(b), obtained by refining the disponent axis in the SD of Figure 8. After the trader has received an order message from the IOSystemDisponent, the calculator computes a bid, respecting the status received. Then the trader conducts the further negotiations with the aid of IOSystemDisponent.

The refined scenarios in Figures 8 and 9 show that every message according to broadcasting is relayed via the IOSystem axis as claimed in Section 3. Our next methodological step is to take the captured scenarios as a starting point for constructively deriving structural and behavioral aspects of the architecture under consideration.

4.2   Component Structure

Recall from Section 1 that an important part of a software architecture is the decomposition of the system under consideration. We use UML 2.0's hierarchic structure diagrams

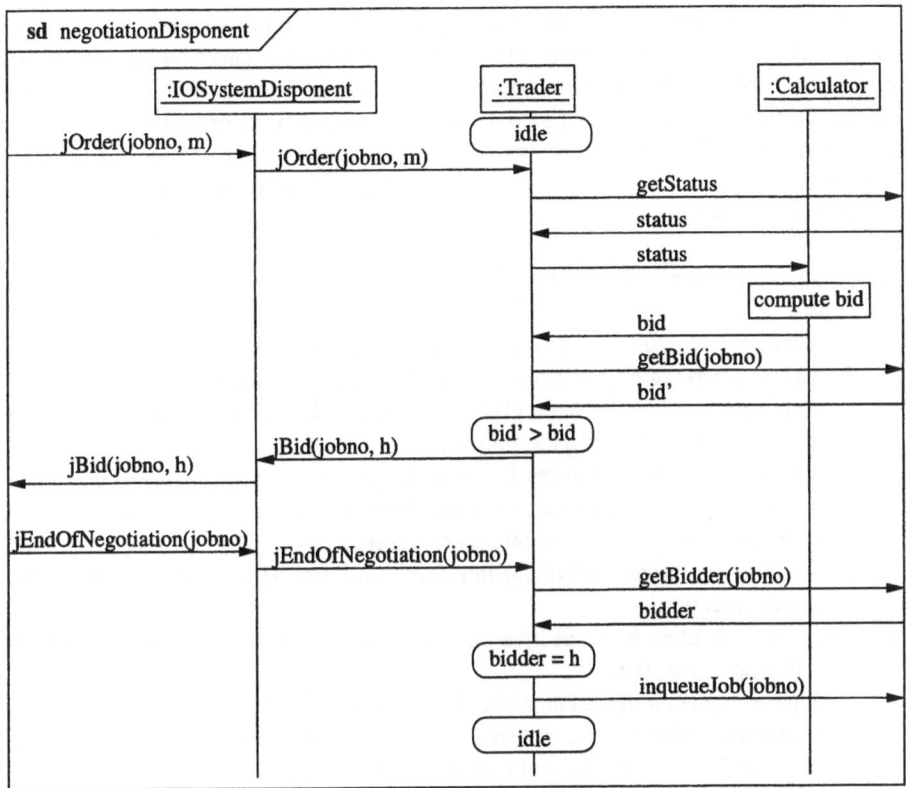

Fig. 9. Refined Disponent axis

for representing system structures. Consider, as an example, the structure diagram of Figure 1; it displays items for the HTSs, the stores, the machine tools, and broadcast system as an exemplary subset of the entities contained in Figure 3. Each member of this set is a part of the structured class ProdSys. Every HTS has connectors to each of the stores, as well as to every machine tool, with corresponding ports. Moreover, there exist connectors between the HTSs and the broadcast system; similar connections exist for the machine tools and the out store.

Systematic generation of component structures. In the following, we suggest a method for developing structure diagrams using the knowledge captured during requirements analysis, and expressed via the domain model and the SDs of Section 4.1. We show how structured classes, its interfaces and its wired parts can be derived systematically and discuss the embedding of broadcast communication using these concepts. The model we obtain serves as a starting point for the development of a system design, which can be completed, generalized, and optimized by subsequent refinement steps. The advantage of the proposed procedure is that we obtain *consistency with the requirements analysis* by construction.

We start with an overview of the steps to get a first sketch of a structure diagram. We assume that, starting from the domain model, the active components have been identified already by capturing interaction scenarios, as shown in Section 4.1. The procedure consists of three phases: First, the container class and its parts describing the system are defined (steps 1+2, below). Second, interfaces are derived from the SDs (step 3). Third, the interfaces are assigned to ports which are linked by connectors (steps 4+5). The methodical steps are as follows:

1. Create a container class which will contain the entire parts identified in the further steps[2].
2. a) Create a part in the container for each class which appears in the SDs as an axis.
   b) Create a part which performs the broadcast message passing, if broadcast communication occurs between axes in the SDs under consideration. We call this part *broadcast system* in the following.
3. a) Create up to two interfaces for each pair of classes which exchange regular messages in SDs. Include all messages belonging to one of the communication directions into one of these interfaces, respectively.
   b) If necessary, create individual interfaces for each class which uses broadcast communication.
4. Assign to each class its respective ports associated with the respective interfaces created in previous step.
5. Establish a connector in the container class between any two ports derived from p2p communication interfaces; establish a connector in the container class between any port derived for broadcasting and the broadcast system.

Steps 3 through 5 are straightforward for p2p communication: After interface generation we just need to create a port which associates a provided or a required role to these interfaces, respectively, and link this port to the port of its communication partner. Unfortunately, we cannot use connectors and ports in such a straightforward way for broadcast communication, because in general there are more than two communication partners involved.

Instead, we handle broadcasting by introducing an explicit class for broadcast communication, in line with the architectural pattern introduced in Section 3. Each class which is involved in broadcast communication is equipped with a port connecting it to this broadcast class (step 3(b)). This approach models broadcasting explicitly.

Example. By means of our running example we illustrate the methodological steps introduced above: First we create the structured class ProdSys which will embed all parts of the system communicating at top level (step 1). Then we derive the parts of type HTS, InStorage, OutStorage and MachineTool from a set of top level SDs[3] to be embedded in the container (step 2 (a)). Since broadcast communication is used in these SDs we create a part of type BroadcastSystem (step 2 (b)). For the generation of interfaces, let us consider the handshake communication HTS ↔ MachineTool. From

---

[2] UML 2.0 requires a top-level container for all parts of the system.

[3] Two examples are shown in the Figures 6, 7.

Table 1. Protocols

«interface» iRequest	«interface» iBroadcastMT
requestWP() : void	jOrder(jobno,m) : void
requestPlace() : void	jEndofNegotiation(jobno) : void

«interface» iRelease	«interface» iBroadcast
releaseWP() : void	jBid(jobno) : void
releasePlace() : void	jTransporting(jobno) : void
(a)	⋮
	jFinished(jobno) : void

(b)

the SDs, the interfaces iRequest and iRelease are created. Table 1(a) depicts these interfaces. Analogously we proceed with other pairs of communicating capsules (step 3a). For broadcast communication we consider every class participating in broadcast communication. We create an individual interface containing messages which each class sends and a common interface which contains all broadcast messages received by all classes. Table 1(b) shows the individual interface iBroadcastMT for class MachineTool and the common interface Broadcast for all broadcasting classes (step 3(b)). Every class gets its ports with appropriate interfaces according to its communication roles, e.g. class MachineTool gets a port providing interface iRequest and requiring interface iRelease and a port providing interface iBroadcast and requiring interface iBroadcastMT (step 4). Finally the connectors between the related handshake ports and between broadcast ports and broadcast system are added in the structure of class ProdSys (step 5). The result is a first prototype of the system's structure diagram. Clearly, we have to adjust the cardinality of the parts HTS and MachineTool to their required number, as given in a concrete instance of the system. The resulting structure diagram is shown in Figure 1.

Hierarchical decomposition. At nested hierarchical levels the generation scheme can be simplified. Step 2(b) and 3(b) are omitted, because broadcast communication is only performed in the top level SDs. In decomposed views broadcast messages are distributed by respective IOSystems. Thereby broadcast communication is transformed to p2p communication and only relevant messages are forwarded. Step 1 is omitted, because the container class with its public ports is already given by the previous generation of the more abstract level.

Example (continued). As an example, we use the SDs of the decomposed HTS view (one of them is depicted in Figure 8) to derive the structure diagram of the class HTS in Figure 10(a). According to step 2(a) we derive the parts of type IOSystemHTS, Disponent, Database and SingleJobControl. Creating interfaces, assigning ports and establishing connectors for internal p2p communication is treated as before. However, there is a new kind of p2p communication between parts and environment

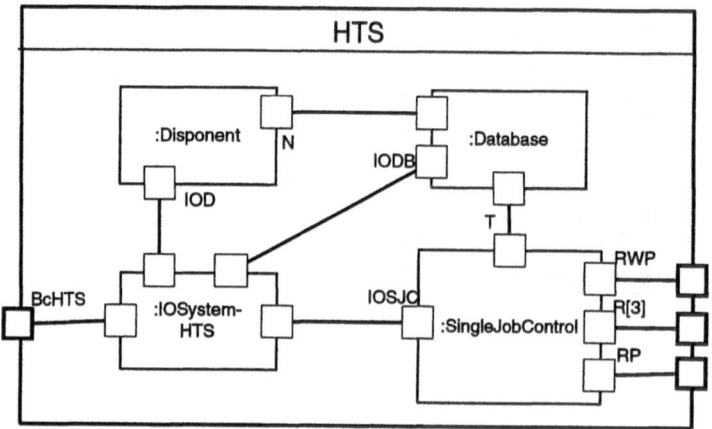

(a) Capsule diagram of HTS

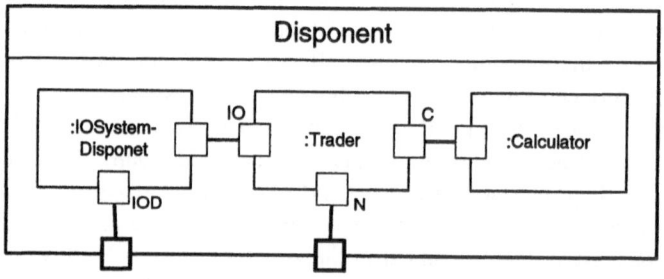

(b) Capsule diagram of Disponent

Fig. 10. Decomposed structure views

of HTS, for example IOSystemHTS↔environment. Hence there must already exist interfaces which contain these messages and public ports associated to the respective interfaces. In fact this is true for the interfaces iBroadcastHTS and iBroadcast (Tab.1(a)) and the respective port in the example under consideration. Thus, we can omit creating interfaces for those communication partners. Only a respective port has to be assigned to the class and in structure of class HTS the port of the corresponding part has to be connected to the respective public port. This works gracefully because we obeyed the rules of structural refinement in developing the SDs.

Analogously we derive the structure of the class Disponent of Figure 10(b) by means of SDs such as the one shown in Figure 9.

4.3   Component Behavior

In this section, we give a rough sketch of the derivation of behavior specifications of the system components from the scenarios collected during the requirements analysis. Again, this development step can be carried out automatically, using the algorithm presented in [13]. This algorithm takes a set of sequence diagrams as input, and generates an automaton specification for the component under consideration as output. This algorithm employs the state labels introduced in Section 4.1 to determine execution orderings between the specified scenarios. It consists essentially of four steps:

1. *Projection*: After having selected the component for which we want to construct an automaton, we project each of the given SDs onto this component,
2. *Normalization*: We determine the transition-path segments defined by the projected SDs, according to the state labels appearing in the SDs; if necessary, we add appropriate state labels at the beginning and at the end of the projected SDs,
3. *Transformation into an automaton*: We turn every message arrow appearing in an SD into a transition of the automaton; if necessary, we add intermediate states to link transitions, such that they correspond to a sequence of messages within a normalized SD,
4. *Optimization*: We apply heuristics, or use algorithms known from automata theory for automaton minimization.

As an example, let us consider the part of type trader appearing in Figure 10(b). The input source for the generation of a statechart of the class is the SD in Figure 9. The states on the axis of the trader express that the execution ends in the same state as it started (named idle). Two further state conditions on bids and names of bidders allow the truncation of the negotiation; they yield a split of the SD into three parts at this point in step (2) of the transformation procedure. These state conditions allow us to specify alternatives at this points which we have omitted here for brevity. For a detailed model, we refer the reader to [14]. An automaton resulting from the generation which does include choices is shown in Figure 11. Note that this statechart has to handle only the messages relevant for the trader.

5   Conclusions and Outlook

We have presented an approach at incorporating broadcast communication into the modeling of architectural design using UML 2.0. To that end, we have introduced and employed an architectural pattern for capturing broadcasting by means of explicit components on all levels of the component hierarchy. This introduces broadcasting seamlessly on the basis of UML 2.0's p2p communication model in the area of composite structures. Dealing with broadcasting explicitly on the level of a logical architecture of the system under consideration has several advantages. It supports classical top-down structural system decomposition, and introduces a flexible, adaptable, and configurable communication mechanism we can exploit during further stages of requirements analysis and specification.

We have also shown that by means of only few syntactic extensions we can employ the UML's sequence diagrams for transparently capturing broadcasting scenarios. This

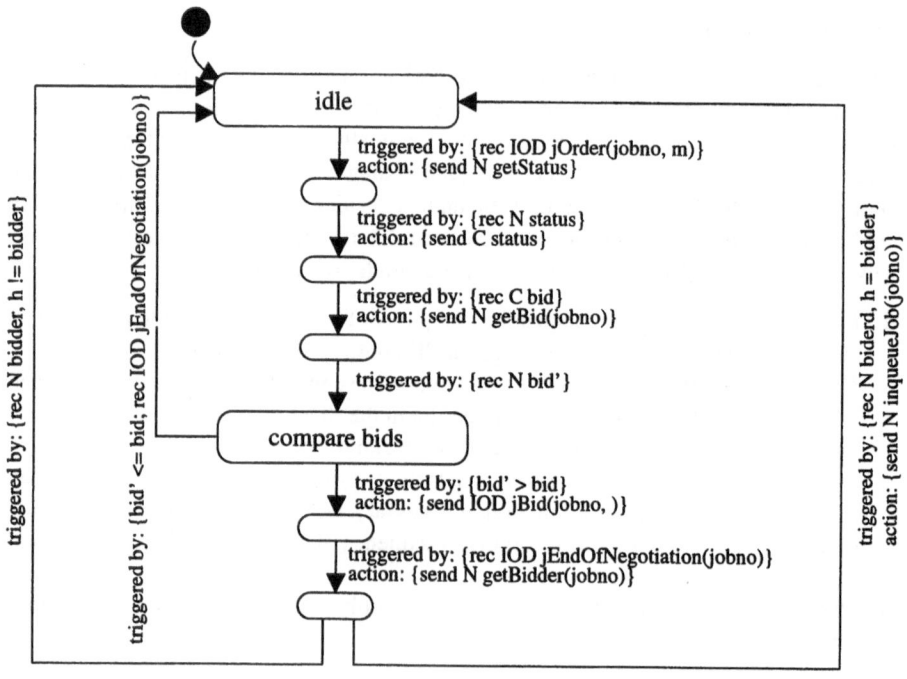

Fig. 11. An optimized statechart for the trader

enables concentrating on use cases and service-oriented specification techniques also in the development process for broadcasting systems. Making these extensions an integral part of the language allows both for a compact modeling of broadcasting and for adopting these aspects systematically into the systems architecture. Furthermore, integration of timing aspects, such as the durations of communications, can be easily integrated along the lines of what is already available for regular sequence diagrams in the UML [1,17].

Prototypical models can be generated automatically from broadcasting scenarios captured by means of SDs. The resulting diagrams provide a high level architecture description and are ideally suited to serve as a starting point for the actual design of the system to be developed, because they guarantee consistency with the requirements analysis by construction. The initial architecture can be refined in subsequent development steps: For example, new messages can be introduced or entire interaction interfaces can be reorganized in order to develop more general interfaces used by strutured classes. A structuring of these development steps can be based on formal notions of refinement, even supported with guidance given by constructive rules (see for instance [11]).

With UML, we have employed a powerful and widely used modeling language to demonstrate the benefits of our approach. Our approach has the potential to support the integration of flexible communication regimes beyond broadcasting into arbitrary software architecture descriptions. Incorporating this support as a general design principle into corresponding case tools is a necessary and promising area of further development of our approach.

References

1. UML 2.0 superstructure. http://www.omg.org/uml/, August 2003.
2. M. v. d. Beeck. A Comparison of Statecharts Variants. In H. Langmaack, W.-P. de Roever, and J. Vytopil, editors, *Proc. Formal Techniques in Real-Time and Fault-Tolearnt Systems (FTRTFT'94)*, volume 863 of *LNCS*, pages 128–148. Springer, 1994.
3. M. Björkander and C. Kobryn. Architecting systems with UML 2.0. IEEE Computer Society, July/August 2003.
4. F. Buschmann, R. Meunier, H. Rohnert, P. Sommerlad, and M. Stal. *A System of Patterns. Pattern-Oriented Software Architecture*. Wiley, 1996.
5. D. D'Souza and A. C. Wills. *Objects, Components, and Frameworks with UML–The Catalysis Approach*. Addison Wesley, 1998.
6. Fraunhofer-Institut für Produktionstechnik und Automatisierung IPA. Referenzfallstudie Produktionstechnik v1.3. http://tfs.cs.tu-berlin.de/SPP/themenbereiche.html, 1999.
7. D. Harel and M. Politi. *Modeling Reactive Systems with Statecharts. The STATEMATE approach*. McGraw-Hill, 1998.
8. ITU-T. *ITU-T Recommendation Z.120 – Message Sequence Chart (MSC 96)*. ITU-T, Geneva, 1996.
9. ITU-T. *ITU-T Recommendation Z.100 – Specification and description language (SDL)*. ITU-T, Geneva, 1999.
10. P. Kruchten. *The Rational Unified Processs. An Introduction*. Addison Wesley, 1999.
11. I. Krüger. *Distributed System Design with Message Sequence Charts*. PhD thesis, Technische Universität München, 2000.
12. I. Krüger. Notational and Methodical Issues in Forward Engineering with MSCs. In T. Systä, editor, *Proceedings of OOPSLA 2000 Workshop: Scenario-based round trip engineering*. Tampere University of Technology, Software Systems Laboratory, Report 20, 2000.
13. I. Krüger, R. Grosu, P. Scholz, and M. Broy. From MSCs to statecharts. In F. J. Rammig, editor, *Distributed and Parallel Embedded Systems*, pages 61–71. Kluwer Academic Publishers, 1999.
14. I. Krüger, W. Prenninger, and R. Sandner. Development of an autonomous transport system using UML-RT. Technical report, Technische Universität München, 2002.
15. I. Krüger, W. Prenninger, and R. Sandner. Semantics of Broadcast MSCs. In *Semantic Foundations of Engineering Design Languages (SFEDL)*, 2002.
16. I. Krüger, W. Prenninger, R. Sandner, and M. Broy. From scenarios to hierarchical broadcasting software architectures using UML-RT. *International Journal of Software Engineering and Knowledge Engineering (IJSEKE)*, 2002.
17. J. Rumbaugh, I. Jacobson, and G. Booch. *The Unified Modeling Language Reference Manual*. Addison-Wesley, Reading, Massachusetts, USA, 1999.
18. B. Selic. Recursive Control. In R. Martin, D. Riehle, and F. Buschmann, editors, *Pattern Languages of Program Design 3*, Software Patterns Series. Addison-Wesley, 1998.
19. B. Selic, G. Gullekson, and P. T. Ward. *Real-Time Object-Oriented Modeling*. Wiley, 1994.

An Engineer's Workstation to Support Integrated Development of Flexible Production Control Systems

Wilhelm Schäfer[1], Robert Wagner[1], Jürgen Gausemeier[2], and Raimund Eckes[2]

[1] Software Engineering Group
Department of Computer Science
University of Paderborn
Warburger Straße 100 D-33098 Paderborn, Germany
{wilhelm|wagner}@uni-paderborn.de
[2] Computer Integrated Manufacturing Group
Heinz Nixdorf Institute
Fuerstenallee 11
D-33102 Paderborn, Germany
{Juergen.Gausemeier|Raimund.Eckes}@hni.uni-paderborn.de

Abstract. Today's manufacturing industry demands flexible and decentralized production control systems to avoid hours of down time of the production line in case of a failure of a single central production control computer or program. Additionally, today's market forces demand smaller lot sizes and a more flexible mixture of different products manufactured in parallel on one production line. These requirements increase the complexity of the control software. Consequently, sophisticated techniques for the development of such production systems are needed. In this paper we present an overview of our seamless methodology for integrated design, analysis, and validation for such production control systems. We illustrate our approach by an existing material flow system which is a major part of a real production system. We show how our modelling approach is used for simulation facilities, code generation for programmable logic controllers, and maintenance purposes.

1 Introduction

Current production control systems for any complex industrial good, e.g. a factory for cars, face two major problems. First, production control systems need to become more decentralized to increase their availability. It is no longer acceptable that a failure of a single central production control computer or program causes hours of down time for the whole production line. Second, today's market forces demand smaller lot sizes and a more flexible mixture of different products manufactured in parallel on one production line. These requirements result in highly complex systems, especially concerning the control software. Consequently, sophisticated techniques to develop such kind of production systems are needed.

H. Ehrig et al. (Eds.): INT 2004, LNCS 3147, pp. 48–68, 2004.

The ISILEIT project aims at the development of a seamless methodology for the integrated design, analysis, and validation of distributed production control systems. Its particular emphasis lies on (re-)using existing techniques, which are used by engineers in industry, and improving them with respect to formal analysis, simulation, and automatic code generation. The methodology defined in the ISILEIT project consists of several consecutive design steps covering all aspects of software and system design.

At the beginning of every system design process a system specification describing the functionality of the system has to be developed. In our case, the engineer uses an intelligent configuration system for the layout of the production system. For the early detection of faults in planning, the configuration system employs rules running in the background. Thus, specification errors are recognized very early in the development process and are eliminated immediately.

The configuration of a production system also requires a specification of the functional requirements for the control software. This specification is done by using a graphical language which integrates SDL block diagrams, UML class diagrams, and UML behaviour diagrams like collaboration diagrams, activity diagrams, and statecharts in a visual specification (or even programming) language. This language is also considered to be a programming language because the code generation algorithm which has been developed within the ISILEIT project produces a complete executable version of the control software of a production control system.

Generally, generating code from UML behaviour diagrams is not well understood. Frequently, the semantics of a UML behaviour diagram depends on the topic and the aspect that is modelled and on the designer that created it. In addition, UML behaviour diagrams usually model only example scenarios and do not describe all possible cases and possible exceptions. To overcome these problems we restrict the UML notation to a subset of the language that has a precise semantics. In addition, we define which kind of diagram should be used for which purpose and how the different kinds of diagrams are integrated to a consistent overall view. This precise semantics allows the automatic translation of the integrated diagrams to object-oriented programming languages like Java and C++ or even non-object-oriented languages for PLCs (Programmable Logic Controllers), which are widely used in the production industry. In this paper we present the PLC code generation for a material flow system used within our ISILEIT case study.

One of the main problems in today's manufacturing industry is long down times of production lines due to long testing phases of newly installed software. Our approach allows to validate the control software and to simulate the production process beforehand in order to shorten software reconfiguration down times of physical assembly lines. The validation and simulation is based on the generation of an executable model using the system design model. The generated executable model is pure Java code, which can be compiled and executed on any computer platform supporting Java. It is used to simulate the system and allows observing and visualizing the resulting system behaviour within a Virtual Reality (VR) application.

Finally, when the manufacturing system is built up and the software is running on the PLCs, an Augmented Reality (AR) tool is used. It augments the engineer's field of view with different states of the manufacturing system, i.e. the user sees the real (physical) manufacturing system plus the digital augmented state information. The states displayed refer to the different components of the system. This includes all components of the production system as developed by the different domains, namely mechanics, pneumatics, electrics and even the software. As every component state is perceived, the engineer is able to see all dependencies between state changes of the different components during operation of the physical system. Such an AR tool provides benefits like online debugging, training, and better maintenance facilities. In the end it leads to a better overall understanding of the system and supports communication between the engineers from the different domains.

The paper is organized as follows. The next section discusses related work in more detail. In section 3 the used case study is described. The defined seamless methodology is addressed in section 4 where the different design phases are described as well. In section 5 the code generation for programmable logic controllers is presented. Our integrated tool support with simulation facilities is introduced in section 6. The following section 7 shows how augmented reality technology is used for the maintenance of the running system. In the last section the paper is concluded.

2   Related Work

Current approaches for the specification of production agents use either SDL [16] or statecharts [11]. SDL is very popular in the electrical and mechanical engineering community. SDL block diagrams are used to specify processes and channels between such processes as well as messages passed via these channels. The behaviour of embedded system processes is specified using either SDL process diagrams or statecharts. Both notations basically model finite state automata which react on signals by executing actions, sending signals, and changing to new states. Both languages have a well defined formal semantics and tool support for analysis, simulation, and code generation [1, 6, 12, 14, 23, 26].

Compared to SDL process diagrams, statecharts provide more expressive language features like nested states, and-states, and history-states. In addition, the modelling of the internal process behaviour becomes the domain of software developers (instead of mechanical or electrical engineers) who are more used to statecharts than to SDL process diagrams. Thus, we decided to adopt statecharts for the purpose of modelling internal process behaviour.

However, statecharts (as well as SDL process diagrams) lack appropriate means for the specification of the actual actions triggered by the received signals. Usually, one has to use pseudocode for this purpose and in case of code generation one actually deals with the nasty details of current textual programming languages. Statecharts provide sophisticated means for the specification of (concurrent) control flows for reactive objects. However, a statecharts purpose is to abstract from the complex application-specific object structures that make up the concrete states of a system. Statecharts do not explicitly deal with the values of attributes or links to other objects nor with the evolution and changes of these object structures caused by the execution of usual methods.

The specification of application-specific object structures is a well-known application area for graph grammars, cf. [24, 25]. Basically, a graph rewrite rule allows the specification of changes to complex object structures by a pair of before and after snapshots. The before snapshot specifies which part of the object structure should be changed and the after snapshot specifies how it should look afterwards, without caring how these changes are achieved. While graph grammars are appropriate for the specification of object structure modifications, they lack appropriate means for the specification of control flows. Even the well-known graph rewrite system PROGRES [25] provides only textual control structures.

To overcome this problem, in previous work we introduced UML activity diagrams as high-level control flow notation for graph rewrite rules, cf. [9, 17]. For the specification of the reactive behaviour of communicating and collaborating production agents we integrated graph grammars, "hiding" them behind a collaboration diagram notation to avoid acceptance problems within industry [20].

3   Case Study: A Flexible Production System

The case study regarded in the ISILEIT project concerns a flexible and autonomous production control system for automated manufacturing. The production system depicted in Figure 1 consists of several NC controlled processing machines, robots, and manual work places which are connected by a rail-bound material flow system. The substantial components of this modular system are self-propelled transportation units[1], switches[2], and fixing stations, as well as straight and curved monorail tracks.

Note that in our case study rail-bound shuttles for the transportation tasks are employed. In contrast to that, in the reference case study *production automation* free-ranging Automatic Guided Vehicles (AGV) are used. However, this does not have any impact on our defined methodology for the integrated design of such systems. Thus, our seamless methodology is also applicable without any restrictions for the reference case study.

The experimental setup made in the mechanical laboratory for computer integrated production implements a manufacturing system for the production of bottle openers. The system consists of four stations which are connected by a material flow system. Figure 2 shows a schematic overview of our case study.

A shuttle is electrically propelled and moves in exactly one direction. It rotates on the main loop until the control assigns a production task to it. If a

---

[1] called shuttles in the following

[2] called transfer gate in the following

Fig. 1. Flexible production system and its components

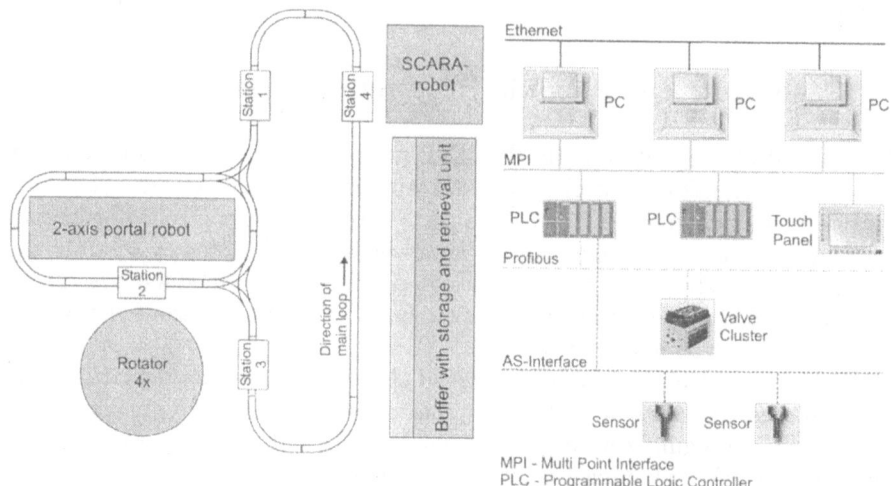

Fig. 2. Schematic overview of our case study

task was assigned to a shuttle, the first step is to move to the manual work place (station 1) where the production starts. There, the shuttle is equipped by a worker with the appropriate material. A touch panel with a display shows the worker which pieces are needed. After the shuttle is completely equipped the worker pushes a button to signal the material flow system to proceed. Now the shuttle moves to the portal robot (station 2) where the actual assembly takes place. The portal robot takes the material from the shuttle and hands it over

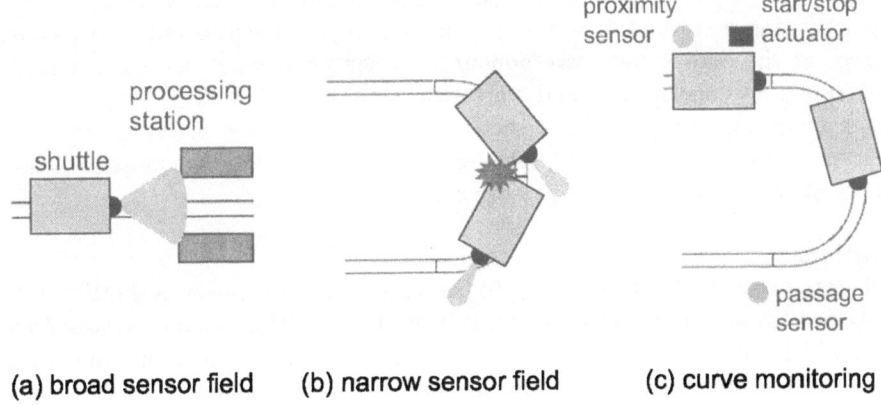

(a) broad sensor field   **(b) narrow sensor field**   **(c) curve monitoring**

Fig. 3. Curve monitoring for collision avoidance

to the rotator, where the required manufacturing step is performed. After that, the portal robot takes the assembled good from the rotator and puts it on the waiting shuttle. The shuttle now moves to the integrated buffer storage (station 4) where it is unloaded by a SCARA[3] robot. Within this buffer, goods, parts, and materials are stored temporarily to ensure a continuous supply of necessary components. If the control does not assign a new task to the shuttle, it will rotate on the main loop until it gets one. Note that, for the moment, station 3 has no task within the current manufacturing process. However, in the near future it will connect this manufacturing system to a second one.

The decentralized production control system consists of PCs on the supervisory control level and Programmable Logic Controllers (PLC) on the cell level. The actuators and sensors are connected to the PLC via an Actuator Sensor Interface (ASI). The communication among PCs and PLCs is implemented by a multi-point interface (MPI, Siemens AG). Higher-level tasks, e.g. planning, order assignment, and coordination of local activities of all controllers are done at the supervisory control level. The PLCs on the cell level are responsible for the control of local components such as stations or robots.

Shuttles
Shuttles are equipped with an opto-electronic distance sensor to prevent rear-end collisions with other shuttles. However, the range noticed by the sensor is reduced laterally in order to prevent unintentional stoppage of a shuttle by objects residing near the track. This leads to the fact that collision avoidance does not work properly within curves.

To prevent rear-end collisions within curves the control has to ensure that only one shuttle enters a curve. This is achieved by the employment of additional sensor and actuator technology (cf. Figure 3). If a shuttle enters a curve the

---

[3] Selective Compliance Assembly Robot Arm

shuttle is detected by a proximity sensor. The control stops all following shuttles by activating a start/stop actuator. This blockage is released only if a passage sensor at the end of the curve announces a shuttle leaving the curve area. In our case study the sensors and start/stop actuators of stations are reused for the monitoring of these critical sections. For example, the presence sensors of station 3 and station 4 serve as curve entrance sensors, while the presence sensor of the station 1 acts as curve passage sensor.

Stations

All stations are built-up according to the same principle. Before a shuttle enters a station the speed of the shuttle is reduced. Each station provides a start/stop unit which consists of a stop pin and a starting actuator. The stop pin ensures that shuttles are stopped. The presence of a shuttle is announced to the control by an inductive proximity sensor. Before any processing starts, the shuttle is fixed by a pressure-controlled mechanical interlock. This is done for a precise positioning of the shuttle. The interlock has to be released before the shuttle is started by the starting actuator.

Transfer Gates

Within our material flow system two types of transfer gates can be identified: those that branch out of a track (Brancher) and those that merge two tracks into one (Joiner). Although they are used differently, they are identical in construction and operate on the same principle. Figure 4 shows a schematic overview of a transfer gate.

A transfer gate consists of an interlock, a double-action pneumatic cylinder, and two proximity sensors, one for each switching direction. For safety reasons the transfer gate is generally locked. The first step for switching into another direction is to disengage the interlock by activating the singleaction pneumatic cylinder. Now the transfer gate can change its direction by turning into the new position.

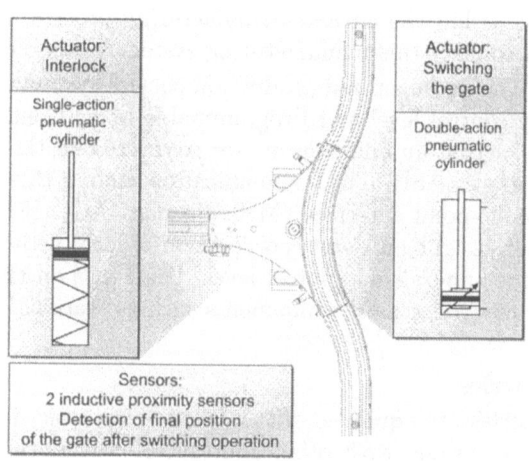

Fig. 4. Transfer Gate

This is done by the double-action pneumatic cylinder. When the switching operation is completed, the final position is detected by one of the proximity sensors. After that, the pressure-controlled mechanical interlock has to be re-engaged. The occurrence of a switching failure can be recognized only by an absent sensor trigger after a predefined timeout. Additionally, before starting the switching process, the control has to guarantee that no shuttles are located on or are entering the transfer gate. This is achieved analogous to the curve monitoring for collision avoidance described previously.

4   Modelling Approach

In this section we give a brief overview about our modelling approach. A more detailed description can be found in [20] and a graphical overview on our software development process in [22]. The software development process for the above mentioned case study is defined by six phases:

Analysis Consolidation Phase. Based on the results of a previous informal requirements- gathering phase which is beyond the scope of this paper, in this phase the topology of the planned production control system is modelled. This includes the identification of the number and types of participating processes as well as the definition of communication channels and of all kinds of interchanged signals.

We use SDL block diagrams for this purpose since SDL block diagrams are very popular in engineering disciplines and this work is done in close collaboration with mechanical and electrical engineers. However, many of the missing concepts for large- scale and complex system development have been integrated into the UML 2.0 proposal of the main tool vendors [21]. Hence, they are likely to become a part of the standard UML and will therefore be widely available in the industry. Thus, in the near future SDL specifications may become obsolete and be replaced by the new UML 2.0 standard for the same purpose.

Design Phase. In the next step, one derives the initial (UML) class diagram of the desired system. Here, each process(type) identified in the SDL block diagram generates a class in the class diagram. In addition, each signal received by a process in an SDL block diagram creates a signal method in the corresponding class.

Reactive Behaviour Modelling Phase. SDL block diagrams (and the derived class diagrams) specify the particular signals which are provided and understood by the different processes. Now we have to define how each process will react on these signals. Thus, for each process class, one has to provide a statechart describing the general process behaviour. These statecharts should at least cover all signals that are understood by / declared in the corresponding process class.

In the engineering field, SDL process diagrams are usually used for this purpose. We chose statecharts due to their additional expressive power over SDL process diagrams provided by nested states and and-states.

Action Modelling Phase. Statecharts specify in which states a certain process reacts to a particular signal. In response to a signal, a process might change its state and execute some additional activities. For a flexible production agent, these activities might again include complex computations. These complex computations might employ or modify complex object-oriented data structures in order to reflect the surrounding world or the execution of manufacturing plans for certain products. For the specification of such complex computations we use UML-like collaboration diagrams with a precisely defined operational semantics based on graph-grammar theory [9]. Consequently, we use collaboration diagrams to specify complex control flows of methods employed as actions within statecharts.

Frequently, one will need more than a single collaboration diagram to model a number of object structure modifications. Therefore, we combine statecharts (and activity diagrams) with collaboration diagrams yielding a powerful visual specification language. Basically, we allow using collaboration diagrams as the specification of activities instead of just pseudocode statements.

Verification. When the system design model, which will be used for code generation, reaches a mature state it will be verified. This proves the correctness of the specified control software. The verification is done by formal model-checking techniques based on ASM and AsmL [22].

Code Generation Phase. Once all aspects of the system are specified, the FUJABA environment is able to generate a complete, executable Java implementation from the class and behaviour diagrams. This implementation is further used for the simulation phase that follows. Furthermore, as will be explained later, generation for PLCs is also possible and supported.

Simulation Phase. One of the main problems in today's manufacturing industry is long down times of assembly lines due to long testing phases of newly installed software. Our approach allows to simulate the production process beforehand in order to shorten software reconfiguration down times of physical assembly lines.

Maintenance Phase. Once the manufacturing system is built and operating, the maintenance phase starts. The aim is to provide an uninterruptible operating process. Causes for interruptions have to be analysed and eliminated as fast as possible. The analysis of causes for an interruption generates down time of the manufacturing system. An AR-tool will support this analysis and shorten down time of the manufacturing system.

In our approach, the different diagrams are mutually dependent on each other. The SDL block diagrams specify the minimum number of (process) classes to be contained in the class diagram and for each such class all its signal methods. In addition, each process class is equipped with one main statechart. This statechart has to define the response to all signals of the corresponding class. In addition to state changes, this response might include actions. Each of these actions is specified using one behaviour diagram (which in turn may apply additional diagrams for sub-activities). Thus, following our seamless methodology, this leads to an overall specification where each aspect of the system is specified by exactly one diagram, e.g. an SDL block diagram defining the overall architectural view and possible communication channels between processes, a class diagram refining the architectural view, and a statechart-based refinement of all communication channels by defining exactly one statechart for each process. A complete syntactic definition of all used diagrams, including static semantics which supports inter-diagram consistency analysis, is explained in [5, 27]. A semantic model integrating all used diagrams is given in [22]. Note that our integrated approach allows an arbitrary number of loops between the different phases. Hence, the incremental development is supported by the corresponding environment.

This section presented a brief overview about the different phases of our modelling approach. For a detailed description of the first four phases see [18, 20], whereas the verification phase and the appropriate semantic integration are presented in [22]. In the following sections we focus on the last three phases starting with a more detailed description of the code generation for programmable logic controllers.

5   Code-Generation for PLCs

Control systems are often complex, safety-critical and expensive. Any failure in the control software might not only result in a financial loss but lead to accidents as well. Therefore, in our methodology we employ validation via simulation and formal verification of the modelled system. After a successful validation and verification, the entire system model needs to be implemented. One way to ensure a correct translation of the model into a program is to generate the code from the model automatically.

In our approach, the defined precise semantics of the used models allows the automatic translation of the integrated diagrams into object-oriented programming languages like Java and C++ [20]. The generated executable code is used for the simulation phase (cf. section 6) and the supervisory control at a higher control level as well. However, in our case study, we use Programmable Logic Controllers (PLC) to execute the control software on the cell level.

5.1   Programmable Logic Controllers

Programmable Logic Controllers (PLC) are microprocessor systems that are widely used in industrial automation. The reason for their popularity in this field is that they are robust and reliable. A PLC is connected to sensors and actuators: the former provide information on the state of the controlled production system while the latter perform the actions prescribed by the control software. Hence, the basic task of the software is to map input information into output commands.

PLCs behave in a cyclic manner where each cycle follows three phases: (1) poll all inputs and store read values, (2) compute new output values, and (3) update all outputs. The repeated execution of this cycle is managed by the built-in real-time operating system. Thus, the programmer has to adapt only the computing phase for the output values.

For the decentralized control of our manufacturing system we use four PLCs of type Simatic S7-300. The controller uses the actuator sensor interface for a continuous interaction with the environment and reacts to events stimulated by the environment in a negligibly short time. Thus, the controller can be seen as a *reactive system* [13]. For the modelling of reactive behaviour, statecharts [11] are used and have to be implemented on the target platform. In the following we give a short impression on the translation of a statechart to Structured Text (ST) for programmable logic controllers by means of an example. Note that the code generation for our UML-like collaboration diagrams employed as actions and activities within statecharts (cf. section 4) was already presented in our previous work [20].

5.2   Implementing Statecharts

There are different programming languages for PLCs, each intended for a specific application domain and based on the background of the control engineer who uses them. In order to achieve more conformity of the different notations the standard IEC 61131- 3 [15] was developed. Each of the standardized languages cover different abstraction levels. Instruction List (IL) for example is a low level assembly language very close to hardware programming, whereas Sequential Function Charts (SFC) describe the sequence of a PLC program as a state transition diagram. For the automatic generation of PLC-code, we adapted the code generation mechanisms to produce Structured Text (ST) instead of Java code. Structured Text is a notation similar to PASCAL. It is a higher level language than IL and provides more structuring and organizing constructs such as if-then-else-conditionals and while-loops. However, as a classical procedural programming language, ST does not support typical object-oriented concepts like inheritance or polymorphism. Thus, a direct mapping of a statechart to an object-oriented implementation, e.g. the state-pattern [14, 10], is not possible. The mapping of object-oriented concepts has to be managed explicitly as described in [20]. For statecharts, we omit this overhead by using a simpler translation based on switch-case statements [4, 23].

Figure 5 depicts a simple statechart of the control software for the transfer gate used in our case study (cf. section 3). The specified statechart switches the transfer gate between the straight and the round direction. Initially, the transfer gate is switched to the straight direction and fixed by a mechanical interlock. When the *round()* event is received, the interlock is disengaged by the exit action *lock:=false*, and state *straight unlocked* is entered. After that, the triggerless transition is fired and the appropriate action *valve_def:=false* is

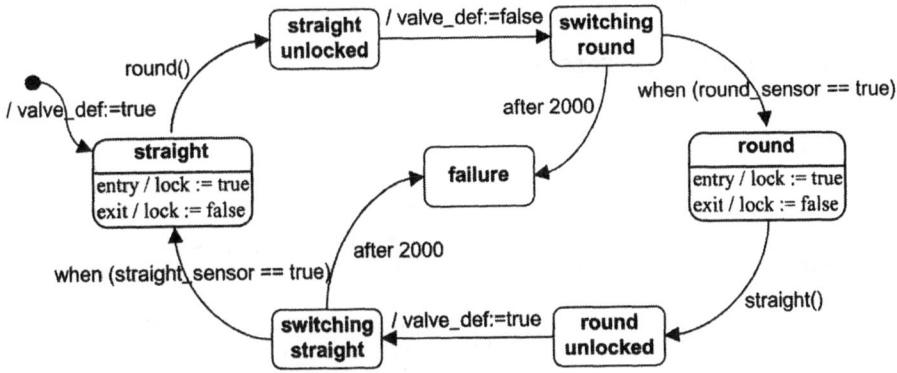

Fig. 5. Statechart of the transfer gate controller

executed. This action triggers a pneumatic cylinder responsible for turning the transfer gate into the round direction. The state *switching round* is left either if the proximity sensor announces that the switching process completed or if a timeout of 2000 milliseconds occurs. In the case of a timeout, a failure state is entered. In the other case, the switching process was successful. Thus, state *round* is entered and the interlock re-engaged. Now the transfer gate can be switched back to the straight direction by sending a *straight()* event. The switching is performed analogous to the described switching process for the round direction.

When implementing a statechart on PLCs, two problems arise. First, there is a problem moving from an event-based statechart world into a signal-based PLC-universe. In contrast to events, signals exist the whole time and are handled by the PLC as boolean values. To overcome this problem, an event can be associated with the rising and falling edges of a corresponding signal. For example, a rising edge can be detected comparing the signal between two cycles. If the signal was low in the previous cycle and is now high, a rising edge is detected [7].

Second, due to the cyclic execution of the three phases, signals and events from the environment can appear to occur simultaneously. Even worse, if a signal does not hold for at least the maximum amount of time needed for a cycle, one cannot be sure that the PLC will ever read the signal. The solution to this problem is to use PLCs which are fast enough.

In our experimental case study the used PLCs run infinitely faster than the environment. Hence, signals are always recognized and do not occur simultaneously. The control system can be seen as a reactive system with a negligibly short reaction time to signals and events stimulated by the environment. Hence, the assumption of the perfect synchrony hypothesis [3] regarding the interaction between the environment and the controller on the cell level is fulfilled. Note that, as mentioned in section 4, this is not true for the decentralized case with a large number of asynchronous communicating control units. This case is still handled as described in [20].

The behaviour of a statechart can be implemented by simple switch-case constructs. The piece of code in Figure 6 is part of the generated program for

```
VAR state: INT := 1;                    /* state = "straight" */
    timer: TIMER;
    expired: BOOL := FALSE;
END_VAR;

CASE state OF
    ...
    3:/* state = "switching round" */
      timer(IN:=TRUE, TV:=T#2000ms);/* start or update timer */
      expired := NOT timer.Q;           /* test for expired timer */

    IF (round_sensor = TRUE) THEN /*when (round_sensor==true) */
       timer(IN:=FALSE, TV:=T#2000ms);/* stop timer */
       state := 4;                      /* state = "round" */
       lock := TRUE;                    /* entry action */

    ELSIF (expired = TRUE) THEN         /* after 2000 */
       timer(IN:=FALSE, TV:=T#2000ms);/* stop timer */
       state := 7;                      /* state = "failure" */
    END_IF;

    4:/* state = "round" */
    IF (straight = TRUE) THEN           /* event: straight() */
       lock := FALSE;                   /* exit action */
       state := 5;                      /* state = "round unlocked" */
    END_IF;
    ...
END_CASE;
```

Fig. 6. Example for generated PLC code

the statechart shown in Figure 5. It gives a short impression on the translation in Structured Text for the states *switching round* and *round*.

We declare an integer variable *state* to keep the current state of the statechart. Each state is encoded by an integer which is handled in a case statement. Events and signals are translated to boolean variables in the symbol table. The symbol table provides a mapping between the program and the sensors/actuators plugged in to the PLC. In each state, the outgoing transitions of that state are treated. Timer events are handled by built in timer functions. If a transition is enabled, the new state is set and the appropriate exit and entry actions are executed. Note that the presented program is executed once in each cycle. Thus, it is the body of an implicit loop-forever statement.

6   Tool Support: An Engineer's Workstation

The engineer's workstation is based on the integrated environment FUJABA [5] including tools which support software specification as explained in the previous sections. Figure 7 gives an overview of the employed tools.

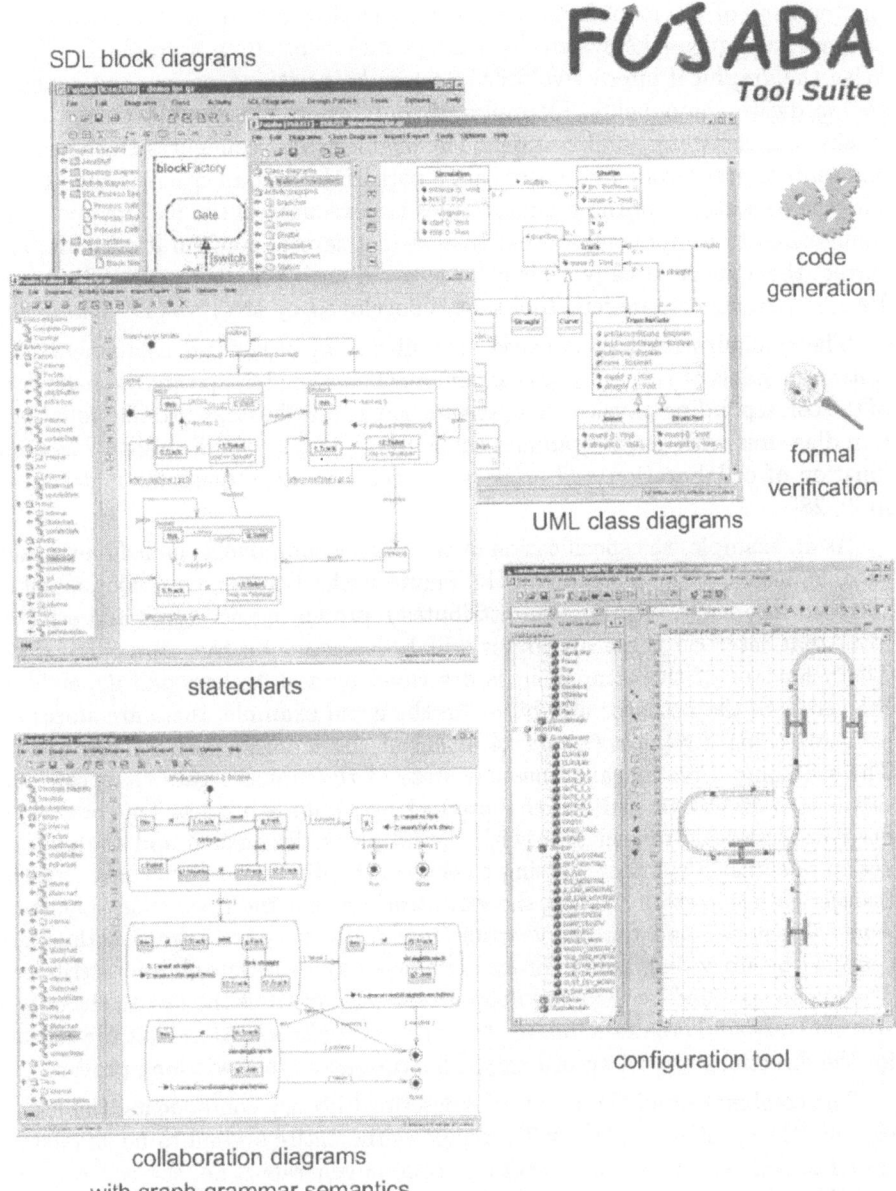

Fig. 7. Engineer's workstation based on the FUJABA Tool Suite integration platform

FUJABA includes editors for SDL block diagrams, UML class diagrams, statecharts and story diagrams as well as tools for code generation and formal verification [18]. In addition, the consolidation phase (cf. section 4) is supported by a configuration tool called PROJECTOR. This tool supports the engineer developing the topology of the manufacturing system including sensors and actuators. The engineer configures the system by taking components from a graphical library. With the graphical interactive user interface he positions, orient, and connects the hardware components. Examples of components are straight tracks, curve tracks, transfer gates, and stations. The engineer also configures the actuators and sensors. Actuators and sensors are a part of the system specification. To ensure the consistency of the topology, rules are executed in the background while configuring its components. These rules detect several configuration faults and correct them automatically. This helps to avoid design faults in the early stages. PROJECTOR is a commercial tool that is developed by the FASTEC GmbH [8].

The configuration tool is based on a library of predefined components, i.e. software models of the real physical devices. These models specify the behaviour of the corresponding physical components using statecharts, UML-like collaboration diagrams with graph grammar semantics, and activity diagrams. The combination of collaboration and activity diagrams to story diagrams is described in [9, 28].

As an example, the specification of one library component, namely a transfer gate, is described in more detail. In Figure 8 the transfer gate component is specified as a class with boolean attributes representing actuators and sensors. Note that later on these attributes will be accessed by the control software. The behaviour of the component is described by a statechart and depends on the values of the actuator attributes. In the given example, there are states for each switching direction (*round*, *straight*) of the transfer gate (cf. section 3). The switching direction and thus the state of the transfer gate changes if the valve attribute is changed and the interlock attribute is not set. This behaviour describes the real transfer gate with the interlock disengaged and the double-action pneumatic cylinder starting to change the direction. For example, if the transfer gate is in state *straight*, the valve *true*, and the interlock *false*, then state *round* is entered and the entry action *round()* is executed. Entry actions are specified by story diagrams in order to change object structures and attributes. The action specified by the story diagram *round()* destroys the link to the object *straightTrack* and creates a link to the object *roundTrack*. After that the sensors for the directions are set accordingly. This completes the switching process.

The combination of the previously described library components, the topology and the specified control software allows the entire system to be simulated. Based on this specification, executable code is generated, i.e. the control code and the code that represents the behaviour of the physical system. In contrast to other tools and simulation environments, the simulation model is not interpreted, but executed. The generated code implies the simulation model and its execution simulates the entire system.

This simulation model is connected to a 3D model that is rendered in real-time using Virtual Reality (VR) technology. The 3D model is based on the topology of the manufacturing system and its object model and it is generated automatically. The animations in the VR environment, e.g. moving shuttle or switching transfer gate, are triggered by the executed code. This means the

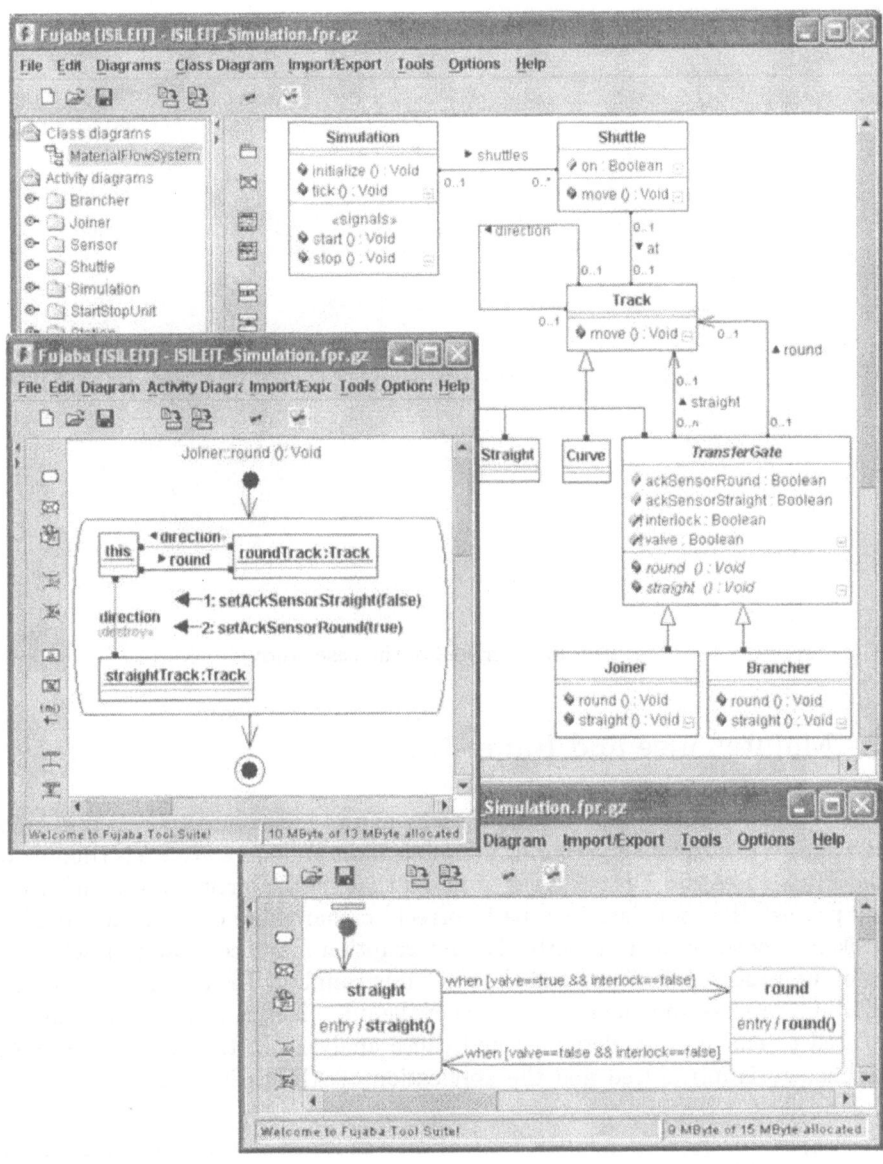

Fig. 8. Software models describing one library component (Joiner)

simulated states of components of the manufacturing system can be visualised. This 3D model is examined using the advantages of immersion and the human machine interaction that is delivered by VR while the simulation is running. A screenshot is shown in Figure 9. It shows an extended 3D model of the complete case study.

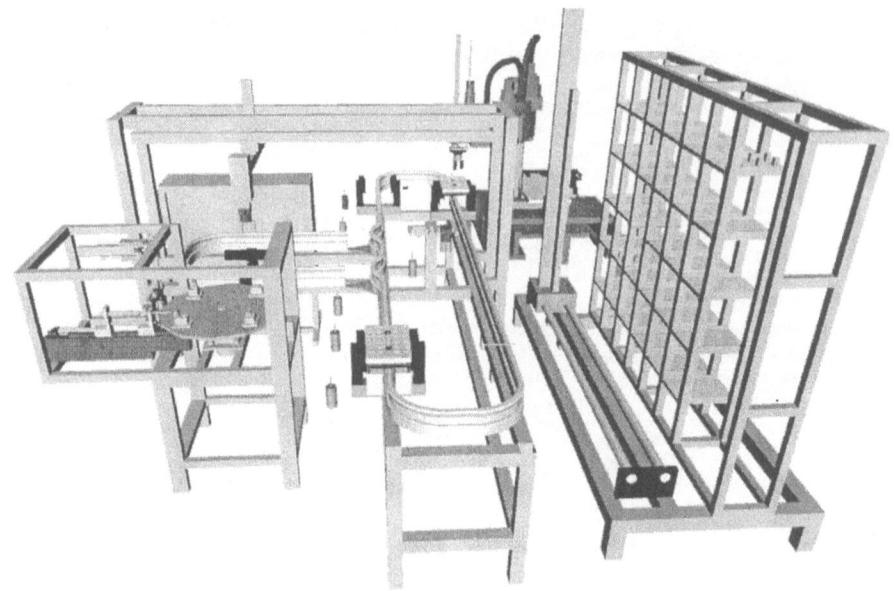

Fig. 9. 3D model of the case study

7   Maintenance and Ramp-Up

The process to build a manufacturing system and put it into operation is called rampup. When the manufacturing system is built and the software is running on the PLCs there can be two types of faults that may interrupt the manufacturing process. The software may be incorrect[4] or hardware components could be broken or not installed properly. The interruption may occur later on when the ramp-up process is finished and the system is running. To support the so-called ramp-up process and the maintenance of the manufacturing system an AR-tool is used to enable fault detection and cause analysis. In the following, the AR technology is introduced and the application of AR in the ISILEIT project is described.

Augmented Reality is a new form of man-machine interface which is closely related to VR [2]. In Augmented Reality the computer provides additional information that enhances or augments the real world. The user can interact with the real world in a natural way, with the AR-system providing information and assistance. Therefore, AR enhances reality by superimposing information rather then completely replacing it, like VR (Virtual Reality) does. The information is inserted in a context-dependent way, i.e. derived appropriately from the perceived real world object. A real world object is recognised and, depending on

---

[4] Due to the complexity of the regarded system, verification is performed for safety-critical software components only. Hence, the software may still contain undetected faults and defects.

the specific object, the content-dependent information will be retrieved and displayed. The motivation is that Augmented Reality enhances a user's perception of and interaction with the real world. The virtual objects display information that the user cannot directly detect with his own senses, e.g. states of sensors or software. The information conveyed by the virtual objects helps a user perform realworld tasks [19].

The man-machine interface AR in ISILEIT supports the integration of the different domains. Connecting the AR tool and the controllers will enable the system to retrieve state information. The states refer to the different components of the system. This includes all components of the manufacturing system as developed by the different domains, namely mechanics, pneumatics, electronics and even the software.

Most states and changes will be seen in reality, e.g. the switching of a transfer gate. The state of a sensor may be indicated by the glow of an LED or a pneumatic cylinder may cause a motion activity. But these real components can be hidden, e.g. the cylinder is integrated into the transfer gate. The user perhaps doesn't know the actuator's position and how it works within the transfer gate. Using the AR tool the cylinder can be displayed as a 3D-object with the active state at a position within the transfer gate. The state change of the actuator can be shown by using a 3D animation. Regarding the realtime aspect, the virtual actuator will change its state while the transfer gate is switching from one to another direction.

In opposition to states that refer to real components, the states referring to electronics and software are not directly perceptible. These states can only be visualised with the real system and the AR tool. The internal computer model receives the software specification from the integration platform. An interface to the PLCs enables the AR tool to retrieve the I/O values of the PLC's ports. This allows the abstract software states to be combined, e.g. statecharts or object diagrams, and the corresponding signals sent or received by the PLC. Dependencies between hardware and software are now identified without reading the control code, but by looking at the real system and receiving augmented information about the states of the system. As every component state is either seen in reality or can be displayed virtually, the engineer is able to see all dependencies between state changes of the different components during operation of the physical system. The described AR tool provides benefits like online debugging, better maintenance, and training. In the end it leads to a better overall understanding of the system and supports communication between engineers from different domains.

In the case of an error the AR tool is used for failure detection. The failure detection is based on the analysis of the dependencies and impacts between hard- and software. By using the AR tool it is possible to explicate states and state changes of mechanics, pneumatics, electronics, and the software.

The regarded component for the above-referenced application scenarios is the transfer gate and the corresponding statechart describing the control software shown in Figure 4 and Figure 5. In this scenario, for instance, one of the inductive proximity sensors is not working correctly. Sometimes it does not detect that the final switching position of the transfer gate has been reached. The result is that the interlock is not re-engaged and the switching process is not finished. No shuttles should now be allowed to pass through this transfer gate. The engineer sees that the transfer gates switches but he can not perceive whether the interlock, the inductive proximity sensor, or the software is causing the problem. In particular, if the inductive proximity sensor fails in only some cases, the reason for the failure is hard to find. Using the AR tool, the engineer can retrieve all states online in real-time. The moment the failure occurs, current states are displayed. The statechart seen in Figure 5 will show him that the current state is *switching round* and the condition is *when (round_sensor==true)* to change into the next state *round* that will re-engage the interlock on entry. The software will switch to the state *failure* after the timeout of 2000 milliseconds. The transfer gate has switched as seen in reality, but the inductive proximity sensor does not detect the final switching position. Hence, the state is not changed. This information is displayed as augmentation in the view of the engineer, i.e. the state of the sensor is shown at its real position. Combining all the given states the engineer infers that either the sensor or the wiring causes the fault. After he verifies that the wiring has no slack joint, the conclusion is that the sensor is the cause for the failure and has to be replaced.

Additional benefits of the AR tool are a better overall understanding and integrating the views of the different domains (literally), e.g. understanding the interrelationship between software, sensors/actuators, and hardware. Regarding the transfer gate as described before, the disadvantage of the built-in switching actuator and the interlock is that they can not be seen while standing in front of the transfer gate. For training and educational purpose this might be explained with the AR tool. The transfer gate is seen in reality. The built-in components like the interlock and the switch actuator are displayed as 3D objects (pneumatic cylinders) at their real position. The user can change position or walk around the transfer gate, if possible, and the 3D objects will remain where their corresponding real counterpart is built-in. The state of the cylinder (extended or not extended) is directly visible. The change of the state is visualised by an animation of the 3D object. Additionally, the states of the other sensors and the software can be used to augment the field of view. All this information, states, and supporting 3D graphics can be taken to develop a didactical guiding AR-system that explains the functionality of the manufacturing system and the interrelationship between the components during operation.

8   Summary

In this paper we presented an overview of our seamless methodology for the integrated design, analysis, validation, and verification of production control systems. The paper focused on code generation for programmable logic controllers, simulation and maintenance. We developed a code generator for implementing statecharts on PLCs. The presented translation of statecharts is based on simple switch-case constructs in the programming language Structured Text.

Due to demanded flexibility in shorter innovation cycles, today's manufacturing industry needs shortened phases for development and ramp-up of the control software. In this paper we presented an approach to simulate the software beforehand. While the simulation is running, faults in the control software are detected by the engineer early in the design phase. Thus, faults in the control software are corrected even before the manufacturing system is built. This significantly reduces the time needed for the final system tests on the real hardware.

Furthermore, we have shown how we incorporated Augmented Reality technology for maintenance of the operating manufacturing system.

The concepts described in this paper were integrated in a tool integration platform called FUJABA Tool Suite. This platform is the basis for the engineer's workstation and supports the described phases of our modelling approach. The release of FUJABA is available via: http://www.fujaba.de

References

[1] J. Ali and J. Tanaka. Implementation of the dynamic behaviour of object oriented systems. In *Proc. of the 3rd Biennal World Conference on Integrated Design and Process Technology*, pages 281-288. ISSN No. 1090-9389, Society for Design and Process Science, 1998.

[2] R. Behringer, G. Klinker, and D. Mizell. Augmented reality - placing artificial objects in real scenes. In *Proceedings of th IWAR, San Francisco, California*, 1999.

[3] G. Berry and G. Gonthier. The esterel synchronous programming language: Design, semantics, implementation. Technical report, Ecole Nationale Superieure des Mines de Paris, 1988.

[4] G. Booch, J. Rumbaugh, and I. Jacobson. *The Unified Modeling Language User Guide*. Addison-Wesley, Reading, Massachusetts, USA, 1st edition, 1999.

[5] S. Burmester, H. Giese, J. Niere, M. Tichy, J. Wadsack, R. Wagner, L. Wendehals, and A. Zündorf. Tool integration at the meta-model level within the fujaba tool suite. In *Proc. of the Workshop on Tool-Integration in System Development (TIS), Helsinki, Finland, (ESEC / FSE 2003 Workshop 3)*, pages 51-56, September 2003.

[6] B. Douglass, editor. *Real Time UML*. Addison-Wesley, 1998.

[7] M. Fabian and A. Hellgren. PLC-based implementation of supervisory control for discrete event systems. In *Proceedings of the 37th IEEE Conference on Decision and Control, Tampa, Florida, USA*, Dec 1998.

[8] G. FASTEC GmbH, Paderborn. http://www.fastec.de.

[9] T. Fischer, J. Niere, L. Torunski, and A. Zündorf. Story diagrams: A new graph rewrite language based on the unified modeling language. In G. Engels and G. Rozenberg, editors, *Proc. of the 6th International Workshop on Theory and Application of Graph Transformation (TAGT), Paderborn, Germany*, LNCS 1764. Springer Verlag, 1998.

[10] E. Gamma, R. Helm, R. Johnson, and J. Vlissides. *Design Patterns: Elements of Reusable Object Oriented Software*. Addison-Wesley, Reading, MA, 1995.

[11] D. Harel and E. Gery. Executable object modeling with statecharts. In *Proc. of the 18th International Conference on Software Engineering, Berlin, Germany*, pages 246-257. IEEE Computer Society Press, May 1996.

[12] D. Harel, H. Lachover, A. Naamad, A. Pnueli, M. Politi, R. Sherman, A. Shtull-Tauring, and M. Trakhtenbrot. Statemate: A working environment for the development of complex reactive systems. In *IEEE Transactions on Software Engineering*, pages 403-414. IEEE Computer Society Press, 1990.

[13] D. Harel and M. Politi. *Modeling Reactive Systems with Statecharts: The Statemate Approach*. McGraw-Hill Companies, Inc., New York, first edition, 1998.

[14] ILogix. *Rhapsody, the Rhapsody case tool. Online at http://www.ilogix.com*.

[15] International Electrotechnical Commission, Technical Commitee No. 65. *Programmable Controllers - Programming Languages, IEC 61131-3*, 1993.

[16] International Telecommunication Union (ITU), Geneva. *ITU-T Recommendation Z.100: Specification and Description Language (SDL)*, 1994 + Addendum 1996.

[17] J. Jahnke and A. Zündorf. Specification and implementation of a distributed planning and information system for courses based on story driven modelling. In *Proc. of Intl. Workshop on Software Specification and Design (IWSSD-9. Kyoto, Japan*, pages 77-86. IEEE Computer Society Press, 1998.

[18] H. Köhler, U. Nickel, J. Niere, and A. Zündorf. Integrating uml diagrams for production control systems. In *Proc. of the 22nd International Conference on Software Engineering (ICSE), Limerick, Irland*, pages 241-251. ACM Press, 2000.

[19] C. Matysczok. Augmented reality - chances and potentials of a new man-machine-interface. In *Proceedings of the International Digital Media Conference, Cairo*, 2004.

[20] U. Nickel, W. Schäfer, and A. Zündorf. Integrative specification of distributed production control systems for flexible automated manufacturing. In M. Nagl and B. Westfechtel, editors, *DFG Workshop: Modelle, Werkzeuge und Infrastrukturen zur Unterstützung von Entwicklungsprozessen*, pages 179-195. Wiley-VCH Verlag GmbH and Co. KGaA, 2003.

[21] OMG. *Unified Modeling Language: Superstructure, Version 2.0, 3rd Revised Submission to OMG RFP ad/00-09-02*. Object Management Group, 250 First Avenue, Needham, MA 02494, USA, April 2003.

[22] F. Rammig and M. Kardos. Model based formal verification of distributed production control systems. In *This volume*, 2004.

[23] Rational. *RR-RT, the Rational Rose Real Time case-tool. Online at http://www.rational.com*.

[24] G. Rozenberg, editor. *Handbook of Graph Grammars and Computing by Graph Transformation*, volume 1. World Scientific, Singapore, 1999.

[25] A. Schürr, A. Winter, and A. Zündorf. Graph grammar engineering with progres. In W. Schäfer, editor, *Proc. of European Software Engineering Conference (ESEC/FSE)*, LNCS 989. Springer Verlag, 1995.

[26] B. Selic, G. Gullekson, and P. Ward. *Real-Time Object Oriented Modeling*. WILEY, 1994.

[27] R. Wagner, H. Giese, and U. Nickel. A plug-in for flexible and incremental consistency management. In *Proc. of the International Conference on the Unified Modeling Language 2003 (Workshop 7: Consistency Problems in UML-based Software Development), San Francisco, USA*, October 2003.

[28] A. Zündorf. *Rigorous Object Oriented Software Development*. University of Paderborn, 2001.

A Formal Component Concept for the Specification of Industrial Control Systems

Benjamin Braatz[1], Markus Klein[1], Gunnar Schröter[1], and Matthias Bengel[2]

[1] Technische Universität Berlin, Germany
[bbraatz,klein,schroetg]@cs.tu-berlin.de
[2] Universität Stuttgart, Germany
Matthias.Bengel@iff.uni-stuttgart.de

Abstract. Motivated by the wide acceptance of component based technologies in software development, a component concept for software engineering is applied to modeling in the field of production automation. Taking the modeling of a holonic transport system as an example, it is shown, how function blocks in the sense of production automation can be understood as software engineering components. Thus, the advantages of component based modeling with respect to structuring, exchange and reuse can be transferred to systems in production automation.

1 Introduction

Component based technologies for the development of complex software systems, e.g. Java Beans and Corba, found a wide acceptance in todays applied software engineering. These technologies ease the development of large scaled software architectures since the abstraction of the realization of the funcionalities to component interfaces minimizes the complexity of architecture building.

In using so called "middleware" it is tried to gain a certain independence of concrete programming languages for the component implementations. But also physical devices with corresponding interfaces can be understood as components, and hence, whole production systems can be described as component architectures.

Not only the improved handling of the structuring of systems, which primary leads to a reduction of the complexity in the design stage, but also reusability and exchangeability are regarded as important advantages of component based technologies. If a component is implemented once, it is possible to use the same component implementation for another project, if the functionality of the component is, maybe partially, relevant for the new project. This means, the new environment of the component imports functionalities, which are offered by the component. Therefore the services, the component expects from its environment, have to be available in the new context. Moreover, components can be replaced within a single system. In this case, the new component has to fulfill the assumptions of the existing system.

In addition, component structures ease the adaption of software systems to changed requirements and environment condidtions, since the system adaption might eventually be limited to single components. If the changed components fulfill their interfaces afterwards, the remaining system components can be left unchanged without any further examiniation.

In order to specify system components before the actual implementation, a suiting component based specification technique is needed. Existing techniques, especially the UML components in [1], lack a means to express abstract interface specifications. The components in the new UML 2.0 specification in [2] are already a lot more elaborated and have notions of explicit export and import interfaces. Unfortunately, the UML diagram element for an interface still has some restrictions that seem to be inappropriate for a usage in our application field (e. g. it is not intended to instantiate interfaces, which stands in conflict to the ideas presented in Sect. 4). For this reason we will still use a special kind of UML subsystems in this paper, which were developed in [3] to integrate function blocks in the sense of production automation into an object oriented method for the development of prodution systems presented in [4].

These subsystems are an instance of the abstract component concept presented in [5]. In this approach a component is defined by three specification parts: export, import, and body specification. The export specification describes, which services the component offers to its environment. The body specification describes the realization of the exported service using the imported services of the component. This approach carries the advantages of component based technologies, i. e. abstraction, reusablility, and exchangeability, to the design stage of the development process.

For several reasons, it is desirable to have specification techniques available, that are equipped with a formally defined semantics, because this enables the (partial) code generation of implementations for the software part of the system. Beyond this, a formal semantics provides additional advantages. The semantics and correctness of a composed system can e. g. be deferred from the semantics and correctness of its components, provided that the used composition operations are compatible with the semantics. In this paper we will use a specification technique consisting of UML class diagrams and UML statecharts as in [1] and a simple action language based on the notations of OCL. For a number of UML techniques a formal semantics based on transformation systems was developed in [6,7], which have been summarized and integrated in [8].

In [9] we have already presented first ideas concerning the correspondence of function blocks according to [10] and software specification components. In contrast to [9] we will give a much more detailed discussion in this paper and we show how the used component framework can be extended by a model based semantics.

The paper is organized as follows: In Sec. 2 we show how function blocks in production automation can be modelled using diagram techniques from the UML. In Sec. 3 we interpret these UML function blocks as components in a formal component concept. In Sec. 4 we sketch a model-theoretic semantics for such components. Finally, in Sec. 5 we conclude by giving some directions of future work.

2   Modelling Function Blocks with UML Subsystems

In this section we show how function blocks according to the IEC/PAS 61499-1 specified in [10] can be modelled by UML subsystems in the sense of [1]. This approach, using the ODEMA[1] method presented in [4,11], was originally introduced in [3].

Figure 1 shows the characteristic elements of a simple function block according to IEC/PAS 61499. These elements are mapped to a UML subsystem function block in the following way: In the specification part of a UML function block we model the event and data flow of the services the subsystem offers to its environment (export interface), while distinguished (proxy) elements in the realization part model the event and data flow of services it assumes from its environment (import interface). The rest of the realization part models internal data, execution control and algorithms of the function block by a class diagram, statecharts and action language expressions.

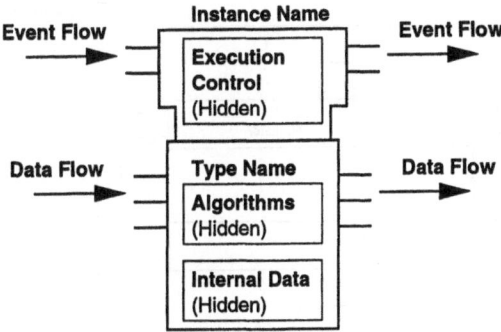

Fig. 1. Function block characterization

The specifications of function blocks shown below are slighlty modified parts of a solution for the reference case study "holonic matererial flow", presented in [12], within the DFG priority program "Software Specification" (see [13]). This solution was developed in the project IOSIP[2] and can be found under [14].

Figure 2 shows the function block structure of the control software of an H-AGV[3], where function blocks are symbolized as UML subsystems. The function block IO reads out the incoming data stream from the CommunicationMedia. Data packages that have to be send to other H-AGVs are transferred through the IO function block, too. Hence, the function block CommunicationMedia, which is a function block realized by an apparat, has to offer features for receiving and

---

[1] Object-oriented method for developing technical multi-agent-systems

[2] Integration of object-oriented software specification techniques and their application-specific extension for industrial production systems on the example of automobile industry

[3] Holonic automated guided vehicle

sending data in its interface. The function block Interpreter analyzes incoming messages that are relevant for the particular H-AGV. If, for example, a machine status was received, a possibly necessary negotiation would be initiated. For this purpose, a calculation of costs and the composition of outgoing messages would be done in the Negotiatior function block. These messages would be put into the used communication protocol in the Mediator function block, before they reach the I/O function block. If the negotioation ends up with transport order, the controlled H-AGV has to drive to the particular workpiece. This happens under the usage of the DrivingControl function block, where the controlling of the driving relevant sensors and actuators in the function block Vehicle is implemented. The function block Handover realizes the loading and unloading of workpieces between H-AGVs and machines by a carrier apparat in the Carrier function block.

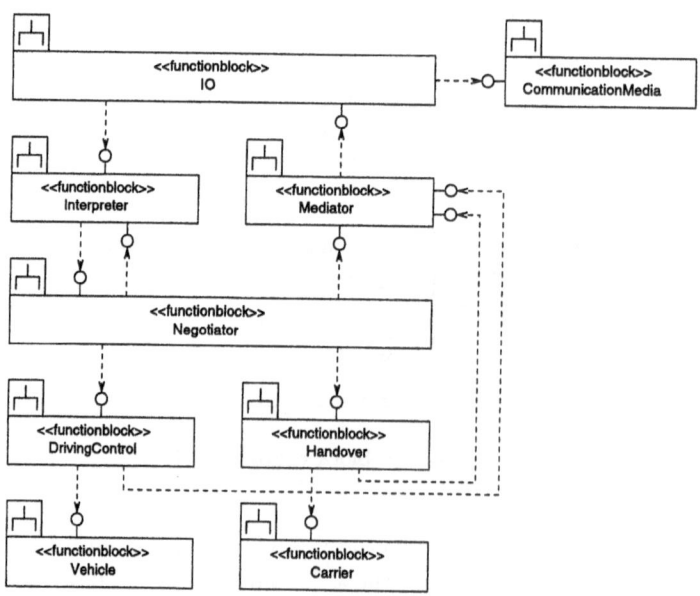

Fig. 2. Architecture of the H-AGV control software

The function block Handover, shown in Fig. 3 uses the sensors and actuators of the workpiece carrier of the H-AGV. Thus, the function block has output events that are used as communication signals for the function block Carrier. The small boxes on the lines modeling the event and and data flow mark synchronization points. For example, the event loadWorkpiece is connected to two data elements, wpt and m of type WorkpieceType and MachineID, respectively. The Return events are meant as signals that report the termination of a corresponding method, where some of them are connected to data flow elements, which means that this method has a return value of that type.

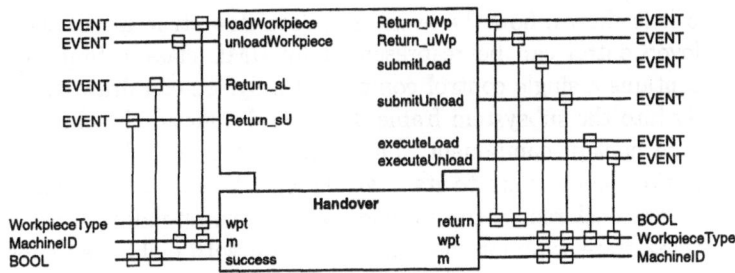

Fig. 3. Function block Handover

This representation style might be very useful for realizing function blocks by physical devices, but if a function block is planned to be realized by a piece of software, it should be expressed in a modeling language which is more common in the software engineering world. We will use UML diagrams and the UML based method ODEMA for this purpose together with a mapping of function blocks to UML subsystems originally presented in [3]. Figure 4 shows the structure of the function block Handover and the function blocks it relies on to provide its funcionality, where the function block Carrier is realized by an apparat and the function block Mediator by a software component. This is represented in the diagram by corresponding UML components with the stereotypes <<embedded>> and <<executable>>, respectively.

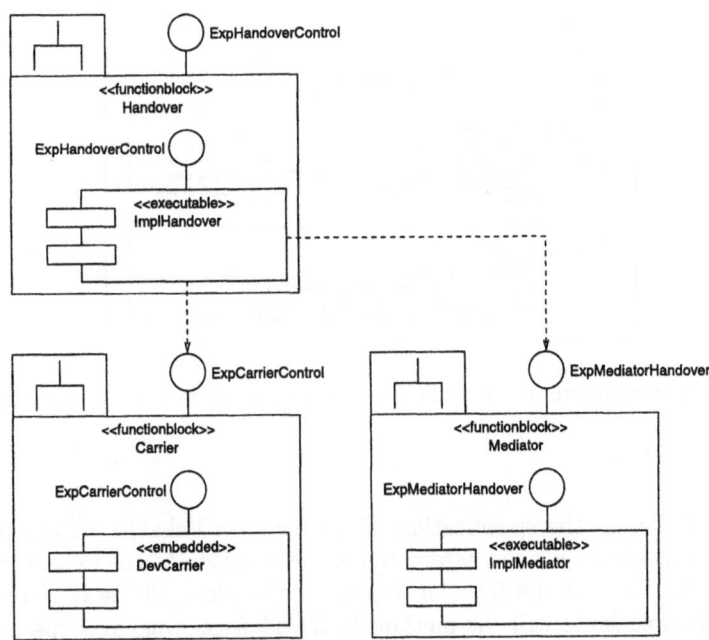

Fig. 4. Subsystem structure of the function block Handover

In Fig. 5 it is shown, how the event and data flow structure of the function block HandoverControl can be respresented by UML classes. Since this function block contains a single control component only, we can draw the class diagram directly into the subsystem frame. In general, function blocks can contain more than one control component. The export interface subsumes the methods, the function block offers to its environment. We use asynchronous signal events which are declared in the inteface of the corresponding function block with a <<com>> stereotype for the communication with embedded subsystems. We use synchronous method calls for the communication between executable software subsystems. Moreover, the dependencies to other subsystems are redirected through interfaces marked with the stereotype <<ODproxy>> in order to make explicit the imports of the subsystem, which leads to a self-contained description of the function block.

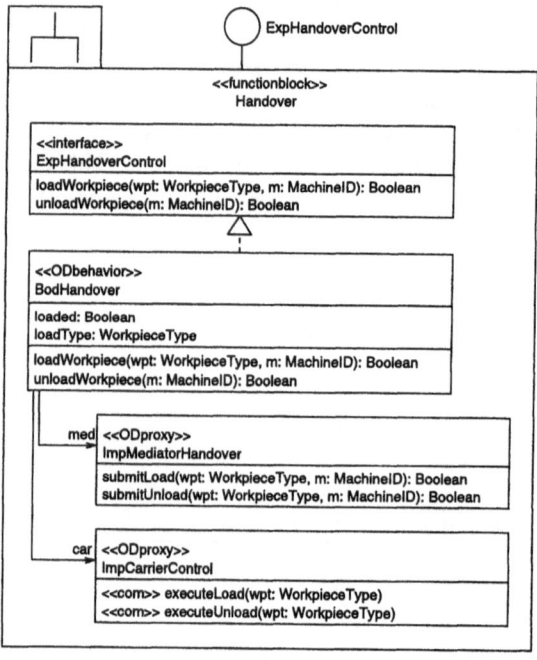

Fig. 5. Detailed structure of the single control component in the function block Handover

In Fig. 6 we see the specification of the reactive behavior of the function block by a statechart. We can regard this as an addition to the export interface as well as the body of the function block specification. The statechart allows other functionblocks to call the method loadWorkpiece, whenever the carrier is empty, and the method unloadWorkpiece, if some workpiece is loaded onto the H-AGV. Both methods non-deterministically choose to either switch the state or stay in the same state, since this choice depends on the success of the imported submit methods of ExpMediatorHandover, which are not visible in the statechart. Other function blocks importing Handover have to ensure, that this protocol is respected.

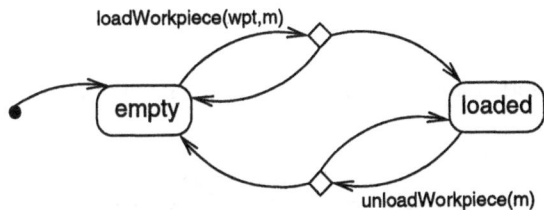

Fig. 6. Statechart of the function block Handover

The specification of the realization of the methods is encapsulated in the body specification of the function block. Figures 7 and 8 show such action language specifications for the methods loadWorkpiece and unloadWorkpiece, respectively, where we use a rather simple ad hoc action language, which is neither part of the UML nor ODEMA at the moment. The description shows the concrete sequence of actions and how other methods, e. g. submitLoad, and signals, e. g. executeLoad, are used in the method.

```
context BodHandover::loadWorkpiece(wpt: WorkpieceType, m: MachineID):
if submitLoad(wpt, m)
then executeLoad(wpt);
     set loaded := true;
     set loadType := wpt;
     return true
else return false
endif
```

Fig. 7. Action language description of the method loadWorkpiece

An addition to the import specification is the protocol statechart in Fig. 9, which constrains the signals executeLoad and executeUnload to be sended alternating. On the other hand the methods of ImpMediatorHandover are not further constrained.

In the next section we will show, how function blocks modelled by UML subsystems as presented in this section can be interpreted as components in a formal specification component concept, and which benefits can be drawn from two kinds of semantics for these components. Especially we will see how architectures of function blocks can be flattened by a composition operation based on a transformation semantics for components.

context BodHandover::unloadWorkpiece(m: MachineID):
if submitUnload(loadType, m)
then executeUnload(loadType);
    set loaded := false;
    unset loadType;
    return true
else return false
endif

Fig. 8. Action language description of the method unloadWorkpiece

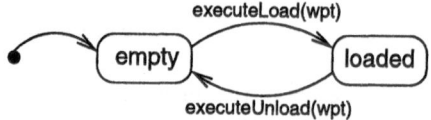

Fig. 9. Statechart of the import ImpCarrierControl

3   UML Subsystems in an Abstract Component Concept

In this section we shortly introduce an abstract component concept based on the ones published in [15] and [5]. Then we show, how UML subsystems can be interpreted as components in the sense of this concept and which semantical implications arise from such an interpretation.

In contrast to software components such as the ones in CORBA, Java Enterprise Edition or .NET, the component concept considered here is concerned with specification components, which are means to structure large specifications into manageable parts. The concept of specification components is orthogonal to the software components in the implementation and deployment structure, i. e. there is not necessarily a bijective correspondence between specification and software components, but there could also be specification components, which specify several software components, and, vice versa, software components, which are specified in several specification components.

A component *Comp* in this framework consists of import and export interface specifications *Imp* and *Exp* and a body specification *Bod*, which is supposed to realize the provisions granted in *Exp* using the requirements stated in *Imp*. Note, that *Imp*, *Exp* and *Bod* are in general supposed to be constructed from the same specification techniques. Hence, the interfaces are not restricted to certain kinds of specifications, unless we explicitly impose such a restriction for an instantiation of the component concept.

In [15] it is additionally assumed, that there is a model-theoretic semantics for the specifications, which induces a model class *Mod(Spec)* for each specification *Spec*. An instantiation of this requirement by models suitable for the specification of object-oriented systems is sketched in Sect. 4. A viewpoint concept used to manage the specification of heterogeneous aspects of such systems is introduced

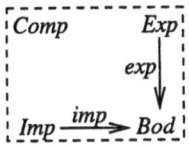

Fig. 10. Specification component

in [16] in this volume, where this concept lies orthogonally to the concepts of parameterization and abstraction realized in components.

An abstract component is shown in Fig. 10. The import specification is connected to the body specification by an import connection $imp: Imp \rightarrow Bod$, where this connection should be a parameterization, i.e. it specifies, how the imported entities are used in the construction of the body. On the other hand, the export is related to the body by an export connection $exp: Exp \rightarrow Bod$, which is an abstraction from the details in the body, i.e. it specifies, how the abstract provisions in the export are realized by the body.

UML subsystems can be seen as an instantiation of this concept, where the operations offered by the interfaces of a subsystem together with its specification elements form the export interface, and the realization elements correspond to the body of the component. The UML does not demand explicit modeling of the import of a subsystem, but we have added this by redirecting dependencies to the environment through interfaces with the stereotype <<ODproxy>>, which have no realization in the subsystem itself but are instantiated by dependencies to the environment. The connections are then given by inclusions of the interface elements into the whole subsystem. The UML subsystem Handover in Fig. 5 can for example be interpreted as a component with the UML interface ExpHandoverControl in its export and the proxy interfaces ImpMediatorHandover and ImpCarrierControl in its import. The body then consists of all three interfaces together with the class BodHandover. This component structure is made explicit in Fig. 11.

There are two approaches to the semantics of components. In [15] a model-theoretic approach is sketched, which can be seen as a generalized version of the algebraic module concept in [17]. In this approach, depicted in Fig. 12, the semantics of an import connection imp is given by a construction $Constr_{imp}: Mod(Imp) \rightarrow Mod(Bod)$, which builds models satisfying the body specification from models satisfying the import specification. An export connection exp is interpreted by a restriction $Restr_{exp}: Mod(Bod) \rightarrow Mod(Exp)$, which abstracts from the details of the realization in models of Bod, leading to models of Exp. Then, the model semantics $ModSem(Comp): Mod(Imp) \rightarrow Mod(Exp)$ of a component $Comp$ is just the composition $ModSem(Comp) = Restr_{exp} \circ Constr_{imp}$. Thus, the model semantics of the subsystem Handover is a function transforming models of the import interfaces into models of the export interface. A model semantics for UML specifications together with constructions and restrictions is sketched in Sect. 4.

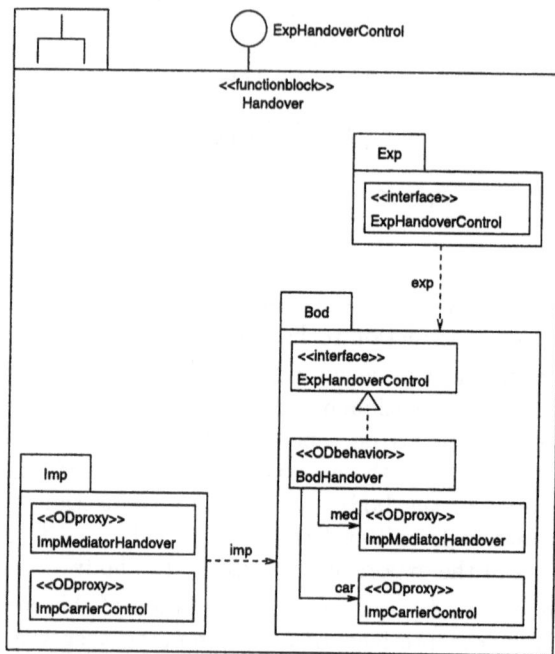

Fig. 11. Component Handover with explicit component structure

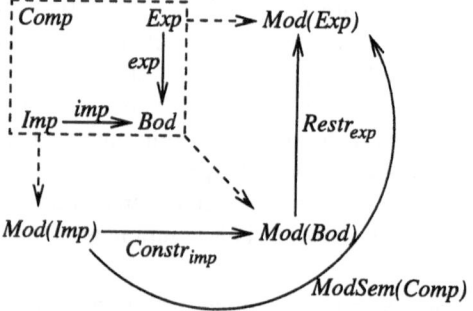

Fig. 12. Model-theoretic semantics of component

The second approach to component semantics, taken in [5], is based on transformations of specifications, where these transformations are supposed to somehow refine the specifications, and a class of inclusions of specifications. The transformation semantics $Trafo(Spec)$ of a specification is then given by the class of all possible tranformations $t: Spec \Rightarrow Spec'$. Transformations and inclusions have to be composable by a composition operator $\circ$. Moreover, the extension property has to be satisfied, i.e. for each inclusion $i: Spec_1 \hookrightarrow Spec_2$ there has to be an extension function $Ext_i: Trafo(Spec_1) \rightarrow Trafo(Spec_2)$, such that for each transformation $t: Spec_1 \Rightarrow Spec_1'$ with extension $Ext_i(t): Spec_2 \Rightarrow Spec_2'$

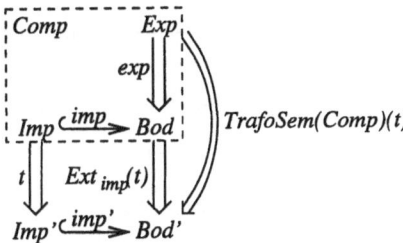

Fig. 13. Transformation semantics of component

there is an inclusion $i': Spec'_1 \hookrightarrow Spec'_2$. The semantics of a component, which now has to have an inclusion as import and a transformation as export connection, is then a function $TrafoSem(Comp): Trafo(Imp) \to Trafo(Exp)$ with $TrafoSem(Comp)(t) = Ext_{imp}(t) \circ exp$, which means that a component can construct transformations of the export specification from transformations of the import specification. This situation is shown in Fig. 13.

A transformation based component concept for UML diagrams has already been examined in [18], where the transformations are inheritance relations between elements in an export package and elements in the corresponding body package and inclusions correspond to the import of the elements in an import package. Considering UML subsystems the transformations correspond to adding the satisfying realization in the realization elements of the subsystem to the specification in the export interface. Especially implementing classes as for example BodHandover in Fig. 11 are added to UML interfaces like ExpHandoverControl. The import inclusions are in this case obviously the inclusion of the elements marked as <<ODproxy>> into the whole subsystem.

The relation between model and transformation semantics could be given by the requirement, that there has to be a construction $Constr_i$ for each inclusion i and a restriction $Restr_t$ for each transformation t and these have to be compatible with composition. This means, for $i_1: Spec_1 \hookrightarrow Spec_2$ and $i_2: Spec_2 \hookrightarrow Spec_3$ we have $Constr_{i_2 \circ i_1} = Constr_{i_2} \circ Constr_{i_1}$ and for $t_1: Spec \Rightarrow Spec'$ and $t_2: Spec' \Rightarrow Spec''$ we have $Restr_{t_2 \circ t_1} = Restr_{t_1} \circ Restr_{t_2}$. Another interesting compatibility condition is compositionality of the model semantics with extension. This means for $i: Spec_1 \hookrightarrow Spec_2$ and $t: Spec_1 \Rightarrow Spec'_1$ with $Ext_i(t): Spec_2 \Rightarrow Spec'_2$ and $i': Spec'_1 \hookrightarrow Spec'_2$ we have $Restr_{Ext_i(t)} \circ Constr_{i'} = Constr_i \circ Restr_t$ (i.e. the outer square in Fig. 14 commutes).

In other words, the inclusions and transformations of the transformation semantics approach, which could in general be interpreted arbitrarily, can be required to be sound w.r.t. the model semantics. After soundness has been proven for inclusions and transformations, the developer using the specification technique does not need to deal with the model semantics directly anymore, but can use the transformation semantics, which enables the refinement of specifications by syntactical transformations.

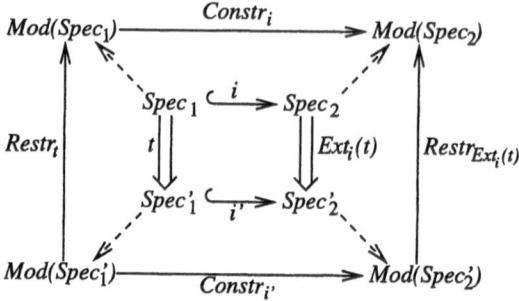

Fig. 14. Compatibility of model semantics with extension

In order to instantiate the requirements requested by the import specification, the composition of components yielding larger components is useful. In Fig. 15 the components $Comp_1$ and $Comp_2$ are composed via the connector $conn\colon Imp_1 \rightarrow Exp_2$ leading to a new component $Comp_3$. Regarding the transformation semantics approach $conn$ has to be a transformation, so that the extension $Ext_{imp_1}(exp_2 \circ conn) = ce'$ exists due to the extension property. Regarding the model semantics, there should be a restriction $Restr_{conn}\colon Mod(Exp_2) \rightarrow Mod(Imp_1)$. Note, that compositionality of the model semantics can be deduced from the compatibility of transformation and model semantics:

$$ModSem(Comp_3)$$
$$= Restr_{exp_3} \circ Constr_{imp_3}$$
$$= Restr_{exp_1} \circ Restr_{Ext_{imp_1}(exp_2 \circ conn)} \circ Constr_{imp_1'} \circ Constr_{imp_2}$$
$$= Restr_{exp_1} \circ Constr_{imp_1} \circ Restr_{conn} \circ Restr_{exp_2} \circ Constr_{imp_2}$$
$$= ModSem(Comp_1) \circ Restr_{conn} \circ ModSem(Comp_2)$$

The composition of components also leads to a composition operation for the instantiation to UML subsystems. With this composition architectures of UML subsystems with dependencies between their respective interfaces can be flattened by removing the redirections and proxy classes for satisfied imports and connecting the contents of the different subsystems directly. For example the architecture shown in Fig. 4 could be flattened to a single subsystem with no imports and just the interface ExpHandoverControl in the export as shown in Fig. 16.

In [19] the concepts of union and multiple interfaces for transformation components based on high-level replacement transformations, a generalization of graph transformations, have been additionally treated. These concepts are also a useful line of future work for this instantiation of the abstract component concept, because especially multiple import and export interfaces arise very naturally from the usage of UML subsystems.

Considering the notion of component in UML 2.0 introduced in the substructure specification in [2], it seems promising to also interpret these as instantiation of the abstract component concept. UML 2.0 components have provided and re-

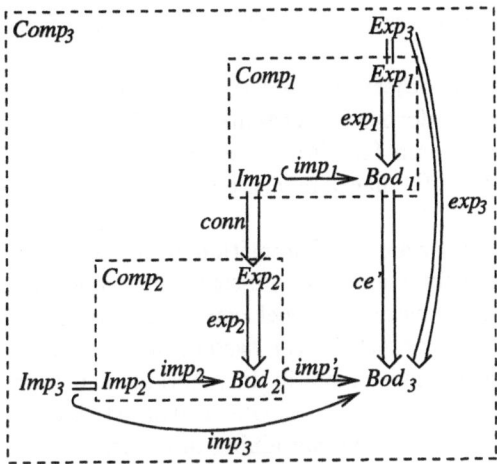

Fig. 15. Composition of components

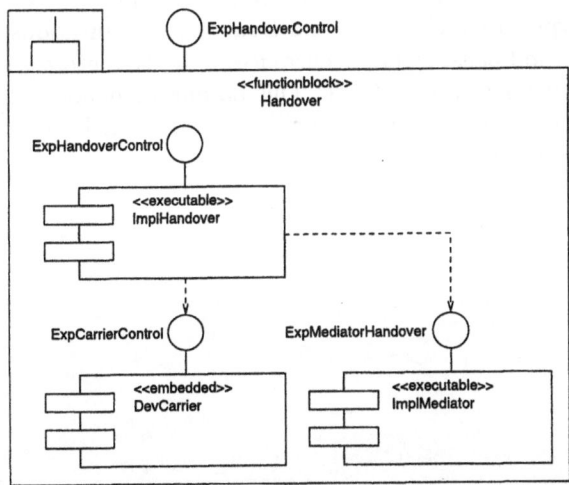

Fig. 16. Composition of Handover

quired interfaces and ports, that can be used as export and import specifications in the sense of the abstract component concept. Moreover, protocol state machines can be assigned to interfaces and ports, which allows to add constraints for the applicability of operations to the export and import specifications. Together with a model-theoretic semantics for (parts of) UML 2.0 similar to the one in the next section a formal notion of correctness could be derived for UML 2.0 components, which could enhance the reliability of specifications significantly, if practicable methods to proof this correctness are provided.

4   A Model-Theoretic Semantics for UML Subsystems

In this section we use object-oriented transformation systems (OOTS), which are variants of the transformation systems of Große-Rhode (see [8]), as a model-theoretic semantic domain for UML subsystems. The structure of OOTS and the specification by UML diagrams are presented in more detail in [16] in this volume.

An OOTS is given by a control transition graph, where the nodes are labeled with object configurations and the transitions are labeled with sets of actions executed during the transition. Object configurations contain the values of attributes for all existing objects of the system, where links between objects are considered as a special case of attributes. Actions can be calls and returns of methods, signal occurrences, and assignments of attribute values. Each OOTS is built over a static algebra St containing data type sorts with corresponding data functions. The entities of an OOTS (data type sorts, data functions, object sorts, attributes, signals, and methods) are declared in a data space signature $DSig$. The possible configurations and actions w.r.t. this data space signature then form the data space $\mathbf{D}_{DSig}$. Figure 17 shows an example OOTS, where we can also see that the actions are parameterized with parameters from the static part for data type sort parameters and from the configurations for object sort parameters. Method calls, signal occurrences and attribute assignments get an additional parameter as the first one. This parameter denotes the receiving object for a method call or signal or the object, whose attributes will be changed, for assignment actions.

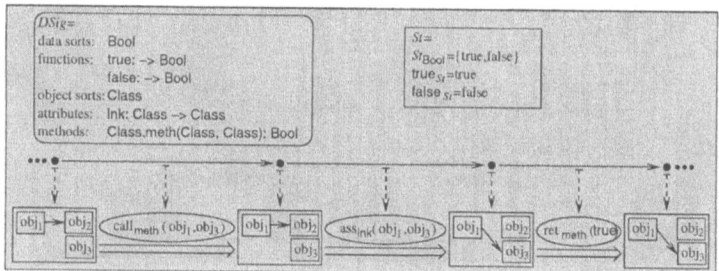

Fig. 17. Object-oriented transformation system

Each specification has an associated signature, which induces the data space of OOTS models for that specification. For example the import specification Imp of Handover as shown in Fig. 11 has the associated data space signature ImpSig given in Fig. 18. Note that we also give abbreviated names (in square brackets), which will be used in the following figures for readability reasons. The configurations of the data space $\mathbf{D}_{Imp\Sigma}$ contain sets of existing objects for the object sorts ImpCarrierControl and ImpMediatorHandover. The actions in the data space are the occurrences $occ_{ICC.eL}$ and $occ_{ICC.eU}$ of the signals and the

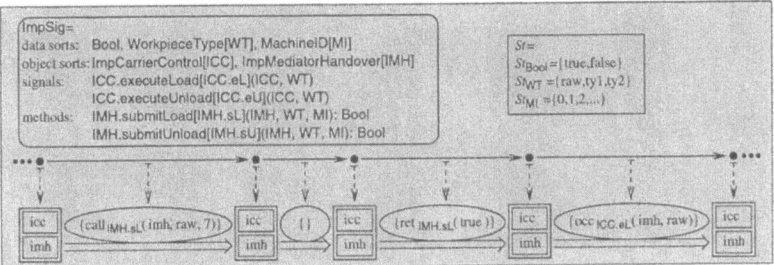

Fig. 18. OOTS for the import specification

call and return actions call$_{\text{IMH.sL}}$ and ret$_{\text{IMH.sL}}$ for the method submitLoad and call$_{\text{IMH.sU}}$ and ret$_{\text{IMH.sU}}$ for the method submitUnload. The models $Mod(\text{Imp})$ of the import specification are now all OOTS for the data space $\mathbf{D}_{\text{Imp}\Sigma}$, for which the statechart in Fig. 9 is satisfied, i. e. the signals executeLoad and executeUnload can be sent alternatingly. Since no statechart is given for ImpMediatorHandover, we assume that both methods are always callable. Because an OOTS for the import specification will in most cases be a restriction (see below) of a refined specification, it will usually contain transitions labeled with an empty set of actions, denoting that the events are not visible w. r. t. ImpΣ. A part of an example OOTS for the import of Handover is given in Fig. 18.

For the body specification from Fig. 11 some entities are added to the data space signature shown in Fig. 19, namely object sorts for the class BodHandover and the interface ExpHandoverControl, the attributes of BodHandover and the methods available for BodHandover and ExpHandoverControl. Now we can construct a minimal model for the body specification, a part of which is shown in Fig. 19. This model is minimal in the sense that the internal structure of imported methods is omitted. This means they are only represented by their call actions and return actions as e. g. the method submitLoad in the example. For each invocation of an imported method it contains all return actions, which an instantiation of the import could possibly generate, since the body model has to be able to interact with arbitrary instantiations.

In Fig. 19 we can also see, how inheritance is represented in an OOTS: Since, the class BodHandover inherits from ExpHandoverControl, each object of BodHandover is also an object of ExpHandoverControl, e. g. the object bh in the object configurations is the object ehc. The call and return actions are included for both, the object and method of the implementing class and the object and method of the abstract class.

According to the model theoretic approach for the semantics of components presented in [15] and discussed in Sect. 3 the semantics $ModSem(Comp)$ is given as composition $ModSem(Comp) = Restr_{\text{imp}} \circ Constr_{\text{exp}}$. The construction $Constr_{\text{imp}}: Mod(\text{Imp}) \to Mod(\text{Bod})$, which is the semantics of the import inclusion imp, can now be obtained by synchronizing any given model in $Mod(\text{Imp})$ with this minimal model leading to a model in $Mod(\text{Bod})$, which uses the im-

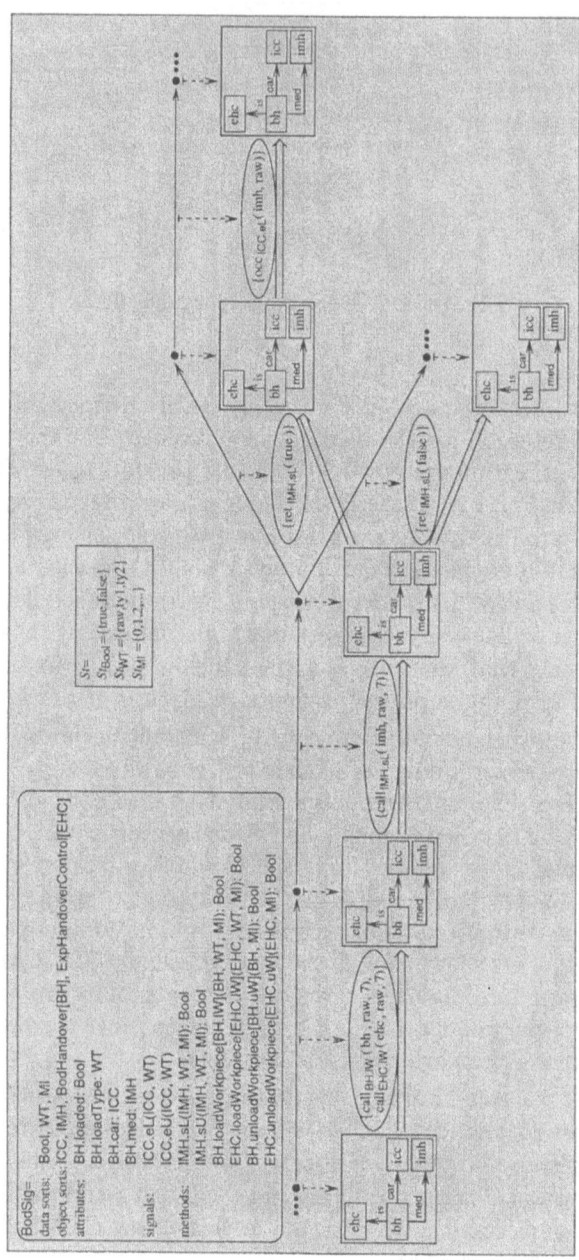

Fig. 19. Minimal OOTS for the body specification

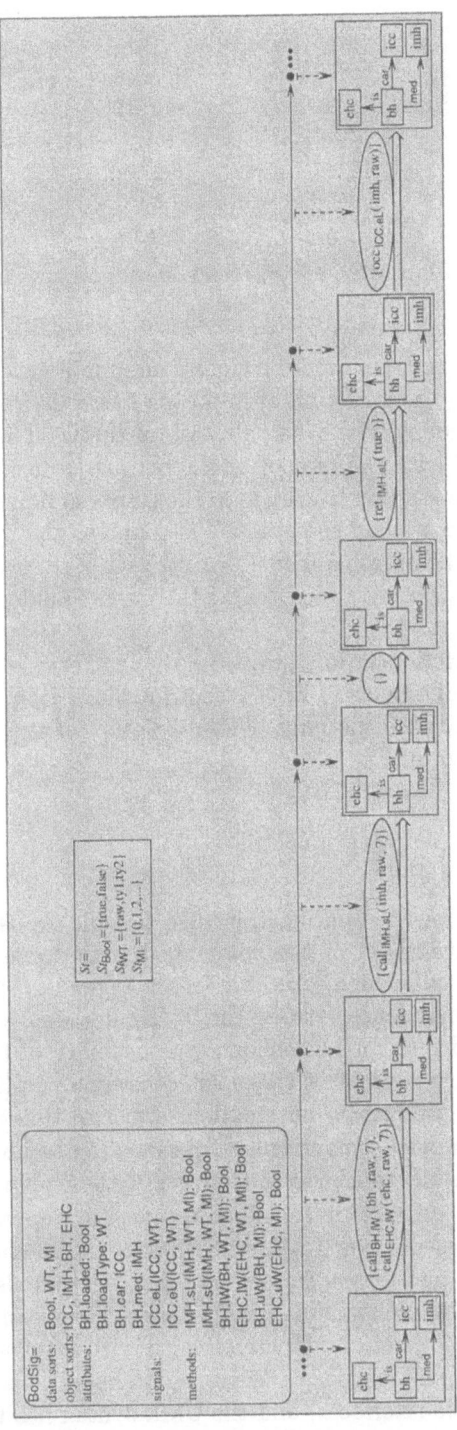

Fig. 20. Constructed OOTS for the body specification

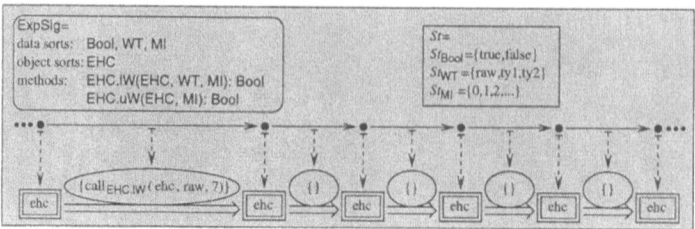

Fig. 21. Restricted OOTS for the export specification

ported model to realize the imported signals and methods. This synchronization is done by inserting the structure of imported methods from the import model into the minimal model. The syncronization of the OOTS part of the minimal model from Fig. 19 with the part of an import model from Fig. 18 is shown in Fig. 20, where the transition labeled with the empty action set, which represents the execution of the method submitLoad, is added to the minimal model of the body. The part of the minimal model dealing with a return value of false is not contained in the synchronization, because the import model returns true for this invocation.

Finally, the restriction $Restr_{exp}$, which is the semantics of the export inclusion exp, hides all parts of models of Bod, except for the object sort of ExpHandover-Control and its associated methods. The restriction of the partial body OOTS from Fig. 20 is shown in Fig. 21.

5   Conclusion

Along the example of the specification of a holonic transport system it was shown, how the advantages of the component notion can be carried over to the development of embedded, object oriented systems. This was achieved by establishing a correspondence between the UML subsystem and the IEC function block notion. In order to further enhance the usability of this concept, as well as the complementary concept of viewpoint consistency in [16], more aspects of specific interest for production automation, e. g. real-time constraints, will be integrated into the model semantics and specification techniques based on, but not limited to, the UML will be examined w. r. t. these aspects.

In order to have available well defined composition operations and a formal semantics we sketched out how UML susbsystems can be understood as components in an abstract and formal framework. This relation also has to be worked out in more detail to make available code generation, correctness notions, etc. for the modeling of components and function blocks with subsystems. Especially the relation between the different formal composition operations (horizontal composition, union, multiple interfaces) and the UML syntax has to be clarified.

Furthermore, the relations to the UML meta-model and components in the sense of UML 2.0 will be examined, in order to develop guide lines for tools supporting the concepts shown in this paper and the orthogonal concepts in [16]. More specifically, the component concept would induce a notion of correctness of components together with administration guidelines for such components, which could e. g. minimize and observe the proof obligations for correctness and composition of components.

Acknowledgements. This work has been supported by the IOSIP project in the DFG priority program SoftSpez. We would like to thank Hartmut Ehrig and Martin Große-Rhode and the referees for their valuable comments on previous versions of the paper.

References

1. Object Management Group: Unified Modeling Language – Version 1.5 (UML 1.5). (2003) Available from http://www.omg.org/.
2. Object Management Group: Unified Modeling Language – Version 2.0 (UML 2.0). (2004) Available from http://www.omg.org/.
3. Braatz, A., Klein, M., Ehrig, H., Westkämper, E.:   Konzeption und Entwicklung eines UML-basierten Funktionsblockmodells für den objektorientierten Steuerungsentwurf. In: Entwicklung und Betrieb komplexer Automatisierungssysteme (EKA 2003), Institut für Regelungs- und Automatisierungstechnik, TU Braunschweig (2003)
4. Westkämper, E., Braatz, A.:   Eine Methode zur objektorientierten Software-Spezifikation von dezentralen Automatisierungssystemen mit der Unified Modeling Language (UML). at – Automatisierungstechnik 5 (2001) 225–233
5. Ehrig, H., Orejas, F., Braatz, B., Klein, M., Piirainen, M.: A Generic Component Concept for System Modeling. In Kutsche, R.D., Weber, H., eds.: Fundamental Approaches to Software Engineering (FASE 2002). Number 2306 in Lecture Notes in Computer Science, Springer (2002) 33–48
6. Parnitzke, D.: On Formal Semantics of Object Systems with Data and Object Attributes. Forschungsbericht 2001/05, Fachbereich Informatik, TU Berlin (2001)
7. Tenzer, J.: A Formal Semantics of UML Class Diagrams based on Transformation Systems. Forschungsbericht 2001/09, Fachbereich Informatik, TU Berlin (2001)
8. Große-Rhode, M.: Semantic Integration of Heterogeneous Software Specifications. Monographs in Theoretical Computer Science. Springer (2004)
9. Klein, M., Braatz, B., Ehrig, H., Schröter, G., Bengel, M.:   Anwendung softwaretechnischer Komponentenkonzepte auf die Produktionsautomatisierung. atp – Automatisierungstechnische Praxis (2004) To appear.
10. International Electrotechnical Commission: IEC/PAS 61499-1 – Function Blocks for Industrial-Process Measurement and Control Systems – Part 1: Architecture. (2000)
11. Braatz, A.: Entwicklung einer Methode zur objektorientierten Spezifikation von Steuerungen. PhD thesis, Universität Stuttgart (2004) submitted.
12. Braatz, A., Ritter, A.: Referenzfallstudie Produktionstechnik (PA) v2.0 (2001) Available from http://tfs.cs.tu-berlin.de/~iosip/.
13. Ehrig, H., Große-Rhode, M.: Integration von Techniken der Softwarespezifikation für ingenieurwissenschaftliche Anwendungen. Informatik Forschung und Entwicklung 16 (2001) 110–117

14. Klein, M., Oezhan, M., Piirainen, M.: IOSIP Case Study Model Files (2002) Available from http://tfs.cs.tu-berlin.de/~iosip/.
15. Ehrig, H., Orejas, F.: A Generic Component Framework for Integrated Data Type and Process Modeling Techniques. Forschungsbericht 2001/12, Fachbereich Informatik, TU Berlin (2001)
16. Braatz, B., Klein, M., Schröter, G.: Semantical Integration of Object-Oriented Viewpoint Specification Techniques. In Ehrig, H., Damm, W., Desel, J., Große-Rhode, M., Reif, W., Schnieder, E., Westkämper, E., eds.: Integration of Software Specification Techniques for Applications in Engineering. Number 3147 in Lecture Notes in Computer Science. Springer (2004)
17. Ehrig, H., Mahr, B.: Fundamentals of Algebraic Specification 2 – Module Specifications and Constraints. Volume 21 of Monographs on Theoretical Computer Science. Springer (1990)
18. Piirainen, M.: Applications of a Generic Component Framework to a UML Case Study in Production Automation. Diploma thesis, TU Berlin (2003)
19. Ehrig, H., Orejas, F., Braatz, B., Klein, M., Piirainen, M.: A Component Framework for System Modeling Based on High-Level Replacement Systems. Software and System Modeling **3** (2004) 114–135

Specification Methodology, Case Studies, and Experiments – An Introduction to the Subject Area of Traffic Control Systems

Eckehard Schnieder

Institute for Traffic Safety and Automation Engineering,
Technical University of Braunschweig,
Langer Kamp 8, 38106 Braunschweig, Germany
E.Schnieder@tu-bs.de

1 Introduction

"Specification" is a very complex concept. This complexity results initially from the questions "What is the purpose of a specification? What is the subject of a specification?" and "Who writes a specification?", which in turn lead to the questions "What methods and processes are used for specification?". Answering these questions in detail and finding a definition for the term "specification" that encompasses the full extent and depth of this term represents an enormous academic challenge; it is also of great practical relevance. Because even if analytical deductions can be made from a specification that provide an understanding in retrospect, the actual milestones of a correct and efficient specification are in fact a goal-oriented synthesis of the subject of specification as a unit and its proper functioning in reality.

There are two sides to a specification. On the one hand, it involves methodically identifying all its objectives correctly and unambiguously and defining them clearly. On the other hand, a specification is a result, a condensed version of deliberations; it is also an independent manifestation of thoughts, methods and a selection of variants in the form of more or less substantial documentation and more or less formal or formalised illustrations that take the form of text or images. A specification is thus also a touchstone and a mirror for the results it generates.

It is impossible to carry out scientific research on the methods and definitions of a specification without taking into account its technical field and area of application, or the people involved in the specification process. Each technical field has developed its own range of methods and definitions; however, these are questioned whenever new technologies and paradigms promise better or new solutions. From a scientific point of view, research about the migration of specifications is very revealing in this respect. Particularly given its place in the starting phase of a project, a specification is crucial to the remaining project process.

H. Ehrig et al. (Eds.): INT 2004, LNCS 3147, pp. 89–95, 2004.

2   Domains Traffic (Control) Systems and Models

The focus research programme "Integration of Software Specification Techniques with Applications in Engineering" has decided to highlight traffic control systems to consider these scientific issues in more detail; this technical field unites different perspectives, hence its attraction for scientific research. Until only a few decades ago, this field had its own established development methods and notations based on electromechanical control and actuators, and wired communication, which meet the very high requirements regarding the safety of the persons involved in this field. Given the opportunities offered today by digital, hardware and software technologies, or mobile radio transmission, as well the traditional engineering skills and innovative computing knowledge we have, we are presented with the challenge to use and further develop the opportunities offered by the new technologies to achieve higher operational performance and efficiency in this safety-relevant field.

Migrating the immense capital spending volume and the installed traffic control systems for road and rail transport is a task of a national economic scale, which concerns the whole continent and will take decades to implement. It started two decades ago with several European programmes such as Prometheus for road transport or ETCS for rail transport, and has been pursued in numerous projects within the european framework research programmes.

The many update issues, ranging from changes to traffic routes, to vehicle procurement or technical equipment, never question the system itself; however, the question generally arises as to whether it is possible to concentrate less on generic models or basically invariable universal domain models, and to shift the focus instead to specific tasks using modularisation and parameterisation. There have been first steps in that direction, such as the European Formal Methods Rail Initiative [Fm], the Open Track Model [Hü1], or the RailML project [Hü2], whose aim it has been to create standard product data models. These have many advantages, such as data exchange, simulation modelling or module integration. Some conceptual approaches are also promising, such as generic models with a wide variety of definitions, as those presented by [Me] or, in this volume, by [RJZ]; these may be developed further to form a standard basis for specifications.

3   Reference Case Study

To study different specification techniques that are crucial to the success of a project, a comparative approach was chosen. This allowed focusing on a highly realistic sample case without digressing into technical detail.

To avoid restricting specification requirements to achieving specific functionalities, we chose a highly topical example as a case study, the level crossing with barriers. It integrates the high demand for safety relevance with the effects and repercussions this would have on the specification by expressly excluding and avoiding requirements that were not permitted. Due to their hybrid dynamics with discrete event and continuous behaviour, level crossings with barriers have frequently been studied and referred to. With the support of Deutsche Bahn AG, we constructed a complex case study and delivered its documentation as a benchmark for this investigation [JS,HPSS,Sc4]. This provided a common basis and reference for the work on specification methods and scientific study. As the papers in this volume show, a wide variety of approaches, in terms of both the methods and the definitions used, has been the result.

To compare the individual approaches, we organised a number of workshops e. g. [Sc4]. Given their common object of reference, the presentations and discussions went into far more depth than is usual. In a collaboration with the FORMS (Formal Methods for Railway Management Systems) series of conferences, our reference case study was also a required reference for conference papers [Sc1,Sc2, Sc3,TS].

Given its accessibility for the scientific community, the reference case study was also widely used internationally. We would like to mention in particular the work carried out by Italian partners [Im], or the French initiative for formal specification techniques, which used our reference case study as a basis for its research [BBM]. Work carried out in this field has also been applied in an international initiative for developing a domain model for the railway sector [Tr]

4   Demonstrator Level Crossing

In order not to limit the scientific treatment of specification techniques to theory and form, an experimental phase provided the opportunity to test, validate and compare their results. For this purpose, a scaled model of a level crossing and a train model were conceived, constructed and validated using simulation [ESSS1, ESSS2,HKSS,HPSS,JS]. This provided a test environment that was affordable, and which was frequently used by the working parties for their experiments on site at the Institute for Traffic Safety and Automation of Braunschweig Technical University.

5   Scientific Methods in Case Studies and Real Experiments

In the natural and engineering sciences, real experiments are an essential part of research, although cost and efficiency constraints have led to a continuous shift in methods towards using digital simulation experiments in these fields, too. But epistemology states that the ultimate validity of a hypothesis or model can only be shown in a direct real experiment. Before implementing a project in real life, experiments are first carried out on a smaller scale using simulators or mock-ups, or on the so-called technical scale. This use of scientific methods is quite established in sciences and engineering; however, it is often still viewed as redundand by computer scientists.

"Integration of Software Specification Techniques with Applications in Engineering" not only means integrating descriptive methods and process models, it also implies addressing the differences in scientific culture there are between these (two) worlds. Real experiments are viewed as normal in physics, biology or chemistry; but engineering science goes even further. Natural scientists are focused on the acquisition and analysis of knowledge. Engineering scientists, on the other hand, strive to achieve real-life goals by applying synthesis in technical facilities. They therefore need to take into account the specific physical laws of a technical field in order to complete a synthesis in the technical constraints given, using their technical expertise. Computer scientists for their part primarily consider formal models and laws as abstract mental constructs. Their "experiments" are not restricted by the inertia of physical processes; computer scientists are therefore surprised by the physical constraints of their engineering counterpart, which responds within the constraints of the inertia inherent in its own laws. Only when the chain of events and effects incorporating physical and data-related factors has been completed with the integration of engineering and information science concepts, can we progress to specifications that are sustainable in practice.

6   Overview

The papers below that use the reference case study Traffic Control Systems have approached the inherent topic in a number of ways and have studied its aspects in detail from their respective points of view.

The first paper by Hänsel, Poliak, Slovák and Schnieder, project KNOSSOS [HPSS], provides a detailed introduction to the reference case study. It starts with the question whether formal specifications are required in railway signalling technology. This is followed by a detailed presentation of the case study including normal functioning and malfunctioning behaviour. The second part presents the concept for and technical implementation of the demonstration model; it also describes integration options for coupling executable specifications.

The paper by Arabestani, Bitsch and Gayen, project SafeRail [ABG], addresses two aspects. Firstly, it shows how the system definition is prioritised using UML descriptive methods. This applies to its structure, the dynamics of the internal control behaviour using state-transition charts, and to the reactions between train, control centre and level crossing control. The authors have used message sequence model scenarios for this purpose. They have also applied the safety pattern concept as an example to explain the methical formalisation of safety requirements as a system.

The paper by Berkenkötter, Bisanz, Hannemann and Peleska, project HYBRIS [BBHP], extends UML by hybrid aspects with real-time properties and semantically defines it to match the special dynamic aspects of this technical field more closely.

Using the highly complex example of a new railway interlocking system, Rástočný, Janota and Zahradník [RJZ] show in their paper how UML expressions can be used for specifications of real industrial and complex tasks in the railway sector. They give details of different UML modelling levels, such as use case, class and sequence diagrams or state charts, and use them for different specification tasks. This is the first time the specification of a signal box has been comprehensively documented in a scientific paper.

In addition to the papers compiled here, which relate directly to the reference case study, the focus programme included other projects (from other subject areas) that also used this study as a reference (project ForMoSA by Reif, Schellhorn, Thums, Ortmeier [OTSR,TSOR], project USE, by Damm, Klose, Westphal [BBDKWW] and also the second contribution of the projekt KNOSSOS [Ei]). These have been published in others sections of this volume, since they have a different focus. The subjects include operational specification methods, fault detection etc.

7   Results

As new and successful results of the subject area Traffic Control Systems the following can be summarized:

- The research programme provided one of the world's first comprehensive *analyses within the railway transportation domain by means of computer science methods*. Its results are an important contribution to the similar oriented European activities FME, FORMS and recently TRain etc.
- A realistic and *full detail reference case study of the level crossing control* was created. It includes all kind of the multifaceted domain system features. Since other international research groups applied the case study too, an *international accreditation and visibility* was achieved.
- To demonstrate experimentally results achieved in the field of computer science a *physical model of the case study* was designed and build. It is directly accessible for experiments by standard interfaces; a remote control via internet is intended.
- The main conclusion of the research is that the *contemporary techniques* (e.g. UML) *are not sufficient* in order to achieve unambiguous and verifiable software specifications for this specific and safety relevant domain. Hence several *formal extensions were developed and investigated*.

References

[ABG]   S. Arabestani, F. Bitsch, J.-T.Gayen: *Precise Definition of the Single-track Level Crossing in Radio-based Operation in UML Notation and Specification of Safety Requirements*. This volume.

[BBHP]   S. Berkenköter, S. Bisanz, U. Hannemann, J. Peleska: *Hybrid UML and its Application to Specification and Test of Train Control Systems*. This volume.

[BBM]   J.-L. Boulanger, P. Bon, G. Mariano : *From UML to B : a level crossing case study*. 8th International Level Crossing Symposium, University of Sheffield, Rail Safety and Standards Board, Sheffield 2004.

[BBDKWW]   M. Brill, R. Buschermöhle, W. Damm, J. Klose, B. Westphal, H. Wittke: em Formal Verification of LSCs in the Development Process. This volume.

[Ei]   S. Einer: *STOP - Specification Technique of Operational Processes.* This volume.

[ESSS1]   S. Einer, H. Schrom, R. Slovák, E. Schnieder: *Experimental validation of train control systems by using a railway model.* In: J. Allan, R. J. Hill, C. A. Brebbia, G. Sciutto, S. Sone, (Eds.): Computers in Railways VIII, S. 925-934, Ashurst Lodge, Ashurst, Southampton, SO40 7AA, UK, 2002. 8th International Conference on Computer Aided Design, Manufacture and Operation in the Railway and Other Advanced Mass Transit Systems (COMPRAIL 2002), Lemnos, Greece, WITPRESS.

[ESSS2]   S. Einer, H. Schrom, R. Slovák, E. Schnieder: *A railway demonstrator model for experimental investigation of integrated specification techniques.* In: H. Ehrig, M. Grosse-Rhode (Eds.): ETAPS 2002 - Integration of Software Specification Techniques, pp. 84-93, Berlin, April 2002. TU Berlin, DFG.

[Fm]   Internet page of the "Formal Methods Europe" http://www.fmeurope.org

[HKSS]   F. Hänsel, S. König, R. Slovák, E. Schnieder: *A Railway demonstrator model for experimental Validation of integrated specification techniques.* In: E. Schnieder (Ed.): Workshop on Software specification of safety relevant transportation control tasks, pp. 23-34, 2003.

[HPSS]   F. Hänsel, J. Poliak, R. Slovák, E. Schnieder: *Reference Case Study "Traffic Control Systems" for Comparison and Validation of Formal Specications Using a Model Demonstrator.* This volume.

[Hü1]   D. Hürlimann: *Objektorientierte Modellierung von Infrastrukturelementen und Betriebsvorgängen im Eisenbahnwesen.* Dissertation, Technische Wissenschaften ETH Zürich, No. 14281, 2001.

[Hü2]   D. Hürlimann: *RailML - ein generelles Austauschformat für Eisenbahndaten.* Special edition in the DVWG series of publications on the occasion of the "transport logistics" international specialist fair, 22-26, DVWG, Berlin, 2003.

[Im]   S. Imastato: *Level Crossing Safety.* 11th International Symposium Zel2004, CETRA University of Zilina, 2004.

[JS]   L. Jansen, E. Schnieder: *Traffic Control Systems Case Study: Problem Description and a Note on Domain-based Software Specification.* In: Ehrig, H.; Große-Rhode, M.; Orejas, F., Hrsg.: INT 2000 Integration of Specification Techniques with Applications in Engineering, pp. 41-47, TU Berlin, July 2000.

[Me]   M. Meyer zu Hörste: *Methodische Analyse und generische Modellierung von Eisenbahnleit- und -sicherungssystemen.* Dissertation, Technische Universität Braunschweig, Institut für Verkehrssicherheit und Automatisierungstechnik, 2004.

[RJZ]   K. Rástočný, A. Janota, J. Zahradník: *The Use of UML for Development of a Railway Interlocking System.* This volume.

[OTSR]   F. Ortmeier, A. Thums, G. Schellhorn, W. Reif: *Combining Formal Methods and Safety Analysis - The ForMoSA Approach.* This volume.

[Sc1]   E. Schnieder (Ed.): *Forms 1998 - Formale Techniken für die Eisenbahnsicherung.* Institut für Regelungs- und Automatisierungstechnik, TU Braunschweig 1998.

[Sc2]   E. Schnieder (Ed.): *Forms 1999 - Formale Techniken für die Eisen-bahnsicherung*. Institut für Regelungs- und Automatisierungstechnik, TU Braunschweig, in: Fortschritt-Berichte VDI 1999.

[Sc3]   E. Schnieder (Ed.): *Forms 2000 - Formale Techniken für die Eisen-bahnsicherung*. Institut für Regelungs- und Automatisierungstechnik, TU Braunschweig, in: Fortschritt-Berichte VDI 2000.

[Sc4]   E. Schnieder (Hrsg.): *International Workshop on Software Specification of Safety Relevant Transportation Control Tasks*. Düsseldorf, 2003. VDI Verlag.

[Tr]   Internet page of the "TRain: The Railway Domain"
            http://www.railwaydomain.org/

[TSOR]   A. Thums, G. Schellhorn, F. Ortmeier, W. Reif: *Interactive Verification of Statecharts*. This volume.

[TS]   G. Tarnai, E. Schnieder (Eds.): *Forms 2003 - Formal Methods for Railway Operation and Control Systems*. L'Harmattan Budapest, 2003.

Reference Case Study "Traffic Control Systems" for Comparison and Validation of Formal Specifications Using a Railway Model Demonstrator

Frank Hänsel, Jan Poliak, Roman Slovák, and Eckehard Schnieder

Institute for Traffic Safety and Automation Engineering,
Technical University of Braunschweig,
Langer Kamp 8, 38106 Braunschweig, Germany
{haensel|poliak|slovak|schnieder}@iva.ing.tu-bs.de

Abstract. As domain modelling has been identified as a key issue for putting formal specification techniques into engineering practice, two reference case studies were elaborated within the research programme "Integration of Software Specification Techniques for Applications in Engineering". One of them, coming from the railway transportation control domain and using an example of a radio based level crossing control system, was developed at the Institute of Traffic Safety and Automation Engineering. A physical railway model demonstrator was designed and developed as a means of comparison and validation for the formal specifications coming from partners involved in the research program.

1 Introduction

With regard to outstanding research issues in software specification, theoretical computer science often demonstrates the applicability of newly developed formalisms by means of small, well defined and easy-to-understand examples. Well known and widely studied problems are a generalized railroad crossing [HJL] and a steam boiler controller [?]. With good reason, the settings of such small-scale examples are generally restricted to the problem characteristics at hand. However, various aspects of practical relevance are commonly neglected and their combination cannot be studied in such settings. Industrial case studies might seem to be a good way out, but on the other hand tend to be complex, i. e., not easy to understand for non-domain experts, and due to their size, often require huge resources to implement. In addition, the settings of industrial case studies for some other good reasons often are not published in complete detail which makes it impossible to apply and compare different specification techniques and approaches for their integration on a common reference. Accordingly there is a need for, one might say, virtual industrial case studies that are realistic, well formed and publicly accessible.

Two case studies have been provided within the focus research programme "Integration of Software Specification Techniques for Applications in Engineer-

H. Ehrig et al. (Eds.): INT 2004, LNCS 3147, pp. 96–118, 2004.
© Springer-Verlag Berlin Heidelberg 2004

ing" of the German Research Council (DFG). They aim to close the aforementioned gap and serve as a reference for the comparison of different approaches. This paper deals with the case study from the traffic control systems domain. The problem is the specification of a radio based railway level crossing control application, which is distributed over a train-borne control system (on-board system), a level crossing control system and an operation centre. The setting described in the next chapter is reasonably realistic, as it is taken from the specification of a new radio based train control system that has been developed for the German Railways [Ff]. It contains various kinds of problems that require the use of different specification techniques and, at the same time, is limited with respect to complexity and work load. It is important to note that the setting of the case study is not intended to resemble a real application and that simplifications have been made on purpose in accordance with the aims of the case study.

To validate the results of the projects, simulation in requirements engineering [Kr] as well as in system design and realization is needed. The problem is that there is no real continuous way from formal work on paper to a real implementation. In other domains, e. g. chemical process technology, an additional step of development, also called "scaling up" is widely accepted to handle this problem. It means to experiment in low scaled processes, before starting the real operation. Such experiments also seem to be necessary in software engineering, but not many experiences have been reported [Sn].

The purpose of validation requires a real testing environment with its specific properties. One of these is a certain degree of inaccuracy in detecting the system's current state. Implementing this in software leads to a high model complexity. This was one reason why it has been decided to build a physical railway model for validating the research results of the focus research programme under nearly real operating conditions. The paper firstly presents the objectives and features of the reference case study (Chapter 2) [SJ]. Secondly (Chapter 3), the functional design of the demonstrator, its implementation and first experiences with the integration of formal control specifications and their validation are presented.

2 Reference Case Study

2.1 Formal Specification in the Railway Signalling Domain

In [Bj] domain engineering is called a prerequisite for a new software engineering paradigm. Domain modelling is the activity of explicating all the generic knowledge of a domain that might ever become relevant for a systems engineering step. In particular, a domain model has to be free of all requirements of the systems to be developed. Thus, domain modelling allows a separation between the explication step and the requirements specification. The necessity to establish consistent relations between a domain model and a software specification motivates the studying of domain modelling and domain-based support for software specification in the context of the DFG focus research programme.

Several domain-oriented approaches are known from software engineering, which may be considered to support other specification techniques. Domain-specific languages [Ni] are tailor-made to express problems of a restricted domain, often in a declarative way. They are easy to use for domain experts and in many cases allow for automatic code generation. A modification or extension of the underlying domain model, however, is expensive and limits flexibility of use.

In [BBM] a formal domain model is presented using the RAISE specification language. In combination with a formal requirements specification the approach allows formal analysis and proofs. However, a formal domain model is difficult to construct, maintain and understand for domain experts. A linguistic approach is described in [OS]. A normative domain-specific language can be constructed on the basis of a lexicon and a set of sentence patterns. The lexicon (expert terminology) defines a list of words together with their meanings, that can be used in a domain (see [Ui] for a lexicon of railway terminology). Schemata for constructing correct sentence patterns ensure an informally but unambiguously defined meaning of complex sentences. The linguistic method seems highly promising for a comprehensible domain approach for software specification. A normative human-style language is easy to learn, adapt and use for domain experts. Moreover, it is independent of a specific domain and not biased towards or against a certain design method.

Specialists in the train control systems domain generally are not familiar with formal software specification techniques. Nonetheless, they are increasingly confronted with the necessity of applying formal methods throughout the entire product life cycle in order to ensure high quality results for problems of growing complexity.

2.2   Regular Behavior Definition

The problem chosen for the reference case study is a decentralized radio-based control system for a railway level crossing, where a single track railway line and a road cross on one level. The intersection area of the road and the railway line is called the danger zone, since trains and road traffic are not allowed to enter it at the same time to avoid collision. The railway crossing is equipped with barriers and road traffic lights. Traffic lights at the level crossing consist of a red and a yellow light. When the yellow light is shown road users (drivers, cyclists, pedestrians etc.) should stop at the level crossing if possible. The red light means that the level crossing is closed for road traffic and road users are not allowed to enter it. The yellow and red lights must never be on together. When both lights are off, road users may enter the crossing area. Half arm barriers are used to block the entry lane on either side of the level crossing. Since there are no barriers for the exit lanes, road users may possibly enter the crossing area on the opposite lane. Although this behaviour constitutes a severe contravention of the traffic regulations, it can be frequently observed due to long waiting times at closed level crossings. This has to be taken into account for the level crossing control system by monitoring a maximum closure time.

The traffic lights and barriers at the level crossing are controlled by the level crossing control system. It is activated when a train is approaching the level crossing (see Figure 1). In the activated mode the level crossing control system

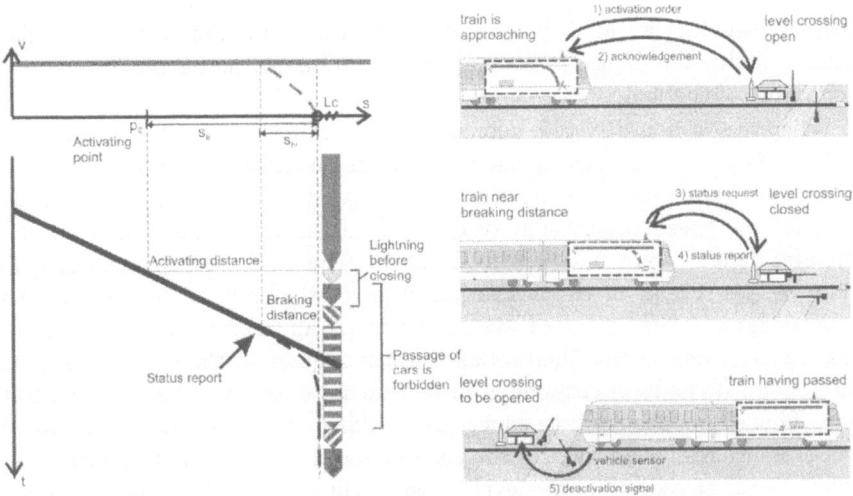

Fig. 1. The regular scenario of the operational railway process

performs a sequence of actions according to a specific timing in order to safely close the crossing and to ensure the danger zone is free of road traffic. First, the traffic lights are switched on to show the yellow light; then after 3 seconds they are switched to red. Approximately 9 seconds later, the barriers start to be lowered. If the barriers have been completely lowered within a maximum time of 6 seconds, the level crossing control system signals that the level crossing is in its safe state, thus allowing the train to pass the level crossing. When the train has completely passed the crossing area the level crossing may be opened for road traffic again and the level crossing control system switches back to the deactivated mode.

The main components of interest for software specification are the train-borne control system, the trackside level crossing control system and the operations centre. These main components can communicate with each other by means of mobile radio communication. Transmission times on the radio network may vary and have to be considered. Radio telegrams even may get lost on the radio network.

The approaching of a train at the level crossing is traditionally detected by trackside equipment or signal staff such that the level crossing can be closed in time to let the train pass through without any delay or braking action. In modern radio-based train control systems the activation of the level crossing is based on continuous self-localization of the train and mobile communication between the train and the decentralized level crossing control system. A route map on board the train contains the positions of potential danger points at level crossings and provides additional information for the train on when or where to send an activation order to the respective level crossing control system.

Self-localization is realized by balises, i. e. small transponders between the rails, transmitting an identification signal to the train. Comparison of this information with the digital route map stored on board the train allows an exact positioning of the train.

When the on-board system detects that the train is approaching a level crossing it sends a radio message to the level crossing control system to switch on the road traffic lights and to lower the crossing barriers. It will also set a braking curve for the speed supervision system, which will make the train stop at the potential danger point in a failure situation. The level crossing control system acknowledges receipt of the activation order to the train. After receipt of the acknowledgment the on-board system waits an appropriate time for the level crossing to be closed and then sends a status request to the level crossing control system. If the level crossing is in its safe state, this will be reported to the train. This allows the train to cancel the braking curve and safely pass over the level crossing while supervising the regular speed profile. The triggering of the vehicle sensor at the end of the level crossing will cause the barriers to be opened again and the traffic lights to be switched off.

2.3   Failure Behavior Definition

Possible failure conditions have to be taken into account to achieve safe control of the level crossing and the train. A main cause of failures is the malfunctioning of sensors or actuators. Faults may also occur in the main physical structures. Failures of communication systems may affect the communication between control systems and devices as described above for radio networks and mobile communication. Last, but not least the control systems themselves may fail.

Defective devices will be repaired after some time so that the occurrences of both failures and repairs have to be taken into account. While failures may occur at any time, repair of defective devices in the case of non-recoverable failures, mostly physical components or sensors and actuators, will not take place when there is a train approaching or passing the level crossing.

In the case study only a limited number of failures are considered (Figure 2): failures of the yellow or red traffic lights (to be considered separately), the barriers, the vehicle sensor and the delayed receipt or loss of telegrams on the radio network. The traffic lights and the vehicle sensor are constantly monitored and defects are immediately reported to the level crossing control system. Failure of the barriers can only be detected by time-out when barriers fail to reach the upper or lower end position in time or at all. The required behaviour of the control systems under failure conditions will be described below according to the time sequence of failure occurrences and control reactions (see also Figure 2).

The level crossing control system is able to detect the occurrence of failures of traffic lights and vehicle sensors. It immediately reports such an event to the operations centre, which is able to have the defective component repaired. After repair, it may be necessary to carry out re-initialisation of the level crossing control system (e. g. barrier failure). This does not imply that train operation

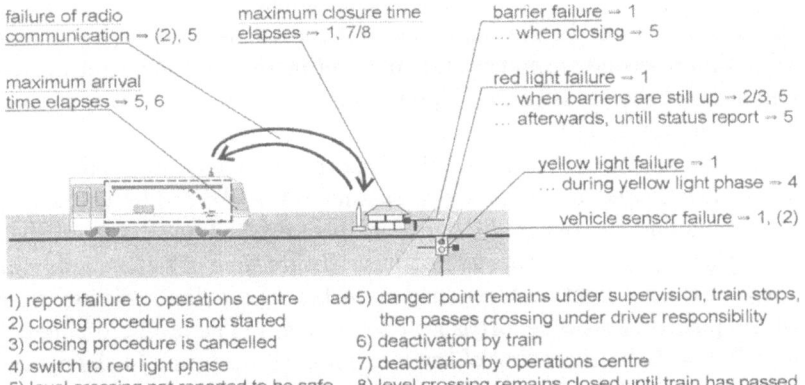

failure of radio
communication → (2), 5

maximum arrival
time elapses → 5, 6

maximum closure time
elapses → 1, 7/8

barrier failure → 1
... when closing → 5

red light failure → 1
... when barriers are still up → 2/3, 5
... afterwards, untill status report → 5

yellow light failure → 1
... during yellow light phase → 4

vehicle sensor failure → 1, (2)

1) report failure to operations centre
2) closing procedure is not started
3) closing procedure is cancelled
4) switch to red light phase
5) level crossing not reported to be safe

ad 5) danger point remains under supervision, train stops,
    then passes crossing under driver responsibility
6) deactivation by train
7) deactivation by operations centre
8) level crossing remains closed until train has passed

Fig. 2. Technical faults to consider within the operational process

is suspended on the affected section of track for the time up until the repair is carried out.

After having sent the activation order to the level crossing, the train waits for an acknowledgment. The train will send no status request until the acknowledgment has been received. The following applies in all cases, whether the train has sent the status request having received the acknowledgment or not. If the train does not subsequently receive the status report indicating that the level crossing is in its safe state before entering its breaking curve, the on-board system will apply the brakes until the status report has been received or the train has come to a standstill. If the status report is received before the train comes to a complete stop, the brakes are released and the train can continue. Otherwise the system causes a message to appear on the driver's display, asking the driver to make sure that it is safe to cross the level crossing and to give confirmation via the display unit that the level crossing is in its safe state. If meanwhile the status report has been received, the message is cancelled from the display, the brakes are released and the driver does not need to give confirmation. Otherwise the driver has to confirm that the level crossing is in its safe state in order to release the brakes and continue the journey.

After receipt of an activation order from a train, the level crossing control system immediately checks if the level crossing control should be activated, and accordingly will or will not send an acknowledgment to the train. The level crossing control system will not be activated if the red traffic lights or the vehicle sensor are defective. If the level crossing control system has been activated, then, after a minimum green time has passed since the last deactivation of the level crossing, the yellow traffic light is switched on for 3 seconds. If the yellow traffic light becomes defective either before or during the yellow light period, the traffic lights are switched to red and the red light period of 9 seconds is extended accordingly by the lost yellow light time. If the red traffic light fails after activation of the level crossing control system the closing procedure has to be cancelled unless the lowering of the barriers has already begun. The level crossing must be reported to be in the failure state if the barriers fail to be completely lowered within 6 seconds from the start of lowering or if in the meantime the red traffic light has become defective. Upon request, the current status of the level crossing will be reported to the train.

If the vehicle sensor becomes defective, the level crossing control system cannot be deactivated anymore by a passing train. Accordingly the barriers remain lowered and the red traffic light remains switched on. However, the level crossing control system monitors a maximum closure time of 240 seconds starting from the time the red lights are switched on. After the maximum closure time has elapsed, no positive status report is sent to the train. The level crossing control system will report the exceeding of the maximum closure time to the operations centre. The operations centre finds out, whether the train has already passed the level crossing or not. In the first case, the operations centre sends a deactivation order to the level crossing. Otherwise the train is still approaching or just passing over the level crossing and the rules for late arrival at the level crossing apply as described above.

Regarding redundancies and symmetries within the geometry and equipment at the level crossing, it was recommended that any multiplicity of devices or processes should be ignored (e. g. number of trains, level crossings or directions of train traffic). For the purpose of specifying non-finite behaviour, the track may be assumed to be virtually circular. However a clear separation of different laps made on the track is recommended, so that no two successive closing procedures of the level crossing overlap. Therefore it might be necessary to synchronize e. g. the opening of the barriers with the next sending of an activation order by the train. Also note that the train driver may slow down, stop or speed up the train at any moment or location. This must not affect the safety of the level crossing control system. The train may be assumed to always run in the same direction. The described reference case study combines different aspects of specification problems from the traffic control system domain and was successfully used for a comparison of properties and practical capabilities of different formal specification techniques. The more detailed reports can be found in the papers of [OTSR,TSOR,BBHP,ABG,BBDKWW,Ei].

3   Model Demonstrator

3.1   Functional Design

Software validation in the context of an assessment process in railway engineering today often requires integration of hardware components (e. g. validation of the European Train Control System in railway laboratories in Germany and Spain). This has the advantage of highly unambiguous and therefore trustworthy results. The requirement for real time operation capability and the specific inaccuracy in behaviour were the main reasons for the chosen hardware realisation of the validation environment.

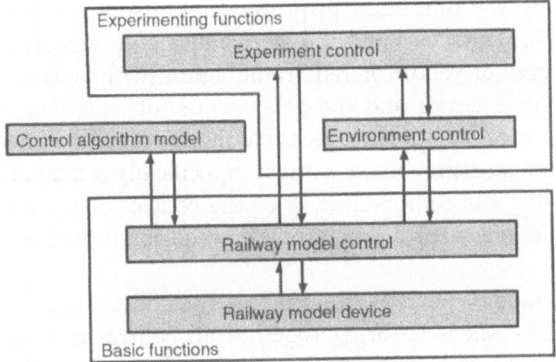

Fig. 3. Functional structure of the demonstrator

To achieve the aim of formal specification validation, several practical problems have to be taken into account. Firstly, the use of the physical model has to be effectively available for all participants of the research programme. To solve this problem an internet connection was included in its functional design.

Secondly, within various research projects of the focus research programme different modelling languages supported by different software tools are used. Some of the applied formal techniques do not allow modelling of all aspects included in the reference case study specification. Thus a suitable tool coupling the concept with a flexible architecture of the railway model control system is required, which will make it possible to join model parts designed by different tools into one virtual model.

In order to meet all requirements mentioned at the outset, a functional structure of the demonstrator control system was derived (Figure 3). The structure consists of three main functional groups. Besides the external control algorithm model, developed according to the case study specification, these are the basic functions of the demonstrator and the group of experimental functions. Additionally a remote control algorithm integration via the internet must be possible. In the following sections a more detailed description of each demonstrator function block will be given. A detailed explanation of the railway model device can be found in chapter 3.3.

The main task of the experiment control is to prepare, configure, start and stop the experiment as well as the data recording and processing and the final visualization of the obtained results. Also a suitable mode of environment control has to be chosen. In order to provide the remote experiment control via the internet, a suitable web interface is needed which supports experiment definition, control, visualization and exporting of results.

The environment control has to simulate the possible influence of the environment of real operating conditions. At the same time the controllability of the environment influences must be guaranteed. On the one hand, these are the inputs resulting from potential train driver behaviour and from possible actions initiated by the operation inspector supervising the functionality of the level crossing. On the other hand, the occurrence of hazardous failures has to be simulated. Failures of yellow or red traffic lights (to be considered separately), barriers, the vehicle sensor and the delay or loss of telegrams on the radio network are considered. One of three possible modes of environment control has to be selected before starting an experiment. Specifically a manual on-line environment control using the command desk or the control computer can be replaced by a concrete definition of an experiment scenario specifying the environment influences.

The railway model control system represents a direct interface to the railway model device. Its task is to bring together all control commands from higher functional layers, to test their admissibility and to adapt them to the model device requirements. Also the actual operating states of the model device components are to be acquired and transmitted in a suitable form to the experiment or environment control as well as to the external control algorithm model.

As already mentioned, the control algorithm models are designed by different external project partners participating in the research program. The model functions, which have to be implemented in accordance with the case study specification, can be dedicated to three functional parts: train-borne control system, trackside level crossing control system and the operations centre. The modelling of these functional blocks can be can be implemented in the form of a single model or as three separate models. A separated solution makes it possible to combine different parts of the control algorithm model from different projects also using formal modelling languages which are not suitable for modelling all required system aspects.

A refinement of the functional structure in Figure 3 and its hardware allocation are shown in Figure 4. It shows one configuration option with the user control algorithm model consisting of three separate parts running on three different computers. To couple the control algorithm models with demonstrator functions, an Inter Tool Communication (ITC) framework for integration of application programming interfaces (API) is required. If the user's modelling language is not able to describe all the functional aspects of the case study specification, it is possible to add the missing functions by activating one of the demonstrator auxiliary functions.

3.2   Experimental Function Implementation

Figure 4 shows the implemented functionality and communication in the experimental functions. It contains the experiment control and environment control which were realised in MATLAB/Simulink® [Ma].

The experiment control can be defined off-line as a scenario before the start of the experiment. For this purpose a special graphical user interface was designed.

Using the interface, a control file is generated which can be directly processed by the environment control. The control file defines train driver and operating inspector actions as well as failure occurrences in relation to the time from the start of the experiment. The experiment can be controlled on-line during the

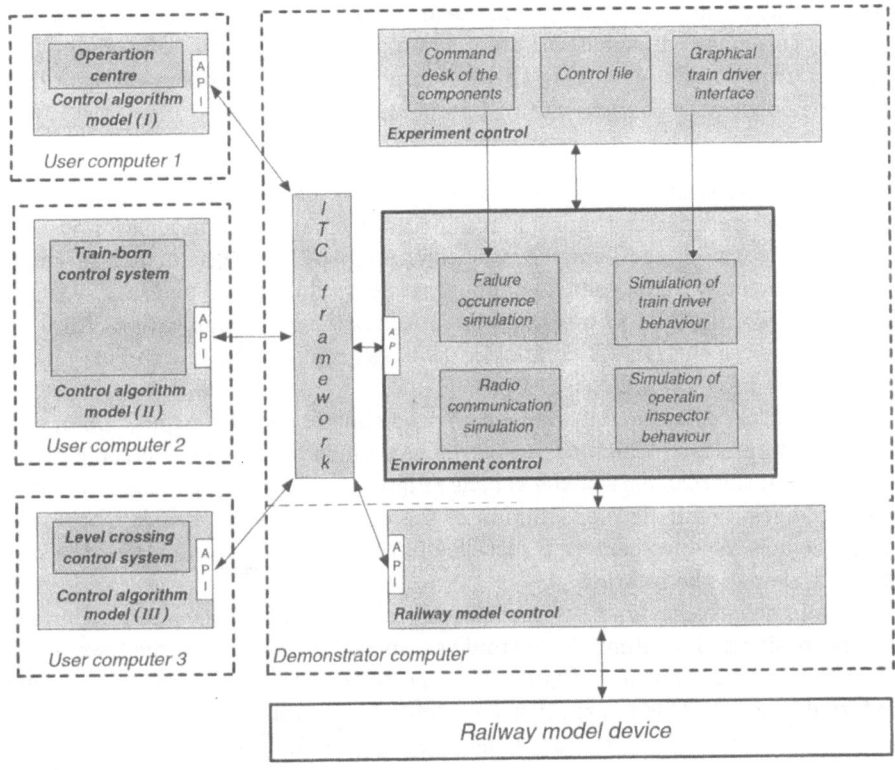

Fig. 4. Realization of the demonstrator control using a distributed control algorithm model

experiment run using a train driver interface. Failures may also be introduced on-line directly from the railway model device.

For remote experiment control, a web interface is being realized (control file generation, train driver interface). It provides video supervision of the whole experiment including a detailed view from the vehicle cab.

All communication activities between the control algorithm model and the demonstrator are stored with the corresponding time stamp in an experiment log. A filtering tool can be used to extract the desired information for post-processing by the experiment evaluation.

3.3 Basic Function Implementation

The basic demonstrator functions (railway model control system and railway model device) were implemented through the development of specific hardware components. The main items are the vehicle (train) and trackside components (traffic lights, barriers, vehicle sensors, balises and switches). Special attention was paid to the design of a suitable communication between static and mobile components of the railway model device and its control system. The implemented concepts are based on a suitable abstraction of properties of specific components of the railway model device. In the following sections the implementation of all basic demonstrator components will be presented in detail.

Vehicle. The train vehicle, the mobile element in the case study, is located on the track and passes the level crossing at intervals. Communication was implemented between the demonstrator computer and the vehicle. The originally considered concept [Bo] used a communication module based on DECT (Digital Enhanced Cordless Telecommunications) for wireless communication. After initial experiences the DECT communication was replaced by a standard module for wireless LAN (WLAN).

The vehicle's functionality includes speed control and the acquisition of positioning information. This functionality is performed by a set of electronic boards mounted on the rear part of the vehicle (Figure 5). This set of electronic boards also provides a realistic reproduction of the acceleration and braking behaviour of the vehicle. A video camera is installed in the vehicle cab to transmit the train driver's view to the internet.

A microcontroller board is used to control the vehicle speed and acquire its precise position. This item of electronic equipment is located on the lower of the electronic boards shown in Figure 5 at the back of the train vehicle. To allow external access to this board, it is connected to a serial port of the PC located on the upper and smaller boards shown in Figure 5. This is an industrial PC

Fig. 5. A train vehicle

running the Linux operating system with a special daemon that provides a TCP service to provide access to the train vehicle via (wireless) LAN.

The absolute position of the train vehicle on the track is acquired using balises, which are installed with small transmitters on the track. They are detected by a receiver on the rear of each train vehicle. Each balise transmits a unique code, thus enabling the application using the demonstrator to determine the correct position of each train vehicle.

The system of balises uses infrared light as its transmission medium. They are spaced at intervals of about 30 cm (12 inches). An incremental encoder fixed to one of the train vehicle's axles provides its relative position between the balises.

The overall positioning information consists of the number (code) of the last balise passed and the distance from it (calculated from counting the impulses from the incremental encoder).

Track side components. Each individual trackside element (barrier, traffic light, axle counter and switch) is able to communicate with the trackside network of the demonstrator and to check that its hardware is functioning correctly.

Each trackside component is equipped with its own controller and control hardware. The controller is exactly the same item of hardware in each of the elements mentioned. It is a small board with a microcontroller that has a built-in CAN unit and four light-emitting diodes, which indicate its current state. Since this board is designed as a generic platform that contains common hardware functions, only the software has to be customized for the functionality required by the specific application.

The control hardware (or baseboard) is specific to each trackside element. All the different control hardware boards have identical sockets that fit the controller board plug.

As an example of the trackside hardware, Figure 6 shows a demonstrator traffic light. The design described made it possible for each component to have only one electrical connection to the rest of the demonstrator system that carries the power and the communication lines.

Communication. A key function of the railway model device is the communication between the different hardware components and the application using the demonstrator (the models and tools). This communication only provides data exchange between hardware components involved in the simulation of the validation environment. It is not a part of the environment control, which is responsible for the generation of different communication failures.

However, highly reliable communication is necessary in order to guarantee controllability of the experiment.

Firstly, the communication inside the railway model device will be described. From a hardware point of view, it consists of two main levels: an upper level, which contains the application using the demonstrator; and a lower level, which contains all the hardware and provides a single point of access to its functionality.

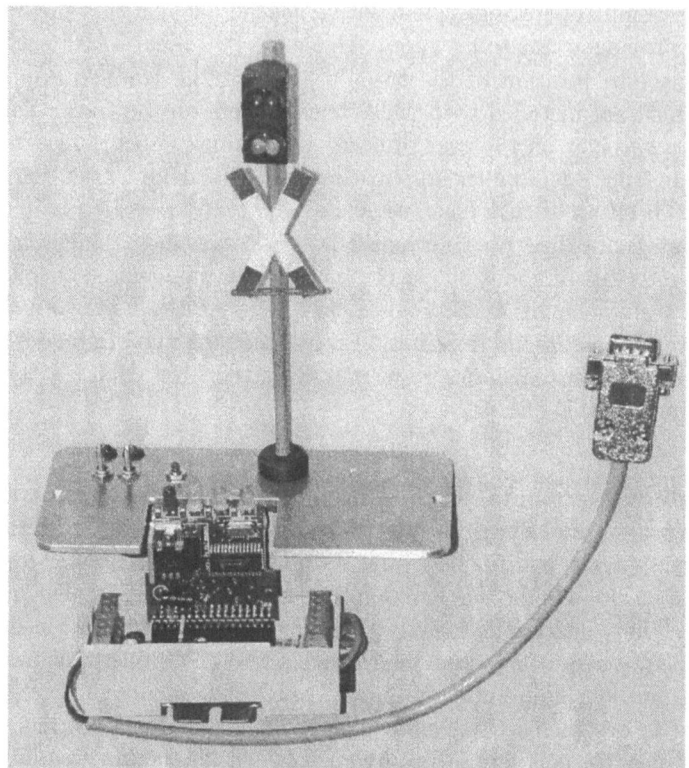

Fig. 6. Traffic light with its electronic

Figure 7 shows the overall communication structure of the demonstrator focusing on this lower level (not on the control models).

The lower (or hardware) level itself can be divided into three different sublevels. The uppermost of these sublevels contains the functions to access the hardware from a single connection. It is implemented as an item of software providing a TCP service and running on a PC called the "central demonstrator server" (CDS) with a Linux operating system. This software uses standard functions for providing this kind of service (e. g. as used by web servers).

The next hardware sublevel down contains the access to the individual train vehicle and to the trackside CAN bus via a serial to CAN converter.

Each train vehicle PC runs a software program providing a TCP service for accessing the individual train vehicle. During startup of the CDS service, it connects to all train vehicles. The CDS itself is connected via a serial cable to the CAN bus of the demonstrator using a serial-to-CAN converter to exchange information. During the initialisation, each component (train vehicle and trackside elements) is assigned an individual number, by which the models can address it. So the CDS service can be seen as a multiplexer/demultiplexer for the different data streams from and to the different hardware components of the demonstra-

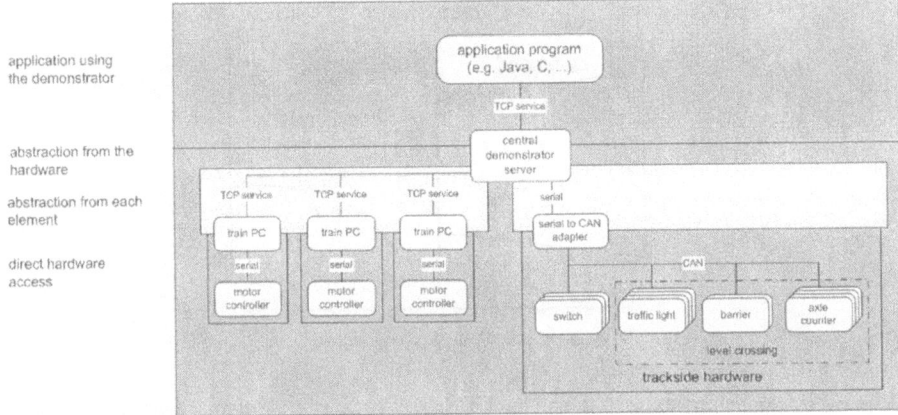

Fig. 7. Communication structure

tor. This encapsulates and abstracts the different technologies and protocols to access individual components from the model level and allows a homogeneous access protocol.

The lowest sublevel contains the direct access to the individual hardware items located in the different (physical) components of the demonstrator.

Communication with the train vehicle. To allow external access, each train vehicle is equipped with a PC and a wireless LAN module, which enable it to be mobile on the track while being connected to the (wired) LAN of the demonstrator.

On the basis of this technical environment, a daemon (server software) was developed to run on the PC of each train vehicle and provide a TCP service on standard network equipment for access to the functionality of the train vehicle. This daemon is also connected to a serial port of the PC where it can communicate with the train vehicle control board.

When an application (in the case study, the CDS is the application using the train vehicle) connects to this service, commands can be sent to the daemon, which transfers them to the control board where they are processed. In the other direction, information sent by the electronic board are received by the daemon and transferred to the connected application. This abstracts from the concrete hardware implementation of the control board.

Figure 8 shows a simple information transfer between the CDS service and the control board of a train vehicle via the PC on the train vehicle. The first part is done via wireless LAN and TCP, the second via the serial line on the train vehicle.

Communication with trackside elements. To access the trackside components of the demonstrator, a cheap and readily available technology had to be

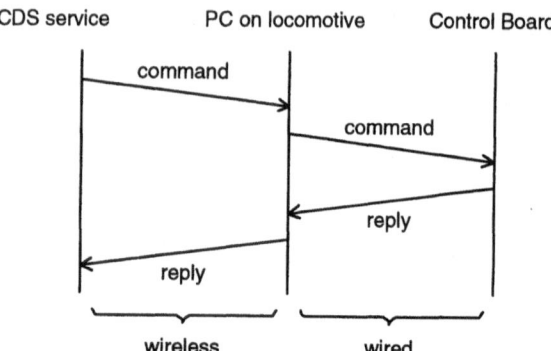

Fig. 8. Information transfer between CDS service and a control board of one train vehicle

chosen. In first trials, a self-developed field bus system was used [SS]. A short time later, very small and quite cheap microcontrollers with built-in CAN interfaces became available, so the decision was made to use this established technology in the further development.

As mentioned above, the CDS is connected to the track's CAN bus via a serial-to-CAN adapter. This allowed us to use a standard PC as CDS with no need for a special CAN interface card. This adapter was built using the same microcontroller board that was used on the above-mentioned trackside components. The CAN data are transferred along the serial line via the serial-to-CAN adapter using a transfer protocol which was developed for this purpose. It has a simple handshake mechanism, error checking and encapsulates CAN messages in single data frames.

For the CAN bus, a set of messages was defined to transfer commands to each specific component (e. g. a barrier or a traffic light of a level crossing), and states as replies from the components.

Figure 9 shows an example of a communication between the CDS service and a trackside component.

3.4   Integration of the Control Algorithm Model

In order to realize the coupling of the user control algorithm models with the demonstrator, an interface definition containing 22 data telegrams has been specified (Figure 10 and Table 1). According to the reference case study the control algorithm model can be dedicated to three functional parts: the train-borne control system, the level crossing control system and the operation centre. These functional parts can be developed as a single model or as a three separate models.

On the middleware level, an API (application programming interface) specification is available in order to establish an on-line connection between different software tools using a special ITC (Inter Tool Communication) framework. For this purpose a tool **EXITE** [EX] was used, working on the basis of the CORBA

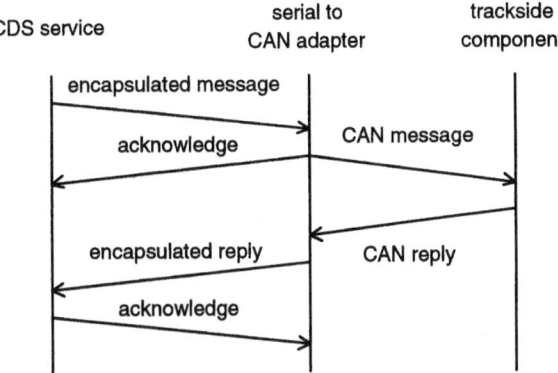

Fig. 9. Communication between CDS service and a trackside component

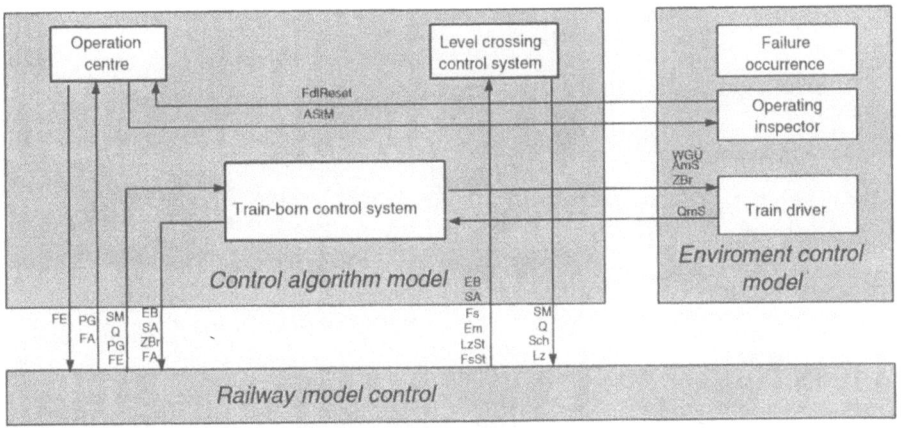

Fig. 10. Interface for the control algorithm model integration

standard technology. **EXITE** provides a server and a client for each connection. It follows an object-oriented philosophy, where a client and a server are software tasks that can run on any operating system for which a CORBA implementation exists. Via CORBA the simulation clients communicate directly with each other, thus avoiding any bottlenecks caused by a central simulation member. This allows communication via continuous and discrete signals. The simulation data are exchanged directly between the client and the server interface.

In order to test the experimental and the basic demonstrator functions, a control algorithm model was designed using the formal Stateflow language (provided as well by MATLAB/Simulink®). Figure 11 shows as an example the control algorithm model of the level crossing control system. The Stateflow language used is equivalent to the finite state machine notation.

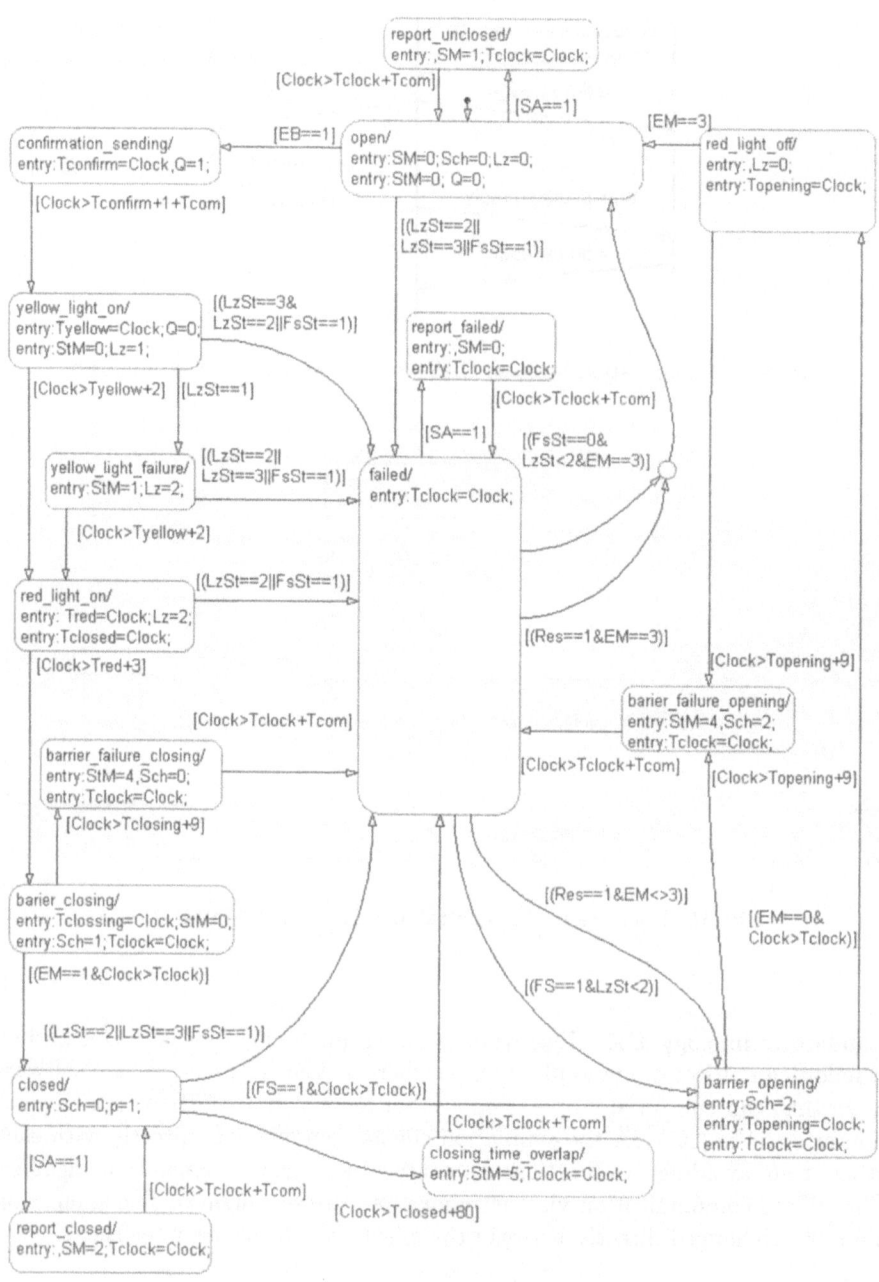

Fig. 11. Stateflow model of the level crossing control algorithm

Table 1. Telegrams used at the model level for the control algorithm interface

AmS	request for manual closing	LzSt	traffic light failure
AO	activating point	PG	position and actual speed of vehicle
AStM	display of crossing failure	Q	acknowledgement
EB	activation order	QmS	acknowledgement for manual closing
EM	final position report	Res	reset
EO	positioning system report	SA	status request
FA	moving authority request	SM	status report
FE	moving authority	Sch	barrier control
FS	vehicle sensor	StM	failure report
FsSt	vehicle sensor failure	WGÜ	speeding warning
Lz	traffic light control	ZBr	automatic brake activation

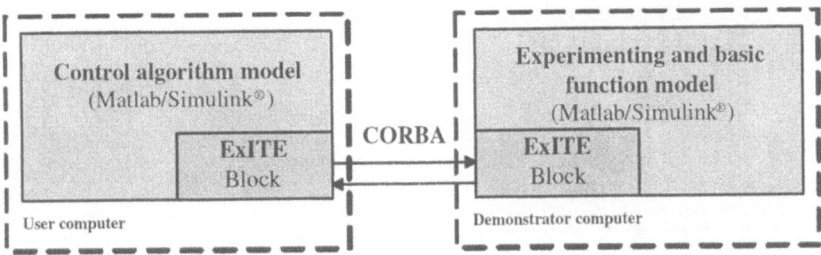

Fig. 12. The concept of inter-tool communication in MATLAB/Simulink®

Inter tool coupling. Application of the tool **EXITE** allows, in the first instance, coupling of the control algorithm model on the level of two identical tools running on the demonstrator computer and on the (remote) user computer. This configuration was applied by integration of control algorithm models designed in MATLAB/Simulink® (test purposes) with the MATLAB/Simulink® implementation of the experimental and basic demonstrator functions (Figure 12). For this purpose **EXITE** provides a block set allowing a direct implementation in the MATLAB/Simulink® models.

Similar to its coupling with a MATLAB/Simulink® control algorithm model, EXITE supports model integration in several other tool environments (Artisan, Rhapsody etc. [EX]).

In the case of an integration control algorithm model not designed in one of the tools supported by **EXITE**, an additional interface interpreter can be used. The interface interpreter provides a connection between **EXITE** and the application programming interface (API) of the connected tool (Figure 13). This solution was applied within the research programme by the coupling of the STATEMATE [HL+] models in project USE [BBDKWW].

C++ code coupling. One of the user requirements was to provide the ability to validate code generated from a formal control algorithm model. The inte-

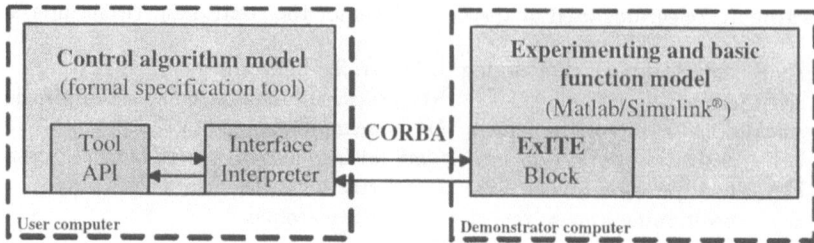

Fig. 13. The concept of possible configurations for on-line simulation with different tools

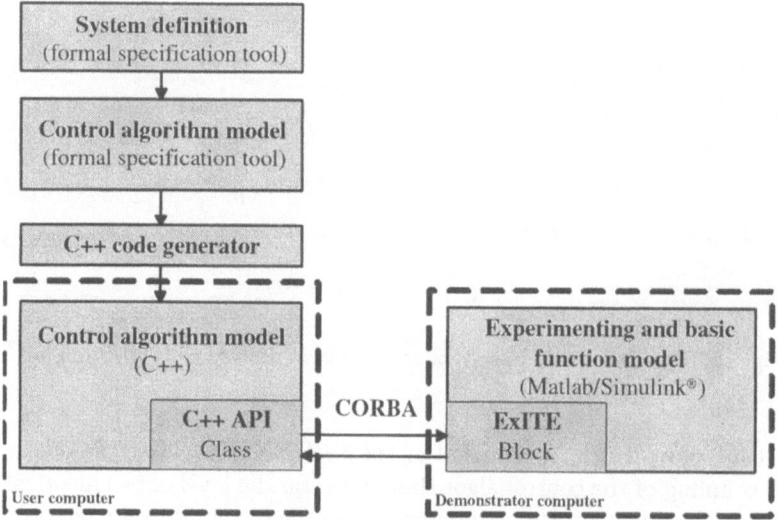

Fig. 14. The concept of possible configurations off-line code generation

gration is realised by a special C++ API class of the demonstrator that can be implemented in the automatically generated code. Figure 14 shows schematically the coupling of a C++ code generated by a formal specification tool. Within the research programme this solution was applied in the case of the tool StP (Software through Pictures) [St] in the project SafeRail [ABG].

Remote control algorithm integration. The design of the control algorithm integration presented here theoretically allows remote operation of the user computer. Practical experiences show that the real time requirements of the model control system limit the distance to several kilometres. For this reason, a local positioning of the user computer seems to be necessary.

The remote control algorithm integration allows the users to transfer a formal control algorithm model to the user computer (positioned locally in the demonstrator area) via the internet. The corresponding formal specification tool must be installed on the user computer. Using the internet interface of the experimental functions (Figure 15) and a remote session with the user computer, it is possible to perform the experiment. The visualization and the experiment log are the basis for a final evaluation of the control algorithm validation.

Fig. 15. Remote visualization of the experiment by static and mobile video cameras

3.5 Experiences with Formal Specification Validation

During the design of the control algorithm model for testing purposes, several imprecise wordings were already identified in the text version of the reference case study. As an example, the necessity for "level crossing re-initialisation" was discovered in the situation after remedying of a barrier failure. In this context the reference case study was refined and updated.

The final fault-free operation of the railway model device confirmed a correct implementation of the defined demonstrator functions. During the testing phase regular mode and failure mode operation were checked with regard to the possible scenarios (Figure 16 shows an example). The validation experiments currently being carried out by the project partners of the research programme will demonstrate how the system fulfills user requirements.

4 Conclusions

A comparative reference case study has been presented that combines different aspects of specification problems from the traffic control systems domain. Domain modelling has been identified as an important field where software specification techniques may be applied for integration. It has been argued that, besides formal correctness, other notions of correctness are relevant for validating a specification, design or implementation.

Fig. 16. Example of validation process: the locomotive waits for manual closing of a defective barrier

A physical railway demonstrator model seems to be a suitable means to depict all aspects of real operational system behaviour required for software validation. The realization of the operational process is a very complex task. It requires a true reproduction of all hardware and software components involved as well as the modelling of non-deterministic environment influences like human behaviour and equipment failures.

A further important aspect is the integration of the validated software specification. On one hand, the presented railway demonstrator offers an opportunity to validate a specification in the form of formal models, providing a coupling with the respective development tool. On the other hand, it supports the integration of C-code, e. g. automatically generated from the formal specification.

Last, but not least, the capabilities of remote experiment configuration, control, visualisation and evaluation make it possible to implement experiments without being bound to a specific location. The designed access by internet will allow a broad utilisation for scientific and educational purposes.

References

[ABG]   S. Arabestani, F. Bitsch, J.-T.Gayen: *Precise Definition of the Single-track Level Crossing in Radio-based Operation in UML Notation and Specification of Safety Requirements.* This volume.

[ABL]   Jean-Raymond Abrial, Egon Börger, Hans Langmaack (editors): *Proceedings of Formal Methods for Industrial Applications: Specifying and Programming the Steam Boiler Control.* Lecture Notes in Computer Science. Volume 1165, Springer-Verlag, October 1996.

[BBDKWW] M. Brill, R. Buschermöhle, W. Damm, J. Klose, B. Westphal, H. Wittke: em Formal Verification of LSCs in the Development Process. This volume.

[BBHP]   S. Berkenköter, S. Bisanz, U. Hannemann, J. Peleska: *Hybrid UML and its Application to Specification and Test of Train Control Systems.* This volume.

[BBM]   Dines Bjørner, Jakob Braad, and Karin S. Mogensen: *Models of Railway Systems: Domain.* Technical report, Dept. of IT, Techn. Univ. of Denmark, 1999. Electronic version available: http://www.ifad.dk/Projects/FMERail/proceedings3.htm.

[Bj]   Dines Bjørner: *Domain engineering: a precursor for requirements engineering and software design.* Technical report, Dept. of Information Technology, Techn. Univ. of Denmark, 1997–1998.

[Bo]   Ulrich Bock: Betriebs- und Kommunikationskonzept für dynamische Rendevous-Manöver von Zügen. Dissertation, Braunschweig, 2001 in J.-Uwe Varchim [Hrsg.]. Berichte aus dem Institut für Elektrische Meßtechnik und Grundlagen der Elektrorechnik, Band 13, ISBN 3980818101.

[Ei]   S. Einer: *STOP - Specification Technique of Operational Processes.* This volume.

[EX]   A product of Extessy AG, Germany.

[Ff]   *Betriebliches Lastenheft für FunkFahrBetrieb.* Stand 1.10.1996.

[HJL]   C. L. Heitmeyer, R. D. Jeffords, and B. G. Labaw: *A benchmark for comparing different approaches for specifying and verifying real-time systems.* Procceedings Tenth International Workshop on Real-Time Operating Systems and Software, May 1993.

[HL+]   D. Harel, H. Lachover, A. Naamad, A. Pnueli, M. Politi, R. Sherman, A. Shtull-Trauring, M. Trakhtenbrot: *STATEMATE: A Working Environment for the Development of Complex.* IEEE Transactions on Software Engineering. Volume 16, 1990, pages 403-414.

[Kr]   M. Krone: *Visual Formal Specification in Railway System Development.* In *Doctoral Consortium of ISRE 97.* Annapolis, USA, 1997.

[Ma]   MATLAB/Simulink® Product of The MathWorks, Inc.

[Ni]   T. Nilsson: *Application Domain Languages: Some Suggestions for Research.* In *CC '96 Workshop on Compiler Techniques for Application Domain Languages and Extensible Languages Models (ALEL '96),* pages 1–4, May 1996.

[OS]   E. Ortner and B. Schienmann: *Normative language approach - a framework for understanding.* In B. Thalheim, editor, *15th Intern. Conf. on Conceptual modeling,* pages 261–276, Berlin, 1996. Springer-Verlag.

[OTSR]   F. Ortmeier, A. Thums, G. Schellhorn, W. Reif: *Combining Formal Methods and Safety Analysis - The ForMoSA Approach.* This volume.

[Pa]   Jörn Pachl: *Systemtechnik des Schienenverkehrs.* Verlag B. G. Teubner, Stuttgart, Leipzig, 1999.

[PS]   S. Parthasarathy and E. Schnieder: *The explication problem: Achille's heel of formal methods.* In *6. Fachtagung Entwicklung und Betrieb komplexer Automatisierungssysteme (EKA '99)*, volume 1, pages 93–103, May 1999.

[SS]   H. Schrom and E. Schnieder: *SCAN - A hardware minimised low cost / low power bus - A functional overview.* MICRO.tec 2000, Volume 1, S. 183-186, Hannover, Februar 2000. Hannover, 25.-27.09.2000, Expo 2000.

[SJ]   E. Schnieder, L. Jansen: *Traffic Control Systems Case Study: Problem.* Description and Note on Domain-based Software Specification, Integration of Specification Techniques with Applications in Engineering. In *Forschungsbericht des Fachbereichs Informatik der TU Berlin*, 2000.

[Sn]   G. Snelting: *Paul Feyerabend und die Softwaretechnologie*, Informatik Spektrum. Oktober 1998, pages 273-276.

[St]   StP: Software through pictures, Product of AONIX.

[Ui]   *Lexique général des termes ferroviaires – Français, Deutsch, English, Italiano, Español, Nederlands.* Union Internationale des Chemins de fer, Paris, 4th edition, 1988.

[TSOR] A. Thums, G. Schellhorn, F. Ortmeier, W. Reif: *Interactive Verification of Statecharts.* This volume.

Precise Definition of the Single-Track Level Crossing in Radio-Based Operation in UML Notation and Specification of Safety Requirements

Saeid Arabestani[1], Friedemann Bitsch[2], and Jan-Tecker Gayen[1]

[1] Institute of Railway Systems Engineering and Traffic Safety (IfEV),
Technical University of Braunschweig, Pokelsstraße 3,
38106 Braunschweig, Germany
{s.arabestani, j.gayen}@tu-bs.de

[2] Institute of Industrial Automation and Software Engineering,
Universität Stuttgart, Pfaffenwaldring 47,
70550 Stuttgart, Germany
bitsch@ias.uni-stuttgart.de
http://www.ias.uni-stuttgart.de/projekte/saferail

Abstract. For developing precise system definitions and for simplifying the evidence of safety, the use of formal methods is highly recommended in the new European CENELEC standards for safe railway systems (EN 50126, EN 50128, DIN EN 61508). But not only in railway sector these methods are difficult to handle and to understand. This contribution introduces a concept for developing precise system definitions based on a notation, which does justice to engineers. A system definition in notation of the Unified Modeling Language (UML) is presented for the reference case study *single-track level crossing in radio-based operation*. On the basis of this system definition, relevant safety requirements are stated. These safety requirements form the basis for formal checks of the system definition for correctness and safety. A precondition for formal checks is that the safety requirements are specified in a logic language. For that purpose the safety pattern concept is presented, which supports and guides the user in selecting and instantiating the correct formal specification of safety requirements.

Keywords: object orientation, UML, safety requirements specification, safety patterns, level crossing, radio-based train control system (FFB)

1 Introduction

Guidance and safety systems of railways are usually very complex. Due to the use of computer systems work done by man is now more frequently being conducted by technical facilities. With regards to the means of safety there evolve special demands because of new CENELEC standards (cf. [11], [12] and [13]), the computing technology and the process of approval.

H. Ehrig et al. (Eds.): INT 2004, LNCS 3147, pp. 119–144, 2004.
© Springer-Verlag Berlin Heidelberg 2004

The development of railway systems starts with the creation of a system requirements specification which is the starting-point for the realization / implementation of a system. The system definition of a safety related signaling system requires the assurance of the safety authority. By giving its consent, the safety authority confirms that the system definition is in accordance with the relevant laws and regulations and that it meets the necessary safety criteria.

Today, system requirements specifications, including those for safety related systems, are mostly written in natural language and completed by diagrams e.g. system requirements specification of the radio-based train control system (FFB) (cf. [1]), which has been the basis for the reference case study (cf. [19]). These are usually easy to comprehend but only with difficulty and enormous efforts can they be tested as to their consistency, unambiguousness, safety conformity and completeness. In this case the new CENELEC standards recommend formal methods but without giving concrete and practical instructions of how to do it. What is needed are method-based means of description. On the one hand these have to be formal and on the other hand they have to be adequate for describing the properties of railway signaling systems. A fundamental property of the railway system as such is that it is possible to regard its parts as objects. From these objects then new and more specialized objects can be derived (e.g. track warrant element → switch or level crossing; level crossing {single-track} → multi-track level crossing; railway vehicle locomotive → shunting locomotive) and some of them can communicate with each other. This leads to the obvious conclusion of using an object-oriented approach for specifying those systems, thus implying object-oriented means of description. UML then was the choice. Its means of description are based on graphics and are easy to understand, thereby meeting another requirement from the engineer's point of view. The UML description tools however are for the most part semi-formal. If in a certain range of application the necessity arises then a proper formal back-up has to follow so that necessary steps of verifying the safety become valid.

Summarized below are the fundamental demands on the methods:

- possibility of presenting different views of the system
- modularity and compositionality, ability to trace the steps so far conducted in the system and to identify single modules
- ability of reuse and application throughout the whole development and approval process
- integration of formal verification into the method
- ability to validate and carry out a simulation of the system to be built
- easier integration of changes
- for the railway engineers easy to learn, work with and understand
- the description has to be easily comprehensible to the safety authority during the approval process necessary with railway systems (proof of safety)
- interface for risk and endangering analysis (cf. [9])

Formal methods do raise the precision of a system definition but they are usually hard to comprehend and work with not only for engineers. Moreover, formal methods do not really support easy implementation of changes and the use throughout the whole development process is not that easy. So far this has been the reason why formal methods have not yet come into use regarding development and approval process of railway systems worth mentioning.

In the first part of this paper we present the construction of the case study transportation domain based on the object-oriented paradigm. Since the Unified Modeling Language (UML) is on its way to become a standard among the object-oriented specification languages we will use UML description means for the system specification. The object-oriented approach offers the possibility to project a system and its characteristics onto a model. The system components can be defined as objects or classes of the model. The relationships between these objects then depict the relationships between the system components. The object oriented model precisely, compactly and comprehensibly represents the static structure and dynamical behavior of the system. Moreover, all system implications can be followed by looking at the relations of the object-oriented approach (cf. [3] and [5]). Transforming the system components into objects represents the point of view of engineers and it yields easier implementation of changes. Due to the selected notations of UML being reusable and consistent this kind of system definition can be used in subsequent development phases.

Another advantage of this model is the ability to transform it into a formally verifiable form (cf. [2]) and by employing model checking it can be verified that safety requirements are met. Consequently, a formal verification can already be conducted during the definition phase.

The advantage of model checking is its easy use since the formal proof is conducted automatically. However, the implementation assumes the existence of an adequate formal specification of the safety requirements which has to be in the form of temporal logic. The second part of this paper is concerned with the safety requirements and their shaping regarding the implementation of a formal verification.

The formal notation of safety requirements as temporal logic formula is difficult and prone to errors (cf. [20]). In order to reduce the possibility of errors when formulating in temporal logic and thereby to make formal formulations of safety requirements easier the concept of safety patterns was developed. With the help of safety patterns the transition from descriptions of safety requirements in natural language to formulations in temporal logic is demonstrated. This transition is necessary for the implementation of the formal verification by means of model checking.

2   Precise System Definition of the Case Study with UML

The system definition of the reference case study *single-track level crossing in radio-based operation* is based on the object oriented paradigm. The system is grasped as a set of interacting objects. Every object is identified by a name and possesses attributes and functions, which are called actions. The data of an object are determined by the attribute values. The object dynamic consists of attribute value changes, which takes place in form of action execution.

For specification of the reference case study, an object oriented model has been created (cf. [4]). It depicts the system structure and the dynamic system behavior. The system components are considered as interacting objects. The static system structure is defined by relations between objects. The dynamic system behavior is described by the local behavior of single objects and by interactions between the objects.

The creation of the object oriented model depends on a procedure, which is described in the next sections. It is also discussed how the requirements of the reference case study has been depicted in the model. The model is presented in notation of the Unified Modeling Language (UML), which is explained in detail in [28].

2.1 Object Oriented Modeling of the Reference Case Study

The object oriented model of the case study consists of 17 classes. These depict the main components of the FFB and their elements. Communication between objects of the classes is event triggered. It takes place by action calls of the respective objects. Time and observing time related actions and events have been modeled explicitly by communication with the object Timer. In this model, the system structure consists of class diagrams. These diagrams describe the order of classes of the whole system and their relations.

For every class a state diagram has been created, which represents the local behavior of objects of this class. The behavior of objects in the faultless case as well as in fault cases is modeled in the corresponding state diagrams. Interactions between objects have been outlined with sequence diagrams. Always one sequence diagram has been created for faultless case and several diagrams for fault cases. Because these scenarios are system requirements, they are partly safety requirements, which are relevant for formal verification of correctness.

2.2 Creation of the Object Oriented Model

Forming the model takes place by identification and depiction of the components, their tasks and their relations among each other. The main components of FFB are radio block center (RBC), trains and state variable track elements. These communicate with each other via radio. Operation handling follows by peripheral track protection and control, train speed supervision and train separation. These tasks are realized by cooperation of system components. Every component executes a set of actions, which in cooperation with actions of other components lead to fulfillment of the intended tasks. The specification of the system structure results from identification of system components and their relations. Specification of the system behavior consists in action descriptions of the several components and their chronological order in the whole system.

2.3 System Structure

When creating the model of the reference case study the three components RBC, trains and track elements are the first classes of the model. The attributes and the actions of these classes are defined with the help of subtasks of the track protection and control, train speed supervision and train separation. A train needs a movement authority to accomplish a train run. The beginning and the end of the requested route is according to the registration in the route map. RBC is competent for issues of movement authority and assignment of tracks. Therefore the actions *request_movement_authority()*, *request_element()*, etc. are defined in class *RBC*. Finally in class *Track Element* the actions *start_protection()*, *report_status()*, etc. are defined, because the track element has to be protected when requested and has to report its status when requested.

For tasks like *refresh_route_map()*, *distribute_route_map()*, etc., which can not be allocated to any of the named classes the class *Administration* is introduced. In addition, the class is responsible for putting into operation and putting out of operation of all objects. In consequence, there is the system structure of Figure 1.

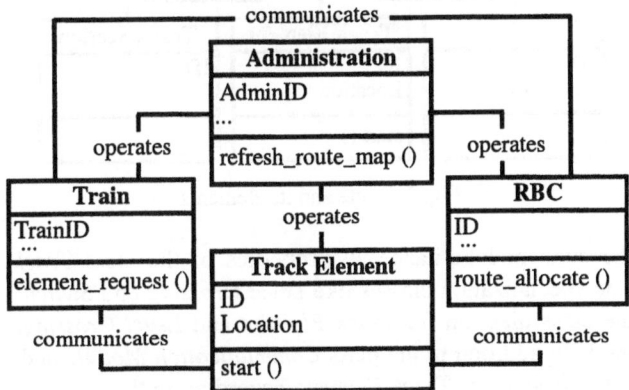

Fig. 1. System structure of FFB

In addition to state variable track elements there are also balises on routes. Balises serve to determine absolute location information. Consequently, a route consists of track sections, balises and state variable track elements like e.g. switches and level crossings. In Figure 2 the relation between the class *Route* and its parts is depicted by means of aggregation. The relations aggregation and composition are used for depiction of whole-part relationship among the objects. In UML (cf. [28]) these relations are used to describe the case when two or several classes belong together. It is claimed, that both kinds of relations define a transitive, non-symmetric relationship. Based on the relationship between the behavioral and structural aspects of system components we have discussed these relations and their properties in [3]. We have shown that aggregation and composition can not be transitive.

In FFB elements like level crossings and switches are state variable track elements. They are protected on demand and they respond their current status on demand. In this paper, it is not dealt with switches and with other kinds of track elements. Every state variable track element communicates with trains or with the RBC via radio communication modules. In addition, every track element is able to detect defects and to report them to the RBC. If a procedure of a track element is not completed in time then a defect is assumed. Therefore, every track element possesses a timer. The timers are necessary for control and observation of temporal sequences. Consequently, the classes *Communication Module* and *Timer* are parts of the *Track Element*. Relation of composition shows in the respectively class diagrams, that these classes are parts of the class *Track Element*.

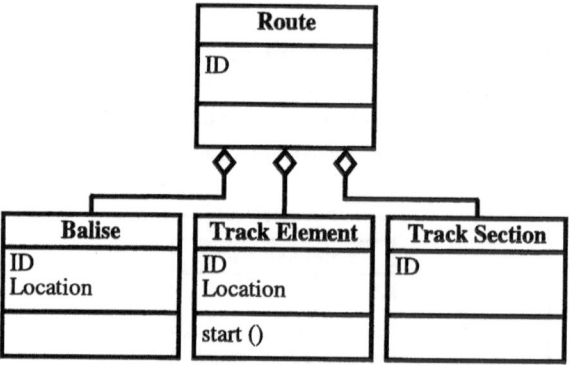

Fig. 2. Route and its elements

By using the concept inheritance all properties of the class *Track Element* are transferred to the specialization classes like *Level Crossing* and *Switch*. Accordingly, there results the class diagram for *Track Element* and *Level Crossing*, which is depicted in Figure 3. In addition to the parts *Communication Module* and *Timer*, which have been adopted from class *Track Element*, according to the radio-based train control system the class *Level Crossing* has the special parts *Wayside Signal*, *Barriers* and *Switch Off Sensor*.

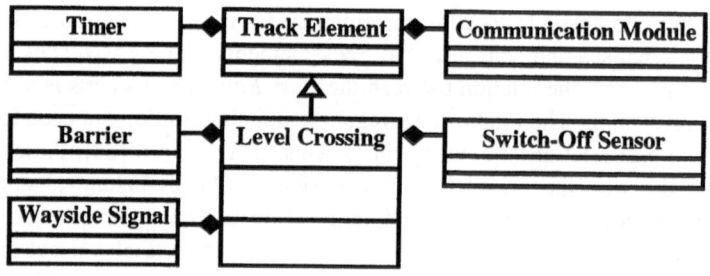

Fig. 3. Class diagram of the classes track element and level crossing

In the object oriented model of the reference case study the objects of class *Train* have as sub-components objects of the classes *Communication Module, Timer, Route Map, Odometer, Brakes*. An object of class *RBC* possesses as sub-components objects of the classes *Communication Module, Timer, Route Map* and *Route*. To an object of the class *Administration* belong objects of the classes *Communication Module, Timer* and *Route* as components. For these classes there are no figures in this paper.

2.4 System Dynamics

System dynamics consists of the internal behavior of several objects and of interactions between objects. In the object oriented model of the reference case study the internal behavior of objects has been specified using UML state diagrams. For describing system scenarios, UML sequence diagrams have been used. In the following, the behavior of the model is explained by means of the main components level crossing, RBC and train.

2.5 Internal Behavior of Objects

In the reference case study, the task track protection is subject to cooperation between RBC, trains and state variable track elements. The train sends in time a request to the track element. The track element has to acknowledge the receiving of the order. After completing the protection procedure, a status report from the track element is given. According to the current state of track element, it has to be decided, if the train is allowed to drive on the track element or if it has to stop before entering the track element.

In the system requirements specification of FFB for every track element it is demanded, that it starts automatically the protection procedure. Every track element has to acknowledge the receiving of a request and has to react to a status request by means of a message on the safe or unsafe state. Track elements have to be able to detect defects by permanently executing tests. Defects have to be reported to the RBC. A defect track element has to react on a request respectively on a status request with a message on its defect status if still possible. Finally, every track element has to offer the possibility of manual control because of reasons of availability. As a consequence the staff is able to operate the track element locally, e.g. if it is defect. The requirements on a track element can be specified in form of a general behavior for all track elements, see Figure 4. There, t_{akt} stands for the current time.

A level crossing is a state variable track element. It performs the protection procedure by setting the wayside signal on red and closing the barriers. Using the concept inheritance all properties of the class *Track Element* are transformed to specialization class *Level Crossing*. Inheritance not only compromises static but also dynamic properties. All functionalities, which have been defined as behavior of track elements are adopted and if necessary extended for the level crossing. We have discussed in [5] this kind of inheritance. We have shown, that the specialization class inherits the

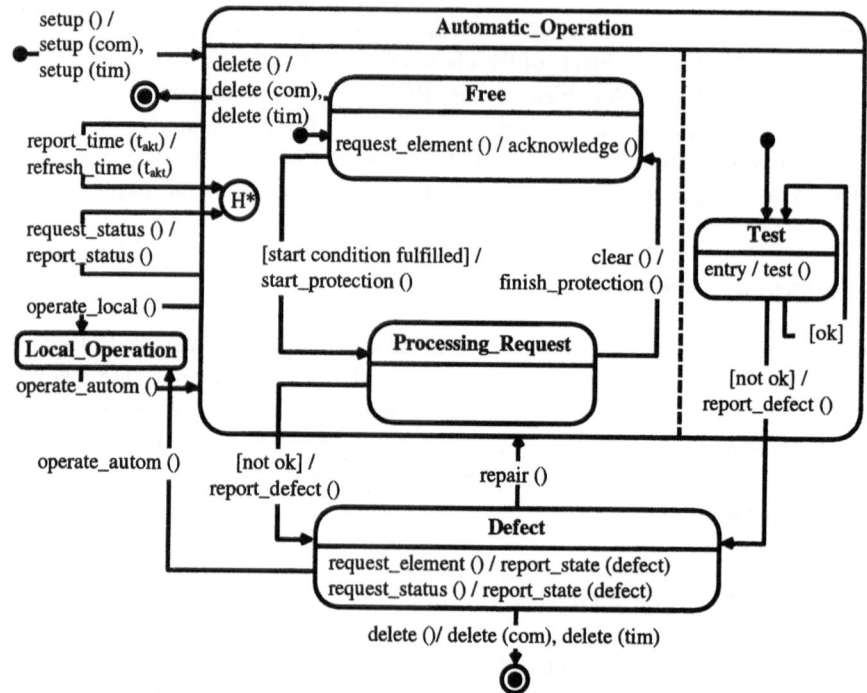

Fig. 4. State diagram of class *Track Element*

dynamic properties in the context of their states in the state diagram. Therefore the specialization class adopts all attributes, actions, states and transitions of the general class as well as all relations to other classes.

The behavior of the objects of class *Level Crossing* is an extension of the behavior of Figure 4. Every time, the objects of this class are in one of the defined state. The extension of this behavior corresponds to the activities in the states *Free* and *Processing_Request* and the transitions of these states. All other states and actions remain unchanged. In Figure 5 the part of the state diagram of class *Level Crossing* is presented, in which the extended behavior of the mentioned states is depicted.

In the depicted states the objects of class *Level Crossing* communicate with its sub-components *Wayside Signal*, *Barrier* and *Switch Off Sensor*. The state diagrams of these classes are not presented in this paper.

In the model the RBC is responsible for assignment and administration of tracks, track sections and for checking and allocation of the movement authority. It passes the messages, which are sent to the RBC in case of fault detection, on the class *Administration*. Figure 6 shows the modeled behavior of class *RBC*. The objects of this class communicate with objects of its sub-components and the objects of the class *Train*. RBC administrates the track sections by comparison of the given movement authority and the already released track section by determining the position of the rear of the train from the received train location and length of the train.

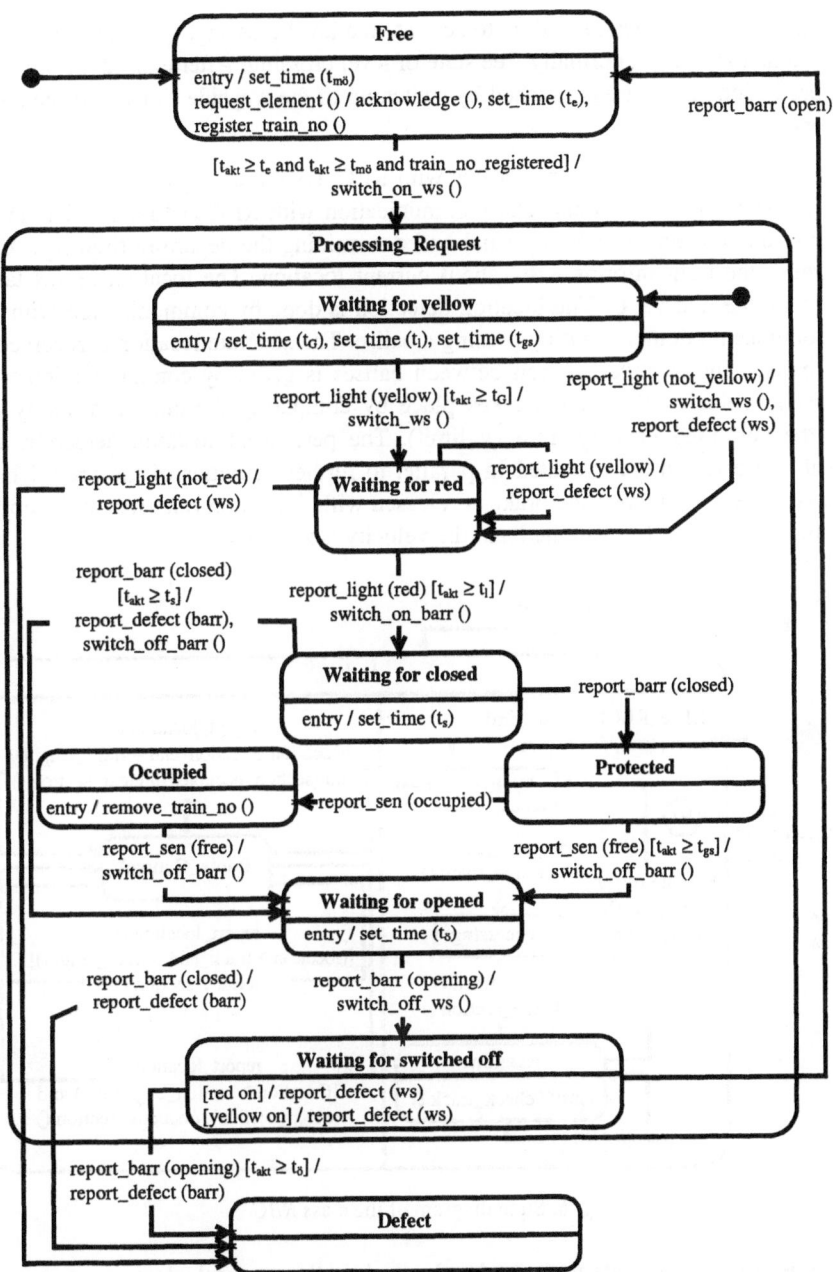

Fig. 5. Extension of the states *Free* and *Processing the Request* at level crossing by inheritance

The abbreviations in Figure 5 have the following meanings:
    ws = wayside signal, barr = barrier, sen = switch off sensor, t_G = duration of yellow light, t_1 = duration of red light before closing the barriers, $t_{m\ddot{o}}$ = minimal duration between two protection processes, t_s = length of time to close, $t_{\ddot{o}}$ = length of

time to open barriers, t_e = time to activate the level crossing, t_{akt} = current time, t_{gs} = time to return to normally free state of level crossing. After expiration of t_{gs}, the protection procedure is finished by switching of the wayside signal and the barriers.

In the model the train communicates with RBC, level crossing (lc) and in addition with its own sub-components. The communication with RBC at first consists in requesting the movement authority (ma) and determining the departure time (t_a). After departure, the train informs RBC about current location. The location report takes place with the interval t_m. The location detection is done by communication with the sub-component odometer and by passing a balise. The absolute location is received at each balise. The relative location between balises is given by communication with odometer. Velocity observation takes place by comparing the current velocity (v) with the permitted velocity limit (v_limit). The permanent location detection and velocity observation are executed in parallel to further activities of the train. These processes are started when the brake is released with the action *release*() and stopped after the brakes have been applied and the velocity is zero (v = 0).

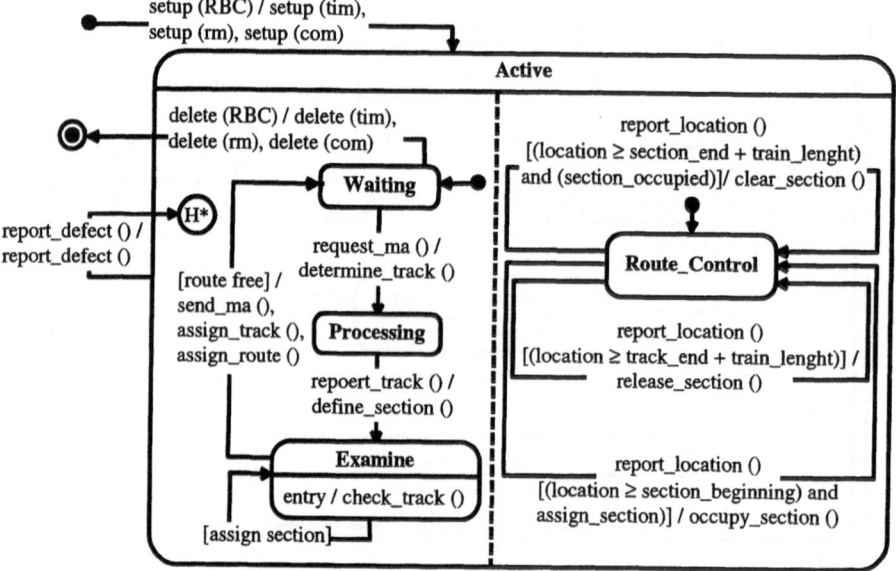

Fig. 6. State diagram of the class *RBC*

In order to communicate with the level crossing, the train calculates according to its current velocity and its current location a point in time (ct) to contact the level crossing. After sending the request, the maximum time for acknowledge receiving (t_q) is calculated. In case of successful protection of the level crossing, the train passes the level crossing and identifies the next hazard point. This might be another level crossing or the endpoint of the movement authority. If the level crossing is defect, then the

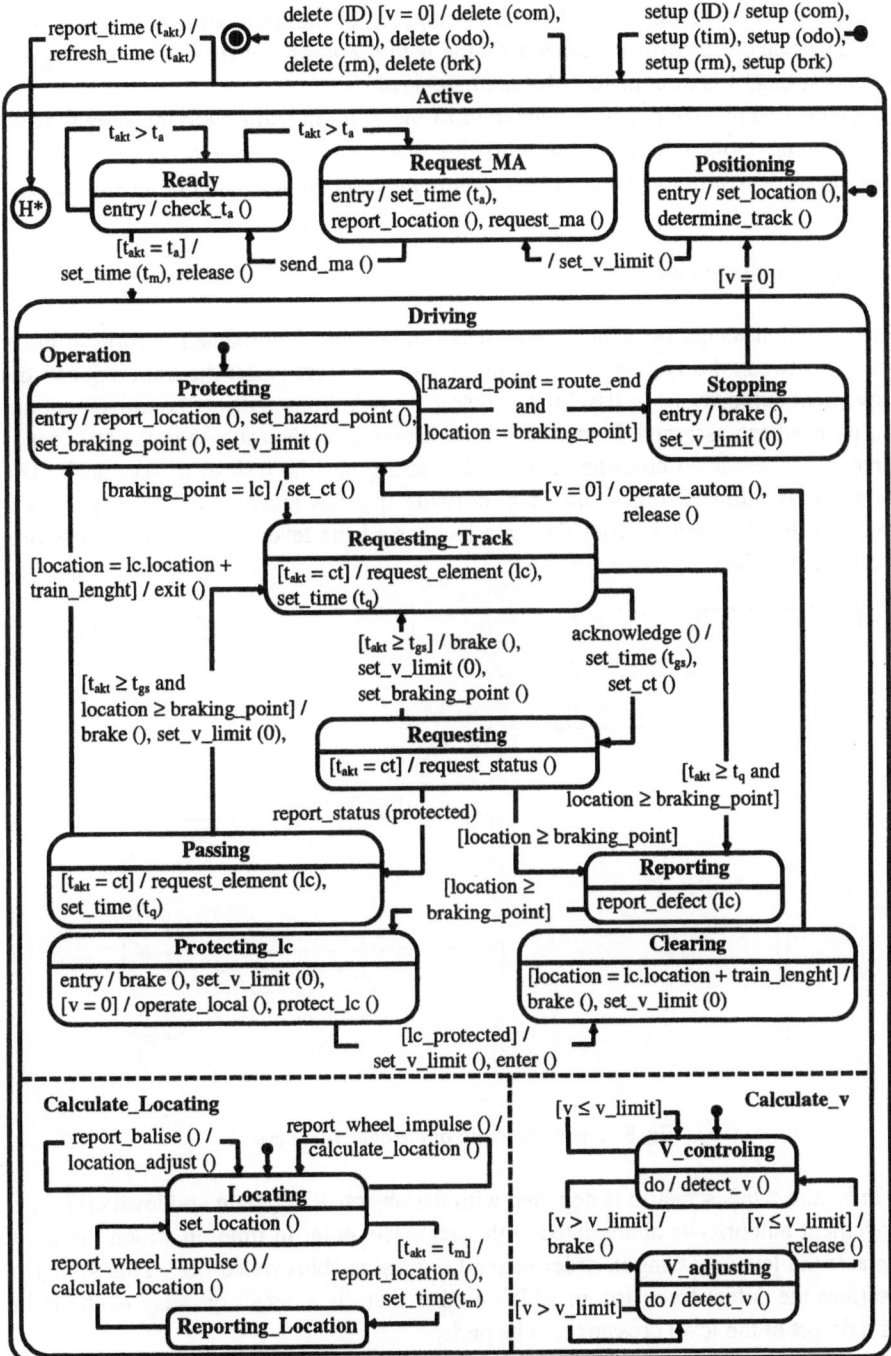

Fig. 7. State diagram of class *Train*

protection has to be done manually after stopping of the train before the level crossing. The manual control is realized by the action *operate_local()*. After passing the level crossing, it is reset in state *Automatic operation*.

Figure 7 shows the dynamic behaviour of the train. In addition to the already mentioned abbreviations there are the following ones: lc stands for level crossing, rm for route map, odo for odometer, com for communication module and brk means brake.

2.6 System Scenarios

The operation scenarios, which are depicted in [19] can be modeled in form of interactions between the system components. A train run starts, after the train requests the movement authority from RBC for a route and if the route is free the movement authority has been assigned. If there is a level crossing on the route then the train sends a request to the level crossing. The level crossing has the task to protect itself. The train is only allowed to pass the level crossing if it has received the message of the protected level crossing. After the train has passed the level crossing, the protection process is finished.

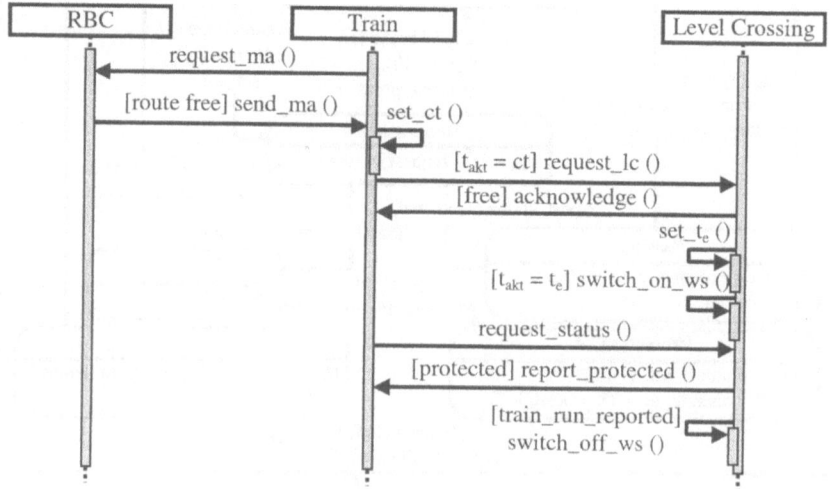

Fig. 8. System scenario of the defect-free case

In Figure 8 this scenario is depicted with the objects RBC, train and level crossing. Movement authority is abbreviated with "ma". The point in time, in which the train contacts the level crossing in order to send request is abbreviated "ct". This scenario describes the defect-free case, in which neither there is a defect or delay of the train nor a defect of the level crossing and its parts.

If the train does not receive the message of the protected state of the level crossing as a consequence of a failure, then the train has to stop before the level crossing. In this case the level crossing has to be protected manually by the staff. After the train has passed the level crossing, then the train is turned back in automatic operation.

This case may happen, if the protected state is not reached because of a failure of the level crossing or of one of its parts. Another possible reason is a failure of a communication module, which cuts off the radio contact between train and level crossing so that the level crossing does not receive the request or does not send the acknowledgement. For all these cases, a separate sequence diagram is necessary. Exemplarily a scenario is depicted in Figure 9. In this case, the level crossing is defect but the communication between train and level crossing takes place.

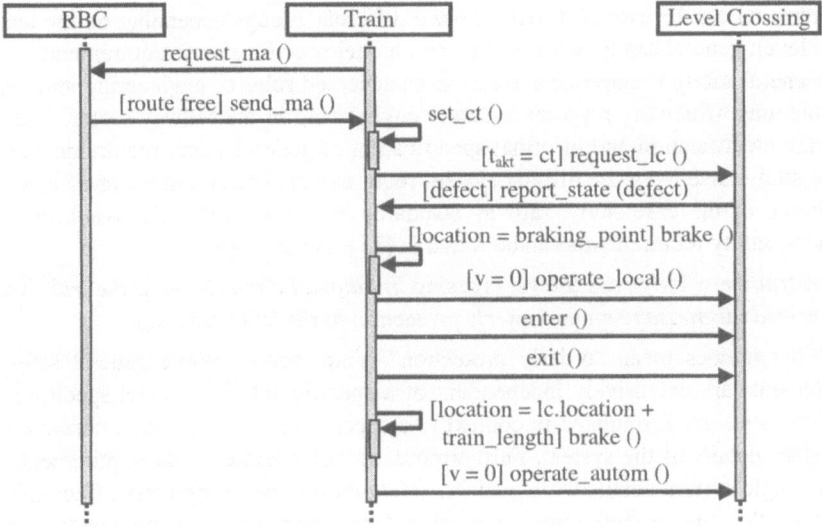

Fig. 9. System scenario with defect level crossing

3 Specification of Safety Requirements

For evidence of safe functionality the safety related correctness of the system definition has to be shown. For that purpose the compliance of safety requirements in the UML model has to be checked. To perform this correctness check sound and to increase trust in the system definition as basis for the development of a safe system, the correctness check should be done with formal exactness. On that score the safety requirements have to be specified formally as basis for formal correctness checks. This section of the paper handles the specification of safety requirements with regard to formal verification of the UML system definition. The concept has been developed in order to avoid mistakes in formal formulations of safety requirements and consequently to simplify formal specification. By means of safety requirements of the reference case study, it is explained how descriptions of safety requirements in natural language can be systematically transformed to formal specifications by using safety patterns.

3.1 Preparation of the Safety Requirements

In order to achieve sensible results of practical relevance for evidence of safe functionality, it is important to derive systematically the safety requirements. There is the problem that safety requirements, which have been formulated independently of the creation of the system model, are too abstract for direct formalization and formal verification. This is a further obstacle in the widespread use of formal verification methods in engineering. The precondition for formalization is that the safety requirements must have reference to the UML system model, see [6] and [23]. Safety requirements can be distinguished into two different groups depending on the abstraction level: general safety requirements and model specific safety requirements.

General safety requirements result from accepted rules of engineering and general regulations, which are relevant to safety engineering in the railway sector. The basis for the identification and informal specification of general safety requirements of the case study have been the official system requirements specifications of FFB, the description of the case study, railway standards and regulations. The resulting list of general safety requirements can be found in [17]. For example:

A train may only pass a level crossing in automatic operation, if the train has received the message on the orderly protection of the level crossing.

What it does mean "orderly protection" is not stated. While general safety requirements are extensively independent of a specific solution, model specific safety requirements are formulated in context to a specific technical solution concept. They consider details of the system. Furthermore, model specific safety requirements deal with single system details while general safety requirements regularly affect different aspects. So, one general safety requirement can have several corresponding model specific safety requirements. Model specific safety requirements are specified in context to a model of the system. Variables of the system model (state, event, action, condition or any other attribute variables) are used in the formulations of model specific safety requirements. By using safety analysis techniques, especially FMEA, the formulation of safety requirements in context to the UML system definition is supported (cf. [6] and [9] for more details). In these analyses, possible failures of system functions and its correlation are analyzed, which lead to operational hazards. The general safety requirements have to be considered. In order to prevent systematic failures, which have been detected in the analyses, safety requirements are formulated for these system details. In order to achieve, that these safety requirements are model specific, the safety analyses have to be performed in context to the UML system model. Then the model structure and model variables are used in the safety analyses. In [16] it is described how the system structure with the system functions can be automatically derived from the UML system definition. In this way not only efficiency of system development is increased but also FMEA is performed consistent to the UML system definition.

Relating to the general safety requirement example it can be analyzed in the FMEA which failures could avoid an orderly protection. In Figure 10 an FMEA detail is shown, which is based on the system definition (cf. Figure 1 and 3). One detected failure function is "switch on barriers is too early". If the barriers are closed too early it could happen that the time is too short to vacate the level crossing. To prevent this operational hazard, which arises from the detected safety relevant failure function the following model specific safety requirement is defined:

Level_Crossing.switch_on_barr is only permitted to be valid when the time Level_Crossing.t, after occurence of Wayside_Signal.switch_on_red_light has been run down.

This model specific safety requirement is specified as relation between the model variables *"switch_on_barr"* of the class *"Level_Crossing"* (cf. Figure 3 and 5), the duration of red light before closing the barriers *"t,"* of the class *"Level_Crossing"* (cf. Figure 5) and the variable *"switch_on_red_light"* of the class *"Wayside_Signal"* (cf. Figure 3).

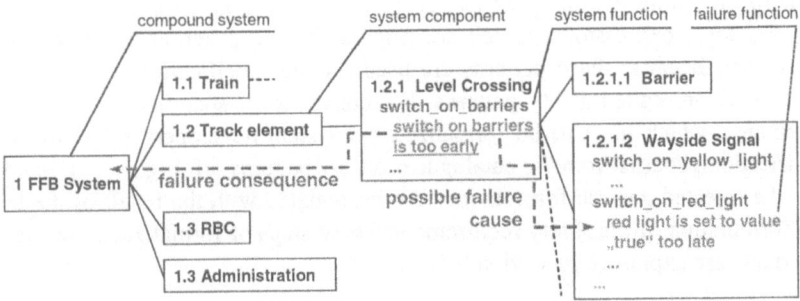

Fig. 10. Detail of FMEA as basis for derivation of model specific safety requirements

3.2 Difficulties of Specifying Safety Requirements Formally

A precondition for formal correctness checks of safe functionality by model checking is the specification of safety requirements in temporal logic. Details on temporal logic can be found in [8]. One reason for the very rare use of model checking is the difficulty of understanding and applying temporal logic, especially for engineers, who are normally not familiar with higher logic. In [21] it is reported from the case study of [14] on model checking, wherein not only model failures are detected but also errors in the formally stated requirements in temporal logic. It is concluded in [20]: "Expressing certain properties in temporal logic is complex and error-prone, not only for practitioners but for formal methods experts as well." In [8] the difficulties are demonstrated to correctly read, interpret and formulate requirements in temporal logic. The difficulty lies in the correct use of the complex semantics of temporal logic with its very expressive power. It easily happens, that a formula is specified, which states something different than it really should. The consequences could be fatal in such a way that the system is unsafe only due to problems related to formal specification.

In the standards DIN EN 61508 [15] and EN 50128 [11] these difficulties have been recognized. For reasons of clarity, in addition to formal specification, the use of a natural language is necessarily required. But this is not a sufficient solution. The problem is that a natural language permits ambiguous formulations. Therefore a possible consequence could be a specified safety requirement, which is interpreted differently with respect to the original intention of the formal specification. Moreover, an equivalent specification of the original intention cannot be guaranteed. A solution to solve these problems of applicable precise specification and interpretation and of specification in a natural language terminology equivalent to formal specification is the safety pattern concept. This is explained in detail in the next section.

3.3 Safety Patterns Concept – The Key to Formal Specification of the Safety Requirements

The core idea of the safety pattern concept is to formalize safety requirements with the help of a finite set of specification patterns. These patterns contain only those temporal logic expressions, which are suitable for the different kinds of safety requirements. Because these patterns are used for the specification of safety requirements, they are called safety patterns. For conventional specifications of safety requirements, which have to be formalized the system developers select the suitable specification patterns from the catalogue of safety patterns (cf. Figure 11). In a further step, the selected generic formulations are instantiated with the result of the instantiated formulation of the safety requirement. These steps of formalization are tool supported and are explained in section 3.4.

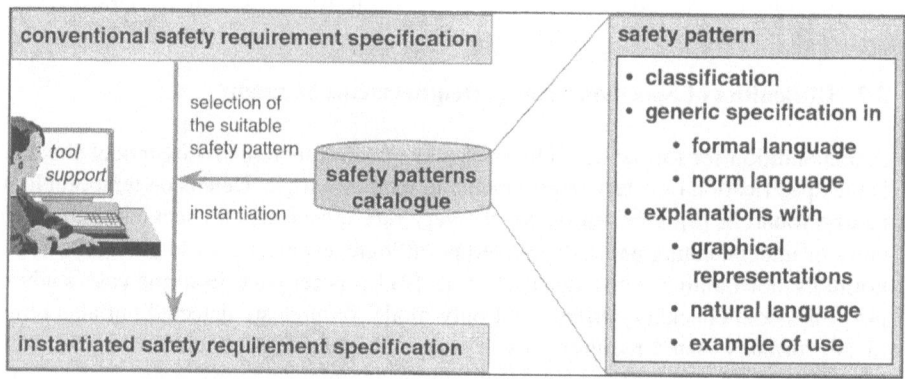

Fig. 11. Overview on the safety pattern concept

In the catalogue, the safety patterns are classified in such a way that every safety pattern has a specific and a clear classification, which enables a definite identification of the safety patterns. Every safety pattern can be found in the formal notations CTL (Computation Tree Logic), LTL (Linear Time Temporal Logic) and μ-Calculus. In this way the developer can choose the formalism required for the verification tool according to his preferences. Every safety pattern is explained in natural language, so that the meaning of the safety patterns is easily understood.

As explained earlier, standards necessarily require for reasons of clarity that in case of formal specification there should be also a formulation in a natural language. For that reason, safety patterns do not only support formal specification of safety requirements but also enable specifications in the terminology of a natural language equivalent to the formal specification. Every safety pattern contains a specification template in a restricted terminology of natural language. The meanings of the allowed structure and terms used for description are fixed, see [7]. This means that a *norm language* for safety patterns is used. A norm language sounds similar to a natural language, but it is a strongly reduced form of a natural language. It is a connecting link between natural languages and formal languages [24]. By the fixed assignment of a formal formulation and a formulation in restricted safety requirements related terminology, the equivalence of formal specification and specification in words of natural language is guaranteed. The demands of the standards are fulfilled and simultaneously the weakness of the standards is resolved. In this manner, a safety pattern can also be used to formulate precisely a safety requirement in natural language. Finally, every safety pattern contains an example of use. Figure 12 shows exemplary a safety pattern.

It is also in progress to enlarge the data in every safety pattern with graphical descriptions. The graphical description contains typical possible sequences of states and also different examples of possible computation paths, see [7].

In teamwork communication and also in communication with approval authorities, the meaning of formal safety requirements is to interpret clearly based on such a safety pattern catalogue.

[9] states the role and the benefits of embedding the safety pattern concept in the process of developing system requirements specifications for railway systems.

3.4   Tool Support for the Selection and Instantiation of Safety Patterns

For developers using the safety pattern concept it would be very hard to select suitable safety patterns only on the basis of a list of safety patterns. To have an overview on the different kinds of classification criteria and of the respective classes, tool support is necessary, which assists in the selection of the correct safety patterns. Furthermore, the software tool guides the system developers at the instantiation of generic formulations to avoid mistakes in this specification step. The tool name is *SAPIS* (Safety Pattern Instantiation System). It is a web-based application, which can be used via the Internet at http://www.ias.uni-stuttgart.de/safety-patterns/.

The safety patterns are catalogued by means of 13 classification criteria. Every classification criterion is decisive for the classification of a safety pattern to one of two or more classes. E.g. one criterion is the **temporal restriction of validity.** The possible classes are *duration of validity, beginning of validity* or *beginning and duration of validity*. A certain combination of classes of different classification criteria describes the different properties of a safety pattern.

Safety Pattern ds-woet-nv-84

Dynamic safety requirement without explicit time, concerning beginning and duration of validity and concerning necessity of validity, safety pattern ID 84

Generic Formulation in Norm Language
If *a* is valid then *b* must be valid permanently until *c* is valid.

Generic Formulation in Formal Languages

CTL: AG (a -> A(b W (c and b)))

LTL: G (a -> (b W (c and b)))

μ-Calculus: nu Z1.((a -> nu Z0.((c and b) or
            (b and [-]Z0))) and [-]Z1)

Explanation in Natural Language

A main characteristic of this safety pattern is that *b* has to be true always from this point in time on when *a* is valid. This has to be valid every time when *a* occurs. Then *b* must be permanently valid until *c* occurs. There must be no interruption in the validity of *b* until *c* occurs. The validity of *b* must neither end anytime before *c* nor in the state directly before *c* but may end first in this state when *c* becomes true. *a* as well as *c* may occur but they do not have to.

Example of Use

System
Level crossing in radio-based operation

Conventional specification of the safety requirement
If the messages `Level_Crossing.report_defect(wayside_signal)` or `Level_Crossing.report_defect(barrier)` are true, then `Level_Crossing.acknowledge = 0` must be true until `Level_ Crossing.repare` occurs.

Safety requirement in norm language
If `Level_Crossing.send_defect(wayside_signal)` or `Level_Crossing.send_defect(barrier)` is valid then from this point in time on `Level_Crossing.acknowledge = 0` must be valid permanently until `Level_Crossing.repare` is valid.

Safety requirement in formal language (CTL)
AG ((Level_Crossing.send_defect(wayside_signal) or Level_
Crossing.send_defect(barrier)) -> A((Level_
Crossing.acknowledge = 0) W (Level_Crossing.repair and
(Level_Crossing.acknowledge = 0))))

Fig. 12. Safety pattern example

Based on this safety patterns classification scheme, it is possible to select the appropriate safety pattern for the safety requirement to be specified. Every classification criterion can be used to characterize a property of the safety requirement to be specified. In this way, the properties of the searched safety pattern are selected and so the searched safety pattern itself is selected. This selection process is tool supported by SAPIS [8]. With the help of the dialog system of SAPIS the system developer selects the suitable safety pattern classes step by step in the form of question-answer-interactions. SAPIS helps to determine, which criteria are relevant for the safety requirement to be specified. It also supports the user to make decisions in a meaningful sequential order. The precondition to avoid specification faults by using SAPIS is the correct comprehension of the safety pattern classes.

SAPIS offers built in search functions enabling one to refer to the exact meaning of safety requirement specifications.

The safety pattern tool set also contains graphical simulations in the form of Java applets to support correct interpretation of safety patterns. As a simulation concept the intuitive interpretable representation of timing diagrams is used (cf. [7]). Every safety pattern has at least one condition variable and one property variable. The property variable depends on the condition variable. The simulation concept is an interactive dynamic visualization in such a manner that the user is able to set step by step any value successions of the conditional variable whereas the value of the property variable is simulated by the tool. With the use of colors, a visual distinction is made between "possible validity", "deterministic validity" and "undefined validity". There is also a visualization feature for compositions of safety patterns. In this way, inconsistencies between formulations can be revealed.

With the help of the instantiation assistant of SAPIS mistakes at instantiation can be avoided. For that purpose, it is checked that the user only uses variables, which have been previously declared. The tool supports the insertion of single system variables, propositional compositions of system variables (by not, and, or, $\rightarrow$) and connectives of comparison ($>$, $<$, $=$, $\neq$). The correct syntax related to the used variable types is checked. The tool supports the specification of complex safety requirements and the storage and the management of instantiated safety requirements. For specification of complex safety requirements several safety patterns have to be combined by and, or or not connectives of propositional logic. In other cases, safety patterns have to be inserted in other safety patterns to specify complex safety requirements, see [8]. In some cases it is also necessary to insert value changes of a variable (e.g. the entrance in or exit of a state; removing signal), which is supported by SAPIS, see [8].

3.5 Derivation of the Safety Pattern Set

A major objective, the safety pattern set has to accomplish, is that all possible safety requirements for automation systems like train control systems have to be specifiable. According to [22, p. 181] and [18] automation systems like traffic control systems are reactive systems. Properties of reactive systems can be specified in temporal logic, see [25]. Safety requirements are the safety relevant subset of the expression possibilities of temporal logic.

Consequently, the specification of temporal relations plays a particular role in the properties of automation systems. Such systems underlie the temporal behavior of the technical process, which is the technical environment in which the automation system operates. Therefore the formulation of temporal relations in requirements of automation systems plays an essential role. Consequently, the safety pattern concept has to support the correct specification of such temporal relations in safety requirements with regard to formal correctness checks of system models.

To fulfill this demand the safety pattern set has been derived according to the following steps:

1. The set of necessary generic formulations for safety patterns is derived:

It is taken into consideration, which atomic syntactical formulation possibilities exist in the common temporal logic languages LTL and CTL. Logic expressions which result from basic combinations of temporal logic operators and which are repeated in complex formulations are considered as atomic. Additionally, only those formulations are taken into account, which possess a meaning, which has not yet occurred in the analysis of expression possibilities. According to [26] and [27] the different linguistic layers at *sentence level* and at *meaning level* need to be distinguished. This means, that there can be several formulations, which are different at sentence level but which are equal at meaning level. Therefore, in our consideration there are different expressions in temporal logic at sentence level, which are equivalent at meaning level. In the analysis of expression possibilities of temporal logic, only expressions, which have not yet been taken into account in the set from the meaning level point of view, are included in the set of necessary generic formulations.

Another part of this analysis is to check whether the considered expressions are meaningful in context to safety in terminology of automation. This implies, that safety means avoidance of danger, cf. [10]. For that purpose, only formulations are suitable for safety requirements, which express a deterministic relation of system variables and which clearly define under which conditions the expressed property has to be valid. Other formulations tolerate undefined behavior which could lead to hazardous system situations. E.g., the CTL formula (1) is not relevant for safety requirements.

$$AF \ (p \ -> \ AX \ EF \ q) \tag{1}$$

The meaning is that anytime a system state has to be reached in which is valid: If p is true, then anytime later q has to be reachable. Thereby not in all but only in some states it has to be true, that if p is true then at anytime later it must be possible that q is true. It is not controlled at which points in time this demand has to be true. It is absolute arbitrary when the attainability property is valid. This non-determinism is not tolerable from the safety point of view.

The analysis result is a set of 32 expressions in temporal logic, which form the set of necessary generic formulations for safety patterns. This set is the basis for specifying all safety requirements by composition and instantiation. E.g. "p must be permanently valid, before q is valid, and must only be valid, before q is valid" can be expressed by the formulations (2) and (3) and a logical AND-composition. The resulting meaning is "p must be permanently valid, before q is valid", and "from this point in time on when q is true p must never be valid".

$$A(p \ W \ q) \tag{2}$$

$$AG \ (q \ -> \ AG \ (not \ p)) \tag{3}$$

2.   The set of useful generic formulations for safety patterns is derived:

This set supports the usability of the safety pattern concept. Firstly, for the purpose of usability the set of necessary generic formulations is analyzed with regard to distinct characteristics of the different generic formulations so that the formulations can be classified. Classification is necessary to select the appropriate generic formulations for the safety requirements to be specified. The sensible organization of the safety pattern set by classification criteria and safety pattern classes leads to additional generic formulations, which could also be created by the combination of basic formulations.

From former experiences with specification difficulties, further safety pattern classes have been added, so that the safety pattern set also contains further non-atomic generic formulations. Such specification problems are caused by:

- non-trivial compositions of safety patterns.
- decisive specification possibilities which are likely to be overlooked. For this reason, rather than using compositions these cases should be part of the safety pattern catalogue.
- specification problems relevant for automation, which are not supported by dedicated language constructs, e.g. safety requirements with explicit time.

As result of this, 13 classification criteria have been identified. The combination of these safety pattern classes produces a set of 454 safety patterns. To prevent the safety pattern set from getting too large in order to keep the selection process simple, a safety pattern can also contain special cases. They contain generic formulations with minor differences the regular generic formulations.

3.6 Example of Safety Requirements Specification with the Help of Safety Patterns

The application of SAPIS will be demonstrated by a brief example. For the safety requirement of the reference case study there is the following model specific safety requirement:

If the class "Train" is in state "Passing" while class "Level_Crossing" is in state "Automatic_Operation", then at the same time class "Barrier" has to be in state "Barrier_Closed".

The property that class *Barrier* is in state *Barrier_Closed* has to be true under certain circumstances. The condition is that class *Train* (cf. Figure 1) is in state *Passing* and class *Level_Crossing* is in state *Automatic_Operation* (cf. Figures 3 and 4). It is easy to formalize this condition with the help of a logical and: `(Level_Crossing.state = Automatic_Operation)` and `(Train.state = Passing)`. But to express the validity of the property depending on this condition, a suitable safety pattern has to be selected. To detect the suitable formal specification in the temporal logic CTL, first the safety requirement has to be assigned to the correct classes of the different classification criteria with the help of SAPIS. In the following the relevant classification criteria, which have to be decided are listed (a) along with the related decision making questions belonging to them (b). Then the decision regarding the correct class the safety requirement belongs to is explained (c). Unlike SAPIS not all decision possibilities are listed here because of lack of space.

1. a. **Existence of a temporal logic aspect in the safety requirement.**
    b. *Does the safety requirement contain any temporal logic aspect?*
    c. Yes, the property has to be true only at certain points in time. It has to be valid always then when class *Train* is in state *Passing* and class *Level_Crossing* is in state *Automatic_Operation*. For that purpose, the suitable safety pattern class is **dynamic safety requirement**.

2. a. **Existence of dependencies between propositions.**
    b. *Should the searched generic formulation contain any logical dependency between propositions?*
    c. There is a logical dependency between ...
        - `((Level_Crossing.state = Automatic_Operation)` and `(Train.state = Passing))` and
        - `Barrier.state = Barrier_Closed` (cf. Figure 3).

        Therefore, the safety requirement belongs to the class **safety requirements with dependencies between propositions.**

3. a. **Type of time specification.**
    b. *Does the safety requirement contain any explicit time specification?*
    c. No, there is no temporal statement dependent on a system clock. For that reason, it is a **safety requirement with implicit time specification only.**

4. a. **Modality of demand.**
    b. *What is the modality of demand?*
    c. The safety requirement does not state a permitted behavior but a necessary one. That is why the class is **necessity**.

5. a. **Type of validity beginning.**
    b. *When exactly should the validity of the demanded property begin?*
    c. The demanded property has to be valid at once, because the condition is non-temporal. In the safety requirement, it is only stated that the property has to be true always at those points in time, in which the condition is fulfilled. It is not stated when the condition, that class *Train* is in state *Passing* and class *Level_Crossing* is in state *Automatic_Operation* is valid. So the class is **property with non-temporal condition.**

Based on this classification the following safety pattern with the appropriate explanations is identified:

Generic formulation in safety pattern norm language:
Always if a is valid then also b has to be valid.

Generic formulation in formal language (CTL):
AG $(a \rightarrow b)$

Specification of the safety requirement in norm language:
Always if `((Level_Crossing.state = Automatic_Operation)` and `(Train.state = Passing))` is valid then also `(Barrier.state = Barrier_Closed)` has to be valid.

Specification of the safety requirement in formal language (CTL):
AG `(((Level_Crossing.state = Automatic_Operation)` and `(Train.state = Passing))` → `(Barrier.state = Barrier_Closed))`

The example shows clearly that the variables of a safety pattern predicates can be substituted by state, event, action, condition, configuration variables or combinations (cf. section 3.4) of the corresponding system model. By using the model checker SMV the fulfillment in the system definition (cf. section 2) safety requirements, which have been formalized in the depicted way has been shown.

3.7 Demonstration of Benefits for Applied Concepts

By means of the demonstrator of the *Institute for Traffic Safety and Automation Engineering* [19], benefits of the used concepts to achieve evidence of safe functionality have been illustrated. It has been demonstrated that the safety requirements, which have been checked by model checking are also preserved at control of the demonstrator. The UML model has been adapted to form the basis for demonstrator control. Therefore it has also been demonstrated that the system definition has been precisely specified. By the safe operation of the demonstrator it has also been pointed out that safety requirements specified with the help of safety patterns have avoided false specifications. For that purpose the demonstration possibilities have been used to cause safety critical situations by setting hardware failures. In this way the correct system behavior can be observed in different safety critical situations. Using the demonstrator it has been also illustrated that the use of model checking and the automatic transformations of the UML model in the entrance language of the model checker has been successful. The verified safety requirements are preserved in operation of the demonstrator.

The demonstrator control has been technically realized by a C++ software program. This has been implemented systematically on the basis of the UML model by using code generation. For that purpose, the code generator of the tool *Software through Pictures* (StP) from the company Aonix has been applied. This code generator allows the specification of the transformation rules in detail. The same kind of transformation has been used to convert the UML model into the entrance language of the model checker SMV. Data interchange between the control software and the software interface of the demonstrator (see [19]) has been manually implemented in C++.

4   Summary

By means of the case study *single-track level crossing in radio-based operation,* a way to develop a precise system definition and to obtain evidence of safe functionality has been depicted. The concept complies with European standards in the railway sector and with the generic safety standard DIN EN 61508 [15]. The UML notation can be used to specify a precise and clearly understandable system definition, which is exact, unambiguous and compact as well as easy to understand by developers, operation authorities and supervising authorities. A precise system model in UML enables correctness and refutation checks related to the fulfillment of safety requirements. The expenditure for creation of an object oriented system definition is considerably higher than a description in natural language but it possesses the named benefits.

Safety patterns have been introduced as pre-specified safety requirements, which convey an expert knowledge on correct specification and interpretation of safety requirements. Applying safety patterns, engineers who are no experts in higher logic, are able to correctly specify and interpret safety requirements in formal specification languages, what is recommended by standards, as well as precise specifications in a natural language. In this way, safety patterns are a connecting link between specifications in a natural language and formal specifications. The concept helps to comply with recommendations and demands of safety standards in specifying safety requirements formally and in describing the formal specification in terms of natural language. Furthermore, it overcomes weaknesses of safety standards. The concept supports the correct use of formal languages for specification and interpretation. Ambiguities in using a natural language to describe formal specifications are avoided. The equivalence of the formal specification and the specification in norm language is guaranteed.

With the help of the demonstrator the benefits of the developed and used concepts has been illustrated.

References

1. Adtranz: Lastenhefte zum Funkfahrbetrieb (FFB), Deutsche Bahn AG (1997)
2. Arabestani, S.: Umschreibung von Zustandsdiagrammen der UML für das Model-Checking. In: Schnieder, E. (Hrsg.): Entwurfsmethodik, Modellbildung, Werkzeuge und Anwendungen, 8. Fachtagung EKA (2003) S. 63-79
3. Arabestani, S.: Relations in Object-Oriented Analysis. In: Ehrig, H., Grosse-Rhode, M. (eds.): Proceedings of 2nd International Workshop on Software Specification Techniques-Satelite Event of ETAPS (2002) pp. 37-47
4. Arabestani, S., Gayen, J.-T.: Objektorientierte Analyse zur Modellierung im Eisenbahnwesen. Signal & Draht 92 (2000) 1+2, S. 20-27
5. Arabestani, S., Gayen, J.-T.: Prinzip der Vererbung bei der objektorientierten Analyse am Beispiel der funkbasierten Bahnübergangssteuerung. In: Schnieder, E. (Hrsg.): Forms 2000 - Formale Techniken für die Eisenbahnsicherung, Fortschritt-Berichte VDI, Reihe 12, Verkehrstechnik/Fahrzeugtechnik, Nr. 441 (2000)

6. Bitsch, F., Canver, E., Moik, A.: Strukturierte Erstellung von Sicherheitsspezifikationen in UML mit Hilfe der FMEA-Methode. In: Schnieder, E. (Hrsg.): Forms '99 - Formale Techniken für die Eisenbahnsicherung, Fortschritt-Berichte VDI, Reihe 12, Verkehrstechnik/Fahrzeugtechnik, Nr.436, VDI Verlag GmbH, Düsseldorf (2000) S. 225-245

7. Bitsch, F., Göhner, P.: Spezifikation von Sicherheitsanforderungen mit Safety-Pattern. Software Engineering in der industriellen Praxis, VDI-Bericht-Nr. 1666, Düsseldorf (2002) S. 29-40

8. Bitsch, F.: A Way for Applicable Formal Specification of Safety Requirements by Tool-Support. In: Tarnai, G., Schnieder, E. (eds.): Proceedings of FORMS 2003 - Formal Methods for Railway Operation and Control Systems, L'Harmattan, Budapest (2003) pp. 175-185

9. Bitsch, F.: Process Model for the Development of System Requirements Specifications for Railway Systems. In: Schnieder, E. (ed.): Workshop on Software specification of safety relevant transportation control tasks, VDI-Fortschrittbericht, Reihe 12, Verkehrstechnik/Fahrzeugtechnik, Nr.535, VDI Verlag GmbH, Düsseldorf (2002) pp. 75-90

10. Bitsch, F.: Safety Patterns - The Key to Formal Specification of Safety Requirements. In Voges, U. (ed.): Proceedings of 20th International Conference SAFECOMP 2001 - Computer Safety Reliability and Security, LNCS, Vol. 2187. Springer-Verlag, Berlin, Heidelberg (2001) S. 176-189

11. CELENEC EN 50126: Railway Applications - The specification and demonstration of Reliability, Availability, Maintainability and Safety (RAMS) (1999)

12. CENELEC EN 50128: Railway Applications - Communications, signaling and processing systems - Software for railway control and protection systems (2001)

13. CENELEC EN 50129: Railway Applications - Safety related electronic systems for signaling (2000)

14. Dill, D.L., Drexler, A.J., Hu, A.J., Yang, C.H.: Protocol Verification as a Hardware Design Aid. Proc. IEEE Int'l Conf. Computer Design: VLSI in Computers and Processors (1992) pp. 522–525

15. DKE Deutsche Kommission Elektrotechnik Elektronik Informationstechnik im DIN und VDE: DIN EN 61508 (VDE 0803) "Funktionale Sicherheit - Sicherheitssysteme (E/E/PES)" (2002)

16. Fingerle, M.: Konzeption zur Auswertung von UML Systemmodellen für die Durchführung von Sicherheitsanalysen. Diplomarbeit IAS, SADA Nr. 1868, Universität Stuttgart (2003)

17. Gayen, J.-T.: Sicherheitsanforderungen/-eigenschaften im FFB. http://ivev8.ivev.bau.tu-bs.de/forschung/dfg-spp/sicherheitsanforderungen/ (1999)

18. Gunzert, M.: Komponentenbasierte Softwareentwicklung für sicherheitskritische eingebettete Systeme. Dissertation, IAS, Universität Stuttgart (2003)

19. Hänsel, F., Poliak, J., Slovák, R., Schnieder, E.: Reference case study "Traffic Control Systems" for comparison and validation of formal specifications using a model demonstrator. In this volume.

20. Heitmeyer, C.L.: On the Need for 'Practical' Formal Methods. In: Formal Techniques in Real-Time and Real-Time Fault-Tolerant Systems, Proc., 5th Intern. Symposium (FTRTFT'98), LICS 1486, Lyngby, Denmark (1998) pp. 18-26

21. Heitmeyer, C., Kirby Jr., J., Labaw, B., Archer, M., Bharadwaj, R.: Using Abstraction and Model Checking to Detect Safety Violations in Requirements Specifications. IEEE Transactions on software engineering, vol. 24, no. 11 (November 1998) pp. 927-948

22. Lauber, R., Göhner, P.: Prozessautomatisierung 1. 3. Auflage, Springer Verlag, Berlin, Heidelberg, New York (1999)

23. Moik, A.: Ingenieurgerechte formale Methoden für die Entwicklung von sicheren Automatisierungssystemen. Dissertation, IAS, Universität Stuttgart (2002)
24. Ortner, E.: Methodenneutraler Fachentwurf - Zu den Grundlagen einer anwendungsorientierten Informatik. Stuttgart, Leipzig: B. G. Teubner Verlagsgesellschaft (1997)
25. Pnueli, A.: The Temporal Logic of Programs. In Proceedings of the 18th IEEE Symposium Foundations of Computer Science (FOCS 1977) pp. 46-57
26. Lakoff, G.: Linguistik und natürliche Logik. Athenäum Verlag, Frankfurt (1970)
27. Schnieder, E.: Methoden der Automatisierung – Beschreibungsmittel, Modellkonzepte und werkzeuge für Automatisierungssysteme. Friedr. Vieweg & Sohn Verlag, Braunschweig, Wiesbaden (1999)
28. OMG *Unified Modeling Language Specification*, Version 1.5, OMG Document formal/03-03-01, (March 2003)

Executable HybridUML and Its Application to Train Control Systems*

Kirsten Berkenkötter, Stefan Bisanz, Ulrich Hannemann, and Jan Peleska

University of Bremen,
P.O. Box 330 440
28334 Bremen, Germany
{kirsten,bisanz,ulrichh,jp}@informatik.uni-bremen.de

Abstract. In this paper, the authors introduce an extension of UML for the purpose of hybrid systems modeling. The construction uses the profile mechanism of UML 2.0 which is the standard procedure for extending the Unified Modeling Language. The "intuitive semantics" of the syntactic extension is based on the semantics for hierarchic Hybrid Automata, as suggested by Alur et. al. In contrast to Alur's formalism, HybridUML allows to label transitions not only with conditions and assignments, but also with signals. Furthermore, our approach associates formal semantics by definition of a transformation from HybridUML specifications into programs of a "low-level" language which is both executable in hard real-time and semantically well-defined. When compared to approaches assigning semantics directly to the high-level constructs of a formal specification language, the transformation approach offers two main advantages: First, semantics can be more easily adapted to syntactic extensions by extending the transformation in an appropriate way. Second, all models are automatically executable, since the low-level language is.

1   Introduction

A real-time system is called *hybrid* if it processes *time-continuous* variables in addition to discrete-range parameters. The (piecewise) continuous evolution over dense time of real or complex observables occurs naturally in physical models and in the development of (embedded) control systems monitoring some continuous observables (e.g. temperature, speed) via analog sensors and setting others (e.g. voltage, thrust) using actuators.

In this paper, the authors introduce *HybridUML*, a novel specification formalism for hybrid systems, and the *Hybrid Low-Level Language Framework HL^3* for generating programs to be executed in hard real-time on cluster hardware architectures.

---

* The work presented in this article has been investigated by the authors in the context of the HYBRIS (Efficient Specification of Hybrid Systems) project supported by the Deutsche Forschungsgemeinschaft DFG as part of the priority programme on *Software Specification – Integration of Software Specification Techniques for Applications in Engineering.*

H. Ehrig et al. (Eds.): INT 2004, LNCS 3147, pp. 145–173, 2004.

As suggested by its name, HybridUML is based on the syntax of the Unified Modeling Language UML 2.0 [OMG03a,OMG03b]. Since core UML does not support the specification of time-continuous behavior, a language extension is required. To this end, the authors introduce a new *profile*, that is, a definition of new UML constructs introduced by means of UML stereotypes applied to existing language elements. In particular, HybridUML extends the UML variant of Statecharts by augmenting state descriptions using *invariants* and *flows* or *algebraic conditions*. The latter ones describe time-continuous variable evolutions taking place while the system resides in the respective state. Transitions may be triggered by conditions and signals (i.e. atomic events) and lead to actions consisting of variable assignments and signal generations. Following the suggestions of existing formalisms [Hen96,AGLS01], transition execution is conceptually performed in zero-time, but with interleaving semantics. Parallel components process signals in a synchronous, but non-blocking way: A signal s generated by some transition is available in multicast-fashion to other agents for their next computation step. Time passes during the phases where agents reside in a given state, and time-continuous variables change according to the flow/algebraic conditions applicable in the current agent states.

The HL^3 framework developed by the authors consists of a re-usable hard real-time runtime environment R and a design pattern P for compilation targets of arbitrary hybrid specifications. Given a high-level formalism H – such as HybridUML – for the description Φ of hybrid systems, transformations Φ_H from high-level specifications S into instances $\Phi_H(S)$ of the HL^3 pattern P can be developed. For $(\Phi_H(S), R)$, a formal semantics $\mathcal{S}(\Phi_H(S), R)$ is defined so that the transformation both provides a semantic definition of S and an executable program whose behavior will be consistent with $\mathcal{S}(\Phi_H(S), R)$. Similar to machine code, HL^3 should not be used for manual programming, but as a target language for automated transformations. In contrast to machine code, the real-time semantics of HL^3 programs can be determined in a direct way, thereby assigning formal meaning to the high-level specification used as the transformation source. This is achieved by using a very limited range of instructions for multi-threading, timing control, and consistent handling of global state in presence of concurrency.

Though today numerous formalisms and verification approaches are available for hybrid systems (see references in the related-work section below), their application in an industrial "real-world"-context is still rare. According to our analysis, two main causes are responsible for this situation:

- The syntax developed for hybrid formalisms within research communities was too specialized and not supported by conventional software engineering tools available to practitioners.
- While the underlying theories supported formal verification by theorem proving or model checking, they did not support the development of optimized code for embedded control systems.

With respect to the first cause we suggest to augment existing well-accepted formalisms of software engineering by new specification constructs describing time-continuous behavior. From today's point of view, the Unified Modeling Language UML 2.0 is the best candidate for such an approach: It is currently the most widely known software-engineering formalism supported by a variety of tools. Furthermore, language extension is an inherent feature of UML, therefore well-constructed UML tools should support this extension as well.

The second cause is related to both practical and theoretical considerations: From a practitioner's point of view, the effort invested into formal specification and verification – which will certainly be considerably higher than the effort spent on elaborating informal conventional specifications – is only justified if the specifications can be easily transformed into executable systems. For example, we do not expect that the amount of time required for developing executable code by step-wise refinement will ever be widely accepted among project leaders and developers of embedded systems.

From a theoretic point of view, the problem is even more subtle: If a transformation into executable code is available, how can the consistency between high-level specification semantics and execution behavior of the low-level implementation using conventional programming languages and operating systems be ensured? A practical consequence of this problem consists in the fact that the simulation facilities provided by many case tools never declare which formal high-level semantics has been used as a reference for the encoded simulation behavior.

In "classical" UML [RJB99,OMG03a,OMG03b], the definition of a universal formal semantics has been deliberately avoided. Instead, the various language constructs are only associated with a general informal meaning so that their purpose in various modeling situations becomes clear. In [RJB99, pp. 105] this approach is motivated by the fact that the semantic interpretation of specification constructs depends on the specific project context, and precise behavior is only obtained by transformation into the target programming language. While this avoids the obligation to prove consistency between executable system and high-level specification semantics, it still poses the problem that in general, it will be infeasible to capture the potential behavior of software written in Java, C/C++, or Ada, when executed in a specific target environment.

Our suggestion to overcome this problem is to restrict the infinite variety of possible compilation targets for hybrid specifications according to the HL^3 framework introduced below: First, the framework fixes a specific hard real-time runtime environment which avoids uncertainties introduced by using arbitrary operating systems. Second, all specifications written in a given hybrid high-level formalism have to be compiled using a transformation function which generates instances of abstract classes pre-defined by the framework. As a consequence, the variable compilation targets depending on formalism and specification are restricted with respect to software architecture and interfaces to the runtime environment. Therefore the behavioral semantics of the executable target can be given more easily than for an unrestricted compilation into a programming language. If the high-level formalisms have been introduced informally, the transformation defines the semantics as well. If, however, the transformation has only been created in order to translate specifications with given high-level semantics into executable code, the consistency between abstract specification behavior and executable compilation target still has to be verified. Due to the restrictive structure of compilation targets and runtime environment, this proof obligation is at least easier to discharge within the HL^3 framework than for arbitrary transformations designed in an intuitive way.

Before presenting a more formal definition, the "look-and-feel" of the new HybridUML profile is illustrated in Section 2 by means of a train control systems case study defined by the DFG priority programme *Software Specification – Integration of Software Specification Techniques for Applications in Engineering* [DFG]. The UML 2.0 profile defining HybridUML in a systematic way is described in Section 3. For illustration purposes, these definitions refer to the case study introduced before. Conforming to the general UML approach, the profile defines some basic semantic features together with the syntax, but is still quite far from a complete formal description of behavioral properties. To achieve this, we first introduce the HL^3 framework in Section 4. This is used in Section 5 to specify the full HybridUML semantics by providing a transformation into HL^3. Apart from describing the specification capabilities offered by the HybridUML profile, this paper focuses on the transformation concept and the semantic model of the HL^3 framework. Other areas of interest – such as hard real-time simulation, automated test data generation against HybridUML specifications, and performance measurements of HL^3 implementations on multi-CPU computer clusters – are briefly discussed in the conclusion (Section 6), with references to current work in progress.

Due to the usual space limitations, the HybridUML profile definition, the HL^3 semantics, and its performance as a time-triggered hard real-time runtime environment on cluster architectures cannot be exhaustively described in this paper. We refer to [BBHP04] for a detailed description of HybridUML profile and [BBH+04] for semantics, implementation, and real-time measurements of HL^3.

Hybrid systems have been studied extensively in various research communities since the early nineties. The definition and investigation of the Duration Calculus (see [ZRH93,RRS03] and further references given there) provided fundamental contributions to understanding Hybrid Systems. The introduction of Hybrid Automata [Hen96] demonstrated the feasibility of verification by model checking for hybrid specifications. The applicability of hybrid automata to large-scale systems was improved by the introduction of hierarchical hybrid specifications [AGLS01]. Alternative hierarchical approaches closer to the Statecharts formalism have been described in [KMP00] (together with a proof theory) and [BBB+99] (verification by model checking).

We mention GIOTTO [HHK03] as today's most prominent example of a hard real-time language with well-defined semantics. Similar to our HL^3 framework, GIOTTO follows the time-triggered systems paradigm described in [Kop97]. The time-triggered approach is particularly well-suited for real-time programs discretising time-continuous evolutions, since it guarantees bounded timing jitter for periodic schedules. In contrast to this, other approaches to hard real-time focus on the fast response to external interrupts, see [RTAI03,Lab04] for popular real-time variants of the Linux operating system.

2   HybridUML by Example: Radio-Based Train Control

In this section, HybridUML is introduced and illustrated by means of an application example – the specification of a radio-based train control system. This is one of two case studies within the scope of the DFG priority programme Software Specification [DFG].

HybridUML as Profile for UML 2.0. One of the mostly critized points of UML 1.4 is the lack of formal specification. Especially the real time community needs this for building safe systems. As this fact has not changed with UML 2.0, another solution must be found for using UML in the real-time domain.

To overcome this deficiency, we propose HybridUML as a UML 2.0 profile. UML 2.0 offers profiles as a powerful extension mechanism for tailoring UML to specific working areas. Based on a metamodel like the Meta Object Facility (MOF) or usually UML itself, a profile specifies new model elements called stereotypes. Each stereotype is dependent on exactly one element of the corresponding metamodel (see Fig. 5 for an example). These stereotypes customize the used metamodel in different ways: introducing a new terminology, e.g. for Enterprise Java Beans, introducing new syntax, either for elements without syntax or new symbols for elements with syntax, introducing new semantics and constraints, or adding further information like transformation rules from model to code. A set of stereotypes forms a profile.

A profile can be applied by a model or a package in a model. All stereotypes can be used as modeling elements. As every stereotype extends an already known element, the model is still a valid UML model if the profile is taken away. Profile application is visualized by a dependency with the keywort ≪*apply*≫ attached. The profile itself is a package and therefore depicted like this with the keyword ≪*profile*≫ above its name. The HybridUML profile thus takes a subset of UML, modifies it according to the requirements on a specification formalism for hierarchical hybrid systems, and associates it with a precise semantics. The most important constraint on applying the HybridUML profile is using only the model elements specified in it.

Radio-Based Train Control. An important part of the specification of the train control system is the coordination of train and railroad crossings in order to ensure that whenever the train crosses the road, the crossing is safe (i.e. it is locked for cars, pedestrians etc.). A special feature is the absence of signals and train monitoring equipment on the track, i.e. train and crossings always guarantee a safe and consistent state of the complete system on behalf of state requests and notifications. Particularly, the train controller continuously (re-)calculates velocity-dependent locations on the track at which requests must be sent, or at

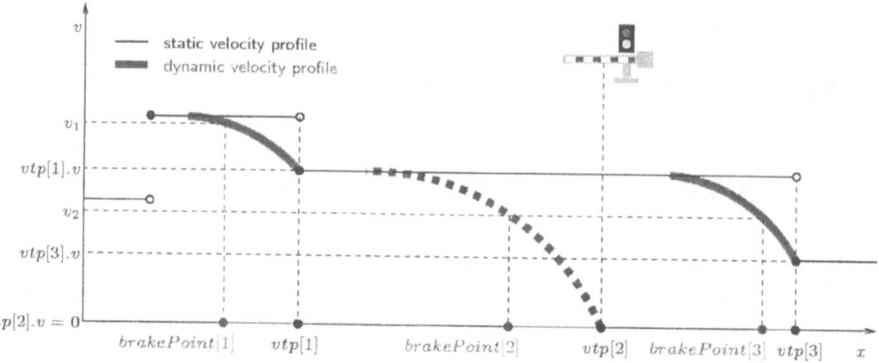

Fig. 1. Dynamic velocity profile defined by velocity target points on the track

which the brake has to be activated. There are related investigations concerning the "generalized railroad crossing" applying a more abstract model of the system, e.g. [HL94].

In this case study, a single train is considered that moves on a single track without switches. There are *velocity target points* on the track with dedicated velocities that the train must not exceed. There are two kinds of velocity target points: (1) *Conditional* velocity target points are assigned to railroad crossings and have a target velocity $v = 0$. If the crossing is not safe, the velocity target point is active and the train has to stop there. (2) The route atlas contains a (piecewise constant) static velocity profile that defines a maximum allowed velocity for each location on the track. Each location for which this velocity gets lower implies a *fixed* velocity target point, denoting a restrictive velocity change. These points are always active.

Figure 1 is an abstract view on a track example with fixed $(vtp[1], vtp[3])$ and conditional $(vtp[2])$ velocity target points. In consideration of the train's maximum deceleration, the static velocity profile and the velocity target points define the *dynamic* velocity profile, resulting in *brake points* – the locations on the track where the train must start braking in order to reach the target velocity at the respective target point. The brake points depend on the train's current velocity; in the diagram, example values for current velocities v_1 and v_2 are given, whereas v_1 leads to brake point $brakePoint[1]$ and v_2 implies $brakePoint[2]$ and $brakePoint[3]$, respectively. A safety-critical aspect of the train control system is to ensure that the speed limit of target velocity points is never broken. The remainder of this section focuses thereon.

Architectural Structure. The main building block for modeling architectural structure within HybridUML is called *agent* in conformance with related work. Agents are concurrently operating entities and can be combined by parallel composition, or grouped together enclosing them with a hiding operator. For precise interface descriptions we distinguish local and global variables and signals. Hy-

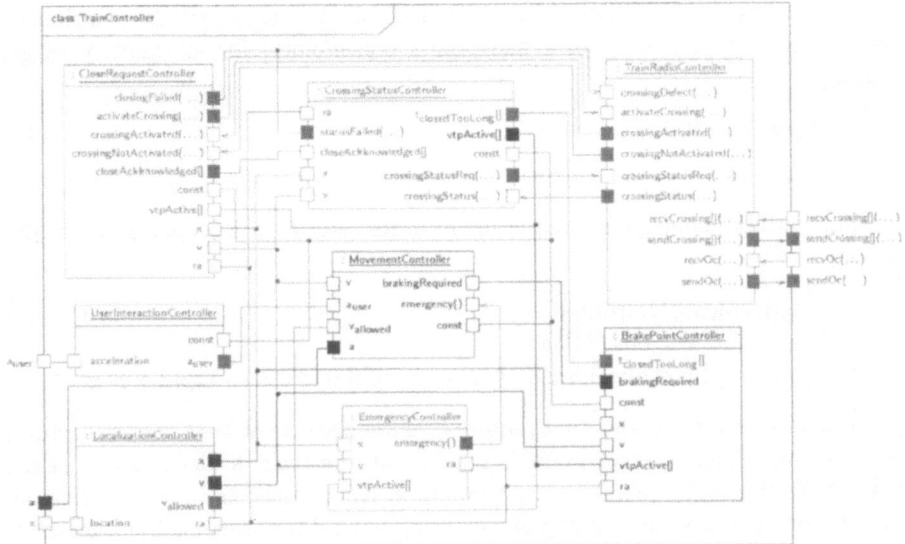

Fig. 2. Structure diagram of agent TrainController.

bridUML allows communication between concurrent agents via shared variables as well as via message passing to model multicasting of signals.

Agent TrainController consists of several (parallel) agents as defined in its structure diagram (Fig. 2), including their interdependencies. It calculates and provides the required acceleration a of the train. Therefore the train's location x and the user-requested acceleration a_{user} from the locomotive driver are read from the environment. These are time-continuously changing variables. Further, several locally defined constants affect the computation of a, like the route atlas ra which is defined as a data structure. It contains the velocity target points vtp that consist of a location x, a target velocity v, and its type (fixed or conditional). Finally, radio messages are received that provide status information about the railroad crossings.

The highlighted basic agents BrakePointController and MovementController are discussed in the following.

Agent BrakePointController provides the boolean variable brakingRequired that denotes that the train has to brake because of any velocity target point. This is determined by the train's location x, its current speed v, and the set of currently active velocity target points (which is defined by vtpActive[] consisting of a boolean variable for each velocity target point).

Behavioral Specification. The behavior of a basic agent is given by an associated hierachical state machine. As typical for hybrid systems, there are basically two ways of acting: either some discrete transition is taken or time passes and the continuous variables change over time according to their specified constraints.

The behavior definition (shown in Fig. 3) is based on the continuous (re-)calculation of the set of brake points brakePoint[i] for all velocity target points:

(1) **algeBrakePoint** $\equiv$
$$\forall i \in \{1..VTP\_COUNT\} \bullet brakePoint[i] = ra.vtp[i].x - \frac{ra.vtp[i].v^2 - v^2}{2 \cdot const.a_{min}}$$

The variable brakingRequired is set in a discrete fashion, dependent on condition:

(2) **condBrakingRequired** $\equiv$
$\exists i \in \{1..VTP\_COUNT\} \bullet$
$vtpActive[i] \wedge brakePoint[i] \leq x \wedge ra.vtp[i].v < v \wedge ra.vtp[i].x > x$

It denotes the situations that require braking because at least one brake point of an active velocity target point is reached by the train while its speed is too high. Note that only velocity target points in front of the train are considered, because particularly the opening of a crossing behind the train shall not affect it.

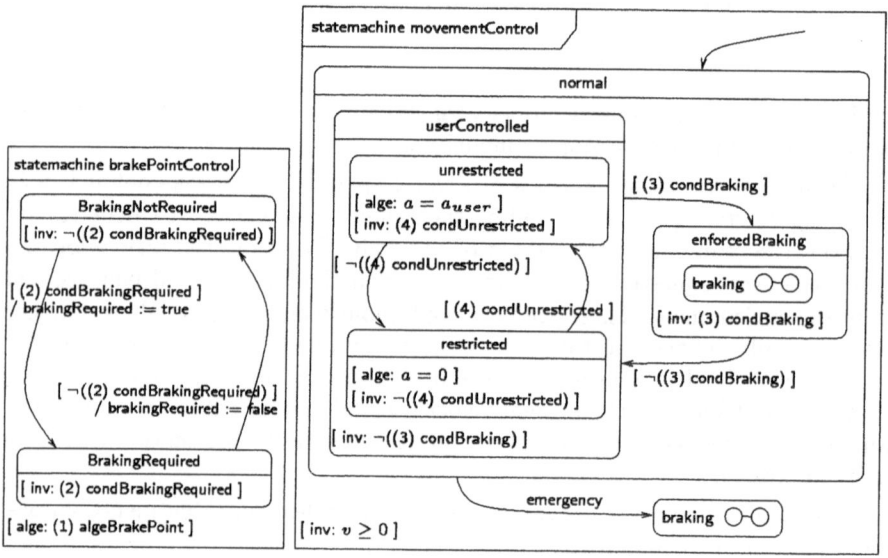

Fig. 3. Behavior of agent BrakePointController.

Fig. 4. Behavior of agent MovementController.

Thus the mode BrakingRequired is active for exactly these situations, whereas the mode BrakingNotRequired is complementary. The transitions in combination with the invariants model the mandatory mode changes according to the condition such that variable brakingRequired is always up-to-date.

The responsibility of agent MovementController (Fig. 4) is to determine the required acceleration a. It constrains the user-requested acceleration a_{user} on behalf of brakingRequired, the current velocity v, the currently allowed velocity $v_{allowed}$, and a special signal emergency. It is modeled strictly hierarchically, initially in mode normal. Submode userControlled maps the user-requested acceleration to a, whereas submode enforcedBraking forces the train to brake. Similarly to BrakingRequired, the active submode directly depends on a condition:

(3)   **condBraking** $\equiv$
$brakingRequired \vee v > v_{allowed}$

In case of enforced braking, the submode braking defines a to be the maximum deceleration until the train stops. Otherwise, there is a distinction between unrestricted and restricted appliance of a_{user}: The mode restricted guarantees that the minimum (0) and maximum ($v_{allowed}$) velocities are not violated, else unrestricted maintains $a = a_{user}$. Again, a condition controls this:

(4)   **condUnrestricted** $\equiv$
$(v < v_{allowed} \vee a_{user} \leq 0) \wedge (v > 0 \vee a_{user} \geq 0)$

Finally, mode braking is re-used in movementControl – if the signal emergency (that is caused by violating a velocity target point) is received, the train is definitely stopped.

3   The HybridUML Profile

In this section we give a brief overview on the most relevant elements of the HybridUML profile, their relation to existing UML constructs, and their intuitive semantics. For a detailed language description we refer the reader to [BBHP04].

Types and Expressions. HybridUML uses typed variables. As UML provides only Integer, String, and Boolean as basic types, we have to extend explicitly PrimitiveType to get the datatype Real. In this way, we can use real-valued variables within the profile. For better separaton of concerns, we also need analog real numbers as extension which can be changed continuously according to flow conditions in Modes while variables of type Real can only be changed discretely by transitions. AnalogReal thus is a specialization of Real. For better readability in large applications, we introduce StructuredDataType as an instance of DataType to define a structure. All StructuredDataTypes of a model are implicitly collected in a package which is imported by all diagrams of this model.

For describing the valuation of AnalogReal variables, specific expressions are needed, i.e. differential expressions and algebraic expressions. Invariant expressions are needed to define state invariants. RTExpression is an instance of Expression (see Fig. 5) which defines mathematical and logical terms that may be dependent on time. RTExpression is an abstract metaclass that cannot be instantiated.

The real-time expression is given as a string, just as in Expression. Furthermore, the expression must be mathematically or logically evaluable. The notation and

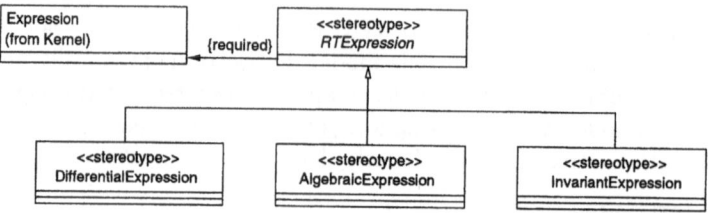

Fig. 5. Stereotypes for RTExpressions

semantics are given by the concrete subtypes, i.e., specializations of RTExpression, which are: *AlgebraicExpression*, to describe algebraic terms dependent on time, *DifferentialExpression*, to describe differential terms dependent on time, and *InvariantExpression*, to describe logical terms used for modeling invariants a variable must fulfill.

Constraints. To describe the restrictions on the valuation of analog variables in modes we introduce RTConstraints. As an instance of Constraint, RTConstraint is a UML constraint which is restricted in order to describe an RTExpression. DifferentialExpressions and AlgebraicExpressions can be attached to AnalogReal variables, InvariantExpressions can be attached to all variable types. RTConstraint is visualized in the same way as UML 2.0 constraints, i.e. an RTExpression term given in curly brackets. In Modes, brackets are used.

Clocks and Timers. We do not use the UML 2.0 time model as it has no formal semantics and as it is not powerful enough for our purposes. A Clock is modeled by a variable of type AnalogReal that uses a DifferentialEquation for modeling the flow of time. Therefore we inherit from AnalogReal to get a clock. The flow of time is specified as a differential equation: Let t be the value of a Clock instance. Then the following expression always holds: $\dot{t} = 1$. As the differential equation is explicitly given, it is not added as a constraint following the variable. Similarly we have timers which are set with a value and count downwards, consequently they are specified by the differential equation $\dot{t} = -1$.

Variables and Signals. Variables in HybridUML can be shared between agents for communication purposes. They are visualized in the same way as UML 2.0 Ports, which are linked by connectors. The shared variable model requires connected interfaces to hold the same value. VariablePorts are depicted as a rectangle on the boundary of the owning classifier. Instead of visualizing the attached interfaces in lollipop-notation, a required interface (corresponding to read-only access) is a white filled rectangle and a provided (corresponding to read/write access) interface is a black filled rectangle. In class diagrams, only the variable owned by the VariableInterface of the port will be shown.

RTSignals are introduced as a different means for communication between Agents, as pure communication via shared variables can be managed when modeling small systems, but tends to be cumbersome for larger systems. RTSignal is an instance of Signal (from Common Behaviors) which defines an asynchronous message. An RTSignal is depicted in composite structure diagrams in correspondence with SignalPorts and SignalInterfaces similar to shared variables.

Using these elements of UML allows to represent the communication structure between agents in a composite structure diagram (see Fig. 2) as far as their shared variables and signals are concerned. In statemachine diagrams, RTSignals are used in combination with SignalEvents and ModeTransitions. SignalEvents carry RTSignals. They are used as triggers in Modes. Nevertheless, we prefer the term event as this is usual for state machine models.

Agents. Agents are stereotypes of classes and consist of VariablePorts, SignalPorts, private variables, Modes, initial states, and parameters. Initial states are specified in Agent instances just as concrete values for parameters. Modes are class variables and cannot be changed by Agent instances. Parameters are used for better scalability. They specify constants that can be used in invariants and other expressions used in the Agent instance and its Mode(s).

An Agent instance can own an internal structure which may consist of Agent instances itself. Agents communicate by shared variables (represented by VariablePorts and VariableConnectors) and signals (as modelled by SignalPorts and SignalConnectors).

In the HybridUML profile we distinguish *basic* Agents which are not nested and own a single top-level Mode, and *composite* Agents which are composed from subagents and have many top-level Modes. Clocks are global for all parts of an Agent. We do not model them as VariablePorts as this would be obfuscating. Parameters are constant global variables for usage in constraints of all kind. The top-level Modes define the behavior of the system. The semantics of a basic Agent are defined by the (trace) behavior of its top-level Modes, constructed from the respective relations describing the continuous behavior and the discrete transitions of a Mode (see below).

The standard operations on concurrent components like the composition of two Agents $A_1 \| A_2$, application of a hiding operator, and renaming of the variables of an AgentInstance, can be reflected in the representation of an Agent's internal structure in a composite strucure diagram. An execution of an Agent A follows a trajectory, which starts in some initial state and is a sequence of flows, i.e. continuous changes to the analog variables, interleaved with discrete steps of agents. While continuous steps are performed simultaneously by all Agents, discrete steps are performed by one Agent at a time, possibly changing variables or taking part in communication via events.

Agents are depicted like UML classes with internal structure. In a class diagram, the internal structure is visualized as aggregated classes. The parameter list of each Agent is given behind its name in parentheses in the first compartment of the class symbol. VariablePorts and their included VariableInterfaces and variables as well as SignalPorts and their included SignalInterfaces and signals are given as attributes in the second compartment of the class symbol. In the class diagram, for variables only the name and type are shown, for signals the name and parameters are given. Optionally, in the third compartment of the class the Mode of the Agent is given. This is the name of the Mode followed by concrete parameters listed inside parentheses. A parameter of a Mode may also be a parameter of the Agent, i.e. the concrete value is given in an Agent instance.

The internal structure of composite Agents is shown in a composite structure diagram (see as example Fig. 2). The name of the Agent is given in the upper left corner with the keyword *class* before it. After that, the concrete parameters of the composite Agent follow. Here read/write access of global variables is shown as ports with required and provided interfaces. The same holds for sending and receiving signals.

Agent instances are visualized as objects in composite structure diagrams. Behind the objects' name and type the concrete parameters are given in parentheses in the first compartment of the object symbol. In the second compartment, optionally the respective initState is given as a constraint, i.e. in curly brackets. The Mode of the Agent is given in a statechart diagram. The name of the Mode with the keywort *statemachine* before it is given in the upper left corner of the diagram.

Modes. Sets of states of a basic agent are described by *Modes* which may contain submodes themselves and transitions. In our profile, Mode is an instance of StateMachine describing an Agent's behavior. As Modes may have flow conditions, they are (hierarchical) hybrid state machines. Each Mode contains exactly one region, i.e. there is no parallel behavior inside a Mode. It is entered and left by control points, which are partitioned into entry and exit points. Top-level Modes are connected to an Agent. They use the global variables and signals defined in this Agent. Modes can have parameters for better scalability. Within Modes, the time-continuous behavior is defined by differential equations and algebraic constraints and limited by invariants. When a mode is executing a continuous step, the hierarchical state machine as a whole is acting, i.e. modes on all levels, from the top-level mode to the leaf modes, have to coordinate for this. Part of this coordination is that any possible valuation of analog variables has to comply to the constraints attached to all active modes on the various levels.

Discrete steps are described by transitions between modes where taking a transition does not take time. Transitions consist of a condition part and an action part. As condition, we can have a boolean expression, i.e. firing that transition depends on the state, or a signal trigger, i.e., an event based invocation, or both. As action of a transition we allow instantaneous operations on variables and sending of a signal. When a transition is taken, discrete variables may be updated or signals can be sent and received. Preemption and interrupts are modeled by using group transitions, i.e. exiting a higher level Mode via some distinguished exit point.

An execution of a Mode consists of a sequence of steps which can be chosen out of three different types: a continuous step according to the respective constraints, a discrete step according to the condition and action of a transition within the mode, and an environment step that can change all but the local variables of that mode. The last variant represents an activity of a different Mode on the same hierarchical level. For a top-level mode no environment steps in this sense are possible, as it is the solitary Mode of that level.

Modes are visualized the same way as UML 2.0 StateMachines (see Fig. 4). Parameters are given behind the name of the Mode in parentheses. The invariant is marked *inv*, the flow conditions with *flow*, and algebraic expressions are marked with *alge*. As these are constraints, they are given in brackets.

Transitions. In order to provide a clear-cut interface of Modes while avoiding inter-level transitions we use control points for Modes as sources and targets of transitons. Entry points are depicted as small circles on the border of a Mode with an optional name attached to it while exit points are depicted as small solid black-filled circles. Every Mode has one default entry point and one default exit point which are not depicted explicitly. We employ ModePseudostate as an instance of Pseudostate to denote control points.

ModeTransition is an instance of Transition depicted by an arrow with open arrowhead. ModeTransitions are taken according to their condition part, i.e., their guard constraints or a triggering SignalEvent. The guard constraint is given in brackets followed possibly by the SignalEvent. The ModeTransitionActivity is separated from the guard by a slash. In UML 2.0, Transitions can only have Activities as effect. As ModeTransitionActivity thus is an instance of Activity, it can be an updateActivity which updates variables according to some instruction, or it can be a sendActivity which emits a SignalEvent.

4 HL^3 – The Hybrid Low-Level Language Framework

As indicated in Section 1, the *Hybrid Low-Level Language Framework* HL^3 is a generic compilation target for hybrid high-level formalisms H. It has been designed to support the transformation Φ_H of specifications S written in H into executable code $(\Phi_H(S), R)$, thereby assigning a formal semantics $S(\Phi_H(S), R)$ to the compilation target. The generated HL^3 program is suitable for hard real-time execution, to be used either for developing embedded applications or for their automated test in hardware-in-the-loop configurations. The concepts described here have been implemented on multi-CPU computers where CPUs can be reserved exclusively for the HL^3 runtime environment. In order to support executability on specific target hardware, high-level specifications S consist of three parts: (1) The *behavioral specification* S_1, written, for example, in HybridUML, (2) the *architectural specification* S_2 describing the available cluster nodes, CPUs, hardware interfaces and the mapping from S_1-objects to concrete hardware, (3) the *physical constraints specification* S_3 describing the required frequencies for the discretization of time-continuous evolutions, writing to/reading from hardware interfaces, as well as the required precision for discrete time-dependent steps.

The framework is sketched in Fig. 6, with additional definitions of basic types shown in Fig. 7. Its underlying idea is to provide a re-usable hard real-time processing infrastructure – the *runtime environment R* – and a design pattern

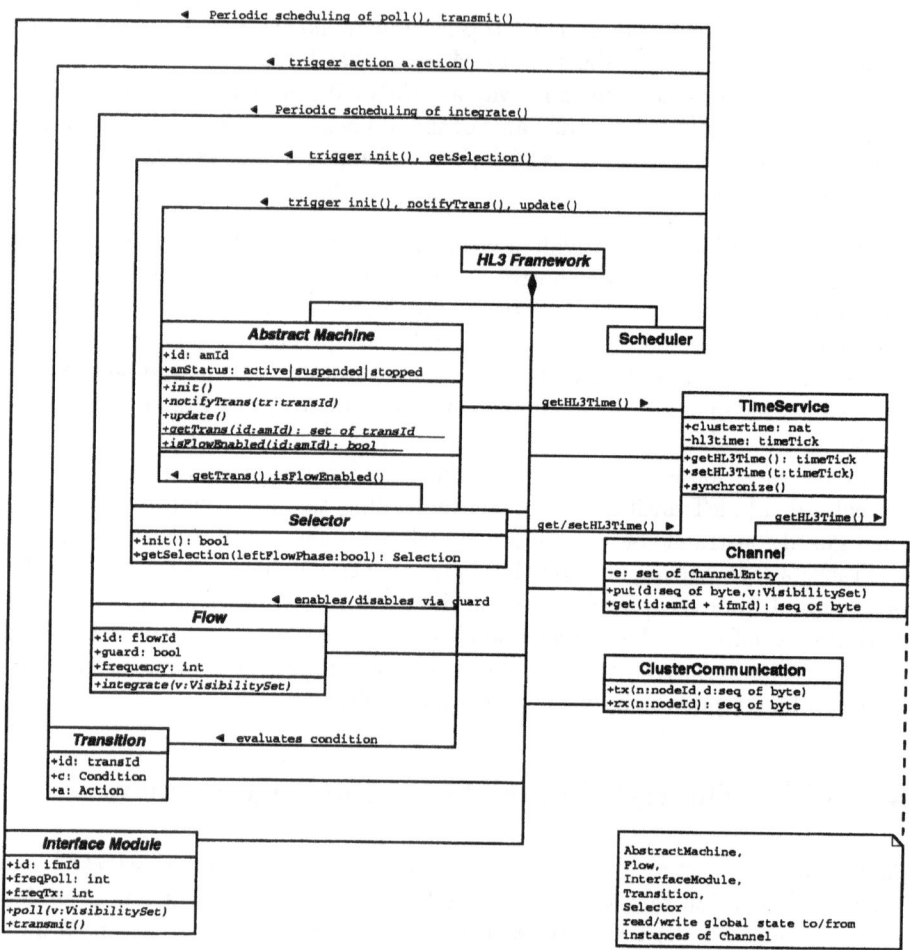

Fig. 6. Design pattern for the HL^3 run-time environment.

P for the formalism- and specification-dependent components to be executed within the runtime environment.

The HL^3 runtime environment R consists of a user space Scheduler running on reserved CPUs without interruptions from the underlying operating system (Linux with a kernel-extension developed by the authors' research group). In addition, TimeService and a communication service (Channel and ClusterCommunication) provide the mechanisms to ensure consistent data views within the cluster configuration. The Scheduler enforces *time-triggered* real-time system behavior [Kop97]: All activities to be performed by the components of a HL^3 instance are scheduled at pre-determined points in time which are multiples of a fixed time unit.

The design pattern P consists of the abstract classes AbstractMachine, Selector, Transition, Flow, Interface Module, and their relations with each other and with the runtime environment R. Pattern P facilitates the development of the transformation Φ_H by defining the abstract interfaces and relationships we regard as essential for creating the full compilation target. Instances of AbstractMachine are used to implement the local behavior of sequential components specified in the high-level formalism. Each new high-level specification S gives rise to a new set $\alpha_H(S)$ of abstract machines, to be generated by a transformation α_H. The Selector enforces global behavioral constraints on the concurrent systems, such as the synchronous execution of transitions. Since these constraints depend on the formalism H, but not on the concrete specifications S, Selector has to be instantiated just once for each new high-level formalism H. As we are dealing with hybrid systems, sequential components may run through discrete and time-continuous processing phases. Discrete steps are represented in HL^3 by instances of Transition, time-continuous ones by instances of Flow.

For handling application-specific hardware interfaces, another abstract specification is given: Instances of Interface Module create a hardware abstraction layer, hiding driver-specific details and the location of hardware interfaces within the cluster from scheduler, flows, and transitions.

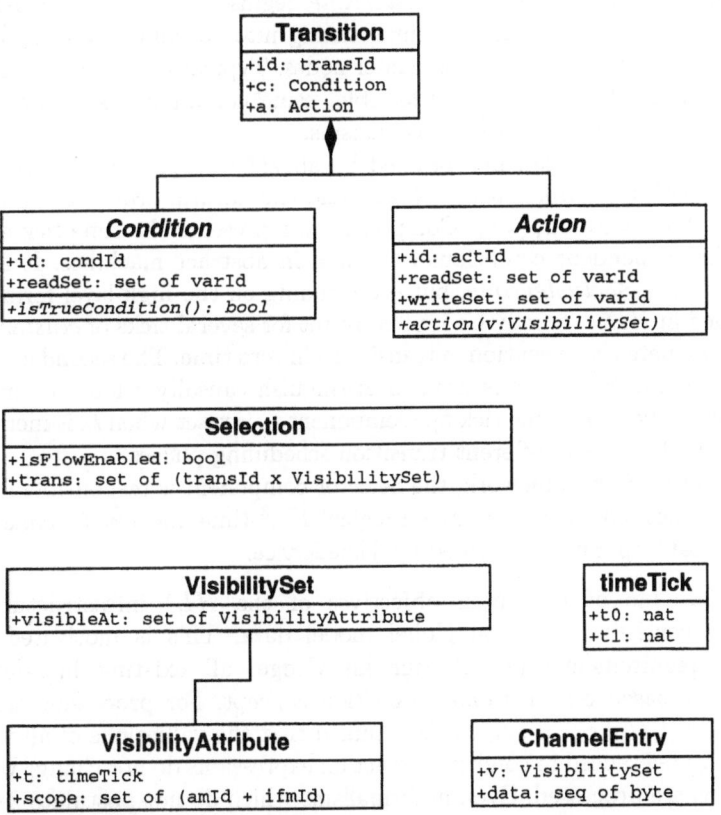

Fig. 7. Basic types referenced in the HL^3 framework.

As a result, the complete transformation Φ_H from H into executable HL^3 instances can always be structured as

$$\Phi_H(S) = (\alpha_H(S), \tau_H(S), \phi_H(S), \iota_H(S), \mathsf{Selector}_H)$$

where α_H, τ_H, ϕ_H, and ι_H generate collections of abstract machines, transitions, flows, and interface modules, respectively.

In the paragraphs below, additional details of HL^3 are presented. For a complete description, the reader is referred to [BBH+04].

TimeService. Executable HL^3 systems are clusters connected by high-speed local area networks. As a consequence, relativistic effects between cluster nodes may be neglected, so we can assume the existence of global physical time, denoted by $@t \in \mathbb{R}_+$ with physical unit [sec]. The HL^3 TimeService provides a *cluster time* value *clustertime* $\in \mathbb{N}$ (corresponding to the notion of *global time* in [Kop97]) which is related to physical time according to

$$@t = \gamma \cdot clustertime + \omega + \pi, \text{ where } \pi \in [-\gamma - \Pi, \gamma + \Pi]$$

Constant $\gamma \in \mathbb{Q}$ is the cluster time *granularity* with physical unit [sec], ω is a constant to be added because *clustertime* begins at 0 on cluster startup, and Π is the precision of the cluster time, taking into account physical clock drift and jitter between clocks at local cluster nodes. Typically, $10^{-9} \leq \gamma \leq 10^{-6}$ and precision values $\Pi \leq 10\mu sec$ are feasible, using combinations of software and hardware clock synchronization mechanisms.

Logical HL^3-time can be obtained by all HL^3 programs as a pair $t_0.t_1 \in timeTick$ with type $timeTick = \mathbb{N} \times \mathbb{N}$, and the natural ordering $a_0.a_1 \leq b_0.b_1$ iff $a_0 < b_0 \vee a_0 = b_0 \wedge a_1 \leq b_1$. Component t_0 represents the time tick as visible to the time-dependent conditions evaluated in abstract machines. It is always ensured that $t_0 \leq clustertime$, but – depending on the high-level formalism to be encoded in HL^3 – t_0 may be kept constant for several ticks of *clustertime*, in order to simulate the execution of transitions in zero time. The second component t_1 of the logical HL^3-time is used to distinguish causally related events which occur during the same time tick t_0. Component t_1 is reset when t_0 is incremented and increased between different transition scheduling phases.

Within the HL^3 framework, the Selector component is responsible for maintaining the desired relation between logical HL^3-time and *clustertime* via the setHL3time() operation provided by TimeService.

Channels. One of the main objectives of the HL^3 infrastructure is to provide a consistent view on global model data. This is motivated mainly by three requirements: (1) To our knowledge, all existing high-level formalisms are based on an *atomic* transition concept: For processing transition $[C(x_1, \ldots, x_n)]e/a(x_1, \ldots, x_n)$, it is assumed that the valuations of all variables $(x_1, \ldots, x_n)$ referenced in condition or action expressions do not change while the expressions are processed. Even in formalisms which do not postulate zero-time for transition execution it is always assumed that the calculation is performed atomically – meaning in zero-time – but time passes before the earliest possible point in time when the next transition can be fired. (2) The discretization of time-continuous flows requires that all flows synchronously performing a Δt integration step view the same pre-state of all observables, even if only one CPU is available for processing quasi parallel integration steps. In particular, state changes performed by one flow must not become visible to other flows referencing the related variables before the actual integration step has been completed. (3) As the HL^3 framework supports cluster hardware architectures, a consistent view of data at all cluster nodes is mandatory.

To implement these requirements, HL^3 uses abstract data types called Channels. Channels are data containers providing two operations (see Fig. 6): The `put(d:seq of byte,v:VisibilitySet)` method stores data items d in the channel c, together with a VisibilitySet v. The elements of v are VisibilityAttributes $a = (t, scope)$, where $t = t_0.t_1$ is a logical HL^3 time tick and $scope$ a set of abstract machine or interface module identifications. The interpretation of a is as follows: When retrieving the data from a channel using the `d = c.get(id)` command, the returned value d satisfies the following constraints:

$$\exists x \in c.e, a \in x.v.visibleAt \bullet (x.data = d \wedge id \in a.scope \wedge a.t \leq \texttt{getHL3Time()}) \wedge$$

$$(\forall y \in c.e, b \in y.v.visibleAt \bullet (id \in b.scope \wedge b.t \leq \texttt{getHL3Time()} \Rightarrow b.t \leq a.t))$$

Intuitively speaking, the identification id of the caller is a member of a scope attribute set associated with d. Among all data items contained in the channel such that id is within their scope, d is the most recent entry associated with a visibility time attribute which is less or equal to the current logical HL^3 time value.

By associating a set of visibility attributes with each data item contained in a channel, it is possible to widen the visibility scope at later points in time. This can be used, for example, in formalisms where changes become immediately visible within the local context of the executing agent, but are published later to other agents (e.g. at the beginning of a new macro step).

Every `put()` operation on a channel leads to immediate distribution of the data within the whole cluster. This is performed by the ClusterCommunication service. If the visibility attributes refer to a future point in time, all cluster nodes will have a consistent view on this data, as long as the distribution is completed before the data becomes visible.

Abstract Machines. Sequential components of a high-level formalism are mapped to Abstract Machines in HL^3. The task of each abstract machine is

- to indicate which transitions might be taken by the sequential component,
- to enable and disable flows according to the current state, and
- to indicate whether a flow phase may be started according to the abstract machines' local state.

While the concrete behavior of an abstract machine depends on the high-level formalism and the concrete high-level specification, the HL^3 framework defines a universal abstract interface for them: Operation `getTrans(id:amId)` returns the list of all transitions which might be performed in the current state. To this end, the abstract machine evaluates both the local static location data and the global state provided by channels. Since abstract machines represent sequential components, all high-level formalisms with a notion of nondeterminism require to select one out of several transitions which might be chosen in a specific state. Observe, however, that abstract machines do not perform this selection and never trigger associated actions. The former task is delegated to the Selector, the latter to the Scheduler.

After some enabled transition has been selected and its action performed, the associated abstract machine is notified by the scheduler (operation notifyTrans()) to trigger changes between locations within that abstract machine. The execution of actions associated with transitions will generally affect the global state encoded in channels. Therefore, the scheduler will call the update() operation of each abstract machine after transitions or flows have been performed. This operation initiates a new evaluation of all invariants and transition conditions applicable in the present state, possibly leading to a new set of enabled transitions within each abstract machine.

We expect that in every conceivable high-level formalism the execution of flows or transitions is mutually exclusive. Otherwise racing conditions might prevent the discrete change of observables due to simultaneous changes by flows. As a consequence, an abstract machine may indicate whether in the current state only transitions, only flows, or one of both may be performed. Depending on the local abstract machine state, the execution of flows may be disabled. This may happen in the case of high-level formalisms based on the maximal progress concept (sequential components with enabled transitions must fire) or allowing the definition of urgent transitions. Flows are also disabled if the abstract machine resides in a location whose invariant has just been violated, so that a transition becomes mandatory. The information whether flows may be performed is obtained via the isFlowEnabled(id:amId) operation.

A technical detail related to distributed execution of HL^3 components is indicated by the fact that the getTrans(id:amId) and isFlowEnabled(id:amId) operations have been declared on class level in Figure 6: While each abstract machine instance is created on a single cluster node only, where also their init(), update(), and notifyTrans() operations are scheduled, getTrans() and isFlowEnabled() may be called anywhere. This is motivated by the fact that the Selector should be able to call these operations from arbitrary nodes. The suggested implementation for abstract machines is to store the actual return values of these operations in associated channels, at the end of each update() operation. Since channel data is consistently available on all nodes, getTrans() and isFlowEnabled() can return these values wherever they are called.

Selector. The Selector is a centralized instance enforcing synchronization conditions for transition execution with respect to the high-level formalism. The abstract interface required by the HL^3 framework offers a getSelection() operation to the scheduler. It returns an indication whether a flow phase may be started and a (possibly empty) set of transition identifications with associated visibility sets. The transitions returned are the result of a selection procedure among all possible transitions offered by the abstract machines in their current state. In formalisms where transition sequences are supposed to be executed in zero time, the Selector keeps the same value for logical HL^3 time t_0 until all transitions within a zero-time step have been performed. Before the next flow phase, logical time is adapted to physical time. The actions associated with these transitions can be concurrently scheduled. Since actions derive pre-state from channels and change global state via channels as well, they may be triggered on arbitrary nodes and CPUs.

Note that even for the same high-level formalism it can be useful to apply different **Selector** instances: For application development, a selector will usually resolve nondeterministic transition selection – which may be allowed according to the high-level formalism – to deterministic execution sequences. In contrast to this, a simulation or testing system will require a selector which is capable of producing all transition schedules possible according to the high-level formalism.

Transitions. Instances of Transition implement atomic state transformers, enabled by abstract machines. In order to support the partitioning of high-level model state into discrete *locations* and additional *variables*, transitions are equipped with a *trigger condition*, represented by Boolean function condition(). In contrast to high-level formalisms allowing condition expressions over global or local variables, HL^3 requires that condition functions retrieve state information from channels. The associated get(id) calls use the identification of the abstract machine owning the transition. Furthermore, each transition is associated with a (possibly empty) Action, implemented as a function reading the same channel data pre-state as the trigger condition, but also setting a post state via channels, to become visible at the point in time and for the indicated scope defined by the input parameter. Observe that HL^3 transitions are not equipped with any signal or event mechanism. We consider these as objects of higher-level formalisms, to be implemented in HL^3 by means of channels, the scheduler, and the selector component. This design decision could be revised as soon as the hardware platforms could provide semantically well-defined and fast signal mechanisms. However, our analysis of current PC or embedded controller hardware indicates that there is no such universally suitable mechanism for the embedded application domain. The concept of locations – if required by the high-level formalism – is encoded inside abstract machines. As a result of an action execution, abstract machines may be suspended, activated, or stopped, and the guards enabling/disabling flow execution may be set.

Flows. Instances of Flow represent integration functions as a result of the discretization of time-continuous evolutions. The scheduler will activate all flows according to their specified frequency, provided that their guard attribute evaluates to *true*. The integration function integrate(v:VisibilitySet) is written in standard C/C++ syntax, but retrieves pre-state from channels instead of global or static local variables. Since flows are executed on behalf of their enabling/disabling abstract machines, they inherit the scope from the abstract machine. Based on current logical HL^3 time, the integrate()-operation reads the latest visible state and writes global data back to channels, to be published according to the visibility set v. Observe that HL^3 flows require integration functions which can be called with regular frequency. If the high-level formalism specifies flows by differential equations, these have to be solved using separate tools – such as Matlab – generating numerical libraries from given differential equations, for the purpose of discrete Δt integration.

Interface Modules. A hardware abstraction layer conforming to the time-triggered system concept is provided by Interface Modules which are software components in one-to-one correspondence with hardware interfaces. Interface modules are scheduled with fixed frequency and perform an abstraction from raw data received on hardware interfaces to channel data and vice versa. When scheduled with the `poll(v:VisibilitySet)` operation, raw data is read from the interface and placed into the abstraction channel, using the visibility set passed by the scheduler with the call. If $t_0.t_1$ is the HL^3 time tick when the data has been received, the visibility set v ensures that the data will have been distributed to all cluster nodes before the earliest publishing time $t'_0.t'_1 > t_0.t_1$ defined by any visibility attribute contained in v. Conversely, each interface module retrieves the latest visible version of the associated channel data when scheduled and transmits this data item via driver and interface hardware. Observe that interface modules allow to use also interrupt-driven hardware devices in a time-triggered system: Interrupt handlers store the received data in intermediate buffers. Interface modules read the buffers when they are scheduled and publish the data via channels for the next periodic point in time, as required for the given interface in the physical constraints specification.

Scheduler. Based on the synchronized cluster time introduced above, the Scheduler dispatches activities according to the following concept: Periodic scheduling of flows and interface polling is pre-planned at compile time, following the principles introduced for GIOTTO [HHK03]. For optimization purposes, activities a whose changes become effective at logical HL^3 time $(u_0.u_1)$ may be scheduled simultaneously with activities b to be published at $(v_0.v_1) \leq (u_0.u_1)$, if the pre-states for a are based on the visibility at an earlier time tick $(w_0.w_1) < (v_0.v_1)$. Since all activities as well as the cluster communication have bounded maximum length, each scheduler instance can determine when to start a new activity whose pre-state depends on the result of preceding ones, without the need to implement a commit protocol between cluster nodes.

5   HybridUML Semantics

The semantics of HybridUML specifications is defined by a transformation Φ_{HUML} to the Hybrid Low Level Language HL^3. As required by the HL^3 framework, a HybridUML specification is mapped to a selector and a collection of flows, transitions, and abstract machines (the aspects depending on architectural and physical constraints specifications are not considered here).

As described in Section 3, the main building block of a HybridUML specification is a set of basic agent instances. Their infrastructure for interaction is provided by connections between sets of variables or signals from different agent instances such that connected variables actually denote the same single shared variable or signal, respectively. For each connected set of variables or signals that cannot be extended we choose a unique Channel in terms of the low-level language HL^3 as representative of this set. This includes singleton sets, i.e. unconnected global variables and signals as well as local variables. As each variable and each signal is mapped to exactly one maximal set of connected variables or signals there is a function $chan : Var \cup Sig \to Chan_{hl3}$ that identifies the corresponding channel of a variable or signal. Signals are represented as channels carrying boolean data.

Transformation ϕ_{HUML} of Algebraic and Flow Constraints. Algebraic and flow constraints of the HybridUML model are distributed over the modes of the basic agents. They define the set of HL^3-Flow instances by a mapping $flow_{hl3} : Flow \cup Alge \to Flow_{hl3}$: (1) The operation integrate() is provided by a mapping $proc : Exp \to op_{hl3}$ that defines an HL^3 operation of the form void op() for each HybridUML expression. The mapping of algebraic expressions is straightforward – variables v are mapped to local HL^3 variables that are read from or written to $chan(v)$, operators are mapped to corresponding HL^3 operators. Flow expressions are transformed by use of an appropriate (numerical) mathematical toolkit like Matlab. (2) For the boolean guard, a separate Channel is created. It is controlled by the abstract machine (described below) that corresponds to the flow constraint of the HybridUML model. (3) The frequency is obtained from the physical constraints specification. (4) A consecutive id is generated.

Transformation τ_{HUML} of Transitions. Transitions in the HybridUML model connect the submodes of basic agents. The Transition instances t as well as the corresponding instances a of Action and c of Condition are given by $trans_{hl3} : Trans \to \{(t, a, c) \in Trans_{hl3} \times Act_{hl3} \times Cond_{hl3} \mid t.a = a \wedge t.c = c\}$.

Transitions. A Transition instance is created that contains one condition and one action as described below. A consecutive transition id is generated.

Conditions. (1) The operation isTrueCondition() evaluates a boolean expression that is given by a mapping $bexp : Exp_{bool} \to op_{hl3}$. Similarly to $proc$, the mapping provides C expressions that directly implement the expression from the HybridUML model; quantifiers on finite sets are realized by for-statements. Additionally, the (optional) signal is incorporated and treated as a conventional boolean variable. (2) The read set is created from the channels of the variables and the signal within the generated expression. (3) A consecutive condition id is generated.

Actions. (1) Similar to the integration operation of flows, action(...) is defined by $proc$; sending of signals is realized by sending true on the corresponding channel. The visibility parameter of action(...) is applied to the channels of the write set exactly as it is received (see below). (2) The writeSet consists of the channel identifiers that correspond to the written variables, i.e. the variables from action(...) that are on the left-hand side of assignments. (3) The variables from the right-hand sides define the channel identifiers in readSet. (4) A consecutive action id is generated.

Transformation α_{HUML} of Sequential Control Components. Sequential control components are exactly the basic agent instances mentioned above. They are represented by instances of AbstractMachine: $am : Agent_{basic} \rightarrow AM_{hl3}$. Note that the arrangement of the basic agent instances to composite agent instances (through some levels of hierarchy) only provides the *distribution* and *renaming* of shared variables and signals, which is completely represented by the channel mapping *chan*.

An abstract machine defines the discrete behavior of a top-level mode, which in turn defines the discrete behavior of exactly one basic agent.

Data structure. The abstract machine defines a (recursive) data structure that maps to the hierarchical structure of the top-level mode, such that the Mode instances form a mode tree. Within the tree, the sequence of active submodes, beginning with the root mode, constitutes the mode configuration, i.e. the set of all currently active modes. Based on the mode tree, the data structure is defined in a straightforward way:
Mode: A Mode consists of a set of control points of type ControlPoint, a set of submodes of type Mode, a set of transitions of type ModeTransition, a set of flow constraints of type FlowConstraint, and a set of invariant constraints of type InvariantConstraint. Additionally, a history variable points to the currently active submode. **InvariantConstraint:** An InvariantConstraint contains a boolean function that evaluates according to a mode's invariant specification. **Flow-Constraint:** A FlowConstraint represents an algebraic or flow constraint from the HybridUML model. It references the low-level Flow according to $flow_{hl3}$. Particularly, the boolean guard is controlled in order to enable or disable the associated integration operation, depending on the current mode configuration. **ControlPoint:** A ControlPoint contains outgoing transitions of type ModeTransition. Furthermore, a reference to its parent mode is included. The distinction between entry and exit control point is included as a flag. **ModeTransition:** A ModeTransition connects a source and a target ControlPoint. It can fire, if its Signal is present, and if its Guard evaluates to true. The firing of a transition (possibly) causes a discrete state change, therefore it is associated with the corresponding low-level transition of type Transition assigned by $trans_{hl3}$ that encapsulates this. Since a transition may affect the history of its containing mode, a reference to the Mode is also contained. **Signal:** A Signal references a boolean flag that denotes if the corresponding signal is currently active. **Guard:** A Guard contains a boolean function that implements the corresponding guard of a transition.

Additional entities exist in the data structure but are not described here. They are used for efficiency; for example, the set of currently enabled transitions is stored explicitly.

Data structure instantiation. A basic HybridUML agent defines an instance of the data structure: For each mode, an instance of Mode exists. Each Mode apart from the top-level mode is inserted into its parent's set of submodes. For its algebraic and flow conditions, FlowConstraint instances are created and linked to the appropriate Flow instances. Every invariant expression is represented by a boolean function `bool exp()` provided by *bexp*. A ControlPoint instance is created for every control point of the specification and linked with the corresponding Mode.

Each transition from the HybridUML model is represented by a ModeTransition instance which is linked to the ControlPoint instances that represent its source and target, respectively, as well as with its parent mode. The transition's parent mode is the mode for that it connects either two submodes or the mode itself with a submode. Every ModeTransition is equipped with a Guard, an optional Signal, and the Transition instance described earlier. The guard, the signal, and the action are taken from the HybridUML model in the same way as described for low-level Action and Condition instances, whereas the guard represents the Condition without signal. Figure 8 shows the data structure instance for the basic agent BrakePointController from Section 2.

(5)   **readSetTransBrakingRequired** $\equiv$
$\{v \mid \exists i \in \{1..VTP\_COUNT\}\bullet$
$v \equiv chan(vtpActive[i]) \lor v \equiv chan(brakePoint[i]) \lor$
$v \equiv chan(ra.vtp[i].v) \lor v \equiv chan(ra.vtp[i].x)$
$\} \cup \{chan(x), chan(v)\}$

The HL^3 operations within guards and invariants (as well as actions and flows) operate on the HL^3 channels (representing the HybridUML variables and signals). Therefore, local HL^3 variables of appropriate types are used and distributed to the respective channels.

Execution semantics. The semantics of the abstract machine is given by the execution of the set of provided operations:
init(): Executes the initialization step of the agent: The top-level mode's default entry point is entered. **notifyTrans(tr:transID)**: Accepts the notification which transition was chosen and executed externally. Internally, the corresponding ModeTransition fires without executing its action, thus here it adjusts its internal state correspondingly by entering a new control point. **update()**: Updates the internal data structure with respect to the current values of the corresponding channels: (1) A flag flowEnabled is set if this abstract machine is in a state that allows time to pass. This is given iff all invariants of the mode configuration are satisfied and there is no mandatory step. Therefore, the invariants of the mode configuration are recalculated. A mandatory step is a step that initially

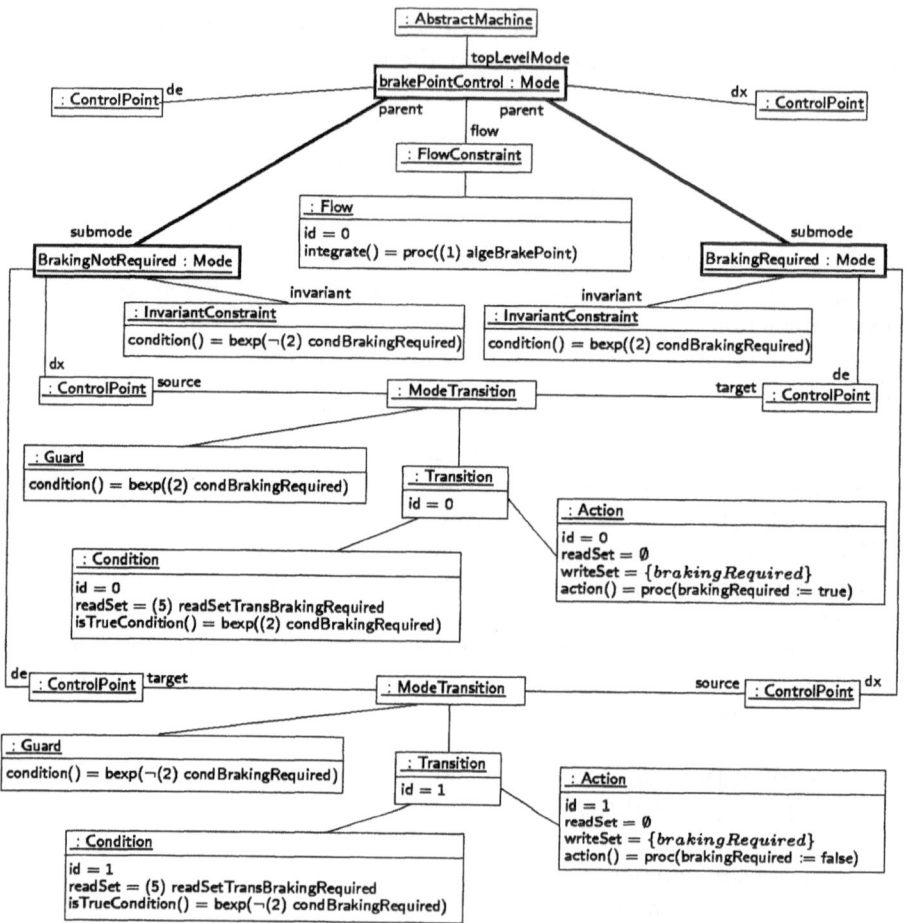

Fig. 8. Instantiated data structure of Agent BrakePointController. The mode tree is highlighted.

consumes a signal (i.e. that is triggered by a signal) or a step that does not start at a default exit point. (2) The set enabledTrans of enabled transitions is generated. (3) The set enabledTrans and the flag flowEnabled are written to respective special channels, such that exactly these values are provided by subsequent calls of getTrans(amId) and isFlowEnabled(amId).

The precise behavioral description of the above operations is given by their implementation. For example, notifyTrans(id:ID) defines a discrete step:[1]

Abstract Machine. The transition itself fires:

```
void AbstractMachine::notifyTrans (transID tr) { m_trans[tr].fire(); }
```

ModeTransition. The transition fires by (1) leaving its source control point, (2) (optionally) resetting a consumed signal, (3) modifying its parent mode's

---

[1] The remaining definitions are omitted because of space restrictions.

history and (4) entering its target control point.

```
void ModeTransition::fire() {
  m_source.leave(); if (m_pSignal != 0) m_pSignal->setActive(false);
  writeHistory(); m_target.enter(); }
```

ControlPoint. When a control point is left, its parent mode has no active control point anymore:

```
void ControlPoint::leave() {getParentMode().setCurrentControlPoint(0);}
```

When a control point is entered, it becomes the active control point of its parent mode:

```
void ControlPoint::enter() getParentMode().setCurrentControlPoint(this);
```

Mode. The setting of a mode's current control point has several implications: (1) The mode's current control point is the new control point. (2) If the control point is the default entry, then the history is resumed recursively for the mode, if possible. (3) If for a leaf mode the control point is the default entry, then it is directly transferred to the default exit. (4) If the control point is the default exit, then all parent modes are also set to their default exits recursively. (5) If the control point is a non-default control point or a default entry that cannot resume a history, then the parent modes are recursively modified such that they have no current control point.

```
void Mode::setCurrentControlPoint(ControlPoint* pControlPoint) {
  m_pCurrentControlPoint = pControlPoint;
  if ((pControlPoint == m_pDe) && (m_pHistory != 0))
    m_pHistory->setCurrentControlPoint(m_pHistory->m_pDe);
  else if ((pControlPoint == m_pDe) && (m_leafMode))
    setCurrentControlPoint(m_pDx);
  else if ((pControlPoint == m_pDx) && (m_pParent != 0))
    m_pParent->setCurrentControlPoint(m_pParent->m_pDx);
  else if (m_pParent != 0) m_pParent->setCurrentControlPoint(0); }
```

In this way, we calculate the set of current control points which is required to determine the set of enabled transitions of the abstract machine. One of the following situations results: *Initialization* – the set consists of exactly one default entry of a non-leaf mode. There is no complete mode configuration, and only a transition that initializes the current mode can be enabled. *Stable* – the set consists of exactly the default exits of all modes of the current mode configuration from the root mode to the leaf mode. This is a (potentially) stable situation that may allow time to pass. Transitions of all hierarchy levels can be enabled. *Unstable* – the set consists of exactly one non-default control point. Steps through non-default control points implicitly make up a compound step that must not be interrupted, therefore only continuation transitions may be enabled next.

HybridUML Simulation Semantics Definition Selector$_{HUML}$. For the coordination of flows, transitions, and abstract machines with respect to the *simulation* semantics of HybridUML, a customized Selector is provided. The selector defines an initialization operation init():bool:

The initial valuation of the channels has to be given by the environment, i.e. from outside the HL^3 specification. Initialization constraints result from the initStates of the agent instances within the HybridUML model. They control if there is an execution of the model for the given valuation. If all these constraints evaluate to true, initialization is completed successfully, otherwise unsuccessfully.

The operation getSelection(leftFlowPhase:bool): Selection is defined as follows:
(1) The logical HL^3 time $hl3time$ is adjusted. If the preceding scheduler phase was a flow phase, i.e. if $leftFlowPhase$, then setHL3Time(clustertime,0) of TimeService is activated and therefore the model time is updated to the cluster time. Since model time has increased, on every channel that represents a HybridUML signal, false is written, and thus signals are reset. Otherwise, after a transition phase ($\neg leftFlowPhase$), the t_1 component is incremented: setHL3Time(getHL3Time().t0,getHL3Time().t1+1);
(2) It is determined if a flow of time would be admissible for the complete model, which is denoted by the conjunction $flowEnabled = \bigwedge_{i=0}^{n} isFlowEnabled(am_i)$ for all abstract machines.
(3) The sets $tr_i = getTrans(am_i)$ of (identifiers of) enabled transitions are requested for all abstract machines.
(4) A set $tr = \{id \in \bigcup_{i=0}^{n} tr_i \mid \forall t_1 \in Transition, t_2 \in Transition \bullet ((t_1.id \in tr_k, t_2.id \in tr_l) \wedge (t_1 \neq t_2 \Rightarrow tr_k \neq tr_l) \wedge (t_1.a.readSet \cup t_1.c.readSet) \cap t_2.a.writeSet = \emptyset)\}$ is chosen non-deterministically. Thus, a set of transition identifiers is chosen that (1) contains up to one transition identifier per abstract machine and that (2) contains only identifiers of transitions that are independent of each other, i.e. every possible execution sequence of these transitions is allowed. Note that $n = |tr| > 1$ is just an optimization of n successive transition phases selecting one transition each. If $\neg flowEnabled$, $tr \neq \emptyset$ is preferred, otherwise the HybridUML model is deadlocked.
(5) If $tr \neq \emptyset \wedge flowEnabled$, then an "almost" non-deterministic choice is made between transitions and flows: Since the scheduler always executes possible transitions, as long as there is enough time left before the next flow phase, $tr = \emptyset$ may be enforced.
(6) A visibility attribute att_v is created that satisfies $att_v.t0 = hl3time.t0 \wedge att_v.t.t1 = hl3time.t1 + 1$, and which has an unrestricted scope $att_v.scope$, i.e. every abstract machine or interface module that reads the channels of the written variables is included. The visibility set $\{att_v\}$ is attached to every transition: $trv = \{(t, v) \in Transition \times VisibilitySet \mid t.id \in tr \wedge v = \{att_v\}\}$.
(7) Finally, a Selection s with $s.isFlowEnabled = flowEnabled$ and $s.trans = trv$ is returned by update.

6   Conclusions

We have introduced HybridUML, a novel specification formalism for the description of hybrid systems. HybridUML was defined as a profile extending UML 2.0. The main intention of this approach is to facilitate the understanding of the formalism for users already familiar with the UML and to utilize existing UML tools for the development of hybrid specifications. The "look-and-feel" of HybridUML was illustrated by means of a case study describing a distributed radio-based train control system. The semantics of HybridUML has been obtained via transformation into the Hybrid Low-Level Language framework HL^3, thereby obtaining semantically well-defined programs which can be executed in hard real-time.

When compared to GIOTTO [HHK03], our HL^3 framework differs in the following aspects: (1) The HL^3 channel concept – corresponding to GIOTTO ports – explicitly supports visibility time stamps and scope. We regard these mechanisms as very helpful for ensuring consistent data views on different cluster nodes in time-triggered systems. (2) The HL^3 framework has been explicitly designed to facilitate the automated generation of compilation targets from higher-level formalisms. This is reflected by the pre-defined roles and interfaces of abstract machines and selector. (3) GIOTTO tasks have a low granularity, corresponding to single flows, transitions or transition collections emanating from the same location. Transitions between locations as, for example, between hierarchic states of a statechart, have to be modeled by GIOTTO mode switches disabling/activating "task vectors". In contrast to this, the HL^3 abstract machines encode behavioral models of complete sequential agents; only the flows and actions are separated from the abstract machines, in order to optimize scheduling.

Our current investigations related to semantic issues focus on the respective advantages and tradeoffs presented by interleaving semantics versus "true parallelism" interpretations for transitions executed in the same "zero-time phase". The interleaving semantics as defined in this paper and suggested in [AGLS01] is compatible with the rely-guarantee verification method [dR+01, pp. 447] developed for shared-variable concurrency. Therefore its utilization gives us the advantage of well-understood formal concepts and proof theories. A major drawback is the fact that interleaved transition execution – while being perfectly well-suited on single-processor platforms – cannot easily be distributed for parallel execution on several processors: The action of one transition may invalidate the firing condition for another transition, so in the worst case – if the write sets of the actions for all available transitions overlap with the read sets of all their conditions or actions – it is mandatory to execute one transition at a time. In contrast to this, Statecharts semantics [DJHP98] defines truly parallel execution rules for transitions simultaneously enabled in parallel components: All transitions available at the beginning of a macro step have the same view on the state components within their scope and may fire simultaneously. Their state changes become visible in subsequent micro or macro steps. Obviously, these execution rules are well-suited for multi-processor scheduling environments. However, this advantage has to be paid by increased verification complexity, as, for example, reflected by the problem of racing conditions occurring due to simultaneous changes to the same variables in the same step.

Apart from facilitating the development of hard real-time target systems, our transformation strategy supports automated testing of hybrid systems. Here, HybridUML agents are used both for the specification of the system under test and for the description of environment behavior to be simulated in specific test executions. While the transformation from HybridUML into the abstract machines of HL^3 is the same for target system development and testing, different selector instances are used in these two situations: For developing target systems, the semantic freedom which could be exploited by the selector in the non-deterministic choice among possible transition interleavings, as well as the decision when to trigger enabled, but non-urgent transitions, should be resolved in a deterministic way which can be relied on to meet all periodic schedules. In contrast to this, a selector for testing hybrid systems may apply strategies to simulate the greatest possible variation of environment behavior, in order to increase the structural coverage of the system under test and to check its robustness. A more detailed description of testing aspects is currently under preparation [BBPT04].

The authors would like to emphasize that HL^3 is not just an experimental runtime environment for research purposes. Its current version is used for embedded systems testing of controllers for the Airbus A380 aircraft family [VS04]. Test engines operate with cluster configurations consisting of 3, 5, or more multi-CPU PC nodes.

Acknowledgements. The authors are indebted to Aliki Tsiolakis for her stimulating comments and suggestions on HL^3, its semantics, and implementation. Christof Efkemann and Kai Thomsen did a formidable job in their development of a Linux kernel patch for CPU reservation and interrupt relaying.

References

[AGLS01]   R. Alur, R. Grosu, I. Lee, and O. Sokolsky. Compositional refinement for hierarchical hybrid systems. In *Proceedings of the 4th International Workshop on Hybrid Systems: Computation and Control, LNCS* vol. 2034, pp. 33–48, 2001.

[BBB+99]   T. Bienmüller, J. Bohn, H. Brinkmann, U. Brockmeyer, W. Damm, H. Hungar, and P. Jansen. Verification of automotive control units. In *Correct System Design,LNCS* vol. 1710, pp. 319–341, 1999.

[BBH+04]   K. Berkenkötter, S. Bisanz, U. Hannemann, J. Peleska, and A. Tsiolakis. The Hybrid Low Level Language HL^3. Technical Report 34, Technologie Zentrum Informatik TZI, Universität Bremen, to appear July 2004.

[BBHP04]   K. Berkenkötter, S. Bisanz, U. Hannemann, and J. Peleska. The HybridUML Profile for UML 2.0. Technical Report 32, Technologie Zentrum Informatik TZI, Universität Bremen, June 2004.

[BBPT04]   K. Berkenkötter, S. Bisanz, U. Hannemann, J. Peleska, and A. Tsiolakis. Automated Test Data Generation for Hybrid Systems.

[DFG]   Priority Programme Software Specification – Integration of Software Specification Techniques for Applications in Engineering. http://tfs.cs.tu-berlin.de/projekte/indspec/SPP.

[RTAI03]   Dipartimento di Ingegneria Aerospaziale Politecnico di Milano. RTAI homepage. http://www.aero.polimi.it/ rtai/about/index.html, 2003.

[DJHP98]   W. Damm, B. Josko, H. Hungar, and A. Pnueli. A compositional real-time semantics of STATEMATE designs. *LNCS* vol. 1536, pp. 186–238, 1998.

[dR+01]   W.-P. de Roever, F. de Boer, U. Hannemann, J. Hooman, Y. Lakhneche,
           M. Poel, and J. Zwiers. *Concurrency Verification*. Number 54 in Cam-
           bridge Tracts in Theoretical Computer Science. Cambridge University
           Press, Cambridge, UK, April 2001.

[Hen96]   T. A. Henzinger. The theory of hybrid automata. In *Proceedings of the
           11th Annual Symposium on Logic in Computer Science (LICS)*, pp. 278–
           292. IEEE Computer Society Press, 1996.

[HHK03]   T. A. Henzinger, B. Horowitz, and C. M. Kirsch. Giotto: A time-triggered
           language for embedded programming. *Proceedings of the IEEE*, 91, pp.
           84–99, 2003.

[HL94]   C. Heitmeyer and N. Lynch. The generalized railroad crossing: A case
           study in formal verification of real-time systems. In *IEEE Real-Time
           Systems Symposium*, pp. 120–131. IEEE Computer Society, 1994.

[KMP00]   Y. Kesten, Z. Manna, and A. Pnueli. Verification of clocked and hybrid
           systems. *Acta Informatica*, 36(11):836–912, 2000.

[Kop97]   H. Kopetz. *Real-Time Systems – Design Principles for Distributed Em-
           bedded Applications*. The Kluwer International Series in Engineering and
           Computer Science. Kluwer Academic Publishers, 1997.

[Lab04]   FSM Labs. RT-Linux homepage. http://www.rtlinux.org, 2004.

[OMG03a]   OMG. UML 2.0 Infrastructure Specification, OMG Adopted Specifica-
           tion. http://www.omg.org/cgi-bin/apps/doc?ptc/03-09-15.pdf, Septem-
           ber 2003.

[OMG03b]   OMG. UML 2.0 Superstructure Specification, OMG Adopted Specifi-
           cation. http://www.omg.org/cgi-bin/apps/doc?ptc/03-08-02.pdf, August
           2003.

[RJB99]   J. Rumbaugh, I. Jacobson, and G. Booch. *The Unified Modeling Language
           – Reference Manual*. Addison-Wesley, 1999.

[RRS03]   M. Rönnkö, A. P. Ravn, and K. Sere. Hybrid action systems. *Theoretical
           Computer Science*, 290:937–973, January 2003.

[VS04]   Verified Systems. RT-Tester 6.x – User Manual. Technical Report
           Verified-INT-014-2003, Verified Systems International GmbH, Bremen,
           2004.

[ZRH93]   C. Zhou, A. P. Ravn, and M. R. Hansen. An extended duration calculus
           for hybrid real-time systems. In *Hybrid Systems*, pp. 36–59. The Computer
           Society of the IEEE, 1993. Extended abstract.

The Use of UML for Development of a Railway Interlocking System

Karol Rástočný, Aleš Janota, and Jiří Zahradník

University of Žilina, Faculty of Electrical Engineering,
Department of Control & Information Systems, Veľký diel, 010 26 Žilina, Slovak Republic
{karol.rastocny, ales.janota, jiri.zahradnik}@fel.utc.sk

Abstract. We present the Unified Modeling Language (UML) and show how it can be applied to development of a new railway interlocking and signalling system. Using a simplified example of an interlocking system, we demonstrate principles of an object-oriented approach to specifying functional safety requirements. Starting from an informal specification we create a semi-formal specification based on the UML model. Within conclusions we resume advantages of the presented approach resulting from practical experiences gained in the project aimed at development of a new computer-based interlocking system.

1 Introduction

The use of electronic components and programmable subsystems changes methods usable for development of railway interlocking systems and approaches applied to reach required safety. Software development came over evolution from machine code through symbolic assembler to high-level procedural and object oriented languages. Unfortunately, concurrently with growing level of abstractness complexity of implemented functions also increased. Higher complexity of systems requires usage of such graphical languages and notations from which text notations in implementation languages could be derived (automatically or manually) and thus system functions described. One of prospective and promising graphical languages is an object-oriented language called Unified Modeling Language (UML). The UML standard [1], [2] offers different modelling and visualisation elements to catch and model (i.e. specify) system requirements. It provides different diagrams for graphical and textual abstract description of system functions, which is independent on hardware/software implementation. With the help of a proper software tool, development of object-oriented software can become more unambiguous, better structured and complete, doing the following:

- *Analyze* (define system requirements, identify necessary objects and define their structure and behaviour using UML diagrams);
- *Design* (trace requirements to the design, taking into account architectural, mechanistic, and detailed design considerations);

H. Ehrig et al. (Eds.): INT 2004, LNCS 3147, pp. 174–198, 2004.

-   *Implement* (automatically generate code from the analysis model, then build and run it from within the software tool);
-   *Test* (animate the application on the local host or a remote target to perform design-level debugging within animated views).

Analysis is the software development activity for studying and formulating a model of a problem domain and focuses on what is to be done; design focuses on how to do it. The paper deals with these first two activities and shows how an object-oriented approach (see e.g. [3], [4]) can be applied to development of railway interlocking systems. Informal requirements for control logic of a railway interlocking system are generally specified by relevant technical national standards and regulations. The model presented in this paper respects basic regulations as given by the Slovak technical standard [5], but its philosophy and build-up comes out from the real project solved by the authors when developing a new railway interlocking system for the applications at the German railways.

The entire model of a real system includes tens of classes and hundreds of states. In an effort to explain the used approach and for the sake of better understanding we extract basic principles of modelling and present partially simplified example showing a framework of the most frequently performed activity in the system – setting and cancelling the main route. Due to introduced simplifications some of functions cannot be considered here, e.g. co-operation with level crossing installations is omitted. Partial views on discussed problems were published in e.g. [6], [7], [8], [9], [10].

2   Modelling of Functional System Requirements

Out-side elements of an interlocking system (signals, point machines, derailer machines, technical means for monitoring vacancy/occupancy of track sections, electromagnetic locks etc.) are connected to the control interlocking logic through appertaining circuits of power interface and the bus as shown in Fig. 1. Interlocking logic on the control level co-operates with a control panel and with other interlocking and signalling systems, e.g. a section blocking system (SBS), work siding etc.

The function requirement specification as given below covers both analysis and design phases of the development cycle and results in the following set of diagrams:

-   Use Case diagrams (describing the functionality of the system - what the system will do for the user);
-   Class / Object diagrams (describing a static structure of the system);
-   Sequential diagrams (behaviour diagrams providing dynamic view at the system, specifically interactions among classes/objects);
-   Statechart diagrams (behaviour diagrams providing dynamic view at the system).

Although the UML provides more possible views at the system, mentioned five types of diagrams were chosen as predicative enough to describe function requirements. The model was created in the software tool Rhapsody™ ver. 4.0 (a trademark of I-Logix) supporting UML standard 1.3. The tool determines graphical representation of visual elements used in diagrams, which is (in some cases) slightly different from a UML standard.

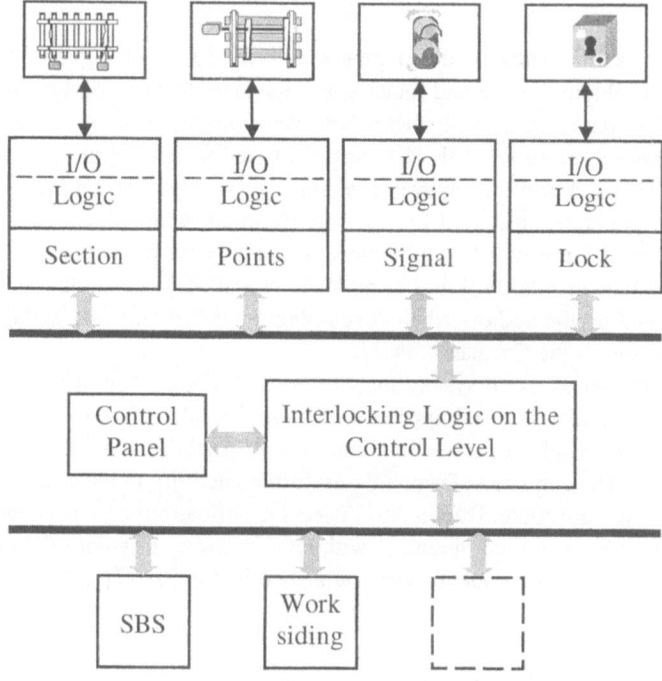

Fig. 1. Static structure of an interlocking system

The following principles have been applied when assigning names to individual model elements:

- cXxxx   .... Class;
- oXxxx   .... Object;
- avXxxx .... Variable attribute; i.e. an attribute that may have different values in time;
- apXxxx .... Project attribute; i.e. an attribute whose value is invariant and depends on an individual application;
- kXxxx   .... Value of an attribute;
- evXxxx .... Event or method triggered by an event with this name;
- mXxxx   .... Primitive operation.

Since presented parts of the model comes out from the real project elaborated for a German customer, the names of classes, objects, attributes, events and states used in the following text have a form of abbreviated original German expressions. Except for the Use Case diagram (described totally in English), the model as it is should be well readable by German speaking professionals from the railway domain. For other English speaking readers key names and/or abbreviations are properly explained continuously in the text.

2.1 Use Case Diagram

Fig. 2 shows the Use Case diagram of the considered interlocking system. The diagram defines a system boundary, use cases, actors and mutual relations between these elements. Actors represent external entities – a Station Dispatcher and co-operating technical systems (SBS, Work Siding, etc.). Relations between a Station Dispatcher and individual use cases (Control of Train Running, Control of Shunting Operation, Control of Points Movement, etc.) are represented as bidirectional communication associations, i.e. a Station Dispatcher can activate these activities and is informed about them. Other actors are cooperating systems that have bidirectional communication association with activity Control of Train Running. Another associations may be defined between individual activities (use cases), e.g. between the Control of Outgoing Routes and the Control of Train Running there is an association relationship <<generalization>>; activity the Control of Entry Routes inherits properties of the Control of Train Running; between activities the Control of Outgoing Routes and the Route Setting there is an association relationship of <<include>> indicating that a use case is also used by other use cases.

2.2 Class Diagram

The Class Diagram makes description of a static structure of the system possible. In Fig. 3 a simplified class diagram for the interlocking logic considered on the control level is shown. For the sake of lucidity and readability only those classes are depicted in the diagram that are necessary for description of activities discussed later in the text without showing their mutual relations and multiplicity.

The package Steuerebene (Control Level) includes packages Bedienung (Operation), Fahrstrasse (Route), Strecke (Line), Weiche (Points), Gleisabschnitt (Track Circuit), Signal (Signal) and Schluesselsperre (Key Locking).

The package Bedienung includes the class cHilfsbedienung (Emergency Operation) and cBedienung (Operation) that generate one object each. These objects enable both standard and emergency operation of an interlocking system (sending messages that contain commands for setting main or shunting routes, commands for changing states of outdoor elements; receiving messages that contain information on conditions of main or shunting routes, information on conditions of outdoor elements etc.).

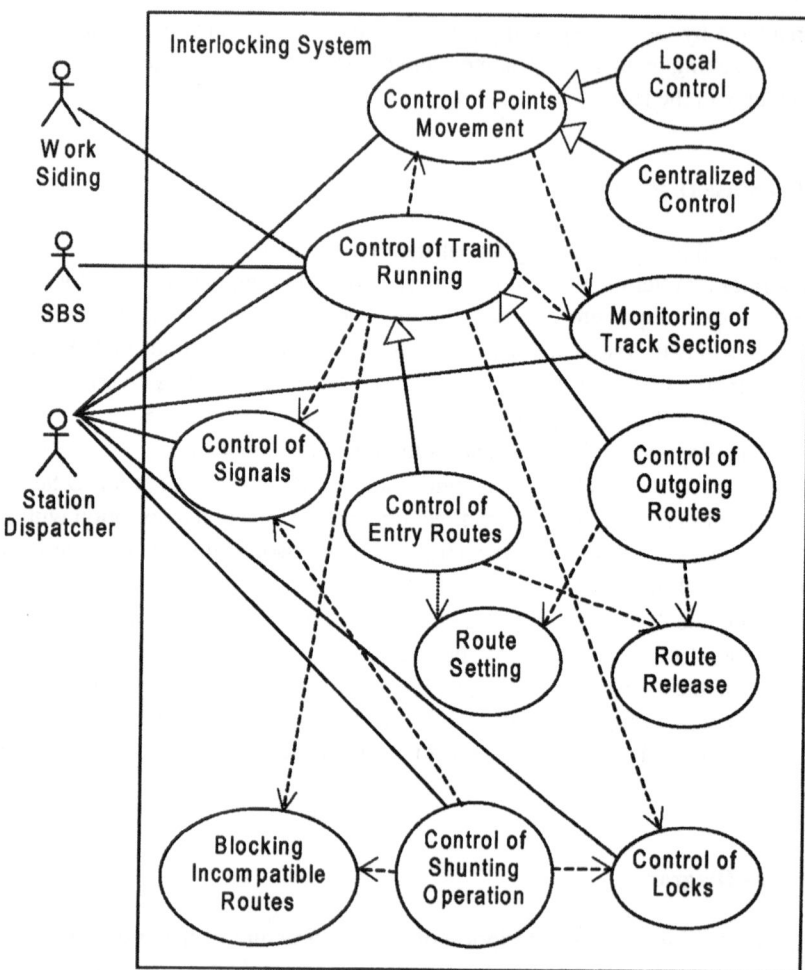

Fig. 2. The Use Case Diagram

In the class cFahrstrasse (Route) the whole process of setting and releasing the main route is implemented. This implementation also includes control of all elements assigned by project (application) to the particular main route. Each entry and outgoing main route is represented by one object of this class.

The class cVWFahrstrasse (Route Management) generates one object that partially realises logical relations between individual main routes with one another and relations between main routes and shunting operation (incompatibility between routes). The object receives and processes demands for setting and releasing the main routes and shunting operation as entered through the control panel. At the same time only one main route may be in the process of setting. If other demands for setting another main routes are received during this process they are memorized and processed later after the setting process of the previous main route is over.

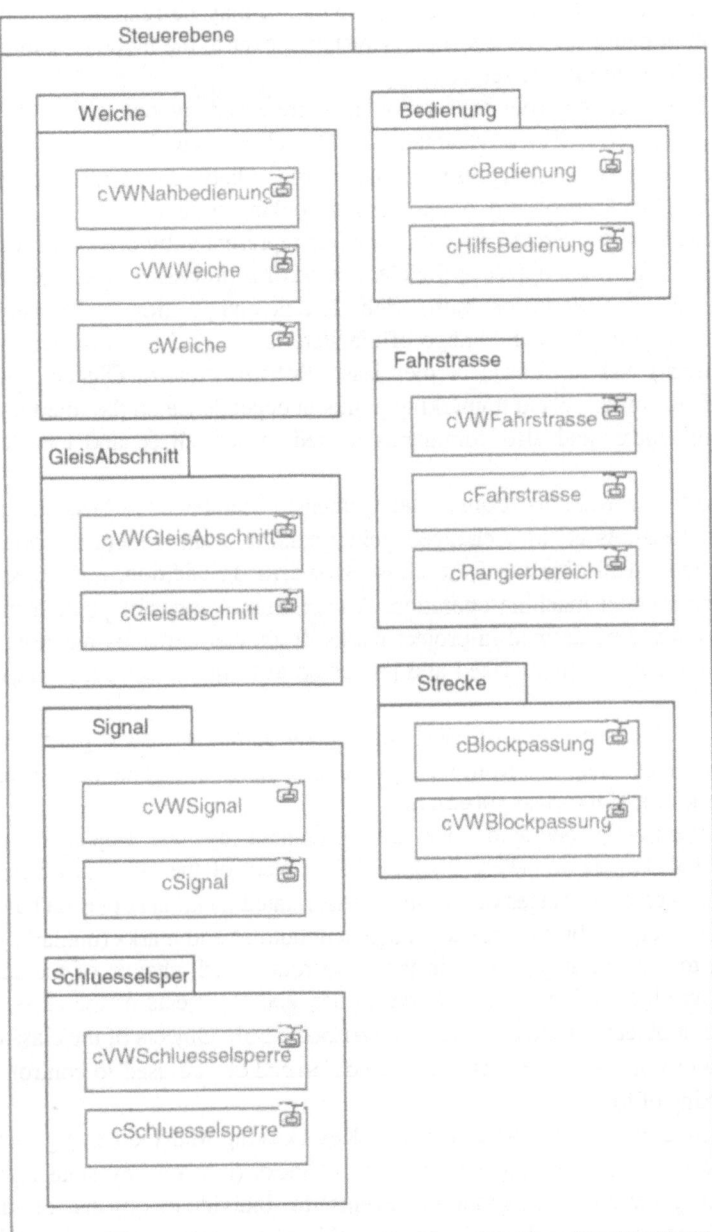

Fig. 3. The Class Diagram

The class cRangierbereich (Shunting) generates as many objects as many shunting areas the railway station is divided to. An object of the class cRangierbereich checks all conditions to be fulfilled to permit or cancel shunting operation in a given part of the station. Shunting operation may be realised only if no main route is set or being set. If the station is switched over to the mode of shunting operation, no main route may be set.

Each line track entering the station is represented by one object of the class cBlockpassung (Block Adaptation). The class cVWBlockpassung (Block Adaptation Management) represents data interface between an interlocking system and a section blocking system, or another interlocking system.

Each electrically operated switch (points) is represented by one object of the class cWeiche (Points). An object of the class cWeiche processes messages on the state of its related points (points position – right, left, no end position, force-opening of the points, points failure). Each change of the state is reported to an object of the class cBedienung and to objects of the class cFahrstrasse. Objects also process commands for marking and unmarking points in dependence on the role they perform in the main route, and also commands related to centralized and local control of points.

The class cVWWeiche (Points Management) generates one object that processes incoming telegrams about a changed points condition and generates corresponding events to individual objects of the class cWeiche. In addition, this object sequentially controls point machine operation. A maximum number of points concurrently being moved can be defined in project works. If another demands for moving points are received they are memorized and processed after the actual points movement is over.

The class cVWNahbedienung (Local Operation Management) generates one object that receives telegrams from locally operated points and generates corresponding events to objects of the class cWeiche.

Each electrically operated lock is represented by one object of the class cSchluesselsperre (Key Locking). An object of the class cSchluessel-sperre processes messages on the state of its related lock, messages on handling the lock buttons (request button, acknowledgement button) and marks (unmarks) the lock according to the role it performs in the main route. Each change of the state is reported to an object of the class cBedienung and to objects of the class cFahr-strasse or objects of the class cRangierbereich. Objects of the class cFahr-strasse or objects of the class cRangierbereich are used to control blocking or unblocking of locks.

The class cVWSchluesselsperre (Key Locking Management) generates one object that receives incoming telegrams from locks (info on key state and buttons state) and generates corresponding events to individual objects of the class cSchluesselsperre. In addition, this object processes commands for blocking and unblocking the keys coming from objects of the class cSchluesselsperre.

Each stand-alone signal is represented by one object of the class cSignal (Signal). An object of the class cSignal processes reports on signal indications given at the related signal; marks (unmarks) the signal according to the role it performs in the main route, controls distant signals in accordance with signal indications of the main signals and also processes commands from objects of the package Bedienung and objects of the class cFahrstrasse for turning on the required indication at the signal. The class also implements processing of messages and commands for different kinds of signals (stand-alone distant signals, main signals, indicators etc.).

The class cVWSignal (Signal Management) generates one object that processes telegrams coming from signals and generates corresponding events to individual objects of the class cSignal. In addition, it receives and processes commands for changing signal indication coming from objects of the class cSignal.

Each track section is represented by one object of the class cGleisabschnitt (Track Circuit). An object of the class cGleisabschnit processes messages on vacancy or occupancy of its related track section; marks (unmarks) a track section according to the role it performs in the main route and blocks a track section (technical occupancy of a track section). Each change of the state of a track section is reported to objects of the classes cFahrstrasse, cBlockpassung and cBedienung.

The class cVWGleisabschnitt (Track Circuit Management) generates one object that processes telegrams coming from technical means used to monitor vacancy of track sections (failure message; a track section has been vacated in a certain direction; a track section has been occupied in a certain direction) and generates events to corresponding objects of the class cGleisabschnitt.

Each class is a category or a group of entities having similar features and the same or similar behaviour. Behaviour of entities in the given class is described by specific operations (methods). Features of entities in the given class are described by attributes. Fig. 4 shows a closer specification of the class cWeiche.

2.3 Sequential Diagram

Sequential diagrams are used to describe co-operation of system objects with respect to time. They should be created for all possible scenarios related to interlocking system operation.

Fig. 5 shows a part of co-operation of objects generated by the class cBedienung, cVWFahrstrasse, cFahrstrasse, cBlockpassung, cWeiche, cGleisabschnitt, cSchluesselsperre and cSignal in the process of setting and releasing the main route. Objects mutually co-operate via message exchange; lines with simple arrows represent asynchronous messages (events) and horizontal lines with filled-in arrowheads represent synchronous messages (primitive operations).

After giving a command for setting the main route an object of the class cBedienung sends the event evFsStellen(pFsNum,pZiel) to an object of the class cVWFahrstrasse. The event contains information on a number of the required main route (parameter pFsNum) and on its destination (parameter pZiel). The received number of the main route is analysed and helps an object of the class cVWFahrstrasse to decide whether a single main route (entry, outgoing) or a complex main route (transit through the station) is concerned. If the complex route is

Fig. 4. The Class cWeiche

the case it is realised by consecutive setting the single routes it consists of. For each single main route an object of the class cVWFahrstrasse generates the event evFsAnforderung(pZiel). If the required route may be set (there is neither another main route nor shunting route to endanger it) then an activated object of the class cFahrstrasse generates events to individual objects of main route elements (objects of the classes cWeiche, cGleisabschnitt, cSchluesselsperre, cSignal) with a command for marking them according to the role that each element plays in the main route. This role is defined in project works (attributes of the class cFahrstrasse) and the transmitted event includes it as a parameter pZweck. For instance, for objects of the class cWeiche the event evWeiKennzeichnung(pZweck) is generated with the parameter pZweck having one of possible values:

- kWeiFweg, for points being a part of the main route;
- kWeiDweg, for points being a part of protection distance of the main route;
- kWeiFwegFlschutz, for points representing flank protection for the main route;
- kWeiDwegFlschutz, for points representing flank protection for protection distance of the main route.

Information on the fact that the process of setting the main route was started is given to an object of the class cVWFafrstrasse by the event evFs-

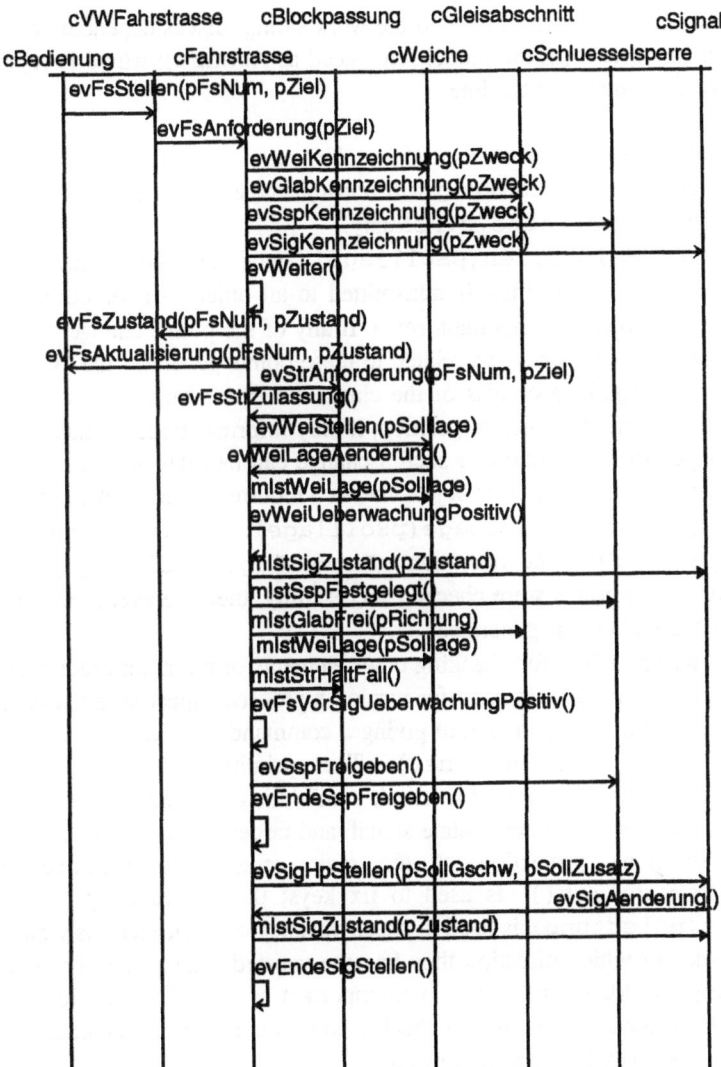

Fig. 5. Example of a Sequential Diagram (*Setting a Main Route*)

Zustand(pFsNum, pZustand) and to an object of the class cBedienung by the event evFsAktualisierung(pFsNum, pZustand).

Setting an outgoing route requires permission from a section blocking system of the target track. For this purpose an object of the class cFahrstrasse generates the event evStrAnforderung(pFsNum,pZiel). The parameter pZiel may get a value:

- kUndefiniert, if a train goes to a work siding, that has no relation to the interlocking system (in the model referenced as Anst) or a train goes to the adjacent station;

- kAwanstN, if a train goes to the work siding, that is dependent on the interlocking system (in the model referenced as Awanst); where N represents an Awanst number at the line.

If conditions required for a train to leave the station are fulfilled then a relevant object of the class cBlockpassung will transmit the event evFsStrZulassung() to the object oFahrstrasse[avFsNum].

The event evWeiStellen(pSolllage) containing a command for switching points to the required position is transmitted to all objects of the class cWeiche, defined by the project for this main route. If any of the points change their position, an object of the class cWeiche related to these points generates the event evWei-LageAenderung() to objects of the class cFahrstrasse. This event doesn't contain information about points position, it only informs about the fact that some of points changed their condition. If such a change can be relevant to an object of the class cFahrstrasse then this object checks a required position of the points by the primitive operation mIstWeiLage(pSolllage). Check of points position is positive (successful) if the operation mIstWeiLage(pSolllage) returns the value true. If all points were checked successfully, then the event evWeiUeberwachungPositiv() is generated.

The similar procedure for checking other elements of the main route must also be realised before giving a command for turning a proceed aspect at the start-signal (or at the intermediate signal) or before giving a command for release of a start-key (in the case of a route to Anst). The primitive operation mIstSig-Zustand(pZustand) is used to check conditions of signals in the station – stop aspect at the start-signal, intermediate signal, and target signal and at signals playing the role of flank protection of the main route. The primitive operation mIstSspFestgelegt() is used to fix keys; the primitive operation mIst-GlabFrei(pRichtung) is used to check vacancy of track sections whilst there is no importance in which direction they became vacated. The value of the parameter pRichtung = kUndefiniert is unimportant as well. The primitive operation mIstStrHaltFall() is used to check a correct position of elements included in the first line section which a train runs on.

In the case of the positive result of these checks (an object of the class cFahrstrasse generates the event evFsVorSigUeberwachungPositiv() to itself) the event evSigHpStellen(pSollGschw, pSollZusatz) is generated to all objects of the class cSignal, that take a share in setting signal aspects for the main route being in the process of setting. The parameter pSollGeschw carries information on velocity required in sections behind the signal; the parameter pSoll-Zusatz carries information on velocity that is to be expected at the next signal.

If a train leaves for the work siding having no relation to the station (Anst), giving proceed aspect at the start-signal must be preceded by a command for unblocking a start-key (evSspFreigeben()) that an engine-drive carries about.

Once proceed aspect is being given at the start-signal, setting the main route is over.

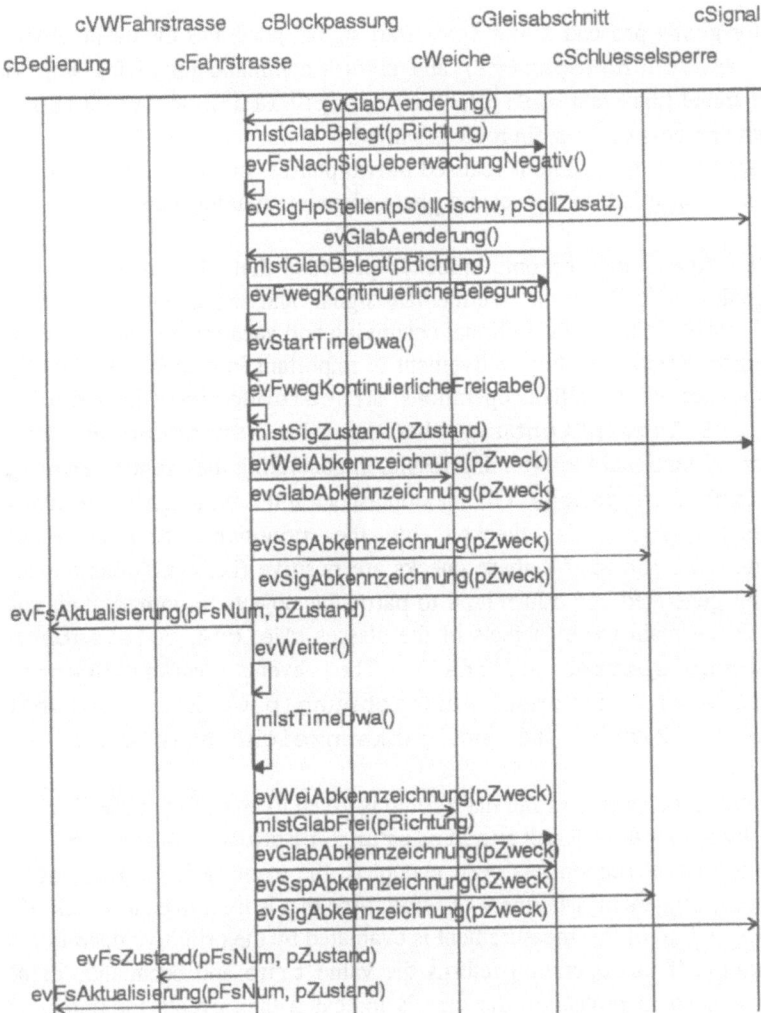

Fig. 6. Example of a Sequential Diagram (*Releasing a Main Route*)

The sequential diagram in Fig. 6 shows a part of how objects of the classes cBedienung, cVWFahrstrasse, cFahrstrasse, cBlockpassung, cWeiche, cGleisabschnitt, cSchluesselsperre and cSignal cooperate in releasing an outgoing main route.

If the main route is being set then continuous check of fulfilment of conditions for giving proceed aspect at the start-signal (eventually at the intermediate signal) must go on, e.g. if a train enters a section behind the start-signal then the state of this track section is changed and an object of the class cGleisabschnitt, assigned to this track section, generates the event evGlabAenderung(). The primitive operation mIstGlabBelegt(pRichtung) returns the value true, an object of the class cFahrstrasse representing the set main route evaluates breaking conditions necessary for giving proceed aspect at the start-signal, generates the event `evFsNach-SigUeberwachungNegativ()` and gives a command for giving stop aspect at the start-signal (the event `evSigHpStellen(pSollGschw, pSollZusatz)` – the release process of the main route is started.

Release of the main route is realised in two phases. In the first phase lock of route elements is cancelled, in the second phase elements making flank protection are released.

Route elements may become unlocked provided that stop aspect is given at the start-signal, eventually at the intermediate signal, and sequential release occurs. Sequential release is based on continual occupying and vacating the track sections of the route. Since direction of train movement is important in evaluation of continuality, the parameter of primitive operations `mIstGlabBelegt(pRichtung)` and `mIstGlabBelegt(pRichtung)` has the value `kSteigend` or `kFallend`. Detection of continual train running results in generating the event `evFwegKonti-nuierlicheFreigabe()`. Giving stop aspect at the start-signal, eventually at the intermediated signal, is checked by the primitive operation `mIstSig-Zustand(pZustand)`. If these checks are positive (i.e. conditions are fulfilled), events are generated and transmitted to particular objects to unmark their roles performed in the main route (objects of the classes `cWeiche`, `cGleisabschnitt`, `cSchluesselsperre`, `cSignal`). The events `evWeiAbkennzeich-nung(pZweck)`, `evSspAbkennzeichnung(pZweck)`, `evGlabAbken-zeichnung(pZweck)` and `evSigAbkennzeichnung(pZweck)` are concerned.

Information on release of the main route is given to an object of the class `cBedi-enung` (by the event `evFsAktualisierung(pFsNum, pZustand)`).

After the target section has been occupied, the event `evStartTimeDwa()` is generated. It triggers measurement of safety time that is used to cancel lock of protection distance. End of this measurement is evaluated by the primitive operation `mIst-TimeDwa()`. If this operation returns the value `true` and occupancy of no track section included in protection distance is indicated then events for unmarking elements in protection distance are generated. If a target track section has been vacated during safety time measurement, measurement is untimely finished, the primitive operation `mIstTimeDwa()` returns the value `false` and lock of protection distance must be cancelled using emergency means.

Information about the main route being released is given to an object of the class `cVWFafrstrasse` by the event `evFsZustand(pFsNum, pZustand)` and to an object of the class `cBedienung` by the event `evFsAktualis-ierung(pFsNum, pZustand)`.

2.4 Statecharts of the Class `cFahrstrasse`

The statechart diagram is another kind of diagram that is used to describe functional properties of the system. The state diagrams use the following convention to specify transition from one state to another: `trigger[condition]/action`

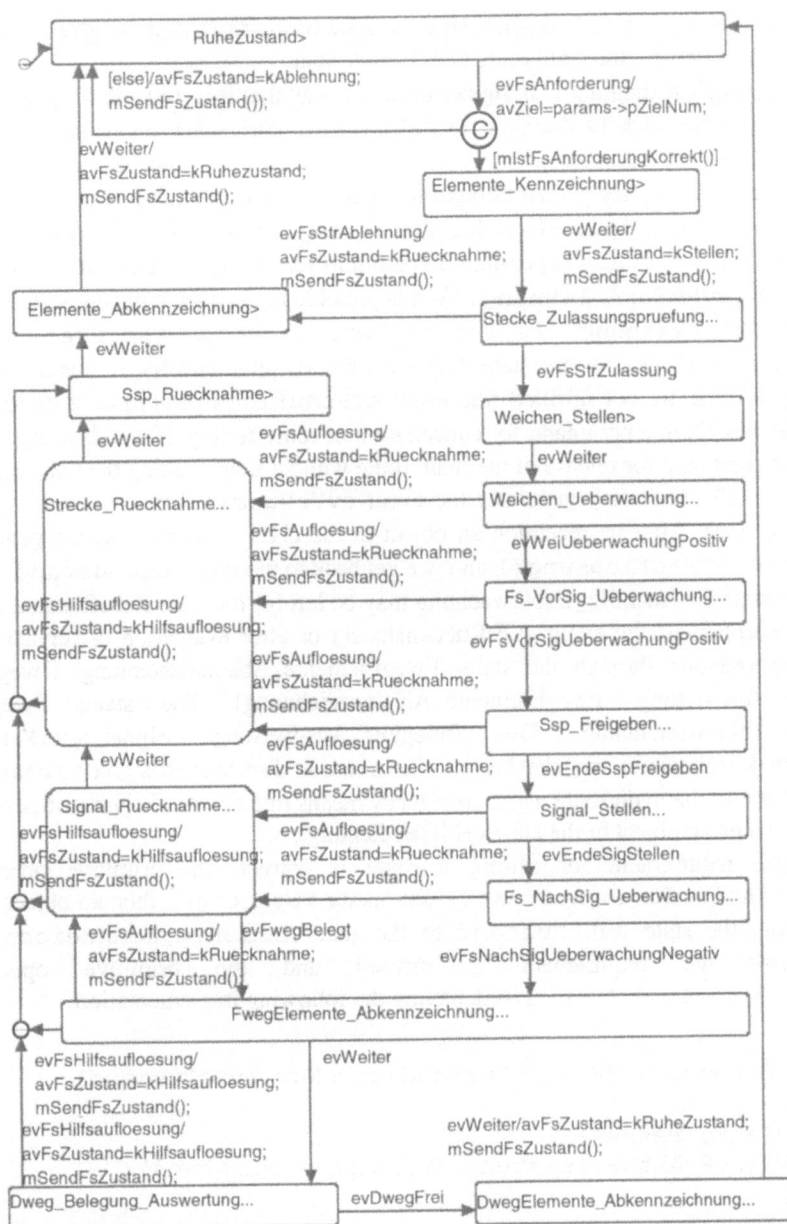

Fig. 7. Example of a Statechart Diagram: Statechart of the class `cFahrstrasse`

Fig. 7 shows the statechart diagram of the class `cFahrstrasse`. After initialisation the system enters the state `RuheZustand` by default. An object of the class `cFahrstrasse` remains in this state when waiting for a command for setting the main route (represented by the event `evFsAnforderung()`). Entering this state, all variable attributes of the class `cFahrstrasse` are set to their default values, e.g. the attribute `avFsZustand` remembering the state of the main route is given the value `kRuhezustand` – the main route is in the idle state.

The statechart diagram is designed in such a way that it is possible to go regularly from any state back to the state `RuheZustand`. The states `Elemente_Kenn-zeichnung`, `Weichen_Stellen`, `SspRuecknahme` and `Elemente_Ab-kennzeichnung` are passed through to the next state executing a code when entering the state. In the state `Strecke_Zulassungspruefung` automatic return to the state `RuheZustand` is possible if conditions for setting the route are not fulfilled (the event `evFsStrAblehnung()`). It is possible to get back from the states `Wei-chen_Ueberwachung`, `Fs_VorSig_Ueberwachung`, `Ssp_Frei-geben`, `Signal_Stellen` to the state `RuheZustand` automatically if conditions for setting a route are not fulfilled (the event `evFsAufloesung()`) or a station dispatcher has given a command for cancellation of route setting. If a station dispatcher gives a command for release of the main route without train running then an object of the class `cBedienung` generates the event `evFsRuecknahme()` (not visible in this diagram). After its reception an object of the class `cFahrstrasse` generates the event `evFsAufloesung()` and we get back to the state `RuheZustand`.

The state Fs_NachSig_Ueberwachung may be left for the state RuheZustand either after reception of the event evFsRuecknahme() or after evaluation of regular train running (passing through the states FwegElemente_Abkennzeichnung, Dweg_Be-legung_Auswertung, FwegElemente_Abkennzeichnung). The states FwegEle-mente_Abkennzeichnung, Dweg_Belegung_Aus-wertung, Signal_Ruecknahme, Strecke_Ruecknahme may also be left after a station dispatcher has given a command for release of the main route using emergency means (the event evFsHilfsaufloesung() generated by an object of the class cHilfsBedienung).

If the requirement for setting a route is correct (the primitive operation `mIstFsAnforderungKorrekt()` returns the values `true`), then an object transits from the state `RuheZustand` to the state `Elemente_Kennzeichnung`, otherwise the requirement is refused and the primitive operation `mSendFsZustand()` is triggered, having the following implementation:

```
oBedienung->GEN(evFsZustand(apFsNum,avFsZustand);

oVWFahrstrasse-
>GEN(evFsAktualisierung(apFsNum,avFsZustand);
```

After entering the state `Elemente_Kennzeichnung`, the events are generated to mark objects of those classes that belong to elements related to the main route, e.g. the following code is used to mark points:

```
BYTE i;
.........
for (i=0; i<kWeiMax; i++)
{
```

```
if(apWeiZweck[i]!=kUndefiniert)
oWeiche[i]->GEN(evWeiKennzeichnung(apWeiZweck[i]);
}
..........
GEN(evWeiter());
```

The constant kWeiMax represents the maximum number of switches in the station and the constant kUndefiniert means the switch is not related to the main route.

When setting an outgoing main route, an object of the class cFahrstrasse must cooperate with an object of the class cBlockpassung. This cooperation can be found in the state Strecke_Zulassungspruefung that comprises other sub-states. In this state conditions for train leaving the station are being checked, i.e. transmission of single-line permission, reception of return indication after the last train, vacancy of the first line section, active giving proceed aspect at the first block signal if it hasn't an individual distant signal. In the case a train leaves for the work siding having dependency on the interlocking system (Awanst), conditions of the work siding are also to be checked. Cooperation with the line is not necessary in this state if an entry main route is being set. If conditions related to the line are fulfilled, the event evFsStrZulassung() is generated and route setting goes on; otherwise the event evFsStrAblehnung() is generated, an object of the class cFahrstrasse enters the state Elemente_Abkennzeichnung (generates commands for unmarking elements) and an object gets back to the state Ruhe-Zustand.

In the state Weiche_Stellen commands are generated to move points relevant to the main route:

```
BYTE i;
for(i=1;i<=kWeiMax;i++)
  {
   if(apWeiLage[i]!=kUndefiniert)
   oWeiche[i]->GEN(evWeiStellen(apWeiLage[i]));
   }
   GEN(evWeiter());
```

The attribute apWeiLage is of the array type. The number of elements represents a number of points operated in the railway station and each element may have a value:

-   kUndefiniert, if points position is not defined for the main route;
-   kRechts, if position "right" is required for a given main route;
-   kLinks, if position "left" is required for a given main route.

Fig. 8 shows the statechart of cFahrstrasse.Weichen_Ueberwachung. In this statechart a correct end position of the points related to the main route is checked. If all relevant points are in the required position, then the primitive operation mWei-FueZ() returns the value true.

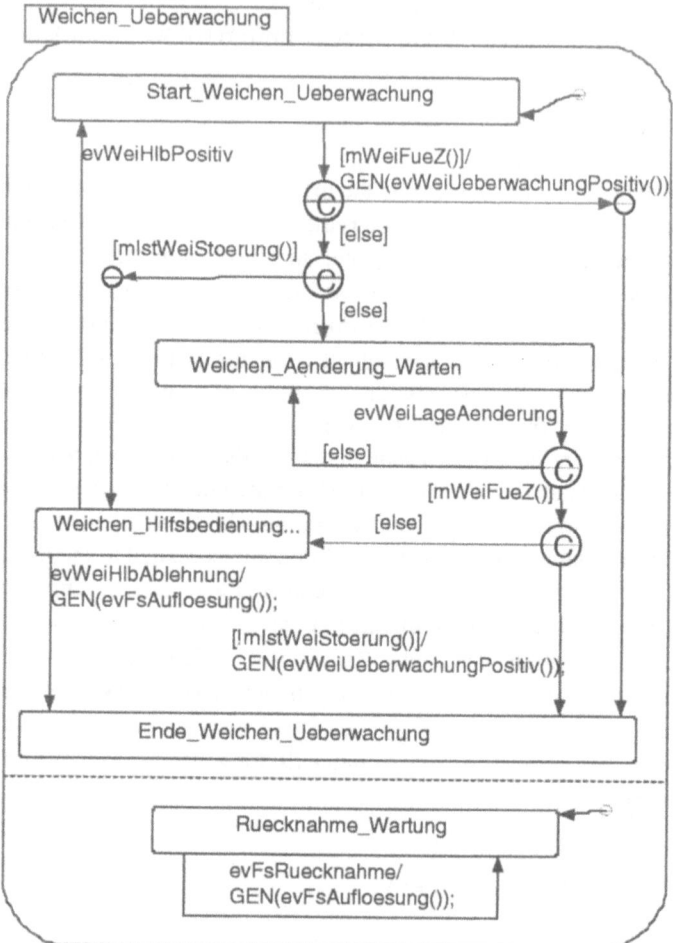

Fig. 8. Statechart of `cFahrstrasse.Weichen_Ueberwachung`

The primitive operation `mIstWeiStoerung()` returns the value `true` provided that some of the points related to the main route are faulty (e.g. end position of points has not been reached within a given time limit). In that case the system enters the state `Weichen_Hilfsbedienung`, where emergency operation of the points is enabled. If emergency operation of the points is successful, the event `evWeiHlbPositiv()` is generated; otherwise the event `evFsAufloesung()` is generated. The serial state `Ruecknahme_Wartung` makes a command for main route release possible (command from a station dispatcher).

In the state `Fs_VorSig_Ueberwachung` (Fig. 7, Fig. 9) those conditions are checked that are necessary for giving proceed aspect at the start-signal, eventually at the intermediate signal. It is checked whether actual state of all elements (signals,

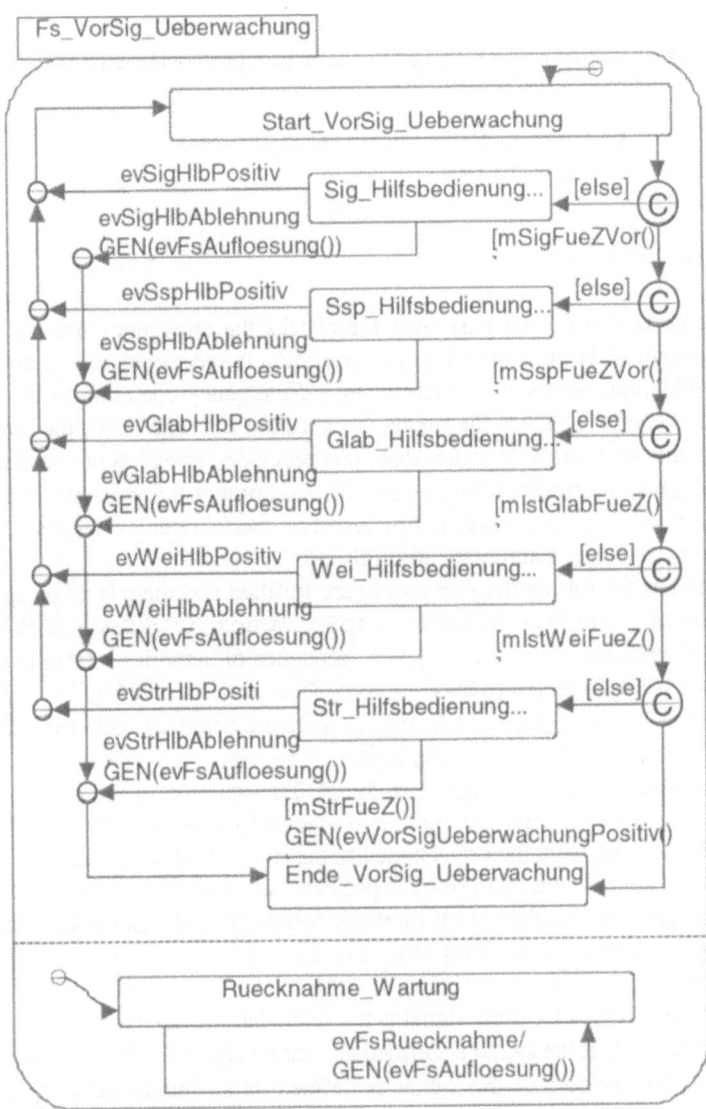

Fig. 9. Statechart of cFahrstrasse.Fs_VorSig_Ueberwachung

locks, track sections, points and line) related to the main route corresponds to the required states. The result of check is positive if the primitive operations mSigFueZVor(), mSspFueZVor(), mGlabFueZ(), mWeiFueZ(), mStrFueZ() return the value true, e.g. the implementation of the primitive operation mWeiFueZ() that checks points conditions is as follows:

```
BYTE i;
for(i=1;i<=kWeiMax;i++)
```

```
{
if((apWeiLage[i]!=kUndefiniert)&&(avWeiHlb[i]==kKeineHl
b))
        {
            if(!rWeiche[i]->mIstLage(apWeiLage[i]))
            return false;
        }
}
return true;
```

For elements that do not pass over the checks the emergency operation is automatically required. If such an emergency operation is successful, then it goes on with another problematic element (if there is any). Emergency operation of the particular element is recorded (e.g. for the points the attribute avWeiHlb of the array type is used; the value kKeineHlb means that emergency operation has not been used) and other emergency operation of this element for a set route is not possible. If emergency operation of some of elements fails (the result of checks remains negative), the process of setting the route is automatically finished.

If conditions for setting the main route are fulfilled and there is a key specified in the project as a constant kStart (apSspZweck[i]=kSspStart), then a command for release of this key is given. Sequence of activities related to release of the start-key is implemented in the state Ssp_Freigeben (see Fig. 7).

In the state Signal_Stellen (Fig. 7) there are activities included that relate to generating commands for giving stop aspect at the target signal and proceed aspect at the intermediate signal and at the start-signal. Transmission of the command is followed by the check whether the command was really executed. These activities are realized sequentially from the target signal to the start-signal (Fig. 10).

The role of signals in a main route is projected as an attribute apSigZweck. It is of the array type and number of its elements corresponds to number of signals in the station, e.g. an element of this array may have the value:

- kUndefiniert , if the signal is not related to the main route;
- kSigZiel, if the signal is defined as a target signal for the main route;
- kSigZwischen, if the signal is defined as an intermediate signal for the main route;
- kSigStart, if the signal is defined as a start-signal for the main route;
- kSigFwegFlschutz, if the signal makes flank protection for the main route;
- kSigFwegFlschutz, if the signal makes flank protection for protection distance of the main route;
- kSigStartVorZiel, if the signal is defined as a start-signal for the main route and concurrently also as a distant target signal;
- ......

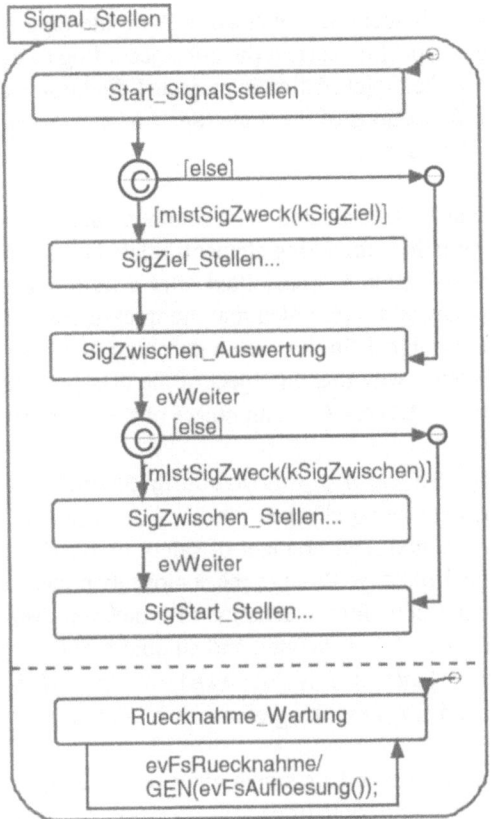

Fig. 10. Statechart of cFahrstrasse.Signal_Stellen

In the state Fs_NachSig_Ueberwachung (Fig. 7) conditions for giving proceed aspect at the start-signal, eventually at the intermediate signal, are being checked. If they are not fulfilled, a command for giving stop aspect at the start-signal is given, the element, which is the cause of difficulties, is identified and its emergency operation is requested, e.g. at the start-signal a call-on aspect may be given. Once proceed aspect is given at the start-signal, no emergency operation of track sections is possible. Occupancy of the section (including a technical occupancy) will cause transition to the state FwegElemente_Abkennzeichnung and the evaluation process of train running continuality is started. If technical occupancy causes stop aspect at the start-signal then the station dispatcher must initiate call-on aspect in order to realize train running. Conditions for giving proceed aspects are checked in two steps:

1st step – when entering the state;

2nd step – after reception of the message about a changed state of some elements in the station.

In the state FwegElemente_Abkennzeichnung those conditions are checked that are necessary to release the main route. Train movement is considered continual if:

- Occupancy of all sections contained in the route (apart from a target section) was recorded respecting correct direction according to the project;
- Occupancy of the target section in projected direction was recorded;
- Vacancy of all sections of the route (apart from a target section) in correct direction was recorded.

If train running has been evaluated to be continual and relevant signals do not give proceed aspects, events for unmarking elements related to the route are generated. For entry routes return indication is transmitted after a train entered the station. Return indication may be transmitted provided that the track section behind the entry signal is vacant and the entry signal (in this case a start-signal) gives stop aspect. Transmission is realised in such a way that an object of the class cFahrstrasse generates the event evStrRueckblock() to an object of the class cBedienung (not visible in the diagram).

In the state Dweg_Belegung_Auswertung conditions for cancellation of protection distance lock are being checked (vacancy of track sections contained in protection distance, completed measurement of safety time). If the target signal is concurrently a start-signal (passage through the station) then measurement of safety time is not required. If conditions for cancellation of protection distance lock are fulfilled, the event evDwegFrei() is generated and an object of the class cFahrstrasse enters the state DwegElemente_Abkennzeichnung, where events are generated containing a command for unmarking elements related to protection distance of the main route.

If the start-signal or intermediate signal gives proceed aspect and a command was given for release of the main route (the event evFsAufloesung()), then an object of the class cFahrstrasse enters the state Signal_Ruecknahme. In this state commands are generated for giving stop aspects at these signals and their execution is checked. The main route becomes released after safety time lapses away (time is different from safety time for protection distance). If all track sections of the locked main route are vacant when safety time has lapsed away, the event evWeiter() is generated and an object of the class cFahrstrasse enters the state Strecke_Ruecknahme. If occupancy of a track section contained in the route is recorded during measurement of safety time, the event evFwegBelegt() is generated and an object of the class cFahrstrasse enters the state FwegElemente_Abkennzeichnung. Release of the main route by train running is expected.

If any activities related to blocking the line or elements in the adjacent station were performed in the process of route setting, now this blocking must be cancelled. Actions related to this activity are performed in the state Strecke_Ruecknahme.

If a start-key was released in route setting, then the main route may be released not earlier than the key was locked and fixed. Actions related to this activity are performed in the state Ssp_Ruecknahme.

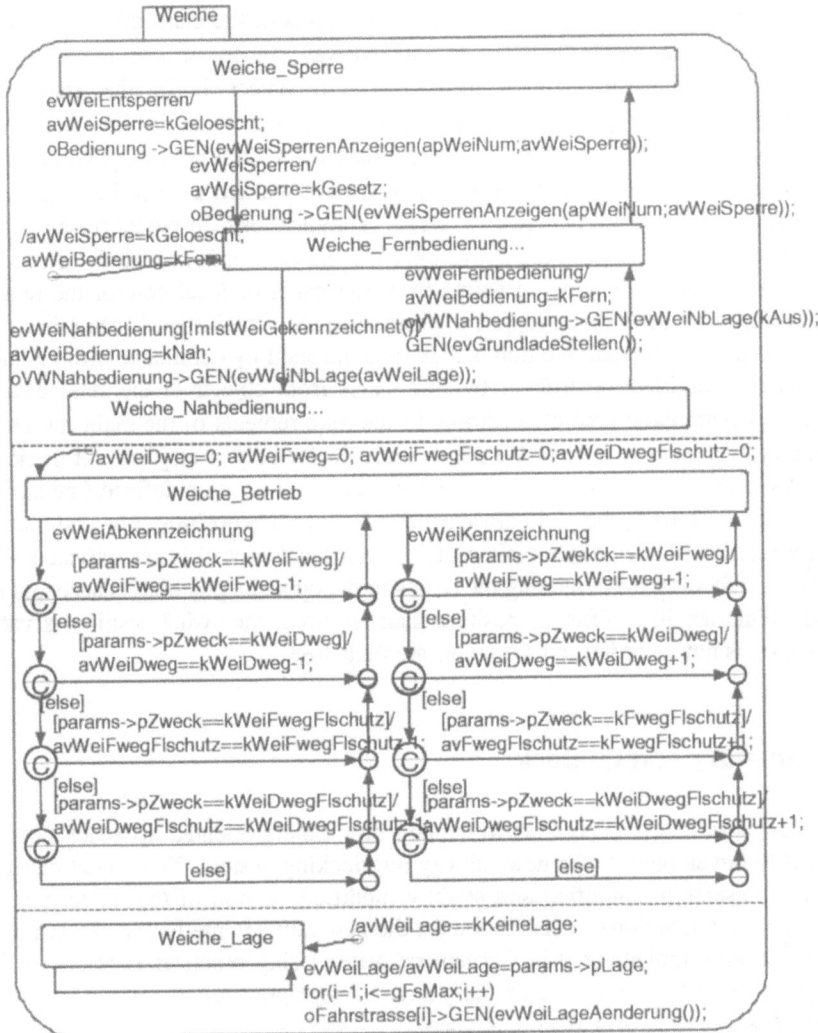

Fig. 11. Statechart of cWeiche

2.5 Statechart of the Class cWeiche

Fig. 11 shows the statechart diagram of the class cWeiche, which consists of three serial states. In the state Weiche_Betrieb there is reception of commands for marking (evWeiKennzeichnung()) or unmarking (evWeiAbkennzeich-nung()) of the points according to the roles played in the main route. The points may concurrently be related to more main routes (e.g. points may be a part of one route and represent flank protection for another route). In the state Weiche_Lage messages about the actual states of points or their failures are received. Information on a changed state of the points is sent to all objects of the class cFahrstrasse. The points may be controlled in a centralized way (an object is in the state Weiche_Fernbedienung), in a local way (an object is in the state Weiche_Nahbedienung) or may be blocked (an object is in the state Weiche_Sperre). If the points are blocked, electrical switching is impossible. Points may become controlled locally only if they are not marked as used in a main route ([mIstWeiGekennzeichnet==false]). Indications on points position given at the panel of local control are active only if local control is activated. After reception of a command for moving points from the panel of local control the required position must be determined (opposite position to the actual one). If centralised control of points is activated, the points may be controlled by commands from a station dispatcher (individual control) or by commands from objects of the class cFahrstrasse (automatic control according to the requirements of the main route). The station dispatcher may control the points individually only if they are not marked as being used in a main route. If the points have a default position defined (the attribute apWeiGrundlage), they will always move back to this position provided that they are not marked for usage in a main route or their local control is not activated. Command for switching over (moving the points to the opposite position) is accepted only if the points are in a different position than required, the switch section is vacant, force open is not recorded and the points are fault-free.

3 Summary and Outlook

The main aim of the paper was to explain how object-oriented approach could be applied to development of a new railway interlocking system. The model discussed above represents a simplified and slightly modified version of the model that was elaborated as a functional specification for the new railway interlocking system being developed and implemented in German railways. Using practical experiences from applying the UML in the field of designing railway applications, we can see several advantages that are worth mentioning here:

At the beginning a customer presented a set of incomplete initial requirements in the form of the "wish list" (ger. Lastenheft) representing an informal function requirements specification. In comparison with this document the final UML-based function requirements specification is more unambiguous, complete and well-structured;

Created model may be used as a basis for communication of (international) development teams working over the common project; this also holds good for subjects active in the process of safety assessment and safety approval of a newly developed system. In our case the UML-based model has been accepted by relevant Railway Authority (EBA);

Creation of the UML-based model is generally unthinkable without support of a proper CASE tool; what's more, created specification is generally independent on particular programming language (linkage will be of use first when source code is automatically generated, i.e. in the process of forward-engineering). Although authors of this paper were not involved in the process of coding (translating semantics into full production-quality code), according to practical experiences of involved software workers at least 90% of the generic core of the interlocking logic was automatically generated using the mentioned software tool. For automatic code generation two types of diagrams were used – sequence and statechart diagrams;

Another advantage consists in tool-supported automatic generation of documents that makes unification of documentation principles possible;

Functionality of the designed model can be verified using animation; with possibility to present a prototype of the system to a customer immediately after the specification phase is completed;

In comparison with informal specifications and/or specifications based on other formalisms, maintenance and realisation of later changes and modifications of UML models is much easier. In addition, general availability and understandability of the standard UML is an undoubted advantage, together with minimum cost needed to learn it and permanent support of the UML standard from the main providers of software tools.

At present support of tools and their implemented methods is quite sufficient for design, simulation and transfer to implementation, unfortunately the same cannot be said about proofs. Much effort is made to solve the task of checking correctness of UML-based specifications and possibilities of their verification. The UML standard still belongs to the group of semi-formal methods that are not able to provide mathematical (calculated) proof about ability or inability of the system to enter a certain hazardous state or recover safety state under abnormal situations. What's more, usability of UML specifications is restricted to modelling safety function requirements, not safety integrity requirements.

References

1. OMG Unified Modeling Language Specification 1.3. Object Management Group. http://www.omg.org/cgi-bin/doc?formal/00-03-01
2. ISO/IEC DIS 19501-1: Information Technology - Unified Modeling Language (UML) - Part 1: Specification. Edition 1 (2000) 1024 p.
3. Coad, P., Yourdon, E.: Object Oriented Analysis. Prentice-Hall, Englewood Cliffs, New Jersey (1990)
4. David E. Monarchi, Gretchen I. Puhr: A Research Typology for Object-Oriented Analysis and Design. Communications of the ACM, 35(9) (1992) 35-47
5. TNŽ 34 2620: Predpisy pre staničné zabezpečovacie zariadenia (Regulations for railway interlocking apparatus). (1996) 23 p.
6. Janota, A., Rástočný, K., Zahradník, J.: UML – a Formal Method Usable in Development of Safety-related Systems. In: The 3rd Int. Workshop on Computer Science and Information Technologies. Vol. 3 – USATU Publishers, Ufa, Russia (2001) 194–198
7. Janota, A., Rástočný, K., Zahradník, J.: The Use of UML in Design of Railway Interlocking Systems. In: Int. Scientific Conference Transport in the 21st Century, Warszawa (2001) 93–100

8. Rástočný, K., Zahradník, J., Janota, A.: An Object Oriented Model of Railway Safety-Related Control System. Communications, No. 4, ŽU in Žilina (2002) 32–39
9. Rástočný, K., Janota, A., Zahradník, J.: The Use of UML to Development of a Railway Interlocking System. Advances in Electrical and Electronic Engineering, Vol. 2, No. 2 (2003) 48-54
10. Zahradník, J., Rástočný, K., Janota, A.: UML - based Specification of a Railway Interlocking and Signalling System. In: Workshop on "Software Specification of Safety relevant Transportation Control Tasks" (E. Schnieder, Ed.), VDI-Report, Düsseldorf (2003) 131-142

Process Description Languages and Methods: Introduction to the Chapter *Petri Nets and Related Approaches in Engineering*

Jörg Desel

Katholische Universität Eichstätt-Ingolstadt
Lehrstuhl für Angewandte Informatik
85071 Eichstätt, Germany
joerg.desel@ku-eichstaett.de

Abstract. This is the introduction to the chapter on the subject area *Petri Nets and Related Approaches in Engineering*. After a short report on experiences in this subject area during the DFG[1] Priority Program we introduce and survey the papers of this chapter. Furthermore, we indicate that the work done in the subject area provided answers to important questions and – more importantly – helped to identify the state-of-the-art in the field as well as gaps to be filled by further research and development activities.

1 The Subject Area

At the beginning of the Priority Program *Integration of Software Specification for Applications in Engineering* five years ago, *Petri Nets* and *Process Description Languages* were installed as two independent subject areas. It turned out after a short time that both areas have a strong intersection. Therefore, these two areas joined soon – resulting in the subject area with the title *Petri Nets and other Process Description Languages*.

The subject area organized (almost) annual workshops, often in connection with a general assembly of the project partners to ensure that many project participants were able to participate. The main issue of these workshops was to exchange ideas rather than to present finished results, thus allowing the researchers from the various project groups to contribute to the development of other approaches, to reflect their ideas with other experts and to mutually profit from the results as early as possible. This way, cooperation and exchange of questions (rather than only answers) was possible. The proceedings of the workshops have not been and will not be published, but most of the presented material is now comprised in the papers of this chapter.

Although Petri nets play a particular role in this subject area, many projects of the priority program not engaged in Petri net research took part in the activities of the subject area. It might be remarkable that in particular the project

---

[1] Deutsche Forschungsgemeinschaft (German Research Council)

H. Ehrig et al. (Eds.): INT 2004, LNCS 3147, pp. 199–205, 2004.

groups from engineering departments were interested in this topic – thinking in processes is apparently more developed in engineering than in computer science. Since not all participating research groups document their work with a paper in this chapter, the groups that contributed to the subject area are listed below (in alphabetic order):

DisPA led by B. Vogel-Heuser (Uni Wuppertal), P. Göhner (Uni Stuttgart)
(see the contribution of K. Fischer et al. in this chapter)

GRASP led by W. Dangelmaier, F.J. Rammig, W.H. Müller (Uni Paderborn), T. Kropf (Uni Tübingen)
(see the contribution of S. Flake et al. in this chapter)

ISILEIT led by J. Gausemeier, U. Glässer, W. Schäfer (Uni Paderborn)

KNOSSOS led by H.D. Ehrich, E. Schnieder (Uni Braunschweig)
(see the paper of S. Einer in this chapter)

SAW led by G. Saake, S. Conrad, D. Ziems (Uni Magdeburg)

SFC-Check led by Y. Lakhnech, W.P. de Roever (Uni Kiel), S. Engell, S. Kowalewski (Uni Dortmund)

SpeciMen led by J. Desel (Kath. Uni Eichstätt-Ingolstadt), H.-M. Hanisch (Uni Halle-Wittenberg)
(see the paper of J. Desel et al. in this chapter)

Additionally, we are happy that a paper from an internationally reputed research group, authored by L.M. Kristensen and K. Jensen, Aarhus University, is included in this chapter.

2   Process Languages and Methods in Computer Science and in Engineering

Process description languages used by engineers and those used by computer scientists have many similarities. Sometimes they share common sources, e.g. automata or Petri nets, that were developed long before software specification techniques were an issue. Some languages have been taken from the other field, e.g. graphical languages from the UML created from software engineers for software engineers are adopted to the engineering field.

The title of this introductory paper does not sufficiently indicate that most of the work done in this subject area deals with *methods* rather than only with *languages*. In other words, not the actual language is most relevant for the success of an apporach but rather the way a model given in terms of a specific language is used within the development process of a dynamic system in engineering or computer science.

Engineering has a remarkable and successful history in methods for system development processes. Moreover, there are various engineering disciplines which share some common principles but which have completely different methods and models. This is mainly due to the different requirements within the disciplines (compare, e.g., architecture with electrical engineering). There seems to be a general agreement that this situation is satisfying in engineering. The traditional approaches are, however, not immediately applicable to technical systems heavily based on complex software.

Conversely, there is a vivid discussion in computer science on process models and methods since years. However, these considerations have only led to standards within single companies or within public administrations but there is no agreement on *the* standard practice. Many different languages were developed and applied in the last decades, leading to a situation where each model (each method, respectively) was understood by only a small number of users although the goal of many modelling languages was quite comparable. The rise of the UML with its various languages (and variants) together with associated methods and tools was motivated by this unsatisfactory situation. Although the UML stems from a particular need to model software systems in a specific domain in a unique and understandable way, the languages of the UML are nowadays applied in almost every domain of computer science and even in engineering. These generalizing approaches are not always successful because often other approaches are more appropriate. Moreover, the UML lacks (by purpose) precise semantics for their languages – or several competing semantics have been published – and models can often be interpreted in more than one way. Although some people claim that the UML is a step towards necessary standards, it turns out that actually some of its languages constitute a step backwards compared with other more traditional standardized notions which are not that widely spread though.

As modelling languages and methods cannot easily be carried over from engineering to computer science, traditional computer science methods are not always appropriate in the engineering field. However, the possible transfer of successful approaches from one discipline to the other is an important research issue – the vision is to participate from long experiences and to avoid errors. Moreover, embedded systems require specifications that address both, engineering and software aspects. These specifications have to be developed and understood by practitioners from both areas.

The aim of the subject area and hence of this chapter is to study relations, intersections, possible generalizations and applications of *process* specification languages and methods applying respective specifications from engineering and computer science. In particular, we consider the methods based on Petri nets, which can be viewed as a quite old "unifying modelling language" for process modelling with sound mathematical semantics, with a uniform graphical notation, with existing analysis tools, and with numerous applications in engineering and in computer science.

3   Articles in This Chapter

In this section we provide a short survey on the papers published in the chapter.

Specification and Verification of Product Automation Systems with Real-Time Properties

The GRASP project is based on a successfully applied specification language for production automation systems, called MFERT[2]. MFERT-models have many similarities with Petri nets. One of the main issues of the GRASP project was to specify and verify formal properties of MFERT models. This includes definition of a formal semantics and identification of relevant properties. The verification is based on efficient model checking. Moreover, for making the results immediately applicable for engineers, tools for graphical animation have been developed.

The first paper of this chapter (after this introduction), *Specification and Formal Verification of Temporal Properties of Production Automation Systems*, authored by Stephan Flake, Wolfgang Müller, Jürgen Ruf, and Ulrich Pape concentrates on *temporal properties*. The specification language RT-OCL is defined as an extension of the language OCL for the specification of constraints in the context of UML diagrams.

On a more formal level, MFERT models are translated to I/O Interval Structures, and RT-OCL-specifications are translated to expressions in a timed variant of the temporal logic OCL, namely Clocked CTL. Fed with this, the model checker RAVEN returns traces of counter examples which are visualized by a 3D animation.

A Formal Specification Technique of Operational Processes Applying Colored Petri Nets

The author of the second contribution, Stefan Einer, is today employed by Swiss Federal Railways. In fact, the railway domain had been his research area before, at the University of Braunschweig, where he was particularly active within the project KNOSSOS. His approach presented in the paper *STOP Specification Technique of Operational Processes* was developed in this context (and also shows a railway crossing example) but is apparently applicable in a more general setting.

As the author writes in his abstract, STOP is a methodical specification and a formal technique, and a specific application of colored Petri Nets. So colored Petri nets serve as the underlying language for processes. The paper distinguishes validation of specifications and verification techniques based on occurrence graphs of colored Petri nets. Surprisingly, Petri nets are used in the paper also to describe the verification process model.

---

[2] Modell der Fertigung (model of manufacturing)

Design and Specification of a Protocol for Mobile Networks

The next paper was written by Lars Michael Kristensen and Kurt Jensen, the latter being well-known for the introduction of colored Petri nets and, together with his research group in Aarhus, development of the CPN tools – the leading academic Petri net tool suite. Their article *Specification and Validation of an Edge Router Discovery Protocol for Mobile Ad-hoc Networks* describes experiences from an industrial case study. Like the previous paper, colored Petri nets and Petri-net-based verification techniques are employed. The domain of the application is again in engineering, but it is completely different from the railway domain of the previous paper. Clearly, the authors use the CPN tools from Aarhus for verification.

Besides the language and the tool, the particular application domain is specific for this paper. Another remarkable point is that Message Sequence Charts have been employed in this project, too. The link between Petri nets and Message Sequence Charts proves that there is not necessarily competition between these notions. Rather the computer scientists and their tools have to adapt to the appropriate and known language of their users, namely the engineers.

Synthesis of Control in Automation Systems

The *Guide to Modelling and Control with Modules of Signal Nets* by Jörg Desel, Hans-Michael Hanisch, Gabriel Juhás, Robert Lorenz, and Christian Neumair has two, more or less independent, parts. Since the results of the project SPECIMEN only fits well in this subject area, two different aspects of the developed concept are combined to one paper; Part 1 surveys the syntax and semantics of modular signal Petri nets whereas Part 2 provides an (informal) illustrative description of the automatic synthesis of control modules from a given specification.

Again Petri nets are applied, but in this approach these nets are elementary, i.e., without *colored* individual tokens. Instead, the application domain of modular automation systems with distributed plant and control modules asked for a modular extension of Petri nets. Since, in reality, physical entities communicate via signals from sensors and to actuators, respective signal arcs are added to Petri nets for allowing a faithful modelling of modules. This way, the advantages of Petri nets, namely their immediate representation of concurrency, conflicts and synchronization, are preserved while the engineering view of blocks communicating by signals is also respected. An important feature of signal Petri nets and their modules is that the numerous analysis methods for Petri nets can still be applied to this extended class of Petri nets.

The control synthesis procedure described in the second part essentially follows the known procedure from supervisory control. The latter is, however, based on automata. So the (more involved) aim of the approach presented here is not only to start with Petri net modules but also to end up with a Petri net module modelling the "maximally permissive" control for a given specification of the output behavior of a plant. This contribution does not contain the full proofs of the necessary results but rather points to the original papers containing these results. It demonstrates the concept in an illustrative way.

Conceptual Models for Product and Plant Automation

The last contribution of this chapter is a bit off-beat in the sense that Petri nets are not mentioned at all. Katja Fischer, Peter Göhner, Felix Gutbrodt, Uwe Katzke, and Birgit Vogel-Heuser from the project DisPA identify in *Conceptual Design of an Engineering Model for Product and Plant Automation* deficits of the UML when applied in engineering. They come up with a draft for an object-oriented approach in the domain of automation and process control. In particular, UML stereotypes for control, configurations of attributes and operations to achieve reusability and real time constraints are considered.

Although this paper does not follow the line of the other papers in this chapter, it nicely complements the view of the other papers. For example, the previously mentioned paper from Desel et al. refers to a black box view of modules in a closed loop to motivate a comprehensive and faithful modelling approach based on Petri nets. Hence modelling principles have been transferred from engineering to computer science, thus modifying the language accordingly. In the present paper, concepts from computer science are transferred to engineering, thus detailing or refining the box models of a closed loop.

4   Resume

A summarizing view at the papers of this chapter and additional work done within this subject area as well as in other subject areas made very clear that there is no *best* or *universal* process description language for software specification in engineering. Instead, there are numerous parameters associated to an application, including in particular

- the area of engineering,
- the particular persons involved in the development and their respective background,
- aspects like real-time and priority,
- dependability and security issues,
- availability of analysis techniques and tools,
- the characteristics of the software and
- the platform under consideration.

Each setting of these parameters may lead to a different appropriate language and method.

Instead of hunting for a perfect language and method, the experience from the research results obtained in the subject area showed that marriage between languages is necessary and – fortunately – possible in various ways. It will rarely be a good idea to try to convert researchers or even practitioners from other areas to the own models. Instead, identifying the appropriate method(s) and the required features of a modelling language in an interdisciplinary field is already a problem that requires research. The work done in the subject area contributes in this direction.

Transformation of models with comparable expressive power but different representations is an issue, as well as dealing with complementary models describing different aspects of the same object. Whereas the contributions show that this kind of transformation and combination is possible for many examples, a more general setting was not obtained in this subject area but can rather be expected in other subject areas of the Priority Program which are concerned with integration aspects.

For ending with a positive statement, the results of this subject area also proved that computer scientists and engineers easily find a cooperative way between their disciplines, although they have quite different general approaches. Even more, looking across the respective borderlines often gives rise to new views, new aspects and new relations between concepts. At least, this was my personal experience from several project meetings on all levels where researchers from computer science worked together with researchers from engineering.

Specification and Formal Verification of Temporal Properties of Production Automation Systems

Stephan Flake[1], Wolfgang Müller[1], Ulrich Pape[2], and Jürgen Ruf[3]

[1] Universität Paderborn
Fürstenallee 11, 33102 Paderborn, Germany
[2] Heinz Nixdorf Institut
Fürstenallee 11, 33102 Paderborn, Germany
[3] IBM Deutschland Entwicklung GmbH
Schönaicher Str. 220, 71032 Böblingen, Germany

Abstract. This article describes our approach for the specification and verification of production automation systems with real-time properties. We focus on the graphical MFERT notation and RT-OCL (Real-Time Object Constraint Language) for the specification of state-oriented real-time properties. RT-OCL is an extension of the Object Constraint Language (OCL) that is part of the Unified Modeling Language (UML). We introduce the formal semantics of RT-OCL based on a formal model of UML Class and State Diagrams and provide a mapping to temporal logics. The applicability of our approach is demonstrated by the case study of a manufacturing system with automated guided vehicles.

1 Introduction

In early stages of development of production automation systems, system model behavior is most frequently analyzed by quantitative and qualitative simulation. However, due to the complexity of those systems, simulation can never provide coverage for complete verification for those systems. In recent years, formal verification with equivalence and model checking has received a wide acceptance in the domain of digital circuit and communication protocol design. A model checker verifies a property specification for a given state-oriented model of a system, typically given as a Kripke Structure. The model checker returns either 'true' or generates a counter example in cases when the model does not satisfy the property. The counter example demonstrates an execution of the model that leads to a situation which falsifies the property. This can be most helpful for detailed error analysis. The most remarkable advantage of model checking is that the task of verifying is fully automated. However, model checking has two main obstacles in practical application. The first one is the *state explosion problem* in dependence to the number of possible inputs. The second one is due to the specification of properties in *temporal logics*, since it often turns out that designers and programmers are not familiar with formal methods and regard it as a task too cumbersome to specify and understand properties in temporal logics.

H. Ehrig et al. (Eds.): INT 2004, LNCS 3147, pp. 206–226, 2004.
© Springer-Verlag Berlin Heidelberg 2004

For production automation systems, the correct *time-critical behavior* of required properties is of particular interest. This is already important in early phases of development to avoid expensive and time-consuming changes to the system under development at later stages. Though classical model checking is mainly for the verification of cycle-accurate behavior *without* timing properties, there are a few tools like the RAVEN model checker [36] that support the formal verification of time-annotated system models and additionally provide basic timing analysis.

In this article, we present the GRASP[1] approach to formal verification of production automation systems. The GRASP approach covers the design flow for the modeling and formal verification of production automation systems by means of the domain-specific modeling language MFERT[2] with complementary visualization through animation of a virtual 3D model (cf. Figure 1). MFERT is a methodology and graphical language for the description and analysis of production automation systems. For analysis, GRASP focuses on model checking and integrates a model checker by seamlessly embedding it into a graphical environment with 3D animation for virtual prototyping, in particular for the animation of counter examples. The main idea was that in a first step the designer specifies a model in a graphical specification language, namely MFERT. The model, i.e., the MFERT description, is then translated into an annotated state machine-based formalism (i.e., I/O-Interval Structures [38]) for model checking. Additionally, properties are specified and translated into temporal logics (i.e., Clocked Computation Tree Logic, CCTL [37]) for formal verification with the RAVEN model checker. Once the objects in the virtual prototype are associated with the system model, the execution of counter examples can be observed in the virtual prototype animation.

One of the main visions of the GRASP approach was to provide practical means to designers with programming skills to facilitate property specification. We investigated existing related work and developed a pattern-based approach in the early phases of the GRASP project (see Section 2.1 for more details). In a second step, we decided to integrate an extension of the Object Constraint Language (OCL) [42,43] with MFERT for the specification of required properties for production automation systems. OCL was introduced as a language for the specification of constraints in the context of the Unified Modeling Language (UML) de-facto standard [29], focusing on Class Diagrams and on guards in behavioral diagrams. The syntax of OCL comes in a 'programmer-friendly' style using dot-notation and operation calls as known from object-oriented languages. With the wide acceptance of UML, OCL has also received a considerable visibility. However, OCL currently lacks sufficient means to specify constraints over the

---

[1] GRASP (GRAphical Specification and Real-Time Verification for Production Automation Systems) is a project within the DFG Priority Programme 1064 'Integration von Techniken der Softwarespezifikation für ingenieurwissenschaftliche Anwendungen'.

[2] MFERT is short for 'Modell der FERTigung' (German for 'Model of Manufacturing').

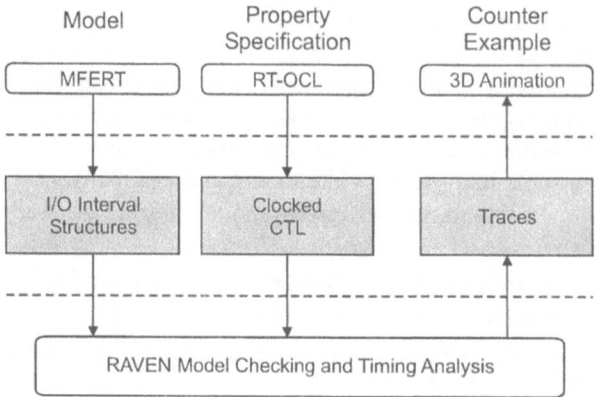

Fig. 1. GRASP Approach to Verification of Production Automation Systems

temporal behavior, i.e., the evolution of state activations and state transitions as well as timing constraints. Since it is essential to be able to specify such timing constraints for time-dependent systems to guarantee correct system behavior, we developed an OCL extension, i.e., RT-OCL, that overcomes this limitation and at the same time keeps compliant with the syntax and semantics of the latest version of OCL, i.e., Version 2.0 [28].

To seamlessly integrate RT-OCL with the domain-specific language MFERT, we defined UML Profiles for both MFERT and RT-OCL and defined mappings to the formal means of I/O-Interval Structures and CCTL, respectively. CCTL was introduced by Ruf and Kropf in [37] for the specification of properties over I/O Interval Structures. CCTL formulae are composed from propositions denoting predicates in combination with Boolean connectives and time-annotated temporal operators. The temporal CCTL operators build upon the common CTL operators and are annotated by timing intervals, such as $AF[a,b]$, where A is a path quantifier ('*on all paths*') and F is the temporal CTL operator ('*eventually in the future*') that is further limited by the timing interval $[a,b]$. For further details of CCTL and its application for real-time model checking we refer to [35,39].

The remainder of this article is structured as follows. The next section discusses related work in the domain of (real-time) property specifications. Section 3 gives an introduction to MFERT with an example. Section 4 introduces syntax and semantics of our temporal OCL extension RT-OCL. Section 5 demonstrates the application of RT-OCL in the context of a production automation scenario with automated guided vehicles. Finally, Section 6 concludes the article and gives an outlook on future work.

2   Related Work

There are already several approaches that make use of graphical captures for model checking, e.g., with Petri Nets or StateCharts [6,3]. Those means are used to define the system by a model. Behavioral property specification, however, is usually still performed by means of temporal logics formulae, mainly in Computation Tree Logic (CTL) or Linear Time Logic (LTL). The most prominent formal method that investigates whether a given model satisfies such property specifications is *model checking* [8]. Model checking takes a set of synchronous finite state machines as a model and (a set of) temporal logic formulae as the specification of required properties. In application, the main obstacles for model checking lie in the *state explosion problem* and in the *adequate specification* of properties by means of temporal logic formulae [33]. Several approaches to support property specification have been developed. In the following subsections, we distinguish the areas of (a) pattern-based specification, (b) graphical property languages, and (c) temporal extensions of OCL.

2.1 Pattern-Based Property Specification

To support temporal logic property specification, some approaches identify *patterns* which provide the user with structured application of formulae. First attempts in pattern classification led to taxonomies that coarsely distinguish between safety and liveness properties. A detailed pattern-based classification is published by Dwyer et al. in [14]. That pattern system is based on the investigation of more than 500 examples for property specification and presents a semantically ordered hierarchy of property patterns. For instance, absence, eventual existence, and global existence of states/events are combined as so-called occurrence patterns.

The idea of patterns was adopted not just to *classify* but also to *construct* specifications for finite state verification. For example, the Testbed Studio is a framework for business process modeling that provides a small set of templates in natural English language for verification with the SPIN model checker [26]. These templates are also denoted as patterns, although they refer to concrete specifications in contrast to the previously mentioned classification patterns. In a more general approach of natural language oriented specification, the PROSPER project aims at the specification through an English language subset [24].

In the early phases of the GRASP project, we developed an interactive visual framework that employs structured English sentences [23] as given in Figure 2. Compared to other pattern-based approaches, we provide a richer set of specifications, in particular, as we additionally cover explicit timing annotations. In contrast to temporal logic formulae-based approaches, non-experts can more easily capture the final sentence in structured English than just by CTL or LTL. Compared to unstructured English, the available structured English fragments give the uneducated user a better guidance through the allowable and non-allowable specifications with less iterations. However, it turned out that this approach leads to quite long sentences and remains too cumbersome for more complex applications, so that we started to investigate alternative approaches.

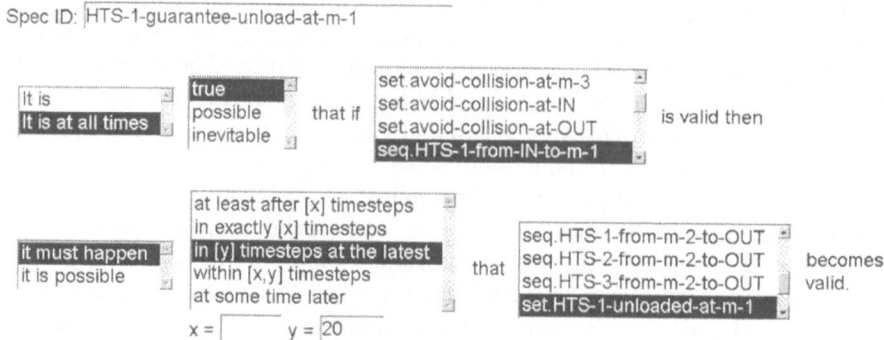

Fig. 2. Specification with Structured English Sentences

2.2   Graphical Property Specification

Regarding property specification by visual means we can distinguish two different kinds of approaches. The first ones are still syntactically based on CTL or LTL specifications. Those frameworks provide support to visually compose segments of specifications, e.g., by enabling and disabling parts of specifications during the development process. In UPPAAL, invariants and reachability properties can be specified using a very limited subset of LTL formulae [27]. To create specifications with this approach, the user must know how to apply and to control temporal logic formulae. Other approaches have an abstract graphical notation, which is translated to temporal logic formulae before checking. Examples are *Symbolic Timing Diagrams (STDs)* [15] and *Life Sequence Charts (LSCs)* [10], which are for StateChart verifications.

2.3   OCL-Based Property Specification

As an alternative to the previous approaches, we investigated UML in combination with OCL for model checking. OCL was originally developed complementary to UML to restrict values of (parts of) a model, e.g., attributes or associations, but has recently been extended towards a more general query and expression language [28]. Several non-commercial OCL tools are currently available that implement syntax and type checks, dynamic constraint validation, test automation, and code generation of OCL constraints. An overview can be found in [31,32][3]. OCL constraints are frequently used in the UML specification documents at the UML metamodel level (M2 layer) to define the static semantics of UML diagrams. Those so-called *well-formedness constraints* specify syntactical restrictions on diagrammatic model elements. There are several approaches

---

[3] See http://www.klasse.nl/ocl and http://www.um.es/giisw/ocltools for updated lists of available OCL tools.

that either extend OCL for temporal constraints specification or introduce alternative UML-based means to express behavioral real-time constraints for UML diagrams.

Ramakrishnan et al. [30] extend the OCL syntax by additional grammar rules with unary and binary future-oriented temporal operators (e.g., `always` and `never`) to specify safety and liveness properties. Ziemann and Gogolla [45] introduce similar temporal operators based on a finite linear temporal logic. Therein, Richter's formal object model [31] is extended to provide a formal definition of system state sequences. However, it is left open *how* system state sequences are exactly derived. A similar approach has been published by Conrad and Turowski in the area of business modeling [9]. Their approach additionally considers past-temporal operators; a formal semantics is not provided.

Distefano et al. [13] define *Object-Based Temporal Logic* (BOTL) to facilitate the specification of static and dynamic properties. BOTL is not directly an extension of OCL. It rather maps a subset of OCL into object-oriented CTL. Bradfield et al. [2] extend OCL by useful causality-based templates for dynamic constraints. A template consists of two clauses, i.e., the *cause* and the *consequence*. The cause clause starts with the keyword `after` followed by a Boolean expression, while the consequence is an OCL expression prefaced by `eventually`, `immediately`, `infinitely`, etc. The templates are formally defined by a mapping to *observational μ-calculus*, a two-level temporal logic with OCL on the lower level.

In the domain of real-time systems modeling, we can find mainly three approaches for temporal constraint specification. Roubtsova et al. [34] define a UML Profile with stereotyped classes for dense time as well as parameterized specification templates for deadlines, counters, and state sequences. Each of the templates has a structural-equivalent dense time temporal logics formula in Timed Computation Tree Logic (TCTL). Sendall and Strohmeier [41] introduce timing constraints on state transitions in the context of a restricted form of UML protocol state machines that define the temporal ordering between operations. Five time-based attributes on state transitions are proposed, e.g., (absolute) completion time, duration time, or frequency of state transitions. Cengarle and Knapp [5] present OCL/RT, a temporal extension of OCL with modal operators `always` and `sometime` over event occurrences. They specify deadlines and time-outs of operations and reactions on received signals. Events are equipped with time stamps by introducing a metaclass `Time` with attribute `now` to refer to the time unit at which an event occurs. In turn, each object can access the set of currently queued events at each point in time.

In contrast to the event-based temporal extensions of OCL, we focus on *state-oriented properties* due to the intended application domain of state-based modeling of production automation systems with MFERT. Note that it is already possible to refer to the states of UML State Diagrams in standard OCL, i.e., the operation `oclInState(stateName)` returns a Boolean value that indicates whether a given state is currently activated or not. However, OCL does not yet integrate the notion of State Diagram states on the language definition level, i.e., the semantics of State Diagram states in the context of OCL expressions is not sufficiently defined so far. To overcome this deficiency, we provided a formal semantics for state-oriented OCL expressions for application with UML State Diagrams in [22].

3   MFERT

Our approach is based on MFERT as the basis for modeling of production automation systems. MFERT is a language and a methodology for the specification and implementation of planning and control assignments in production processes. MFERT is basically a universal approach which has been successfully applied in various projects with different industrial partners [12,11], additionally acknowledged by the German science award of logistics [40]. An MFERT model is based on *production elements* and *production processes*. Production elements represent objects whose properties are changed by processes and transformations. Properties of production elements are described by attributes. A production element obtains its own identity, composed out of the description and the element's correlative status. Using this identity, the different states during the production can be associated to production elements. An MFERT model is a directed bipartite graph of *E-nodes* for elements and *P-nodes* for processes. The graphical notation of an E-node is a triangle. P-nodes are represented as rectangles. Each E-node represents a specific state and can be seen as a container for elements in the respective state. P-nodes represent transformations on elements, performed by the corresponding processes. Nodes are connected by edges that describe exchange relations between two nodes. Edge annotations define if a predecessor is bringing, providing, or waiting for elements and processes, as well as that a successor is fetching, receiving, or waiting for elements. Interface edges are for connecting different levels of hierarchy. They additionally allow the coupling to a real production environment. MFERT-Elements and MFERT-Processes are in certain states, which are characterized by attributes. An attribute denotes a property of an element and assigns a value to a relation. Constructors for the definition of discrete time modes are available. In practice, different time models are required for the definition of production assignments, e.g., the provision of the source materials for an assembly line may take place non-recurringly at the beginning of a shift, while the mounted end products are transported every hour to the delivery store. For implementation, model nodes are equipped with functions and their process control is carried out by means of message exchange between nodes and by a so-called *global manager* that coordinates the computations in the model.

Figure 3 gives the MFERT example of a subsystem for the production of engines with processing steps Milling, Drilling, and Washing. The primary input of the example is modeled by the E-nodes RawEngines and RawShafts. Corresponding processes are used to supply these items into E-nodes EnginesSupplied and ShaftsSupplied. Input and output buffers of processes are modeled by the corresponding E-nodes like ItemsBeforeMill,

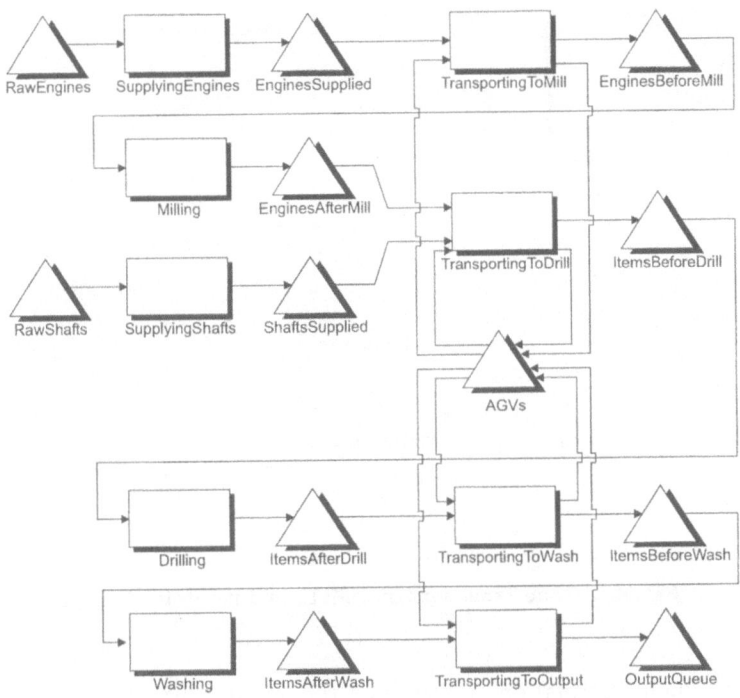

Fig. 3. MFERT Graph of the Case Study

`ItemsAfterMill` etc. The transport between stations and the primary output is modeled by different transport processes like `TransportingToMill` and `TransportingToOutput`. Automated guided vehicles (AGVs) transport items between the different production steps, where the AGV resource management is modeled as a separate E-node.

The input/output behavior of P-nodes is basically defined as time-annotated finite state machines whose graphical presentation is not given in MFERT. For P-node representation, we thus developed a variant of timed UML State Diagrams in [17] to define the local functionality of P-nodes.

In order to be able to give a formal semantics, we have to limit the set of actions and activities of standard UML State Diagrams. We only consider actions and activities that perform (a) requests of P-nodes to put and get elements to and from E-nodes, (b) transfers of production elements between MFERT nodes, and (c) local transformations with a duration. Due to the limited space, we give just a a small example and refer to [17] for more details about the graphical notation, the formal model, and the dynamic semantics of MFERT.

Consider the P-node `TransportingToMill` and its corresponding State Diagram given in Figure 4. The diagram specifies that a transport requires an `AGV` and either an `Engine` or a `Shaft`, where the movement between stations is expected to be executed within 20 to 50 time units. Such basic timing declarations

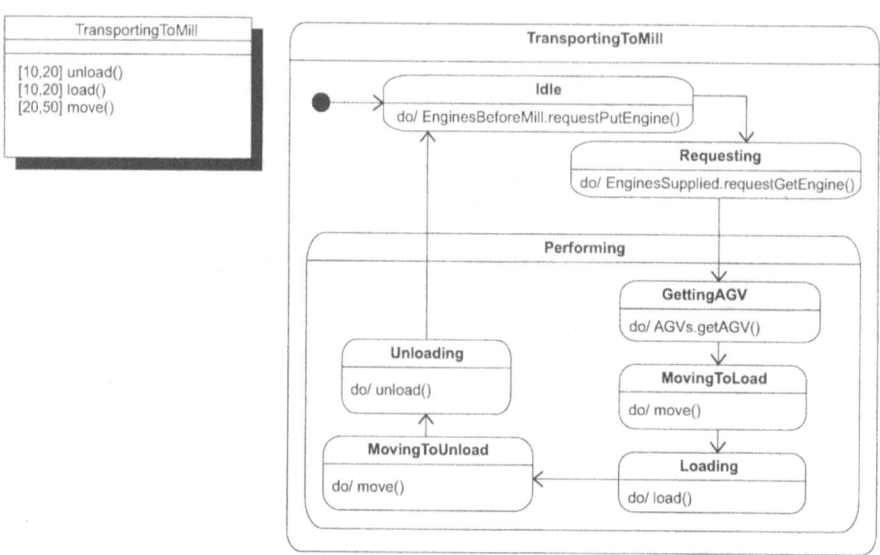

Fig. 4. P-node `TransportingToMill` and its State Diagram

are based upon information gained from the actual physical alignment of the production system.

4   RT-OCL

Figure 5 gives an overview of our formalization approach in the domain of modeling production automation systems. We decomposed the whole approach into four different activity parts. Figure 5 also illustrates the dependencies among the different activities.

First, we integrated the notational concepts of UML State Diagrams into the existing formal description of Class Diagrams by Richters [31]. Basically, the resulting so-called *extended object model* is based upon a set-theoretic definition of the UML metamodel parts for Class Diagrams and State Diagrams. In parallel, we developed a timed variant of UML State Diagrams. Note that this activity is at a lower position in Figure 5 to indicate it as a more domain-specific task, because timing issues are a non-standard concept of UML State Diagrams, while the extended object model basically concerns standard UML. Integrating the two formal models and applying further restrictions leads to our domain-specific notation MFERT, which is provided as a domain-specific UML Profile with stereotypes, e.g., for P-nodes and E-nodes [22]. Additionally, we defined a mapping to the semantic domain of *I/O-Interval Structures* [17].

We have also defined an extension of OCL called RT-OCL that allows for specification of temporal state-oriented properties. For such OCL expressions, we provide a mapping to CCTL formulae. The semantics of the combination of

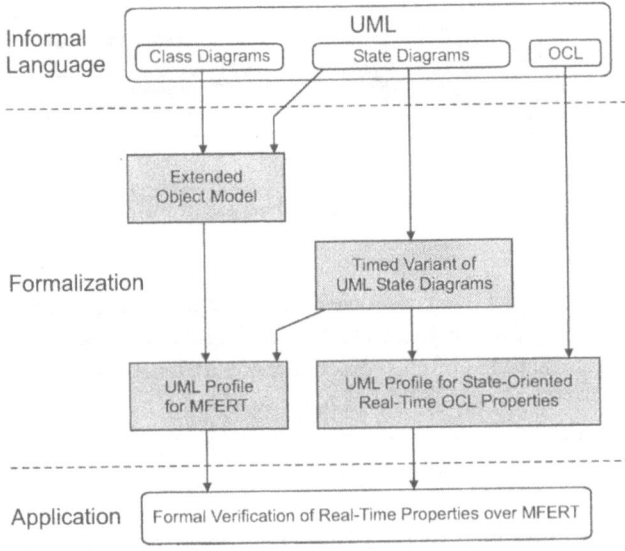

Fig. 5. Overview of the Formalization Approach [16]

MFERT notation and temporal state-oriented OCL expressions is then automatically available, as the two formal target languages already have a well-defined formal relationship, i.e., CCTL formulae have a well-defined semantics over *execution runs* of I/O-Interval Structures. In that context, recall that the model checker RAVEN is able to verify whether a model (a set of I/O-Interval Structures) satisfies a given property (a CCTL formula) [36].

The reminder of this section sketches some details of the definition of RT-OCL and its semantics. But first, we give an introduction to standard OCL in the next subsection.

4.1   OCL

The Object Constraint Language is an integral part of UML [29, Chapter 6]. OCL constraints are defined over a given UML model to restrict the values of object properties. OCL is mainly applied to define invariants for classes and pre- and postcondition of operations. As OCL is a declarative expression-based language, evaluation of OCL expressions does not have side effects on the corresponding UML model.

Each OCL expression has a type. Beyond user-defined model types (e.g., classes or interfaces) and predefined basic types (e.g., `String`, `Integer`, `Real`, or `Boolean`), OCL has a notion of object collection types, i.e., sets, ordered sets, sequences, and bags. Collection types are homogeneous in the sense that all elements of a collection have a common type. A standard library is available with operations to select, access, and manipulate values and objects.

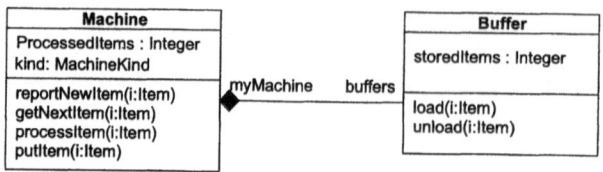

Fig. 6. Sample Class Diagram

Assume, for example, that we have a model with classes `Machine` and `Buffer` and an association between these classes (cf. Figure 6). The following invariant defines that each instance of class `Machine` has at least one associated buffer:

```
context Machine
inv: self.buffers->notEmpty()
```

We briefly outline how to read this OCL constraint. The identifier following the **context** keyword specifies the class for which the constraint is defined. The keyword **inv** specifies that this is an invariant, i.e., for each object of the context class the following expression must evaluate to true 'at any time'[4]. The (optional) keyword **self** refers to the object for which the constraint is evaluated. Attributes, operations, and associations can be accessed by dot notation, e.g., evaluation of `self.buffers` results in a (possibly empty) set of instances of `Buffer`. The arrow operator indicates that a collection of objects is manipulated by one of the predefined OCL collection operations. For example, operation `notEmpty()` returns 'true' if the accessed set is not empty.

Standard OCL currently lacks means to specify constraints over the dynamic behavior of a UML model. Constraints covering the consecutiveness of states and state transitions as well as time-bounded constraints cannot be defined. However, since those are essential to specify a correct system behavior, we have developed a temporal OCL extension that enables modelers to specify state-oriented real-time constraints [19,20]. Because the official UML 1.5 specification [29] did not come with an OCL metamodel, our first idea was to develop an extension of the OCL type metamodel that was presented by Baar and Hähnle in [1]. More recently, in reply to the OMG's OCL 2.0 Request for Proposals, the extensive OCL 2.0 language proposal by Ivner et al. [25] became available, which addresses a seamless integration of OCL to relevant parts of UML. In October 2003, this proposal has been adopted by the OMG as the official OCL 2.0 Specification [28]. Based on the metamodel provided in these documents, we developed a more lightweight approach by defining a UML Profile for our temporal OCL extension [22]. The syntax and semantics of this extension are briefly described in the following two subsections.

---

[4] Note that an invariant may be violated during execution of an operation. The term 'at any time' has therefore to be refined by a dynamic OCL semantics. See our proposal in [18].

4.2 OCL Syntax Extension

The concrete syntax of OCL 2.0 is defined by an attributed grammar in EBNF (Extended Backus-Naur Form) with inherited and synthesized attributes as well as disambiguating rules. *Inherited attributes* are defined for elements on the right hand side of production rules. Their values are derived from attributes defined for the left hand side of the corresponding production rule. For instance, each production rule has an inherited attribute env (environment) that represents the rule's namespace. *Synthesized attributes* are used to keep results from evaluating the right hand sides of production rules. For instance, each production rule has a synthesized attribute ast (abstract syntax tree) that constitutes the formal mapping from the concrete to the abstract syntax. *Disambiguating rules* allow to uniquely determine a production rule in the case of syntactically ambiguous production rules.

The following rule gives the main production rule for temporal expressions we introduced for our RT-OCL extension. The idea is to interpret a future-oriented temporal expression as a kind of operation call. Future temporal OCL expressions map to a new stereotype FutureTemporalExp that is a specialization of OperationCallExp on the abstract syntax level (i.e., the OCL metamodel). For temporal OCL expressions, we introduce a temporal operator '@' to distinguish temporal expressions from OCL's common dot and arrow notation for accessing attributes, operations, and associations.

```
FutureTemporalExpCS ::= OclExpressionCS '@'
                                    simpleNameCS '(' argumentsCS? ')'
Abstract Syntax Mapping:
   FutureTemporalExpCS.ast : FutureTemporalExp
Synthesized Attributes:
   FutureTemporalExpCS.ast.source         = OclExpressionCS.ast
   FutureTemporalExpCS.ast.arguments      = argumentsCS.ast
   FutureTemporalExpCS.ast.referredOperation =
      OclExpressionCS.ast.type.lookupOperation(
                              simpleNameCS.ast,
                              if argumentsCS->notEmpty()
                                 then argumentsCS.ast->collect(type)
                                 else Sequence{}
                              endif )
Inherited Attributes:
   OclExpressionCS.env = FutureTemporalExpCS.env
   argumentsCS.env     = FutureTemporalExpCS.env
Disambiguating Rules:
   -- Operation name must be a (future-oriented) temporal operator.
   [1] Set{'post'}->includes(simpleNameCS.ast)
   -- The operation signature must be valid.
   [2] not FutureTemporalExpCS.ast.referredOperation.oclIsUndefined()
```

Note that an operation call in the abstract syntax has a source, a referred operation, and operation arguments. In this case, the variable ast is re-typed to `FutureTemporalExp` and thus inherits the features `source`, `arguments`, and `referredOperation` from the metatype `OperationCallExp`. These features get the evaluation results of the corresponding parts of the right-hand side of the production rule (cf. the section 'Synthesized Attributes' above).

Additional temporal operations can easily be introduced at a later point of time, as just the disambiguating rule [1] has to be modified in such cases. For instance, `next()` can be introduced as a shortcut for `post(1,1)`, or `post()` as shortcut for `post(1,'inf')`.

4.3 Semantics

While the syntactic integration of the temporal OCL extension is straightforward, the definition of the semantics needs more investigation. The OCL 2.0 specification provides extensive semantic descriptions by both a metamodel-based as well as a formal mathematical approach, but unfortunately, those are currently neither consistent nor complete [18].

In the metamodel-based approach, the semantics of an OCL expression is given by associations between the different modeling layers M1 (user model layer) and M2 (metamodel layer). On the one hand, each value defined in the semantic domain on layer M1 is associated with a type defined in the abstract syntax on layer M2. On the other hand, each evaluation is associated with an expression on the abstract syntax. Given a snapshot of a running system, the associations yield to a unique value for an OCL expression, which determines the result value of expression evaluation.

The second approach gives the *formal semantics* of OCL and is based on set-theory using the notion of an *object model* [28]. An object model is a tuple

$$\mathcal{M} = \langle\, CLASS, ATT, OP, ASSOC, \prec, associates, roles, multiplicities \,\rangle$$

with a set $CLASS$ of classes, a set ATT of attributes, a set OP of operations, a set $ASSOC$ of associations, a generalization hierarchy $\prec$ over classes, and functions *associates*, *roles*, and *multiplicities* that give for each $as \in ASSOC$ its dedicated classes, the classes' role names, and multiplicities, respectively.

The formal semantics of that object model, however, lacks descriptions of ordered sets, global OCL variable definitions, OCL messages, and states of UML State Diagrams. Especially the latter are needed for our RT-OCL semantics. In the remainder, we call an instance of an object model a *system*. A system changes over time, i.e., the (number of) objects, their attribute values, and other characteristics change during system execution. This information is stored in *system states*, i.e., a system state represents a snapshot of the running system that is used to evaluate OCL expressions.

In OCL 2.0, a system state $\sigma(\mathcal{M})$ is formally defined as a triple $\sigma(\mathcal{M}) = \langle \Sigma_{CLASS}, \Sigma_{ATT}, \Sigma_{ASSOC} \rangle$ with a set Σ_{CLASS} of currently existing objects, a set Σ_{ATT} of attribute values of the objects, and a set Σ_{ASSOC} of currently established links that connect the objects. However, this information is not sufficient to evaluate OCL expressions, as system states do not comprise currently activated states and messages that have been sent. We therefore have to extend the formal model and system states accordingly, such that the resulting *extended object model* $\mathcal{M}$ with

$$\mathcal{M} = \langle\ CLASS, ATT, OP, paramKind, isQuery, SIG,$$
$$SC, ASSOC, \prec, \prec_{sig}, associates, roles, multiplicities\ \rangle$$

additionally includes

- functions that give a parameter kind $\in \{in, inout, out\}$ for each operation parameter,
- functions that indicate whether an operation is a query operation without side-effects or not,
- signal receptions for classes with corresponding well-formedness rules, and
- State Diagrams and their association with classes[5].

The formalization of the extended object model is completed by a formal definition of state configurations[6] and an extension of the formal descriptor of a class.

Furthermore, the following information has to be added to system states to be able to evaluate OCL expressions that make use of state-related and OCL message-related operations:

- for each object, the input queue of received signals and operation calls that are waiting to be dispatched[7],
- the state configurations of all currently existing active objects,
- the currently executed operations, and
- for each currently executed operation, the messages sent so far.

The resulting tuple of a *system state* over an extended object model $\mathcal{M}$ is

$$\sigma(\mathcal{M}) = \langle\ \Sigma_{CLASS}, \Sigma_{ATT}, \Sigma_{ASSOC}, \Sigma_{CONF}, \Sigma_{currentOp}, \Sigma_{currentOpParam},$$
$$\Sigma_{sentMsg}, \Sigma_{sentMsgParam}, \Sigma_{inputQueue}, \Sigma_{inputQueueParam}\ \rangle\ .$$

With those extensions, it is possible to define *execution traces* that capture all of those system changes that are relevant to evaluate OCL constraints (see [18] for details). The final formal semantics for our temporal OCL expressions is given in [22,17]. While those articles also provide a general mapping to CCTL formulae, we here give some typical specification examples in the next section.

---

[5] Note that no specific execution semantics for State Diagrams has to be assumed here.

[6] UML only informally defines *active state configurations*. This results in some shortcomings, e.g., it is not considered that final states can be part of state configurations.

[7] As we only need to consider those events that are *relevant* for the evaluation of OCL constraints, implicit events such as completion events generated by State Diagram executions do not have to be considered in this context.

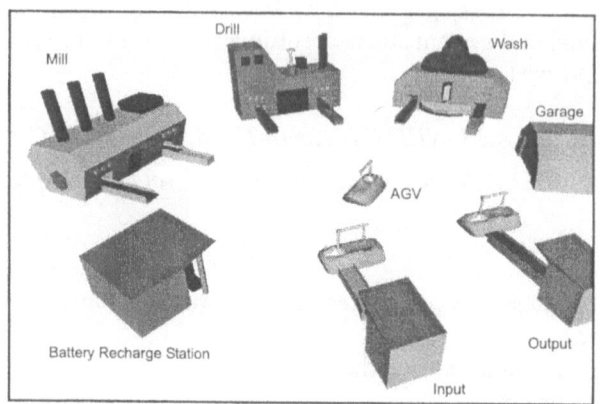

Fig. 7. Virtual 3D Model of the Holonic Manufacturing System

5   Application

We applied the GRASP approach to the case study of a Holonic Manufacturing System (HMS). The HMS case study was introduced by the IMS Initiative in [44]. The HMS is composed of a set of different manufacturing stations and a transport system as it is illustrated by the virtual 3D model in Figure 7. The different manufacturing stations transform items, e.g., by milling, drilling, or washing. Additional input and output storages are for primary system input and output. The flexible transport system consists of a set of automated guided vehicles (AGVs), i.e., autonomous vehicles that carry items between stations. We considered that stations have an input buffer for incoming items and that each AGV can take only one item at a time.

In the following, we provide some typical time-bounded constraints that refer to the MFERT model given in Section 3. We here just refer to the P-node TransportingToMill; similar constraints can be defined for other P-nodes. To outline the mapping, the following also gives the corresponding temporal logic formula in CCTL [35] for each RT-OCL constraint.

1. When TransportingToMill is in state Idle, we require that it gets a grant to put an engine into the subsequent E-node EnginesBeforeMill within the next 100 time units.

```
context TransportingToMill
inv: self.oclInState(TransportingToMill::Idle)
     implies
     self@post(1,100)->forAll(p:Sequence(OclState) |
                         p->includes(TransportingToMill::Requesting))

// CCTL formula:
AG ( (TransportingToMill.state==TransportingToMill.idle)
```

```
        -> AF[1,100](TransportingToMill.state==
                                        TransportingToMill.requesting))
```

2. A transport – once started after the acknowledgments have been received –
   has to be completed within 300 time units.

```
context TransportingToMill
inv: self.oclInState(TransportingToMill::Performing)

        implies
        self@post(1,300)->forAll(p:Sequence(OclState) |
                p->exists(s:OclState | s = TransportingToMill::Idle))

// CCTL formula:
AG ( (TransportingToMill.state==TransportingToMill.performing)
    -> AF[1,300](TransportingToMill.state ==
                                    TransportingToMill.idle))
```

3. The acknowledgment for an available AGV within composite state TransportingToMill::Performing must be received within 150 time units.

```
context TransportingToMill
inv: self.oclInState(TransportingToMill::Performing::GettingAGV)
        implies
        self@post(1,150)->forAll(p:Sequence(OclState) |
            p->exists(s:OclState |
                    s <> TransportingToMill::Performing::GettingAGV))

// CCTL formula:
AG ( ((TransportingToMill_performing.state==
                            TransportingToMill_performing.gettingAGV)
        & (TransportingToMill_performing.activated))
    -> AF[1,150]( (TransportingToMill_performing.state==
                        TransportingToMill_performing.movingToLoad)
            & TransportingToMill_performing.activated
            )
    )
```

Note here, that for technical matters, the activation of composite substate
Performing has to be considered explicitly in the CCTL formula, as explained in [17, Section 7.3].

4. To enforce the production flow, it has to be guaranteed that the mill station
   is continuously served, i.e., at each point of time, state Performing will
   eventually be entered, and at each point of time, state Idle will eventually be
   entered. (The latter condition guarantees that state Performing is eventually
   left again.)

```
context TransportingToMill
inv: self@post()->forAll(p:Sequence(OclState) |
                    p->includes(TransportingToMill::Performing))
```

```
and
self@post()->forAll(p:Sequence(OclState) |
                      p->includes(TransportingToMill::Idle))
```

```
// CCTL formula:
AG AF (TransportingToMill.state==TransportingToMill.performing)
&
AG AF (TransportingToMill.state==TransportingToMill.idle)
```

Further examples of time-bounded state-oriented OCL constraints in the context of other UML and MFERT models can be found in [20,4,17]. In [21], we additionally demonstrated that it is possible to express the property specification patterns of Dwyer et al. [14].

For formal verification of MFERT models and RT-OCL/CCTL specifications, we apply the RAVEN model checker. In RAVEN, additional timing analysis queries help users to extract important time bounds from formal system descriptions. For instance, one might be interested in the maximal number of time steps an item is waiting until it is processed. Other typical problems are minimal and maximal delay times between events, e.g., the maximal time until the first item leaves the process. For intuitive interpretation of counter examples, RAVEN generates execution runs to give the example of a violating path in the state transitions. Additionally, we have extended RAVEN to automatically generate traces which trigger the animation of the virtual 3D model (cf. Fig. 7).

6   Conclusion

We have presented the GRASP approach for the specification and verification of production automation systems combining the domain-specific language MFERT and a temporal OCL extension, i.e., RT-OCL. For application in the context of model checking with the real-time model checker RAVEN, we have defined the semantics of RT-OCL by means of a mapping to Clocked Computational Tree Logic. The approach demonstrates that an OCL extension by means of a UML Profile towards temporal real-time constraints can be seamlessly applied on the M2 layer of UML, i.e., the OCL metamodel. Nevertheless, some extensions have to be made also on the user model level (i.e., M1 layer) in order to enable modelers to use our temporal OCL extensions. The presented extensions are based on a future-oriented temporal logic. However, current work additionally investigates the extension to past-oriented and additional logics.

We have implemented an editor and simulator for MFERT as given in Figure 8. Efficient code generation for RAVEN is currently investigated and under implementation. The code is generated with respect to efficient runtime in BDD composition and model checking considering optimized module and variable orders. The temporal OCL extensions as presented here are integrated into our OCL parser and type checker, which translates constraints with temporal operations to CCTL formulae.

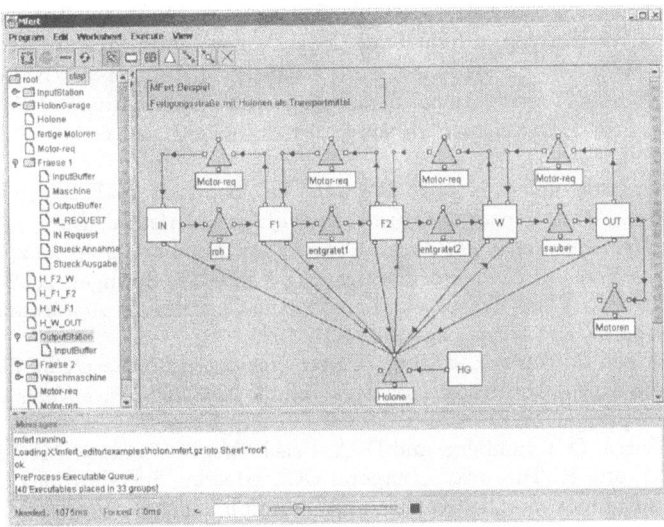

Fig. 8. MFERT Editor and Simulator

Acknowledgements. We thank Henning Zabel for his work on the MFERT editor and simulator.

The work described in this article receives funding by the DFG project GRASP within the DFG Priority Programme 1064 'Integration von Techniken der Softwarespezifikation für ingenieurwissenschaftliche Anwendungen'. In the final phase, the GRASP project received partial contributions from the DFG Special Research Initiative 614 'Selbstoptimierende Systeme des Maschinenbaus'.

References

1. T. Baar and R. Hähnle. An Integrated Metamodel for OCL Types. In R. France, B. Rumpe, J.-M. Bruel, A. Moreira, J. Whittle, and I. Ober, editors, *OOPSLA'2000 Workshop Refactoring the UML: In Search of the Core, Minneapolis, MN, USA*, 2000.

2. J. C. Bradfield, J. Küster Filipe, and P. Stevens. Enriching OCL Using Observational Mu-Calculus. In R.-D. Kutsche and H. Weber, editors, *5th International Conference on Fundamental Approaches to Software Engineering (FASE 2002). Part of the Joint European Conferences on Theory and Practice of Software (ETAPS 2002), Grenoble, France, April 2002*, volume 2306 of *Lecture Notes in Computer Science*, pages 203–217. Springer, 2002.

3. U. Brockmeyer and G. Wittich. Tamagotchis Need Not Die — Verification of STATEMATE Designs. In B. Steffen, editor, *Proceedings of TACAS '98, Lisbon, Portugal, March/April 1998*, volume 1384 of *Lecture Notes in Computer Science*, pages 217–231. Springer, 1998.

4. S. Burmester, S. Flake, H. Giese, W. Schäfer, and M. Tichy. Towards the Compositional Verification of Real-Time UML Designs. In P. Inverardi and J. Paakki, editors, *Joint 9th European Software Engineering Conference (ESEC) and 11th ACM SIGSOFT International Symposium on the Foundations of Software Engineering (FSE-11), Helsinki, Finland, September 2003*, pages 38–47. ACM Press, 2003.

5. M. V. Cengarle and A. Knapp. Towards OCL/RT. In L.-H. Eriksson and P. Lindsay, editors, *11th International Symposium of Formal Methods Europe (FME 2002), Formal Methods: Getting IT Right, Copenhagen, Denmark, July 2002*, volume 2391 of *Lecture Notes in Computer Science*, pages 389–408. Springer, 2002.

6. A. Cheng. Petri Nets, Traces, and Local Model Checking. In *Algebraic Methodology and Software Technology*, pages 322–337, 1995.

7. T. Clark and J. Warmer, editors. *Object Modeling with the OCL. The Rationale behind the Object Constraint Language*, volume 2263 of *Lecture Notes in Computer Science*. Springer, 2002.

8. E. M. Clarke, O. Grumberg, and D. A. Peled. *Model Checking*. MIT Press, 1999.

9. S. Conrad and K. Turowski. Temporal OCL: Meeting Specifications Demands for Business Components. In K. Siau and T. Halpin, editors, *Unified Modeling Language: Systems Analysis, Design, and Development Issues*, pages 151–165. IDEA Group Publishing, 2001.

10. W. Damm and D. Harel. LSCs: Breathing life into message sequence charts. *Formal Methods in System Design*, 19(1):45–80, 2001.

11. W. Dangelmaier and H.-J. Warnecke. *Fertigungslenkung: Planung und Steuerung des Ablaufs der diskreten Fertigung*. Springer, 1997.

12. W. Dangelmaier and H. Wiedenmann. *Modell der Fertigungssteuerung*. Beuth Verlag GmbH, Berlin, Wien, Zürich, 1st edition, 1993.

13. D. Distefano, J.-P. Katoen, and A. Rensink. On a Temporal Logic for Object-Based Systems. In S. Smith and C. Talcott, editors, *Fourth International Conference on Formal Methods for Open Object-Based Distributed Systems (FMOODS 2000), Stanford, CA, USA, September 2000*, pages 305–326. Kluwer Academic Publishers, 2000.

14. M. B. Dwyer, G. S. Avrunin, and J. C. Corbett. Patterns in Property Specifications for Finite-State Verification. In *21st International Conference on Software Engineering (ICSE 99), Los Angeles, CA, USA, May 1999*, pages 411–420. ACM Press, 1999.

15. K. Feyerabend and B. Josko. A Visual Formalism for Real Time Requirement Specifications. In *4th International AMAST Workshop on Real-Time Systems and Concurrent and Distributed Software (ARTS'97)*, Lecture Notes in Computer Science, pages 156–168. Springer, 1997.

16. S. Flake. Modeling and Verification of Manufacturing Systems: A Domain-Specific Formalization of UML. In M. Hamza, editor, *7th IASTED International Conference on Software Engineering and Applications (SEA 2003), Los Angeles, CA, USA, November 2003*, pages 580–586. ACTA Press, Calgary, Canada, 2003.

17. S. Flake. *UML-Based Specification of State-oriented Real-time Properties*. PhD thesis, Faculty of Computer Science, Electrical Engineering and Mathematics, Paderborn University, Shaker Verlag, Aachen, Germany, December 2003.

18. S. Flake. Towards the Completion of the Formal Semantics of OCL 2.0. In V. Estivill-Castro, editor, *27th Australasian Computer Science Conference (ACSC 2004), Dunedin, New Zealand, January 2004*, volume 26 of *Australian Computer Science Communications*, pages 73–82. Australian Computer Science Society, Sydney, Australia, 2004.

19. S. Flake and W. Müller. An OCL Extension for Real-Time Constraints. In Clark and Warmer [7], pages 150–171.

20. S. Flake and W. Müller. Specification of Real-Time Properties for UML Models. In R. Sprague, Jr., editor, *35th Hawaii International Conference on System Sciences (HICSS-35), Big Island, HI, USA, January 2002*. IEEE Computer Society Press, 2002.

21. S. Flake and W. Müller. Expressing Property Specification Patterns with OCL. In *The 2003 International Conference on Software Engineering Research and Practice (SERP'03), Las Vegas, NV, USA, June 2003*, pages 595–601. CSREA Press, Las Vegas, NV, USA, 2003.

22. S. Flake and W. Müller. Formal semantics of static and temporal state-oriented OCL constraints. *Software and Systems Modeling (SoSyM), Springer*, 2(3):164–186, October 2003.

23. S. Flake, W. Müller, and J. Ruf. Structured English for Model Checking Specification. In K. Waldschmidt and C. Grimm, editors, *Methoden und Beschreibungssprachen zur Modellierung und Verifikation von Schaltungen und Systemen, Frankfurt/M., Germany, February 2000*, pages 251–262. VDE Verlag, Berlin, Germany, 2000.

24. A. Holt and E. Klein. A Semantically-Derived Subset of English for Hardware Verification. In *37th Annual Meeting of the Association for Computational Linguistics (ACL'99), University of Maryland, College Park, MD, USA*, pages 451–456, June 1999.

25. A. Ivner, J. Högström, S. Johnston, D. Knox, and P. Rivett. Response to the UML2.0 OCL RfP, Version 1.6 (Submitters: Boldsoft, Rational, IONA, Adaptive Ltd., et al.). OMG Document ad/03-01-07, January 2003. ftp://ftp.omg.org/pub/-docs/ad/03-01-07.pdf.

26. W. Janssen, R. Mateescu, S. Mauw, P. Fennema, and P. van der Stappen. Model Checking for Managers. In D. Dams, R. Gerth, S. Leue, and M. Massink, editors, *Theoretical and Practical Aspects of SPIN Model Checking, 5th and 6th International SPIN Workshops, Trento, Italy, July 1999, and Toulouse, France, September 1999*, volume 1680 of *Lecture Notes in Computer Science*, pages 92–107. Springer, 1999.

27. K. G. Larsen, P. Pettersson, and W. Yi. UPPAAL in a Nutshell. *Springer International Journal of Software Tools for Technology Transfer*, 1(1+2), 1997.

28. OMG, Object Management Group. UML 2.0 OCL Final Adopted Specification. OMG Document ptc/03-10-14, October 2003. ftp://ftp.omg.org/pub/docs/ptc/-03-10-14.pdf.

29. OMG, Object Management Group. Unified Modeling Language 1.5 Specification. OMG Document formal/03-03-01, March 2003. ftp://ftp.omg.org/pub/-docs/formal/03-03-01.pdf.

30. S. Ramakrishnan and J. McGregor. Extending OCL to Support Temporal Operators. In *21st International Conference on Software Engineering (ICSE 99), Workshop on Testing Distributed Component-Based Systems, Los Angeles, CA, USA*, May 1999.

31. M. Richters. *A Precise Approach to Validating UML Models and OCL Constraints*. PhD thesis, Universität Bremen, Bremen, Germany, Logos Verlag, Berlin, BISS Monographs, No. 14, 2002.

32. M. Richters and M. Gogolla. OCL: Syntax, Semantics, and Tools. In Clark and Warmer [7], pages 42–68.

33. D. Rosenblum. Formal Methods and Testing: Why State-Of-The-Art is not State-Of-The-Practise. In *ISSTA'96/FMSP'96 Panel Summary*, ACM SIGSOFT Software Engineering Notes, 21(4), July 1996.

34. E. E. Roubtsova, J. van Katwijk, W. Toetenel, and R. C. de Rooij. Real-Time Systems: Specification of Properties in UML. In *7th Annual Conference of the Advanced School for Computing and Imaging (ASCI 2001), Het Heijderbos, Heijen, The Netherlands, May/June 2001*, pages 188–195, 2001.

35. J. Ruf. *Techniken zur Modellierung und Verifikation von Echtzeitsystemen*. PhD thesis, Universität Karlsruhe, Karlsruhe, Germany, March 2000. (in German).

36. J. Ruf. RAVEN: Real-Time Analyzing and Verification Environment. *Journal on Universal Computer Science (J.UCS)*, Springer, 7(1):89–104, February 2001.

37. J. Ruf and T. Kropf. Symbolic Model Checking for a Discrete Clocked Temporal Logic with Intervals. In E. Cerny and D. Probst, editors, *Correct Hardware Design and Verification Methods (CHARME'97), 9th IFIP WG 10.5 Advanced Research Working Conference, Montreal, Canada, October 1997*, pages 146–166. Chapman and Hall, 1997.

38. J. Ruf and T. Kropf. Modeling and Checking Networks of Communicating Real-Time Systems. In L. Pierre and T. Kropf, editors, *Correct Hardware Design and Verification Methods (CHARME'99), 10th IFIP WG 10.5 Advanced Research Working Conference, Bad Herrenalb, Germany, September 1999*, pages 265–279. Springer, 1999.

39. J. Ruf, T. Kropf, and R. Weiss. Modeling and Formal Verification of Production Automation Systems. (in this volume).

40. U. Schneider. *Ein formales Modell und eine Klassifikation für die Fertigungssteuerung – Ein Beitrag zur Systematisierung der Fertigungssteuerung*. PhD thesis, Heinz Nixdorf Institut, HNI-Verlagsschriftenreihe, Band 16, Paderborn, Germany, 1996. (in German).

41. S. Sendall and A. Strohmeier. Specifying Concurrent System Behavior and Timing Constraints Using OCL and UML. In M. Gogolla and C. Kobryn, editors, *UML 2001 – The Unified Modeling Language. Modeling Languages, Concepts, and Tools. 4th International Conference. Toronto, Canada. October 2001*, volume 2185 of *Lecture Notes in Computer Science*, pages 391–405. Springer, 2001.

42. J. Warmer and A. Kleppe. *The Object Constraint Language: Precise Modeling with UML*. Addison-Wesley, 1999.

43. J. Warmer and A. Kleppe. *The Object Constraint Language – Getting Your Models Ready for MDA*. Object Technology Series. Addison-Wesley, 2nd edition, 2003.

44. E. Westkämper, M. Höpf, and C. Schaeffer. Holonic Manufacturing Systems (HMS) – Test Case 5. In *Proceedings of Holonic Manufacturing Systems, Lake Tahoe, CA, USA*, February 1994.

45. P. Ziemann and M. Gogolla. An Extension of OCL with Temporal Logic. In J. Jürjens, M. Cengarle, E. Fernandez, B. Rumpe, and R. Sandner, editors, *Critical Systems Development with UML – Proceedings of the UML'02 Workshop*, pages 53–62. Technische Universität München, Institut für Informatik, Munich, Germany, 2002.

STOP – Specification Technique of Operational Processes

Stefan Einer

SBB – Swiss Federal Railways, Infrastructure, Bümplizstrasse 45, CH-3000 Bern 65
stefan.einer@sbb.ch

Abstract. The formal technique STOP is a specific application of Coloured Petri Nets [1]. It serves as a methodical specification of operational processes in automation systems. Each concrete specification made by using STOP can be verified with regard to relative completeness and correctness. The present paper introduces the approach and the application domain of STOP as well as its technical characteristics. By discussing experiences made in application of STOP the theoretical introduction of STOP is additionally practically substantiated.

1 Introduction

STOP stands for Specification Technique of Operational Processes. It has been developed at the Institute for Traffic Safety and Automation Engineering, which is a department of the Technical University of Braunschweig in Germany. STOP is one contribution to the priority programme of the German research council which sets up priorities within this LNCS volume and which is called *Integration of Software Specification Techniques for Applications in Engineering.*

STOP is a partial result of the main challenge to develop technical systems continuously in a formal way, which also means to use formalisms for more than software aspects. In order to take up this challenge a set of general methodology concepts called BASYSNET ([2], [3]) has been developed at the above-mentioned institute. By intensifying BASYSNET a framework for defining formal techniques as a specific application of formalisms has been introduced in [4]. STOP is an exemplary result of successful usage of this framework. All technical characteristics of STOP as well as all aspects of the previously raised motivation and used frameworks etc. has been published within the German PHD Thesis [5]. The present paper summarizes the technical part of this work in order to introduce it to a broader community.

In detail, STOP is a formal technique for specification and analysis of operational processes within the field of automation systems. The specification shall show the behaviour of the automation system in all cases of its operation.

The significance of STOP is that it divides the set of scenarios, which make up an operational process, into concurrent processes. The idea of this wellknown principle of concurrency is to compress the complexity of the model as opposed to an explicit specification of all scenarios, but still capturing all scenarios implicitly within the model, so that it is possible to derive them automatically. The specific approach of STOP is to classify each of the concurrent processes either as a so-called *essential*

H. Ehrig et al. (Eds.): INT 2004, LNCS 3147, pp. 227–247, 2004.

process, as a *supervision process* or as a *safety process*. This abstract view is different from the more obvious decomposition of a model into such concurrent processes, which are only classified by the physical component they belong to. The specific approach of STOP was chosen because for capturing the operational process of a complex system the detailed modelling of components-behaviour leads to models with non-suitable information, which are too complex for handling them easily.

The analysis-methods of STOP firstly allow checking the completeness of a model, which is here meant as proving, that each scenario derived from the model ends up in a specified manner. Secondly the analysis-methods allow checking the correctness, which means to prove, that no state of the derived scenarios is an udesired one.

Because Petri nets are a suitable formalism for concurrent modelling they are used as the basis of STOP. To be exact, the formalism is CPN (Coloured Petri Nets) [1]. There is no reason that Petri nets must be the only formalism for putting the idea of STOP into service. Comparable formalisms, which support concurrency, e.g. MSC (Message Sequence Charts) [6], might be used as well. However, as written in [7], Petri nets are developed on a strong mathematical base, which leads to different basic analysis-methods ([8]). Therefore Petri nets are very universal and some of the more specific formalisms fallback on the theory of Petri nets, as e.g. MSC do in [9].

CPN are well known and are also intuitively understandable so they would not be introduced here in detail.[1] Rather, in the following chapter, the application domain of STOP will be explained. Then in chapter 3 and 4 the technical characteristics of STOP separated into notations and methods will be described. Chapter 5 devotes itself to the practical experiences made with STOP by specifying and analysing the operational process of the radio based railway crossing, which is known as one of the two case studies provided from the above mentioned priority programme and which is generally introduced also within this LNCS volume. Finally this paper presents the conclusions.

2   Specifications of Operational Processes

There are different possibilities for dividing automation systems. An overview of technologies of automation systems is given by [10]. From the technological point of view engineering and computer science are joining each other very tightly, which can be seen clearly by terms as e.g. *process informatics* ([11], [12]). Therefore the automation science has to take care of complex tasks in information theory [13]. That leads to the neccessity to combine the engineering sciences and the computer science also at a theoretical level. STOP is such a combination because it supports the engineering task of abstract process design by using computer aided modelling and analysis. The following subchapters explain the named engineering task by firstly introducing the term *operational process* and secondly by describing the task of specifying the operational process. Then the approach in formalising this specification process will be shown.

---

[1]   In order to get a close description also for readers beeing not familiar with CPN essential aspects of this formalism are explained by footnotes if it is needed for understanding a certain statement.

2.1 The Operational Process in Automation Systems

One possible functional division of automation systems is to differentiate between: 1. *process* 2. *command and control functions* and 3. *environment* ([2]). The scope of automation systems defined by this concept is the same that is used within the present paper, but the process term is used differently here. The notion *process* within this paper describes not only the behaviour of the part of the system that is to be controlled and what can be called the process in a closer sense, but also the behaviour of the control system itself. This holistic view is sensible, because the general objective of the automation system integrates two different objectives. These two objectives are firstly the objective of the process in the closer sense, which is generally the transport or transformation of energy, material, or information ([14]) and secondly the objective of the automation which is the economy and quality of the process. To limit the scope of the automation system to only one of these objectives can lead to the missing of optimisation of the whole system. Therefore by definition a view of the whole system must include the holistic behaviour. This behaviour is here called *the operational process*. It terms the process in broader sense integrated within its environment and therefore the behaviour of the whole automation system. But merging the different views cannot be done without using another structuring approach, because operational processes are too complex to handle them trivially in a holistic way. Therefore STOP introduces the approach to divide the operational process into concurrent parts, which are either so-called *essential* or which are serving the *supervision* or the *safety*. This concept follows the objective that beside the objective of the automation system the operational process also has to guarantee the safety of the system and its environment ([15]).

2.2 Aspects of Specification of Operational Processes

Specifying is principally an evolutionary process. Especially the non-standardised part of this process falls within the field of creative activity [16]. So the focus of standardisation of the process shall be to guide and support the creative activity and not to replace it. Because of that it is assumed that the basis of the specification of the operational process is a concept of the operational process that is principally sufficient for reaching the objective of operation.

First of all the concept of the operational process intends target behaviour under ideal conditions, here called *normal behaviour*. Moreover with the concept it is regularly known which states of the system are generally prohibited because they are dangerous or otherwise undesired. Additionally the concept tells us which behavioural aspects of the operational process cannot be specified deterministically. On the one hand these aspects are failures, because it happens always spontaneously. On the other hand it can be events within the environment that can take place due to being out of focus of the control from the control system. This includes the operational behaviour of humans within the automation system, because their handling includes lot of potential variations.

Coming from the concept the first task in order to specify the operational process is to analyse how the normal behaviour is influenced by the nondeterministic properties of the system. Because of these properties states regularly become possible which are prohibited or miss the possibility to progress to target states. In this case the specification must determine the system behaviour which prevents the prohibited states and which closes the gap between the dead end and the target states. Therefore alternative scenarios that include processes of supervision and safety supplement the straight lined normal scenario. At the end the specification of the operational process is a set of scenarios. It is closed if all possible system states in which the ongoing behaviour is undetermined or inadmissible can be excluded with certainty.

2.3 Approach of Formalising the Specification

The motivation in formalizing the specification is caused by the difficulties of the conventional specification process. One main direct problem is to proof conventional specifications to its correctness and completeness.

Within the present paper completeness is meant as the property that in every state of the system that is reachable because of the specification the ongoing states are also defined by the specification. Correctness of the specification means here that the system will not come in states, which are forbidden, if it behaves in accordance to the specification. Therefore, in order to check the correctness, forbidden states must be defined, for example from a safety point of view.

Checking out the completeness and correctness of the specification is difficult because automation systems have a wide range of possible behaviour and therefore the size of information for the specification is also a wide range. This is mainly because the fact those deviations from the ideal behaviour of the system are appearing nondeterministically. The deviations firstly lead to behavioural variations because of the direct changing of the essential process and secondly because of the changing of the supervision and safety processes which has to be specified as a result of the first changing. All in all, the nondeterministic deviations lead to an exponential increasing of the amount of possible system behaviour.

Because of the wide range of the possible system behaviour the specification consists of a set of scenarios that cannot be easily overlooked. However, today the engineers decide about the completeness and correctness of this set mostly only by their experience. This weak situation would be improved if the engineers were supported in their specification and proving tasks by a computer aided method.

To reach this goal it is necessary to form the process and the result of the specification that the completeness and correctness of the specification can be verified automatically. The approach used here in realising such ability is a step-by-step specification process shown in fig. 1.

The first step of the proposed specification process is *the modelling*. Firstly it serves the purpose to bring methodically the application knowledge into a formal model, which describes the operational process holistically. This model is then a first design of the correct and complete specification of the operational process. Moreover the modelling serves secondly as the *specification of the model requirements*. The latter specification possibly contains requirements that originate from the application knowledge of the engineer like the model of the operational process does. The other parts of the Specification of the model requirements are related to the form of the model of the operational process. This part can be automatically derived for each single case from generic requirements valid for all models, which are created by using STOP. That is the main gain in using STOP because the latter requirements are also specific for the application but they are not needed to be known explicitly for each single application by the engineer but only in general as knowledge about formal marks.

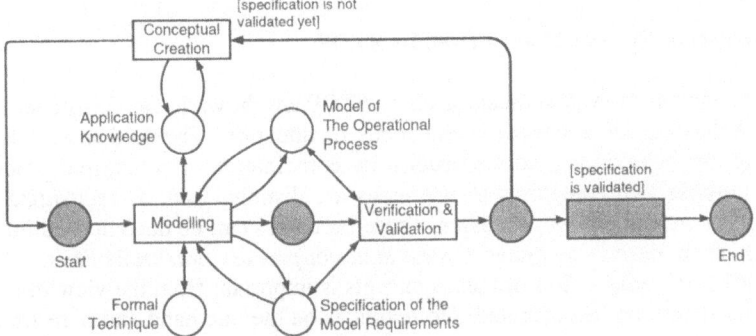

Fig. 1. Approach of the formal specification process

Formal verification of the model of the operational process against the specification of the model requirements is a part of the second step within the specification process. In case of success the verification is followed by a more or less informal validation of the model of the operational process. The validation is a proof of the model against the complete concept. In difference to the verification it is not the proving of completeness of the already specified parts of the operational process but the proving if all parts have been specified.

If the present state of the model of the operational process cannot be verified or if the validation reveals a not completly sufficient specification this result must be interpreted related to the application. Then the concept of the operational process must be supplemented. Followed by that the model of the operational process and the specification of the model requirements will be methodically supplemented as well, this means an iterative cycle of the specification process.

Once the verification and validation leads to success the specification process is done. In this case the model of the operational process is the complete and correct specification of the operational process.

The following chapters show how the presented approach of formal specification is realised by the formal specification technique STOP.

3 The Notation of STOP

The notation of STOP, i.e. the notation of a formal technique, is more than the notation of the basically used formalism. The notation of STOP includes a specific definition and interpretation of elements or constructions of the formalism CPN from a view of a general system theory ([11], [17], [18]). Therefore concepts of system theory can be identified which are typical of STOP as well as the familiar formalism.

The next subchapter gives an overview about the concepts of system theory used by STOP. In the first place these concepts are described independently from the formalism. Then, within the following subchapter, it is shown, how the used concepts of system theory are realised as modelling concepts by the utilisation of CPN. The generic patterns used to explain the modelling concepts are called *design patterns* within the present paper.

3.1 Concepts of System Theory Used by STOP

The basic concepts of system theory used by STOP are shown in fig. 2. Altogether the potential behaviour of a system is the focus of attention. The further approach in structuring this behaviour is to construct it by combination of concurrent processes. For that purpose two categories of processes are distinguished: 1. *sequential processes* and 2. *communication processes*. These processes can be decomposed into elements, which are describing either *process states* or *process state transitions*.

The further decomposition of these concepts is important from the view of causality. Process states can be separated into *activities* on the one hand and pure *states* on the other hand. Activities are focussing continuous subprocesses onto a discrete abstraction level, but pure states are static.

Process state transitions are distinguished between *events* and *reactions*. Furthermore events are separated into *endogenous* and *exogenous events*. Endogenous events occur within the system, while exogenous events are related to the system environment.

Process elements can be further specialised. The sort of specialisation depends on the process category to which the process element belongs. It is exemplary shown in fig. 2 but shall not be discussed here in more detail.

Last but not least, uncoupled from the previously described aspects of structure, decomposition and causality, the temporal concepts shall be added. The basic statement concerning this is that process states have duration, while process state transitions occur in an instantaneous moment.

3.2 Basic Desing Patterns

Two kinds of design patterns have been developed during the development of STOP. Firstly such design patterns, which define the basic approach in actually putting in service the concepts of system theory. Secondly there are such design patterns, which serve the purpose of optimising the basic design patterns in order to reach goal-directed model behaviour. Concretely speaking these design patterns serves the limitation of the state space of the model and the control of conflicts between subscenarios. In order to point out the main aspects of STOP the following paragraphs describe only the basics of the firstly mentioned design patterns. They are structured by the aspects: *structure* (including *decomposition*), *causality* and *temporality*, because these are suitable aspects in differentiating special features of Petri nets.

3.2.1 Model – Structure Composed by Coupled Processes. Each specification built by using STOP is described through one single Petri net. As previously described by explaining the concepts of system theory such a net consists of sequential processes and communication processes. Fig. 3 shows an example design pattern, in which two sequential processes are connected by one communication process.

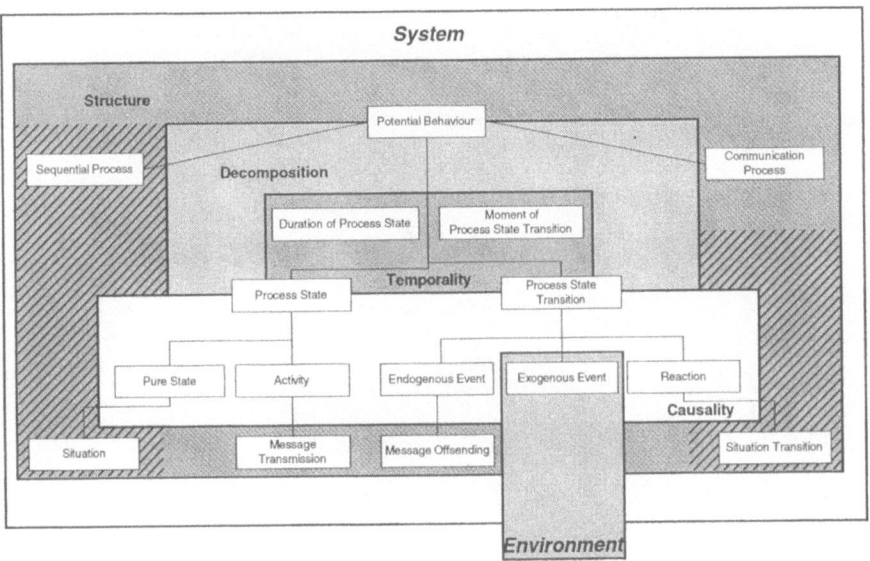

Fig. 2. Concepts of system theory used by STOP

The sequential processes are constructed as an example, i.e. their inner structure can be different. The essential point is that every sequential process is a state machine, i.e. there is never a branching at a transition.[2] A sequential process has one *starting place* and at least one *ending place*. All elements of the sequential process are connected in a unique running direction. The starting place of a sequential process is provided with the *initial marking* of the process, which is a local part of the global *initialisation marking*.

Aside from the communication processes there is another kind of coupling sequential processes named *feedbackfree statecoupling*. It is also shown in fig 3. The coupling element between the sequential processes of such coupling is a so-called *status place*. The token providing the status place is carrying the information of the present status of a certain sequential process (here sequential process 1). By connecting the status place to other sequential processes (here sequential process 2) the behaviour of the latter processes can be conditioned by the first one.

3.2.2 Causal Meaning of Model Elements. A transition belongs to one sequential process either exclusively or to one or more communication processes additionally (fig. 4). In each case a transition has exactly one pre-place and exactly one post-place of the sequential process it belongs to. Further more it has at most one pre-place of a communication process and maybe one or more post-places of communication processes, which then each of them must belong to different communication processes.

---

[2] A *transition* is one from the two disjunctive kinds of nodes of a Petri Net. Considering CPN the other one is called *place*. Places, mostly visualised as circles or ellipses, describe potential local states, which are reached, if the places are provided with a certain set of tokens. Transitions are able to change the marking of the places which surrounding them, i.e. they describe potential transitions from one local state of the Petri Net to one other. Transitions are mostly visualised by rectangles.

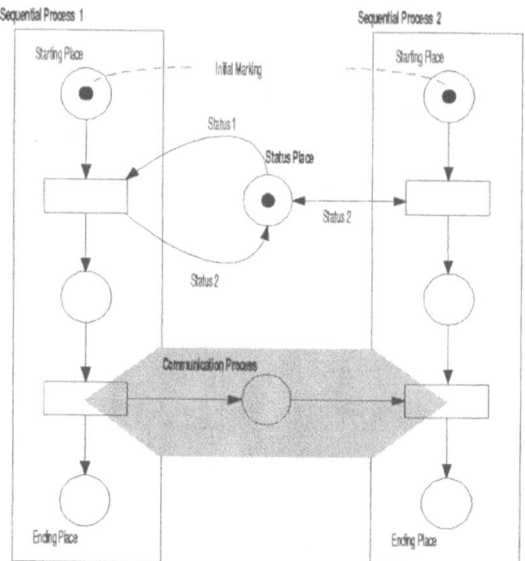

Fig. 3. Basic design pattern of an example model-structure

Within the above-described concept of system theory used by STOP on the one hand process states have already been distinguished between activities and states and on the other hand process state transitions have been distinguished between events and reactions. These differentiations determine the causality of the model of the operational process and leads to the corresponding interpretation of the meaning of CPN-elements, i.e. places on the one hand and transitions on the other hand. As well as events reactions are described by transitions. Activities and states are described by places. In more detail each transition depicts exactly one event and possibly one or more reactions relating to the other processes that are containing the transition.

3.2.3 Temporal Meaning of Model Elements.

The duration of a process state and the time of a process state transition are generally not modelled absolutely, but they are fixed by two aspects: Firstly by the temporal aspects of some concrete model elements, which are modelled as a part of the model structure and secondly by the concrete model dynamics. The latter one is not determined by some single elements, but by all of them and by the initialisation marking of the Petri net.

Within the present subchapter the temporal aspects described by the structure of the model is been shown. Events and therefore also reactions of exogenous events have no temporal marks of their own. Their occurring time is determined by the elements surrounding them. Endogenous events are determined by the duration of that one process pre-state, which is an activity. Analogously the occurring time of exogenous events is determined by the duration of their single process pre-state.

The temporal marks of activities are shown in fig. 5. Because of the attributing of the input-arc of the place describing an activity the time stamp of that token which starts the activity gets a value that differs from the starting time of the activity by as much as the activity lasts. So this value, which is the number within the attribution of the input-arc, describes the duration of the activity (fig. 5(a)).

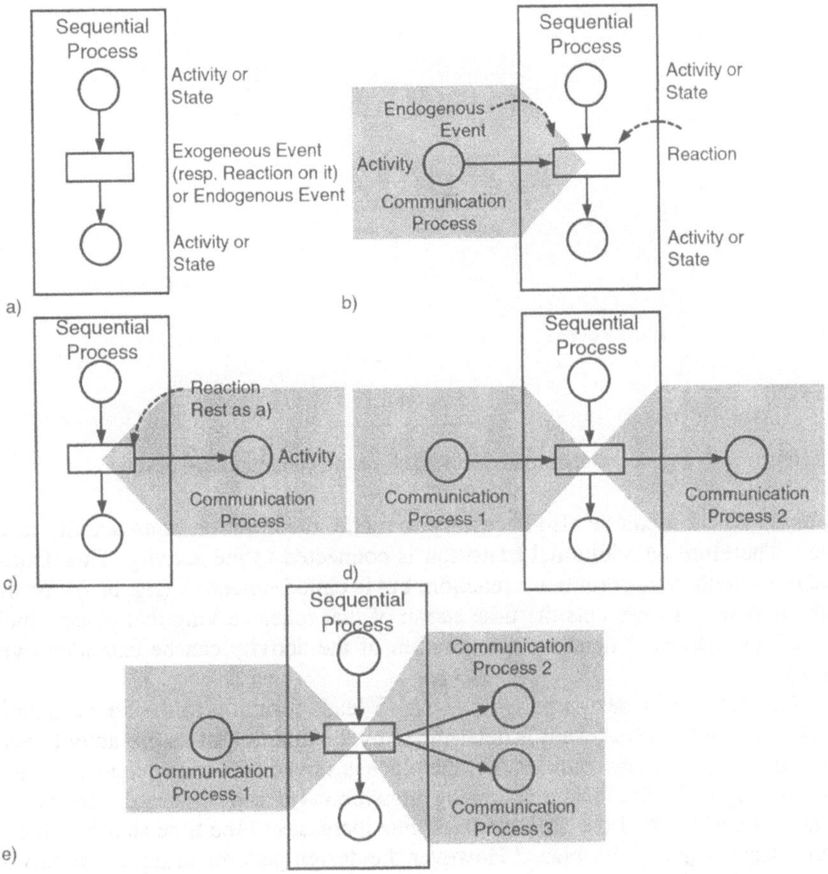

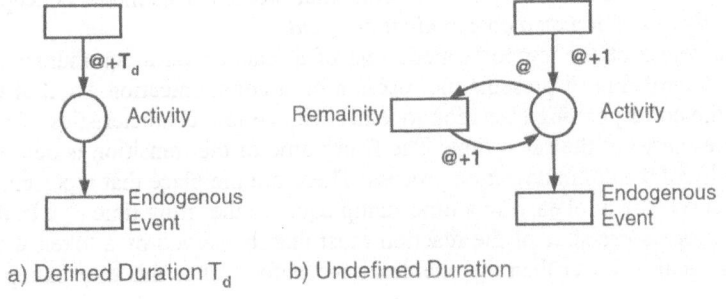

Fig. 4. Design patterns of causality

Fig. 5. Temporal marks of activities

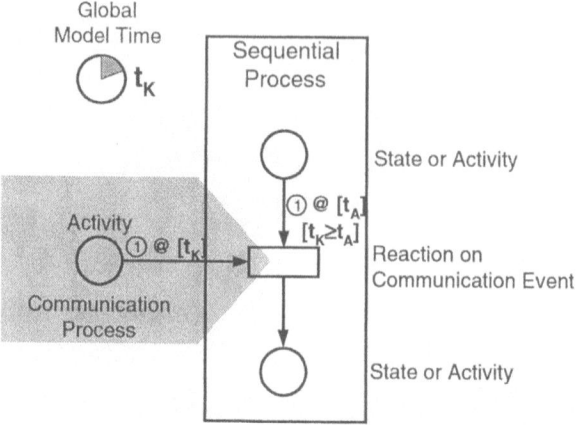

Fig. 6. Temporal marks of reactions on communication events

Using STOP it can be also necessary to model the duration of an activity as unde-fined. Therefore an additional transition is connected to the activity. This Transition describes neither an event nor a reaction, but is called *remainity* (fig. 5(b)). By firing[3] it the remainity increments the time stamp of that token serving that place which de-scribes the activity. Therefore the duration of the activity can be extended dynami-cally.

Using the shown design patterns in fig. 5 leads formally to the above mentioned fact that an endogenous event is determined by the duration of its pre-activity because if the activity is actually running, i.e. the place is served by a token, the only condition for enabling the firing of the following transition which describes the following en-dogenous event is that the *global model time* increases to the time stamp of the token which serves the activity-place.[4] However the design patterns in fig. 5 are only valid, if the endogenous event is part of a sequential process. If the endogenous event is part of a communication process the statements relating to fig. 5 are still true but they have to be extended (fig. 6). In such case the endogenous event as part of a communication process is causally connected to a reaction on this event, which is described by the same transition and which is part of a sequential process. This model concept shall be shortly called *reaction on a communication event*.

In the centre of the temporal modelling of a reaction on a communication event stands a guard[5]. Fig. 6 presents the reaction on a communication event at the firing time of the corresponding transition together with certain characteristics of the tokens of the pre-places at the same time. The firing time of the transition is determined by the activity of the communication process. Therefore the place that represents this ac-tivity is served by a token with a time stamp equal to the firing time (t_K). In this situa-tion the process-pre-state of the reaction must than be served by a token whose time stamp is equal or lower than the one described before. Thus this time stamp does not

---

[3] Firing of a transition names the actual changing of tokens by a transition in a running Petri Net.

[4] In theory of CPN the global model time is incremented if no transitions is enabled to fire at the present global model time

[5] A guard is an additional firing condition of a transition.

prevent the firing of the transition and above all it is not a contribution to the triggering of the firing at any time. Otherwise the transition would lose its role as a reaction on side of the sequential process and act as an event. The aforesaid guard ($[t_K \bullet t_A]$) prevents such behaviour in any case.

4 Methodology of STOP

The methodology of STOP is fixed by a process-model that combines elementary methods. Within the present paper firstly the elementary methods will be introduced separated as methods of modelling and methods of proving. Secondly the process-model will be sketched. All methods are discussed in general, because in detail they are more related to implementation of STOP than to scientific knowledge.

4.1 Methods of Modelling

STOP comprises the following methods of modelling: 1. *modelling of scenarios*, 2. *modelling of restrictions* and 3. *modelling of potential deviations*.

The modelling of scenarios serves the systematical transformation of the scenario knowledge into the Petri net model that bases on concurrent processes. This method is mostly made of a set of transformation rules but it also includes the automatic configuration of some temporal aspects of the Petri net model and includes therefore also analytical parts. Considering the modelling of scenarios, not only the concepts of system theory but also the domain specific basis of STOP is important to be looked at. It says that each sequential process within the model is either a so-called *essential process* or a *supervision* or a *safety process*. Models built by using STOP are therefore abstract objects, which include processes that do not need to be structurally equal to physical processes.

Also the modelling of restrictions serves the transformation of application knowledge into the Petri net model. But in contrast to the modelling of scenarios this method is not focused to sequential process but to certain functional requirements, which necessity will be revealed by the model proving.

The modelling of potential deviations exists because STOP intends to increase the scope of a model stepwise. This is to be done by supplementing a present model by variation of some local behaviour aspects, which is supported by the named method. The effects of these variations then will be proved analytically by one certain method of proving, as described in the following subchapter.

4.2 Methods of Proving

Model Proving comprises two methods of verification that have been already mentioned in chapter 2.3. On the one hand the proving of admissibility of each global state of the model, which is termed by *correctness* within the present paper, and on the other hand the proving of a correct termination of the model-behaviour, which is herein termed *completeness*.

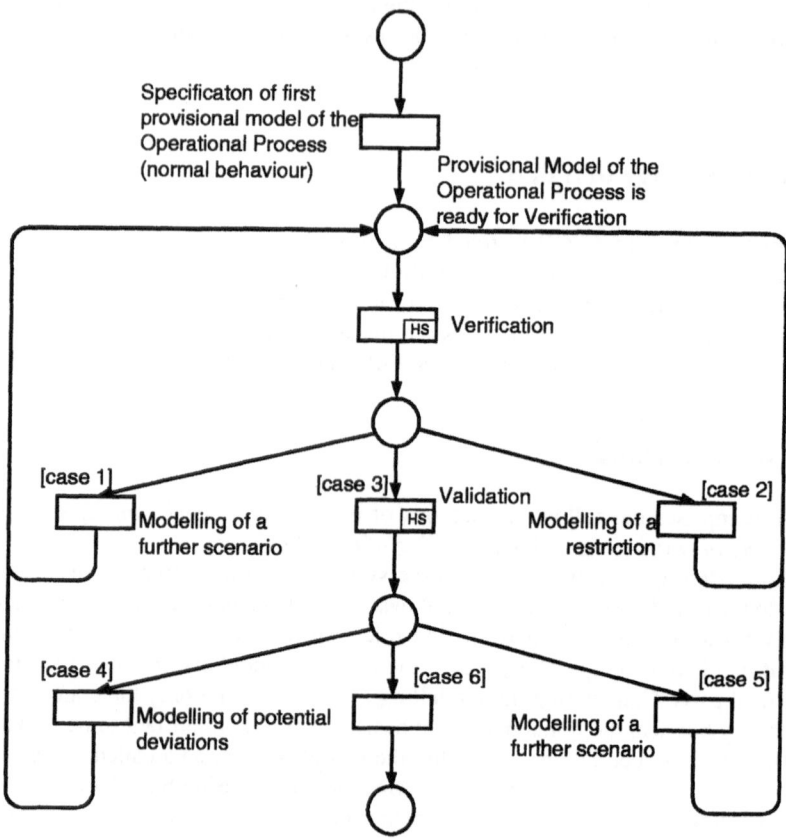

Specification is initiated

Specificaton of first provisional model of the Operational Process (normal behaviour)

Provisional Model of the Operational Process is ready for Verification

HS   Verification

[case 1]

[case 3]   Validation

[case 2]

Modelling of a further scenario

Modelling of a restriction

[case 4]

[case 6]

[case 5]

Modelling of potential deviations

Modelling of a further scenario

Specification is finished

Fig. 7. The process-model of STOP in a top level view

Both methods of verification prove global effects on local changes of a model. The proofs are based on analysis of the occurrence graph[6] of the Petri net model.

For proving the correctness, permitted global states must be specified beforehand. Against which the criteria of verifying the relative completeness can be derived from the form of the model. Like this a model would be discovered as incomplete. For example if the guard that describes the temporal condition of a transition, which again describes a reaction in application, prevents the firing of the transition in certain possible running sequences of the model. This reveals that the specified reaction, which

---

[6] The occurrence-graph of a petri net is the transformation of the potential behaviour of the petri net into a static view. The initialisation marking and each possible global marking of the Petri Net, which can be reached from the initialisation marking by any sequences of transition firing is a so-called *global-state* and is in each single case represented by one node in the occurrence-graph. The orientated connections from one node to another in the occurrence graph then show the possible changes of one global-state into some other by firing in each case a certain transition, whose identity is related to the corresponding connection.

is represented by the transition, cannot occur in each case when the pre-places of the transition have been served by tokens. That means that an alternative reaction to the first one also has to be specified and has been missed until now.

Beside the verification the methodology of STOP also supports validation. However the validation is not really formal but is supported by the formal representation of the model. The validation also serves the completeness of the model. Related to this aspect, as mentioned in chapter 2.3, the difference between verification and validation is here that by validation the model is proved to aspects which completely has not been modelled up to now, whereas the verification proof the completeness of already modelled aspects.

4.3 The Process-Model of STOP

Fig. 7 shows the process-model of STOP in the top-level view. It is a specialisation of the process-model in fig. 1, which is describing the approach of the formal specification process. In this view each method of modelling of STOP can be found explicitly, while the methods of proving are only shown by their differentiation in verification and validation.

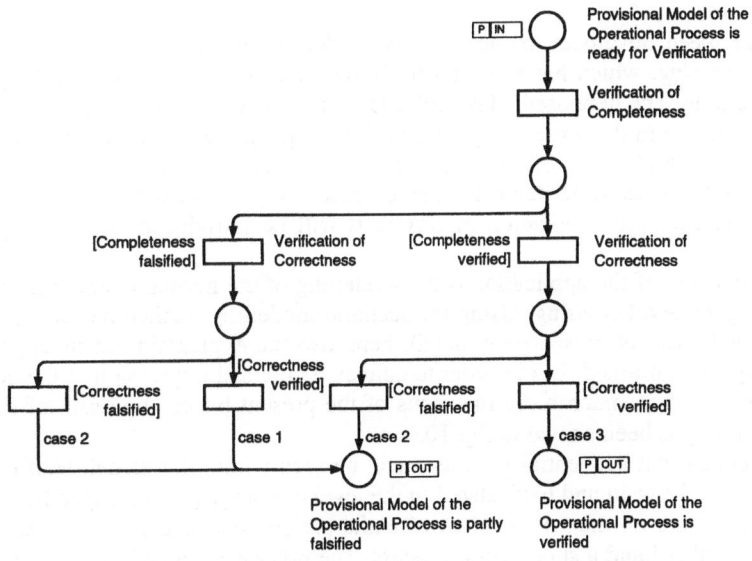

Fig. 8. The verification-process-model of STOP

Therefore fig. 8 shows a refinement of the verification-process and fig. 9 is detailing the validation-process. Both pictures are self-explanatory related to the question of which method is used when. Why the methods are used in that order will not be discussed in more detail here, because it depends much more on technical aspects than on scientific effort.

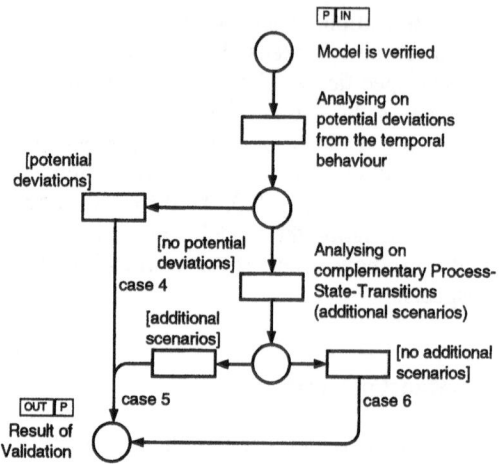

Fig. 9. The validation-process-model of STOP

5   Experiences in Application of STOP

STOP has been developed inductively by modelling of the case study *radio based railway crossing*, which has been generally introduced separately within the present LNCS volume. The here used CPN tool is DesignCPN, Version 4.0 ([19]).

However within the present paper we will not explain the experience of developing STOP but the application of STOP as a fully developed method. Therefore after finishing STOP for the time being the named case study has also been used for documenting an example application of STOP. It will be introduced within the present chapter.

The first step of the application is the modelling of the normal operational process of passing the level crossing. Using the scenario modelling method has done this. As this method was not presented in detail, here also the explanation of its application shall only be mentioned. But in order to convey a practical impression of the notation of STOP, which is much more the focus of the present paper, the result of the first modelling step is been shown in fig. 10.

Four concurrent sequential processes can be seen within the model. Half of them are related to the train and half related to the level crossing. The train specific sequential processes are on the one hand an essential process that is called *train movement* and on the other hand a supervision-process. The processes related to the level crossing cover one supervision- and one safety-process, which are named *lc-supervision* and *lc-safety*. The reason for the difference between the process categories of the train and the level crossing is that the train passes the railway crossing unhindered within the normal operational process, i.e. without using safety functions, while otherwise the level crossing has no other essential functionality as the saving of the train by itself. By using the communication processes the concrete model dynamics, i.e. the order of events and reactions are coordinated.

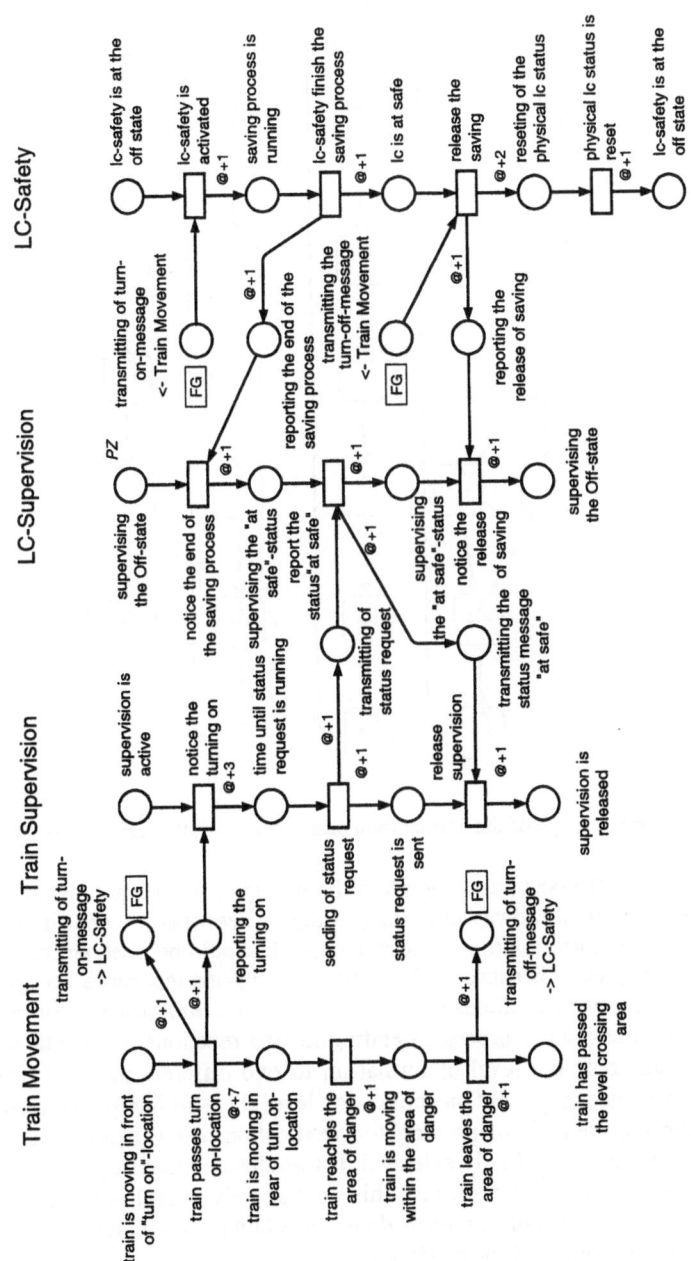

Fig. 10. Model of the normal operational process of passing the railway crossing

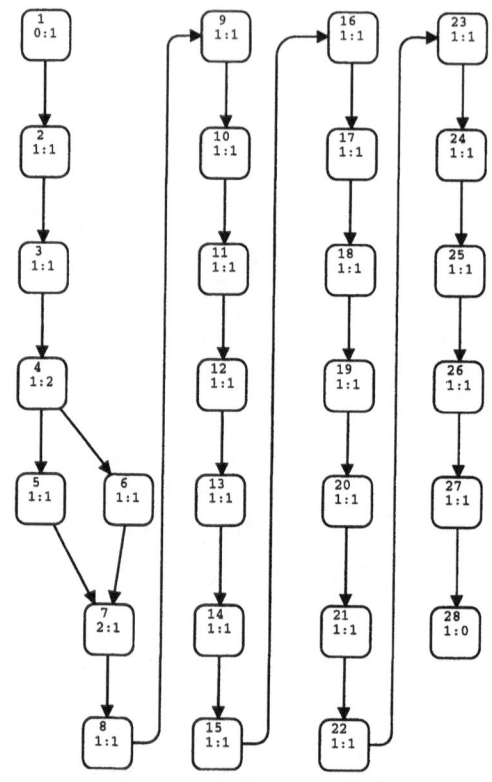

Fig. 11. Occurrence graph of the normal train passage through the railway-crossing model

Fig. 11 presents the occurrence graph of the model of the normal operational process. Because the normal railway crossing passage is described by one single scenario the structure of the corresponding occurrence graph should be a sequence. In fact it is only nearly a sequence because CPN as interleaving-models serve no global state transition by firing two transitions at once. But the event *train passes turn-on location* causes two communication processes ending in two reactions that occur simultaneously. This leads onto the level of formalism to two different paths of firing order within the occurrence graph, but on application level it is still interpreted a sequence.

After using the methods of proving for verification and validation the model of normal behaviour has been firstly extended. It was changed that way that the train can change its speed at any times because this corresponds to real potential behaviour. The extension of the model has been done by adding *remainities* to each activity within the Train Movement Process (fig. 12[7]).

Considering the extension of its possible behaviour the system can reach the forbidden state that the train is moving within the area of danger while the level crossing is not at safe. This can be found by trying to verify that the model behaviour never reach a global state where the place *lc at safe* is not served by a token while the place

---

[7] Grey colored parts have been modelled before.

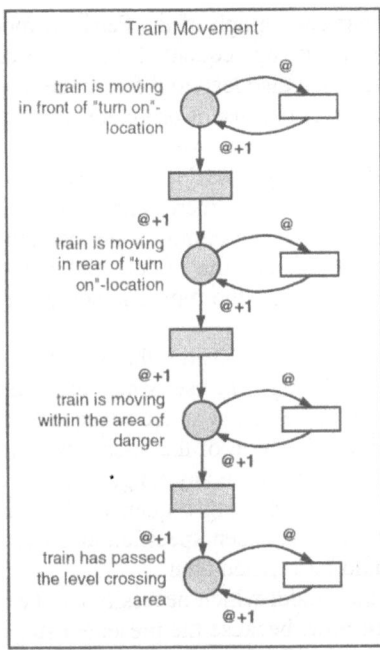

Fig. 12. Modelling of the potential temporal deviations in train movement

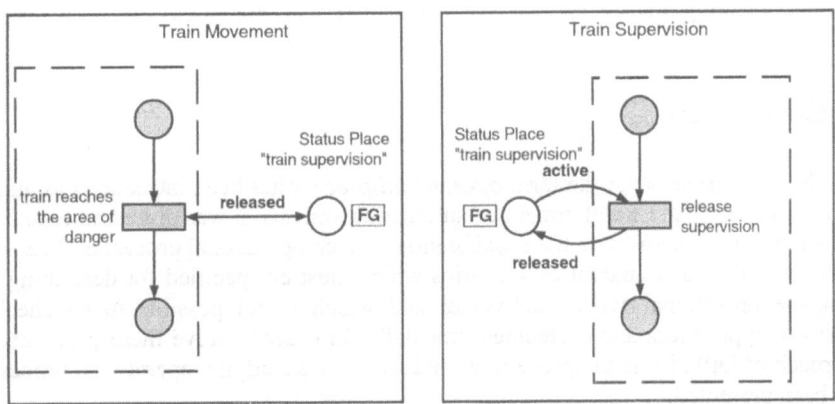

Fig. 13. Modelling of the restriction related to the train entry

train is moving within the area of danger is. This verification failed for the moment, so a further extension of the model, i.e. an extension of the specification, must have been done by modelling a restriction. This restriction describes the functional requirement that the train is to be hindered in running into the area of danger if the level crossing is not at safe or the other way round that the supervision of the train must be released before the train is running into the area of danger in every case. This restriction is modelled by a feedbackfree status coupling as shown in fig. 13.

Fig. 14 shows the occurrence graph of the Petri net model after modelling the restriction. Its character is still being sequential, but some branches can be seen which partly join again but which can also lead to different dead ends. This is not fully interpretable onto application level because it originates from different concepts of STOP like the herein introduced *remainity* as well as the just mentioned concept of limiting the state space. All in all, by using STOP it is not useful to analyse occurrence graphs by its shapes visually, but the evident increasing of possible paths through the occurrence graph is comparable to the increasing of the potential behaviour of the system. One benefit of STOP is that this amount of potential behaviour must not be specified explicitly, i.e. that the extension of the model is not as large as the increasing of the occurrence graph.

The next modelling step was to consider the potential temporal delay in transmitting the *turn-on message*. Putting it in use is not really different from what we have seen before so that it is not presented here. However the result is different because the verification revealed that the reaction of the lc-supervision-process *reports the status "at safe"* cannot be sent in every case any longer, i.e. the corresponding transition is no longer able to fire in every running sequence of the model. Therefore a further scenario, called *status unsafe* has been specified and was integrated into the model. The integrated model could be verified then.

Further extension of the model which necessity can be revealed by further validation has not be done until now, because the presented steps in modelling and proving covers the whole spectrum of STOP and reaches the goal of approving the soundness of this formal technique in principle. However, the state space of the specified operational process was grown from 28 states of the *normal train passage*-model to more than 800 states after adding the described changes, so that maybe methods in more efficient computing must be applied to make STOP applicable in real industrial usage.

6 Conclusions

Within the present paper the term *operational process* has been introduced as an important subject in the development of automation systems. It was discussed especially in relation to problems with the specification of such operational processes. The main problem is the huge amount of scenarios which must be specified for describing the complete operational system behaviour and which is not possible to be checked against completeness and correctness manually. In order to solve these problems an approach of formalising the procedures and results in specifying operational processes has been presented.

Afterwards it was shown how the named approach was put into use by a formal technique called STOP, which has been developed especially for fitting this purpose. The notation as well as the methods of STOP has been described by their main technical characteristics.

The definition of the notation of STOP has been presented by design patterns, which create a relation between certain concepts of system theory and the used formalism Coloured Petri Nets (CPN). The methods of STOP, including methods of modelling as well as methods of verification and validation, has been introduced by explaining their intention and their composing into process models.

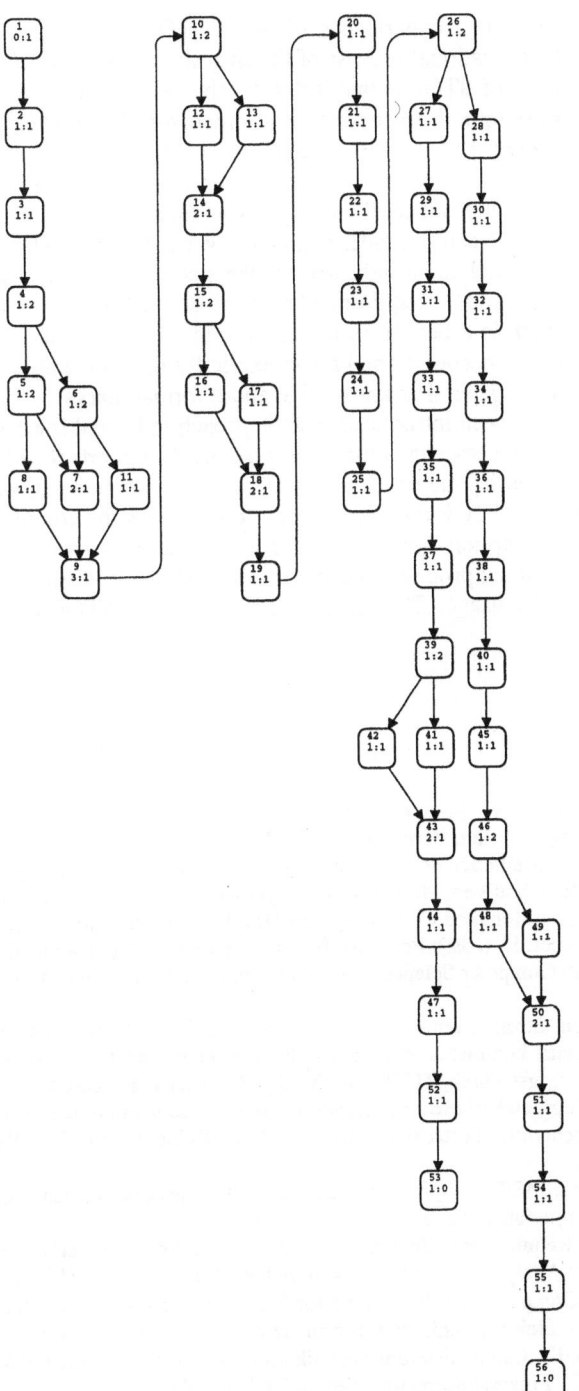

Fig. 14. Occurrence graph of the model supplemented by the restriction

At least the practical experiences of using STOP were presented by specifying some parts of the operational process of the case study *radio based railway crossing*.

The significance of STOP is that it divides the set of scenarios, which make up an operational process into abstract concurrent processes classified as so-called *essential* processes and *supervision* as well as *safety processes*. Following this approach STOP allows that the amount of operational behaviour of a automation system must not be specified total explicitly but can be partly derived analytically, i.e. that the number of elements of the specification model is much lower than the number of elements of its occurrence graph which is an indicator for the size of the explicit specification. Also certain application specific requirements can be derived automatically from the form of the model which is a benefit in automating the development process because the requirements are not needed to be known explicitly for each single application by the engineer but only in general as knowledge about formal marks.

All in all STOP has been introduced as an approach in formal specification and analysis of operational processes in automation systems. It supports the idea of concurrency and proposes to classify the concurrent processes in so-called *essential, supervison* or *safety processes*. So STOP reaches the goal to compress the complexity of the model as opposed to an explicit specification of all scenarios. However, even if the state space of an operational process is derived automatically, it is still too complex to handle it for industrial usage. The further development of STOP must especially deal with this problem.

References

1. Jensen, K.: Coloured Petri Nets; Basic Concepts, Analysis Methods and Practical Use, Vol. 1. Springer Verlag, Berlin Heidelberg New York (1992)
2. Schnieder, E.: Methoden der Automatisierung, Vieweg, Braunschweig, Germany (1999)
3. Schnieder, E., Chouikha, M., Einer, S., Meyer zu Hörste, M.: BASYSNET – An Integrated Approach for Automated Control System Development. In: Ehrig, H., Reisig, W., Rozenberg, G., Weber, H. (eds.): Petri Net Technology for Communication-Based Systems. Lecture Notes in Computer Science, Vol. 2472, Springer Verlag, Berlin Heidelberg New York (2003)
4. Einer, S.: Ein Strukturierungsansatz für formale Techniken. In: Schnieder, E. (ed.): EKA 2003 – Entwurf komplexer Automatisierungssysteme., Institut für Verkehrssicherheit und Automatisierungstechnik, TU Braunschweig, Braunschweig (2003)
5. Einer, S.: Petrinetzbasierte Spezifikation und Analyse operationaler Prozesse am Beispiel Eisenbahnsicherung. Fortschritt – Berichte VDI, Reihe 20, Nr. 373, VDI-Verlag Düsseldorf (2003)
6. ITU-T SG 10: MSC 2000, Recomendation Z.120 : Message Sequence Charts (MSC). ITU General Secretariat, Geneva (1999)
7. Partsch, H.: Requirements Engineering systematisch. Springer Verlag (1998)
8. Starke, P.H.: Analyse von Petri-Netz-Modellen. Teubner Verlag (1990)
9. Kluge, O.: Compositional Semantics for Message Sequence Charts based on Petri Nets. Fakultät IV – Elektrotechnik und Informatik der Technischen Universität Berlin (2000)
10. Zacher, S. (ed.): Automatisierungstechnik kompakt Vieweg Verlag (2000)
11. Schnieder, E.: Prozessinformatik. Vieweg Verlag (1986)
12. Heidepriem, J. Prozessinformatik. Oldenbourg-Verlag (2000)
13. Balzer, D., May, V., Müller, R., Schulze, K.-P.: Wissensbasierte Systeme in der Automatsierungstechnik. Carl-Hanser Verlag (1992)

14. DIN 19222: Leittechnik; Begriffe. Beuth Verlag (1985)
15. Litz, L.: Grundlagen der sicherheitsgerichteten Automatisierungstechnik. Übersichtsaufsatz in : at – Automatisierungstechnik 46 (1998) 2, R. Oldenbourg Verlag (1998)
16. Grams, T.: Grundlagen des Qualitäts- und Risikomanagements. Vieweg-Verlag (2001)
17. Ropohl, G.: Allgemeine Technologie – Eine Systemtheorie der Technik. Hanser (1999)
18. van Schrick, L.: Entepetives Management – Konstrukt, Konstruktion, Konzeption. Habilitationsschrift, Fachbereich Sicherheitstechnik der Bergischen Universität-Gesamthochschule Wuppertal (2001)
19. http://www.daimi.au.dk/designCPN/

Specification and Validation of an Edge Router Discovery Protocol for Mobile Ad Hoc Networks

Lars Michael Kristensen* and Kurt Jensen

Department of Computer Science, University of Aarhus
IT-parken, Aabogade 34, DK-8200 Aarhus N, DENMARK,
{lmkristensen,kjensen}@daimi.au.dk

Abstract. We present an industrial project at Ericsson Telebit A/S where Coloured Petri Nets (CP-nets or CPNs) have been used for the design and specification of an edge router discovery protocol for mobile ad-hoc networks. The Edge Router Discovery Protocol (ERDP) supports an edge router in a stationary core network in assigning network address prefixes to gateways in mobile ad-hoc networks. This paper focuses on how CP-nets and the CPN computer tools have been applied in the development of ERDP. A CPN model has been constructed that constitutes a formal executable specification of ERDP. Simulation and message sequence charts were used for initial investigations of the protocol's behaviour. Then state space analysis was applied to conduct a formal verification of the key properties of ERDP. Both the modelling, simulation, and subsequent state space analysis helped in identifying several omissions and errors in the design, demonstrating the benefits of using formal modelling and analysis in a protocol design process.

1 Introduction

The specification and development of communication protocols is a complex task. One of the reasons is that protocols consist of a number of independent concurrent protocol entities that may proceed in many different ways depending on when, e.g., packets are lost, timers expire, and processes are scheduled. The complex behaviour makes the design of correct protocols a challenging task.

The specification of communication protocols is, in many cases, based on natural language descriptions. One example of this is the Request for Comments (RFC) documents published by the Internet Engineering Task Force (IETF) [17]. Natural language specifications of protocols have several weaknesses. Firstly, they are inherently ambiguous making it difficult to achieve inter-operability between independent implementations. Secondly, they are often incomplete in the sense that the behaviour of the protocol is not completely described for all cases. This has motivated the use of formal description techniques [3] for the specification and validation of protocols.

An advantage of many formal description techniques is that they are based on the construction of executable models that make it possible to observe and

---

* Supported by the Danish Natural Science Research Council.

H. Ehrig et al. (Eds.): INT 2004, LNCS 3147, pp. 248–269, 2004.

experiment with the behaviour of the protocol prior to implementation using, e.g., simulation. This typically leads to complete specifications since the model will not be fully operational until all parts of the protocol have been specified. Another advantage of formal modelling languages is that they support abstractions, making it possible to specify the operation of the protocol without being concerned with irrelevant implementation details. Furthermore, the use of formal description techniques results in models that are amenable to verification using, e.g., state space methods where the basic idea is to compute all reachable states and state changes of the protocol and represent these as a directed graph. State space methods make it possible to automatically (i.e., algorithmically) check whether a protocol has the desired set of properties. In addition, state space methods have the advantage that counter examples (error-traces) can be automatically synthesised if the protocol does not satisfy a given property. Other examples of verification techniques for Petri nets [25, 10] includes structural and invariant methods [8, 26], and partial-order and unfolding methods [9, 13].

We present a case study from a joint research project [20] between the Coloured Petri Nets Group [6] at University of Aarhus and Ericsson Telebit A/S [12]. The research project applies formal description techniques in the form of Coloured Petri Nets (CP-nets or CPNs) [18, 21] and the supporting CPN computer tools [5, 11] in the development of Internet Protocol Version 6 (IPv6) [15] based protocols for ad-hoc networking [23]. An ad-hoc network is a collection of mobile nodes, such as laptops, personal digital assistants, and mobile phones, capable of establishing a communication infrastructure for their common use. Ad-hoc networking differs from conventional networks in that the nodes in the ad-hoc network operate in a fully self-configuring and distributed manner, without any preexisting communication infrastructure such as base stations and routers. Network layer and routing protocols for ad-hoc networking are under development by the IETF Mobile Ad-hoc Networks working group [14].

The CPN modelling language combines Petri nets and programming languages. Petri nets [25, 10] provide the foundation of the graphical notation and the semantical foundation for modelling concurrency, synchronisation, and communication in systems. The functional programming language Standard ML [27] provides the primitives for compactly modelling the sequential aspects of systems (such as data manipulation) and for creating compact and parameterisable models. State space methods are the main verification techniques for CP-nets. The CPN modelling language is supported by two computer tools: CPN Tools [5] and Design/CPN [11].

This paper shows how CP-nets and the CPN computer tools have been used and integrated in the development of the Edge Router Discovery Protocol (ERDP). ERDP is a protocol for connecting gateways in mobile ad-hoc networks to edge routers in stationary core networks. ERDP allows gateway nodes to discover and create an attachment to the core network, and it allows edge routers to configure gateways with a globally routeable IPv6 address prefix. This address prefix can, in turn, be used by the gateway to configure global IPv6 unicast addresses for the mobile nodes in the ad-hoc network. CP-nets have previously been applied in a number of industrial projects for the specification and analysis of protocols and systems [16].

The paper is organised as follows. Section 2 gives a brief introduction to ERDP explaining the basic operation of the protocol. Section 3 presents selected parts of the CPN model specifying ERDP, and Sect. 4 shows how the protocol was analysed and verified using state spaces. Finally, in Sect. 5 we sum up the conclusions. The reader is assumed to be familiar with the basic ideas of Petri nets, high-level Petri nets, and state space methods. The paper [21] gives an introduction to CP-nets sufficient to understand the results presented in this paper. The reader is referred to [18] for a complete introduction to CP-nets, their analysis methods, and applications.

2   The Edge Router Discovery Protocol

This section gives a brief introduction to the Edge Router Discovery Protocol (ERDP). The aim is not to give a complete description of ERDP, but to provide sufficient information to understand the CPN model and the state space analysis results presented in the later sections.

Figure 1 shows the IPv6-based network architecture considered in the project. The network architecture consists of an IPv6 stationary core network connecting a number of mobile ad-hoc networks on the edge of the core network. The project focuses on IP routing in this hybrid network architecture. A number of *edge routers* reside on the edge of the core network, and an ad-hoc network may contain one or more nodes capable of acting as *gateways* for communication with nodes outside the ad-hoc network. The edge routers and the gateways handle the connection between the core network and the ad-hoc networks, and an edge router may serve multiple ad-hoc networks. The core network is a classical wired IP network with stationary nodes, whereas wireless communication is used for communication between the mobile nodes in the ad-hoc networks. The edge routers and the gateways are also connected via wireless links that may be different from the wireless link technology used internally in the ad-hoc networks.

The network architecture also encompasses mobility. The nodes in the individual ad-hoc networks may move within the ad-hoc network or between the ad-hoc networks. It is also possible for an entire ad-hoc network, including its

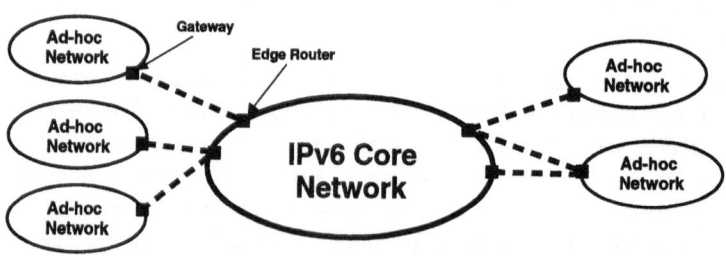

Fig. 1. IPv6-based Networking Architecture.

gateways to move from one edge router to another edge router, and possibly be within reach of several edge routers simultaneously.

ERDP is used between the gateways in the ad-hoc networks and the edge routers in the core network. ERDP supports gateways in discovering edge routers and supports edge routers in configuring gateways with a globally routeable IPv6 address prefix. This address prefix can then be used to configure global IPv6 unicast addresses for mobile nodes in the ad-hoc networks. This has the effect that all nodes in a given ad-hoc network will have addresses based on the same IPv6 address prefix, and entries in the routing tables in the core network can therefore be based on address prefixes rather than having to contain the individual addresses of the ad-hoc network nodes. This ensures that the network architecture scales with respect to the number of entries in the routing tables. When an ad-hoc network moves from one edge router to another edge router, it must be configured with a new topologically correct IPv6 address prefix for the same scalability reasons. Gateway discovery and selection by nodes in the ad-hoc networks are handled by protocols executed internally in the ad-hoc networks and is outside the scope of ERDP.

ERDP is based on extending the Neighbour Discovery Protocol (NDP) [22] which is part of the IPv6 protocol suite. The intended use of NDP is for hosts to discover neighbouring nodes and routers on a local area network, and conduct address configuration. In the IPv6-based networking architecture in Fig. 1, gateways acts as hosts and edge routers acts as routers from the point of view of NDP. Standard NDP can however not be used for configuration of gateways with address prefixes in the above network architecture since it must be ensured that a given address prefix is only assigned to a single gateway. This is required to ensure that routing of packets from edge routers to gateways is well-defined in case an ad-hoc network splits into two ad-hoc networks each with their own gateway.

Figure 2 shows the basic way that an edge router configures a gateway with an address prefix using ERDP. The message sequence chart was generated automatically from the CPN model to be presented in Sect. 3. The column labelled GWBuffer represents packet buffers between the gateway protocol entity and the underlying protocol layers. Similarly, the ERBuffer column represents packet buffers in the edge router.

An edge router periodically multi-casts unsolicited router advertisements (RAs) to announce its presence to any gateways that may be within reach of the edge router. When an unsolicited RA is received by a gateway, it will reply with its list of currently assigned address prefixes in a unicast router solicitation (RS). In this example, the gateway has no current prefixes and hence it sends an RS with no prefixes (indicated by the empty list [ ]). When the edge router receives the RS it will consult its lists of available prefixes and in this case select a new address prefix (P1) to be assigned to the gateway. This newly assigned prefix will then be sent back to the gateway in a unicast RA. When the unicast RA containing the prefix is received by the gateway, it will update its lists of currently assigned prefixes to contain the new prefix P1. Prefixes assigned to

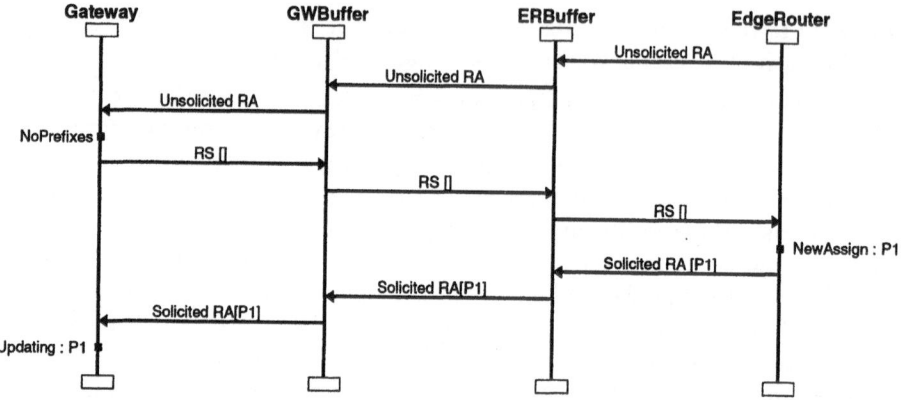

Fig. 2. Message sequence chart for basic prefix configuration with ERDP.

gateways have a limited lifetime, and hence either will expire or will have to be refreshed by the edge router.

CP-nets were integrated in the design and specification of ERDP by developing a CPN model of ERDP together with a conventional natural language specification. In the following sections we will refer to the natural language specification of ERDP as the *ERDP specification*.

3   CPN Modelling

Figure 3 shows the *hierarchy page* of the CPN model providing an overview of the *pages* (modules) constituting the CPN model. Each node in Figure 3 represents a page in the CPN model, and is labelled with a page name and a page number. As an example, the page node at the top left is named ERDP and has page number 1. Page ERDP is the most abstract page in the CPN model. An arc between two nodes indicates that the destination page is a subpage (submodule) of the source page. The arc label(s) specifies the name of the *substitution transition(s)* representing the corresponding subpage at the source page.

The CPN model consists of three main parts. Page Gateway and its four subpages model the operation of the gateway. Page EdgeRouter and its five subpages model the operation of the edge router. Page GW_ER_Link models the wireless communication link between the gateway and the edge router. We consider a system consisting of one gateway and one edge router as this is sufficient for specifying the protocol itself, and for investigating its basic operation. Validation of ERDP in an environment with multiple gateways and edge routers is beyond the scope of this paper.

Figure 4 depicts page EDRP. It corresponds to the ERDP page node in Fig. 3. The substitution transition Gateway represents the gateway, and the substitution transition Edge Router represents the edge router. The communication link

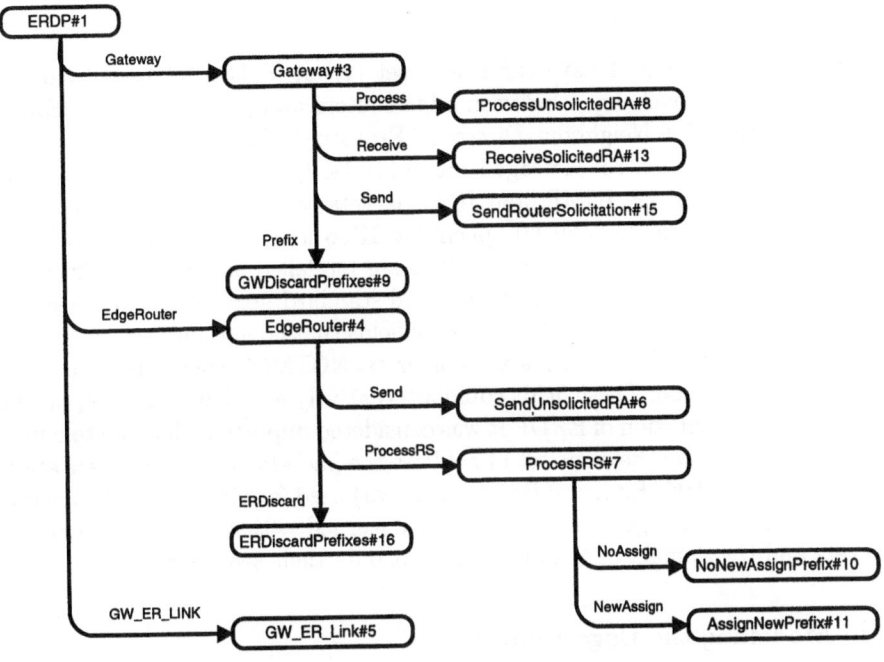

Fig. 3. Hierarchy page - overview of CPN model.

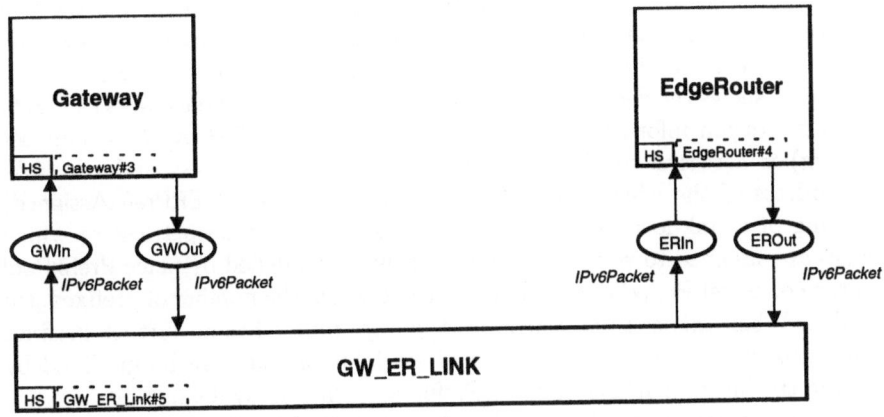

Fig. 4. The ERDP page - top level page in the CPN model.

between the edge router and the gateway is represented by the substitution transition GW_ER_LINK. The four places GWIn, GWOut, ERIn, and EROut model packet buffers between the link layer and the gateway and edge router. Both the edge router (ER) and the gateway (GW) have an incoming and an outgoing packet buffer.

3.1   Modelling Packets

All four places in Fig. 4 have the colour set (type) IPv6Packet used to model the IPv6 packets exchanged between edge routers and gateways. Since ERDP is based on the IPv6 Neighbour Discovery Protocol (NDP) [22], the packets are carried as Internet Control Message Protocol (ICMP) [4] packets. The definitions of colour sets for NDP, ICMP, and IPv6 packets are given in Fig. 5 and have been derived from RFC 2460 [7] specifying IPv6 and RFC 2461 [22] defining NDP. IPv6 addresses and address prefixes are modelled as strings. This makes it possible to use both mnemonic names and standard hexadecimal notation for IPv6 addresses in the CPN model. Protocol fields that do not affect the operation of ERDP have been defined using the colour set NOTMOD containing the single dummy value notmod. These fields could alternatively have been omitted, but for the later implementation of ERDP it was considered important that the tokens in the CPN model have the same set of fields as the packets in the implementation. The colour sets UInt8, Bit4, and Bit8 (not shown) used for bit fields in the packets are all defined as integers, as we are not concerned with the specific layout of packets and the domain of the bit fields, but only their semantics.

3.2   Modelling the Edge Router

Figure 6 shows the page EdgeRouter modelling the edge router. The *port* places ERIn and EROut are assigned to the similarly named *socket* places on page ERDP (see Fig. 4). The place Config models the configuration information associated with the edge router, and place PrefixPool models the number of prefixes still available in the edge router for distribution to gateways. The place PrefixAssigned is used to keep track of which prefixes are assigned to which gateways.

Figure 7 shows the declarations of the colour sets for the three places in Fig. 6. The configuration information for the edge router (modelled by the colour set ERConfig) is a record consisting of the IPv6 link-local address and the link-layer address of the edge router. A list of pairs (colour set ERPrefixAssigned) consisting of a link-local address and a prefix is used to keep track of which prefixes are assigned to which gateways. A counter modelled by place PrefixPool with the colour set PrefixCount is used to keep track of the number of prefixes still available. When this counter reaches 0, the edge router has no further prefixes available for distribution. The number of available prefixes can be modified by changing the initial marking of place PrefixPool which is by default set to 1.

The substitution transition SendUnsolicitedRA (in Fig. 6) corresponds to the multi-cast of periodic unsolicited Router Advertisements (RAs) by the edge router. The substitution transition ProcessRS models the reception of unicast Router Solicitations (RSs) from gateways, and the sending of a unicast RA in response. The substitution transition ERDiscardPrefixes models expiration of prefixes on the edge router side.

The marking shown in Fig. 6 has a single token on each of the three places used to model the internal state of the edge router protocol entity. This is shown by the small circles positioned on top of these places and containing the integer

```
color IPv6Addr = string; (* IPv6 addresses *)

(* --- Router Soliciations --- *)
color RSOption = union RS_SrcLinkAddr        : NDLinkAddrOption +
                       RS_PrefixInformation : NDPrefixInformationOption;
color RSOptions = list RSOption;

color RouterSolicitation = record Options : RSOptions *
                                  NU      : NOTMOD;

(* --- Router Advertisements --- *)
color RAOption = union RA_SrcLinkAddr        : NDLinkAddrOption +
                       RA_MTU                : NDMTUOption       +
                       RA_PrefixInformation  : NDPrefixInformationOption;
color RAOptions = list RAOption;

color RouterAdvertisement = record CurHopLimit  : UInt8  *
                                   M            : Bit    *
                                   O            : Bit    *
                                   RouterLifetime : UInt16 *
                                   ReachableTime  : UInt32 *
                                   RetransTimer   : UInt32 *
                                   Options        : RAOptions;

(* --- ICMP messages --- *)
color ICMPBody = union RS : RouterSolicitation    +
                       RA : RouterAdvertisement;
color ICMPMessage = record Type : UInt8 *
                           Code : UInt8 *
                           Message : ICMPBody;

(* --- IPv6 packets --- *)
color IPv6Payload = union ICMP : ICMPMessage;
color IPv6Header = record Version         : Bit4    *
                         TrafficClass    : NOTMOD  *
                         Flowlabel       : NOTMOD  *
                         PayloadLenght   : NOTMOD  *
                         NextHeader      : Bit8    *
                         HopLimit        : Bit8    *
                         SourceAddress   : IPv6Addr *
color IPv6Packet = record header    : IPv6Header *
                          extheaders : NOTMOD *
                          payload    : IPv6Payload;
```

Fig. 5. Declarations for IPv6 and ICMP packets.

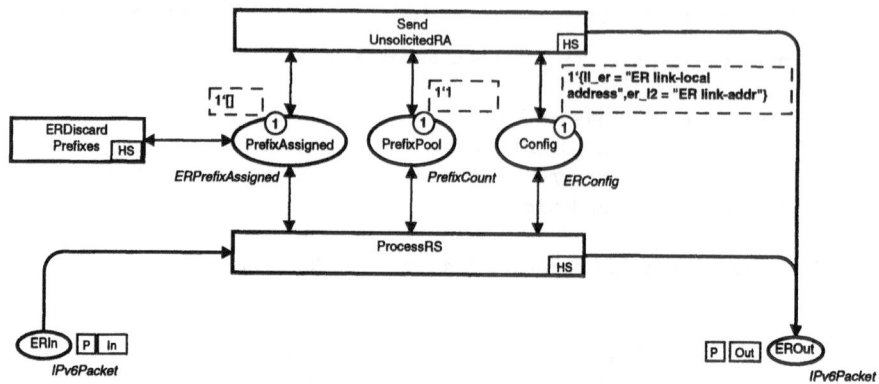

Fig. 6. The EdgeRouter page.

```
color LinkAddr = string;
color PrefixCount = int;

color ERConfig = record ll_er : IPv6Addr * (* link-local address of ER  *)
                        er_12 : LinkAddr;  (* link-addr (layer 2) of ER *)

color ERPrefixEntry = product  IPv6Addr * IPv6Prefix;
color ERPrefixAssigned = list ERPrefixEntry;
```

Fig. 7. Declarations for modelling edge routers.

1. The dashed box positioned next to each of the small circles gives information about the colour of the token. In the marking shown, the token on place
PrefixAssigned with the colour [] (empty list) corresponds to the edge router not
having assigned any prefixes to the gateway. The token on place PrefixPool with
colour 1 indicates that the edge router has a single prefix available for distribution. Finally, the colour of the token on place Config specifies the link-local and
link address of the edge router. In this case the edge router has the symbolic
link-local address of ER link-local address, and the symbolic link-address of ER
link-addr.

Figure 8 depicts page SendUnsolicitedRA which is the subpage of the substitution transition SendUnsolicitedRA in Fig. 6. The transition SendUnsolicitedRA
models the sending of the periodic unsolicited router advertisements. The variable erconfig is of type ERConfig (see Fig. 7) and the variable prefixleft is of type
PrefixCount (see Fig. 7). The transition SendUnsolicitedRA is only enabled if the
edge router has prefixes available for distribution, i.e., prefixleft is greater than 0.
This is ensured by the function SendUnsolicitedRA in the guard of the transition.

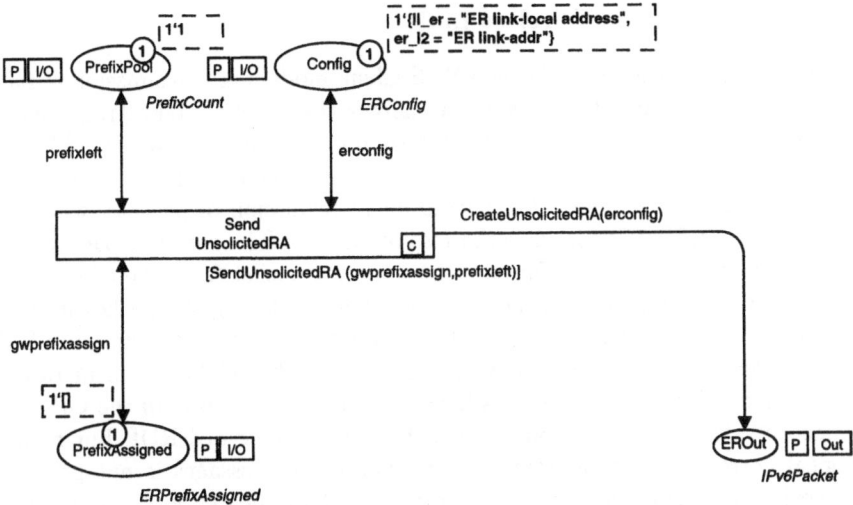

Fig. 8. Page SendUnsolicitedRA - initial state.

Figure 9 depicts the marking of page SendUnsolicitedRA after the occurrence of the transition SendUnsolicitedRA in the marking shown in Fig. 8. An unsolicited router advertisement has been put in the outgoing buffer of the edge router. It can be seen that the unsolicited router advertisement is sent to the all-nodes multi-cast address, and that it carries the link-local and link-layer address of the edge router as part of the options in the router advertisement.

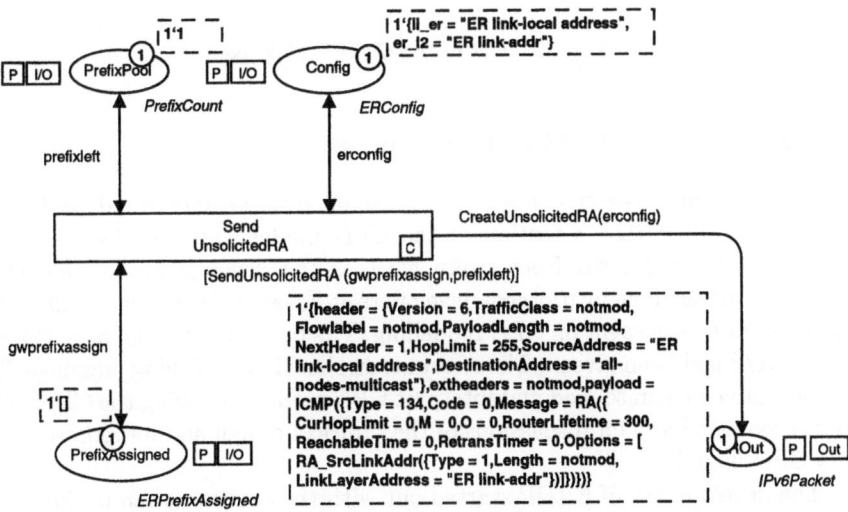

Fig. 9. Page SendUnsolicitedRA - after occurrence of SendunsolicitedRA.

3.3 Modelling the Wireless Link

Figure 10 shows the part of page GW_ER_Link modelling transmission of packets from the edge router to the gateway across the wireless link. Transmission of packets from the gateway to the edge router is modelled similarly. The places GWIn and EROut are linked to the similarly named socket places in Fig. 4. The transition ERtoGW models the successful transmission of packets, whereas the transition LossERtoGW models the loss of packets. The variable ipv6packet is of type IPv6Packet. A successful transmission of a packet from the edge router to the gateway corresponds to moving the token modelling the packet from place EROut to GWIn. If the packet is lost, it will only be removed from place EROut.

Wireless links in general have lower bandwidth and higher error-rate than wired links. These characteristics have been abstracted away in the CPN model since our aim is not to reason about the performance of ERDP but rather its logical correctness. Duplication and reordering of messages is not possible on typical 1-hop wireless links since detection of duplicates and preservation of order will be handled by the data-link layer. The modelling of the wireless link does allow overtaking of packets, but this overtaking will be eliminated in the analysis phase described in Sect. 4 where we impose bounds on the capacity of the input and output packet buffers.

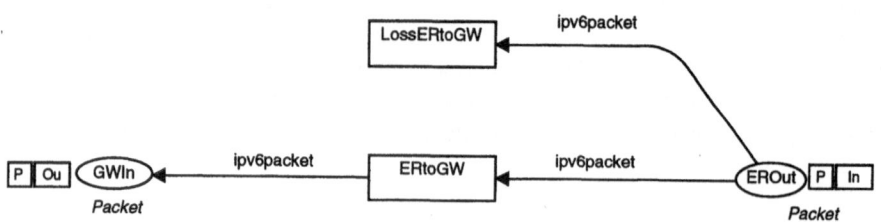

Fig. 10. Part of the GW_ER_Link page.

3.4 Summary of the Modelling Process

The CPN model presented above was developed as an integrated part of the development of ERDP. Creation of the CPN model was done by researchers from the Coloured Petri Nets group whereas the development of the ERDP specification was done by protocol developers at Ericsson Telebit A/S. Altogether 70 man-hours were spent on CPN modelling. The protocol developers at Ericsson Telebit A/S had been given a 6 hour course on the CPN modelling language. This course enabled them to read and interpret CPN models, allowing the CPN model to be used as a basis for discussions of the protocol design and its representation as a CPN model.

The development of ERDP started out with the creation of an initial ERDP (natural language) specification. Based on this specification, a first version of the CPN model was created. The act of creating this initial CPN model and

Table 1. Summary and categorisation of issues encountered in the modelling phase.

Category	Rev 1	Rev 2	Total
Incompleteness and ambiguity in specification	3	6	9 issues
Errors in protocol specification/operation	2	7	9 issues
Simplifications of protocol operation	2	0	2 issues
Additions to the protocol operation	4	0	4 issues
Total	11	13	24 issues

discussing it (in the following referred to as Review 1) lead to the identification of several issues related to the design and operation of ERDP. This included design errors, incompleteness and ambiguity in the specification, and ideas for simplifications and improvements of the protocol design. Based on the issues discovered in Review 1, the ERDP specification was revised and extended. A second review (Review 2) was then conducted by revising the initial CPN model according to the modified ERDP specification and then discussing the CPN model. Review 2 lead to further identification of issues which were eventually resolved and the ERDP specification was modified accordingly. The CPN model was then modified again to reflect the revised ERDP specification. At this stage, no further issues were discovered in the process of revising the CPN model.

Table 1 categorises and enumerates the issues encountered in each of the two reviews (Rev 1 and Rev 2). These issues were identified in the process of constructing the CPN model, single step execution of the CPN model, and discussions of the CPN model among the project group members. Altogether 24 issues were identified in the process of constructing and simulating the model.

Message Sequence Charts (MSCs) (such as the one shown in Fig. 2) integrated with simulation was used in both review steps to investigate the behaviour of ERDP in detail. The basic idea in this integration is to use MSCs to provide visual feedback from simulations of the CPN model. Visual feedback in the form of MSCs is supported by the MSC library [1] available for the CPN computer tools. Technically the integration of MSCs and simulation is achieved by the modeller attaching code segments to the transitions of the CPN model. The code segments invoke primitives in the MSC library. When a transition occurs in a simulation the associated code segment (if any) is executed causing the MSC to be accordingly updated. The visualisation at the level of the CPN model provides a state-based view whereas MSCs provides an event-based view that includes history. The two forms of feedback therefore complements each other.

4   State Space Analysis and Verification

State space analysis was pursued after the three iterations of modelling summarised at the end of the previous section. The purpose of the state space analysis was to conduct a more thorough investigation of the operation of ERDP, including verification of its key properties.

4.1   Analysis Preparations and Approach

The first step towards state space analysis of the CPN model was to obtain a finite state space. The CPN model presented in the previous section has an infinite state space since an arbitrary number of tokens (packets) can be put on the places modelling the packet buffers. As an example, the edge router may initially send an arbitrary number of unsolicited router advertisements. To obtain a finite state space, an upper bound of one token was imposed on each of the places GWIn, GWOut, ERIn, and EROut (see Fig. 4) modelling the packet buffers. This has the effect of also preventing reordering of the packets when transmitted across the wireless link. Furthermore, the number of packets simultaneously in the input and output buffers of the two protocol entities was limited to 2. Technically this was done by using *branching options* available in the CPN state space tool to not explore enabled transitions whose occurrence in a given marking would violate the above bounds.

Figure 11 shows the initial part of the state space in the case where we assume that packets cannot be lost when transmitted across the wireless link. Each of the nodes 1-7 represent a state of the CPN model, and each of the arcs represent an occurrence of an enabled transition. The labels on the arcs give the name of the transition occurring. Node 1 represents the initial state of the CPN model. The two dashed boxes associated with nodes 1 and 2 show the marking of each of the places in the CPN model in the corresponding state. It can be seen that initially (node 1) all packet buffers are empty, the edge router has one prefix to assign, and the gateway is not configured with any prefixes. Sending of an unsolicited RA by the edge router is the only possible event in the initial state. If this event occurs, the state corresponding to node 2 is entered. The state represented by node 2 is identical to the state represented by node 1, except that an unsolicited RA is now in the output buffer of the edge router. In state 2 the unsolicited RA can be sent to the gateway leading to state 3 in which either another unsolicited RA can be sent by the edge router or the gateway can process the unsolicited RA.

The state space analysis was based on first generating the state space for the considered configuration of the protocol. This was followed by generation of the *state space report* and the use of *query functions* to investigate the properties of the protocol. The state space report can be generated automatically by the CPN state space tool, and it contains information about a set of standard properties of the CPN model such as *integer bounds* (minimal/maximal number of tokens on places), *dead markings* (states without enabled transitions), and *home markings* (states that can always be reached). These properties are system independent in that the properties that can be investigated for any CPN model.

The query functions in the CPN state space tool support verification and analysis of system dependent properties. The query functions provide a set of primitives for traversing the state space in various ways, such as visiting all states. The analysis of ERDP relied mainly on the use of the *Strongly Connected Component* graph (SCC-graph) derived from the state space. The SCC-graph is generated by the CPN state space tool and is derived from the state space by considering states to be equivalent if they are mutually reachable. The SCC-

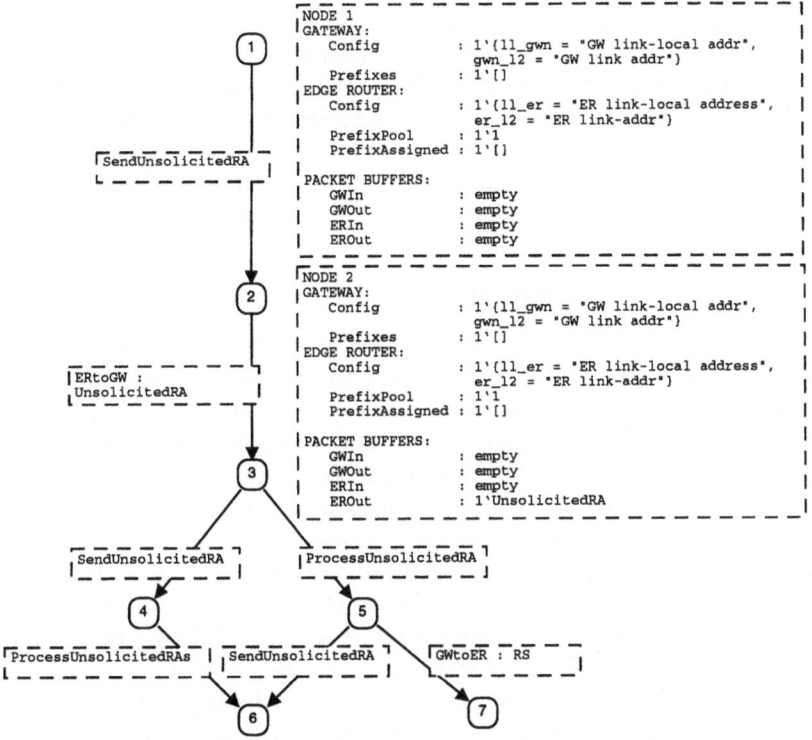

Fig. 11. Initial fragment of state space.

graph has a node for each such equivalence class containing the subgraph of the state space determined by the states in the equivalence class. A node in the SCC-graph is called a *Strongly Connected Component* (SCC). The SCC-graph is an acyclic graph, and two states s_1 and s_2 are in the same SCC S in the SCC-graph if and only if there is a path from s_1 to s_2 and a path from s_2 to s_1 in the state space. There is an arc in the SCC-graph between two SCCs S_1 and S_2 if there is a state s_1 in S_1 with an outgoing arc in the state space leading to a state s_2 contained in S_2. The *terminal SCCs* are the nodes in the SCC-graph without outgoing arcs. A SCC is *trivial* if it contains one state and no arcs. A number of query functions are available in the CPN state space tool for inspecting and traversing the SCC-graph.

The key property of ERDP is the proper configuration of the gateway with prefixes. By this we mean that for a given prefix and state where the gateway has not yet been configured with that prefix, the protocol must be able to configure the gateway with the prefix. Furthermore, when the gateway has been configured with the prefix, the edge router and the gateway should be properly synchronised, i.e., the assignment of the prefix must be recorded in the gateway protocol entity as well as in the edge router protocol entity. In the following we will refer to a state where the gateway is configured with a prefix and the edge router and gateway is synchronised as a *consistently configured state* for that prefix. Whether a state represents a consistently configured state for a given prefix can be checked by inspecting the marking of the place PrefixAssigned in the edge router and the marking of the place Prefixes in the gateway.

The state space analysis was conducted in three steps starting with the simplest configuration of the protocol where no packet loss and no expiration of timers are allowed. The simplifications were then gradually lifted.

4.2   Step 1: Basic Configurations

The first step was to consider the simplest possible configurations of ERDP starting with a single prefix and assuming that there is no loss of packets on the wireless link and that prefixes do not expire. The full state space for this configuration has 46 nodes and 65 arcs and was generated in less than one second on a Linux PIII PC with 1Gb of memory. The SCC-graph has 36 nodes and 48 arcs. Having constructed the state space and computed the SCC-graph, the standard state space report can be generated. Inspection of the state space report showed that there was a single dead marking (a state without enabled transitions) represented by node 36. Hence the state represented by node 36 corresponds to a state where the protocol has terminated. Inspection of node 36 showed that it corresponded to a state where all the packet buffers were empty, but where the edge router and gateway are unsynchronised in the sense that the edge router is in a state where the gateway is assigned prefix P1 (the single prefix), but the gateway is not configured with that prefix. This is an error in the protocol. To locate the source of the problem, query functions in the state space tool were used to obtain a path (i.e., an error-trace or counter example) leading from the node representing the initial state to node 36. Figure 12 shows this error-trace visualised using a MSC. The integration of message sequence charts in the CPN computer tools makes it possible to automatically display a path in the state space as an MSC. The problem is that the edge router sends two unsolicited RA. The first one gets through and the gateway is configured with the prefix (Event A). However, when the second RS (Event B) without any prefixes is received by the edge router, the corresponding solicited RA will not contain any prefixes. Because of the way the protocol was specified, the gateway will therefore update its list of prefixes to the empty list (Event C), and the gateway is no longer configured with a prefix.

To fix the error identified, the protocol was modified such that the edge router always replies with the list of all prefixes that it has currently assigned to the gateway. The state space for the modified protocol contains 34 nodes and 49 arcs, and there are no dead markings in the state space. The state space report specifies that there are 11 *home markings*. Hence, the protocol has the property that any of the corresponding 11 states can always be reached. Inspection of these 11 states showed that they all represented consistently configured states for the prefix P1. The states are contained in the single terminal SCC of the state space. When the SCC-graph has a single terminal SCC, it is always possible to reach one of the states in that terminal SCC and once having entered a state in the

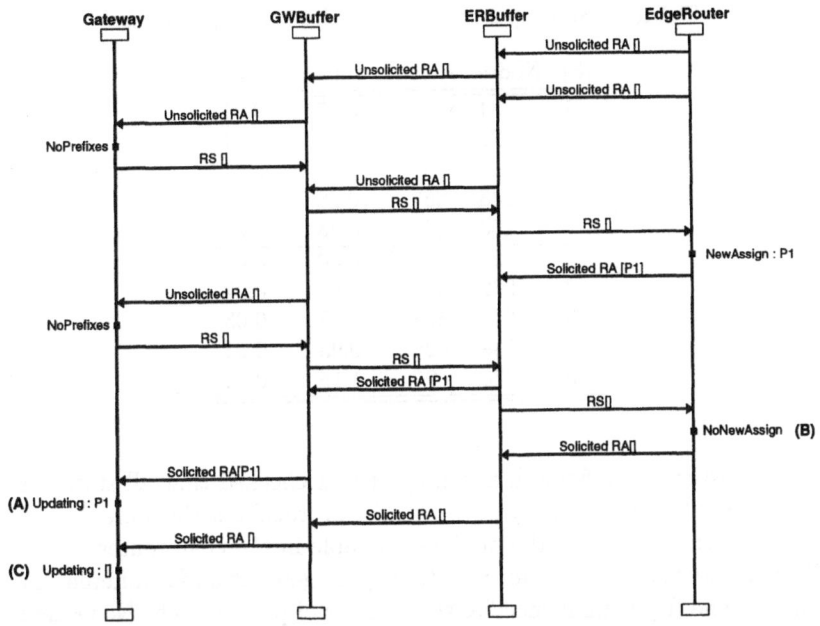

Fig. 12. MSC showing execution leading to undesired terminal state.

terminal SCC, the system can only enter states in the terminal SCC. This shows that when executing ERDP starting from the initial state it is always possible to reach a consistently configured state for the prefix, and when such a state has been reached, the protocol entities will remain in a consistently configured state. To verify that a consistently configured state will eventually be reached, it was checked that the single terminal SCC was the only non-trivial SCC. This shows that all cycles in the state space (which correspond to non-terminating executions of the protocol) are contained in the terminal SCC which (from above) contains only consistently configured states. The reason why the protocol is not supposed to terminate in a consistently configured state represented by a dead marking is that the gateway may at any time when it is configured send a router solicitation back to the edge router to have its prefixes refreshed. Since we ignore expiration of prefixes, the edge router will always refresh the prefix.

The number of prefixes was increased once the correctness of the protocol was established for a single prefix. When there is more than one prefix available it no longer holds that a state will *eventually* be reached where *all* prefixes are consistently configured. The reason is that with more than one prefix, the edge router may at any time decide not to configure the gateway with additional prefixes. Hence, a state where all prefixes have been consistently configured may not eventually be reached. Instead it was verified that there was a single terminal SCC of which all states are states where all prefixes have been consistently configured. This shows that it is always possible to reach such a state, and when the protocol has consistently configured all prefixes, the protocol entities will

Table 2. State space statistics for basic configurations.

|P|	Nodes	Arcs	G-time	A-time
1	34	49	0.05	0.01
2	72	121	0.11	0.01
3	110	193	0.18	0.01
4	148	265	0.28	0.01
5	186	337	0.38	0.01
6	224	409	0.50	0.02
7	262	481	0.62	0.02
8	300	553	0.76	0.03
9	338	625	0.93	0.03
10	376	697	1.15	0.04

remain consistently configured. Secondly, it was checked that all states in each non-trivial SCC represented states where the protocol entities were consistently configured with a subset of the prefixes available in the edge router.

Table 2 lists the statistics for the state space generation for different number of prefixes. The |P| column specifies the number of prefixes. The Nodes and Arcs columns give the number of nodes and arcs in the state space, respectively. The G-time column gives the time in seconds used to generated the state space, and the A-time column gives the time in seconds used to conduct the verification of properties presented above. It can be observed that 38 states are added for each additional prefix. The reason for this is that ERDP proceeds in phases where the edge router assigns prefixes to the gateway one at a time. Configuring the gateway with an additional prefix follows exactly the same procedure as the assignment of the first prefix. It can be seen that once the state space has been generated, the verification of properties could be done in less than one second.

4.3   Step 2: Adding Packet Loss

Next we considered state space analysis in presence of packet loss on the wireless link between the edge router and the gateway. First we considered the case where there is only a single prefix for distribution. The state space for this configuration has 40 nodes and 81 arcs. Inspection of the state space report showed that there was a single dead marking. This state represented an undesired terminal state where the prefix was assigned by the edge router according to its internal state, but the gateway was not configured with this prefix. Figure 13 shows an MSC corresponding to the path in the state space from the initial state to the undesired terminal state. The problem is that when the unsolicited RA containing the prefix is lost, the edge router will have assigned its last prefix and is no longer sending any unsolicited RAs. Furthermore, there are no timeouts in the protocol entities that can trigger the retransmission of the prefix to the gateway.

The problem identified above was fixed by ensuring that the edge router will resend an unsolicited RA to the gateway as long as it has prefixes assigned to the gateway according to its internal state. The state space of the revised CPN

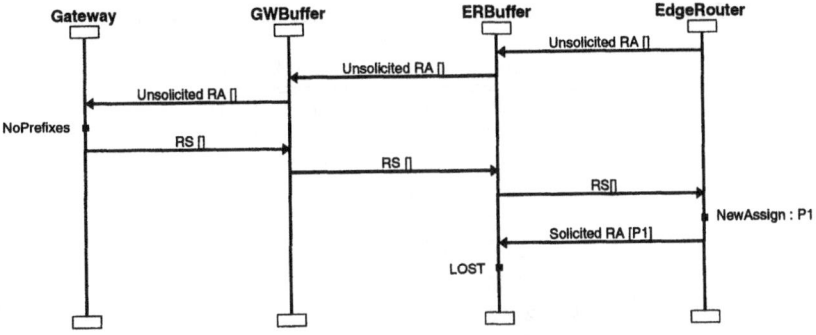

Fig. 13. MSC showing execution leading to undesired terminal state.

model has 68 nodes and 160 arcs. Inspection of the state space report showed that there were no dead markings and no home markings. Investigation of the terminal SCCs showed that there were two terminal SCCs each containing 20 states. The nodes in one of them all represented states where the edge router and gateway were consistently configured with the single prefix P1, whereas the nodes in the other terminal SCC all represented states where the protocol entities were not consistently configured. The states in the undesired terminal SCC hence represent a livelock in the protocol, i.e., if one of the states in the undesired terminal SCC is reached, it is no longer possible to reach a state where the protocol entities are consistently configured with the prefix. The source of livelock was related to the control fields used in the router advertisements for refreshing prefixes and their interpretation in the gateway. This was identified by obtaining the MSC for a path leading from the initial state to one of the states in the undesired terminal SCC. As a result, the processing of router advertisements in the gateway was modified. The state space for the protocol with the modified processing of router advertisements also has 68 nodes and 160 arcs. The state space has a single terminal SCC containing 20 nodes which all represents states where the protocol entities are consistently configured with the single prefix.

When packet loss is present, it is not immediately possible to prove that the two protocol entities will eventually be consistently configured. The reason is that any number of packets can be lost on the wireless link. Each of the non-trivial SCCs were inspected using a query function to investigate the circumstances under which the protocol entities would not eventually be consistently configured. The query function checked that either all nodes in the non-trivial SCC represented consistently configured states or none of the nodes in the SCC represented a consistently configured state. For those non-trivial SCC where no node represented a consistently configured state, it was checked that all cycles contained the occurrence of a transition corresponding to loss of a packet. Since this was the case, it can be concluded that the absence of reaching a consistently configured state is due to packet loss and nothing else. Hence, if only finitely many packets are lost, a consistently configured state will *eventually* be reached. Table 3 gives statistics on the state space for verification of properties.

Table 3. State space statistics for packet loss configurations.

|P|	Nodes	Arcs	G-time	A-time
1	68	160	0.11	0.01
2	172	425	0.34	0.02
3	337	851	0.87	0.08
4	582	1489	1.48	0.16
5	926	2390	2.67	0.32
6	1388	3605	4.48	0.67
7	1987	5185	6.66	1.34
8	2742	7181	9.99	2.65
9	3672	9644	14.15	4.86
10	4796	12625	19.93	10.17

4.4 Step 3: Adding Expire of Prefixes

The final step in the analysis was to allow prefixes to expire. The analysis was conducted first in the configuration where the edge router has only a single prefix to distribute. The state space for this configuration has 173 nodes and 513 arcs. The state space has a single dead marking, and inspection of this dead marking showed that it corresponded to a state where the edge router has no further prefixes to distribute, it has no prefixes recorded for the gateway, and the gateway is not configured with any prefix. This marking is a desired terminating state of the protocol, as we expect prefixes to eventually expire. Since the edge router has only finitely many prefixes to distribute the protocol should eventually terminate in such a state. The single dead marking is also a home marking, meaning that the protocol can always enter the expected terminal state.

When prefixes can expire the two protocol entities may never enter a consistently configured state. The reason is that a prefix may expire in the edge router (albeit unlikely) before the gateway has successfully been configured with the prefix. Hence, we are only able to prove that for any state where a prefix is still available in the edge router, it is possible to reach a state where the gateway and the edge router are consistently configured with this prefix. Table 4 lists the statistics for the state space generation and verification of properties in the case where expire of prefixes is also taken into account.

5 Conclusions

We have described how CPN modelling and state space analysis have been applied in the process of developing ERDP. Already the act of constructing the CPN model based on the ERDP specification provided valuable input to the ERDP specification, and the use of simulation added further insight into the operation of the protocol. State space analysis starting with the simplest possible configuration of the protocol identified additional errors in the protocol. The state space analysis succeeded in establishing the key properties of ERDP. The main drawback of verification based on state spaces is the state explosion

Table 4. State space statistics for prefix expire configurations.

$|P|$	Nodes	Arcs	G-time	A-time
1	173	531	0.34	0.02
2	714	2404	1.80	0.17
3	2147	7562	6.34	0.67
4	5390	19516	18.65	2.09
5	11907	43976	48.56	6.39
6	23905	89654	121.07	15.36
7	44550	169169	289.91	33.14
8	78211	300072	671.24	64.12
9	130732	505992	1560.73	123.81
10	209732	817903	3586.23	229.70

problem [28]. However, for the verification of ERDP presented in this paper the state explosion problem was not encountered and we succeeded in verifying the key properties of the ERDP protocol for the configurations that are envisioned to occur in practice. The verification presented in this paper considered the case with one gateway and one edge router. As part of future work we plan to consider verification in the presence of multiple gateways and edge routers. When considering multiple gateways and edge routers we are likely to encounter the state explosion problem. The symmetry method [19] and sweep-line method [2] are promising candidates for alleviating the state explosion problem in that case.

It can be argued whether or not the issues and errors discovered in process of modelling and conducting state space analysis would have been identified if additional conventional reviews of the ERDP specification had been conducted. Some of them probably would, but more subtle problems such as the synchronisation issues discovered during state space analysis would probably not have been discovered until a first implementation of ERDP was operational. The reason for this is that discovering these problems requires one to consider subtle execution sequences of the protocol, and there are too many of these to do it in a systematic way. This demonstrates the value of being able to conduct state space exploration of the CPN model and in this way cover all execution sequences.

The construction of a CPN model can be seen as a very thorough and systematic way of reviewing a design specification of a protocol. Using an iterative process where both a conventional natural language specification and a CPN model is developed (as in this project) appears to be an effective way of integrating CPN modelling and analysis into the development of a protocol. In general, we believe that a combination of an executable formal model (such as a CPN model) and a natural language specification is a useful specification of a protocol. One reason that both are required is that the people who are going to implement the protocol may not be familiar with CP-nets. Secondly, there are important parts of the ERDP specification that are not reflected in the CPN model, such as the layout of packets. Similar observations were also made in [24] for the design of a security system.

In the project, we have demonstrated the use of message sequence charts (MSCs) for visualising the behaviour of the protocol based on simulations and based on paths in the state space. The automatic creation of MSCs based on executions of a CPN model is different from the conventional use of MSCs as a specification technique. The event-based graphical feedback in the form of MSCs has the advantage that it provides a compact view of the steps, i.e., how the current state of the protocol was reached. In contrast, the conventional state-based visualisation of the token distribution on the CPN model only shows the current state and it is distributed across several pages (modules). The use of MSCs in this project was of particular relevance since it presented the operation of the protocol in a form well-known to protocol developers.

We consider the application of CP-nets in the development of ERDP a success for three main reasons. Firstly and as in earlier case studies [16], we have demonstrated that the CPN modelling language and supporting computer tools are powerful enough to specify and analyse a real-world communication protocol. Secondly, the act of constructing the CPN model, executing, and discussing it lead to the identification of several non-trivial design errors and issues that under normal circumstances would not have been discovered until at best in the implementation phase. Finally, the effort of constructing the CPN model and conducting the state space analysis was approximately 100 man-hours. This is a relatively small investment compared to the many issues that were identified and resolved early as a consequence of constructing and analysing the CPN model.

Acknowledgements. The authors would like to acknowledge Nis A. Clausen, Rolf Christensen, and Shahrokk Sheik-El-Ameh from Ericsson Telebit A/S for their significant contributions in the project. The work on the design and specification of ERDP has been carried out on the Building Blocks for Network Centric Warfare (B2NCW), EUCLID/Eurofinder programme, Project RTP6.22, Contract No. 02/EF 6.22/012, with support from the UK, Swedish and Danish MoDs and the participating companies. The authors are grateful for this support and would like to acknowledge the contributions of all the B2NCW team members.

References

1. S. Christensen. *Message Sequence Charts. User's Manual*, January 1997. Available via www.daimi.au.dk/designCPN.
2. S. Christensen, L.M. Kristensen, and T. Mailund. A Sweep-Line Method for State Space Exploration. In *Proc. of 7th International Conference on Tools and Algorithms for the Construction and Analysis of Systems*, volume 2031 of *Lecture Notes in Computer Science*, pages 450–464. Springer-Verlag, 2001.
3. E. M. Clarke and J. M. Wing. Formal Methods: State of the Art and Future Directions. *ACM Computing Surveys*, 28(4):626–643, 1996.
4. A. Conta and S. Deering. Internet Control Message Protocol (ICMPv6) for the Internet Protocol Version 6 (IPV6) Specification, December 1998. RFC 2463. Work in progress.
5. CPN Tools. www.daimi.au.dk/CPNtools.

6. The CPN Group at University of Aarhus. www.daimi.au.dk/CPnets.
7. S. Deering and R. Hinden. Internet Protocol, Version 6 (IPV6) Specification, December 1998. RFC 2460. Work in progress.
8. J. Desel. Basic Linear Algebraic Techniques for Place/Transition Nets. In *Lectures on Petri Nets I: Basic Models*, volume 1491 of *Lecture Notes in Computer Science*, pages 257–308. Springer-Verlag, 1998.
9. J. Desel. Validation of Process Models by Construction of Process Nets. In *Business Process Managements - models, techniques and empirical studies*, volume 1806 of *Lecture Notes in Computer Science*, pages 110–128. Springer-Verlag, 2000.
10. J. Desel and W. Reisig. Place/Transition Petri Nets. In *Lecture on Petri nets I: Basic Models*, volume 1491 of *Lecture Notes in Computer Science*, pages 122–173. Springer-Verlag, 1998.
11. Design/CPN. www.daimi.au.dk/designCPN.
12. Ericsson Telebit A/S. www.tbit.dk.
13. J. Esparza. Model Checking using Net Unfoldings. *Science of Computer Programming*, 23:151–195, 1994.
14. Internet Engineering Task Force. Mobile ad-hoc networks. www.ietf.org/html.charters/manet-charter.html.
15. C. Huitema. *IPv6: The New Internet Protocol*. Prentice-Hall, 1998.
16. Examples of Industrial Use of CP-nets. www.daimi.au.dk/CPnets/intro/example_indu.html.
17. The Internet Engineering Task Force. www.ietf.org.
18. K. Jensen. *Coloured Petri Nets - Basic Concepts, Analysis Methods and Practical Use. Vol. 1-3*. Springer-Verlag, 1992-1997.
19. K. Jensen. Condensed State Spaces for Symmetrical Coloured Petri Nets. *Formal Methods in System Design*, 9(1/2):7–40, 1996.
20. L.M. Kristensen. Ad-hoc Networking and IPv6: Modelling and Validation. www.pervasive.dk/projects/IPv6/IPv6_summary.
21. L.M. Kristensen, S. Christensen, and K. Jensen. The Practitioner's Guide to Coloured Petri Nets. *International Journal on Software Tools for Technology Transfer*, 2(2):98–132, 1998.
22. T. Narten, E. Nordmark, and W. Simpson. Neighbor Discovery for IP Version 6 (IPv6), December 1998. RFC 2461. Work in progress.
23. C.E. Perkins. *Ad Hoc Networking*. Addison-Wesley, 2001.
24. J.L. Rasmussen and M. Singh. Designing a Security System by Means of Coloured Petri Nets. In *Proc.of 17th International Conference on Application and Theory of Petri Nets*, volume 1091 of *Lecture Notes in Computer Science*, pages 400–419. Springer-Verlag, 1996.
25. W. Reisig. *Petri Nets*, volume 4 of *EACTS Monographs in Theoretical Computer Science*. Springer-Verlag, 1985.
26. M. Silva, E. Teruel, and J. M. Colom. Linear Algebraic and Linear Programming Techniques for the Analysis of Place/Transition Net Systems. In *Lectures on Petri Nets I: Basic Models*, volume 1491 of *Lecture Notes in Computer Science*, pages 309–373. Springer-Verlag, 1998.
27. J.D. Ullman. *Elements of ML Programming*. Prentice-Hall, 1998.
28. A. Valmari. The State Explosion Problem. In *Lectures on Petri Nets I: Basic Models*, volume 1491 of *Lecture Notes in Computer Science*, pages 429–528. Springer-Verlag, 1998.

A Guide to Modelling and Control
with Modules of Signal Nets

Jörg Desel[1], Hans-Michael Hanisch[2], Gabriel Juhás[1],
Robert Lorenz[1], and Christian Neumair[1]

[1] Lehrstuhl für Angewandte Informatik
Katholische Universität Eichstätt-Ingolstadt, Germany
name.surname@ku-eichstaett.de
[2] Lehrstuhl für Automatisierungstechnik
Martin Luther Universität Halle-Wittenberg, Germany
hans-michael.hanisch@iw.uni-halle.de

Abstract. In this paper we summarize syntax and semantics of modules of elementary signal nets and explain how to synthesize the control for discrete event systems modelled by such modules.

Signal nets, introduced in [8,9,10,12], are based on Petri net modules which communicate via signals. Two kinds of signals are employed, namely active signals which force occurrence of (enabled) events, and passive signals which enable/prohibit occurring of events. Modelling with such modules appears to be very natural from an engineering perspective. It enables hierarchical structuring and supports the locality principle.

Given an uncontrolled system (a plant), modelled by a module of an elementary signal net, and a control specification, given as a regular language representing the desired signal output behavior of this system, we show step-by-step how to automatically synthesize the maximally permissive and nonblocking behavior of the plant respecting the control specification. Finally, we show how to synthesize the controller (as a module of an elementary signal net) forcing the plant to realize the controlled behavior.

1 Introduction

In complex applications, models are usually constructed in several steps and are described on several levels of abstraction. Systems are parts of bigger systems, such as a robot is a part of a manufacturing cell. Conversely, many systems are composed from subsystems. This fact motivates the principle of modularity and compositionality. Considering a certain level of abstraction, one does not need to reason about all details of subsystems which were taken into consideration on a sublevel. It is usually sufficient to consider just those parts of subsystems which are in contact with the environment, i.e. the "input/output" parts and to consider the "inside" of the subsystems being a "black box". Such an approach supports local changes in the whole system, i.e. it enables the replacement of one subsystem by another with the same "input/output"-functionality.

Considering discrete event systems (DES), Petri nets are a very successfully successfully used modelling formalism [13,29]. The main reason is that they offer both,

H. Ehrig et al. (Eds.): INT 2004, LNCS 3147, pp. 270–300, 2004.

nice graphical representation and formal background. In addition, modelling with Petri nets is popular because Petri nets usually allow a more compact and structured representation of the system behavior than automata. There are many case studies using Petri nets in modelling and control and many tools supported by sophisticated analytical methods. However, Petri nets (at least in their basic version) do not support the above mentioned features which are very essential for engineering applications: The absence of input/output structure seems to be a strong limitation. Additionally, the important feature of hierarchical structuring is not directly supported by Petri nets.

There are many compositional frameworks for Petri nets, mostly based on gluing common places and/or transitions. However, it is desirable that the composition of modules preserves the structure of modules. Modules of signal nets constitute an extension of Petri nets which supports input/output structuring, modularity and compositionality in an intuitive graphical way. This formalism was developed in a series of papers under the name *net condition/event system* and is widely used for modelling of complex DES, see e.g. [9,10,12]. A signal net is a Petri net enriched by *event signals*, which force the occurrence of (enabled) events, and *condition signals* which enable/prohibit the occurrence of events. Adding input and output signals to a signal net, one gets a *module of a signal net*. Modules of signal nets can be composed by connecting their respective input and output signals.

In the first part of this paper we summarize syntax and semantics of modules of elementary signal nets, where the underlying Petri nets are elementary Petri nets. In the second part, we give a survey on control synthesis for DES modelled by modules of elementary signal nets. In this part technical details are replaced by illustrations (for a detailed presentation see [18,19]). Furthermore, a brief comparison to the supervisory control synthesis approach based on automata is provided.

In the problem of control synthesis for DES, a system is given which can interfere with its environment via inputs and outputs. This is the object to be controlled, and it is called "plant". The goal of control is to ensure a specified behavior of this plant which is given as a set of desired sequences of inputs and outputs. The plant is therefore equipped with sensors that provide information about some (usually not all) so called *observable* states and state transitions of the plant. It is also equipped with actuators that allow to control the behavior of the plant by enforcing or preventing some (usually not all) so called *controllable* state transitions in the plant. The central idea is that plant and control build a so called *closed loop* (or *feedback loop*) which means, roughly speaking, that the control gives inputs to the actuators of the plant based on the observed sensor outputs of the plant.

Modelling a plant by a module of a signal net, sensors in the plant may provide condition signals to give information about a reached observable state to the control. For example, a condition signal can indicate that a process variable of the plant is within a given range of its value. Sensors in the plant may also provide event signals to give information about the occurrence of an observable state transition to the control. For example, it can be indicated by an event signal that a process variable in the plant is just reaching a threshold.

A controller that controls the plant may use both types of signals as well. Via condition signals, the controller prohibits/enables controllable state transitions in the plant whereas via event signals, the controller tries to force controllable state transitions in the plant to occur.

In [18,19], we identify which event signal inputs have to be sent to the plant module in order to observe only such sequences of event signal outputs which are prefixes of and can be completed to sequences of event signal outputs belonging to the control specification. This control specification is given as a regular language. The resulting output behavior of the plant is maximal with this properties. In other words, we construct a language over event signal inputs and outputs of the module of the plant which represents the maximally permissive nonblocking controllable behavior satisfying the control specification. Finally, we show in [19] that for such a behavior there exists a control module (of a signal net) which, composed with the plant module, realizes this behavior. As the main result of [19], we construct such a control module.

The formal definitions in [18,19] are based on low-level Petri nets, where tokens carry no data structure. In particular, the interfaces and the communication between modules are low-level. These elementary signal net models are close to the physical level (similar to assembler code in the area of programming languages). Of course, one can achieve more compact representations (for example of protocols, services, data types et cetera) by using appropriate high level concepts (such as high-level Petri nets in this case). However, the fundamental problems arising in controller synthesis considered in [18,19] (such as observability and controllability of behavior) are of low-level nature. For real applications, a higher-level modelling language would be more suitable. In [5] we present such a language based on signal nets extended by high-level features (such as data types, annotated condition signals, timers etc.) and employed it in a case study from automotive industry (modelling of controllers for the new AUDI A8 model).

Several related work employs modules of signal nets in the control of discrete event systems. In [9,10,12] effective solutions for particular classes of specifications, such as forbidden states, or simple desired and undesired sequences of events are described. An approach for control specification given by cycles of observable events was presented in [21]. Up to recent time, the problem of control synthesis for the general class of specifications given by regular languages (as in supervisory control theory for systems modelled by automata) remained open for modules of signal nets. In [19], we filled this gap.

The paper splits into two parts: In the first part we present *modules of elementary signal nets* with definition of step semantics, composition rules and input/output behavior. In the second part we illustrate control synthesis of DES with modules of elementary signal nets: In Subsection 3.1 we show how to automatically synthesize the maximally permissive nonblocking controllable behavior of a module of a signal net (representing the plant) respecting a given regular specification language. In Subsection 3.2 we present how to construct the controller as a module of a signal net. Finally, we take a short view on methods that use the structure of some models rather than the complete enumeration of the state space in Subsection 3.3. A conclusion and an outlook on further work is given in Section 4.

Part I

2   Modules of Signal Nets

As mentioned in the introduction, we use an extension of elementary Petri nets (1-safe Petri nets) which allows to model condition and event signals, supports modularity, and preserves the essential benefits of Petri nets. We assume the underlying elementary Petri nets to be equipped with the so called *first consume, then produce* semantics (since we allow loops, see e.g. [16]). The first step of the extension is to add two kinds of signals, namely active signals which force the occurrence of (enabled) transitions, and passive signals which enable/prohibit the occurrence of transitions. These signals are represented respectively by two kinds of arcs. A Petri net extended with such signals is simply called a *signal net*.

Active signals, also called event arcs, are represented by arcs connecting transitions. They are interpreted in the following way: An *event arc* leading from transition t_1 to transition t_2 specifies that, if transition t_1 occurs and transition t_2 is enabled to occur then the occurrence of t_2 is forced (synchronized) by the occurrence of t_1, i.e. then transitions t_1 and t_2 occur in one (synchronized) step. If t_2 is not enabled, t_1 occurs without t_2, while an occurrence of t_2 without t_1 is not possible. As an example, an event turning on a switch would be modelled via transition t_1, while the event lighting the bulb would be modelled via transition t_2.

In general, (synchronized) steps of transitions are defined inductively in the above way. Every step starts at one so called *spontaneous* transition which is not synchronized by another transition. It is required that there are no cycles of event arcs.

Consider a transition t which is synchronized by transitions $t_1, \ldots, t_n, n \geqslant 2$. Then there are two dialects in the literature to interpret such a situation. For simplicity we consider the case $n = 2$. In the first approach [9,10,12] both transitions t_1 and t_2 have to agree to synchronize t. Thus the only possible step of transitions involving t has to include transitions t_1 and t_2, too. We call this dialect AND-semantics (see Figure 1, part (b)). In the second one [4] the occurrence of at least one of the transitions t_1 and t_2 synchronizes transition t, if t is enabled. We call this dialect OR-semantics (see Figure 1, parts (a) and (c)).

In general, the relation given by event arcs builds a forest of arbitrary depth. We introduce the most general interpretation, where we distinguish between OR- and AND-synchronized transitions. An OR-synchronized transition demands to be synchronized by at least one of its synchronizing transitions, whereas an AND-synchronized transition demands to be synchronized by all of its synchronizing transitions. Since we allow loops w.r.t. single transitions, i.e. transitions connected to a place with flow arcs in both directions, we also allow loops w.r.t. steps of transitions (see Figure 2, part (a)).

Passive signals are expressed by so called *condition arcs* (also called read arcs or test arcs in the literature) connecting places and transitions. A condition arc leading from a place to a transition models the situation that the transition can only occur if the place is in a certain state but this state remains unchanged by the transition's occurrence (read operation) (see Figure 2, part (b)). There are no condition arcs leading from a transition to a place. Several transitions belonging to a synchronized step can test a place to be in a

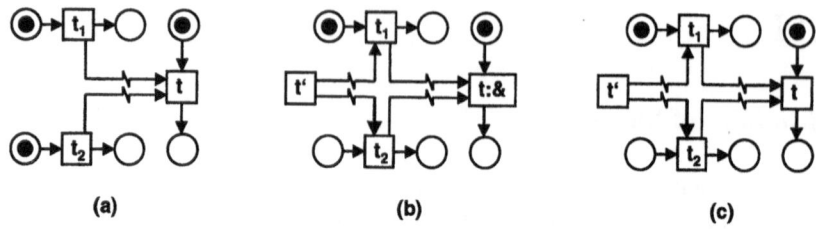

Fig. 1. In (a) the enabled steps are $\{t_1, t\}$ and $\{t_2, t\}$. (b) shows a signal net with AND-semantics: Here the only enabled step is $\{t', t_1\}$, i.e. t is not synchronized. In (c) the same net is shown in OR-semantics: Here we have the enabled step $\{t', t_1, t\}$, i.e. t is synchronized.

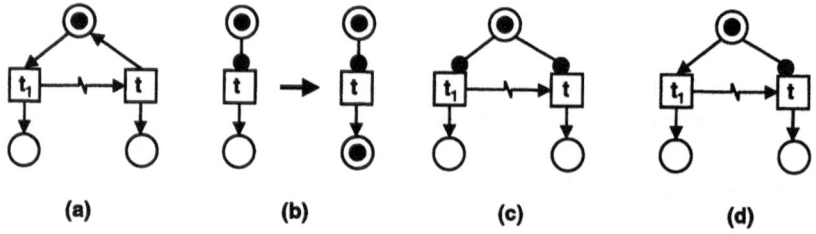

Fig. 2. (a) shows an enabled step $\{t_1, t\}$. The left part of (b) shows an enabled transition t which tests a place if it is marked. The occurrence of t leads to the marking shown in the right part of (b). Figures (c) and (d) again present situations of an enabled step $\{t_1, t\}$.

certain state via passive signals simultaneously since the state of this place is not changed by their occurrence (see Figure 2, part (c)). We also allow that a transition belongs to a synchronized step of transitions testing a place to be in a certain state via a passive signal, whereas the state of this place is changed by the occurrence of this or of another transition in this step. That means we use the so called *a priori* semantics [15] for the occurrence of steps of transitions, where testing of states precedes changing of states by occurrence of steps of transitions (see Figure 2, part (d)).

As usual, places, transitions and the flow relation are drawn using circles, boxes and arrows respectively. To distinguish between OR- and AND-synchronized transitions, AND-synchronized transitions are additionally labelled by the symbol "&". Event arcs and condition arcs are visualized using arcs of a special shape, as shown in Figure 1 and Figure 2.

Let x be a place or a transition: ${}^\bullet x$ is the set of transitions (places) connected with x by an arc ingoing to x, called *preset* of x. $x^\bullet$ is the set of transitions (places) connected with x by an arc outgoing from x, called *postset* of x. For a transition t, we denote in a similar fashion: ${}^+t$ is the set of places which are tested on presence of tokens by t (via a condition arc), called the *positive context* of t. Given a set $\xi \subseteq T$ of transitions, we extend the above notations to ${}^\bullet\xi$, $\xi^\bullet$ and ${}^+\xi$ via the union of sets.

A transition t is *enabled* at a marking m if all places in ${}^\bullet t$ and ${}^+t$ are marked and the places in $t^\bullet \setminus {}^\bullet t$ are unmarked at m.

A *(synchronized) step* of transitions is a set of transitions which can be constructed inductively in the following way: For each spontaneous transition t the set $\{t\}$ is a step. If ξ is a step, t is an OR-synchronized transition not in ξ and ξ contains at least one synchronizing transition of t, then $\xi \cup \{t\}$ is a step. If ξ is a step, t is an AND-synchronized transition not in ξ and ξ contains all synchronizing transition of t, then $\xi \cup \{t\}$ is a step.

A step ξ is *potentially enabled* at a marking m if

- all places in ${}^{\bullet}\xi$ and ${}^{+}\xi$ are marked at m,
- the places in $\xi^{\bullet} \setminus ({}^{\bullet}\xi \cup {}^{+}\xi)$ are unmarked at m, and
- all transitions $t_1, t_2 \in \xi$ are not in conflict w.r.t. to their pre- or postsets, i.e. ${}^{\bullet}t_1 \cap {}^{\bullet}t_2 = \emptyset$ and $t_1^{\bullet} \cap t_2^{\bullet} = \emptyset$.

From all steps potentially enabled at a marking m only those are *enabled* which are maximal with this property.

The *occurrence* of an enabled step ξ removes a token from each place of the preset of ξ and adds a token to each place of the postset of ξ. A sequence of steps which are enabled subsequently from the initial marking is called an *occurrence sequence*.

We add to a signal net an *input/output structure*. This structure consists of sets of event signal inputs and outputs, condition signal inputs and outputs, and arcs connecting these inputs and outputs with places and transitions of the signal net. The event signal inputs and outputs are connected via event arcs with transitions of the signal net. The condition signal inputs are connected with transitions of the signal net via condition arcs. The condition signal outputs are connected with places of the signal net via condition arcs. For the condition signal inputs, their initial states are fixed (either in *on-* or *off-state*). A signal net together with such an input/output structure defines a *module of a signal net* (see Figure 3).

We extend the notions of preset, postset and positive context to the added event and condition signal inputs and outputs in the obvious way.

Two modules A and B can be composed by identifying event resp. condition inputs of module A one by one with event resp. condition outputs of module B, and vice versa, employing a composition mapping Ω (see Figure 4). The identification of inputs and outputs via Ω is required to satisfy the following properties:

- A place of A connected to a transition of B via a condition signal output of A which is identified with a condition signal input of B is initially marked if and only if the condition signal input is in on-state, and vice versa.
- No cycles of event arcs are generated.

The connections of places and transitions of one module to places and transitions of the other module via identified inputs and outputs are replaced by direct signal arcs (see Figure 5). The *composition of A and B w.r.t.* Ω is denoted by $A *_{\Omega} B$.

We are interested in the behavior of a module of a signal net A w.r.t. a given environment: Transitions connected by an event signal input to the environment are not able to occur spontaneously but need to be synchronized by the event input in order to occur. Similar, a transition connected by a condition signal input to the environment is only able to occur if the condition signal input is in on-state. In the most general case, this

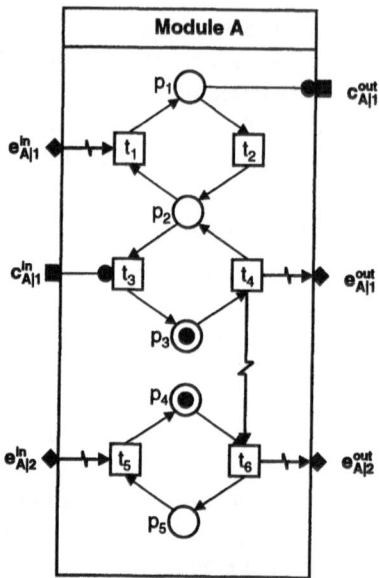

Fig. 3. A module of a signal net with condition inputs $C^{in} = \{c^{in}_{A|1}\}$, event inputs $E^{in} = \{e^{in}_{A|1}, e^{in}_{A|2}\}$, condition outputs $C^{out} = \{c^{out}_{A|1}\}$ and event outputs $E^{out} = \{e^{out}_{A|1}, e^{out}_{A|2}\}$.

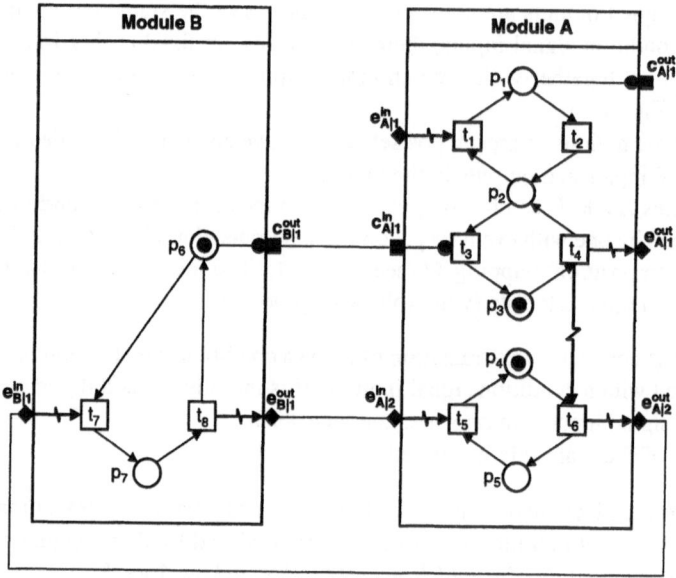

Fig. 4. The composition of two modules.

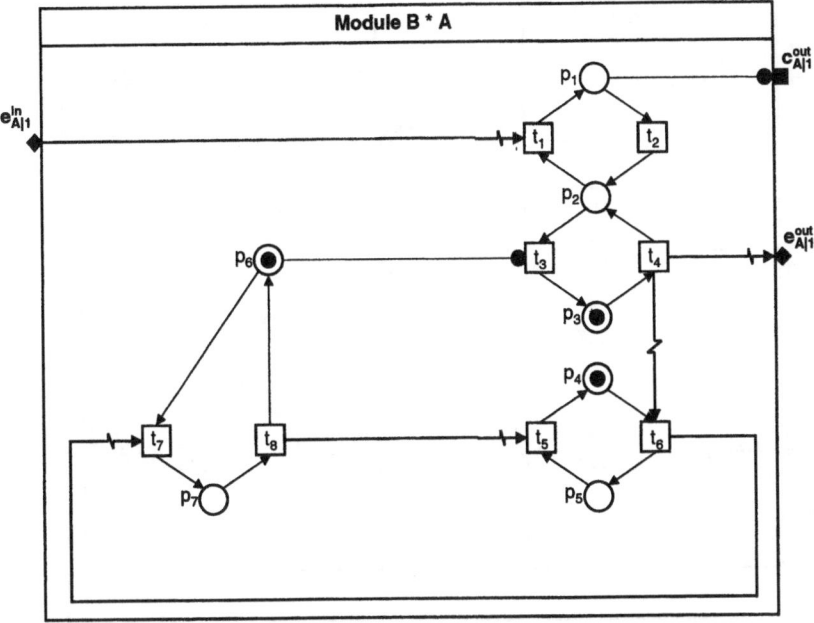

Fig. 5. The result of the composition of the modules from Figure 4.

environment is assumed to be maximally permissive in the sense that there are no causal dependencies between sending event signal inputs and switching on and off condition signal inputs. We model such an environment as a module $\mathcal{E}$ of a signal net and then compose the environment module appropriately with the module A such that $\mathcal{E}$ realizes a *maximally permissive environment* in the following sense (see Figure 6):

- At any moment, $\mathcal{E}$ can send event signal inputs to A: each event signal input of A is synchronized by a corresponding so called *input transition* in $\mathcal{E}$ that is always enabled;
- at any moment, $\mathcal{E}$ can send condition signal inputs to A: Each condition input of M is switched on resp. off by marking resp. unmarking a corresponding so called *input place* in $\mathcal{E}$;
- $\mathcal{E}$ can observe signal outputs of A: Every event signal output of A synchronizes a corresponding so called *output transition* in $\mathcal{E}$ that is always enabled. Every condition signal output enables resp. disables a corresponding *output transition* in $\mathcal{E}$ that is always enabled.

By this definition, in $\mathcal{E}$ no synchronization between its transitions is allowed. In particular, input signals can not be sent in steps from $\mathcal{E}$ to A, and output signals of A can only be observed by $\mathcal{E}$ and not synchronize input signals of A via $\mathcal{E}$.

The assumption that the environment (which later becomes the controller) changes at most one of its inputs to the plant at each moment does not always hold in practice. A controller might change more than one input to the plant within one cyclic run of its control program. In such a case, an environment enabling steps of input signals has to be

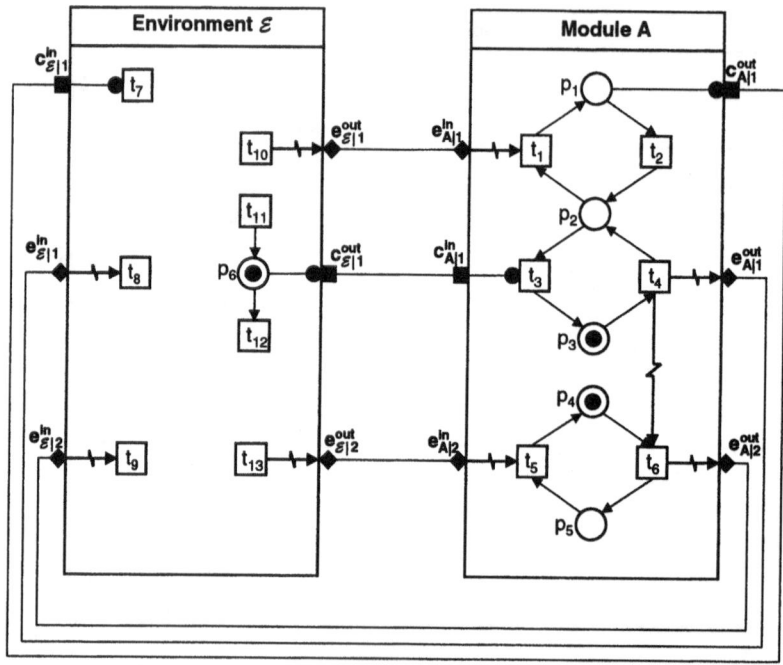

Fig. 6. The composition of the module in Figure 3 with its maximally permissive environment module.

considered. It is straightforward to modify all synthesis algorithms presented in the next part of this paper in order to deal with an environment allowing such steps of inputs.

The composition of A with its maximally permissive environment $\mathcal{E}$ is called the *standalone of A*. This composition has empty input/output structure. As an example, see Figure 7. The standalone is a model representing the uncontrolled behavior of the plant. The set L_A of all occurrence sequences of the standalone of A is called the *behavior of A*.

Since the underlying Petri net is assumed to be 1-safe, the behavior L_A of A is a regular language and can be represented as a finite automaton.

In [17] we introduced the *input/output behavior* of A as the set of all occurrence sequences of the standalone of A in which the transitions of A are hidden. Further, we defined two modules to be *input/output equivalent* if they have the same input/output structure and identical input/output behavior. By defining an appropriate composition operation for standalones, we showed that input/output equivalence is preserved by the composition of modules. This is a crucial concept for hierarchical modelling which allows to replace a module by a more abstract/concrete module with the same "input/output" functionality. Moreover, using the composition operation for standalones, it can easily be seen that the input/output behavior of the composition of two modules A and B can be represented by the composition of the standalones of A and B.

Summarizing, modules of signal nets are an extension of Petri nets supporting input/output structures, modularity and compositionality in an intuitive graphical way with precise syntax and semantics. This fact gives a motivation for a more detailed theoretical

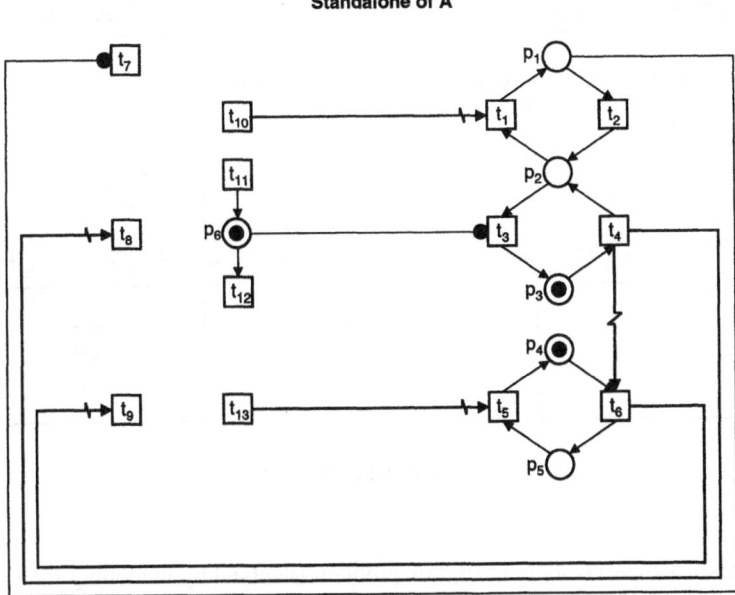

Standalone of A

Fig. 7. The standalone of the module of a signal net in Figure 3.

investigation of this extension of Petri nets. In the following part of the paper we discuss the role of both kinds of signals in control tasks and we focus on control aspects in general.

Part II

3 Controller Synthesis

As mentioned in the introduction, the aim in control synthesis of DES is to influence the behavior of a system by a control via passive and active signals in order to get a specified desired behavior. In principle, there are two possibilities to specify a desired behavior (see [2] for an actual survey, and [1,28] for recent developments):

- The event-based approach used in the seminal work of Ramadge and Wonham on supervisory control of DES [23]. In this framework, automata are used to model the behavior of the plant and of the control. The desired behavior is given by legal sequences of events.
- The state-based approach [13], where Petri nets are used to model plant and control. The desired behavior is derived from a set of legal resp. forbidden states.

In both approaches, the main problem is that the considered modelling formalism (languages, automata, Petri nets) does not provide a straightforward mechanism for enforcing events in the plant.

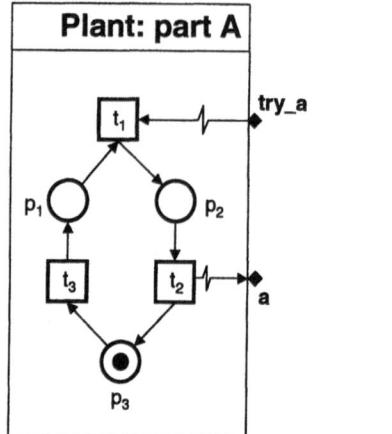
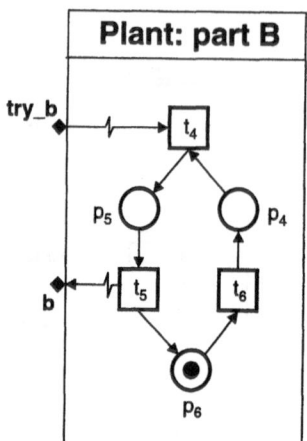

Fig. 8. Model of the plant.

In classical supervisory control, this problem is solved by modelling the enforcing of an event in the plant via prohibiting all other possible events [6]. As a consequence, the behavior of the plant cannot be forced by the control, now called supervisor, but only be restricted. Formally, a regular prefix closed language over a set of events representing the uncontrolled behavior of the plant and a regular subset of this language representing the restricted desired behavior is given. In the most general case, one distinguishes between controllable events (which can be prohibited by the supervisor) and uncontrollable events, and between observable events (which can be observed by the supervisor) and unobservable events. The question is, which controllable events should be prohibited by the supervisor after observing a certain sequence of observable events in order to disable all undesired behavior in a *minimal restrictive way*.

We present an alternative to the existing approaches to control of DES, employing *direct enforcing of events* in our models. The aim of control is to *maximally force* the behavior of the plant in order to ensure the specified desired behavior. Our formalism is suitable for both kinds of specifications of the desired behavior. In the literature, the event-based approach is further developed than the state-based approach in the sense that it allows more general specifications [30]. Therefore, we concentrate in this paper on an event-based specification of the desired behavior.

As an illustrative running example, consider the model of a plant consisting of two modules A and B given in Figure 8. The modules are independent. Each module models a task. The behavior of a module is cyclic and consists of three events. The event t_1 (resp. t_4) occurs if it is synchronized by the event signal try_a (resp. try_b) and if the module is ready to start (place p_1 (resp. p_4) is marked). The event t_2 (resp. t_5), which represents that the task is finished, is spontaneous but can be observed through occurrence of the event signal a (resp. b). Finally, the event t_3 (resp. t_6), which initializes the module to be ready to start, is spontaneous and unobservable.

In the figures we draw the two modules separately but we understand them as one module, obtained by a composition with an empty composition mapping. In other words,

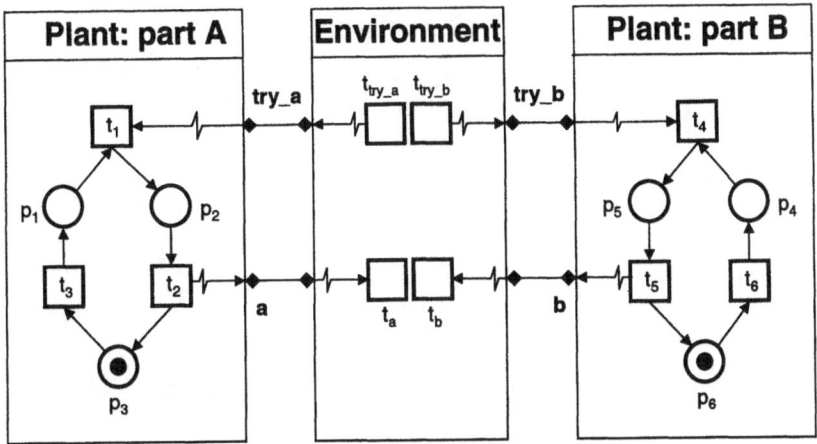

Fig. 9. Model of the plant together with its environment.

we consider the module obtained by putting the both modules side-by-side without connections between their input/output signals. We call this module $\mathcal{P}$.

The aim of the control specification is to coordinate the behavior of both modules in order to ensure the following behavior: Both tasks alternate strictly, starting with the task of module A and ending with the task of module B. More precisely, since only output behavior is relevant, the aim is to observe desired sequences of event output signals. The set of desired sequences is given by the regular language $L_c = (ab)^*$. In general, the desired behavior is given by a regular language which involves event signal inputs. Moreover, since the event arc relation produces a semantics of (synchronized) steps of transitions, the desired behavior must be specified as a regular language over steps of event signal inputs and outputs.

Let $T = \{t_1, \dots, t_6\}$ be the set of transitions and $P = \{p_1, \dots, p_6\}$ be the set of places of the plant. To denote a marking in figures, we use the vector-like notation, which is more usual in control literature.

Consider the maximally permissive environment $\mathcal{E}$ of $\mathcal{P}$, shown in Figure 9, and the standalone of $\mathcal{P}$, shown in Figure 10, which is a composition of $\mathcal{P}$ and $\mathcal{E}$ w.r.t. to a composition mapping Ω. We denote by $I = \{t_{try\_a}, t_{try\_b}\}$ the set of input transitions of $\mathcal{E}$ corresponding to the event signal inputs try_a, try_b and by $O = \{t_a, t_b\}$ the set of output transitions of $\mathcal{E}$ corresponding to the event signal outputs a, b. The behavior $L_{\mathcal{P}}$ of $\mathcal{P}$ is given as the set of all occurrence sequences of the standalone of $\mathcal{P}$. It can be represented by the finite automaton shown in Figure 11. In order to be able to compare $L_{\mathcal{P}}$ with the specification $(ab)^*$, we restate the specification in the form $L_c = (t_a t_b)^*$, replacing event signal outputs by the corresponding output transitions in $\mathcal{E}$.

A sublanguage K of $L_{\mathcal{P}}$ *satisfies the specification* if each occurrence sequence of K is a prefix of an occurrence sequence of K whose projection onto the set O of output transitions of $\mathcal{E}$ is a string in L_c. In particular, each projection of an occurrence sequence of K onto O is required to be a prefix of a string in L_c. The above condition implies that K represents a nonblocking behavior where the tasks specified by L_c always can

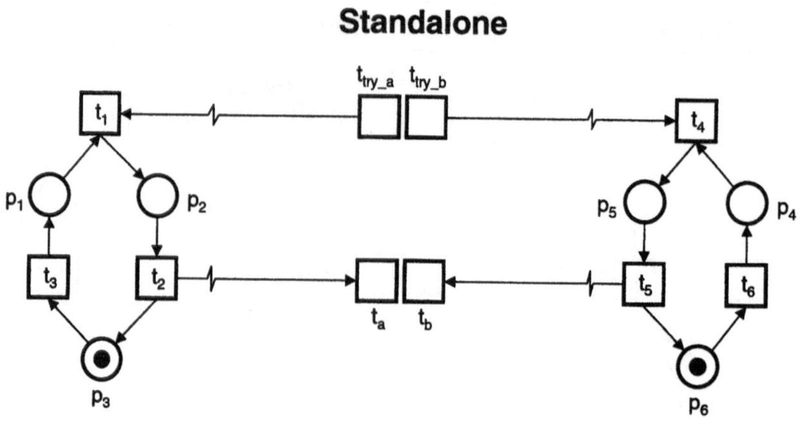

Standalone

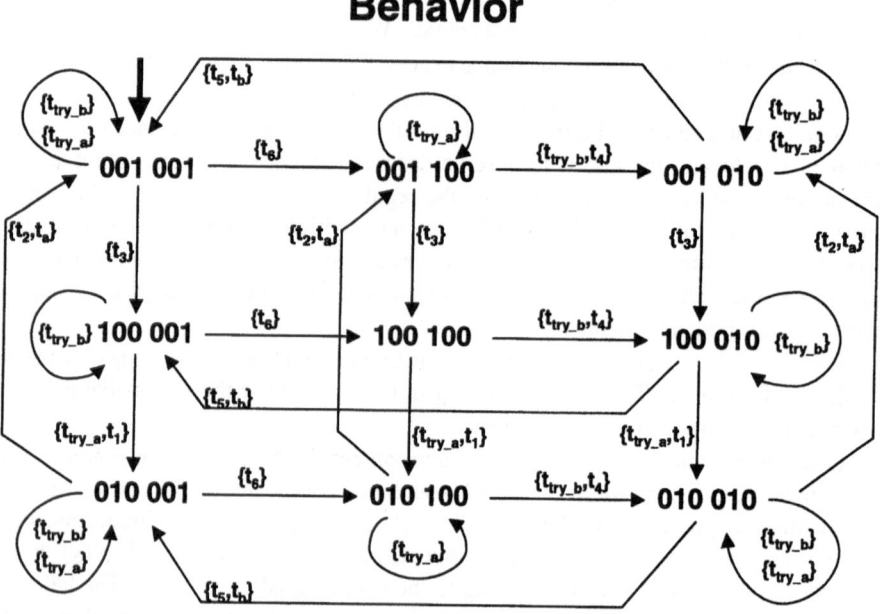

Fig. 10. Standalone of the plant.

Behavior

Fig. 11. Behavior of the standalone of the plant.

be completed. If L_P already satisfies the specification, $\mathcal{E}$ is the desired control module $\mathcal{C}$. Therefore, $\mathcal{E}$ can be seen as a first approximation of $\mathcal{C}$.

In our example, the projection of the occurrence sequence $\{t_6\}\{t_{try\_b}, t_4\}\{t_5, t_b\}$ onto O yields the string $\{t_b\}$, which is not a prefix of a word in $L_c = (t_a t_b)^*$. In such cases, the aim is to add new net elements to $\mathcal{E}$, thus defining causal dependencies between input and output transitions of $\mathcal{E}$ to prohibit such undesired occurrence sequences.

To summarize, the aim is to construct from $\mathcal{E}$ a control module $\mathcal{C}$ which composed with $\mathcal{P}$ by the same composition mapping Ω defining the composition of $\mathcal{P}$ and $\mathcal{E}$ satisfies: Each occurrence sequence of the underlying signal net of $\mathcal{C} *_\Omega \mathcal{P}$ respects the desired behavior in the sense that this occurrence sequence can be completed to another occurrence sequence of this underlying signal net whose projection onto (input and) output transitions of $\mathcal{C}$, which replace event signal (inputs and) outputs of $\mathcal{P}$, is a string of the desired behavior.

We synthesize $\mathcal{C}$ in two steps. First, we define conditions of *controllability* of a regular sublanguage of $L_\mathcal{P}$ (analogously to [23]) and compute the maximally permissive controllable nonblocking subbehavior L_{nbsafe} of $L_\mathcal{P}$ satisfying L_c as a finite automaton. This is done by manipulating regular languages in subsection 3.1. Second, we synthesize a signal net simulating the control structure given by this automaton and add this signal net to $\mathcal{E}$. By this signal net the input and output transitions of $\mathcal{E}$ are coordinated in such a way that L_{nbsafe} is realized.

3.1 The Behavior of the Controlled Plant

We formulate our approach similar as it is done in classical supervisory control. The main technical differences to the classical supervisory control approach are due to the mentioned step semantics. Nevertheless, some algorithms of classical supervisory control can at least be adapted to our framework. While omitting therefore most details of these algorithms, our paper remains self contained, i.e., it can be understood without previous knowledge of supervisory control.

As mentioned in the last section, our aim is to compute a regular sublanguage L_{nbsafe} of $L_\mathcal{P}$ representing the maximally permissive controllable nonblocking subbehavior of $L_\mathcal{P}$ satisfying the specification. Roughly speaking, controllable means that L_{nbsafe} can be realized by a control.

The computation of L_{nbsafe} is done in several steps by manipulating regular languages. For this we need a special projection operator λ_Y. Applying λ_Y to a language over an alphabet of the form 2^X means to project each word in this language onto $2^{X \setminus Y}$. In [18,19] we showed that projection operations of the form λ_Y and pumping operations of the form λ_Y^{-1} preserve the regularity of languages.

"Good" occurrence sequences. In a first step we delete all occurrence sequences w from $L_\mathcal{P}$ satisfying $\lambda_{I \cup T}(w) \notin \overline{L_c}$, i.e. whose projections onto output transitions are not prefixes of L_c ($\overline{L_c}$ denotes the prefix closure of L_c). We call such occurrence sequences *"bad" occurrence sequences* and the remaining ones *"good" occurrence sequences*.

For example, $w = \{t_3\}\{t_{try\_a}, t_1\}\{t_2, t_a\}$ is a good occurrence sequence since $\lambda_{I \cup T}(w) = \{t_a\} \in \overline{L_c}$, and $v = \{t_3\}\{t_{try\_a}, t_1\}\{t_2, t_a\}\{t_3\}\{t_{try\_a}, t_1\}\{t_2, t_a\}$ is a bad occurrence sequence since $\lambda_{I \cup T}(v) = \{t_a\}\{t_a\} \notin \overline{L_c}$.

The set of all good occurrence sequences is denoted by L_{psafe}. It can formally be computed by

$$L_{psafe} = \lambda_{I \cup T}^{-1}(\overline{L_c}) \cap L_\mathcal{P},$$

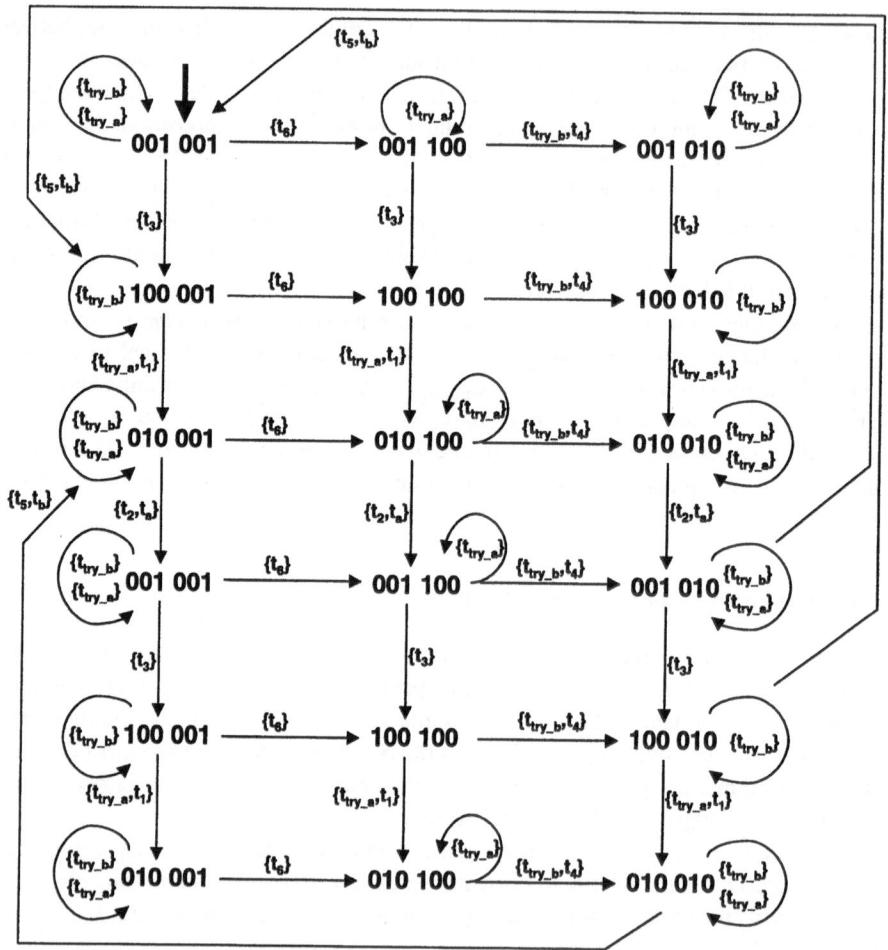

Fig. 12. Automaton recognizing the language L_{psafe}.

and is therefore regular. For our running example, Figure 12 shows a representation of L_{psafe} as a finite automaton.

Controllable occurrence sequences. In L_{psafe} there may exist good occurrence sequences which can be extended within $L_{\mathcal{P}}$ to bad occurrence sequences. For example, the good occurrence sequence $w = \{t_6\}\{t_{try\_b}, t_4\}$ can be extended by the step $\{t_5, t_b\}$ to the bad occurrence sequence $v = w\{t_5, t_b\} = \{t_6\}\{t_{try\_b}, t_4\}\{t_5, t_b\}$. If this extension is not controllable, i.e. contains no controllable transition, it can not be avoided by the control. In our example, once w is allowed, v can not be avoided: The step $\{t_5, t_b\}$ is not controllable, but can only be observed by the control. Therefore, we require L_{nbsafe} to satisfy the property

(1) *What cannot be prevented, should be legal*

which we call the *first condition of controllability*. It corresponds to the classical notion of *controllability* in supervisory control.

Good occurrence sequences which can be extended by uncontrollable steps to bad occurrence sequences are called *dangerous occurrence sequences*. They must be cut off at the last possibility of control, i.e. the last possible signal input (if there is one). In our example, after the step $\{t_6\}$, sending a signal input via occurrence of the transition t_{try_b} should be forbidden, so w is cut after $\{t_6\}$. By this, all dangerous occurrence sequences ending with a step containing an input and their futures are deleted from L_{psafe}.

Due to unobservable transitions, there may remain good occurrence sequences which cannot be distinguished by the control from dangerous occurrence sequences deleted in the last computation step. For example, the control can not decide whether the occurrence sequence $\{t_6\}$ has occurred or not since t_6 is an unobservable transition. Therefore, forbidding the occurrence sequence $\{t_6\}\{t_{try\_b}, t_4\}$ means to forbid also the occurrence sequence $\{t_{try\_b}\}$. This follows the rule

(2) *What cannot be distinguished, cannot call for different control actions,*

called the *second condition of controllability*. It corresponds to the notion of *observability* in supervisory control.

In our example, since the signal input $\{t_{try\_b}\}$ is forbidden after the occurrence of $\{t_6\}$ according to the last computation step, it must also be forbidden from the initial marking (after the empty occurrence sequence). The cutting off of appropriate inputs can be represented by deleting corresponding edges in the automaton representing L_{psafe}, see Figure 13.

Deleting all dangerous occurrence sequences and all occurrence sequences which are undistinguishable to a dangerous occurrence sequence L_{psafe} gives the language L_{safe}.

L_{safe} again can be expressed by a closed formula over regular languages, and is therefore regular. Moreover, it was proven to be the maximally permissive controllable sublanguage of $L_{\mathcal{P}}$ in [19]. For our running example, Figure 14 shows a representation of L_{safe} as a finite automaton.

In general, there can be an occurrence sequence w from $L_{\mathcal{P}}$ which contains no input transition and whose projection onto O is not a prefix of a string in L_c. In this case we cannot control the plant in such a way that no undesired behavior will happen. Thus, only if there is no such sequence, the maximally permissive controllable sublanguage of $L_{\mathcal{P}}$ exists.

Blocking occurrence sequences. By construction, every projection of an occurrence sequence in L_{safe} onto O is a prefix of a string in L_c. However, it might happen that there are occurrence sequences that cannot be completed within L_{safe} to an occurrence sequence whose projection onto O is in L_c, i.e. the desired behavior is blocked. We call such occurrence sequences *blocking*.

In our example, L_{safe} does not contain blocking occurrence sequences and therefore is already the searched language L_{nbsafe}. Therefore, we illustrate the existence of

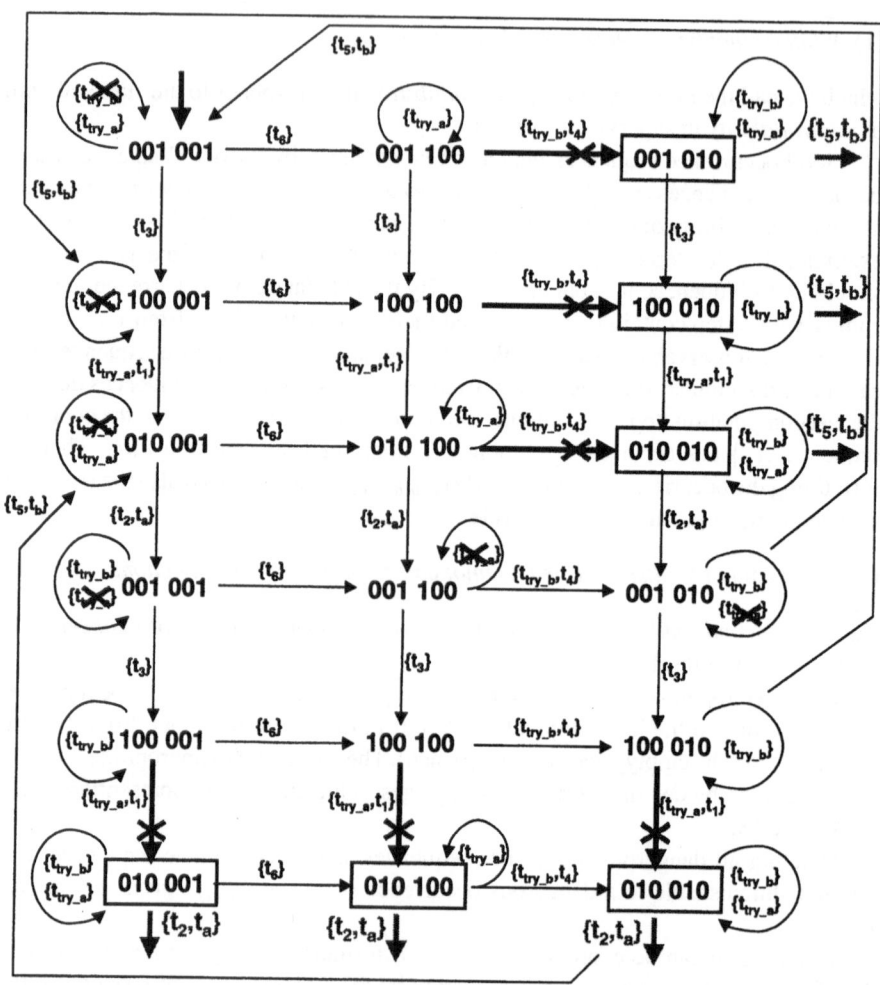

Fig. 13. Removing dangerous occurrence sequences and their future from the language L_{psafe}.

blocking occurrence sequences by another example of the standalone of a module of a plant $\mathcal{P}'$ given in Figure 15. The behavior $L_{\mathcal{P}'}$ of $\mathcal{P}'$ is given by the automaton in Figure 16. The automaton in Figure 17, also representing $L_{\mathcal{P}'}$, is more appropriate to illustrate the procedure of deleting blocking occurrence sequences.

The control specification is given again by the regular expression $(t_a t_b)^*$. All projections of occurrence sequences of the standalone onto $O = \{t_a, t_b\}$ are prefixes of strings in L_c. Thus, $L_{safe} = L_{\mathcal{P}'}$. However, the occurrence sequence

$$\{t_4\}\{t_{i\_1}, t_1\}\{t_5, t_7, t_a\}\{t_{i\_3}, t_3\}\{t_6, t_8, t_b\}\{t_5, t_9, t_a\}$$

is blocking.

Since every future of a blocking occurrence sequence is also blocking, we can delete blocking occurrence sequences by cutting them off at the last possible input (if there

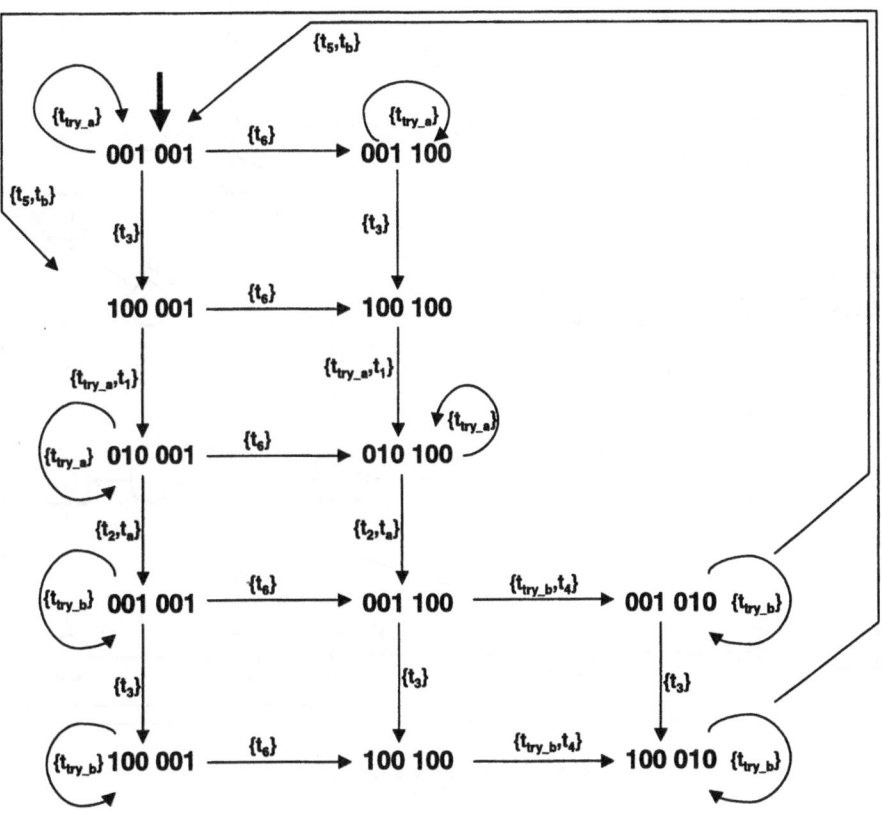

Fig. 14. Automaton recognizing the language L_{safe}.

is one). The prefixes ending with these inputs are called *real bad choices*. In the above example, the last possible input is $\{t_{i\_3}, t_3\}$ and

$$\{t_4\}\{t_{i\_1}, t_1\}\{t_5, t_7, t_a\}\{t_{i\_3}, t_3\}$$

is the corresponding real bad choice (see Figure 17).

Due to the second condition of controllability, such an input must be forbidden for all occurrence sequences which are undistinguishable to a real bad choice. Such occurrence sequences are called *bad choices*. In our example,

$$\{t_{i\_1}, t_1\}\{t_5, t_a\}\{t_{i\_3}, t_3\}$$

is a bad choice undistinguishable to the previous real bad choice (see Figure 17).

Deleting all bad choices and their futures from L_{safe} possibly produces new blocking occurrence sequences. For example, after deleting the real bad choice

$$\{t_4\}\{t_{i\_1}, t_1\}\{t_5, t_7, t_a\}\{t_{i\_3}, t_3\}$$

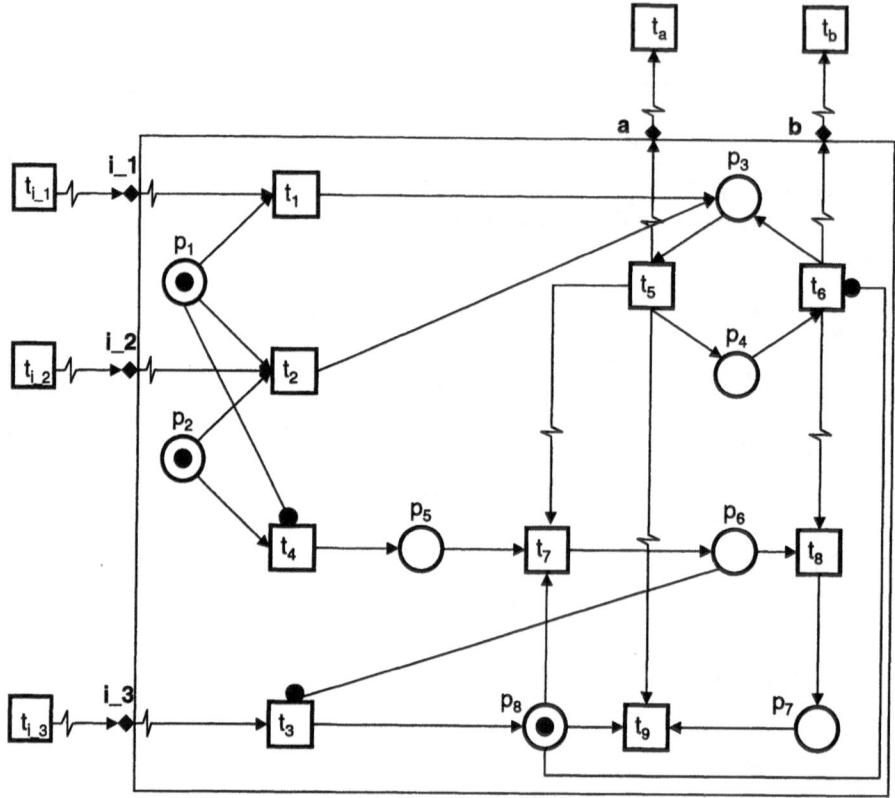

Fig. 15. Standalone of a module.

and its future produces the new blocking occurrence sequence

$$\{t_4\}\{t_{i\_1}, t_1\}\{t_5, t_7, t_a\}.$$

Therefore we have to iterate this procedure (see Figure 17).

To state the algorithm, we denote for any sublanguage K of L_{safe} by $K_{blocking}$ the set of all blocking words of K and by $K_{badchoice}$ the corresponding bad choices in K. We showed in [19] that if K is regular then also $K_{blocking}$ and $K_{badchoice}$ are regular, since they can then be expressed by a closed formula over regular languages. The following algorithm deletes subsequently all blocking words from L_{safe}:

Input: Language $K^0 = L_{safe}$, Integer $i = 0$.

Step 1:
Compute $K^i_{blocking}$.

Step 2:
If $K^i_{blocking}$ contains at least one word without any input **return** *"L_{nbsafe} does not*

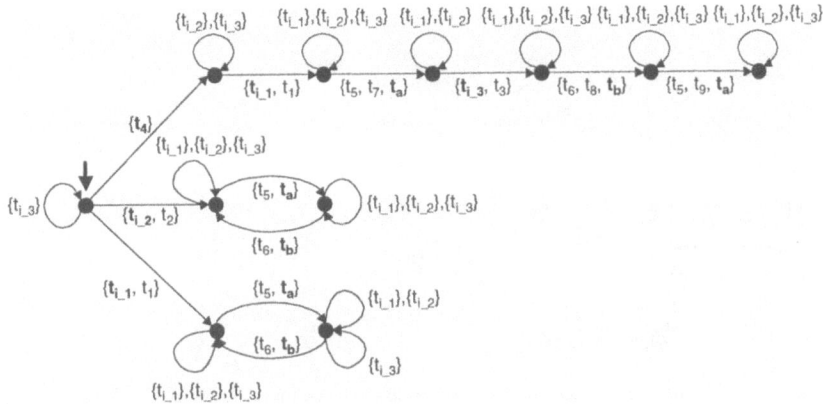

Fig. 16. Automaton representing the behavior of the standalone from Figure 15.

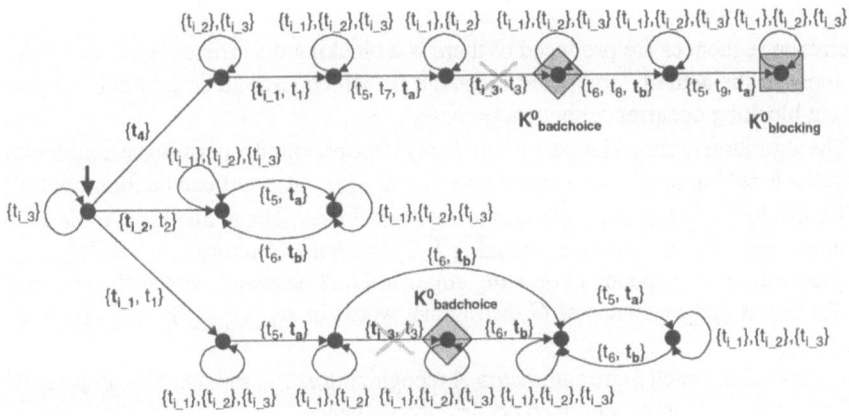

Fig. 17. Automaton representing the behavior of the standalone from Figure 15 which splits the bad choices from other words.

exist" (because there is no possibility to avoid this word by control).
If $K^i_{blocking}$ is empty **return** K^i.

Step 3:
Compute $K^i_{badchoice}$.
Set K^{i+1} by removing all words of $K^i_{badchoice}$ and their future from K^i.
Set $i = i + 1$.
Goto Step 1.

Starting with $K^0 = L_{safe}$ the algorithm iteratively deletes blocking occurrence sequences by cutting them off at the last possible inputs and by additionally deleting all undistinguishable occurrence sequences. This is done until either no new blocking

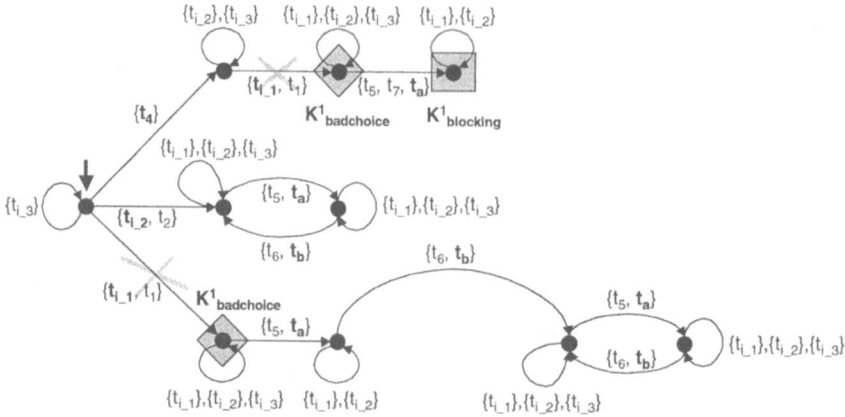

Fig. 18. Automaton obtained by deleting edges representing bad choices from automaton in Figure 17.

occurrence sequences are produced or there is a blocking occurrence sequence without any input in the actually computed language (in which case no controllable language without blocking occurrence sequences exists).

The algorithm returns a language if and only if the maximally permissive nonblocking controllable sublanguage exists, which we call L_{nbsafe}. A proof can be found in [19].

We briefly show that the algorithm always terminates. The main idea is to find a deterministic finite automaton G recognizing L_{safe} such that *deleting words* of $K^i_{badchoice}$ and their future corresponds to *deleting edges* in G. A necessary *and* sufficient condition for this is that the states of G distinguish words in $K^i_{badchoice}$ from words not in $K^i_{badchoice}$.

In general, not each finite automaton A recognizing L_{safe} satisfies this property. For example, the previously mentioned occurrence sequence

$$\{t_{i\_1}, t_1\}\{t_5, t_a\}\{t_{i\_3}, t_3\}$$

is a bad choice. However, in the automaton representing L_{safe} from Figure 16 the occurrence sequence

$$\{t_{i\_1}, t_1\}\{t_5, t_a\}\{t_6, t_b\}\{t_5, t_a\},$$

which is no bad choice in K^0, leads to the same state. In this case, deleting the corresponding edge would cut also nonblocking behavior off, i.e. it would cut too much.

In [19] we showed that such an automaton G always exists by an effective construction.

Figure 17 shows an automaton recognizing the same behavior as the automaton in Figure 16 which distinguishes between bad choices. In the automaton of Figure 17 the bad choice (of the language K^0)

$$\{t_{i\_1}, t_1\}\{t_5, t_a\}\{t_{i\_3}, t_3\}$$

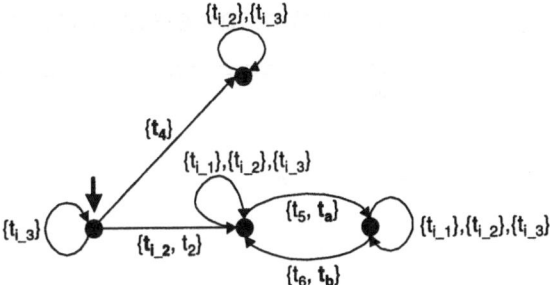

Fig. 19. Automaton obtained by deleting edges representing bad choices from automaton in Figure 18.

is now recognized by a different state as the occurrence sequence

$$\{t_{i\_1}, t_1\}\{t_5, t_a\}\{t_6, t_b\}\{t_5, t_a\}.$$

The application of the algorithm to the automaton in Figure 17 is illustrated in Figures 18 and 19. In the resulting automaton in Figure 19 the transition t_4, which can occur spontaneously, leads to a deadlock in the module. However, this is an "allowed" deadlock because the control specification "if a happens then b must happen too" is still satisfied.

3.2 Synthesis of Control Modules

In this subsection we show how to synthesize a control module C from the controllable subbehavior L_{nbsafe} (see Figure 14) of L_P (see Figure 11) by adding new net elements to the environment module $\mathcal{E}$ (see Figure 9). The composition of the resulting control module C with the plant module $\mathcal{P}$ has exactly the behavior L_{nbsafe}, in the following sense: The projection of the behavior of this composed module onto the set $I \cup O \cup T$ equals L_{nbsafe}.

To synthesize C, we consider the observable part of L_{nbsafe}, i.e. its projection $\lambda_T(L_{nbsafe})$ onto input and output transitions. Figure 21 shows a possible automaton A recognizing $\lambda_T(L_{nbsafe})$. This automaton can be computed in two steps: First take the automaton recognizing L_{nbsafe} from Figure 14 and hide all transitions of T. The result is the nondeterministic ϵ-automaton shown in Figure 20 (ϵ is the empty word). This automaton can be transformed by a standard procedure into an equivalent deterministic automaton. The main idea for the construction of C is to simulate the control flow given by A by a signal net and to add this signal net to $\mathcal{E}$.

For an automaton with states drawn as filled circles and with labelled directed edges between states drawn as arrows with annotation, an edge leading from state s to state s' with label x is denoted by $s \xrightarrow{x} s'$.

In our example, it is quite straightforward to compute a signal net which simulates A: Every state s becomes a place p_s, and every edge $s \xrightarrow{x} s'$ becomes a transition $t_{s \xrightarrow{x} s'}$. In case $s \neq s'$, $t_{s \xrightarrow{x} s'}$ has the preset $\{p_s\}$ and the postset $\{p_{s'}\}$. In case $s = s'$, $t_{s \xrightarrow{x} s'}$ tests p_s to be marked by a condition arc. Initially the place corresponding to the initial

$\lambda_T(L_{safe})$: nondeterministic ε-automaton

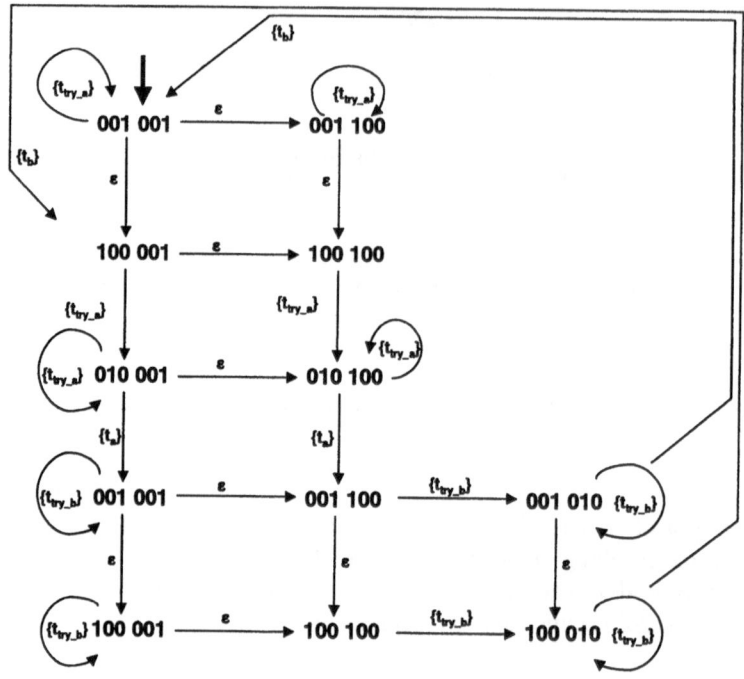

Fig. 20. The nondeterministic ε-automaton recognizing $\lambda_T(L_{safe})$ computed from the automaton recognizing L_{safe} from Figure 14.

state is marked. The procedure is illustrated in Figure 22. For convenience, we use a slightly simpler notation for the transitions. In case $x = \{t_{try\_a}\}$ we write $t_{to\_try\_a}$ for $t_{s \xrightarrow{x} s'}$. This illustrates the intended meaning of $t_{to\_try\_a}$ to send the input signal try_a to the plant. In case $x = \{t_a\}$ we write t_{from_a} for $t_{s \xrightarrow{x} s'}$. This shows the intended meaning of t_{from_a} to observe the output signal a sent from the plant. The labels $x = \{t_{try\_b}\}$ and $x = \{t_b\}$ are treated analogously. Each state s of the automaton corresponds to the marking in the signal net where exactly p_s is marked.

When the resulting signal net is connected with the input and output transitions of $\mathcal{C}$ inherited from $\mathcal{E}$, the control module shown in Figure 23 is obtained. Using the connections between the plant and its environment $\mathcal{E}$, we get the controlled composed module shown in Figure 24. The control module formalizes the intuition of how to send inputs in order to observe prefixes of the desired output behavior $(t_a t_b)^*$: First the input try_a is sent at least once. It is sent as long as one observes the output a. After that it is no longer possible to send try_a. Then try_b is sent at least once. This input is sent as long as one observes the output b. Finally the behavior starts from the beginning.

In general, the automaton A is more complicated because the arc labels are steps consisting of more than one transition. Therefore, the construction of $\mathcal{C}$ is more sophisticated. In [19] the construction of $\mathcal{C}$ for general automata A is presented. This paper

$\lambda_T(L_{safe})$: deterministic automata

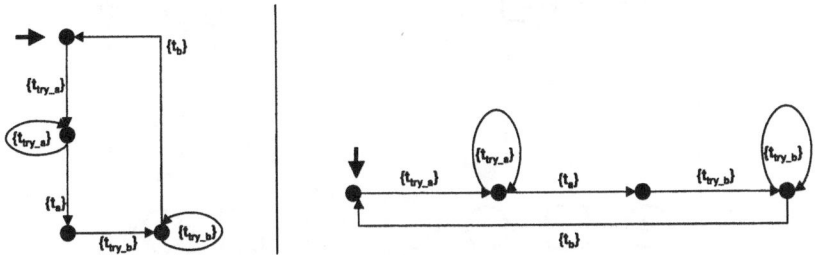

Fig. 21. The deterministic automaton recognizing $\lambda_T(L_{safe})$ computed from the nondeterministic ϵ-automaton from Figure 20. It is drawn in two different forms: The left Figure corresponds to the shape of the automaton recognizing L_{psafe} from Figure 12. The right Figure is convenient to deduce the signal net representing the control flow.

Associated signal net

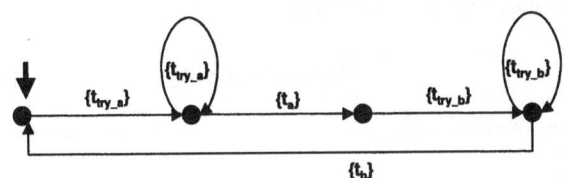

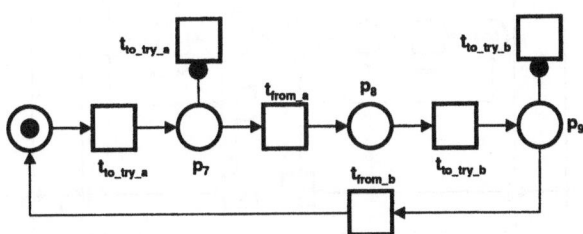

Fig. 22. The signal net simulating the control flow given by the automaton shown above.

contains a proof that the projection of the behavior of the composition of $\mathcal{P}$ and $\mathcal{C}$ onto the set $I \cup O \cup T$ equals L_{nbsafe}. Since the general construction is very involved, we only give some examples for possible problems and their solutions.

Basically, each state s of A can be modelled as a place p_s, and each labelled edge $s \xrightarrow{x} s'$ of A as an AND-synchronized transition $t_{s \xrightarrow{x} s'}$. In the case $x \subseteq O$, the transition $t_{s \xrightarrow{x} s'}$ is intended to observe the step of outputs x. It is therefore synchronized by all

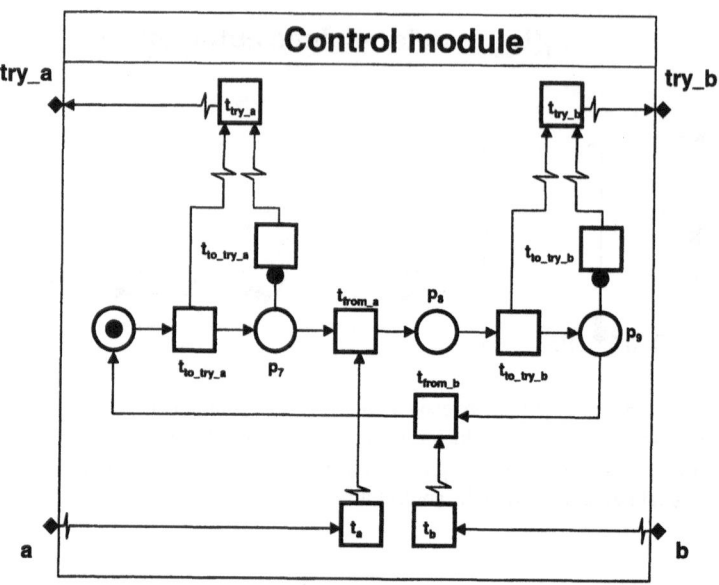

Fig. 23. The resulting control module given by the signal net from Figure 22 connected with the input and output transition from the environment.

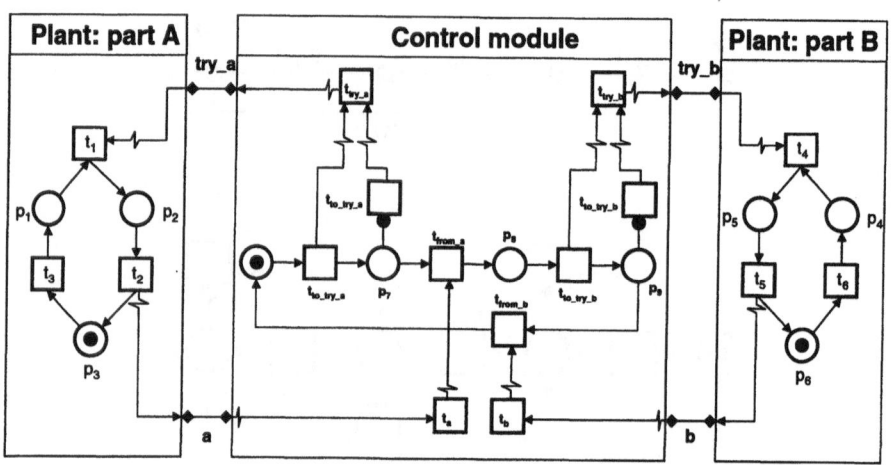

Fig. 24. The control module connected with the two plant modules. The composed module satisfies the specification in a minimal restrictive way.

output transitions in the set $\{t_a \in O \mid a \in x\}$. If x contains signal inputs, the situation is more complicated. Each state is represented by a marking which consists in general of more than one place.

Avoiding undesired conflicts caused by shared pre-places. Consider the automaton A shown in the left part and the signal net simulating A in the middle part of Figure 25

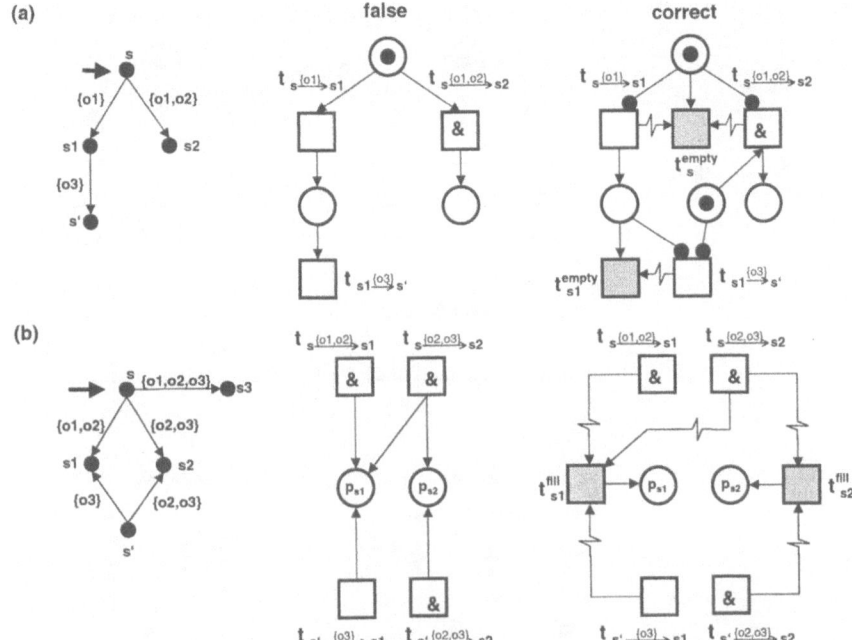

Fig. 25. Part (a): Avoiding undesired conflicts caused by shared preplaces and checking exact markings. Part (b): Avoiding undesired conflicts caused by shared postplaces.

(a). Since the transitions $t_{s \overset{\{o1\}}{\to} s1}$ and $t_{s \overset{\{o1,o2\}}{\to} s2}$ share a pre-place, the occurrence of the step of output signals $\{o1, o2\}$ either synchronizes $t_{s \overset{\{o1\}}{\to} s1}$ or $t_{s \overset{\{o1,o2\}}{\to} s2}$. That means, in the marking corresponding to state s two steps are in conflict. Moreover, one of the steps (when $t_{s \overset{\{o1\}}{\to} s1}$ is synchronized) does not correspond to the control flow.

The right part of Figure 25 (a) shows a signal net simulating A, where the mentioned conflict is avoided. To this end, a transition t_s^{empty} removing the token from the place p_s is introduced. It is synchronized by both transitions $t_{s \overset{\{o1\}}{\to} s1}$ and $t_{s \overset{\{o1,o2\}}{\to} s2}$. Both transitions have empty preset and test the place p_s to be marked via condition arcs. The occurrence of the step of output signals $\{o1, o2\}$ now synchronizes both transitions $t_{s \overset{\{o1\}}{\to} s1}$ and $t_{s \overset{\{o1,o2\}}{\to} s2}$.

Checking exact markings. In the last example, the occurrence of the step of output signals $\{o1, o2\}$ produces the follower marking $\{p_{s1}, p_{s2}\}$. Therefore, the marking corresponding to the state $s2$ is $\{p_{s1}, p_{s2}\}$. The occurrence of the step of output signals $\{o1\}$ produces the follower marking $\{p_{s1}\}$, which therefore is the marking corresponding to the state $s1$.

Since the transition $t_{s1 \overset{\{o3\}}{\to} s'}$ should only be enabled under the marking $\{p_{s1}\}$, but not under the marking $\{p_{s1}, p_{s2}\}$, $t_{s1 \overset{\{o3\}}{\to} s'}$ has to test the place p_{s2} not to be marked.

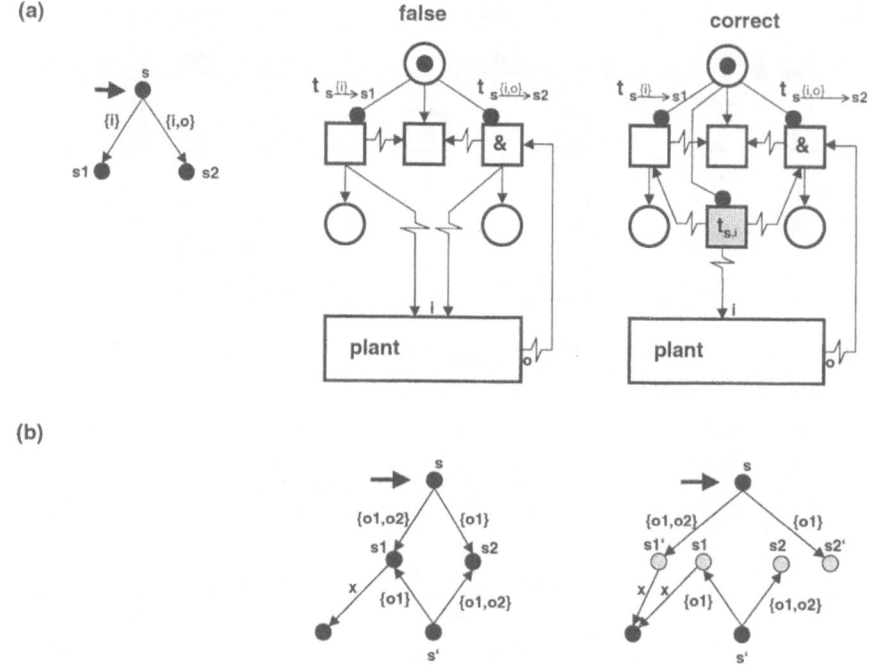

Fig. 26. Part (a): Avoiding cycles of event arcs caused by signal inputs. Part (b): Distinguishing states by markings.

This can be achieved by introducing a complementary place to p_{s2} and to test this place to be marked.

Avoiding undesired conflicts caused by shared post-places. Consider the automaton A shown in the left part and the signal net simulating A in the middle part of Figure 25 (b). The occurrence of the step of output signals $\{o2, o3\}$ in the marking corresponding to state s' synchronizes both transitions $t_{s' \overset{\{o3\}}{\to} s1}$ and $t_{s' \overset{\{o2,o3\}}{\to} s2}$. Therefore, the marking $\{p_{s1}, p_{s2}\}$ corresponds to the state $s2$. Since the occurrence of the transition $t_{s \overset{\{o2,o3\}}{\to} s2}$ must lead to the same marking $\{p_{s1}, p_{s2}\}$, the transitions $t_{s \overset{\{o2,o3\}}{\to} s2}$ and $t_{s \overset{\{o1,o2\}}{\to} s1}$ share a post-place. Therefore, the occurrence of the step of output signals $\{o1, o2, o3\}$ in the marking corresponding to state s either synchronizes $t_{s \overset{\{o2,o3\}}{\to} s2}$ or $t_{s \overset{\{o1,o2\}}{\to} s1}$. That means, in the marking corresponding to state s two steps are in conflict.

The right part of Figure 25 (b) shows a signal net simulating A where the mentioned conflict is avoided. For this, transitions t_{s1}^{fill} resp. t_{s1}^{fill}, which mark the places p_{s1} resp. p_{s2}, are introduced in a similar way as the transitions t_s^{empty} which unmark places.

Avoiding cycles of event arcs caused by signal inputs. Consider the automaton A shown in the left part and the signal net simulating A in the middle part of Figure 26 (a). By the occurrence of transition $t_{s \overset{\{i,o\}}{\to} s2}$ input i is sent to the plant. This produces a cycle of event arcs, since i possibly synchronizes the step of outputs $\{o\}$, which again synchronizes $t_{s \overset{\{i,o\}}{\to} s2}$.

The right part of Figure 26 (a) shows a signal net simulating A, where such cycles are avoided. For this inputs are modelled by additional transitions as shown.

Distinguishing states by markings. Consider the automaton A given in the left part of Figure 26 (b). On the one hand, the occurrence of the step of output signals $\{o1, o2\}$ in the marking $\{p_s\}$ synchronizes the transitions $t_{s \overset{\{o1,o2\}}{\to} s1}$ and $t_{s \overset{\{o1\}}{\to} s2}$. Therefore, the follower marking is $\{p_{s1}, p_{s2}\}$. On the other hand, the occurrence of the step of output signals $\{o1, o2\}$ in the marking $\{p_{s'}\}$ synchronizes the transitions $t_{s' \overset{\{o1,o2\}}{\to} s1}$ and $t_{s' \overset{\{o1\}}{\to} s2}$ and the follower marking is also $\{p_{s1}, p_{s2}\}$. Therefore it corresponds to both states $s1$ and $s2$. That means that the control does not distinguish between observable different states of the plant.

This situation can be avoided if we modify the automaton A such that the states of A distinguish words according to their last character. More formally, we require $x = y$ for all edges of the form $s' \overset{x}{\to} s$ and $s'' \overset{y}{\to} s$. As long as this is not the case for a state s of A, i.e. $x \neq y$, one can split s into two copies, one for words ending with x and one for words ending with y.

3.3   Alternative Techniques for Synthesis

An approach that uses complete enumeration of the whole controlled behavior will obviously reach its limitation if the systems are large. It therefore makes sense to consider methods that use structural properties of the model instead. At the current state of research, a general approach for models without structural restrictions is unlikely. If one restricts, however, to models with simple structures, formal techniques for synthesis are possible. This holds in particular for pure Petri net models of the plant.

Methods for controller or supervisor synthesis for Petri nets are well developed. This holds especially for specification in terms of forbidden states. A comprehensive review can he found in [13]. Synthesis methods for sequential specifications, however, are yet rather sparse. One significant contribution in this area is the work of Giua [7], who studied an alternative design to Ramadge and Wonhams monolithic supervisor. His method entails the Petri net modelling of subsystems and specifications, which are then combined through a "concurrent composition" operation. Then, a "refinement" step of the combined model ensures the non-blocking and controllable properties. In this case, the existence of the Petri net supervisor is guaranteed whenever the given Petri net subsystems are conservative, although additional structure may be needed in the refinement step. The main distinction to [7] in the method described in [21] is the connection of the plant and specification models, which is done through the condition and event signals of Signal nets. This is also the case when we consider systems where plant and controller interact with each other in a closed loop. So, the model of the admissible behavior will not be a classical Petri net but a Signal Petri net. The framework [21] can also be applied as long as the Petri net model of the plant is safe.

The scope of [21] is limited to solving the problem of preventing an uncontrollable event at a specific "controller state." The method starts with a safe Petri net model of the system and a sequential specification that is modelled with a special state machine. A more general modelling framework for sequential specifications is currently under investigation, where a temporal logic formula can be mapped to a signal net model. An initial discussion is given in [20]. The main contribution in [21] can be described as follows: The condition and event signals of Signal nets are used to combine the plant and specification models. Then, the structure of this combined model allows to determine which controllable events need to be restricted by the controller, and at what states they need to be restricted in order to obtain the legal or admissible behavior of the system. Thus, a complete description of the state space is avoided, and control of the system is performed in a minimally restrictive way.

Another issue that is currently under investigation is how to extend the method to reach some "target events" in the plant model. First results are presented in [22]. The major drawback, however, is that in general the set of all reachable markings are required to determine all feasible processes that lead to this target events. This means that even if a process exists that drives the plant model towards the target event, the process might be not feasible since it requires a marking that is not reachable from the initial marking.

4   Conclusion

In this paper we have illustrated methodologies for synthesis of control for DES with input and output structure. For input/output communication, we employ active signals which try to force events and passive signals which prohibit resp. enable event occurrences. As a modelling formalism, we use modules of signal nets. Signal nets offer a direct way to model typical actuators behavior. Another advantage of such modules consists in supporting input/output structuring, modularity, and compositionality in an intuitive graphical way.

Given a control specification in form of a regular language over output signals of the system, we showed how to automatically synthesize the control module. This forces the system to maximally permissive behavior preserving the control specification, in the sense that only sequences of outputs which respect the specification will be observed.

In the paper we did not focus on complexity issues. It is known that the complexity of the supervisory control problem is PSPACE-hard in general, and sometimes even undecidable ([28], pp. 15 - 36). For efficient algorithms, the setting must be restricted in some way, for example by considering only very special classes of control specifications.

We restricted our approach in several aspects: As a control specification, only sequences of signal outputs were considered. Moreover, the synthesized controller changes at most one of its inputs to the plant at each moment. An extension of our methodology to control specifications including signal inputs and to controllers sending steps consisting of more than one signal input to the plant is a straightforward exercise.

The presented approach considers only Petri nets on an elementary level. For complex industrial-size systems, these nets tend to be either very large or too abstract. In particular, data and time aspects cannot be modelled in a natural way. Therefore, we are working on an extension of the control methodology for modules of signal nets with special high-level Petri net features.

References

1. B. Caillaud, P. Darondeau, L. Lavagno and X. Xie (Eds.). Synthesis and Control of Discrete Event Systems. Kluwer Academic Press, 2002.
2. C. G. Cassandras and S. Lafortune. Introduction to Discrete Event Systems. Kluwer, 1999.
3. H. Cho and S.I. Marcus. On supremal languages of classes of sublanguages that arise in supervisor synthesis problems with partial observation. em Mathematics of Control, Signals, and Systems, Vol. 2, No. 2, pp. 47–69, 1989.
4. J. Desel, G. Juhás and R. Lorenz. Input/Output Equivalence of Petri Modules. In *Proc. of IDPT 2002*, Pasadena, USA, 2002.
5. J. Desel, V. Milijic and C. Neumair. Model Validation in Controller Design. In J. Desel, W. Reisig and G. Rozenberg (Eds.) *Lectures on Concurrency and Petri Nets*. Springer, LNCS 3098, 467 – 495, 2004.
6. P. Dietrich, R. Malik, W.M. Wonham and B.A. Brandin. Omlementation Consideration in Supervisory Control. In [1].
7. A. Giua. Petri Nets and Discrete Event Models for Supervisory Control. Ph.D. Thesis. Dept. of Computer and Systems Engineering, Rensselaer Polytechnic Institute. Troy, NY, 1992.
8. H.-M. Hanisch, A. Lüder. Modular Modeling of Closed-Loop Systems. Colloquium on Petri Net Technologies for Modeling Communication Based Systems, Berlin 1999, pp. 103–126.
9. H-M. Hanisch and A. Lüder. A Signal Extension for Petri nets and its Use in Controller Design. *Fundamenta Informaticae*, 41(4) 2000, 415–431.
10. H.-M. Hanisch, A. Lüder, M. Rausch. Controller Synthesis for Net Condition/Event Systems with Incomplete State Observation. European Journal of Control, Nr. 3, 1997, 292–303.
11. H.M. Hanisch, M. Rausch: Netz-Condition/Event-Systeme, 4. Fachtagung Entwurf Komplexer Automatisierungssysteme, Braunschweig, Germany, June 1995, Proceedings, pp. 55-71 (in German).
12. H.-M. Hanisch, J. Thieme and A. Lüder. Towards a Synthesis Method for Distributed Safety controllers Based on Net Condition/Event Systems. *Journal of Intelligent Manufacturing*, 5, 1997, 8, 357–368.
13. L.E. Holloway, B.H. Krogh and A. Giua. A Survey of Petri Net Methods for Controlled Discrete Event Systems. *Discrete Event Dynamic Systems: Theory and Applications*, 7, 1997, 151–190.
14. J.E. Hopcroft, R. Motwani and J.D.Ullman. Introduction to Automata Theory, Languages, and Computation. Addison Wesley, 2001.
15. R. Janicki and M. Koutny. Semantics of Inhibitor Nets. *Information and Computations*, 123, 1–16, 1995.
16. G. Juhás. On semantics of Petri nets over partial algebra. In J. Pavelka, G. Tel and M. Bartosek (Eds.) *Proc. of 26th Seminar on Current Trends in Theory and Practice of Informatics SOFSEM'99*, Springer, LNCS 1725, 408–415, 1999.
17. G. Juhás and R. Lorenz. Modeling with Petri Modules. In [1].
18. G. Juhás, R. Lorenz and C. Neumair. Synthesis of Controlled Behavior with Modules of Signal Nets. In J. Cortadella and W. Reisig (Eds.) *Proc. of 25th International Conference on Application and Theory of Petri Nets*, Springer, LNCS 3099, 238 – 257, 2004.
19. G. Juhás, R. Lorenz and C. Neumair. Modeling and Control with Modules of Signal Nets. In J. Desel, W. Reisig and G. Rozenberg (Eds.) *Lectures on Concurrency and Petri Nets*. Springer, LNCS 3098, 585 – 625, 2004.

20. L.E. Pinzon, H.-M. Hanisch and M.A. Jafari. Sequential Control Specifications with TL and NCES. Rutcor Research Report 4–98, RUTCOR, Rutgers University, Piscataway, NJ, 1998.
21. L.E. Pinzon, M.A. Jafari, H.-M. Hanisch and P. Zhao. Modeling admissible behavior using event signals. To be published in: IEEE Transactions on Sytems, Man and Cybernetics, Part B, 2004.
22. L.E. Pinzon, M.A. Jafari and H.-M. Hanisch. Controller Synthesis for Target Events. Submitted to Wodes 2004.
23. P.J. Ramadge, W.M. Wonham. The Control of Discrete Event Systems. Proceedings of the IEEE, 77 (1989) 1, 81–98.
24. G. Rozenberg, and J. Engelfriet. Elementary Net Systems. In W. Reisig and G. Rozenberg (Eds.) *Lectures on Petri Nets I: Basic Models*, Springer, LNCS 1491, 12–121, 1998.
25. R.S. Sreenivas und B.H. Krogh. On Condition/Event Systems with Discrete State Realizations. *Discrete Event Dynamic Systems: Theory and Applications*, 2, 1991, 1, 209–236.
26. R. S. Sreenivas and B. H. Krogh. Petri Net Based Models for Condition/Event Systems. In *Proceedings of 1991 American Control Conference*, vol. 3, 2899–2904, Boston, MA, 1991.
27. P. H. Starke. Das Komponieren von Signal-Netz Systemen. In Proc 7. Workshop Algorithmen und Werkzeuge für Petrinetze AWPN 2000, Universität Koblenz - Landau, 1–6, 2000.
28. P. Darondeau and S. Kumagai (Eds.). Proceedings of the *Workshop on Discrete Event System Control*. Satellite Workshop of ATPN 2003.
29. M.C. Zhou und F. DiCesare. *Petri Net Synthesis for Discrete Event Control of Manufacturing Systems*. Kluwer Adacemic Publishers, Boston, MA, 1993.
30. Zhonghua Zhang and W.M. Wonham. STCT: An Efficient Algorithm for Supervisory Control Design. In [1].

Conceptual Design of an Engineering Model for Product and Plant Automation

K. Fischer[1], P. Göhner[2], F. Gutbrodt[2], U. Katzke[1], and B. Vogel-Heuser[1]

[1] Chair of Automation and Process Control Engineering
University of Wuppertal, Germany
[2] Institute of Industrial Automation and Software Engineering
University of Stuttgart, Germany

Abstract. Common engineering approaches and modelling approaches from software engineering are brought together. For the domain of process automation, i.e. product and plant automation, an implementation oriented approach for an object oriented software development for heterogeneous distributed systems is introduced. Model elements for control are added to UML as well as small-scale patterns for plant automation. Besides large-scale patterns are introduced as well as implementational models. The adoption of UML regarding applied diagrams and stereotypes for process automation will be introduced and structured components, an idiom for product automation software development, will be compared to other software engineering notations.

1 Introduction

Engineering approaches from the domain of engineering will be merged with advancements in modelling from software engineering. On the one hand process automation traditionally has focussed on implementation issues and on the other hand computer science has neglected the application domain to some extend by focussing on embedded systems in automotive and avionics.

Software development in process automation (plant and product automation) has many deficiencies in procedures, notations and tool support. As a result, modern software engineering concepts and notations, like object oriented approaches or UML, are not wide spread in this field. Hence, drawbacks regarding start-up times, additional costs and low software quality are immense. This paper will derive a draft for an object oriented approach for this domain focussing on implementation aspects. This approach includes UML stereotypes. Besides, constraints for real time applications are necessary. For embedded systems, an implementation oriented approach will be discussed with restrictions of the object oriented constructs to meet constraints in storage and timing.

2 Characteristics and Requirements of Embedded Systems

The general requirements of embedded systems in process automation will be discussed. According to [1] embedded systems are automation (computer) systems,

H. Ehrig et al. (Eds.): INT 2004, LNCS 3147, pp. 301–321, 2004.

which are integrated into a technical process. With this definition, every computer system ranging from tiny microcontroller units up to powerful multiprocessor servers is an embedded system as long it is integrated into a technical process. Examples for embedded systems in product automation are electric razors, washing machines or digitally programmed machine-tools as well as plant automation systems.

In product and plant automation embedded systems are used, which differ from standard (industrial) PCs. It is examined what has to be considered when designing software for embedded systems. In [2] embedded systems are characterized by

- the environment they work in,
- the performance expected of them, and
- the interfaces to the outside world.

This article will only consider environment and performance of embedded systems, because they determine the constraints to software for these systems. An important aspect of the environment of an embedded system is the size and weight admitted to the system. For product automation system engineers, these can be the crucial issue to deal with. These factors are also limiting factors to software design, because they may result in only very few memory and very low computational performance of the device to use. Figure 1 shows the general purpose computing elements of embedded systems. Opposed to general purpose elements, there are also specialized computing elements (e.g. digital signal processors, mixed signal processors, or special system-on-chip designs), which are not covered by this paper.

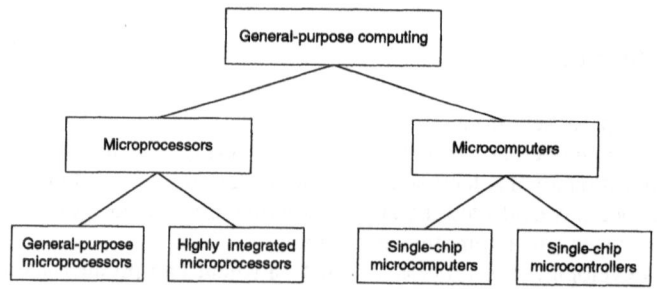

Fig. 1. General purpose computing elements of embedded systems

An overview of requirements of process automation is listed in table 1. The criteria can be structured regarding process requirements, automation system architecture, and project. In process automation, different kinds of processes are possible. In the following, a brief overview of those categories is given. A process automation system represents a type of process, e.g. batch, continuous, or discrete. Sometimes processes are composed of different process types. They are called hybrid, due to the fact, that they consist of different process kinds. These process types require different control strategies (closed and open loop control) and by that they require different modelling notation features, e.g. block diagrams or state charts.

In addition overall requirements are real time requirements, including timers, the integration of I/O peripherals directly via a backplane bus system or a field bus, interrupts from the process and the necessity to describe the automation architecture and the mapping from software to hardware. Multiprocessor systems like VMEbus may be included as well.

Regarding an automation project, there are typically different engineers or technicians involved with different qualification levels and subjects. By that fact, the notation has to be easy to use to a certain level for process, mechanical, and electrical engineers as well as for technicians. A more visionary requirement is to support the entire life cycle with one consistent model, but appropriate notation for each phase of the project.

Table 1. Overview of requirements in process automation

categories/ criteria		functionality / notation aspects
process	batch (continuous)	transfer functions, block diagrams, differential equation
	discrete	status model, flow chart, continuous function chart, Petri net
	hybrid	continuous and discrete process
automation system	heterogeneous or homogeneous	distribution, communication, network / central unit
		different hardware platforms
		different software platforms
		HMI, diagnostics, no screen
	time	hard and soft real time; time and event controlled systems
	implementation	IEC 61131-3 for PLC (embedded system), Proprietary for DCS; C, C++, Personal Java, Embedded Java, RT Java, Ada95
	level of automation	in product automation 100%
project	qualification	easy to handle for engineers and technicians
	system life cycle	top down design
		modularity, component base, object orientation
		Reusability
	tool support	along entire life cycle

The projects approach has been twofold in a differentiated manner. According to different tasks during the process of development it embraces different levels of abstraction. Concomitant it differs between plant and product automation. On one hand, there is the specification oriented approach, for which UML has been adapted by developing special stereotypes. On the other hand, there is an implementation oriented approach, which focuses on embedded systems constraints and derived requirements for an object oriented modelling and programming. Additionally modularity was aimed at [10].

Among object oriented programming languages the implementation oriented approach investigates structured programming languages using object oriented concepts. The reason for consideration of structured programming languages is due to the fact, that in embedded systems structured programming languages are wide spread. In the field of plant automation mainly languages of the IEC 61131-3 are used whereas C is very common in product automation. The programmable controllers and runtime environments of plant and product automation differ in the same way. For that in the following requirements and implementation are separately worked out.

3   Plant Automation

3.1   Requirements

The range of branches and technologies in plant automation varies in batch, discrete and continuous processing. Each branch has its own notations for the description of requirements, i.e. the documentation of given hardware and manufacturing processes. Despite these differences they have a lot of similarities. Very often the engineering of the automation system starts with the documentation of the plant construction and process engineering. Further on these information is used to extract sensors and actuators as inputs and outputs for the automation software and to create raw descriptions of the automation process. Finally they use the same type of automation devices. During the process of developing executable software the given information (user requirements) are detailed in terms of implementation requirements. The description of devices and behaviour changes from an abstract level to executable code.

Today plant manufacturing industry requires standardized automation devices for automation systems, e.g. PLCs (Programmable Logic Controller), which are programmed in IEC 61131-3 [3] Therefore, the transfer of modelling results into IEC 61131-3, which is standardised by the International Electrotechnical Commission (IEC) [16], is   necessary. The IEC 61131-3 contains languages, which follow a function-oriented or procedural-imperative paradigm. The increasing use of these languages causes a growing dependency on the accepted standard, because existing implemented systems must be expanded and the developers are familiar with the practice of "accustomed" programming techniques. The accumulated expertise about home made modules allows a limited reuse and orientation. Without the knowledge of the experience from building modules, the acceptance of reusable modules is very low [17].

For special tasks such as safety related tasks or hard real time requirements additional automation devices may be used, e.g. process control computers with a real time operating system (RTOS). For hard real time systems specific requirements need to be realized. A list of implementation oriented real time requirements is depicted by table 2. Aspects of real time development like reactivity, multi-threading, time-based behaviour and real time environment need to be met. In the past efficient and machine-intimate but Gordian programming was necessary to fulfil these requirements. Actual controllers better their predecessors with a multiplicative computing performance.

In plant automation, communication between several (embedded) systems is realized via different bus systems and in the following explained with the automation pyramid. In the level of field control buses like PROFIbus and Interbus [4] are deployed. Whereas the communication between and inside the level of process control, plant management, and enterprise administration normally is based on Ethernet and TCP/IP. For operation and maintenance, a PC-based human machine interface is used. By that fact the architecture of the automation system is heterogeneous.

Table 2. Real time requirements (functional /implementational model) [46]

Useful Language Constructs for Real Time Programming	Useful Description of Hardware Architecture
task dispatch	connection between peripheral device and technical process
transition control between different states of a task/ state diagram	
Scheduling /EDF	Process peripheral/ modelling of input/ output
synchronisation of tasks /Semaphores, rendevous	Architectural description of differentprocess computer units
task activation / event handling (timer/ interrupts)	
communication between tasks (sent/receive events)	connection between different computers/ network

Another criterion for a successful project is to develop the automation system precise to customer requirements even if this functionality is mechanically under development. During design re-use of developed modules needs to be enabled. The test of this functionality prior to the start-up on plant site is next challenge. Therefore the specification, which should include testing requirements for soft- and hardware, is most important for each project.

Plant automation is currently challenged by the demand of handling a growing complexity. New requirements push the boundary of former approaches for engineering hard- and software systems. New expansion space for a new, extended functionality has resulted from the fact that Moore's law [11] is still valid [12] and performance of logic controllers is still rising. New field buses redefine the boundaries of distributed and centralized systems [13]. The power, given through these improvements stimulates the demand for implementing new functions. In plant automation huge application software and hardware for production and process engineering is developed often with much more than 3000 input / output points (process variables). These input / output points represent sensors and actuators.

More than ever reuse is desired [table 1, 17, 18]. But reuse demands compliance of certain criteria. In [17] usability, suitability for adaptation and portability are mentioned. In [10, 18] modules are regarded differently, dependent on their grade of adjustment. This view differentiates between basic modules, which are implemented without changes of code and application modules which are derived from standardized templates. In both cases criteria like encapsulation and parameterisation target a reduced complexity of modules and systems to keep it clear and to raise the efficiency of changes [17, 18].

An efficient building of variants requires structures and methods which exceed the capabilities of function oriented or procedural-imperative languages defined in the IEC 61131-3. The prevalent practice of "copy, paste & modify" leads to scarcely manageable systems. Clear interfaces are highly demanded, but seldom found. The effort for design and change of complex requirements is very high, reliable prognoses about the completion of software systems are missing. All these occurrences are well known in conventional software development. Now automation systems have reached a grade of complexity which was first described as a software crisis [20, 21]. The existence of powerful hardware allows applications with complex tasks. With an increasing performance of computing and communication, the classical software engineering has born methods and paradigms to profit from progress power with powerful software. It is expected, that the increase of computing power will continue [12, 22]. Thus the facilities of hardware will remain one step ahead the complexity which can be handled with structures and operations of state of the art software engineering. But the solutions, which are already found, extend the range of possibilities to handle complex tasks in a clear and structured way. One essential contribution is offered by the approaches of object oriented software development and programming. It is also convenient for the automation industry.

3.2   Object Oriented Software Development

3.2.1 Overview

Object oriented concepts, notations and procedures have been developed to meet the requirements of complex software running on performant computer systems. The UML, as an object oriented notation, is no exception to that fact. Especially when it comes to code generation, nearly every UML code generation tool assumes a PC environment (e.g. integer size is supposed to be 32 bit) [7]. However, UML's advantages, e.g. applicability across different development phases or degree of familiarity among developers as well as users, are also of value in embedded software engineering. To identify UML elements, that do (or do not) comply with microcontroller software constraints, an implementation driven approach has been chosen to assess the impact of object oriented elements on device resources.

In the following other approaches should be introduced in comparison with this paper. ISILEIT [8] integrates SDL as an extended specification formalism into UML and realises code generation to Structured Text. The application is neither decentralised nor distributed and the real time requirements are compared with this report weak or soft.

ODEMA [24] provides a UML-based concept without a special focus on distributed real-time systems or the domain of process automation. Braatz strengthened the necessity of automatic code generation for industrial automation as introduced in this paper.

AUTOFOCUS [9] provides a concept of a component oriented architecture combined with a model driven, incremental development process. This approach is dissociated from UML as a complete set of diagram types. Instead the "AutoFocus modeling language & framework" has been created using parts of UML, UML-RT and other common notations. The development process and language support an incremental refinement combined with an increasing detail level of the model. Indeed the targeted industry (automotive) differs from the requirements of plant automation, especially the point of reuse is not worked out.

UML 2.0 specifies with the Profile for Schedulability, Performance and Time Specification some useful constructs for real time systems. The UML 2.0 time model has no formal semantics as Berkenkötter et al. [43] analysed. Licht [44] proposed the integration of timed automata, which seems to be a very promising approach, regarding comprehensibility for engineers and formal specification.

Giotto is a programming language for embedded hard-real time control systems with periodic behaviour. "Giotto is a domain-specific high-level programming language: domain-specific, as it addresses embedded control applications; high-level, as it abstracts platformdependent implementation details... Giotto-based control systems separate the two concerns (reactivity vs. scheduling; timing vs. functionality)" [41]. The concepts for scheduling and timing aspects need to be evaluated for this project. Giotto worked also on distributed systems, but didn't focus on process automation specific requirements or large scale software for plants.

Ptomely [45] facilitates functional description by providing various models of computations and hence allowing different domains, but up to now process automation is not included.

3.2.2 UML Diagram Types
One of the working points in the research and development project DisPA is the analysis of existing UML diagram types concerning applicability in process automation [23]. The large number of different diagram types is sensed confusing and complicates the adjustment in UML. In particular, it is desirable for the acceptance in industry to choose an as small as possible number of diagram types. Especially for application in process automation [10, 18] it is necessary to proof the assignment of use case diagrams for description of requirements. In addition, the adoption of activity and collaboration diagrams concerning usage of redundant diagram types should be analysed.

A first step is the evaluation of the experience of all DisPA project agents. As a result class, component, deployment, states, and sequence diagrams are chosen as adequate diagram types. Basis of this discussion is UML 1.4. In addition a combination of deployment and component diagram, which is offered in UML 2.0, is reasonable. Furthermore the timing diagram (UML 2.0), which is developed according timing diagrams in process automation, should be analysed, too.

Current research investigates the evaluation of UML in software development with a typical automation process with electrical engineers in education [23]. A third aspect is the analysis of the agile UML method [25, 26]. Both evaluations are not complete, but seem to approve the application results of project agents.

3.2.3 Designed UML Modelling Elements and Patterns
The following chapters describe the new elements, which should complete the basis of the UML-PA subset (UML for Process Automation). These chapters include also their deduction from typical control automation notation.

Designing UML-PA elements as a subset of the UML is oriented on the needs of users for intuitive programming complex distributed real-time systems. Regarding the requirements, which are listed at the beginning of this article, elements for modelling open and closed loop control, reconfiguration services (redundancy, diversity), time constraints and their reliability are needed. They should look like elements, which are used in automation engineering today. This is necessary for acceptance and consequently its adoption in industry.

On this account we look at a one-to-one description in control engineering. Open loop control is the interaction of all output variables of a process by all input signals in a formal defined way. It is described with block diagrams. A block diagram is a .

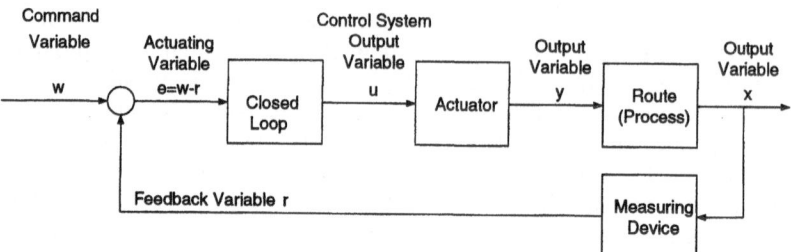

Fig. 2. Ideal block diagram of closed loop control

graphical description of information flows of control system models. Each block is a graphic figure of a functional correlation.

The special focus of the research and development project DisPA lies on the application oriented aspects. On this account UML-PA elements are developed to describe this typical control automation correctly in form and content. In the following a generic closed loop control is described with the UML-PA elements.

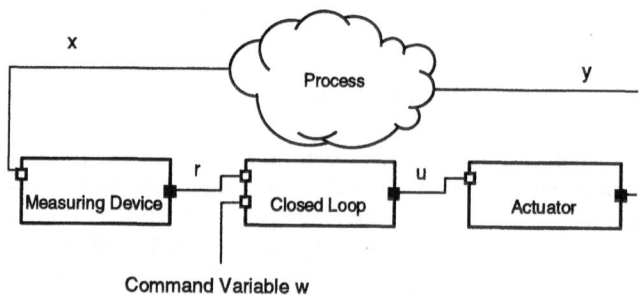

Fig. 3. Corresponding use of UML-PA elements. The process is not part of the model.

Based on these fundamentals a new stereotype named *LoopControl* is defined in UML. It is based on the stereotype *Capsule* [28]. All necessary attributes, operations, and a port are predefined. In addition the underlying state chart is predefined. It includes two sub-states (*idle*, *active*) as symbol for the activation of a loop control system. The real control takes place in the operation *ControlFunction()*. The command variable and the output variable can be written only via the defined port.

Furthermore a closed loop control needs the definition of the actuating variable. Different controller types need specific data as parameter. One way is the definition of a new stereotype. This stereotype would include the transfer of constraints also like attributes, operations, and ports. Another possibility for realisation is the inheritance mechanism. The class *ClosedLoopControl* inherits from the class *OpenLoopControl*. *ClosedLoopControl* is the abstract super class for specialized controllers like P, PI, PID or PD. With it we have got first elements and we can combine them in the same way like blocks (figure 3).

A flow control executes unavoidable stepwise. To continue into a next step a transition has to be fulfilled. These transitions can depend on time or signals from the

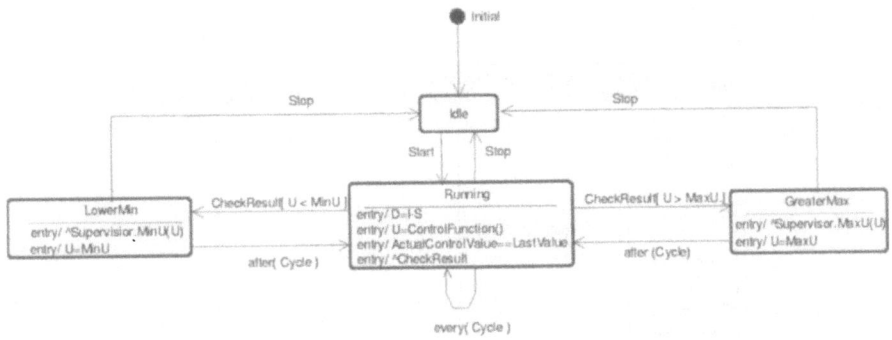

Fig. 4. State machine of the control cycle of the abstract class *ClosedLoopControl*

process (figure 4), whereas the logic control is characterised by the allocation of the input signals to specific states of output signals. This mapping happens in the realisation of the abstract function *ControlFunction()*. It is defined in the inherited controller classes. Figure 5 shows the state machine which implements the *ControlFunction* of a P-Controller.

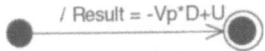

Fig. 5. P-Controller as an example for a *ControlFunction*

The reconfiguration service can be used in new or already existing models to improve the functionality (i.e. safety) of target systems. A controller pattern consists usually of a sensor, an actuator and a controller device. The failure of one of the components results in failure of the entire control chain. This safety problem can be avoided by usage of redundant devices. However, the integration of redundant devices into an existing model is one of the main challenges, often the model structure and also already implemented code have to be changed. An inherited reconfiguration class is designed to solve this problem. It is a virtual representation of a defective device. Any deviation is corrected by an adjustment function (figure 6).

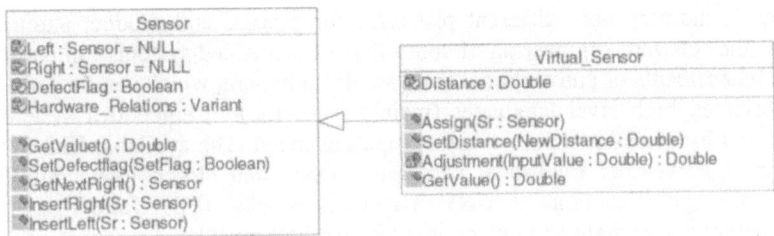

Fig. 6. *Virtual_Sensor* as an inherited reconfiguration class

As an example we suppose an additional sensor or an already existing is needed to improve the steadiness of a system, e.g. a sensor. In this case the reconfiguration class will simply replace the primary sensor device. The whole procedure is shown in figure 7.

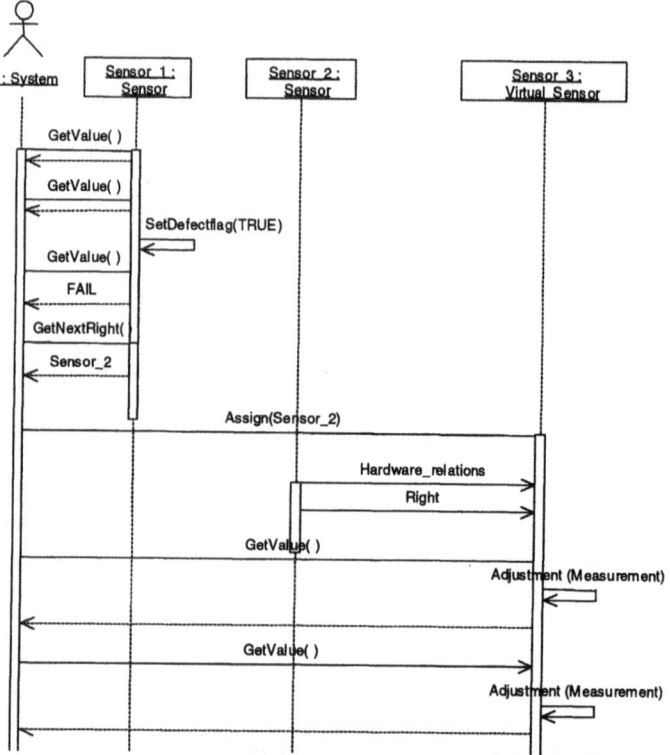

Fig. 7. Sequence diagram: replacement of a defective sensor

The configuration class *Virtual_Sensor* instantiates the physically existing device *Sensor_2*, but it corrects the measurement in a way, that the system's handling of the substitute is identical to the original device. Therefore the reconfiguration class uses the mechanisms of inheritance and overriding.

3.3   Implementation with IEC 61131-3

Automation industry uses different platforms for process and product automation. Whereas the software engineering of controllers of embedded systems can participate in the advancements of conventional software development, which can be done using object oriented high level languages (mainly C++, EC++), embedded systems are only limited by available memory and computing speed. The available IEC 61131-3 languages follow more traditional paradigms. Open and closed loop controls are realised through Functions (FUN), Function Blocks (FB) follow a procedural/imperative paradigm and object oriented concepts must be mapped.

In plant automation existing software and the skills of specialists for plant commissioning still determine the software construction at implementation level. At this phase of development it is unavoidable to remain within established standards. Existing experience and the uncertainty of grave changes conserve the importance of the IEC 61131-3. With more distance to the placing into operation engineering is done on a more abstract level.

Some concepts target the mapping of a reduced UML to IEC languages [29]. Single extensions of PLC-toolsets, which are also function-oriented, allow extended modelling features, but they are isolated and don't actually deliver concepts for reuse.

Nevertheless we developed a toolset for automatic depiction (conversion) of a reduced UML model using an enlarged agile concept [27] to an implementation of IEC 61131-3 (TwinCAT based on CoDeSys [30]). TwinCAT was chosen as a wide spread IEC 61131-3 implementation for PCs and embedded systems, which refer to the standard. The diagrams for automatic conversion have been restricted to class diagrams, state charts, and system architecture diagrams, which is sufficient to model the automation of a lab model.

The class diagram is used to realise the programme structure of the IEC 61131-3 programme and by that the necessary Functions (FUN), Function Blocks (FB), and a Main Programme (PROG) are generated. The state charts are converted into Sequential Function Charts (SFC). This automatic conversion uses SFC and Structured Text (ST). The system architecture diagrams are used to design the hardware aspects, including automatic mapping of hardware addresses. The bi-directional mapping will not be adequate because this conversion uses IEC 61131-3 without any enlargement. The most important result is the ability to include tasks and hardware aspects in this model [26], which is required (see table 1 and 2).

3.3.1 Proposal of Object Oriented Enhancement

The IEC 61131-3 languages are convenient to build block structures and this is the way, the agile concept can be mapped. A complete object oriented model requires more facilities, which are beneficial in automation industry to build variants (see requirement modularity, component base, reusability). Components, which will be reused need to match the following variations (figure 8).

- reduction of a pattern
- enhancement of a pattern
- appendix of a functionality to a pattern
- component should be appropriate for a pattern, i.e. through predetermined changes may be applied in another context

It is important that the developer keeps the control whether a function is overridden [14] or not. Therefore the new keyword virtual initiates the overriding mechanism.

The mechanisms of inheritance and overriding offer an opportunity for building variants with respect to the module characteristics encapsulation and parameterisation. Targeting plant automation these variation requirements on one hand, and respects the experience obtained by the familiar mode of operation on the other hand will be implemented using a design model. Therefore the object oriented structures and mechanisms of inheritance need to be added to the IEC 61131-3. A draft proposal for the languages of the IEC 61131-3 will be supplemented by enhancements.

The syntax enhancements are keywords, which allow the definition of classes and controlling the mechanism of inheritance. Figure 9 shows this as an example for the IEC 61131-3 language ST (Structured Text [19]). The supplemented keyword CLASS is alike the existing keyword STRUCT, but it offers the encapsulation of declarations

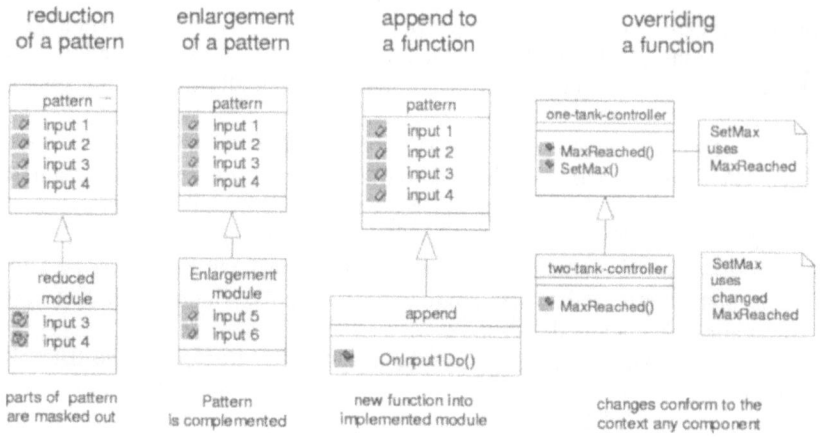

Fig. 8. Target properties of variants (UML-syntax is used for model presentation)

```
TYPE
    OneTankController : CLASS
        VIRTUAL FUNCTION MaxReached: BOOL
        END_FUNCTION;
        FUNCTION_BLOCK SetMax
        END_FUNCTION_BLOCK;
    END_CLASS;

    TwoTankController : CLASS (OneTankController)
        OVERRIDE FUNCTION MaxReached: BOOL
        END_FUNCTION;
    END_CLASS;
END_TYPE;
```

Fig. 9. Proposal for enhancements of the language ST (Structured Text). (The enhancements are marked bold.)

for operations and attributes. Other IEC 61131-3 languages can be enhanced in the same way. The mapping of the enhancements to the standards of IEC 61131-3 needs to be elaborated in a next step.

3.3.2 Modelling of Hardware Aspects

Prior research worked on a comparison of modelling techniques for distributed process control engineering and analysed UML and Idiomatic Control Language (ICL) regarding cognitive models and user acceptance (table 1)[23]. The results of these approaches show the lack in an appropriate accepted modelling technique for

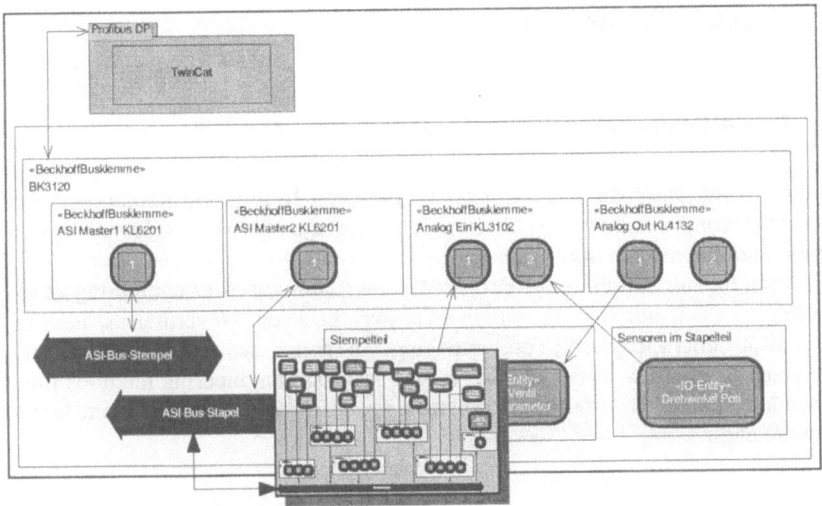

Fig. 10. System architecture as deployment diagram

the design of plant automation integrating hardware and software as well as architectural aspects (table 2)[10].

For modelling hardware aspects UML provides the deployment diagram. For embedded systems usually standard UML diagrams are used, e.g. class diagrams for modelling the system and its environment. In a pragmatic manner some constructs, which are well known from SA/RT are used as *architecture interconnection diagram*, *architecture flow diagram* or *architectural dictionary*, which map the components of the model to architectural components. This idea is integrated into agile UML [27] without any formal or semi-formal basis.

Based on this idea, the system architecture could be modelled as an enlargement of the component diagram using the ARTiSAN tool *Real Time Studio* [31] and applying a top-down design [25]. To model I/O peripherals, subsystems and interfaces are used. Stereotypes for different subsystems are defined, e.g. bus coupler, bus I/O, actuator/sensor, etc. Actuators and sensors may be arranged as a subsystem and are modelled as a subsystem with interfaces. This is realised with the definition of a new stereotype *IO-Entity*.

This stereotype can refer to an attribute of a class, which is used to implement the hardware address. The stereotype of this attribute is called *hardware address*, which is the real physical address on the field bus or the I/O card of a PLC.

For this reason, sensors and actuators are connected with real physical hardware address. This is one prerequisite to close the gap between hardware and software engineering.

The engineering of I/O peripherals, i.e. the acquisition of the real hardware address into the programming environment, will be realized automatically on this basis.

4   Product Automation

4.1   Product Automation Versus Plant Automation

While product automation is strongly demarcated from plant automation, there are also some commonalities, which form a connection between software modelling / implementation in both domains.

In product automation, microprocessors are mainly used as computing devices, as opposed to plant automation, where PCs may be used. Nevertheless, also in plant automation microprocessors are used e.g. in smart sensors / actuators that are connected to field bus systems. That is why software engineering methods that target embedded devices in product automation are also imperative for plant automation software engineering.

4.2   Specific Requirements

Since microprocessors are only one element of embedded systems in product automation, we will focus rather on microcomputers than on "pure" microprocessors. Single chip microcomputers include the following core elements: Microprocessor, memory, address decoder and external bus interface. Additional elements include (real-time) clock, hardware timers, communication controllers and I/O peripherals.

The main difference between single-chip microcomputers and single-chip microcontrollers are the additions to I/O interfacing at microcontrollers, which are usually aiming at the embedded control market. Possible additions include field bus (often CAN) network interfacing, analogue-to-digital converters (ADCs), digital-to-analogue converters (DACs), digital input and output channels. However, this distinction is blurred [2], because also single-chip microcomputers may include above mentioned additions. An example would be the Renesas M16C/6N group of single-chip microcomputers [5]. Embedded systems are often equated with single-chip microcomputers / microcontrollers. Hence, the term "embedded system" will denote a single-chip microcomputer / microcontroller in this article.

The performance of embedded systems is varying strongly. While in PC systems 32 bit bus width is common (currently migrating to 64 bit), in the embedded world, there exist bus widths from 4 bit over 8 bit and 16 bit up to 32 bit. While 4 and 8 bit microcontrollers usually have to be programmed in assembly language, their software is not complex enough to require object oriented development methods. 16 or 32 bit devices can be programmed in high-level languages, e.g. C [6]. These devices enable the use of more complex software, so that object oriented methods may become necessary. In product automation, 16 bit devices are usually sufficient, so they are to be preferred to 32 bit systems due to their lower price. Hence, this chapter focuses on 16 bit microcontroller systems.

Compared to standard PCs, 16 bit microcontrollers have very little memory: usually 5 - 30 *kilo*bytes as opposed to ~ 512 megabytes. Additionally, their computational performance is by factor $100 - 1000$ lower than that of PCs, due to their bus width and lower clock frequency, approx. $10 - 30$ megahertz (PCs: $1 - 3$

gigahertz). To work under such conditions, microcontroller software has to be an order of magnitudes smaller in size and more efficient than PC software.

4.3   C++ in Product Automation

4.3.1 Introduction

The most common high level language for embedded system programming is C. The object oriented language C++ [32] emanated from C, being enhanced with object oriented constructs. While C++ permits the programmer a high degree of freedom concerning object oriented implementation, i.e. from using no object orientation at all to using "unsafe" techniques like multiple inheritance, everything is allowed. Therefore, a consortium of Japanese microcontroller manufacturers has defined a subset of C++, which meets the terms of embedded devices: Embedded C++ (EC++) [33].

EC++ strives to fulfil the following requirements of embedded systems design:

- Avoiding excessive memory consumption
- Taking care not to produce unpredictable responses
- Making code ROMable
- Easy applicability

Therefore, some object oriented features have been omitted from the EC++ specification:

- Software design with multiple inheritance is difficult even for experienced developers. Structural diagrams using multiple inheritance tend to be less readable, the software tends to be less reusable and less maintainable. To avoid the aforementioned drawbacks, multiple inheritance has been omitted from the EC++ specification.
- Generic classes (template classes) may cause unexpected growth of code size if used carelessly. Since program size is critical for embedded systems applications and efficient use of generic elements requires a high level of experience, this feature has been left out from the EC++ specification.
- Namespaces correspond closely with the UML package concept. Due to the limited memory of embedded systems, the size of embedded applications cannot be very large. So, names will seldom, if ever, come into conflict and namespaces are not needed for embedded software development.
- Runtime type identification (RTTI) will result in program size overhead, because the compiler has to add type information for polymorphic classes. Additionally, RTTI is only of advantage, if polymorphism is heavily used. Since program size is critical and complexity is too low to require intensive use polymorphism, RTTI is not present in EC++.
- Exceptions are useful for dealing with errors, but it is difficult to estimate time between exception occurrence and exception handler start. It is as well difficult to determine memory consumption for exception handling. Thus, exceptions are not present in EC++.

Comprising, it can be stated that some features of object orientation should be left out to develop software for embedded devices. When it comes to the definition of a UML based notation for modelling embedded software, this should be regarded. Hence, multiple inheritance, generics, namespaces (provided by UML packages) (figure 11), and heavy use of polymorphism ought to be omitted from that definition. Exceptions are no object oriented concept per se, but most object oriented languages include exceptions and a catch/throw-mechanism. Additionally, some UML tools allow the specification of exceptions [34].

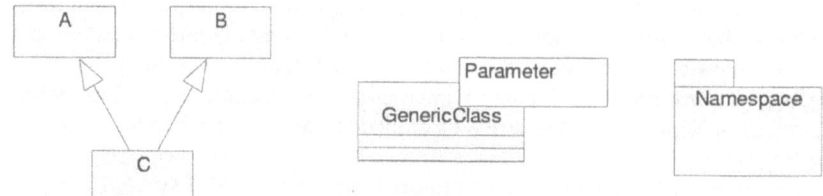

Fig. 11. Multiple inheritance, parameterised class, package with namespace in UML notation

4.3.2 Structured Programming Languages for Product Automation

While object oriented development methods are considered very sceptical by most embedded software developers, they could hardly prevail against traditional, structured methods. Even low footprint OO languages like Embedded C++ are mainly targeting 32 bit MCU applications [33], being still too memory consuming for 16 bit devices. Another approach to access the advantages of object orientation and according notations like the UML are Structured Components [35]. Structured Components are a programming idiom that uses a structured programming language (here: C) to develop flyweight components for embedded systems. Components generally have 8 attributes: functional closeness, structural independence, uniqueness, adaptability, ability of combination, concurrency, immutability (by a third party), and openness. Some of this attributes correspond with OO features (e. g. functional closeness). The difference to object orientation manifests mainly in the improved reusability of components compared to OO structures.

As well as object orientation, component orientation is hardly used in embedded systems development, because "traditional" component models (e.g. COM, CORBA) require overhead due to middleware that is needed to employ component technologies. Structured Components do not have need of middleware and they can be modelled using OO notations. This chapter evaluates Structured Components modelling in order to find additional OO/UML features that do (or do not) comply with embedded systems constraints.

Structured Components do strictly distinguish between internal states and interfaces that display functionality to the outside world. Three parts can be differentiated: the structured component itself (active and passive), service interfaces and event interfaces, which can be modelled using UML class diagrams. The detailed principle of function of Structured Components can be found in [36]. The interesting fact is, that there are some modelling elements allowed, that are considered inappropriate for embedded software development by EC++: multiple inheritance and parameterisation (figure 12).

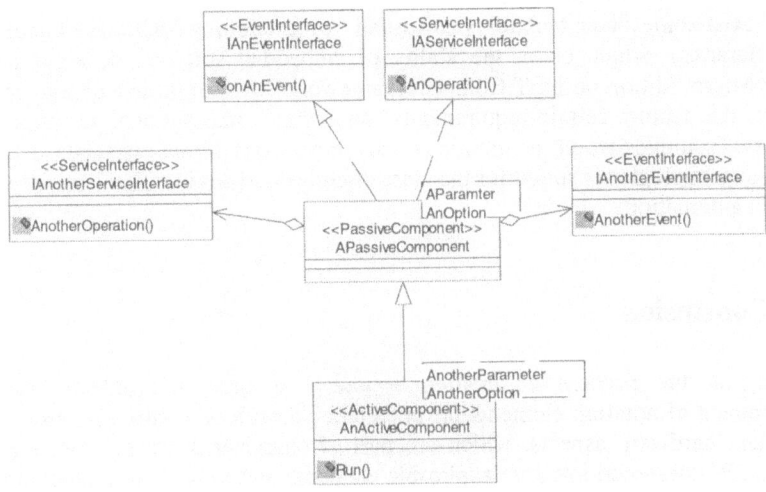

Fig. 12. Structured Components Structure

However, it must be noticed, that the Structured Component principle does also comprise of an idiom, how a diagram is to be converted into source code. This idiom is tailored to the needs of embedded systems:

- Multiple inheritance is allowed as long as it is only realisation, i. e. one component may possess multiple interfaces. This technique is very close to traditional C programming for embedded systems, where functions are often called not "directly" but via function pointers. These function pointers are registered with an application, which later employs them to call a function. Structured Components interfaces bundle groups of functions and allow registration of multiple functions with one call as well as dynamic exchange of the actual implementation.
- Parameterisation is only possible with constant values, e.g. the maximum amount of memory a component may possess. OO-like parameterisation, where the parameter usually consists of a type of a variable, is prohibited.

Structured Components are a powerful method to develop embedded software. Structural independence and adaptability make them reusable without the need of manually altering code inside of a component (copy, paste and modify). Their capability of concurrency (active components) is significant for embedded steering and control tasks. The ability of combination and the differentiation of interfaces and implementation allow dynamic exchange of the actual functionality of a component, e.g. to adapt to different hardware parts. This dynamic exchange enables also dynamic reloading of Structured Components into embedded devices. Since Structured Components can be written in C, they are both lightweight and efficient.

4.3.3 Additional Possibilities

There exist some other technologies (usually programming languages bundled with class libraries), which claim the ability of embedded software development, e. g. Java 2 Micro Edition or .NET Compact Framework. Most of these technologies target systems that feature certain requirements concerning computational performance and memory. Examples would be mobile phones or personal digital assistants. Thus, none of these technologies is suited for the class of embedded devices that is mostly used in product automation.

5   Conclusion

Looking at the process automation approach at first we find the successful development of notation elements for open and closed loop control, interlocking and redundant hardware aspects, which are part of characteristic aspects of embedded systems. We designed intuitive applicable elements on the basis of typical modelling constructs in control automation. In addition we show a possibility to bridge the gap between the function oriented paradigm used in plant automation industry (IEC 61131-3) and the object oriented approach, which is an important aspect for adoption in industry. This aspect is not at least shown by the usage of reusability.

Regarding the product automation approach the comparison of EC++ and the Structured Components displays, that there is no UML element that is per se suited or not suited for embedded software development. While parameterised classes are considered ineligible for EC++ development, they are welcome for Structured Component implementers. The crucial issue is neither the modelling element nor the object oriented concept modelled by the very element, but rather how efficient it is transformed into source code. Willert [38] states, that experienced embedded developers instantly know, how a high level programming language statement is compiled into machine language by the respective compiler. According to that knowledge, they choose constructs that compile efficiently for the target platform. This exactly is the task of UML design tools, to define the mapping rules from model to code according to the target system. Structured Components are a very good starting point, because they incorporate attributes of object orientation (which allows UML modelling), but are implemented using a structured language (which render possible efficiency).

The discussed embedded software engineering methods are relevant to both product and plant software development. They can be used to model traditional product automation software as well as control or (field bus) connectivity software that is used in plant automation. Hence, the presented "embedded capable" UML elements should be used to model the depicted control patterns for plant automation.

At this point the presented parts of UML-PA may look fragmental, but the complete UML-PA will bridge the gap between process automation and computer science. The composition of these parts is the result of the detailed requirements analysis, which was made already in the forefront of the UML-PA elements' development. These requirements based on one hand on different interviews with software developer and user [10, 18] and on the other hand on the evaluation of presently offered UML tools [37, 39].

6   Outlook

While exemplary artefacts of embedded software have been developed using UML-PA and Structured Components, a "real world" example of appliance is still to be elaborated. Therefore, two case studies have been designed to serve as evaluation environment for the embedded software designed with UML-PA. The practicability of UML-PA, as well as the code size and the required computational performance of the software will be evaluated.

As one case study is the demonstrator "single-track level crossing in radio based operation" [47] will be used. This demonstrator contains multiple devices with comparable functionality. This comparable functionality should be dealt with one single Structured Component type that is accordingly parameterised. One component type driving several different systems is a strong indicator for the reusability of software components, which have been developed with UML-PA.

The other case study ,the demonstrator "continuous hydraulic press", represents a process from timber industry: a plant which produces fibreboards. The press has got most restrictive requirements. Time critical closed loop control has to be combined with open loop control and switching to other control loops. This demonstrator is built of several single board computers (SBC) with a real-time operating system connected via a fieldbus.

To meet real time criteria of technical processes, UML-PA has to support real time concepts.The OSEK[1] [48] guidelines have been established as a standard for real-time operation systems in the embedded domain. The OSEK Implementation Language (OIL) allows specifying real-time aspects. So it is obvious to introduce OIL constructs to UML-PA.

Outside the scope of this project, but never the less an interesting enhancement of software, that is designed using UML-PA and implemented with Structured Components, are the aspects dynamic reloading during runtime, automatic (re-) configuration and decoupling of software fragments. Both UML-PA and Structured Components offer promising fundaments to realise such features, due to their supported characteristics concurrency, structural independence, and immutability (by a third party). The challenge to realise the above mentioned abilities is the required communication infrastructure of the software components. Today, this is usually accomplished by communication interfaces, which are also supported by UML-PA. Unfortunately, these interfaces must be known and implemented at compile time, determining the communication structure is static, i.e. it must be known, which component communicates with which other components. Since automation systems usually have not only a high degree of complexity, but also a very long life span (may be up to 30 years), changes while prosecuting the system are difficult at best. Software that supports such dynamic behaviour could be developed using UML-PA and Structured Components as a basis, but this software would need additional features like the ability to negotiate with other parties and to dynamically adapt to given needs. Therefore, continuative methods for software development are necessary.

---

[1] Open systems and the corresponding interfaces for automotive electronics

References

[1] Lauber, R., Göhner, P.: Prozessautomatisierung 1. Springer-Verlag, Berlin, 1999.

[2] Cooling, J.: Software Engineering for Real-Time Systems. Addison Wesley, Harlow, 2003.

[3] Bonfatti, F., Monari, P. D., Sampietri, U.: IEC 1131-3 Programming Methodology. CJ International, Seyssins, 1997.

[4] Heck, B. S., Wills, L. M., Vachtsevanos, G. J.: Software Technology for Implementing Reusable Distributed Control Systems, IEEE Control Magazine, February 2003.

[5] Renesas Technology Corporation: M16C/6N Datasheet, 2003.

[6] Kernighan, B., Ritchie, D.: The C Programming Language. Prentice Hall PTR, Upper Saddle River, 1988.

[7] Brinksma, E. et. al.: Component-based design and integration platforms: a roadmap, Technical Report IST-2001-34820, The ARTIST consortium, April 2003

[8] Nickel, U., Schäfer, W., Zündorf, A.: Integrative Specification of Distributed Production Control Systems for Flexible Automated Manufacturing. In: Nagl, M., Westfechtel, B. (Eds.): Modelle Werkzeuge und Infrastrukturen zur Unterstützung von Entwicklungsprozessen. Symposium, Wiley-VCH Verlag, Weinheim, 2003. pp. 179ff

[9] Huber, F., Schätz, B.: Integrated Development of Embedded Systems with AutoFocus, Technical Report TUM-I0107, TU München, Institut für Informatik, Munich, December 2001

[10] Katzke, U., Vogel-Heuser, B., Fischer, K.: Analysis and State of the Art of Modules in Industrial Automation. In: atp international, 1(2004), issue 1, Oldenbourg Verlag, Munich, 2004.

[11] Moore, G. E.: Cramming more components onto integrated circuits, Electronics Magazine, vol. 8, April 1965, p. 114-117.

[12] Hamilton, S.: Semiconductor Research Corporation: Taking Moore's Law Into the Next Century, IEEE Computer, volume 32, 1999, p. 43-48.

[13] Iwanitz, F.: Horizontale und vertikale Integration durch den Verbund von PROFInet und OPC, In: Automatisierungstechnische Praxis (atp) 45 (2003); issue 1, Oldenbourg Verlag, Munich, 2003, p. 39-69.

[14] Kniesel, G.: Type-Safe Delegation for Dynamic Component Adaptation. LNCS, 1543: p. 136-137, 1998.

[15] Lewis, R. W.: Programming industrial control systems using IEC 61131-3. IEE, Herts, 1998.

[16] www.iec.ch, September 2003.

[17] Stützle, R.: Wiederverwendung ohne Mythos: Empirisch fundierte Leitlinien für die Entwicklung wiederverwendbarer Software, Munich, 2002.

[18] Katzke, U., Fischer, K., Vogel-Heuser, B.: Entwicklung und Evaluation eines Modells für modulare Automatisierung im Anlagenbau. In: P. Holleczek, B. Vogel-Heuser (Ed.), Verteilte Echtzeitsysteme PEARL 2003, Springer Verlag, Berlin, Heidelberg, 2003, p. 63-69.

[19] www.plcopen.org, June 2004.

[20] Göhner, P.: Komponentenbasierte Entwicklung von Automatisierungssystemen, GMA-Kongress 98, Ludwigsburg, June 1998, http://opus.uni-stuttgart.de/opus/volltexte/1999/451/, March 2004.

[21] Mahoney, M.: The Roots of Software Engineering CWI Quarterly volume 3, number 4, 1990, www.princeton.edu/~hos/mike/articles/sweroots.pdf, March 2004.

[22] Mehrgardt, S.: Moore's Zukunftsformel: Wo liegen die Grenzen der Mikroelektronik C, changeX Partnerforum, 11.09.2002, http://www.changex.de/pdf/d_a00767.pdf, March 2004.

[23] Friedrich, D., Vogel-Heuser, B., Bristol, E.: Evaluation of Modeling Notations for Basic Software Engineering in Process Control. In: 29 th Annual Conference of the IEEE Industrial Electronics Society (IECON 03) in Roanoke, Virginia, USA, November 2003.

[24] Braatz, A.: Entwicklung eines UML-basierten Funktionsblockmodells für den objektorientierten Steuerungsentwurf. In: Automatisierungstechnische Praxis (atp) 45(2003) issue 6. P. 38 – 44.

[25] Witsch, D., Vogel-Heuser, B.: Automatische Codegenerierung aus der UML für die IEC 61131-3. Accepted paper in Eingebettete Systeme, Workshop of the GI-Fachgruppe Echtzeitprogrammierung, 2004.

[26] Bartels, J., Vogel, B.: Systementwicklung für die Automatisierung im Anlagenbau. In: at-Automatisierungstechnik, 49 (2001); issue 5, Oldenbourg Verlag, Munich, 2001, p. 214-224.

[27] Hruschka, P., Rupp, C.: Agile Softwareentwicklung für embedded Real-Time Systems mit der UML. Hanser Verlag, Munich, Vienna, 2002

[28] Selic, B., Rumbaugh, J.: Using UML for Modeling Complex Real-Time Systems. www.rational.com\whitepapers, 1998.

[29] Bonfe, M., Fantuzzi, C.: Design and Verification of Industrial Logic Controllers with UML and Statecharts. In: Proceedings CCA 2003, IEEE, Istanbul, Turkey, 2003.

[30] www.3s-software.com, March 2004.

[31] www.artisansw.com, March 2004.

[32] Stroustrup, B.: The C++ Programming Language. Addison-Wesley, Reading, 1997.

[33] Embedded C++ Technical Committee: Rationale for the Embedded C++ Specification. http://www. Caravan.net/ec2plus/rationale.html, 1998.

[34] Pender, T.: UML Bible. Wiley Publishing, Indianapolis, 2003.

[35] Eberle, S., Göhner, P.: Softwareentwicklung für eingebettete Systeme mit Strukturierten Komponenten. In: Teil 1, Automatisierungstechnische Praxis (atp) 46 (2004); issue 3, Oldenbourg Verlag, Munich, 2004.

[36] Eberle, S., Göhner, P.: Softwareentwicklung für eingebettete Systeme mit Strukturierten Komponenten. In: Teil 2, Automatisierungstechnische Praxis (atp) 46 (2004); issue 4, Oldenbourg Verlag, Munich, 2004.

[37] Fischer, K., Vogel-Heuser, B.: UML in der automatisierungstechnischen Anwendung – Stärken und Schwächen, In: Automatisierungstechnische Praxis (atp) 44 (2002); issue 10, Oldenbourg Verlag, Munich, 2002, p. 63-69.

[38] Willert, A.: Zwischen Theorie und Praxis. (atp) 45 (2003); issue 9, Oldenbourg, 2003 Industrieverlag, Munich 2003.

[39] Fischer, K., Hordys, G: Evaluation of an UML Software Engineering Tool by Means of a Distributed Real Time Application in Plant Industry. In: Proceedings of the Modellierung 2004, Marburg, 24.-26.03.2004.

[40] Braatz, A.:Entwicklung eines UML-basierten Funktionsblockmodells für den objektorientierten Steuerungsentwurf. In: Automatisierungstechnische Praxis (atp) 45(2003) issue 6, Oldenbourg Verlag, Munich, 2003,. p. 38 – 44.

[41] Henzinger, T.A., Kirsch, C.M., Sanvido, M.A.A., Pree, W.: From Control Models to Real-Time Code Using Giotto.IEEE Control System Magazine 23(1), P. 50-64, 2003.

[42] http://wwwcs.upb.de/fachbereich/AG/schaefer/ag_dt/ISILEIT/

[43] Berkenkötter, B., Bisanz, S., Hannemann, U., Peleska, J.: HybridUML Profile for UML 2.0, SVERTS, workshop hold in conjunction with UML 2003, San Francisco, 10/2003

[44] Licht, T.: Ein Verfahren zur zeitlichen Analyse von UML-Modellen beim Entwurf von Automatisierungssystemen. Doctoral Thesis, Faculty of computer science and automation at the Technical University of Ilmenau, April 2004.

[45] Overview of the ptolemy project. Technical Memorandum UCB/ERL M03/25 http://ptolemy.eecs.berkeley.edu

[46] Lauber, R.: Prozessautomatisierung, Vol. 1, issue 2, Springer-Verlag, 1989

[47] http://www.ias.uni-stuttgart.de/projekte/saferail/animation/ref.html

[48] http://www.osek-vdx.org/

Introduction to Subject Area "Charts"

Werner Damm and Bernd Westphal

Carl von Ossietzky Universität Oldenburg
Department für Informatik, PO Box 2503, 26111 Oldenburg, Germany
{damm,westphal}@informatik.uni-oldenburg.de

The subject area 'Charts' groups together those projects that study visual specification formalisms or *charts*. Visual formalisms promise to support the use of formal methods in the engineering process of (embedded) software systems by being high-level languages that are equipped with a formal semantics in the elementary formalisms like temporal logic or finite state machines.

The use of chart languages has a long tradition in the domain of systems engineering as a means to support the intuition of the designer and thereby to allow to cope with the complexity of systems under design. For example, the domain of programmable logic controllers (PLC's) has a long history of graphical "programming languages", from ladder diagrams to sequential function charts [1], in the domain of reactive systems Harel's Statecharts [2] find widespread use, and also object-oriented analysis and design are accompanied by multiple visual formalisms, some of which finally merged into the Unified Modeling Language [3].

The aim of the DFG focus area program is the integration of software specification techniques for the application in the engineering sciences. As just pointed out, many specification techniques are visual formalisms hence the study of the exact formal semantics of existing charts languages and their integration are a prominent part of the focus area program.

The chart languages considered in the subject area comprise Statecharts in the UML semantics [4] and also the classical Statemate semantics [5], Sequential Function Charts (SFC) [6], and Live Sequence Charts [7]. Hence the range is from languages that describe models of a system under design (Statemate Statecharts, UML, SFC's) to more declarative languages that specify behavioural requirements (LSC's [8]).

A prime topic of the subject area is the definition of a rigorous semantics of the considered charts languages. Without a formal semantics, the use of visual formalisms is merely illustrative and hence lacks the advantages of formal methods: the possibility to *unambiguously* determine the meaning of a document and the possibility to apply automatic or semi-automatic formal verification technology. Verification in the sense that a model is checked for satisfying a specification, that is, it is proven that the model satisfies the specification, allows to detect errors in a design as early in the development process as possible and hence reduces costs and efforts to revise the design. For these reasons the verification of charts is the other prime topic of the subject area.

H. Ehrig et al. (Eds.): INT 2004, LNCS 3147, pp. 322–324, 2004.
© Springer-Verlag Berlin Heidelberg 2004

The results presented in the following articles range from a semantics of UML Statecharts as used by the design tool Rhapsody [4], over a formal semantics for Sequential Function Charts that allows to capture semantical deviations between commercial tools supporting SFC's as a standardised "graphical programming language" for PLC's [6], a formal semantics of the specification language of Live Sequence Charts [7], to an approach for formal verification of Statecharts in an interactive way using a theorem-prover [5].

The invited contribution by *D. Harel* and *H. Kugler* [4] provides an in-depth discussion of the semantics of Statecharts as implemented by the UML tool Rhapsody that was among the first executable semantics for object-oriented Statecharts.

The main difference to classical Statemate Statecharts, where events, i.e. stimuli issued and processed, are only visible for a single step, lies in the introduction of event queues. In the UML semantics, events are stored in an event queue and processed one after another.

The contribution of project *ForMoSA* (W. Reif, G. Schellhorn, A. Thums, F. Ortmeier (Augsburg)) [5] reports on a theorem-proving based procedure to formally verify Statecharts (in the Statemate semantics) against properties in Interval Temporal Logic in order to overcome the limitation finite-state methods pose on the data domains. That is, the goal is to be able to reason about models without imposing the assumption that all domains are finite. The proof strategy is symbolic execution for which the proof conditions are presented.

This provides the basis for the aims of ForMoSA concerning formal fault tree analysis, a combination of formal models with safety analysis techiques from engineering.

The topic of the project *USE* (Damm, J. Klose, B. Westphal, M. Brill (Oldenburg)) is the assessment of the application of Live Sequence Charts (LSC's) as a specification language for communication between sub-systems. This comprises the development of a complete formal semantics with the aim to provide developers with tools for automatic formal verification of LSC specifications against system models. In the contribution to the subject area "Charts" they provide the formal semantics of LSC's in terms of timed automata [7].

Sequential Function Charts (SFC's) are a graphical formalism for writing concurrent control programs, in particular targeted on PLC automata. The syntax of SFC's is given by an international standard yet a survey of the semantics implemented by a number of programming tools provided by PLC suppliers unveiled significantly different interpretations of the standard.

The associated project *SFC-Check* (Y. Lakhnech, W. P. de Roever, B. Lukoschus, R. Huuck (Kiel), S. Engell, S. Kowalewski, N. Bauer (Dortmund)) contributes a formal semantics of SFC's that is as flexible to formally capture the complete range of semantical deviations found in the survey [6]. This semantics in particular provides the basis to, for example, automatically check SFC's for different notions of well-formedness.

References

1. International Electronical Commission: Programmable controllers – programming languages, IEC 61131-3 (1998)
2. Harel, D.: Statecharts: A visual formalism for complex systems. Science of Computer Programming **8** (1987) 231–274
3. OMG: Unified Modeling Language Specification, ad/01-09-67 (2001)
4. Harel, D., Kugler, H.: The Rhapsody semantics of statecharts (or, on the executable core of the UML). In: this volume. (2004)
5. Thums, A., Schellhorn, G., Ortmeier, F., Reif, W.: Interactive verification of statecharts. In: this volume. (2004)
6. Bauer, N., Huuck, R., Lukoschus, B., Engell, S.: A unifying semantics for sequential function charts. In: this volume. (2004)
7. Brill, M., Damm, W., Klose, J., Westphal, B., Wittke, H.: Live Sequence Charts. In: this volume. (2004)
8. Damm, W., Harel, D.: LSCs: Breathing life into message sequence charts. Formal Methods in System Design **19** (2001) 45–80

The Rhapsody Semantics of Statecharts
(or, On the Executable Core of the UML)*

(Preliminary Version)

David Harel and Hillel Kugler

Department of Computer Science and Applied Mathematics
The Weizmann Institute of Science, Rehovot, Israel
{dharel,kugler}@wisdom.weizmann.ac.il

Abstract. We describe the semantics of statecharts as implemented in the current version of the Rhapsody tool. In its original 1996 version this was among the first executable semantics for object-oriented statecharts, and many of its fundamentals have been adopted in the Unified Modeling Language (UML). Due to the special challenges of object-oriented behavior, the semantics of statecharts in Rhapsody differs from the original semantics of statecharts in Statemate. Two of the main differences are: (i) in Rhapsody, changes made in a given step are to take effect in the current step and not in the next step; (ii) in Rhapsody, a step can take more than zero time. This paper constitutes the first description of the executable semantics of Rhapsody, highlighting the differences from the Statemate semantics and making an effort to explain the issues clearly but rigorously, including the motivation for some of the design decisions taken.

1   Introduction

In this paper we describe the semantics of statecharts as implemented in the Rhapsody tool. Some early work on incorporating statecharts into an object-oriented framework appears in [11,1,12]. However, the detailed basis for a semantically solid OO version of the language of statecharts first appeared in [5]. Two consequences of [5] were (i) the development of the Rhapsody tool to support object-oriented statecharts, and (ii) the essential adoption by the UML developers of its underlying semantics. As a result, Rhapsody [9] can be viewed as the tool that captures the executable kernel of the UML [13].

This having been said, and despite extensive UML documentation, it is also commonly known that there has never been a responsibly detailed description of the executable semantics of the OO statecharts language of [5], as captured by

---

* This research was supported in part by the John von Neumann Minerva Center for the Verification of Reactive Systems and by the European Commission project OMEGA (IST-2001-33522).

H. Ehrig et al. (Eds.): INT 2004, LNCS 3147, pp. 325–354, 2004.

Rhapsody. This we take upon ourselves here, making an effort to explain the issues clearly, including the motivation for some of the design decisions taken. We focus on the differences between the object-oriented nature of Rhapsody compared to the original non-OO statecharts in Statemate. The general spirit and structure of this paper are similar to the paper that described the Statemate semantics [6], and occasionally we even borrow some of the phrases from there. This is done not out of laziness, but to allow readers familiar with statecharts to easily focus on the novel aspects in the new approach. Still, the paper is self-contained, and so is accessible to readers who are not familiar with Statemate semantics or with [6].

The current version of the semantics is a result of much experience gained by users of the Rhapsody tool over the years, which led to modifications and adjustments. Rhapsody executable models can be run in different modes of operation: regular mode, trace mode or animation mode. In the trace and animation modes the user can test the model's behavior by simulating the environment. After each step, the user can generate events and invoke triggered operations that will influence the run of the system. In trace mode, textual information about the system behavior is displayed, while in animation mode a visual graphical representation is displayed showing how the active configuration of each object's statechart changes, by highlighting states entered and transitions taken. The animator can also show inter-object behavior, by creating animated message sequence charts that show graphically how messages are sent between objects during runtime. These can then be compared with previously prepared sequence charts that capture requirements on behavior. There are many interesting issues related to the animation of executable models, but they are beyond the scope of this paper. An important fact that should be stressed is that in contrast to Statemate, the trace and animation modes in Rhapsody use code generated by Rhapsody with additional instrumentation, so that the behavior of the system in these modes is the same as that of the actual production code. This is one of the basic principles that gives added power to executable object modeling.

2   The Basics

An object-oriented system is composed of **classes**. A statechart describes the modal behavior of the class, that is how it reacts to messages it receives by defining the actions taken and the new mode entered. A class can have an associated statechart describing its behavior. These classes are called **reactive classes**. Simple classes that are data driven do not necessarily have statecharts. During runtime there can exist many **objects** of the same class, called **instances**, and each can be in a different **active configuration** — a set of states in which the system resides. Thus, a new statechart is "born" for each new instance of the class, and it runs independently of the others.

The statechart itself is similar to the original description in [4], and to that of Statemate [6,7], in that there are three types of states, OR-**states**, AND-**states** and **basic states**. The OR-states have substates related to each other by "exclusive or", AND-states have orthogonal components that are related by "and", while basic states have no substates, and are the lowest in the state hierarchy. Fig. 1 shows the hierarchy and the three types of states that can be used in a statechart. States S, B, C, D are OR-states, state A is an AND-state and states $B1$, $B2$, $C1$, $C2$, $D1$, $D2$, E are basic states. When building a statechart in RHAPSODY an additional state is created implicitly, the **root** state, which is the highest in the hierarchy, in this case the root state has state S as a substate.

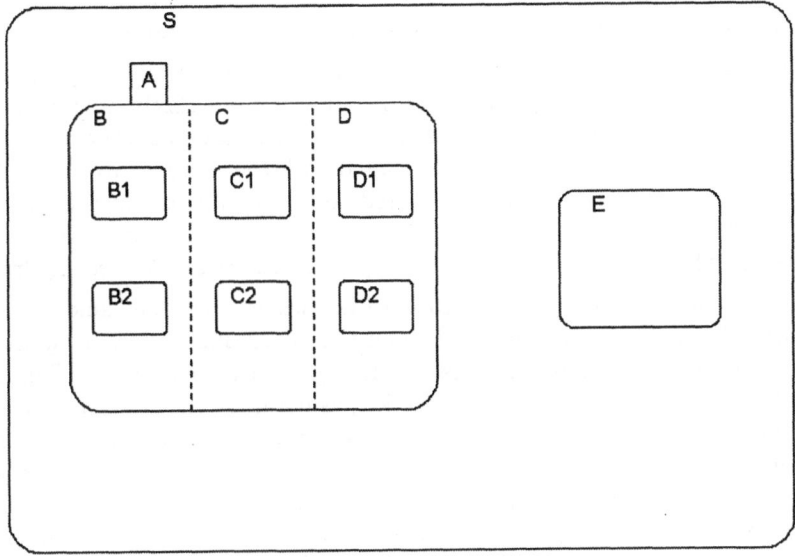

Fig. 1. A small hierarchy of states

The active configuration is a maximal set of states that the system can be in simultaneously, including the root state, exactly one substate for each OR-state contained, all substates for each AND-state contained and no additional states. An example of an active configuration of the statechart in Fig. 1 is :
$\{B1, B, C1, C, D2, D, A, S, root\}$.

The general syntax of an expression labelling a transition in a statechart is "$m[c]/a$" where m is the **message** that triggers the transition, c is a **condition** that guards the transition from being taken unless it is true when m occurs, and a is an **action** that is carried out if and when the transition is taken. All of these parts are optional.

In RHAPSODY, there is a single trigger, which can be an **event** or a **triggered operation**. Events mean asynchronous communication and triggered operations mean synchronous communication. This issue is discussed in greater length in a separate section. It is also possible to have a transition without a trigger, called a **null transition**. Another kind of message that is used in RHAPSODY is a **primitive operation**, which corresponds to an invocation of a method call in the underlying programming language. A primitive operation cannot be used as the trigger of a transition in a statechart, but it can be used in the action part. A trigger can also be a special event timeout, abbreviated $tm(t)$, where t is the time in milliseconds until the event occurs (measured from the time the relevant source state was entered). In RHAPSODY, the guard and action are written in the implementation language[1] and in contrast to STATEMATE there is no special action language. This is a practical design decision, but it should be emphasized that in principle it would be no problem to incorporate such a language. In fact, once the community agrees upon an abstract action language, this could be integrated into the RHAPSODY tool semantics in a natural way.

Besides actions that appear along transitions, they can also appear associated with the entrance to (**Entry action**) or exit from (**Exit action**) a state (any state, on any level). Like actions on transitions, these too are written in the implementation language. Actions associated with the entrance to a state S are executed in the step in which S is entered, as if they appear on the transition leading into S. Similarly, actions associated with the exit from S are executed in the step in which S is exited, as if they appear on the transition exiting from S.

A state can have **static reactions** (SRs), which have the same format as transition labels, i.e., "$m[c]/a$", and again the guard and action are written in the implementation language. Consider the statechart appearing in Fig. 2 (a). State W is associated with a static reaction, as noted by the $>$ symbol attached to its name in the statechart. The actual static reaction $f/act()$ is shown in the state menu at the bottom of the figure. The object is now in state W and in its substate U, and if method f occurs this causes the static reaction to be taken, which involves performing action $act()$. The active configuration of the object does not change, and it remains in U. Semantically, each static reaction in a state can be regarded as a transition in a virtual substate that is orthogonal to its ordinary substates and to the other SRs of the state. Thus, the statechart of Fig. 2 (b) describes the same behavior of that of Fig. 2 (a).

STATEMATE is based on the structured analysis paradigm, where the functional capabilities of the system are captured by activities that are dynamically linked to states in the statechart. Linking states to activities is not relevant to RHAPSODY. As mentioned before, in RHAPSODY the mode of an object of a reactive class is the active configuration of the object's statechart.

The behavior of a system described in RHAPSODY is a set of possible **runs**. A run consists of a series of detailed snapshots of the system's situation. Such a snapshot is called a **status**. The first in the sequence is the initial status, and each subsequent one is obtained from its predecessor by executing a **step** (see Fig. 3). The heart of the semantics, and the main goal of this paper, is to define the effect of a step.

Each step is composed of **microsteps**, as is shown by "zooming-in" on one of the steps in Fig. 3. The system, being in a certain status and as a response to

---

[1] The original version of RHAPSODY used C++ as the implementation language, but current versions support also C, Java and Ada.

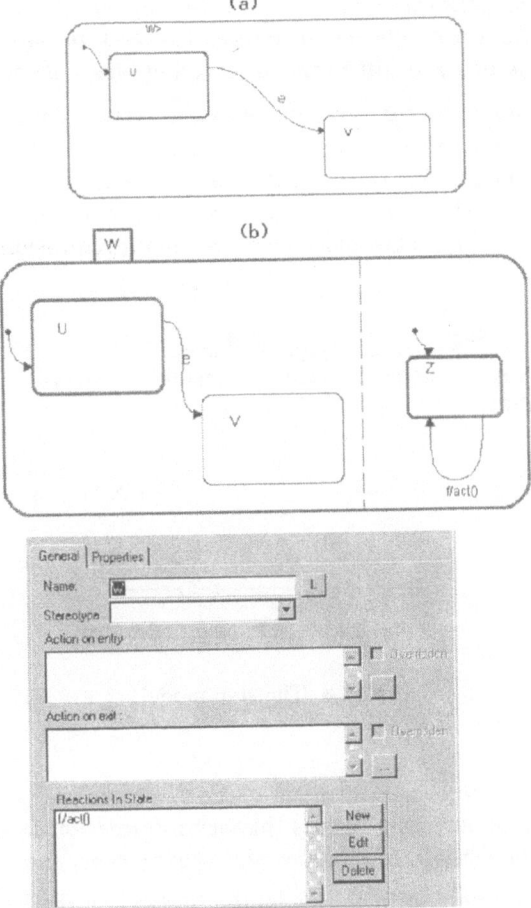

Fig. 2. Static reaction

an occurrence, undergoes a series of microsteps as part of the run-to-completion principle, until it reaches a final status, and at which point it is ready for the next occurrence. Thus the run-to completion principle applies to a step, and it means that as a response to some external occurrence a sequence of microsteps is performed leading to a final status for this step, at which point a new occurrence is considered, initiating a new step. A special case is that of null transitions, that is, transitions without a trigger, and these can be taken spontaneously. A loop of null transitions could in principle cause an infinite number of microsteps to be taken in a single step. However, in RHAPSODY this is avoided by the system setting a maximum value for the number of null transitions that can be taken as part of a step, and informing the user if this bound is violated.

Certain invariants regarding the system's behavior (e.g., being in an OR-state requires being in exactly one of its substates) hold at the beginning and end of a step, but not necessarily in each of the microsteps. Also, a microstep can correspond to performing an action in the implementation language, which can take time. As a consequence, in RHAPSODY a statechart may reside in an OR-state for some non-zero time prior to entering one of its substates.

RHAPSODY supports the development of reactive multi-threaded applications. In such applications each **thread** can perform steps in parallel to the other threads, which makes the definition and behavior more complicated. This topic will be discussed in Section 10, by explaining how threads are introduced into statechart-based systems and how the semantics are defined for them.

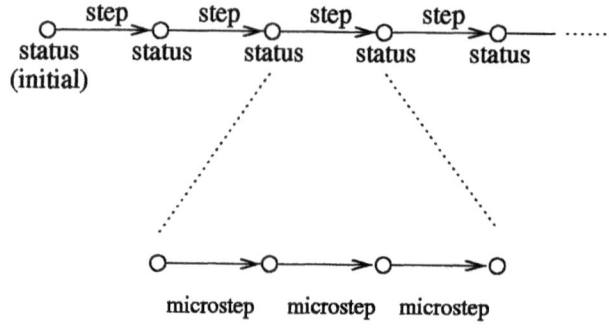

Fig. 3. The step model

A status contains information about all the objects in the system — the states in which the object currently resides, history information for states, values of data members, connections of relations and aggregations and event queues.

Here are some general principles adopted in defining the RHAPSODY semantics:

1. Changes that occur in a step may be sensed in the same step. There is no double buffering to prevent effects from being sensed immediately. This approach is the one more suited to the RHAPSODY context, since a system consists of classes, not all of which have statecharts, and the guards and actions are written in the implementation language. Double buffering would have entailed a high overhead.

2. In RHAPSODY, unlike the situation in STATEMATE, it is possible that many steps will be executed between the time an event is generated and put in the proper event queue and the time it is dispatched to the statechart. Once an event is dispatched to the statechart it will "live" for the duration of one step only, and will not be remembered in subsequent steps.

3. Calculations in one step are based on the current values of data members and the state configuration. When performing a microstep, first the set of relevant transitions is computed and only then are these transitions actually taken. Since there is no buffering as in STATEMATE, the calculation itself can effect

the data members; an evaluation of a guard that has side effects can affect the system. It is not considered good practice to use guards with side effects.

4. A maximal subset of nonconflicting transitions and static reactions is always executed. We refer to this as the "greediness property" of the semantics.

5. The execution of a step does not necessarily take zero time. The time a step will take depends on the actions that are performed while taking the step, mainly those actions corresponding to method calls in the implementation language, and thus are not zero time. RHAPSODY supports two models of time, real and simulated. More on these in section 9.

3   Basic System Reaction

A statechart describes the behavior of all instances of a class, but each instance (i.e., each instance's statechart) can be in a different active configuration. After the instance is created a special method, *startBehavior*, is invoked, initializing the behavior of the reactive object and causing its statechart to enter an active configuration according to the default transitions taken from the root. The active configuration can change according to the messages received by the object and the transitions that are performed. The object terminates its life-cycle if it is explicitly deleted or its statechart enters a termination connector.

Statecharts can react to messages by performing a transition from an active configuration to a new active configuration and possibly performing an action.

We now define the reaction of the system during a simple step: how the status of the system changes when performing a single transition between two OR-states with the same parent state. Assume that the object in question is in state A in the statechart of Fig. 4(a), and message m (event or triggered operation) is dispatched to the statechart of the object.

The response of the system will be as follows: (*i*) The exit action of state A is performed. (*ii*) The action *act* specified by the transition is performed. (*iii*) The

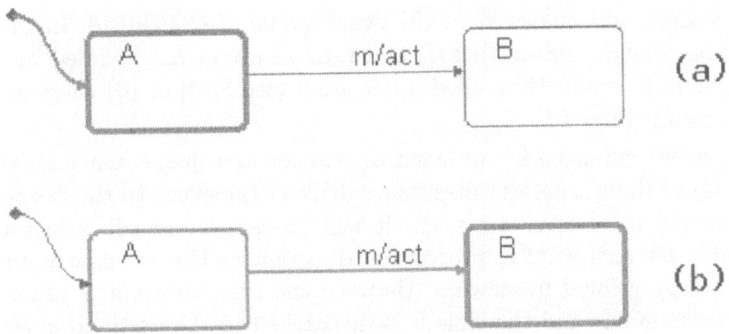

Fig. 4. A simple transition

entry action of state B is performed. (*iv*) The active configuration is updated, and the object is 'placed' in state B. The new active configuration of the example is shown in Fig. 4(b).

The action *act* may be of the form *act1*; *act2*; ... *act$_i$*. In RHAPSODY, actions are guaranteed to be performed in sequential order, each action being executed after the previous has terminated. This in itself does not cause a racing condition. The motivation for this semantics is that actions are written as code in an object-oriented programming language and thus sequential ordering without any double buffering is a natural choice.

The behavior described in Fig. 4 could actually be part of a larger step, during which in some microstep the triggered operation m occurs and activates the response described above.

Statecharts can communicate via an asynchronous communication mechanism that uses events and a synchronous communication mechanism that uses triggered operations. In Fig. 4, for example, the message m can be either an event or a triggered operation. We now discuss the two cases and the differences between them.

3.1   Events

Events are used to describe asynchronous communication. They are entities of the model and are defined as part of a *package*. Each class defines the set of events it can receive. The main motivation for using events is that the sender object can continue its work without waiting for the receiver to consume the event. Events can also be used early in the system development process, and later, when a better understanding of the system is gained and decisions regarding synchronization are made, some of these events can be converted to triggered operations.

Events are sent by applying the GEN method to the destination object: $O \rightarrow GEN(event(p_1, p_2, \cdots p_N))$ The sending object should be able to refer to the destination object O (possibly using a navigation expression based on relations in the model). Here $p_1, p_2, \cdots p_N$ are event parameters that match the event's formal arguments (data members). The GEN method creates the event instance and queues it in the event queue of O's thread. In this section we assume a single system thread, and thus all events are handled by the same event queue. In a multi-threaded application (see Section 10) there is an event queue for each thread.

Events are managed by an event dispatcher in a queue. Once an event gets to the top of the queue, the dispatcher delivers the event to the proper object. When an object receives an event, it will process it according to the run-to-completion semantics. After processing, the event no longer exists and is deleted by the computational framework. Between the time an event is generated and put it in the queue and the time it is dispatched to the destination object, the destination object could be destroyed, in which case all events that were sent to it will be deleted and will have no effect.

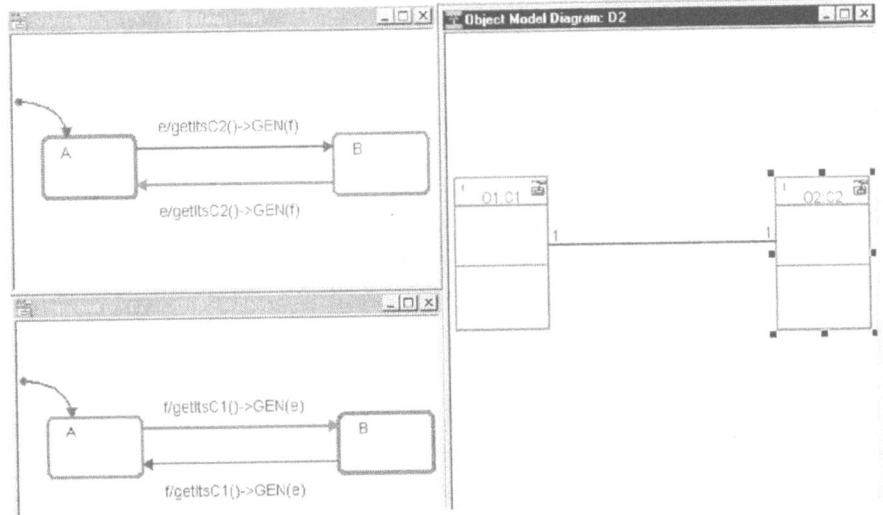

Fig. 5. Communication using events

Consider the system in Fig. 5, with objects O_1 and O_2 of classes C_1 and C_2, respectively, and with a one-to-one relationship between the objects. If object O_1 receives event e (say, from the user), the transition from state A to state B is taken, involving sending event f to object O_2 (by placing a new event f in the event queue), as specified by the action $getItsC2() \rightarrow GEN(f)$, since O_2 is the object that it recognizes from class C_2. Once the transition to state B of O_1 is completed, event f is removed from the event queue, and is dispatched to object O_2, causing it to take the transition from its state A to state B. In a similar way, object O_2 now sends event e to O_1, and the process repeats itself. In this way, a feedback loop is created, with objects O_1 and O_2 repeatedly moving between states A and B, and sending events e and f to each other, ad infinitum.

Unlike STATEMATE, there is no special treatment of internal events in RHAPSODY. Sending events internally is done simply by omitting the destination object from the send operation, as follows:

$GEN(event(p_1, p_2, \cdots p_N))$

Consider Fig. 6. On creation of an object of this class the statechart is initiated, and the default transition to state A is taken, performing the action $GEN(e(1))$, which causes the internal event e with parameter value 1 to be sent. Only after the object has completed the transition and is in state A, is the event e dispatched to the statechart. Processing this event causes a transition to state C, since of the two outgoing transitions from the condition connector, the guard of the transition to state C is satisfied (the parameter of the event in the transition is referenced using the $params \rightarrow$ command, and here the value was 1).

Events are independent entities of the model and can be sub-classed like inherited objects, a mechanism that can be used in order to add attributes —

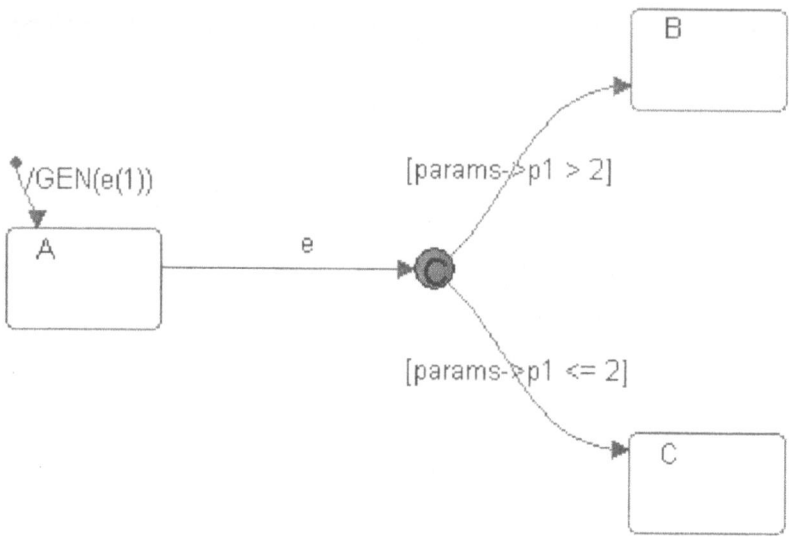

Fig. 6. More communication using events

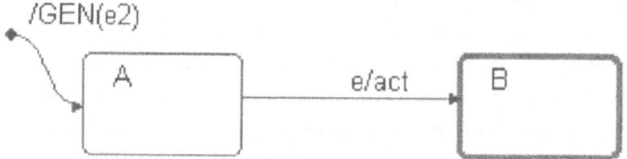

Fig. 7. Event $e2$ inherits from e

event parameters. In particular, if event $e2$ is derived from event e in this way, $e2$ will trigger any transition that has e as a trigger. For example, in Fig. 7, after taking the default transition into state A and sending event e_2 to itself, the transition to state B is taken, since e_2 inherits from event e.

3.2   Triggered Operations

Triggered operations are services provided by a class, and are defined as part of the serving class. They are a synchronous communication means between a client and the server object. A triggered operation may return a value to the client object, since its activation is synchronous.

Unlike events, triggered operations are not independent entities; rather, they are part of the class definition, and are not organized in hierarchies. The use of a triggered operation corresponds to the invocation of a class member function. The main reason that triggered operations were integrated into the RHAPSODY framework was to allow the usage of statecharts in architectures that are not

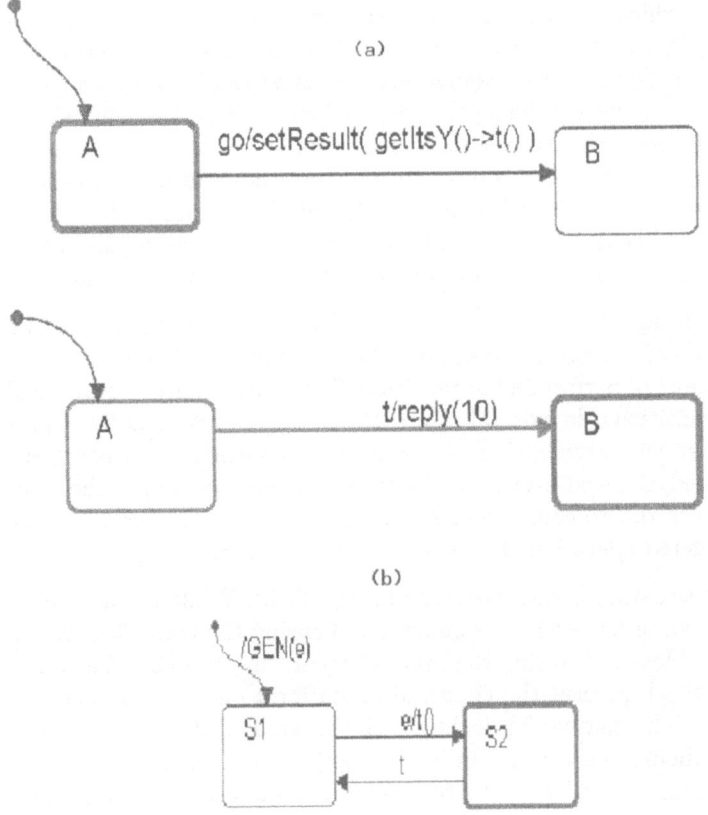

Fig. 8. Using triggered operations

event-driven, and thus to specify the behavior of objects in the programming sense of operations and object state. Triggered operations also provide means for late design decisions to optimize execution time and sequencing, by converting event communication into direct triggered operation invocation.

A triggered operation is invoked like a primitive operation in the underlying implementation language:

$$result = O \rightarrow t(p_1, p_2, \cdots p_N)$$

A triggered operation may return a value whose type is the one defined in the object model, where the operation interface is defined. The return value for a triggered operation must be set within the transition. Replying to a triggered operation is done by calling the reply method defined for the class. The following transition label specifies a reply to the operation t:

$t/reply(17)$

Consider the two statecharts of classes X and Y, described in Fig. 8 (a). If an object of class X receives the event go, a transition from state A to state B

is taken, which invokes the triggered operation t in the relevant object of class Y, as specified by the action $getItsY() \to t()$. The transition to state B of X is not completed before t is processed, causing the Y object to move from state A to state B, with 10 being the returned value of t. The figure shows the active configuration of the statecharts in animation mode, at a point when the Y object has completed its transition to state B, and the X object is in the midst of the transition. The X object's transition is completed after *setResult* is called with the value 10 that was returned by the triggered operation, and the value of the data member *result* of X is updated. Only then is state B entered.

One thing that has to be resolved here is the reaction of an object to an invocation of a triggered operation when it is not in a **stable** state, i.e., when it is in the midst of performing a transition. This is especially relevant in RHAPSODY, since transitions do not take zero time. This would not be a problem if we considered only events, since events represent asynchronous communication and are queued; the next event is taken from the queue only after the step completes, so that the run to completion semantics assures the object is in a stable state. For triggered operations there is no such assurance.

This situation is demonstrated in Fig. 8 (b). While taking the default transition to state $S1$, event e is generated, causing the transition from state $S1$ to state $S2$. However, during the process of carrying this out, the action $t()$ is performed which invokes the triggered operation t on this statechart. There are a number of alternatives for dealing with this kind of situation: One is to treat this as a deadlock, and a problem in the design. Another is to allow the transition to be completed and state $S2$ to be entered, and only then to process t, causing a transition to be taken back to state $S1$.

In RHAPSODY, a different choice was made: the invocation of a triggered operation t in the midst of a transition causes no effect, and the return value from such a call is undefined. In the above example, the object completes its transition to state $S2$ and remains there. The semantics is implemented by a locking mechanism that causes an object to ignore the invocation of triggered operations while in the middle of a step. A self call such as that in the example is a special case, but in general this can also occur as the result of a chain of calls between different objects, ending in a triggered operation invocation to one of the objects that is still in the process of performing a transition.

Earlier, in Fig. 5, we showed an example of a feedback loop between two statecharts. If we modify this example so that e and f are triggered operations instead of events, as shown in Fig. 9, then the result of invoking e on O_1 is that both objects enter state B. In this case, the feedback loop does not close, since when O_2 takes the transition to state B and invokes e on O_1, O_1 is still in the middle of the transition between A and B; hence e is ignored. Once both objects are in state B, if e is externally invoked on O_1 (or, alternatively, f is invoked on O_2), both objects take transitions to state A and remain there. Notice that had we changed only one of the two events to a triggered operation and left the other as an event, the feedback loop would have remained.

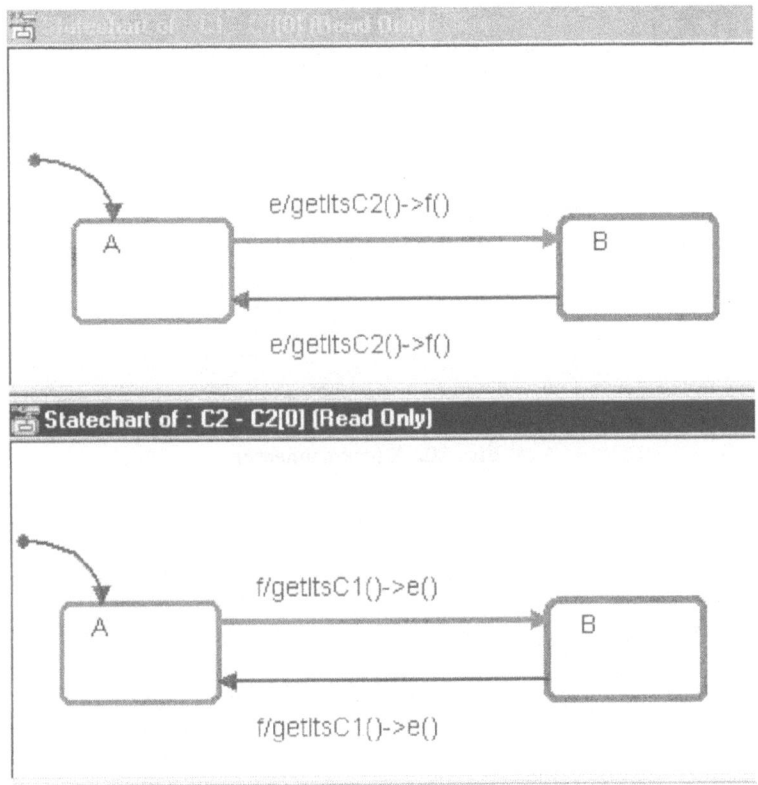

Fig. 9. Coordinated transitions

4   Compound Transitions

Statecharts allow defining transitions in a richer way then just by the simple directed arrow that connects two states, of the kind shown in Fig. 4. This general construct is called a **compound transition** (CT) and may consist of a number of separate transitions appearing in different orthogonal state components. Each of these, in turn, may consist of a number of linked **transition segments**, which are the labeled arrows that connect states and connectors of various kinds. This section explains how transition segments are combined to form a compound transition (CT). We explain the semantics of the different types of connectors and restrictions on how they are used.

The connectors come in two different types: AND and OR. The **fork** and **join** are AND connectors. The transition segments connected to an AND connector will all participate in the same CT. Consider the statechart appearing in Fig. 10. It the object is in state A and the trigger e occurs, the CT transition is taken, causing entrance to state $C1$ in orthogonal component C and entrance to $D1$ in orthogonal component D. The fact that the fork is an AND connector

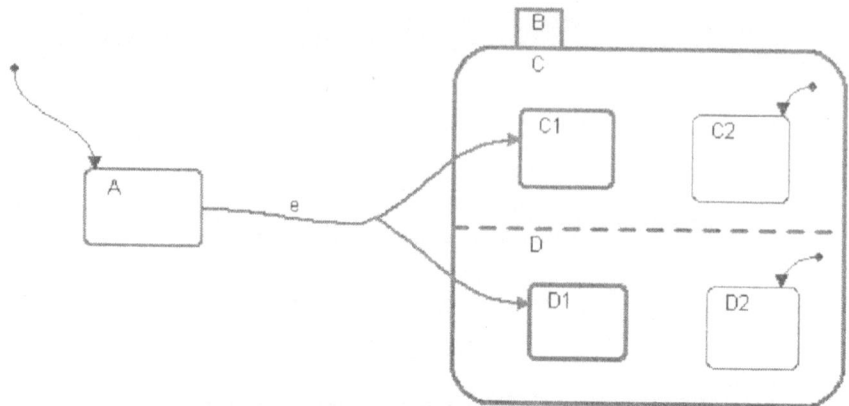

Fig. 10. A fork connector

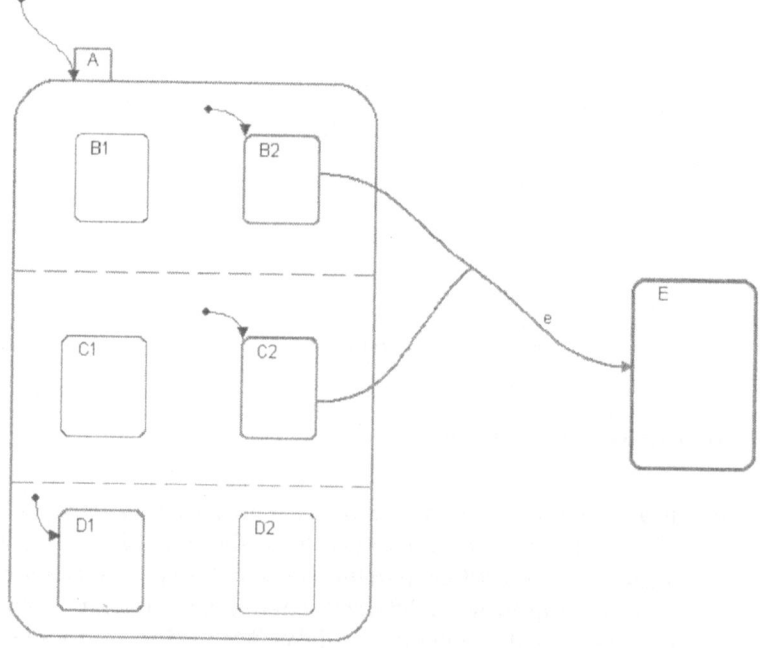

Fig. 11. A join connector

implies that both the transition segment leading to state $C1$ and the one leading to $D1$ must be taken as part of the CT. The destination of a fork segment must be a state or a history connector and the segment cannot have a label.

An example of a join connector is shown in Fig. 11. If the object is in states $B2$ and $C2$ and in either $D1$ or $D2$ and the trigger e occurs, the CT is taken, which causes a transition to state E. The fact that the join is an AND connector

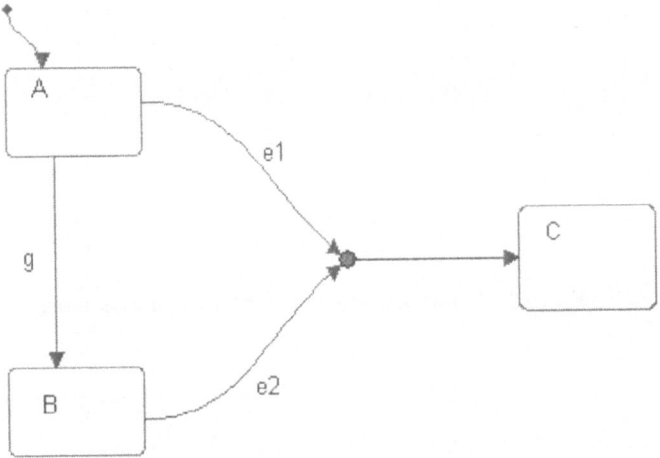

Fig. 12. A junction connector

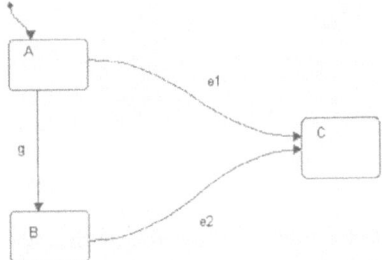

Fig. 13. A construct equivalent to a junction connector

implies that both the transition segment leading from state $B2$ and the one leading from state $C2$ must be taken as part of the CT. The transition segments entering the join connector cannot have labels.

The **junction** and **condition** are OR connectors. Of the transition segments connected to an OR connector exactly one incoming transition segment and exactly one outgoing transition segment must participate in the CT.

An example of a junction connector is shown in Fig. 12. If the object is in state A and the trigger $e1$ occurs, or it is in state B and the trigger $e2$ occurs, a transition to state C is taken. In terms of the active configuration of the statechart, an equivalent statechart has two separate transitions, one from state A and one from state B, as shown in Fig. 13. The label is either written on each of the transition segments entering the junction connector, as in Fig. 12, or on the common transition segment exiting the junction connector, as shown in Fig. 14.

A **condition** connector has one incoming transition and can have several outgoing transition segments called **branches**. Branches are labeled with guards

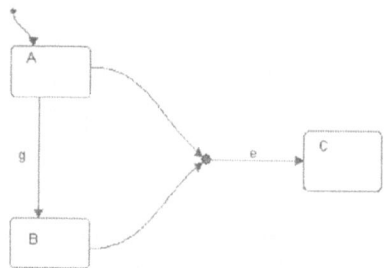

Fig. 14. A junction connector with a common label

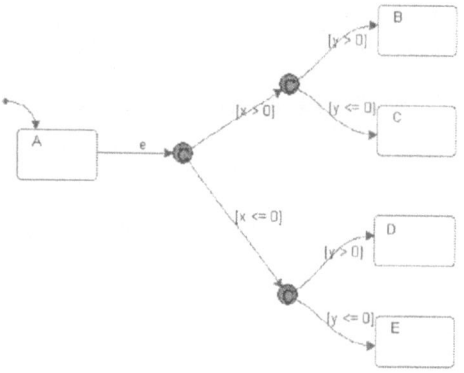

Fig. 15. Nested condition connectors with a common label

that determine which one is to be actually taken. Since the condition connector is an OR connector, only one of the branches can be taken. If the guard of more than one of the branches holds then one is chosen arbitrarily. Each condition connector can have one special branch with a guard labeled *else*, which is taken if all the guards on the other branches are false. Branches cannot contain triggers, but in addition to a guard they may contain actions. A branch can enter another condition connector, thus providing for the nesting of branches. An example is shown in Fig. 15.

When taking a transition, first the guards are all evaluated, and only then are the actions performed. In the statechart described in Fig. 16, for example, the state that is reached is B. The reason is that first the transition to be taken is selected by evaluating the guard, and in this stage $x = 1$; only when performing the transition is the action $x = 2$ performed, but it cannot influence the transition taken.

A step always leads from one legal state configuration to another. A statechart can not remain "stuck" at a connector (with the exception of a termination connector). Similarly, a statechart cannot be in a non-basic state without the ability to enter appropriate substates. For this reason, every OR state with more

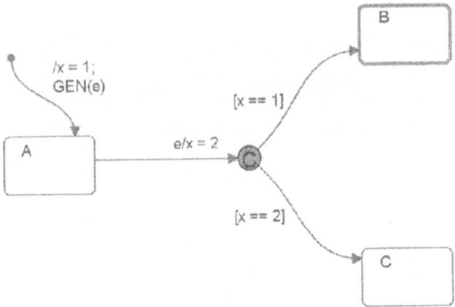

Fig. 16. A condition connector

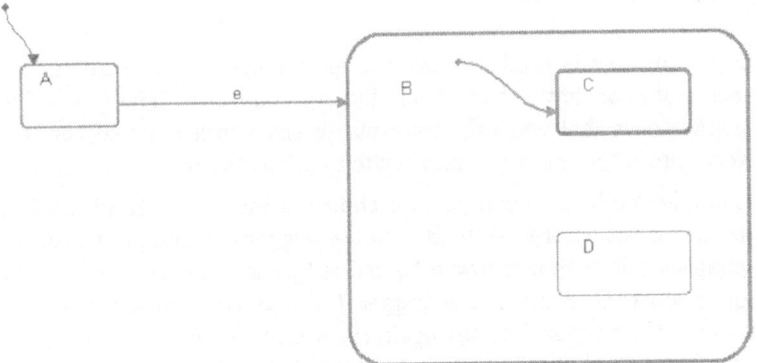

Fig. 17. A default connector

than one substate must have a *default connector* with a transition to one of the OR state's substates. If a destination state of a CT causes a statechart to enter a non-basic state, the default transition associated with this state will be taken. For example, if the object in Fig. 17 is in state A and e occurs, the transition to state B is taken, followed by the default transition to state C.

Taking a default transition is considered to be a microstep. Attributes get their values just prior to the microstep and not the values present at the beginning of the entire step. Thus, in Fig. 18, if the object is in state A and e occurs, the transition to state B is taken, and this is followed by the default transition that leads to state C, since the action $x = 1$ is performed before the default transition's microstep is taken.

As part of a CT, it is possible that several default transitions are taken, each one leading to a deeper state in the hierarchy until finally a basic state is reached. Each such default transition is a microstep and actions performed in the previous microsteps are taken into account.

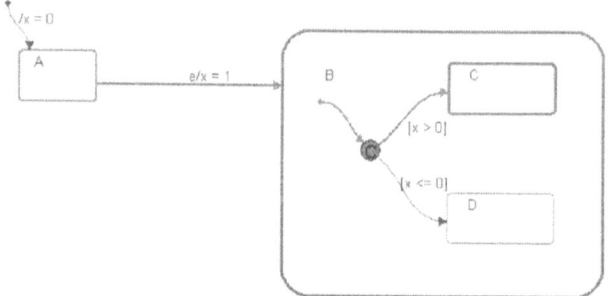

Fig. 18. A default transition as a microstep

5   Dealing with History

A **history** connector is used to store the most recent active configuration of a state. Each state can have at most one history connector. The semantics of the history connector is that when the connector is the source of a CT, the statechart transitively enters the most recently visited active states.

An example of a history connector is shown in Fig. 19. If the object is in state A, but has never yet entered state B, and the trigger e occurs, a transition to the history connector is taken, followed by the outgoing transition from the history connector to state D. Next, if the trigger f occurs the transition to state F is taken. Later, if the trigger f occurs again the active configuration is stored by the history connector and the transition to state A is taken. Finally, if the trigger e occurs, state D and then its substate F are entered, since they constituted the last active configuration prior to state B being exited. States D and F are entered without taking the outgoing transition from the history connector and without performing default transitions or any actions associated with them.

Unlike STATEMATE, the semantics of the history connector in RHAPSODY is the "deep history" semantics (in [4] this is associated with the special notation H*), which entails entering the substates of the most recent active configuration

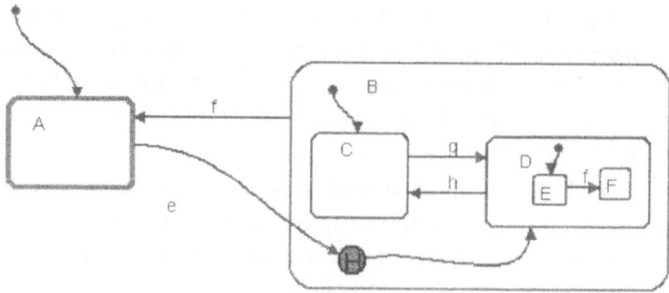

Fig. 19. A history connector

recursively, until basic states are entered. The shallow semantics of STATEMATE is not supported in RHAPSODY.

Also unlike STATEMATE, currently RHAPSODY does not support the *history−clear(S)* operation, which erases the history of state S, thus causing the next transition to the history connector in S to proceed via the default transition as if it were the first time S is entered.

6   The Scope of a Transition

In taking a transition from a source to a target, a CT will often pass through different levels of the statechart hierarchy. As part of performing the CT this causes exiting some of the states and entering others, and performing the appropriate exit and entry actions.

The goal of this subsection is to define the **scope** of a transition, thus determining which states should be exited and which entered while taking a CT. The definition of the scope is the same as in STATEMATE, and we repeat it here for self containment. There are some differences in the usage of the definition, which are discussed later.

Before presenting the definition, consider the simple case of the statechart in Fig. 20. Taking the transition with trigger e causes exiting state B and entering state C. Any relevant entry and exit actions are performed. The scope of this transition is state A.

The scope of a CT is the lowest OR state in the hierarchy of states that is a proper common ancestor of all the source and target states. Taking the CT will result in a change of the active configuration involving only substates in the scope. When the CT is taken, all the proper descendants of its scope in which the system resided at the beginning of the step are exited, and all proper descendants of that scope in which the system will reside as a result of executing *tr* are entered. Thus, the scope is the lowest state in which the system stays without exiting and reentering when taking the transition.

We now illustrate the notion of scope by some examples. Consider the statechart of Fig. 21 (a). If the associated object is in state W and message e occurs,

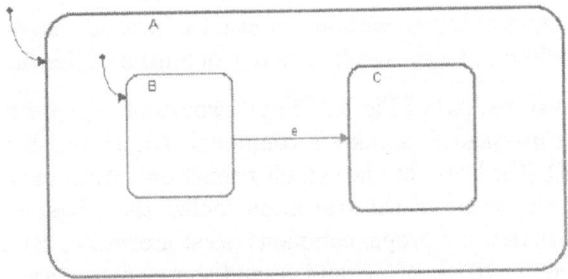

Fig. 20. The scope of a transition

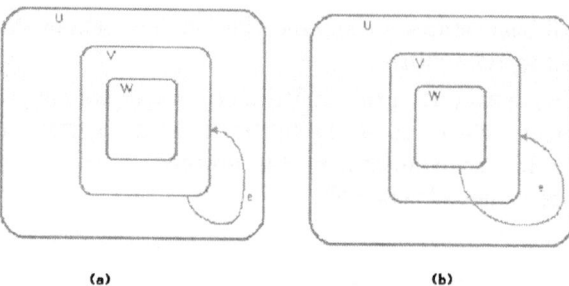

Fig. 21. The scope of a transition

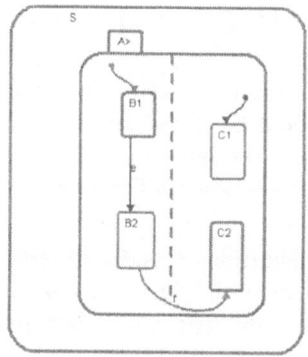

Fig. 22. More on the scope of a transition

the transition with scope U is to be taken, since according to the previous definition U is the lowest OR state in the hierarchy that is a proper common ancestor
of V. Thus, taking the transition implies exiting states W and V and entering
states V and W. We defined U to be the scope of the transition since we consider state V to be both the source and the target of the transition. Notice that
although the (implicit) default transition to state W is taken, we still consider
V to be the transition's target since the default transition is taken as part of a
new microstep. This is important, since if the statechart was modified so that
the source of the transition becomes W, as shown in Fig. 21 (b), considering W
to be also the target of the transition would have implied that V is the scope of
the transition, while in fact according to our definitions U is the scope.

Consider the statechart of Fig. 22. If the associated object is in states $B2$ and
$C1$ and receives message f, it takes a compound transition, causing it to enter
states $C2$ and $B1$ (the latter by the default transition). According to the previous
definition, S is the scope of the transition, being the lowest OR state in the
hierarchy of states that is a proper common ancestor of states $B1, B2, C1$ and $C2$.
The states exited are $B2, B, C1, C$ and A, and those entered are $A, B, B1, C$ and
$C2$. Notice that the notion of scope does not depend on the way the transition
itself is drawn, but on its sources and targets only: the transition in Fig. 22 is

drawn inside state A but this does not cause A to be the scope of the transition rather than S. Even if the transition would have be drawn as exiting the contour of S, the scope would still be S.

7 Conflicting Transitions (Nondeterminism)

We say that two transitions are in **conflict** if there is some common state that would be exited if either of them were to be taken. Consider the statechart in Fig. 23 (a), the two outgoing transitions from state A labeled e are in conflict because they would each imply exiting state A. The transition from state U to state D is in conflict with the two outgoing transitions from state A and also with the transition from state B to state C, since if the transition from U to D is taken it implies also exiting whatever substate of U the object was in.

Two conflicting transitions cannot be taken in the same step. If they are both enabled only one will be taken. We now explain how this choice is made.

The two types of conflicts in Fig. 23 (a) are treated differently. If the object was in state A and message e occurred the system is faced with nondeterminism, since there is no reason to prefer a transition to one of the states B and C over the other. RHAPSODY detects such cases of nondeterminism during code generation and does not allow them. The motivation for this is that the generated code is intended to serve as a final implementation and for most embedded software systems such nondeterminism is not acceptable.[2]

The second case of conflict in Fig. 23 (a) is that between the transition from A to B (assume that the transition between A and C has been removed) and the transition from U to D. In RHAPSODY, when a message can trigger several conflicting transitions priority is given to lower level source states. Hence, here the transition from A to B takes priority over the one from U to D, and there is no nondeterminism. At the end of the step the object will be in state B. Join transitions get priority according to their lower source state. If there is no hierarchal relation between the source states no priority is defined between the transitions. This priority strategy is different than that of STATEMATE, which determines priorities outside-in; in our case according to STATEMATE the object will end up in state D. The strategy in RHAPSODY is more object-oriented, since it enables substates to override transitions in higher states in a way similar to that in which operations in subclasses can override those of the superclass.

Another technical difference between STATEMATE and RHAPSODY is that in STATEMATE we determine priorities outside-in according to the scope of the

---

[2] We suggest that an option be provided to the user to allow such nondeterminism, which can be useful in certain development stages where the model is not yet complete. In any case, the current implementation cannot block all nondeterminism when performing code generation, since we may have conflicting transitions with the same trigger but with different guards, and in general it is impossible to detect at compile time whether both guards will evaluate to true.

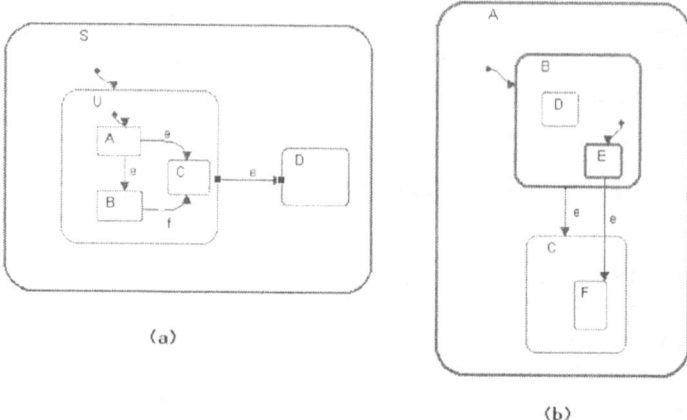

Fig. 23. Conflicting transitions

transition, while in RHAPSODY we determine priorities inside-out according to the source state. Consider the statechart in Fig. 23 (b). If the object is in state E and message e occurs, then in RHAPSODY we take the transition to state F, since the source of this transition E is lower than the source of the transition to state C which is B. In STATEMATE the scope of both transitions is A, resulting in nondeterminism.

The priority of a static reaction is determined according to the state in which it is defined, giving high priority to lower-level states. If a CT and a SR are in conflict, the one with lower source state will be taken and the other will not. If the CT and SR have the same source state, as in Fig. 24, the CT has higher priority, thus the transition to state B will be taken and the static reaction will not be carried out. This is different from the STATEMATE approach, were an enabled static reaction defined in state S is executed if the system was in S at the beginning of the step but S was not exited by any CT during the step.

8   The Basic Step Algorithm

In this section we present a schematic description of the algorithm that executes a step. For a single threaded application, we do the following repeatedly:

If the event queue is not empty, get the next event and its destination from the queue. If the destination object still exists dispatch the event to that object's statechart. The event invocation may cause taking SRs or CTs and all the relevant default transitions, as explained in earlier sections. At the end of the run-to-completion the statechart of the object is in a (possibly new) active configuration. If the statechart does not specify a transition in response to the event, the active configuration remains unchanged. The loop can now be continued, processing the next event.

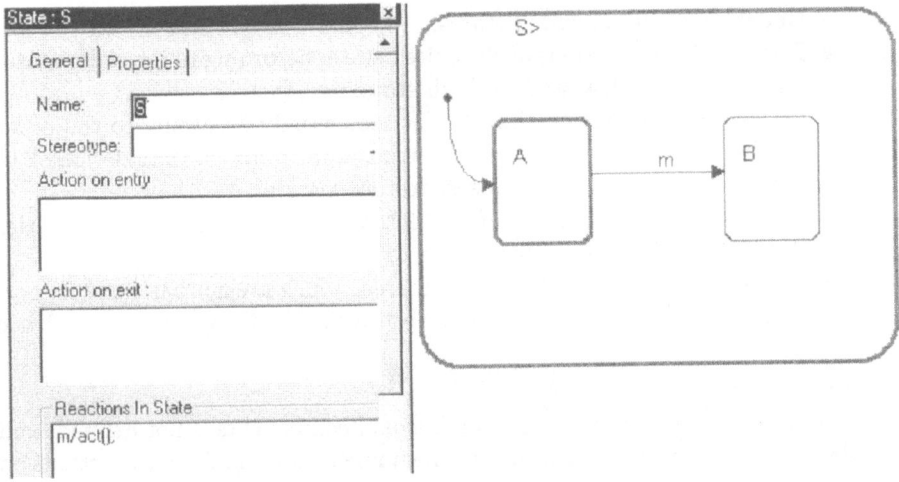

Fig. 24. Conflict between transition and static reaction

A pseudocode description of the procedure is:

```
procedure StepCycle ()
begin
  loop forever
    while Event-Queue ≠ empty do
      ev ← Get-Event-From-Queue
      dest ← Get-Destination-Of-Event
      if dest still exists then
        dest → takeEvent(ev)
      else
        Ignore ev
      end if
    end while
  end loop
end
```

Here now are the details of the main part of this procedure (*takeEvent*), in which an event is processed by the statechart.

– *Determine the CTs/SRs that will fire in response to the message:* Traverse the states in the active configuration from lowest states in the hierarchy upwards. A CT/SR is enabled if its trigger is the dispatched event *ev* or a super-event of *ev*, and the guard evaluates to true. Since for a given state CTs have priority over SRs, they are considered first. Once an enabled transition is found with a given source state stop traversing the states that are higher than this state in the hierarchy. States in orthogonal components are still considered since they may be taken without necessarily causing a conflict.
– *Perform the CTs/SRs that we found should fire:*
  For each transition do:

- Update histories of exited states.
- Perform the exit actions of the exited states according to the order states are exited, from low state to high state.
- Perform the actions on the CT/SR sequentially according to the order in which they are written on the transition, from the action closest to source state to the action closest to target state.
- Perform the entry actions of the entered states according to the order states are entered, from high state to low state.
- For lowest level states that were entered, which are not basic states, perform default transitions (recursively) until the statechart reaches basic states.
- Update the active configuration.

The order of firing transitions of orthogonal components is not defined, and depends on an arbitrary traversal in the implementation. Also, the actions on the transitions of the orthogonal components are interleaved in an arbitrary way.

- *Deal with null transitions:* After reacting to a message, the statechart may reach a state configuration where some of the states have outgoing enabled null transitions — transient configurations. In such a case further steps need to be taken until the statechart reaches a stable state configuration where no null transitions are enabled. Null transitions are triggered by null events that are dispatched to the statechart whenever a transient configuration is encountered. Null events are dispatched in a series until a stable configuration is reached. It is possible that the statechart will never reach a stable configuration; for example when there is a loop of null transitions. In RHAPSODY the infinite loop is detected during runtime and execution is halted. It is possible using the execution framework to set a maximum value for null transitions. When performing the null transitions, each one is taken separately and the values used in the computation are the values after the previous null transition and not the values before the entire step.
- *Wrap up:* Once a stable configuration is reached, the reaction to the message is completed, control returns to the dispatcher and new messages can be dispatched.

9   The Time Model

The RHAPSODY time model is more complex than that of STATEMATE, since RHAPSODY allows describing both synchronous and asynchronous behavior in the same model. Moreover, a step does not necessarily take zero time. Due to these facts, the synchronous time model of STATEMATE is not relevant here. RHAPSODY supports two different modes of handling the progress of time: real time and simulated time. In real time mode time advances according to the actual underlying operating system clock. In simulated time the user of RHAPSODY can control the progress of time in an interactive way, thus enabling effective debugging and testing of the model. A detailed description of the RHAPSODY time model will appear in the full version of the paper.

Recall that all aspects of the execution of a RHAPSODY model, and this includes timing aspects too, are carried out via the generated code. This is important in RHAPSODY, since one of the main goals is to develop production-code. However, there are many interesting opportunities for further research on the timing aspects of modeling object-oriented systems, especially regarding the simulated time mode. In fact, we predict that analytic techniques could be modified to apply to timed behavior, in ways that do not depend directly on the generated code and are thus more robust.

10   Multi-threaded Systems

RHAPSODY supports the development of reactive multi-threaded applications. In such applications each **thread** can perform steps in parallel to the other threads. Obviously, this makes the definition and behavior more complicated. We now discuss this topic in some detail, by explaining how threads are introduced into statechart-based systems and how their semantics is defined. A detailed description of this topic will appear in the full version of the paper.

An object-oriented system consists of objects exchanging messages. The ideal analysis view of such a world is that each object is an autonomous entity executing concurrently with all other objects. In order to have a more realistic and concrete model, this general abstraction can be given various interpretations, regarding the synchronization between objects and the semantics of messages.

In the *synchronous model* objects execute on a clock edge, and the period between two clock edges is called a step. This model is similar to digital hardware systems, where all components are synchronized by a clock. It is also the model implemented in STATEMATE, and although STATEMATE is executed on a sequential machine and concurrency is achieved by simulation, messages sent at a certain step being processed in the next step. The major advantage of this model is that it is deterministic and simple. However, it does not fit software systems for the following reasons: Software systems have a very limited form of concurrency, since in general they run sequentially on the same CPU. Also, in the case of concurrent software, tight synchronization is an undesired overhead, so that concurrent software components are by default asynchronous unless they are explicitly synchronized.

Since real concurrency does not exist in most software applications, the CPU is shared by all software objects. The sequence in which software functions execute is known as the thread of control, which can be thought of as a token (representing the CPU) passed between objects in the system, enabling them to execute. Initially, the token is given to the main program, and it is typically passed along by method activation. A client object sending a message to a server object actually gives up its control of the CPU in favor of the server object. This passing along can be nested, with $o1$ calling $o2$, who calls $o3$, and so forth.

In the general case, a system will have more than one thread, which means that conceptually it has multiple tokens, and this is a far more complicated setup than a single-threaded one. We now discuss the way RHAPSODY deals with some of the major issues in multi-threaded systems: thread creation and destruction, associating objects with threads, and communication and synchronization between threads.

Object/thread relationship: An important issue in a multi-threaded system has to do with which objects belong to which thread. In RHAPSODY, a class can be defined as an **active class** and then each of the instances of this class will have its own thread of control. Another way of defining the object/thread relationship is through composition. Instances that are components of a composite class run on the thread of the composite class, unless they are instances of an active class, in which case they have their own thread.

Instances of classes that are not designated as active classes run on the unique system thread, which is the default thread used by the main program.

It is also possible to set the thread of an object explicitly, by calling the *setThread*() command. This gives developers more control over threading policies. However, it also introduces many delicate issues, such as thread destruction policy, and how to transfer events to the new event queue after an object changes its thread. Some of these issues of dynamic object/thread relationship require further research to enable automatic support for more complicated groupings.

Creation and destruction of threads: The special system thread is created when the main program for the executable model is started. This thread will be destroyed only when the application terminates. Creating an object that is an instance of an active class causes the creation of a thread on which this object runs. This thread is destroyed when the object is destroyed, which can happen explicitly from the outside, or by the object's statechart entering a termination connector. In the case where components of a composite class run on the thread of that composite class, destroying a component does not cause the destruction of the thread; the thread will be destroyed when the composite class object is destroyed.

Automatic support for thread destruction in the case of explicit setting of an object's thread is not currently supported by RHAPSODY. A possible solution is to destroy the thread only when the last object running on the thread is deleted.

Communication and synchronization between threads: As discussed previously, the statechart of an object can deal with asynchronous communication using events and synchronous communication using triggered operations. In the multi-threaded case, an object can receive messages from different objects, each having its own thread of control and therefore running concurrently with other objects.

The case of asynchronous communication using events is simpler: The generated events are put in the event queue of the receiving object and are later dispatched to the statechart. In the case of synchronous communication using triggered operations, the sending object is blocked until the receiving statechart completes its response to the triggered operation. Hence, if different threaded objects invoke a triggered operation on the same statechart they will be posted to the statechart one at a time and each sending object is blocked until its invocation is completed. Situations of deadlocks and starvation are possible, and must be avoided as part of the model design.

Classes can also communicate by calling member functions; i.e., primitive operations. Since synchronization in multi-threaded applications is important, RHAPSODY allows the definition of *guarded* primitive operations. All the guarded primitive operations of a class are mutually exclusive, in that only a single operation can run at any given time and the other invocations are blocked. Operations that are not defined as guarded can run in parallel. Triggered operations can also be defined as guarded, thus causing all guarded operations (primitive or triggered) of the class to be mutual exclusive.

The step algorithm for a multi-threaded system consists of performing the step cycle described in the basic step algorithm for each thread. There are several complications in the semantics relative to the single-threaded case. For example, when one thread is in the middle of performing a step (and as explained earlier, this might take more than zero time), a second thread can interact with it by invoking primitive or triggered operations or sending events. For events, the RHAPSODY execution framework guarantees that the event queue is not corrupted by different threads interacting with it simultaneously, and that events are not lost. This is achieved in RHAPSODY by locking mechanisms. Before accessing the event queue a *lock()* command is invoked, which prevents other threads from interfering with the queue. Only after the interaction with the event queue is over does the *unlock()* command allow other threads to lock the queue and use it. The code generation framework in RHAPSODY implements the *lock()* and *unlock()* commands using a mutual exclusion mechanism in the underlying operating system. In the multi-threaded case, these locking mechanisms can prevent an object attempting to send an event from proceeding until it manages to perform the lock. In contrast, the single-threaded case allows the sending object to generate an event and continue progress immediately.

11   Racing Conditions

A **racing condition** occurs when the execution of transitions in two different legal orders would cause the system to end up in two different configurations. In STATEMATE, the semantics and execution model were simpler, and this allowed the tool to detect and report such conditions. The fact that RHAPSODY deals with synchronous and asynchronous communication and well as with multi-threaded applications, and the fact that a step does not take zero time, make automatic detection and reporting of racing conditions a much harder task, and RHAPSODY does not attempt to undertake it. Developing tool support to handle these issues requires further research. Until this situation changes, users of tools that deal with such advanced features are advised to make efforts to avoid racing conditions by improving and tightening their models.

12   Comparison with Other Work

Readers interested in comparing the RHAPSODY semantics of statecharts with non-OO approaches to statechart semantics are referred to the discussion in Appendix A of [6]. We now briefly discuss appropriate object-oriented approaches.

ROOM: The ROOM method of [12], and its supporting tool OBJECTIME (which later evolved into Rose-RT) were the first to introduce extended state-machines into an object-oriented paradigm in a way that allows development of fully executable models. The main formalism for describing behavior in ROOM is called ROOMcharts, which was inspired by the original statechart formalism [4]. ROOMcharts allow hierarchal nesting of OR-states but not orthogonality (AND-states), which thus renders the language much simpler. The semantics of the language is based on the run-to-completion principle, and an assumption is made that the time taken to process any single event should not exceed the maximum latency requirements of the object. The communication between objects implemented as ROOMcharts can be carried out using asynchronous events and triggered operations of RHAPSODY, and there is a mechanism for defining event priorities.

UML 2.0: In the very recent UML 2.0 there is a distinction between two kinds of state machines (both are variants of statecharts): **behavioral state machines** and **protocol state machines**. Behavioral state machines are really the original OO statecharts of [5] and the present paper, and they are used to describe the behavior of an object. In contrast, protocol state machines describe usage protocols, and are thus geared to specifying requirements of classes, interfaces and ports, rather then defining the entire behavior of an object. In the behavioral statecharts of UML 2.0 shallow history is allowed too, in addition to deep history. Triggers can be signals (corresponding to events in our paper) or operations (corresponding to our triggered operations). The semantics is that of run-to-completion [5], and the way conflicting transitions are handled is by a selection algorithm similar to the one introduced in RHAPSODY and reported upon here. UML allows deferred events, which are not lost if dispatched to the object and the event is not enabled. This extension is currently not part of RHAPSODY statecharts. The UML allows the definition of submachines, which is a syntactic way to break up a statechart and describe some of the more complex hierarchal states in different diagrams. This is also supported by RHAPSODY, but is not essential to this paper because it is essentially a syntactic extension with virtually no impact on the semantics.

It should be noted that the UML standard leaves certain semantical options open, thus allowing "semantic variation points", that can be implemented differently by the tool vendors or according to the application domain.

Semantics for formal verification: Following the publication of [5] and the release of RHAPSODY, and aided by the growing popularity of the UML [13], its application to safety-critical systems, and advances in the field of formal verification, extensive research efforts have been invested in formalizing the UML.

The main goal is to develop formal semantics for the UML, which will make it possible to apply formal verification methods and tools.

In Damm et al. [3] a kernel of the UML is defined and formalized, by associating a model with a symbolic transition system. Semantics of a richer UML subset is then defined by compiling it into that kernel. The rich subset covers such features as active objects, dynamic object creation and destruction, dynamically changing communication topologies in inter-object communication, asynchronous signal based communication, synchronous communication using operation calls, and shared memory communication through global attributes. While the semantic model of [3] is quite general, the paper suggests certain restrictions on the communication scheme between objects, in order to optimize the verification process.

In contrast, RHAPSODY takes a more general approach: rather than imposing restrictions, it allows users to make their own design decisions and supports powerful execution semantics through code generation capabilities. As the impact of formal verification methods increases and verification engines scale up to handle larger systems, we believe that tools like RHAPSODY will be modified to support and take advantage of certain restrictions and semantic idiosyncracies, of the kinds adopted in [3].

A more abstract version of the semantics of [3] appears in [8] by formalization in the langauge of the PVS theorem prover. For more details on other UML verification-driven semantics, e.g., [10,2] see [3].

Acknowledgements. We would like to express our deepest gratitude to Eran Gery and Yachin Pnueli for many helpful discussions on RHAPSODY and its semantics. Thanks also to the entire Rhapsody development team at I-Logix Israel, Ltd. Finally, we thank one of the referees for his/her helpful comments.

References

1. G. Booch. *Object Oriented Analysis and Design with Applications.* Benjamin/Cummings, California, 1994.
2. E. Borger, A. Cavarra, and E. Riccobene. Modeling the Dynamics of UML State Machines. In *Int. Workshop on Abstract State Machines (ASM'00)*, volume 1912 of *Lect. Notes in Comp. Sci.* Springer-Verlag, 2000.
3. W. Damm, B. Josko, A. Pnueli, and A. Votintseva. Understanding UML: A Formal Semantics of Concurrency and Communication in Real-Time UML. In *Formal Methods for Components and Objects (FMCO'02)*, volume 2852 of *Lect. Notes in Comp. Sci.* Springer-Verlag, 2003.
4. D. Harel. Statecharts: A visual formalism for complex systems. *Science of Computer Programming*, 8:231–274, 1987. (Preliminary version: Technical Report CS84-05, The Weizmann Institute of Science, Rehovot, Israel, February 1984.).
5. D. Harel and E. Gery. Executable Object Modeling with Statecharts. *IEEE Computer*, 30(7):31–42, July 1997. (Also in *Proc. 18th Int. Conf. Soft. Eng.*, Berlin, IEEE Press, March, 1996, pp. 246–257.).

6. D. Harel and A. Naamad. The STATEMATE semantics of statecharts. *ACM TRANS. Software Engineering and Methodology*, 5(4):293–333, October 1996.

7. D. Harel and M. Politi. *Modeling Reactive Systems with Statecharts: The STATE-MATE Approach*. McGraw-Hill, 1998.

8. J. Hooman and M. Van Der Zwaag. A Semantics of Communicating Active Objects with Timing. In *Specification and Validation of UML Models for Real-Time and Embedded Systems (SVERTS'03)*, 2003. Available from the European Project OMEGA homepage http://www-omega.imag.fr.

9. I-logix,inc., products web page. http://www.ilogix.com/fs_prod.htm.

10. G. Reggio, E. Astesiano, C. Choppy, and H. Husmann. Analysing UML active classes and associated statecharts - a lightweight formal approach. In *Proceedings Fundamental Approaches to Software Engineering (FASE'00)*, volume 1783 of *Lect. Notes in Comp. Sci.* Springer-Verlag, 2000.

11. J. Rumbaugh, M. Blaha, W. Premerlani, F. Eddy, and W. Lorensen. *Object Oriented Modeling and Design*. Prentice - Hall, New York, 1991.

12. B. Selic, G. Gullekson, and P. Ward. *Real-Time Object-Oriented Modeling*. John Wiley & Sons, New York, 1994.

13. UML. Documentation of the unified modeling language (UML). Available from the Object Management Group (OMG), http://www.omg.org.

Interactive Verification of Statecharts

Andreas Thums, Gerhard Schellhorn, Frank Ortmeier, and Wolfgang Reif

Lehrstuhl Softwaretechnik,
Universität Augsburg, 86135 Augsburg, Germany
{thums,schellhorn,ortmeier,reif}@informatik.uni-augsburg.de

Abstract. In this paper, we present an approach to the interactive verification of statecharts. We use STATEMATE statecharts for the formal specification of safety critical systems and Interval Temporal Logic to formalize the proof conditions. To handle infinite data, complex functions and predicates, we use algebraic specifications.

Our verification approach is a basis for the aim of the project ForMoSA to put safety analysis techniques on formal grounds. As part of this approach, fault tree analysis (FTA) has been formalized yielding conditions that can be verified using the calculus defined in this paper. Verification conditions resulting from the formal FTA of the radio-based level crossing control have been successfully verified.

1 Introduction

We present an approach which aims to support the interactive verification of (safety) properties for concurrent, reactive systems.

We chose STATEMATE statecharts as modeling notation since they have a formal semantics, are broadly accepted, and STATEMATE [HLN+90] is widely used in industrial practice as a specification tool. Our use of statecharts overcomes the problem that typically engineers use more complex semi-formal languages than the fully formal models (usually automata) used by verification engineers.

Safety properties are stated in a first-order variant of Interval Temporal Logic (ITL, [Mos85,CMZ02]). This logic is expressive enough to describe most safety relevant properties. In particular a standard safety analysis technique - fault tree analysis (FTA) - has been formalized [STR02]. Formal FTA allows to rigorously prove cause-consequence relationships between individual component faults and failure of the whole system (see also [OTSW04] in this volume and [OT02]). Statechart verification is the basis for proving such dependencies.

We use the KIV system [BRS+00] as an implementation platform for the developed proof calculus. The proof strategy in KIV is symbolic execution. Symbolic execution is an intuitive proof method widely used for the interactive verification of sequential programs. KIV supports Dynamic Logic (DL, [Har84]) for proving properties of sequential programs by symbolic execution. This proof method has been extended to interval temporal logic and parallel programs [BDRS02] as well. The main contribution of this paper is to integrate proof

H. Ehrig et al. (Eds.): INT 2004, LNCS 3147, pp. 355–373, 2004.

support for STATEMATE statecharts. This allows us to directly use the model of the engineers as the formal system model.

In Sect. 2 we present a small example to explain the basics of STATEMATE statecharts. This example is also used in Sect. 3 to demonstrate the proof strategy of symbolic execution informally. The logical foundations of ITL are given in Sect. 4. They form the basis for embedding statecharts in Sect. 5. The main part of this paper is the presentation of the proof calculus for statecharts in Sect. 6. Sect. 7 gives a statechart model of a radio-based level crossing control. Algebraic specifications over integers are used to specify the velocity and braking behavior of a train. For this specification we have verified the proof obligations of a formal FTA for the hazard "collision on crossing". Finally, Sect. 8 concludes the paper and gives an outlook to future work.

2   Example: Automated Light Control

In the following, the example of an automatic light control will be used to explain important statechart terminology.

The statechart in Fig. 1 models an automated light control, which switches off the light k minutes after the light has been switched on. Initially, the light is *Off*, the timer is *Idle*, and $x = 0$. When the *press* event is active, the transition t_1 switches the light on, generates the event *set* to enable transition t_3, and starts the timer. In state *Cnt*, the timer x is incremented through the *tick* event (*tick* is generated, when the system clock advances) and finally, when x is greater or equal to k, the timer leaves *Cnt* and generates a *sw_off* event (t_4), to switch off the light (t_2).

The model of light control *SYS* consists of an *and*-state *System*, which executes the *or*-states *Light* and *Timer* in parallel. *Off*, *On*, *Idle*, and *Cnt* are *basic*-states, which do not encapsulate any sub-charts. *states(SC)* is the set of states of a statechart *SC* and *states(SYS)* = {*System, Light, On, Off, Timer, Idle, Cnt*} the states of the light control. Sub-charts of a state are computed by the function *childs* : *states(SC)* → ℘(*states(SC)*), so the *childs* relation describes a tree of states, with the root *root(SC)* (*root(SYS)* = *System, childs(System)* = {*Light, Timer*}). Statecharts define *termination*-states, as well. *Termination*-states stop the execution of the statechart, but are not used in the example. The

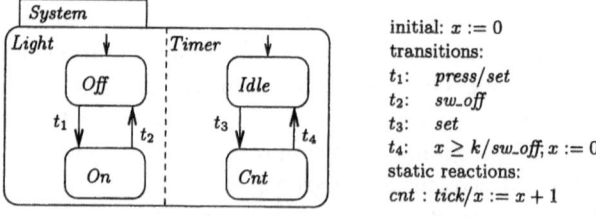

Fig. 1. Automated Light control

mode of a state is computed by $mode : states(SC) \rightarrow \{and, or, basic, term\}$, e.g. $mode(System) = and$.

The structure of a statechart defines a consistency predicate $cons(SC)$ over states. If an and-state is active, every sub-state is active, as well, and if an or-state is active, exactly on of its sub-states is active. A configuration which fulfills this requirement is called $consistent$. E.g., a configuration, where Off and On is active, is inconsistent, but Off and Cnt describe a consistent configuration.

A transition is labeled with a guard and an action. $trans(SC)$ is the set of all transitions of a statechart SC. $source(t)$ computes the source state of a transition t, $target(t)$ the target state, $guard(t)$ the guard and $action(t)$ the action. A transition can be executed, if $source(t)$ is active and $guard(t)$ holds. Then $action(t)$ is executed and the state $target(t)$ is entered. For t_4, $source(t_4) = Cnt$, $target(t_4) = Idle$, $guard(t_4) = x \geq k$, and $action(t_4) = sw\_off; x := 0$.

The state transition from Off to On describes a so called $micro$-step. This micro-step triggers the transition t_3 and a second micro-step is executed. The event $press$ activated a $chain\ reaction$ of micro-steps. If no more micro-steps are possible, a $macro$-step, marked with the $tick$ event, reads in new input values from the environment and time passes. While micro-steps are executed, no input events are considered.

In state Cnt, the timer x is incremented in every macro-step through a static reaction. The set of all static reactions is $sreactions(SC)$. Static reactions are assigned to a state and $sreact : states(SC) \rightarrow \wp(sreactions(SC))$ computes all static reactions of one state. Like transitions, static reactions sr are labeled with a guard $guard(sr)$ and an action $action(sr)$. The action is executed, if the corresponding state of the static reaction is active, not exited, and the guard holds.

3   Symbolic Execution

In this section we give an informal description of the proof strategy $symbolic\ execution$ to prove properties of statecharts. If we want to prove a temporal logic property for the light control, e.g. that the counter is never greater than k, we execute the statechart and show, that in every (reachable) configuration the property holds. With an inductive argument we prove the property for infinite system traces (see Sect. 4 for details). We describe valuations of variables symbolically by equations, e.g. $x \leq k$, and therefore call the proof strategy $symbolic\ execution$. In our approach, states and events are boolean variables and their values are described symbolically, as well. A state or an event is active, if the corresponding variable is true.

Let us consider the statechart of the light control. In Fig. 2 we execute the statechart and compute the successor configurations, depending on the active events. The stars $\star$ mark the currently active states, the equations beneath the chart the values of the variable x, and the transitions between state configurations the active events.

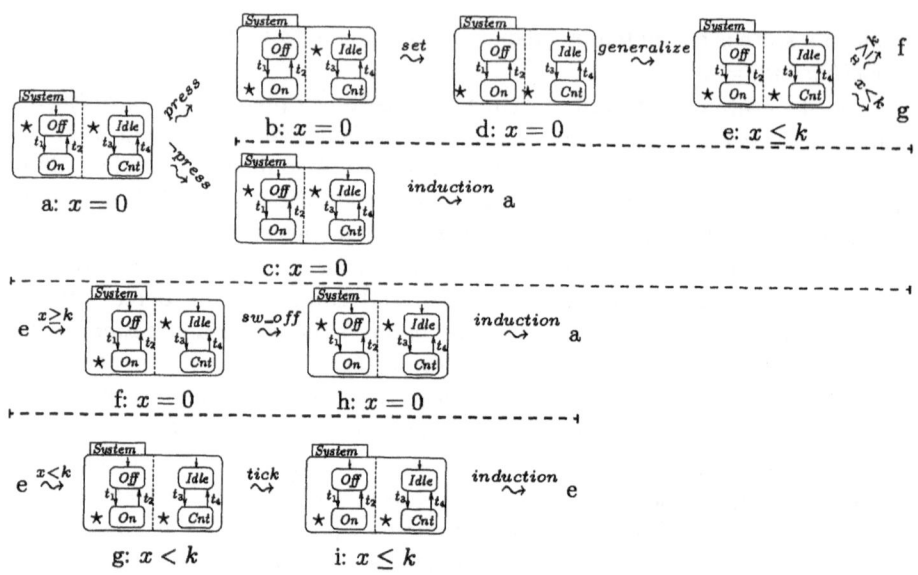

Fig. 2. symbolic execution of statecharts

If we start in an initial state configuration, we have two successors, depending on the *press* event. If *press* holds we step into the state *On* (chart b) and generate the event *set*. Otherwise, we stay in *Off* and get the initial configuration, again (chart c). With an inductive argument, we close this branch of the proof. In chart b, again $x = 0$ and the generated *set* event causes a state transition to chart d. In chart d, the state *Cnt* is active and increases x until $x \geq k$. We generalize $x = 0$ to $x \leq k$ (chart e) to prove that the invariant $x \leq k$ holds for the state *Cnt*. This condition allows two transitions. If $x < k$, we stay in *Cnt*, no further micro-step is possible and a macro-step generates the *tick* event (chart g). The *tick* event enables the static reaction *cnt*, which increases x. After increasing $x < k$, $x \leq k$ holds, chart i equals to chart e, and we can close this proof branch by induction. Otherwise, if $x \geq k$, state *Cnt* will be exited, state *Idle* entered (chart f), the event *sw_off* generated, and x set to 0 by transition t_4. Finally, *sw_off* triggers transition t_2 to enter state *Off*. We reach chart h, which is equal to chart a and again use induction to finish the proof. Because $x \leq k$ holds from chart a to chart i, the property "x is never greater than k" is proven.

Partially specified State Configurations. In the previous proof, we generalized the condition $x = 0$ to $x \leq k$. Analogously, we often want to prove properties over statecharts, where the current state configuration is not unambiguously given. We call such configurations *partially specified state configurations*.

Again, we want to prove the condition, that x is never greater than k. Because x only changes in the chart *Timer*, it is no difference, if *On* or *Off* is active. Because active (and inactive) states are described symbolically (e.g. $On = true$), we can generalize state configurations by omitting informations about states. If we prove conditions with partially specified state configurations (no information, if On or Off are active or not), a generalized induction hypothesis is possible (we can apply it in On and Off) resulting in shorter proofs. However, the computation of successor states gets more complex, since we have to consider transitions for both source state On and Off (see Sect. 6.1).

4   The Temporal Logic Framework

The basis of our approach is Interval Temporal Logic (ITL, [Mos85]). We use a first order extension based on algebraic specifications [Wir90] and consider finite and infinite intervals as described in [CMZ02]. The semantics is based on intervals I (in the following also called traces) which are finite or infinite sequences of states (also called valuations) $I = (\sigma_0, \ldots)$. Every valuation σ_i maps unprimed variables $\sigma_i(x)$ and primed variables $\sigma_i(x')$ to values of our domain. In a trace, the values of the primed variables are equal to the values of the unprimed variables in the next state $\sigma_i(x') = \sigma_{i+1}(x)$. Flexible variables may have different values in each state, while for rigid variables $\sigma_i(x)$ must be the same for all i. Function and predicate symbols are rigid and are interpreted using algebras (see for example [SA91]). Possible algebras are given as the (loose) semantics of algebraic specifications.

As temporal operators we use φ ; ψ (chop - the interval can be split in two subintervals, such that φ holds in the first one and ψ holds in the second), $\square\varphi$ (always), $\diamond\varphi$ (eventually), $\circ\ \varphi$ (strong next - there exists a next state and φ holds then), $\bullet\ \varphi$ (weak next - if there exists a next state, then φ holds there)), φ **until** ψ (until), and others with their standard semantics in ITL. Given an algebra, the semantics of a formula is a set of traces $I = (\sigma_0, \sigma_1, \ldots)$ for which the formula holds. E.g., $\mathcal{A}, I \models \square\varphi$, if and only if for every $i \leq length(I)$ and $I_i := (\sigma_i, \sigma_{i+1}, \ldots)$: $\mathcal{A}, I_i \models \varphi$. This allows to view statecharts as a special kind of formula, because they define sets of traces, as well. Predicate logic formulas Φ only depend on the first state of an interval and $\mathcal{A}, I \models \Phi :\Leftrightarrow \mathcal{A}, \sigma_0 \models \Phi$. If the algebra $\mathcal{A}$ is not relevant for the current consideration, we omit $\mathcal{A}$.

Sequential Programs. To define transactions and static reactions we use abstract sequential programs. Their effects are expressed using Dynamic Logic (DL, [Har84]) in combination with the temporal logic framework. In the following example we require variable x' to be equal to the value of variable x after a program has been executed.

$$\langle \text{if } y = 0 \text{ then } x := 1 \text{ else } x := 2 \rangle\ x' = x$$

Here, x' is either 1 or 2 depending on y. Parallel assignments will be used in the following. A valid formula is e.g.

$$x = 1 \wedge y = 2 \rightarrow \langle x, y := y, x \rangle\ x = 2 \wedge y = 1.$$

Semantically, the program of a DL operator is used to modify the first valuation σ_0 of a trace, the following valuations $\sigma_1, \ldots$ (if any) are untouched.

$$(\sigma_0, \sigma_1, \ldots) \models \langle \alpha \rangle \varphi \; :\Leftrightarrow \quad \text{there exists } \tau \text{ with } \sigma_0 [\![\alpha]\!] \tau \text{ with } (\tau, \sigma_1, \ldots) \models \varphi$$

where $\sigma_0 [\![\alpha]\!] \tau$ is the input/output semantics of program α with input valuation σ_0 and output valuation τ.

Sequent Calculus. We construct proofs using a sequent calculus. Proof rules for predicate logic are standard. For DL we employ rules to symbolically execute the sequential programs. For example the two rules

$$\frac{\varphi_x^\tau, \Gamma \vdash \Delta}{\langle x := \tau \rangle \, \varphi, \Gamma \vdash \Delta} \; assign\ left \qquad \frac{\varepsilon, \langle \alpha \rangle \, \varphi, \Gamma \vdash \Delta \quad \langle \beta \rangle \, \varphi, \Gamma \vdash \varepsilon, \Delta}{\langle \text{if } \varepsilon \text{ then } \alpha \text{ else } \beta \rangle \, \varphi, \Gamma \vdash \Delta} \; if\ left$$

are used to execute assignments and conditionals by reducing the conclusion to the premise. Here, Γ denotes all other premises and Δ the rest f the conclusions. For a full set of rules for Dynamic Logic see for example [HRS88].

Rules for Temporal Logic. The same strategy of symbolic execution is applied to temporal operators. Our first goal is to construct – for each temporal formula – separate formulas restricting the first valuation and the rest of the trace. For example $\Box \varphi$ in the succedent is treated as follows.

$$\frac{\Gamma \vdash \varphi, \Delta \quad \Gamma \vdash \bullet \, \Box \varphi, \Delta}{\Gamma \vdash \Box \varphi, \Delta} \; always\ right$$

In the first premise, we prove that φ holds in the first state, in the second, we establish the property for the rest of the trace. Application of *always right* can be viewed as unwinding (the recursive definition of) the temporal operator. It is comparable to executing programs. Unwinding $\Box \varphi$ and $\Diamond \varphi$ is straightforward, for more details on unwinding $\varphi \, ; \, \psi$ and others, see [BDRS02].

We unwind temporal operators until every temporal formula Γ and Δ is prefixed with a next operator and all other formulas γ and δ are formulas in predicate logic involving unprimed and primed variables. Then we can advance one step in the trace by applying rule *step*.

$$\frac{\gamma_0, \Gamma \vdash \delta_0, \Delta}{\gamma, \circ \, \Gamma \vdash \delta, \bullet \, \Delta} \; step$$

Here γ_0 and δ_0 are obtained from γ and δ by replacing all unprimed variables v with new rigid variables v_0 and all primed variables v' with their unprimed version v. The leading next operators are removed. Thus we have stored the values of variables of the initial state of the trace in new variables v_0 and advanced one step in the trace by removing all primes and next operators.

Induction. Since traces may be arbitrary long or even infinite, it is not feasible, to execute the whole trace. Therefore, we need induction. The basic idea is to advance in the trace until a state of the statechart is repeated and some value decreased. In this case we have executed a loop and if we can show an invariant property, the proof can be finished by induction. To prove a safety property $\Box\varphi$, we use the following induction rule

$$\frac{N = N' + 1 \ \mathbf{until} \ \neg \ \varphi, n = N, \text{IndHyp}(n), \Gamma \vdash \Delta}{\Gamma \vdash \Box\varphi, \Delta} \quad ind. \ always$$

where the induction hypothesis is

$$\text{IndHyp}(n) :\equiv \forall \ m < n. \ Cl_\forall^m (\bigwedge \Gamma \wedge m = N \to \bigvee \Delta)$$

and $Cl_\forall^m(\varphi)$ denotes the universal closure of φ except m. The rule is based on the equivalence

$$\neg \ \Box\varphi \leftrightarrow (\exists \ N. \ N = N' + 1 \ \mathbf{until} \ \neg \ \varphi)$$

and wellfounded induction over N. Informally the proof is by contradiction: if $\Box\varphi$ is false, then there exists a number of steps after which the formula φ becomes false for the first time. This number is the initial value of N, which is decremented (note that $N = N' + 1$ is equivalent to $N' = N - 1 \wedge N \neq 0$) until a state with $\neg \ \varphi$ is reached. For more details on inductive proofs see [Bal04].

5   Embedding Statecharts in ITL

In this section we describe the integration of statecharts into the ITL framework. The key idea is to treat a statechart SC as a formula, with the idea that I $\models$ SC holds if I is a trace of SC. A configuration of a statechart is represented as a valuation of statechart variables $variables(SC)$. The statechart variables are flexible variables and, therefore, additional primed variables v' exists for every $v \in variables(SC)$. In addition to the data variables $vars(SC)$, boolean variables for each state $states(SC)$ and each event $events(SC)$ are required, describing whether the corresponding state/event is active or not. The input variables $events_{env}(SC) \cup vars_{env}(SC)$, with $events_{env}(SC) \subseteq events(SC)$ and $vars_{env}(SC) \subseteq vars(SC)$, are variables, which the systems environment may modify. Local events are $events_{loc}(SC) := events(SC) \setminus events_{env}(SC)$, local variables are $vars_{loc}(SC) := vars(SC) \setminus vars_{env}(SC)$. A statechart step describes a transition from one valuation to another, corresponding to the transition relation of the statechart. A trace of a statechart is a sequence of valuations $(\sigma_0, \sigma_1, \ldots)$ where all relations $\sigma_i \ \rho \ \sigma_{i+1}$ correspond to the transition relation ρ described by the statechart. The semantics of a statechart is defined as all such sequences of states.

Semantics. The statechart semantics depends on the definition of a statechart step. Our formalism supports the STATEMATE semantics of statecharts [HN96] and is based on the operational semantics presented in [DJHP98]. Two important extensions are necessary to integrate statecharts into our ITL framework. In [DJHP98], a statechart step directly computes the successor valuation of the statechart, whereas in our setting, a step has to compute the values of the primed variables. Then the *tl step* rule computes the actual transitions to the successor valuations. The second extension is the following: [DJHP98] defines the semantics of statecharts as the set of traces $(\sigma_0, \ldots, \sigma_n)$, where the transition relation of the statechart ρ holds for every step, i.e. $\sigma_i \rho \sigma_{i+1}$, and the valuation σ_0 is an initial valuation (the initial states are active). Traces are required to be maximal, i.e. for finite traces: $\sigma_n \notin dom(\rho)$. This is not sufficient for our calculus, since symbolic execution leaves the initial state. Therefore, we generalize the definition of the statechart semantics to traces with a *consistent* initial valuation σ_0. A valuation is consistent, if it assigns true to exactly one sub-chart of every or-state. The set of all maximal statechart traces is defined as

$$traces_A(SC) := \{(\sigma_0, \ldots, \sigma_n) \mid n \in \mathbb{N}_\infty, \sigma_i \rho \sigma_{i+1}, \sigma_n \notin dom(\rho), \sigma_0 \text{ consistent}\}$$

Note, that the algebra A used in the definition makes it dependent on the underlying algebraic specification which defines the data part of the statechart. Because all initial valuations are consistent, every initial trace is in $traces_A(SC)$. This definition enables us to prove properties for statecharts, which do not start in an initial configuration. Such properties are often useful as lemmas.

Embedding. The semantics of statecharts is the set of maximal traces of the statechart and the semantical integration into the ITL framework is straightforward.

$$A, I \models SC :\Leftrightarrow I \in traces_A(SC)$$

In this paper, we will not present the definition of ρ, because it basically depends on the definitions in [DJHP98]. Instead, we show in Sect. 6 how to compute the successor valuations in the calculus. A formal definition of ρ and a correctness proof for the calculus is given in [Thu04].

6   Statechart Calculus

Unwinding a statechart step can be split up into two tasks. First, we have to compute all possible steps by $Steps(SC, \Gamma \vdash \Delta)$. Second, for each possible step $stp \in Steps(SC, \Gamma \vdash \Delta)$ we have to compute the effects of the active transitions and static reactions contained in stp. These actions modify variables and generate events. Because transitions leave and enter states, the state configuration changes, too. The rule scheme for unwinding statecharts is defined as

$$\frac{\bigvee_{stp_i \in Steps(SC, \Gamma \vdash \Delta)} exec(stp_i), \Gamma \vdash \Delta}{SC, \Gamma \vdash \Delta} \quad sc \text{ unwind,} \tag{1}$$

with $exec(stp) := cond(stp) \wedge step(stp) \wedge \circ nxt(stp)$. Because our approach allows complex predicates over algebraic specifications as guards, we cannot always determine automatically if a guard is satisfied or not. This is in contrast to approaches which allow finite data structures only, where a model checker can decide such conditions. Therefore, we compute activation conditions $cond(stp)$ for a possible statechart step. Only if $cond(stp)$ holds, the step is executed. Otherwise, the condition is contradictory to the other preconditions.

$step(stp)$ executes a single statechart step and $nxt(stp)$ computes the active states of the successor valuation. Together, they implement the transition relation ρ, defined by the statechart. The formal definitions of $cond(stp)$, $step(stp)$, and $nxt(stp)$ follow in Sect. 6.2.

6.1 Computing Possible Steps

A step consists of maximal sets of non-conflicting active transitions. Transitions are in conflict, if they leave the same state. We require that the sets of transitions are maximal to guarantee, that an active transition is actually executed, unless a conflicting transition is executed in this step. Because of concurrent states (and-states), a maximal set of non-conflicting active transitions is not necessarily a singleton.

The STATEMATE semantics of statecharts defines a top-down priority for conflicting transitions: assume an active or-state s with an active sub-state s_1 and two active transitions t with source state s and t_1 with source state s_1. Because the execution of t leaves s and all its sub-states (even s_1), t and t_1 are in conflict. The priority rule of STATEMATE statecharts solves this conflict in favor of t.

Analogously to [DJHP98], we present a computation of steps, which respects all these requirements. Roughly speaking, the algorithm computes the transition set in a top-down fashion. For an and-state, all possible steps from the sub-states have to be considered. The algorithm computes the Cartesian product of the steps from the sub-states. For an or-state, the algorithm computes a set of active transitions. If this set is empty, the transitions of the active sub-state are considered (the priority rule is respected), otherwise all these transitions are in conflict and the result is a set of steps, where every step is a singleton set of one active transition (non-conflicting is respected). Finally, a basic-state yields an empty step.

Depending on the current sequent $SC, \Gamma \vdash \Delta$, a state s and an activation condition g the function

$$steps : Sequent \times states(SC) \times Fma \to (Fma, \wp(trans(SC)))$$

computes all possible steps $stp = (g_T, T)$ with activation condition g_T for the maximal non-conflicting transitions T. Here, Fma denotes the set of all interval temporal logic formulae. Based on this auxiliary function

$$Steps(SC, \Gamma \vdash \Delta) := steps(\Gamma \vdash \Delta, root(SC), \text{true})$$

computes all possible statechart steps. $steps(\Gamma \vdash \Delta, s, g)$ is defined as

1. $mode(s) \in \{basic, term\}$:

   $steps(\Gamma \vdash \Delta, s, g) := \{(g, \emptyset)\}$

2. $mode(s) = and$:

   Let $\{s_1, \ldots, s_n\} = childs(s)$, then

   $$steps(\Gamma \vdash \Delta, s, g) :=$$
   $$\{(g_1 \wedge \ldots \wedge g_n, \bigcup_{i=1}^{n} T_i) \mid (g_i, T_i) \in steps(\Gamma \vdash \Delta, s_i, s_i \wedge g)\},$$

3. $mode(s) = or$: Let

   - $S' = \{\tilde{s} \mid \tilde{s} \in childs(s) \text{ and } \Gamma \vdash \Delta, \neg \tilde{s} \text{ is not provable}\}$,
   - $T_{\tilde{s}} = \{t_{\tilde{s}_1}, \ldots, t_{\tilde{s}_k}\} = \{t \mid source(t) = s\}$ and
   - $T = \{t_1, \ldots, t_k\} = \bigcup_{\tilde{s} \in S'} T_{\tilde{s}}$.

   Every transition in T has the same priority and they are in conflict.

   $$steps(\Gamma \vdash \Delta, s, g) :=$$
   $$\{(g_t, \{t\}) \mid t \in T \text{ and } g_t := g \wedge guard(t) \wedge source(t)\} \cup$$
   $$\bigcup_{s' \in S'} steps(\Gamma \vdash \Delta, s', g \wedge s' \wedge \neg guard(t_{s'_1}) \wedge \ldots \wedge \neg guard(t_{s'_k})) \quad (2)$$

A basic state cannot execute any transition, so the result is a set of an empty set. An and-state executes every transitions of its sub-states in parallel, so we have to compute the Cartesian product of the transitions from the sub-states. The main difference to the step computation in [DJHP98] is in item 3., where an or-state is considered. First, it has to be determined, which states are possible source states for active transitions. Since we allow partially specified state configurations, active states cannot be determined fully automatic. We approximate the set by collecting those states $\tilde{s}$ in S' where $\Gamma \vdash \Delta, \neg\tilde{s}$ is not provable using the simplifier of KIV. The set $T_{\tilde{s}}$ computes the transitions with source state $\tilde{s}$ and the set T contains all possibly active transitions.

All transitions in T are in conflict (in an or-state, only one transition can be executed) and can be executed, if the guard is evaluated to true and its source state is actually active. Therefore, the activation condition g_t for a transition t is $g_t := g \wedge guard(t) \wedge source(t)$. The precondition g describes, that no transition of a super-state is active.

If a state $\tilde{s}$ is active, but none of the guards of any transitions $t \in T_{\tilde{s}}$ holds, transitions from sub-states of $\tilde{s}$ can be executed. We add the condition, that no guard of $t \in T_{\tilde{s}}$ is enabled to the activation condition for the recursive call of $steps$ in equation (2).

Example 1. Step Computation (I)

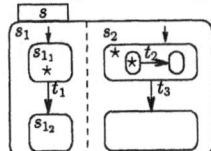

Consider the statechart on the left where $\star$ marks active states. Let $guard(t_1) = g_1$, $guard(t_2) = g_2$, and $guard(t_3) = g_3$ be the guards of the transitions. We only add active states to the activation condition, if necessary.

$$steps(\Gamma \vdash \Delta, s_1, \text{true}) = \{(g_1, \{t_1\}), (\neg g_1, \emptyset)\}$$
$$steps(\Gamma \vdash \Delta, s_2, \text{true}) = \{(g_3, \{t_3\}), (\neg g_3 \wedge g_2, \{t_2\}), (\neg g_3 \wedge \neg g_2, \emptyset)\}$$
$$Steps(SC, \Gamma \vdash \Delta) = steps(\Gamma \vdash \Delta, s, \text{true}) =$$
$$\{(g_1 \wedge g_3, \{t_1, t_3\}), (\neg g_1 \wedge g_3, \{t_3\}), (g_1 \wedge \neg g_3 \wedge g_2, \{t_1, t_2\}),$$
$$(\neg g_1 \wedge \neg g_3 \wedge g_2, \{t_2\}), (g_1 \wedge \neg g_3 \wedge \neg g_2, \{t_1\}), (\neg g_1 \wedge \neg g_3 \wedge \neg g_2, \emptyset)\}$$

Now, let us consider the state s with a generalized state configuration. We abstract from the active states in s_1. If either s_{1_1} or s_{1_2} is active, we get:

$$steps(\Gamma \vdash \Delta, s_1, \text{true}) = \{(g_1 \wedge s_{1_1}, \{t_1\}), (\neg g_1 \wedge s_{1_1}, \emptyset), (s_{1_2}, \emptyset)\}$$
$$steps(\Gamma \vdash \Delta, s_2, \text{true}) = \{(g_3, \{t_3\}), (\neg g_3 \wedge g_2, \{t_2\}), (\neg g_3 \wedge \neg g_2, \emptyset)\}$$
$$Steps(SC, \Gamma \vdash \Delta) = steps(\Gamma \vdash \Delta, s, \text{true}) =$$
$$\{(g_1 \wedge s_{1_1} \wedge g_3, \{t_1, t_3\}), (\neg g_1 \wedge s_{1_1} \wedge g_3, \{t_3\}), (s_{1_2} \wedge g_3, \{t_3\}), (g_1 \wedge s_{1_1} \wedge$$
$$\neg g_3 \wedge g_2, \{t_1, t_2\}), (\neg g_1 \wedge s_{1_1} \wedge \neg g_3 \wedge g_2, \{t_2\}), (s_{1_2} \wedge \neg g_3 \wedge g_2, \{t_2\}), (g_1 \wedge$$
$$s_{1_1} \wedge \neg g_3 \wedge \neg g_2, \{t_1\}), (\neg g_1 \wedge s_{1_1} \wedge \neg g_3 \wedge \neg g_2, \emptyset), (s_{1_2} \wedge \neg g_3 \wedge \neg g_2, \emptyset)\}$$

Example 2. Step Computation (II)

Consider the statechart SYS of the timer example and assume that the initial states Off and $Idle$ are active. If we want to prove $\Box x \leq k$, we get the sequent $SYS, On, Idle \vdash \Box x \leq k$ and the step algorithm computes the following possible steps:

$$steps((On, Idle, \vdash \neg \Box x \leq 6), \text{true}) := \{(press \wedge set, \{t_1, t_3\}),$$
$$(press \wedge \neg set, \{t_1\}), (\neg press \wedge set, \{t_3\}), (\neg press \wedge \neg set, \emptyset)\}$$

The presented step computation extends the one, presented in [DJHP98]. We added the possibility to compute and return activation conditions for steps. This extension is necessary, because we have to consider guards for transitions, which cannot be decided automatically. A second extension is the possibility to cope with partially specified state configurations. Therefore, we have to add the source state of a transition to its activation condition.

We also consider static reactions and inter level transitions in our approach, but omitted these concepts for this presentation. For details we refer to [Thu04].

6.2   Step-Execution

We define the execution of a statechart step with sequential programs. The programs 'implement' the step semantics. We sequentialize the execution of parallel transitions according to the semantics from Damm et al. [DJHP98]. We respect the execution of parallel transitions, although we implement the step execution with sequential programs. To solve read conflicts, where an action reads a variable already changed by a parallel action, we copy variables v in a copy $\tilde{v}$. In the following, we assume for every flexible variable $v \in variables(SC)$ an additional auxiliary variable $\tilde{v}$ and that the actions of transitions assign their values to these auxiliary variables.[1] To solve write conflicts, where different actions change the value of one variable, we introduce nondeterminism, where every action 'wins' once (see below).

We distinguish between micro- and macro-steps. A macro-step is executed, if an empty set of enabled transitions is computed.

$$step((g,T)) := \begin{cases} T = \emptyset, & step_{makro}(T) \\ \text{otherwise,} & step_{mikro}(T) \end{cases}$$

Micro-Step. A micro-step $step_{mikro} : trans(SC) \to Fma$ is defined as

$$step_{mikro}(T) := \bigvee\nolimits_{\underline{\alpha} \in perm(T)} \langle copy; reset^l; reset^e; exec(\underline{\alpha}) \rangle set.$$

As described above, we respect write conflicts through nondeterminism by executing every possible sequence of actions ($\underline{\alpha} \in perm(T)$, $perm$ computes the permutations of the transition set T).

To solve read conflicts, we copy variables from $\underline{v} = vars(SC) \cup events(SC)$ to $\underline{\tilde{v}}$ with $copy$. Then, we reset every event with $reset^l$, by assigning false to the boolean variable, representing an event. To observe generated environment steps at the end of a macro-step, we reset them only in the first micro-step after a macro-step. Then $tick$ holds. Resetting environment events is done with $reset^e$. Now, we can execute the actions. Because we already considered read and write conflicts, the execution can be sequential. Finally, set requires, that the primed variable (unprimed ones in the next configuration) get the values, computed before. The corresponding programs are defined as

$$
\begin{aligned}
copy &:= \underline{\tilde{v}} := \underline{v} \text{ for } \underline{v} = vars(SC) \cup events(SC), \\
reset^l &:= \underline{\tilde{e}} := \text{false, for } \underline{e} = events_{loc}(SC) \cup \{tick\}, \\
reset^e &:= \text{if } tick \text{ then } \underline{\tilde{e}} := \text{false for } \underline{e} = events_{env}(SC), \\
exec(\underline{\alpha}) &:= \alpha_1; \ldots; \alpha_n \text{ for } \underline{\alpha} = \alpha_1, \ldots, \alpha_n, \text{ and} \\
set &:= \underline{\tilde{v}} = \underline{v}' \text{ for } \underline{v} = vars(SC) \cup events(SC).
\end{aligned}
$$

In addition to the given step computation, STATEMATE statecharts generate also events when states are entered and exited. We consider these events in our calculus, too, but have omitted this detail here (see [Thu04]).

Macro-Step. A macro-step $step_{makro} : trans(SC) \to Fma$ is defined as

$$step_{makro}(stp) := \langle copy; reset^l \rangle set^e \wedge set^l$$

---

[1] Reading context variables $v from STATEMATE corresponds to reading $\tilde{v}$, reading 'normal' STATEMATE variables, corresponds to reading v in our setting.

Analogous to a micro-step, we copy the variable values and reset the events. Then, we label the macro-step with the *tick* event and require, that the primed variables for local events and variables values get the current values.

$$set^e := tick' = \text{true}$$
$$set^l := \tilde{\underline{v}} = \underline{v}' \text{ for } \underline{v} = events_{loc}(SC) \cup vars_{loc}(SC)$$

A macro-step does not restrict the primed variables of environment events. A temporal logic step assigns arbitrary values to them to model new input to the environment variables.

State Configuration. In addition to the step computation, we have to compute the active states for the successor valuation. They depend on the current transition set T. Let $S := entered(T) \cup active(T)$ be the set of active states in the next configuration, $\overline{S} := states(SC) \backslash (entered(T) \cup active(T))$ the set of inactive states. *entered* computes the states which will be entered by executing the transitions T, *active* the states, which were neither entered nor exited and *entered*, the states, which were entered through the current step. Then

$$nxt(T) := \bigwedge_{s \in S} s \wedge \bigwedge_{\overline{s} \in \overline{S}} \neg \, \overline{s} \wedge SC$$

computes the active states of the next configuration and requires that statechart formula SC holds again (and can be executed further).

Example 3. Step Execution
Let us consider the timer example once again and denote the statechart SYS. We want to prove the sequent $SYS, Off, Idle \vdash \Box x \leq k$, which we abbreviate to $SYS, \Gamma \models \varphi$. Then the step computation computes four possible steps and therewith four possible premises for the *sc unwind* rule.

(1) $(press \wedge set) \wedge step((press \wedge set, \{t_1, t_3\})) \wedge onxt(\{t_1, t_3\}), \Gamma \vdash \varphi$

(2) $(\neg press \wedge set) \wedge step((\neg press \wedge set, \{t_3\})) \wedge onxt(\{t_3\}), \Gamma \vdash \varphi$

(3) $(press \wedge \neg set) \wedge step((press \wedge \neg set, \{t_1\})\}) \wedge onxt(\{t_1\}), \Gamma \vdash \varphi$

(4) $(\neg press \wedge \neg set) \wedge step((\neg press \wedge \neg set, \emptyset)) \wedge onxt(\emptyset), \Gamma \vdash \varphi$

$$\overline{\qquad\qquad\qquad SYS, \Gamma \vdash \varphi \qquad\qquad\qquad}$$

We only consider the cases 3 and 4 in detail. The 3rd case is a micro-step and the 4th case a macro-step. Copying variables and resetting the events is independent from the concrete step.

$$copy \;= \widetilde{tick}, \widetilde{set}, \widetilde{sw\_off}, \tilde{x} := tick, set, sw\_off, x$$
$$reset^l = \widetilde{tick}, \widetilde{set}, \widetilde{sw\_off} := \text{false}, \text{false}, \text{false}$$
$$reset^e = \textbf{if } tick \textbf{ then } \widetilde{press} := \text{false}$$

The micro-step has to execute the transition t_1 and assign the computed values from the step to the primed variables, to describe the valuation of the next step.

$$exec(<set>) = \widetilde{set} := true$$
$$set \qquad = \widetilde{tick}, \widetilde{set}, \widetilde{sw\_off}, \widetilde{press}, \widetilde{x} = tick', set', sw\_off', press', x'$$

The whole micro-step results in

$$step_{mikro}((press \wedge \neg set, \{t_1\})) = \langle copy; reset^l; reset^e; exec(<set>)\rangle set.$$

The macro-step in the 4th premise resets every event and generates the *tick*-event. Because we do explicitly not assign any value to primed variables for environment variables and events, the following temporal logic step assigns an arbitrary value to environment variable *press*.

$$set^e = tick' = true$$
$$set^l = \widetilde{set}, \widetilde{sw\_off}, \widetilde{x} = set', sw\_off', x'$$

We get the following macro-step.

$$step_{makro}((\neg press \wedge \neg set, \emptyset)) = \langle copy; reset^l \rangle set^e \wedge set^l.$$

6.3   Tool Support

We implemented specification and proof support for statecharts in KIV. The specifications are incorporated into the correctness management of the KIV system. If a statechart specification is changed, every lemma based on this specification becomes invalid.

Because our statechart semantics does not require to specify lemmas for statecharts, which start execution in an initial state, we are able to specify and prove lemmas for intermediate states. E.g., we can prove something like "if we are in state *Cnt*, we will stay there for k macro-steps, at most". We can use this statement in other proofs as a lemma and apply it, if we reach the state *Cnt*.

The proof strategy of symbolic execution leads to diagrammatic proofs. We have to unwind the statechart and execute the statechart step. Thereafter, we unwind the temporal operator, get a predicate logic proof condition for the current valuation and a temporal logic proof condition for the rest of the trace. If we have proven the condition for the current valuation, we turn to the successor valuation, where we can unwind the statechart again. This leads to proofs, following the execution of the statechart. This means, that we do not translate a statechart into a flat transition system, but preserve the structure of the statechart.

We automated this sequence of rule application through heuristics in the KIV system. We extend the heuristics for ITL verification, to apply the *sc unwind* rule. The resulting heuristics enable us to automate simple statechart proofs. As an example, the proof for the property $\Box x \leq t$ of the light control, as shown in Fig. 2 of Sect. 2, can be automated except for the generalization step from $x = 0$ to $x \leq k$. If a concrete k is given, e.g. $k = 6$ the proof is fully automatic.

7   Example: Radio-Based Level Crossing Control

In this section we will describe the application of the presented calculus on a real world case study. This case study is a reference case study of the German research councils priority program 1064. we will briefly describe the problem, then present how it is modeled in statechart notion and finally give some verification results.

The German railway organization, Deutsche Bahn, prepares a novel technique to control level crossings: the decentralized, radio-based level crossing control (FunkFahrBetrieb, FFB [FFB96]). The main difference between this technology and the traditional control of level crossings is, that signals and sensors on the route are replaced by radio communication and software computations in the train and in the level crossing.

Instead of detecting an approaching train by a sensor, the train computes the position where it has to send a signal to secure the level crossing. Therefore, the train has to know the position of the level crossing, the time needed to secure the level crossing, and its current speed and position. When the level crossing receives the 'secure' command it switches on the traffic lights and closes the barriers. When they are closed, the level crossing is 'safe' for a certain period of time. The stop signal, indicating an insecure crossing, is also substituted by computation and communication. The train requests the status of the level crossing. Depending on the answer the train will brake or pass the crossing. A STATEMATE reference model for the radio based crossing control is presented in [KT02] and a safety analysis with fault trees in [TO03,RST00].

7.1   Specification with Statecharts

We specified a version of the radio-based crossing control with statecharts in KIV.

Fig. 3 shows the graphical representation of the specification, that focuses on the problem of closing the barriers early enough and braking in time, if something went wrong (the reference model also considers traffic lights, etc.). We also modeled faulty behavior, highlighted by the gray box, but concentrate on the functional behavior, at first.

The whole setting is specified with three parallel statecharts, one chart for every system component. The chart *train* specifies the behavior of the train. An approaching train sends a closing request to the crossing, if the predicate $close(pos, v, a_{brk}, lc)$ holds. pos indicates the current position of the train, v the current speed, a_{brk} the maximal deceleration, and the level crossing lc. The closing request $close_{snd}$ will be received ($close_{rcv}$) by the crossing if no communication error has happened. Then the crossing closes the barriers within tc_{cl} time units. Thereafter, the barriers are closed for maximal t_{max} time units or until the train passes the crossing.

The train sends a status request $status_{snd}$, which will also be delayed by the communication, and awaits an answer within a certain amount of time. If the crossing receives the status request $status_{rcv}$ and the barriers are closed (the state *closed* is active), the crossing acknowledges the status request (ack_{snd}). If

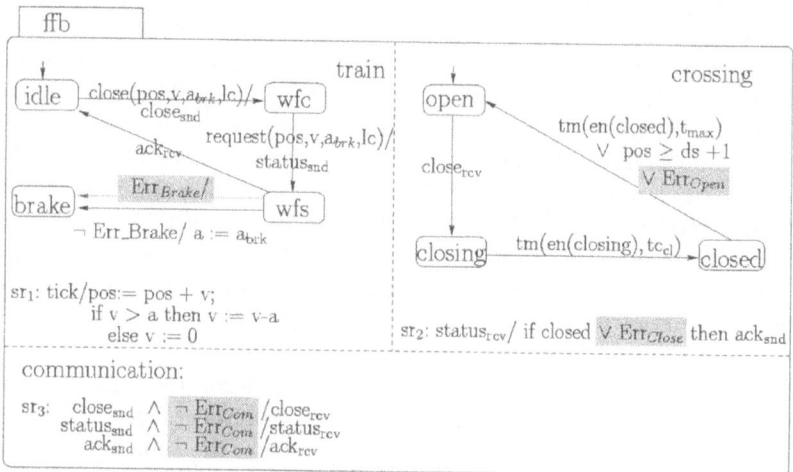

Fig. 3. Radio-Based Level Crossing Control

the train receives ack_{rcv} in time, it will pass the crossing, otherwise the train will brake and stop before the level crossing lc.

Now, let us consider faulty behavior. We modeled the failure of brakes (Err_{Brake}), the break down of the communication channel (Err_{Com}), a faulty acknowledgment of a status request (Err_{Close}) and an undesired opening of the barriers (Err_{Open}). Every fault is modeled by an indeterministic choice. E.g., the failure of the brakes are modeled by an additional transition from the state *wfs* to *brake*. In contrast to the 'correct' transition, this additional one does not set the deceleration to a_{brk}, so the train does not brake. The other failures are modeled analogously.

7.2   Algebraic Specification

The underlying data types for the radio-based crossing control system are algebraically specified using natural numbers. In addition, we specified the predicates $close(pos, v, a_{brk}, lc)$ and $request(pos, v, a_{brk}, lc)$ to compute the optimal time for closing the barriers and requesting the status of the crossing. These predicates rely on the braking distance $brake_d(v, a_{brk})$. Within each macro-step, the static reaction sr_1 computes the position and velocity of the train.

$$tick/pos := pos + v; \textbf{if } v > a \textbf{ then } v := v - a \textbf{ else } v := 0$$

With the deceleration $a > 0$ and the initial velocity v_0, the distance until the train stops is

$$brake_d(v_0, a) := v_0 + \left(\sum_{i=0}^{\lceil v_0/a \rceil} v_0 - i * a \right) \tag{3}$$

(with the distance $v_0 \frac{m}{s} * 1s = v_0 m$). Based on $brake_d$, we can define the predicates $close$ and $request$

$$close(pos, v, a_{brk}, lc) := pos \geq lc - (brake_d(v, a_{brk}) + tc_{cl} * v) \text{ and} \qquad (4)$$

$$request(pos, v, a_{brk}, lc) := pos \geq lc - brake_d(v, a_{brk}). \qquad (5)$$

7.3 Formal Safety Analysis and Verification

In the ForMoSA project, we developed the safety analysis technique formal fault tree analysis (formal FTA, [STR02]). Formal FTA integrates classical fault tree analysis (FTA, [VGRH81]) with formal methods. For the radio-based crossing control we analyzed the hazard "collision of the train on crossing". A detailed fault tree is described in [Thu04]. 10 verification conditions are attached to this fault tree. Altogether they guarantee that the hazard can happen only if one of the causes described by the leaves of the fault tree (e.g. failure of brakes Err_{Brake}) happens. Informally, each verification condition is a temproal formula that intuitively says: "if some consequence happens, then the cause must have happened before or at the same time" (for a formal definition of the conditions, see [OTSW04] in this volume).

All verification conditions could be verified with KIV. The proofs typically proceed by induction over the number of steps it takes to reach the consequence (if the consequence is never reached on a trace, the condition is trivially true).

Some conditions are trivial to prove, but most have rather complex proofs with several hundred proof steps, so they are too complex to show them in detail. Two reasons contribute to the complexity: one is the indeterminism inherent in statecharts, the other is a lack of modular proofs: even though most conditions give properties of only one component (e.g. the train), all properties must still be proved over the full statechart. Research in modular proofs is still an important topic for further research.

As subtasks of the proofs algebraic properties of the definitions (3), (4) and (5) have to be shown: thereby it is proved that the requests to close the gates and the distance where to brake (when the crossing does not acknowledge closing of the gates) are indeed a safe distance away from the crossing, such that the train is able to stop in time.

8 Conclusion and Future Work

We developed interactive proof support for statecharts with infinite data structures. We consider statecharts with finitely many states, but specify data, functions, and predicates by algebraic specifications. Guard conditions of transitions refer to data types using first-order logic. Statechart actions are described by sequential programs and proof conditions for statecharts are interval temporal logic formulas.

We support STATEMATE statecharts with their asynchronous macro-step semantics. As far as we know, this is the first approach which offers proof support for infinite statechart models. We defined a sequent calculus for verifying statechart properties, which is implemented in the KIV system. The calculus has been successfully applied on the radio-based level crossing control.

Up to the present, we considered the verification of statecharts. Damm et al. [DJHP98] gave a modular semantics based on activities, where complex systems can be decomposed in modular sub-activities. Each activity is controlled by a statechart. Modularization is a prerequisite for proving properties for complex systems. Future work will be to extend our approach to modular statechart verification.

References

[Bal04]   M. Balser. *Verifying Concurrent System with Symbolic Execution – Temporal Reasoning is Symbolic Execution with a Little Induction.* PhD thesis, University of Augsburg, Augsburg, Gemany, 2004. (to appear).

[BDRS02]   M. Balser, C. Duelli, W. Reif, and G. Schellhorn. Verifying concurrent systems with symbolic execution. *Journal of Logic and Computation*, 12(4):549–560, 2002.

[BRS+00]   M. Balser, W. Reif, G. Schellhorn, K. Stenzel, and A. Thums. Formal system development with KIV. In T. Maibaum, editor, *Fundamental Approaches to Software Engineering*, number 1783 in LNCS, pages 363–366. Springer-Verlag, 2000.

[CMZ02]   A. Cau, B. Moszkowski, and H. Zedan. *ITL – Interval Temporal Logic.* Software Technology Research Laboratory, SERCentre, De Montfort University, The Gateway, Leicester LE1 9BH, UK, 2002. www.cms.dmu.ac.uk/~cau/itlhomepage.

[DJHP98]   W. Damm, B. Josko, H. Hungar, and A. Pnueli. A compositional real-time semantics of STATEMATE designs. In W.-P. de Roever, H. Langmaack, and A. Pnueli, editors, *COMPOS' 97*, volume 1536 of *LNCS*, pages 186–238. Springer, 1998.

[FFB96]   Betriebliches Lastenheft für FunkFahrBetrieb, 1996. Stand 1.10.1996.

[Har84]   D. Harel. Dynamic logic. In D. Gabbay and F. Guenther, editors, *Handbook of Philosophical Logic*, volume 2, pages 496–604. Reidel, 1984.

[HLN+90]   D. Harel, H. Lachover, A. Naamad, A. Pnueli, M. Politi, R. Sherman, A. Shtull-Trauring, and M. Trakhtenbrot. Statemate: A working environment for the development of complex reactive systems. *IEEE Transactions on Software Engineering*, 16(4), 1990.

[HN96]   D. Harel and A. Naamad. The statemate semantics of statecharts. *ACM Transactions on Software Engineering and Methodology*, 5(4):293–333, October 1996.

[HRS88]   M. Heisel, W. Reif, and W. Stephan. Program Verification Using Dynamic Logic. In E. Börger, H. Kleine Büning, and M. Richter, editors, *1st Workshop on Computer Science Logic. Proceedings*, Springer LNCS 329, 1988.

[KT02]   J. Klose and A. Thums. The STATEMATE reference model of the reference case study 'Verkehrsleittechnik'. Technical Report 2002-01, Universität Augsburg, 2002.

[Mos85]   B. Moszkowski. A temporal logic for multilevel reasoning about hardware. *IEEE Computer*, 18(2):10–19, 1985.

[OT02]   F. Ortmeier and A. Thums. Formale Methoden und Sicherheitsanalyse. Technical Report 15, Universität Augsburg, 2002. (in German).

[OTSW04]   F. Ortmeier, A. Thums, G. Schellhorn, and W.Reif. Combining formal methods and safety analysis - the ForMoSA approach. In *this volume*. Springer LNCS, 2004.

[RST00]   W. Reif, G. Schellhorn, and A. Thums. Formale Sicherheitsanalyse einer funkbasierten Bahnübergangsteuerung. In E. Schnieder, editor, *Forms2000 – Formale Techniken für die Eisenbahnsicherung*, volume Reihe 12, Nr. 441 of *Fortschritt-Bericht VDI*, 2000.

[SA91]   V. Sperschneider and G. Antoniou. *Logic: A Foundation for Computer Science*. Addison Wesley, 1991.

[STR02]   G. Schellhorn, A. Thums, and W. Reif. Formal fault tree semantics. In *Proceedings of The Sixth World Conference on Integrated Design & Process Technology*, Pasadena, CA, 2002.

[Thu04]   A. Thums. *Formale Fehlerbaumanalyse*. PhD thesis, Universität Augsburg, Augsburg, Germany, 2004. (in German).

[TO03]   A. Thums and F. Ortmeier. Formal safety analysis in transportation control. In E. Schnieder, editor, *International Workshop on Software Specification of Safety Relevant Transportation Control Tasks*, volume 12 (no. 535) of *VDI Fortschritt-Berichte*. VDI Verlag GmbH, 2003.

[VGRH81]   W. E. Vesely, F. F. Goldberg, N. H. Roberts, and D. F. Haasl. *Fault Tree Handbook*. Washington, D.C., 1981. NUREG-0492.

[Wir90]   M. Wirsing. *Algebraic Specification*, volume B of *Handbook of Theoretical Computer Science*, chapter 13, pages 675 – 788. Elsevier, Oxford, 1990.

Live Sequence Charts*

An Introduction to Lines, Arrows, and Strange Boxes in the Context of Formal Verification

Matthias Brill[1], Werner Damm[1], Jochen Klose[2], Bernd Westphal[1], and Hartmut Wittke[3]

[1] Carl von Ossietzky Universität Oldenburg, Department für Informatik,
PO Box 2503, 26111 Oldenburg, Germany
{brill,damm,westphal}@informatik.uni-oldenburg.de
[2] Bombardier Transportation, Braunschweig,
Wolfenbüttler Straße 86/Obergstraße 5, 38102 Braunschweig, Germany
jochen.klose@de.transport.bombardier.com
[3] OFFIS, Escherweg 2, 26121 Oldenburg, Germany
wittke@offis.de

Abstract. The language of Message Sequence Charts (MSC) is a well-established visual formalism which is typically used to capture scenarios in the early stages of system development. But when it comes to rigorous requirements capturing, in particular in the context of formal verification, serious deficiencies emerge: MSCs do not provide means to distinguish mandatory and possible behavior, for example to demand that a communication is required to finally occur.

The Live Sequence Chart (LSC) language introduces the distinction between mandatory and possible on the level of the whole chart and for the elements messages, locations, and conditions. Furthermore they provide means to specify the desired activation time by an activation condition or by a whole communication sequence, called pre-chart.

We present the current stage of LSC language and a sketch of its formal semantics in terms of Timed Büchi Automata.

1 Introduction

Message sequence charts (MSCs) are a well established visual formalism for the description of inter-working of processes or objects. There is also a standard for the MSC language, which has appeared as a recommendation of the ITU [1]. The standard defines the allowed syntactic constructs, and is also accompanied by a formal semantics [2] that provides unambiguous meaning to basic MSCs. Despite the widespread use of MSCs and the foundational efforts cited above, several fundamental issues have been left unaddressed. One of the most basic of

---

* This research was supported by the German Research Council (DFG) within the priority program Integration of Specification Techniques with Engineering Applications under grant DA 206/7.

H. Ehrig et al. (Eds.): INT 2004, LNCS 3147, pp. 374–399, 2004.

these is, quoting [3]: *"What does an MSC specification mean: does it describe all behaviors of a system, or does it describe a set of sample behaviors of a system?"*.

In this paper we will provide an introduction to the Live Sequence Chart language, introduced by Damm and Harel in [4], as a conservative extension to the standard MSC language. In the first section, we will motivate the need for another visual formalism and describe the basic features of the LSC language informally. In the second section we will sketch the formal semantics of LSCs in terms of timed automata, and furthermore provide an idea of the relation between LSCs and a compatible reference system. The underlying complete syntax and rigorous semantics of the LSC language can be found in [5].

1.1   Shortcomings of Message Sequence Charts

Typically MSCs are used to capture sample scenarios corresponding to use-cases. While the system model becomes refined and conditions characterizing use-cases evolve, the intended interpretation often undergoes a metamorphosis from an *existential* to a *universal* view: earlier one wants to say that a condition can become true and that when true the scenario can happen, but later on one wants to say that if the condition characterizing the use-case indeed becomes true the system must adhere to the scenario described in the chart.

While the distinction between *mandatory* and *possible* behavior is one of the most urging deficiencies which needs to be addressed in order to construct semantically meaningful computerized tools for describing and analyzing use-cases and scenarios, the formal semantics for MSCs as described in [2] leave a good deal of questions beyond unanswered:

Existential or universal view. An MSC shows only one sample run of the system, one scenario, i.e. it is not possible to specify a mandatory protocol between the communicating entities.

Safety and Liveness properties. The MSC semantics offers no distinction, whether progress is enforced or not, i.e. The semantics in [2] only define permitted sequences of events; the occurrence of an event can not be enforced. Using the terms coined by Lamport in [6] MSCs can only express *safety* (nothing bad ever happens), but not *liveness* properties (something good will happen eventually).

Semantics of Conditions. Conditions in MSCs have no formal semantics. In the words of [2]: *"The semantics of a chart containing conditions is simply the semantics of the chart with the conditions deleted from it."*. This is obviously not the way to treat conditions from a more formal point of view.

Simultaneous events. MSCs do not allow more than one event to happen exactly at the same time, i.e. there is no notation of simultaneity.

Activation time. An MSC does not state explicitly when the behavior it describes should be observed, i.e. there is no indication of when the MSC should be activated during a system run.

Time treatment. The treatment of time is only rudimentary, since quantitative timing is not covered by the semantics, i.e. timer durations are ignored. Only the correct sequence of timer events, respectively intervals is enforced.

The LSC language as described in [5] is a extension to the MSC language which addresses these shortcomings and provides a fully worked out formal semantics. LSCs can therefore accomplish the requirements for the application to more advanced use cases like formal verification as discussed in the companion paper [7].

1.2   Basic LSC Features

This section presents the key elements of the Live Sequence Chart language. The basic idea of LSCs is to allow a distinction between *mandatory* and *possible* behavior, i.e. most LSC elements can be designated to belong to either one category or the other. This distinction is also expressed graphically, which contributes largely to the easy understanding of LSC specifications. Mandatory elements are depicted by solid lines, possible ones by dashed lines.

Instances and Messages. Instances and messages are the elementary building blocks of LSCs. The graphical representation for instances has been adopted from MSCs, i.e. LSC instances consist of an instance head carrying the instance name, an instance axis and an instance end, as the example LSC in figure 1 shows.

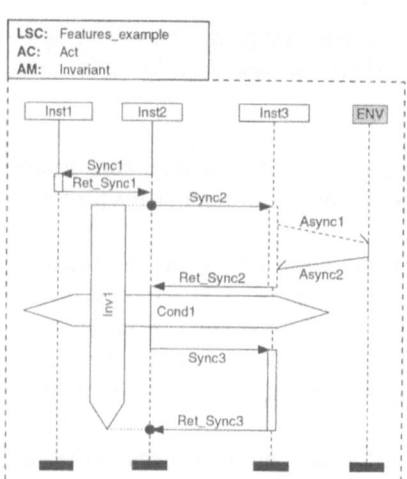

Fig. 1. Kernel LSC features example.

As for MSCs, the horizontal dimension is the structural dimension and the vertical dimension corresponds to the time dimension. Deviating from MSCs we depict the environment by an instance of its own rather than the border of the LSC. When using LSCs for formal verification, an explicit environment instance offers the possibility of expressing assumptions on the behavior of the environment within the LSC by employing the same elements as for the other instances.

Concerning messages we consider two kinds: asynchronous and instantaneous ones. Asynchronous messages are visualized by half stick arrows, instantaneous messages by arrows with solid heads, as shown in figure 1. Instantaneous messages have to be drawn horizontally to indicate simultaneity of sending and receiving, while asynchronous ones are drawn slanted to indicate the passage of time between sending and receipt.

Operation calls, are represented by two instantaneous messages: the method call and the return of the method call. For method calls in LSCs we require the return message to be stated explicitly, because otherwise confusion arises whether messages and other elements following a method call receipt are part of the method body. The pairing of operation call and return is indicated graphically by widening the instance axis on the receiver side into a thin rectangle which marks the operation body; see Sync2 and Ret_Sync2 in figure 1 for example.

Liveness and Temperatures. One deficiency of MSCs is their inability to enforce progress, as mentioned in section 1.1. LSCs overcome this drawback by associating a *temperature* with both locations[1] and messages. The temperature can be either *hot* or *cold*, the former indicating that progress is enforced. The analogy here is that one cannot remain at a hot location for an infinite amount of time, because then one would burn ones feet. This obviously requires that a hot location has to be left, i.e. the following location has to be reached. At a cold location one can stay forever without harming ones feet, i.e. the following location need not be reached. In terms of messages this means that a hot message has to be delivered, whereas a cold message may be lost along the way. Progress information is thus expressed by the temperatures of the messages and along the instance lines.

Graphically hot temperatures are represented by solid lines, cold ones by dashed lines. This means that e.g. a hot location is depicted by a solid instance axis segment, which starts at this location and ends either at the next cold location or the instance end. In figure 1 for example the location of the sending of message Sync2 is cold and the next location (the receipt of the return message) is hot, so that the instance axis segment in between them is dashed.

Conditions and Local Invariants. In order to make statements about the state of the system boolean conditions referring to attributes or data items of the involved entities are used. Graphically, conditions are represented as in MSCs by an elongated hexagon (cf. figure 1). Conditions also come in two variants: *mandatory* and *possible*. A mandatory condition must be satisfied, i.e. the boolean expression associated with it has to hold; violation of the condition is considered an error. Possible conditions do not generate an error when they are not satisfied, but merely constitute an exit from the enclosing LSC. Mandatory conditions are denoted by solid lines (e.g. Cond1 in figure 1) and possible ones by dashed lines.

Conditions constrain attributes or data items of entities at one point in time, but often it is desired to express validity of a condition over a period of time. This observation motivates the introduction of a fitting feature: *local invariants*, which come in two flavors: possible and mandatory, with the same interpretation as for conditions. Since local invariants cover a period of time, they need reference points for start and end and should thus always be bound to observable events. Graphically, local invariants are depicted by a condition symbol, which is rotated

---

[1] Locations are those points on an instance axis, where some event is attached, e.g. sending or receipt of a message, conditions, etc. In section 2.2 we give a formal definition of a location.

by 90°. A pointed end of the invariant symbol indicates the exclusion of the corresponding reference point while a planar end denotes the inclusion (e.g. in figure 1 the local invariant Inv1 includes message Sync2 but excludes message Ret_Sync3).

Simultaneous Regions and Coregions. We now have assembled all basic elements of our kernel LSC language. The default ordering of these basic elements is one after the other from top to bottom along the instance axis. Ordering between instances is induced only by messages and conditions ranging over more than one instance. *Simultaneous regions* allow to group several elements, which should be observed at the same time. This is essential for determining reference points for conditions, local invariants and timers. Graphically they are represented by enlarging the location in question into a small filled circle; see figure 1 for examples.

A coregion is used to indicate that no ordering is imposed on the events it contains, i.e. they may occur in any order. This corresponds to the classical MSC view of a coregion with the exception that – as a consequence of the simultaneous region construct – we also allow events in a coregion to take place simultaneously.

Coregions are represented graphically by a dotted line running in parallel to the instance axis. This differs from the representation in MSCs, where they are depicted as dashed portions of the instance axis.

Activation, Quantification, and Pre-charts. In the preceding paragraphs the graphical elements describing the communication behavior of several interacting entities are presented. This paragraph adds information about when this behavior should be observed and whether it specifies a sample behavior or a protocol to be obeyed, therefore addressing the primary criticism outlined before.

The quantification information represents the distinction between mandatory and possible behavior on the chart level. The sample-run or scenario view of MSCs, i.e. the interpretation that there *exists* a run, which fulfills the LSC, is covered by the possible mode, which we call *existential*. The mandatory mode, which is missing in MSCs as laid out in section 1.1, expresses that the behavior specified in the LSC must be fulfilled by *all* runs, for which reason it is called the *universal* view. Graphically, the quantification information is depicted by the border style of the LSC: a solid border indicates a universal chart, a dashed border an existential one.

For universal LSCs it is vital to be able to characterize the activation point. If every run has to fulfill the universal LSC, it must be possible to state at which point(s) of the run the LSC should be considered, otherwise the behavior of the entire system has to be specified in one LSC, which is clearly undesirable. The activation point of an LSC is characterized by two complementary concepts: *activation condition* and *activation mode*. The activation condition is a boolean condition, which expresses the activation point for a chart. The activation mode specifies, how often an LSC should be activated; the offered modes are *initial*, *invariant* and *iterative*. The initial mode indicates that the LSC is activated at system start only, i.e. it is intended to describe a start-up or initialization sequence. The other two modes indicate that the LSC is activated whenever the activation condition holds. The difference between an invariant and an iterative LSC is that the invariant mode allows a reactivation of the LSC while another incarnation of the same chart is still active, while the iterative mode allows only one incarnation of the chart at a time.

It turns out that activation condition and mode do not always sufficiently characterize the activation point of a property specification. Often it is necessary to know more about the history of a run, before being able to decide, whether the LSC should be activated. There may be e.g. more than one way for a run to arrive at a certain system state (characterized by a condition), but the LSC should only be activated, if the run has followed a specific "route". We are for instance only interested in activating an LSC, when no errors have occurred so far. This motivates the introduction of *pre-charts* which allow to specify a prefix of a run acting as a trigger for the actual LSC. Pre-charts allow to specify a prefix or history, which must be fulfilled by a run in order to activate the LSC. A pre-chart is essentially an LSC, i.e. all language constructs can be used in a pre-chart, but its semantics is different, since the message sequence of the pre-chart is not required to hold in the system, but rather must be observed before activating the actual LSC. Pre-charts do not replace the activation condition, but extend it; the activation condition in the presence of a pre-chart indicates the starting point of the prefix.

The informal semantics of an LSC with pre-chart is consequently: If the activation condition holds *and* afterwards the pre-chart is *completed*, then the LSC is activated.

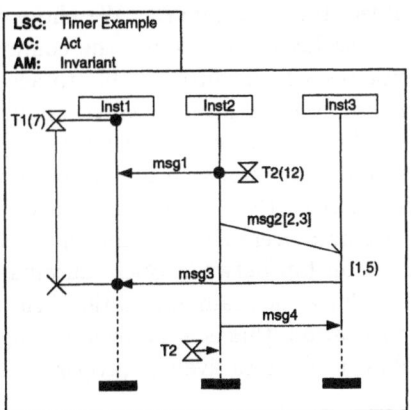

Fig. 2. Examples of LSC timing constraints.

Time. LSCs allow the specification of time constraints either in form of an MSC-style timer or in interval notation, with a lower and an upper bound. The graphical representation of timers is identical to the one given in MSC-96, i.e. the setting of a timer is represented by an hour glass symbol, which is annotated by a name and a duration and is connected to the instance axis by a simple line; a timeout symbol is represented by an hour glass symbol, which is connected to the instance axis by an arrow; a timer reset is represented by a ×-symbol, which is connected to the instance axis by a simple line; see figure 2 for examples.

Timing intervals express quantitative local liveness properties, since they refer to neighboring atoms[2]. They are used to give both a minimum and a

---

[2] Atoms are the most basic building blocks of an LSC, e.g. instance heads, instance ends, sending a message or receiving a message. In section 2.2 we give a formal definition of an atom.

maximum delay between two directly consecutive atoms. The delimiting atoms can either be located on the same instance axis, or be the sending and receipt of an asynchronous message. The intervals are placed next to the instance axis between the two locations which delimit them or are attached to the identifier of the constrained asynchronous message (cf. msg2 in figure 2).

2   Semantics of the LSC Language

The semantics for the behavior of an LSC is defined in terms of a symbolic timed Büchi automaton in [5]. The procedure of deriving an automaton from an LSC, which is called *unwinding*, is inspired by the semantics definition for Symbolic Timing Diagrams presented in [8], which has been taken as a blue print for the first version of the LSC semantics in [4].

Before describing the the unwinding procedure we introduce timed Büchi automata and define the formal syntax of LSC elements, which is the starting point for the translation from an LSC into a timed symbolic automaton.

2.1   Automata-Theoretic Foundation

The base for the definition of the formal semantics of LSCs is a variation of timed Büchi automata. We chose Büchi automata for several reasons: First, we use LSCs to describe the communication behavior of reactive systems, i.e. systems which must be able to accept and react to input signals at any time. These systems are typically designed to operate forever, at least theoretically, which means that runs of reactive systems are infinite. Therefore classical finite automata are not sufficient for our purpose. Büchi automata ([9]) are one possible solution as they accept infinite words. The second reason for choosing Büchi automata over other variants of automata on infinite words is that there is a close relationship between Büchi automata and linear time temporal logic (LTL) [9, 10]. Since the main application field for LSCs is property specification for formal verification, this is a major advantage. The third reason is that Büchi automata allow to express liveness properties easily via their acceptance criterion.

Timed Büchi Automata. The acceptance criterion for Büchi automata (and other automata on infinite words) needs to take the infiniteness of the words into account. Informally an infinite word is accepted by a Büchi automaton if its run passes infinitely often through (at least) one of the accepting states of the automaton; these states are also called *fair* states.

When the occurrence times of the letters of words are important, timed languages are used and consequently a corresponding type of automaton is needed: a timed Büchi automaton. For the definition of timed Büchi automata we loosely follow the lead of [11] here, inasmuch as we associate an occurrence time to each symbol of a word, yielding timed words. In contrast to [11], however, we only consider discrete time instead of dense time. Time is represented by a sequence of time values from the set of non-negative natural numbers: $\tau_i \in \mathbb{N}$, which has to satisfy two constraints: time is non-decreasing and time always progresses:

Definition 1 (Timed Word). *A time sequence $\tau = \tau_0 \tau_1 \tau_2 \ldots$ is an infinite sequence of time values $\tau_i \in \mathbb{N}$ for which the following holds:*

1. *$\tau_i \leq \tau_{i+1}, \forall i \geq 0$ (τ is monotonically increasing)*
2. *$\forall t \in \mathbb{N} \; \exists i \geq 1 : \tau_i > t$ (time always progresses)*

A timed word over an alphabet Σ is then a pair (σ, τ), where $\sigma = \sigma_0 \sigma_1 \ldots$ is an infinite word and $\tau = \tau_0 \tau_1 \ldots$ is a time sequence. The time value τ_i denotes the occurrence time of input symbol σ_i.

In the untimed case the behavior of the automaton only depends on the input symbols, i.e. being in some state the next states of an automaton are determined by the current input symbol. In order for an automaton to also accept timed words it needs a means to count time, since the choice of the next states also depends on the occurrence time of the input symbols in question. This is realized by *clocks*, which can be set to zero on any transition of the automaton and count the time since their last reset. This allows for the introduction of clock constraints on transitions – i.e. a transition may only be taken, if all its clock constraints are satisfied – forcing the input word to obey certain timing requirements. Thus time is introduced into an automaton by adding a (finite) set of clocks and augmenting transitions by clock resets and clock constraints formulated over this set of clocks.

In the following the definition of a timed Büchi automaton, the set of clocks used in the clock constraints of the automaton is added and the transitions between states are augmented by clock resets and constraints. The acceptance criterion is adjusted accordingly, so that fair states are defined in terms of timed words.

Definition 2 (Timed Büchi Automaton). *A timed Büchi automaton $\mathcal{TBA}$ is a tuple*

$$\mathcal{TBA} := (\Sigma, Q, q_0, C, \longrightarrow, F), \text{ where}$$

- *Σ is a finite alphabet of input symbols,*
- *Q is a finite set of states,*
- *$q_0 \in Q$ is the initial state,*
- *C is a finite set of clocks*
- *$\longrightarrow \subseteq Q \times \Sigma \times \mathcal{P}(C) \times \Phi(C) \times Q$ is the transition relation. A transition $(q, \sigma, \rho, \gamma, q') \in \longrightarrow$ represents the change from state q to state q' on input symbol σ. The set $\rho \in \mathcal{P}(C)$ indicates which clocks are reset when taking the transition, the set $\Phi(C)$ is the set of clock constraints over C and $\gamma \in \Phi(C)$ is a clock constraint over C, which has to be fulfilled.*
- *$F \subseteq Q$ is the set of fair (accepting) states.*

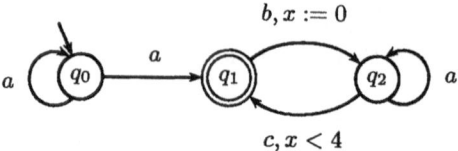

Fig. 3. Example timed Büchi automaton.

Let $(\sigma, \tau) = (\sigma_0, \tau_0)(\sigma_1, \tau_1) \ldots$ be a timed word over Σ. A timed run tr of a timed Büchi automaton $\mathcal{TBA}$ over timed word (σ, τ) is an infinite sequence of configurations q_i, ν_i, where $q_i \in Q$ is the i-th state of the automaton along the run and $\nu_i \in I$ is the clock interpretation in this state:

$$tr : (q_0, \nu_0) \xrightarrow[\tau_0]{\sigma_0} (q_1, \nu_1) \xrightarrow[\tau_1]{\sigma_1} (q_2, \nu_2) \xrightarrow[\tau_2]{\sigma_2} \ldots, \quad with$$

- *$\forall x \in C : \nu_0(x) = 0$, (initially all clocks are zero)*
- *$\forall i \geq 0 \exists (q_i, \sigma_i, \rho_i, \gamma_i, q_{i+1}) \in \longrightarrow : [\![\gamma_i]\!](\nu_i) = true \wedge \forall x \in \rho_i : \nu_{i+1}(x) = 0 \wedge \forall x \notin \rho_i : \nu_{i+1}(x) = \nu_i(x) + \tau_i - \tau_{i-1}$*
  (the target state of each transition is the source state of the following transition, the transition respects all its clock constraints, resets all appropriate clocks and all clocks, which are not reset, correctly advance the time).

Let $inf(tr) \subseteq Q$ denote the set of states of $\mathcal{TBA}$ which are visited infinitely often by timed run tr, i.e. $inf(tr)$ consists of those states $q \in Q$ such that $q = q_i$ for infinitely many $i \geq 0$. The language accepted by $\mathcal{TBA}$ is defined as the set of timed words, for which there is an accepting run of $\mathcal{TBA}$:

$$\mathcal{L}(\mathcal{TBA}) := \{(\sigma, \tau) \mid \exists tr = (q_0, \nu_0) \xrightarrow[\tau_0]{\sigma_0} (q_1, \nu_1) \xrightarrow[\tau_1]{\sigma_1} \cdots : inf(tr) \cap F \neq \emptyset\}$$

Example 1. Figure 3 shows an example of a timed Büchi automaton, which accepts the language $\{(\sigma, \tau) \mid \sigma \in a^+(ba^*c)^\omega \wedge \forall i \exists j > i : \sigma_i = b \Rightarrow \sigma_j = c \wedge \tau_j < \tau_i + 4\}$.

Symbolic Timed Automata. The timed Büchi automata described so far operate on single input symbols only, since they allow but one element of Σ per transition. In order to be able to describe the communication behavior of a system, it is necessary to allow more than one observation at a time.

Symbolic Timing Diagrams (STDs) faced a similar problem, which in [8] is solved by the extension of Büchi automata to *symbolic automata*, where a run is extended to a *computation sequence* referring to valuations of system variables and formulas are allowed as transition annotations in the automaton. We adopt this strategy for the LSC semantics definition and therefore use symbolic automata.

In [8] Schlör does not consider quantitative timing for STDs, so that symbolic automata are untimed. We consequently extend the definition of symbolic automata to also encompass (discrete) time, similar to timed Büchi automata. First, we extend the notion of a timed word to a timed symbolic word (called a computation sequence in [8]).

Definition 3 (Timed Symbolic Word).
Let AP be the set of atomic propositions. A symbolic word is an infinite sequence $\theta = \theta_0 \theta_1 \theta_2 \dots$, where $\theta_i : AP \longrightarrow \mathbb{B}$ is a valuation, which assigns to each $v \in AP$ a boolean value. Let τ be a time sequence. A timed symbolic word then is a pair $(\theta, \tau) = (\theta_0, \tau_0)(\theta_1, \tau_1)(\theta_2, \tau_2) \dots$, where τ_i denotes the occurrence time of valuation θ_i.

In order to refer to the occurrence of several communication events it is necessary to extend the timed Büchi automata to allow formulas:

Definition 4 (Formula over AP). *Let AP be a set of atomic propositions. A formula ψ over AP is a boolean expression produced by the following rules:*

$$psi := \sigma \mid \psi \mid \neg\psi \mid \psi_1 \wedge \psi_2 \mid \psi_1 \vee \psi_2 \text{ , with } \sigma \in AP.$$

The set of all formulas over AP is denoted by $BExpr_{AP}$.

We can now define in extension of definition 2 on page 381 a timed symbolic automaton:

Definition 5 ((Non-deterministic) Timed Symbolic Automaton).
A timed symbolic automaton $\mathcal{TSA}$ is a tuple

$$\mathcal{TSA} := (AP, Q, q_0, C, \longrightarrow, F), \text{ where}$$

- *AP is a finite alphabet of input symbols (atomic propositions),*
- *Q is a finite set of states,*
- *$q_0 \in Q$ is the initial state,*
- *C is a finite set of clocks*
- *$\longrightarrow \subseteq Q \times BExpr_{AP} \times \mathcal{P}(C) \times \Phi(C) \times Q$ is the transition relation. A transition $(q, \psi, \rho, \gamma, q') \in \longrightarrow$ represents the change from state q to state q' while satisfying formula ψ. The set $\rho \in \mathcal{P}(C)$ indicates which clocks are reset when taking the transition, the set $\Phi(C)$ is the set of clock constraints over C and $\gamma \in \Phi(C)$ is a clock constraint over C, which has to be fulfilled.*
- *$F \subseteq Q$ is the set of fair states.*

A timed run tsr of a timed symbolic automaton $\mathcal{TSA}$ over a timed symbolic word (θ, τ) is an infinite sequence of configurations (q_i, ν_i), where $q_i \in Q$ is the i-th state of the automaton along the run, $\nu_i \in I$ is the clock interpretation in this state:

$$tsr : (q_0, \nu_0) \xrightarrow[\tau_0]{\theta_0} (q_1, \nu_1) \xrightarrow[\tau_1]{\theta_1} (q_2, \nu_2) \xrightarrow[\tau_2]{\theta_2} \dots, with$$

- *$\forall x \in C : \nu_0(x) = 0$, (initially all clocks are zero)*

- $\forall i \geq 0 \exists (q_i, \psi_i, \rho_i, \gamma_i, q_{i+1}) \in \longrightarrow: \theta_i \models \psi_i \wedge [\![\gamma_i]\!](\nu_i) = true \wedge \forall x \in \rho_i :$
  $\nu_{i+1}(x) = 0 \wedge \forall x \notin \rho_i : \nu_{i+1}(x) = \nu_i(x) + \tau_i - \tau_{i-1}$
  (the target state of each transition is the source state of the following transition, the boolean expression annotating the transition is evaluated to true,
  the transition respects all its clock constraints, resets all appropriate clocks
  and all clocks, which are not reset, correctly advance the time).

Let $inf(tsr) \subseteq Q$ denote the set of states of $\mathcal{TSA}$ which are visited infinitely
often by timed run tsr, i.e. $inf(tsr)$ consists of those states $q \in Q$ such that
$q = q_i$ for infinitely many $i \geq 0$. The language accepted by $\mathcal{TSA}$ is defined as:

$$\mathcal{L}(\mathcal{TSA}) := \{(\theta, \tau) \mid \exists \ tsr = q_0 \xrightarrow[\tau_0]{\theta_0} q_1 \xrightarrow[\tau_1]{\theta_1} q_2 \xrightarrow[\tau_2]{\theta_2} \cdots : inf(tsr) \cap F \neq \emptyset\}$$

2.2 LSC Syntax

In order to introduce the unwinding procedure we define the formal syntax of
LSC elements, which is the starting point for the translation from an LSC into
a timed symbolic automaton.

  An LSC consists of several components: the body of the LSC – i.e. the instances and events defined on it —, the activation condition and mode, the quantification and the pre-chart While the complete LSC Syntax is defined in [5], the
focus in the remainder of this section is on the body of the LSC.

Definition 6 (LSC). *An LSC is a tuple*

$$L = (l, ac, pch, amode, quant)$$

*with 'l' the body of the LSC, 'ac' the activation condition, 'pch' the pre-chart,
$amode \in \{initial, invariant, iterative\}$ the activation mode and $quant \in \{existen-
tial, universal\}$ the quantification.*

  An LSC body consists of a number of instances, which are collected in the
set $Inst(l)$. In the following let l denote the body of an LSC L, and let $i \in
Inst(l)$ denote some instance of l. The basic blocks (*atoms*) of which an LSC
body is comprised are the following: *instance heads, instance ends, sending a
message, receiving a message, condition atom* (local to one instance), *start of a
local invariant* and *end of a local invariant*.

  The atoms carry the progress information of each instance (cf. section 2.3)
and are organized according to their positioning on the instance axes. The atoms
are thus instance-wise collected in sets:

$$Msgsnd(i), Msgrcv(i) : \text{sets of message send/receive atoms}$$
$$Conds(i) : \text{set of condition atoms}^3$$
$$LI\_starts(i), LI\_ends(i) : \text{sets of start/end atoms of local invariants}$$

  There is only one instance head atom, denoted by $\perp_i$, and one instance end
atom, denoted by $\top_i$, for each instance i, so that it is not necessary to have

sets for these atoms on the instance level. Collecting all atoms of the LSC body according to type yields the following sets:

$$Instheads(l) := \cup_{i \in Inst(l)} \{\bot_i\}, \;\; Instends(l) := \cup_{i \in Inst(l)} \{\top_i\},$$
$$Msgsnd(l) := \cup_{i \in Inst(l)} Msgsnd(i), \;\; Msgrcv(l) := \cup_{i \in Inst(l)} Msgrcv(i),$$
$$Conds(l) := \cup_{i \in Inst(l)} Conds(i),$$
$$LI\_starts(l) := \cup_{i \in Inst(l)} LI\_starts(i), \;\; LI\_ends(l) := \cup_{i \in Inst(l)} LI\_ends(i)$$

Collecting all atoms of an instance, resp. of the entire body yields the sets:

$$Atoms(i) := \{\bot_i\} \cup Msgsnd(i) \cup Msgrcv(i) \cup Conds(i)$$
$$\cup \; LI\_starts(i) \cup LI\_ends(i) \cup \{\top_i\}$$
$$Atoms(l) := Instheads(l) \cup Msgsnd(l) \cup Msgrcv(l) \cup Conds(l)$$
$$\cup \; LI\_starts(l) \cup LI\_ends(l) \cup Instends(l)$$

The atoms of each instance are ordered from top to bottom as drawn in the LSC[4] and thus have a graphical position, given by the function $position(a)$ for $a \in Atoms(i)$.

Definition 7 (Atom Position). *Let $a, a', a'' \in Atoms(i)$ and $a \prec_i a'$ denote the order of a and a' as drawn on instance i. The function $position(\cdot)$ assigns a natural number to each atom $a \in Atoms(l)$ of LSC body l. This number is called position of a.*

$$position : Atoms(l) \longrightarrow \mathbb{N}_0$$

$$position(a) := \begin{cases} 0 & if \; \forall a' \neq a : a' \not\prec_i a \\ 1 + position(a') & if \; a' \prec_i a \wedge \neg \exists a'' \in Atoms(i) : \\ & \qquad a' \prec_i a'' \prec_i a \end{cases}$$

Remark 1 (Atom Positions). The definition of the position of an atom does not assign a unique number to each atom, but allows several atoms of one instance to share one position. This is necessary in order to correctly describe simultaneous regions (see below), which are characterized by the fact that more than one atom occupies the same position.

Atoms $a \in Atoms(i)$ are grouped into *clusters*, which are characterized by the fact that all atoms contained in them are observed simultaneously and therefore have the same position. This concept is needed to express simultaneous regions.

---

[3] Note that a condition atom is local to one instance. A condition shared by several instances consists of one condition atom on each participating instance.

[4] This total order can be disrupted by a coregion as discussed later.

Definition 8 (Cluster). *The set of clusters of an instance $i \in Inst(l)$ is defined by the maximal set*

$$Clusters(i) := \{cl \subseteq Atoms(i) \mid \forall a, a' \in cl : \; position(a) = position(a')\}.$$

The set of clusters of an LSC body l is defined by

$$Clusters(l) := \bigcup_{i \in Inst(l)} Clusters(i).$$

The position function is extended to cover clusters as well:

$$position(cl) := position(a), a \in cl, cl \in Clusters(l).$$

Remark 2 (Clusters). Note that each atom is contained in exactly one cluster, but that each cluster may contain several atoms. The latter case only arises, if the cluster corresponds to a simultaneous region; atoms outside of a simultaneous region result in a singleton cluster.

The clusters on each instance as defined so far are totally ordered; as introduced in chapter 1.2, coregions allow to suspend this total order. A coregion cr is thus a set of unordered clusters and contains all those clusters, which are covered by the dotted line next to the instance axis. Each coregion consists of a set of unordered clusters: $cr := \{cl_1, \ldots, cl_n\} \subseteq Clusters(i)$. The set of all coregions of instance i is given by $Coregions(i)$ and the set of all coregions of an LSC body l by $Coregions(l)$. For each cluster $cl \in Cluster(l)$ we define the function $coreg(cl)$, which returns the coregion cl is part of:

$$coreg(cl) := \begin{cases} \emptyset & , \text{if } \neg \exists cr \in Coregions(l) : cl \in cr \\ cr & , \text{else} \end{cases}$$

The position does not reflect the relaxed ordering requirement imposed by a coregion: the sending of msg3 and the receipt of msg4 on Inst1 in figure 4 on the facing page are still ordered according to their positions. In order to correctly capture the coregion semantics a *logical* position, called *location* is needed:

Definition 9 (Location). *The location of a cluster $cl \in Clusters(i)$ is given by the function*

$$location(cl) := \begin{cases} position(cl), & if \; coreg(cl) = \emptyset \\ min(\{position(cl_i) \mid cl_i \in coreg(cl)\}), & if \; coreg(cl) \neq \emptyset \end{cases}$$

$Locations(i) := \{ location(cl) \mid cl \in Clusters(i)\}$ *is the set of locations of instance i and $Locations(l) := \bigcup_{i \in Inst(l)} Locations(i)$ the set of all locations of LSC body l.*

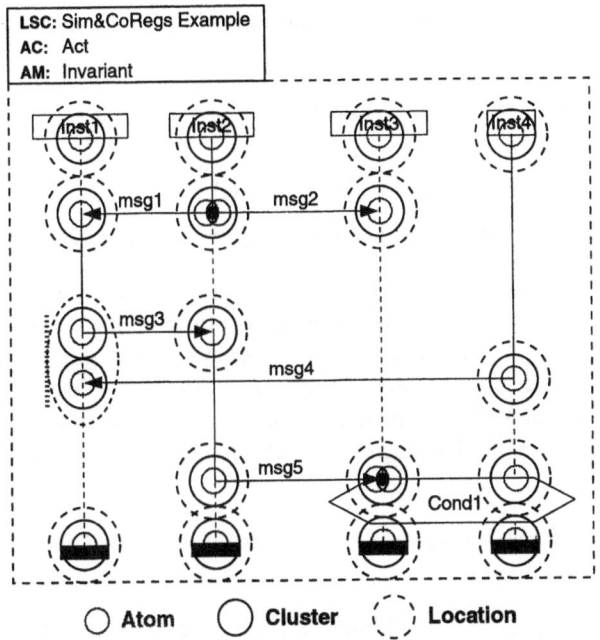

Fig. 4. The Sim&Coregs Example LSC with highlighted atoms, clusters and locations.

Remark 3 (Locations). The locations are unique only on one instance, since *location*(·) relies on *position*(·). The location of a cluster which is not part of a coregion is equal to its position and unique on its instance. All clusters in a coregion share the same location but have different positions. While Clusters on instances without coregions are totally ordered, Clusters on instances with coregions are only partially ordered.

Example 2 (Locations). Figure 4 illustrates the location concept. Notice that the location of a cluster is identical to its position, except for clusters in coregions. All clusters in the coregion share one location.

The atoms introduced above are local to one instance. In order to be able to refer to the graphical elements used in the LSC it is necessary to establish the connection between atoms, which belong to the same LSC element but are located on different instances. Each message e.g. is made up of two atoms, the send and the receive atom, which are located on different instances. Likewise, conditions, which involve more than one instance are comprised by one condition atom on each participating instance. The relation between such atoms is established by the identifier, which designates the graphical element. For an LSC body l there are the following disjunct sets of unique identifiers: *Instances*(l) the set of instance identifiers in l, *Messages*(l) the set of message identifiers in l, *Conditions*(l) the set of condition identifiers in l, *Local_Invariants*(l) the set of identifiers of local invariants in l. The following functions associate an atom with its identifier:

$$instID : Inst(l) \longrightarrow Instances(l)$$
$$msgID : Msgsnd(l) \cup Msgrcv(l) \longrightarrow Messages(l)$$
$$condID : Conds(l) \longrightarrow Conditions(l)$$
$$liID : LI\_starts(l) \cup LI\_ends(l) \longrightarrow Local\_Invariants(l)$$

The identification of the send and receive part of a message is achieved by the $msgID(\cdot)$ function. In the transition annotations of the automaton generated from an LSC body (cf. section 2.3) it is necessary to distinguish send and receive atoms, therefore the set of message labels $MsgLabels(l)$ is introduced, including the function $msgLabel(m)$, which associates a message label with each $m \in Msgsnd(l) \cup Msgrcv(l)$. Sending of message $m1$ is represented by the label $!m1$, receipt by $?m1$.

$$msgLabel : Msgsnd(l) \cup Msgrcv(l) \longrightarrow MsgLabels(l)$$

$$msgLabel(m) := \begin{cases} !msgID(m) & \text{if } m \in Msgsnd(l) \\ ?msgID(m) & \text{if } m \in Msgrcv(l) \end{cases}$$

Furthermore it is necessary to access the properties of messages, conditions and local invariants. For messages the relevant properties are temperature and type (instantaneous or asynchronous), for conditions and local invariants the mode (mandatory or possible). The progress information along each instance is associated with the atoms of this instance, so that the domain of function $temp(\cdot)$ below is the union of message identifiers and atoms. The properties for messages and conditions on the other hand pertain to the LSC elements, represented by the corresponding identifiers, and not the atoms. The situation for the mode of local invariants is identical to that of conditions, i.e. this information is tied to the LSC element.

$$temp : Messages(l) \cup Atoms(l) \longrightarrow \{hot, cold\}$$
$$sync\_type : Messages(l) \longrightarrow \{async, instant\}$$
$$mode : Conditions(l) \cup Local\_Invariants(l) \longrightarrow \{mandatory, possible\}$$

2.3   LSC Semantics

In this section we define the semantics of an LSC in terms of the language accepted by an automaton which is generated from the LSC. We first construct a proto-automaton called *unwinding structure* from the LSC body, which is then completed into a symbolic timed automaton (cf. section 2.1). The semantics of the LSC language in terms of a thorough description of the unwinding algorithm is defined in [5].

The central idea is to define a *cut* through the LSC starting at the top and moving this cut downward until we reach all instance ends, while respecting the partial order imposed by the LSC. Cuts become states in the automaton and the transition relation of the automaton encodes the successor relation among the cuts. Ordering among the atoms in an LSC is induced by the following rules:

1. atoms (clusters) along each instance axis are totally ordered (unless they are part of a coregion)
2. a message has to be sent before it can be received
3. conditions ranging over several instances (*shared conditions*) enforce synchronization between the involved instances

In order to be unwound an LSC element has to be *enabled*. An atom is enabled when:

1. all its predecessors along the instance axis have already be unwound
2. the corresponding message send atom has already been unwound (if the atom is a message receive atom of an asynchronous message) or is being unwound simultaneously (if the atom is part of an instantaneous message)
3. all other condition atoms belonging to the same condition are also enabled (if the atom is a shared condition)

The first condition demands a computation of all predecessors on the instance axis for each atom. It is actually sufficient to only conduct a local computation of the *immediate* predecessor of each atom, since this relation is transitive: If the immediate predecessor of a cluster cl has been unwound, then immediate predecessor of cl must have been unwound, and so on. The formal definition of the function computing the immediate predecessor is:

Definition 10 (Immediate Predecessor).

$$predecessor : Clusters(i) \longrightarrow \mathcal{P}(Clusters(i))$$

$$predecessor(cl) := \begin{cases} \emptyset & , if \, \exists \, a \in cl : a = \bot_i \vee a = \top_i \\ CL & , else \end{cases} , where$$

$$CL := \{cl' \in Clusters(i) \mid location(cl') < location(cl) \wedge \neg \exists \, cl'' \in Clusters(i) :$$
$$location(cl') < location(cl'') < location(cl) \}$$

The function *predecessor*(cl) looks along one instance for the location, which is immediately above the cluster cl and returns the clusters bound to that location. If the element bound to the predecessor location is not a coregion, the returned set of clusters contains a single cluster. Otherwise all clusters of the coregion are returned. For clusters containing instance head or end atoms no predecessor is returned, since an instance head does not have a predecessor and instance end atoms are not unwound by the algorithm (see below).

The second and third rule above involve more than one instance and thus require to also take clusters of other instances into account. The message send and receive atom for an instantaneous message have to be unwound simultaneously, and all condition atoms of a condition must be unwound at the same time. This synchronization of clusters is expressed by the relation $\approx$.

Definition 11 (Equivalence of Clusters). *Let* $cl, cl' \in Clusters(l)$. *The relation* $\approx$ *on* $Clusters(l)$ *is defined as:*

$$cl \approx cl' \Leftrightarrow \exists\, a \in cl\ \exists\, a' \in cl' :$$
$$cl = cl' \vee sharedConds(a, a')\ \vee instMsgs(a, a')$$
$$\vee\ transitivity(a, a')$$

where

$$sharedConds(a, a') := a, a' \in Conds(l)\ \wedge\ condID(a) = condID(a')$$
$$instMsgs(a, a') := a \in Msgsnd(l)\ \wedge\ a' \in Msgrcv(l)$$
$$\wedge\ msgID(a) = msgID(a')$$
$$\wedge\ sync\_type(msgID(a)) = instant$$
$$transitivity(a, a') := a, a' \in syncAtoms(l)$$
$$\wedge\, \exists cl'' \in Clusters(l)\ \exists a_i, a_j \in cl'' : |cl''| > 1$$
$$\wedge\, (sharedConds(a, a_i) \vee instMsgs(a, a_i))$$
$$\vee\, (sharedConds(a', a_j) \vee instMsgs(a', a_j))$$
$$syncAtoms(l) := \{a \in Atoms(l) | a \in Conds(l)\ \vee$$
$$(a \in Msgsnd(l)\ \vee\ a \in Msgrcv(l))$$
$$\wedge\ sync\_type(msgID(a)) = instant\}$$

The classes defined by $\approx$ *are called simultaneous classes.* $SimClasses(l) := \{\, scl\ \subseteq\ Clusters(l)\ |\ \forall\ cl, cl' \in scl : cl \approx cl'\ \}$ *is the set of simultaneous classes of* l.

The simultaneous classes are the basic elements, which the unwinding algorithm operates. Similar to the case for clusters it is necessary to determine whether it is the predecessor(s) of a simultaneous class in order to determine, if it is enabled or not. This gives rise to the definition of the function $prerequisite(\cdot)$, which uses the $predecessor(\cdot)$ function defined for clusters:

Definition 12 (Simultaneous Class Prerequisite).

$$prerequisite : SimClasses(l) \longrightarrow \mathcal{P}(SimClasses(l))$$

$$prerequisite(scl) := \begin{cases} \emptyset & , if\ \exists\ cl \in scl : \exists a \in cl : a \in Instheads(l) \\ SCL & , else \end{cases}, where$$

$$SCL := \{scl' \in Sim\_Classes(l) \,|$$
$$\exists cl \in scl\ \exists cl' \in scl' : (cl' \in predecessor(cl)\ \vee$$
$$\exists a \in cl\ \exists a' \in cl' : a \in Msgrcv(l)\ \wedge$$
$$a' \in Msgsnd(l)\ \wedge msgID(a) = msgID(a')\ \wedge$$
$$sync\_type(msgID(a)) = async)\}$$

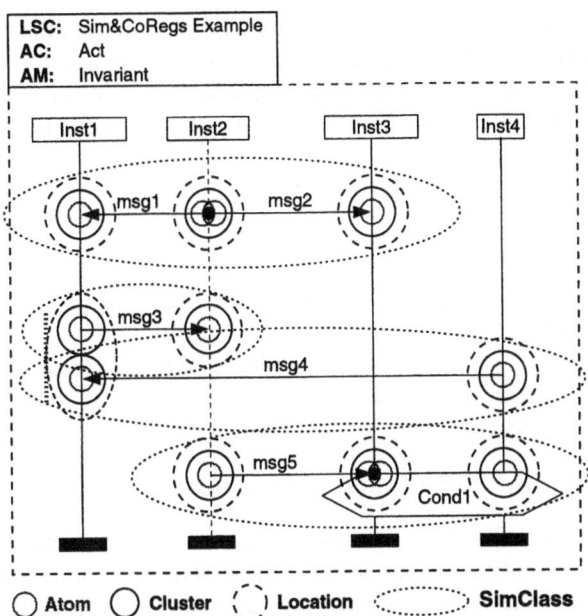

Fig. 5. The `Sim&Coregs Example` LSC with highlighted atoms, clusters, locations and SimClasses.

The *prerequisite*(·) function is similar to the *predecessor*(·) function. It looks for the immediate predecessors of all clusters contained in the considered simultaneous class and collects the simultaneous classes for all predecessor clusters. If the current simultaneous class contains an asynchronous message receive atom, the simultaneous class containing the corresponding message send atom is added as well. It returns the empty set, if the considered simultaneous class contains an instance head atom.

Example 3 (Simultaneous classes). Figure 5 illustrates the concepts of positions, clusters, locations and SimClasses. We have omitted the SimClasses for instance heads and ends for readability's sake.

A *cut* through the LSC is used to keep track of the progress of the unwinding procedure. It represents the borderline between already unwound elements and those which still have to be considered. The elements directly below the cut are those, which are currently enabled. Cuts are represented by a tuple containing one cluster of each instance:

Definition 13 (Cut). *A cut* $Cut \subseteq Clusters(i_1) \times \cdots \times Clusters(i_n)$, *for* $Inst(l) = \{i_1, \ldots, i_n\}$ *is a tuple* $(cl_{i_1}, \ldots, cl_{i_n})$, $cl_{i_j} \in Clusters(i_j)$, $1 \leq j \leq n = |Inst(l)|$.

Let $Cuts(l)$ *be the set of all possible cuts of LSC body* l.

The unwinding algorithm requires a number of other auxiliary sets and constructs, which are collected in a tuple called *phase*. Each phase characterizes one unwinding step and consequently corresponds to a state in the resulting automaton. Possible transitions from one phase to another correspond to transitions of the automaton.

Definition 14 (Phase). *A phase is a tuple Phase := (Ready, History, Cut), with*

- *$History \subseteq SimClasses(l)$: the set of simultaneous classes which have already been unwound*
- *$Ready \subseteq SimClasses(l)$: the set of simultaneous classes, which are currently enabled to be unwound*
- *Cut : the current cut.*

Let $Phases(l)$ be the set of all phases of LSC body l.

Since several simultaneous classes may be enabled concurrently, e.g. due to a coregion, each ready set may contain more than one simultaneous class. In this case all combinations of elements of the ready set lead to valid successor phases and thus have to be taken into consideration. All possible combinations correspond to the powerset of the ready set; the set of simultaneous classes, which is currently chosen to be unwound, is called the *fired set* $Fired \subseteq \mathcal{P}(SimClasses(l))$. Thus, for each phase $Phase_i$ there exist k fired sets $Fired_{i_k}$, with $k = |\mathcal{P}(Ready_i)|$. Let $Firedsets(l)$ be the set of all fired sets in l.

The unwinding algorithm starts at the top of the LSC body and computes the initial phase $Phase_0$, which is given by

$$Phase_0 = (Ready_0, History_0, Cut_0), \text{ with}$$
$$Ready_0 := \Big\{ scl \in SimClasses(l) \mid prerequisite(scl) \in$$
$$\{\mathcal{P}(\{scl' \in SimClasses(l) \mid \forall cl \in scl' : \forall a \in cl :$$
$$a \in (Instheads(l) \cup LI\_starts(l))\}) \setminus \emptyset \Big\}$$
$$History_0 := \{\cup_{i \in Inst(l)}\{\{\bot_i\}\}\}$$
$$Cut_0 := (\{\bot_1\}, \dots, \{\bot_n\})$$

Starting with the initial phase the construction of the automaton considers every phase and computes the fired set(s) for it. For each phase a state is generated in the automaton and for each fired set of the current phase the successor phase is computed and the corresponding state is generated. For each fired set a transition is inserted, which is annotated with the simultaneous class(es) of the fired set. The successor phases for a phase is computed by the function $Step(\cdot, \cdot)$:

Definition 15 (Step).

$$Step : Phases(l) \times Firedsets(l) \longrightarrow Phases(l)$$

$$Step(Phase_i, Fired_{i_k}) = Phase_j$$

where

$$History_j := History_i \cup Fired_{i_k}$$
$$Ready_j := \{scl \in SimClasses(l) \setminus \{\cup_{i \in Inst(l)} \{\{\top_i\}\}\} \mid$$
$$\forall scl' \in prerequisite(scl) : scl' \in History_j \wedge scl \notin History_i\}$$
$$Cut_j := (cl'_1, \ldots, cl'_n), \ with$$
$$cl'_t = \begin{cases} cl''_t & \exists f \in Fired_{i_k} \ \exists scl \in f : cl''_t \in scl \\ cl_t & else \end{cases}, for \ t = 1, \ldots, n$$

The $Step(\cdot, \cdot)$ function is applied to all phases until the entire LSC body has been unwound, i.e. until the final phase is reached:

$$Phase_{final} = (Ready_{final}, History_{final}, Cut_{final}), \ with$$
$$Ready_{final} := \emptyset$$
$$History_{final} := SimClasses(l) \setminus \{\cup_{i \in Inst(l)} \{\{\top_i\}\}\}$$

Example 4 (Primitive unwinding structure). Application of the $Step(\cdot, \cdot)$ function to the LSC in figure 5 on page 391 results in the (incomplete) automata shown in figure 6 on the next page. The sets of the corresponding phases are listed in the following:

$q_0 : History_0 = \{\{\{\bot_{Inst1}\}\}, \{\{\bot_{Inst2}\}\}, \{\{\bot_{Inst3}\}\}, \{\{\bot_{Inst4}\}\}\}$
$\quad Cut_0 = (\{\bot_{Inst1}\}, \{\bot_{Inst2}\}, \{\bot_{Inst3}\}, \{\bot_{Inst4}\})$
$\quad Ready_0 = \{\{\{?msg1\}, \{!msg1, !msg2\}, \{?msg2\}\}\}$
$q_1 : History_1 = History_0 \cup \{\{\{?msg1\}, \{!msg1, !msg2\}, \{?msg2\}\}\}$
$\quad Cut_1 = (\{?msg1\}, \{!msg1, !msg2\}, \{?msg2\}, \{\bot_4\})$
$\quad Ready_1 = \{\{\{!msg3\}, \{?msg3\}\}, \{\{?msg4\}, \{!msg4\}\}\}$
$q_2 : History_2 = History_1 \cup \{\{\{!msg3\}, \{?msg3\}\}\}$
$\quad Cut_2 = (\{!msg3\}, \{?msg3\}, \{?msg2\}, \{\bot_4\})$
$\quad Ready_2 = \{\{\{?msg4\}, \{!msg4\}\}\}$
$q_3 : History_3 = History_1 \cup \{\{\{!msg4\}, \{?msg4\}\}\}$
$\quad Cut_3 = (\{?msg4\}, \{!msg1, !msg2\}, \{?msg2\}, \{!msg4\})$
$\quad Ready_3 = \{\{\{?msg3\}, \{!msg3\}\}\}$
$q_4 : History_4 = History_2 \cup \{\{\{!msg4\}, \{?msg4\}\}\}$
$\quad Cut_4 = (\{?msg4\}, \{?msg3\}, \{?msg2\}, \{!msg4\})$
$\quad Ready_4 = \{\{\{!msg5\}, \{?msg5, cond1\}\}\}$
$q_5 : History_5 = History_1 \cup \{\{\{!msg3\}, \{?msg3\}\}, \{\{!msg4\}, \{?msg4\}\}\}$
$\quad Cut_5 = (\{!msg3, ?msg4\}, \{?msg3\}, \{?msg2\}, \{!msg4\})$
$\quad Ready_5 = \{\{\{!msg5\}, \{?msg5, cond1\}\}\}$
$q_6 : History_6 = History_3 \cup \{\{\{!msg3\}, \{?msg3\}\}\}$
$\quad Cut_6 = (\{!msg3\}, \{?msg3\}, \{?msg2\}, \{!msg4\})$
$\quad Ready_6 = \{\{\{!msg5\}, \{?msg5, cond1\}\}\}$
$q_7 : History_7 = History_4 \cup \{\{\{!msg5\}, \{?msg5, cond1\}\}\}$

$Cut_7 = (\{?msg4\}, \{!msg5\}, \{?msg5, cond1\}, \{!msg4\})$
$Ready_7 = \emptyset$
$q_8 : History_8 = History_5 \cup \{\{\{!msg5\}, \{?msg5, cond1\}\}\}$
$Cut_8 = (\{?msg4\}, \{!msg5\}, \{?msg5, cond1\}, \{!msg4\})$
$Ready_8 = \emptyset$
$q_9 : History_9 = History_6 \cup \{\{\{!msg5\}, \{?msg5, cond1\}\}\}$
$Cut_9 = (\{?msg4\}, \{!msg5\}, \{?msg5, cond1\}, \{!msg4\})$
$Ready_9 = \emptyset$

A closer look at the automaton reveals some redundant states and transitions: The phases for states q_7, q_8, q_9 are identical and could therefore be represented by a single state. The same is true for the phases for states q_4, q_5, q_6, with the exception that their cuts differ. The cuts are not directly relevant for the $Step(\cdot, \cdot)$ function, thus these states could be merged into one as well. The rule for being able to combine states is thus that they have identical history and ready sets.

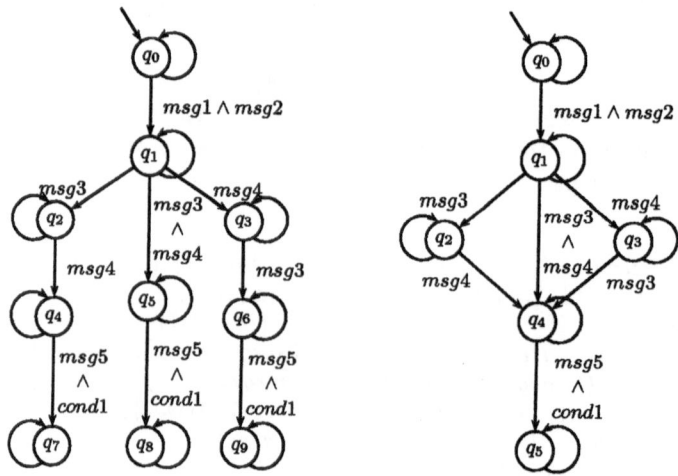

Fig. 6. Incomplete automata for Sim&Coregs Example LSC (c.f. figure 5 on page 391). The left automaton is gained directly from the primitive unwinding structure above; for the right automaton, the identical phases for states q_7, q_8, q_9 and q_4, q_5, q_6 are unified.

Self loop annotation and Interpretation. The question of how to annotate the self loops is influenced by the question whether duplicate messages are allowed, i.e. should it be considered an error, if a message, which is contained in an LSC body, is observed more than once during the activation of the LSC? The interpretation assumed in [4] is that duplicate messages result in an error and are thus prohibited. Applying this *strict* interpretation to the incomplete automaton generated so far results in an automaton where every self loop is annotated with the conjunction of the negation of all messages of the LSC; all non-self-loop messages similarly need to be extended by the conjunction of the negation of all messages of the LSC, which are not unwound in the current step. It is not immediately clear if this interpretation is too restrictive.

This motivates a second interpretation, which we call *weak* and which allows duplicate messages as long as the messages contained in the LSC are observed also at the correct times. This corresponds to annotating the self loops in the automaton only with the conjunction of the negation of all messages, which are in the ready set associated with the current state.

Both interpretations remove the non-determinism in the automaton due to the empty self loop annotation. The annotation for the self loop of the final state is identical for both variants: *true*, because once the behavior specified in the LSC has been observed entirely no further restriction applies to the system.

Example 5 (Sim&Coregs LSC and the corresponding symbolic automaton).

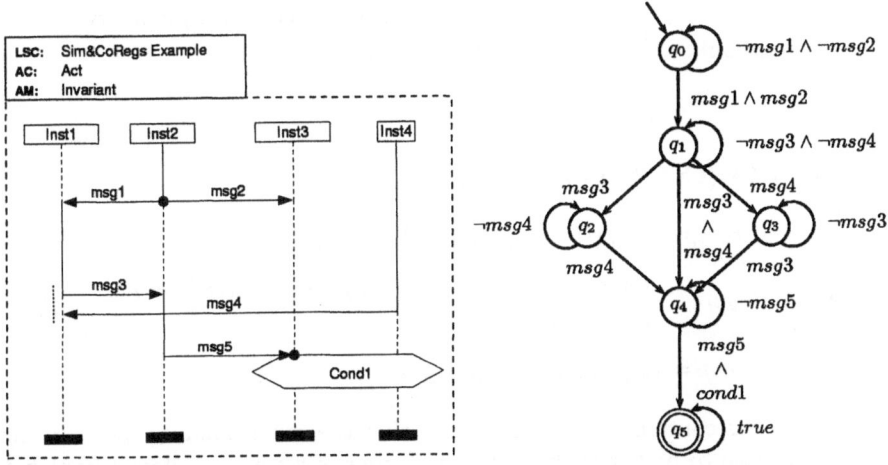

Fig. 7. The Sim&Coregs Example LSC and the corresponding symbolic automaton with annotated self loops using weak interpretation.

Treatment of Liveness and Temperatures. So far the location temperatures, i.e. the progress requirements on the instance axes, have not been considered. This information is collected by the cuts, which indicate up to which locations the unwinding has progressed. The local liveness information of each instance, given by the location temperature, is used to compute the global liveness requirements, which is expressed by the cut temperature defined below.

The LSC syntax as presented in section 2.2 needs to be extended in order to propagate the local temperature of the observed atoms. The atom temperature is first lifted to the cluster level and thereafter to the location level. Analogously to the cut temperature computation below, one hot atom overrides the temperature of all other atoms in a simultaneous region.

$$temp : Clusters(l) \longrightarrow \{hot, cold\}$$

$$temp(cl) := \begin{cases} cold, & \text{if } \forall a \in cl : temp(a) = cold \\ hot, & \text{else} \end{cases}$$

The temperature function is extended analogously to locations, so that coregions can be treated correctly. Since no ordering exists between the atoms of a coregion, no progress between them can be enforced, so that a single temperature is associated with a coregion.

$$temp : Locations(l) \longrightarrow \{hot, cold\}$$

$$temp(loc) := \begin{cases} cold, & \text{if } \forall cl \in Clusters(l) : location(cl) = loc \land \\ & \qquad temp(cl) = cold \\ hot, & \text{else} \end{cases}$$

Definition 16 (Cut Temperature).

$$cut\_temp : Cuts(l) \longrightarrow \{hot, cold\}$$

$$cut\_temp(cut) := \begin{cases} hot & \text{if } \exists \, cl_j \in cut : temp(location(cl_j)) = hot \\ cold & \text{else} \end{cases} \text{, with}$$

$$cut = (cl_1, \ldots, cl_n), 1 \le j \le n$$

Thus phases containing a hot cut mean that the corresponding states in the automaton have to be left within a finite amount of time — analogously to hot locations on an instance. A cold cut indicates that the corresponding state needs not to be left. In conjunction with the self loop this means that such a state is fair in the sense of the Büchi acceptance criterion. Note that the final and the exit state are always fair, since no further requirements are posed by the LSC once it has been completed or exited.

Treatment of possible Conditions. Up to now conditions are only partly treated by the unwinding procedure. The unwinding so far only covers the case that the condition is fulfilled, violations are not considered.

For mandatory conditions no further steps are necessary, since evaluating a condition to false results in a non-accepting run (there exists no transition in the automaton for this case). As illustrated by the automaton in figure 7 condition **Cond1** must be satisfied, when message **msg5** occurs. For possible (cold) conditions, whose violations should result in an exit from the LSC, a special *exit state* is introduced, which is entered whenever a possible condition is violated. This state is similar to the final state inasmuch as no further restrictions apply after entering this state, i.e. the self loop annotation is *true* as well[5].

Treatment of Time Constraints. So far the semantics of the presented LSC elements were expressible in an untimed symbolic automaton, whereas a timed symbolic automaton (c.f. section 2.1 on page 382) is needed when dealing with time constrained LSCs.

The idea is to associate a clock in the symbolic automaton with every timer and timing interval in the LSC, which is set to zero when the corresponding timer is set or the location of the timing interval is reached. When the timer is either reset or a timeout is observed or the location following the one with the timing interval is reached, a clock constraint is placed on the corresponding transitions in the automaton, which reflects the nature and duration of the timer or timing interval. For a timeout atom this means that the value of the associated clock must be equal to the duration of the timer. For a timer reset atom the clock must be strictly less than the timer duration, because no timeout has been observed so far, i.e. the clock must not have reached its maximal value. For timing intervals the clock must be equal to or greater than the lower bound and less than or equal to the upper bound depending on the type of interval (open, closed).

2.4   Relating LSCs to a Reference System

Informally the semantics of an LSC L is defined in terms of the timed runs (cf. definition 5 on page 383), which are produced by the reference system S and accepted by the automaton of L. The unwinding algorithm operates on the identifiers, which are associated with the unwound LSCs elements, and therefore the generated symbolic automaton is annotated with formulas over these identifiers. The final step in relating the LSC to the reference system is taken by mapping identifiers to concrete design elements.

Each *mapping function* for an LSC L and a reference system S, $map \in Maps(S, L)$, assigns a functional unit of S to each instance identifier, and a proposition over signals of S to each message label and condition and local invariant identifier. The concrete definition of $map(\cdot)$ depends on the reference system. If the reference system has a *static* structure, that is, the number and inter-relation of functional units is fixed in all system runs, then $Maps(S, L)$ is a singleton set. Otherwise, $Maps(S, L)$ provides a means to explain *dynamic binding*, i.e. having symbolic instance lines which do not have a one-to-one correspondence to a functional unit but represents *all* functional units of a kind.

For a symbolic automaton $\mathcal{TSA}$ we thus denote the substitution of all identifiers by their corresponding proposition by $map(\mathcal{TSA})$, the accepted language is consequently denoted by $\mathcal{L}(map(\mathcal{TSA}))$.

---

[5] Exit and final state can effectively be merged as a further optimization of the symbolic automaton.

The definition of *Satisfaction* for LSCs depends on the activation mode and quantification. Initial LSCs are activated at system start, whereas invariant and iterative LSCs are activated whenever the activation condition is true. Iterative LSCs allow only one incarnation of an LSC at a time, i.e. such an LSC may not be reactivated.

Definition 17 (Satisfaction of an LSC).

Let $L = (l, ac, pch, amode, quant)$ be an LSC, $\mathcal{TSA}_l$ the timed symbolic automaton generated for LSC body l by the unwinding algorithm, and S the corresponding reference system.

L is existentially satisfied by S, denoted $S \models_\exists L$, iff quant = existential $\wedge$ $\exists tr = tr_0, tr_1, \ldots \in Runs(S) : tr \models_\exists L$, where $tr \models_\exists L$ iff

$$\exists map \in Maps(S, L) : \begin{cases} tr_0 \models ac \wedge \\ \quad \overrightarrow{tr_1} \in \mathcal{L}(map(\mathcal{TSA}_l)) & amode = initial \\ \exists i : tr_i \models ac \wedge \\ \quad \overrightarrow{tr_{i+1}} \in \mathcal{L}(map(\mathcal{TSA}_l)) & amode = invariant \\ \exists i : tr_i \models ac \wedge \neg active(L) \wedge \\ \quad \overrightarrow{tr_{i+1}} \in \mathcal{L}(map(\mathcal{TSA}_l)) & amode = iterative \end{cases}$$

L is universally satisfied by S, denoted $S \models_\forall L$, iff quant = universal $\wedge \forall tr = tr_0, tr_1, \ldots \in Runs(S) : tr \models_\forall L$, where $tr \models_\forall L$ iff

$$\forall map \in Maps(S, L) : \begin{cases} tr_0 \models ac \Rightarrow \\ \quad \overrightarrow{tr_1} \in \mathcal{L}(map(\mathcal{TSA}_l)) & amode = initial \\ \forall i : tr_i \models ac \Rightarrow \\ \quad \overrightarrow{tr_{i+1}} \in \mathcal{L}(map(\mathcal{TSA}_l)) & amode = invariant \\ \forall i : tr_i \models ac \wedge \neg active(L) \Rightarrow \\ \quad \overrightarrow{tr_{i+1}} \in \mathcal{L}(map(\mathcal{TSA}_l)) & amode = iterative \end{cases}$$

By $\overrightarrow{tr_i}$ we denote the suffix of the run tr starting at index i. The predicate active(L) is true if there is another active incarnation of L, which has not yet reached its final or exit state.

3   Conclusion and Related Work

In the paper at hand, we have pointed out the deficiencies of the current state of the MSC language and emphasized the need for a formally well founded visual formalism. We presented the LSC language introduced by Damm and Harel in [4], which overcomes the observed shortcomings. We have sketched a part of the formal semantics of the LSC language as defined in [5] by providing the unwinding procedure, which generates a symbolic timed automaton from an LSC body, and have given an idea of the relation between LSCs and reference systems.

While our primary objective is the application of LSCs in the context of formal system verification, Harel and Marelly have proposed a different use case for LSCs described in [12]. The basic idea of this approach, called *Play-In/Play-Out*, is to play-in the desired interactions and use LSCs to record them. The key point is that no model representation exists at this time, so that the play-in procedure is carried out via a mock-up graphical user interface. Once a set of LSCs has been recorded in this way they can be used as behavior specifications, which monitor a user-guided simulation (*play-out*). This approach is intended to be used at the beginning of the development process to generate the basic system interactions in an easy and intuitive way. The view of this approach is an operational one, whereas the purpose of LSCs as presented here is a denotational description of the behavior of system.

Another advanced use case for LSCs, described by Harel and Kugler in [13], is bridging the gap between requirements, specified by LSCs, and a behavioral model by automatically synthesizing a first-cut model from LSCs.

References

1. ITU-T: ITU-T Recommendation Z.120: Message Sequence Chart (MSC). ITU-T, Geneva (1993)
2. ITU-T: ITU-T Annex B to Recommendation Z.120: Algebraic Semantics of Message Sequence Charts. ITU-T, Geneva (1995)
3. Ben-Abdallah, H., Leue, S.: Expressing and analyzing timing constraints in message sequence chart specifications. Technical Report 97-04, Department of Electrical and Computer Engineering, University of Waterloo (1997)
4. Damm, W., Harel, D.: LSCs: Breathing life into message sequence charts. Formal Methods in System Design 19 (2001) 45–80
5. Klose, J.: Live Sequence Charts: A Graphical Formalism for the Specification of Communication Behavior. PhD thesis, Carl von Ossietzky Universität Oldenburg (2003)
6. Lamport, L.: Proving the correctness of multiprocess programs. IEEE Transactions on Software Engineering 3 (1977)
7. Brill, M., Buschermöhle, R., Damm, W., Klose, J., Westphal, B., Wittke, H.: Formal verification of LSC's in the development process. In: this volume. (2004)
8. Schlör, R.: Symbolic Timing Diagrams : A Visual Formalism for Model Verification. PhD thesis, Carl von Ossietzky Universität Oldenburg (2000)
9. Thomas, W.: Automata on infinite objects. In van Leeuwen, J., ed.: Handbook of Theoretical Computer Science, Volume B: Formal Models and Semantics. Elsevier Science Publishers (1990)
10. Emerson, E.A.: Temporal and modal logic. In van Leeuwen, J., ed.: Handbook of Theoretical Computer Science, Volume B: Formal Models and Semantics. Elsevier Science Publishers (1990) 995–1072
11. Alur, R., Dill, D.: A theory of timed automata. Theoretical Computer Science 126 (1994) 183–236
12. Harel, D., Marelly, R.: Come, Let's Play: Scenario-Based Programming Using LSCs and the Play-Engine. Springer Verlag (2003)
13. Harel, D., Kugler, H.: Synthesizing state-based object systems from LSC specifications. International Journal of Foundations of Computer Science 13 (2002) 5–51

A Unifying Semantics for Sequential Function Charts

Nanette Bauer[1], Ralf Huuck[2], Ben Lukoschus[3], and Sebastian Engell[4]

[1] BASF Aktiengesellschaft
67056 Ludwigshafen, Germany
nanette.bauer@basf-ag.de
[2] National ICT Australia Ltd (NICTA),
The University of New South Wales, Sydney, Australia
rhuuck@cse.unsw.edu.au
[3] Institute of Computer Science and Applied Mathematics
University of Kiel, 24098 Kiel, Germany
bls@informatik.uni-kiel.de
[4] Process Control Laboratory (BCI-AST)
University of Dortmund, 44221 Dortmund, Germany
s.engell@bci.uni-dortmund.de

Abstract. Programmable Logic Controllers (PLC) are widely used as device controllers for assembly lines, chemical processes, or power plants. Sequential Function Charts (SFC) form one of the main programming languages for PLCs and, therefore, the correctness of the PLC software implemented as SFCs is crucial for a safe operation of the controlled process. A prerequisite for reasoning about program correctness is a clear understanding of the program semantics. As we show in this work, this is currently not the case for SFCs. Although syntactically specified in the IEC 61131-3 standard, SFCs lack an unambiguous, complete semantic description. We point out a number of problems and explain how these lead to different interpretations in commercial programming environments. To remedy this situation we introduce a parameterized formal semantics for SFCs including many high-level programming features such as parallelism, hierarchy, actions and activity manipulation. Moreover, we show how to extend the semantics to include time, clocks, and timed actions. The presented semantics is general enough to comprise different existing interpretations while at the same time being adjustable to precisely represent each of them.

1 Introduction

Programmable Logic Controllers (PLCs) are widely used for automation in process industry, transportation and manufacturing. Their hard- and software is defined in the standard IEC 61131. Concerning the software different programming languages are standardized, one of them is Sequential Function Charts (SFC). SFCs are graphical high-level notations for PLC programs. They allow

H. Ehrig et al. (Eds.): INT 2004, LNCS 3147, pp. 400–418, 2004.

the decomposition and structuring of program parts including interesting concepts like parallelism, activity manipulation and hierarchy. Moreover, there is the notion of time and timers, which allows to test and reason about the amount of time a program part has been active and to start program parts after a delay or for some limited time only. All these features can, however, again aggravate the understanding of SFCs.

As PLC software often performs safety-relevant functions, its formal analysis is crucial, and for this a formal semantics is required. However, the standard only gives an informal description of the semantics of the PLC languages. The semantics of SFCs given in IEC 61131-3 is ambiguous and erroneous, and PLC programming tool developers interpret the ambiguities posed by the standard in different ways, which results in a variety of different tool semantics. Although there exist a few approaches to formalize SFCs [1,2,3] none of them addresses all of the concepts which are crucial for SFCs, such as parallelism, hierarchy, their action concept, and timing aspects, and none of them considers tool-specific interpretations.

To remedy this situation a formal semantic is defined which includes all language concepts and furthermore tool-specific implementations. This semantics makes formal analysis possible and may also be helpful as a unifying basis for further tool developments.

The remainder of this work is organized as follows: First we introduce the basic concepts of SFCs informally in Sect. 2. In Sect. 3 we show ambiguities arising from the IEC 61131-3 definitions for SFCs and define a formal syntax and semantics for untimed SFCs which considers these ambiguities by the introduction of adaptable parameters. In Sect. 4 it is shown how this semantics can be augmented to timed aspects. Section 5 shows how the semantics can be adapted to the behavior of different tools. The contribution closes with conclusions given in Sect. 6.

2   Sequential Function Charts

2.1   Basic Structure

Sequential function charts are defined in [4] as elements of a graphical programming and structuring language for programmable logic controllers. The SFC definitions in IEC 61131-3 (in the following referred to as "the standard") are based on IEC 60848 [5], which defines the specification language Grafcet. Grafcet in turn is strongly related to Petri nets [6].

Basically, SFCs are transition systems consisting of *steps* (the locations) and *transitions*. For every SFC there exists exactly one *initial step*. Every transition is labeled with an associated transition condition, called *guard*. Moreover, one or more *actions* may be associated to each step. Actions are again SFCs or programs in one of the other programming languages proposed by the standard. Since the actions associated to steps can also be SFCs themselves, a concept of hierarchy is provided. An example of a sequential function chart is depicted in Fig. 1.

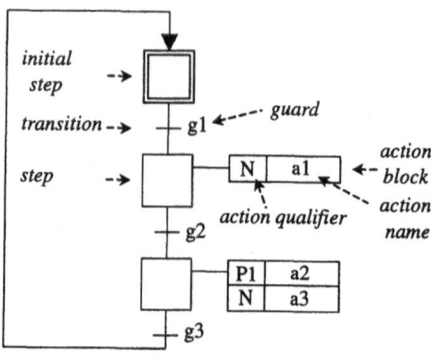

Fig. 1. Elements of SFCs

The *action blocks* shown in Fig. 1 are a graphical means to associate actions to steps. An action block consists of an *action qualifier*, which can be used to specify the activity of the respective action, and the *action name*. Concerning the action qualifiers defined in the standard, we focus on those without an associated duration of time (considered later in Sect. 4). These are the following:

qualifier	meaning
N	Non-stored
S	Set or Stored
R	Reset
P1	Pulse – rising edge (activation of corresponding step)
P0	Pulse – falling edge (deactivation of corresponding step)

Intuitively, the non-stored actions are always active while control resides in the corresponding step, i.e., as long as it is active. In contrast the stored actions remain active even outside their step of activation until the corresponding reset action is called. The actions with the pulse qualifier are performed only once when entering (P1) or exiting (P0) a step.

An SFC does not necessarily have to be a single sequence of steps and transitions. For SFCs we can identify a number of different transition types (cf. Fig. 2). Transition (1) denotes a *simple transition* between two steps, (2) describes *alternative branching*, i.e., the choice between several transitions, (3) *divergence*, (4) *convergence*, and (5) a simultaneity of both of the latter. In this context divergence means a parallel branching from one step to a set of next steps while convergence means the synchronization of several steps in parallel to a single one. Furthermore, direct combinations of both as depicted in (5) are allowed. Moreover, the standard refers to transitions like the one guarded by g_3 in Fig. 1 as *loops*. From our point of view loops as well as alternative branching belong to the same class, namely (sets of) simple transitions.

An additional feature of SFCs is to explicitly assign priorities to alternative branches. This means, when firing transitions the one which has the highest

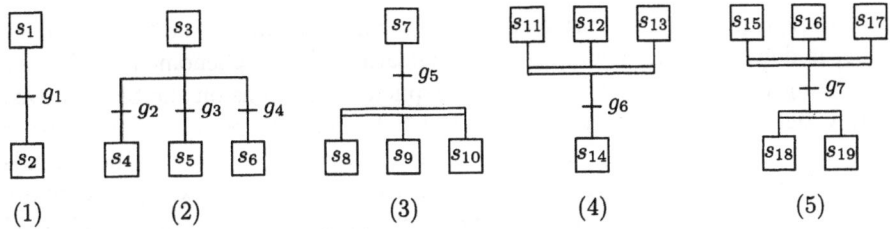

Fig. 2. Basic transition types

priority among the enabled ones will be taken. If there are no priorities given, SFC programming tools often implement the implicit rule that the transitions are ordered "from left to right" in decreasing priority, i.e., in Fig. 2 the transition guarded by g_2 has priority over those guarded by g_3 and g_4, and the one guarded by g_3 has priority over the one guarded by g_4.

The basic transition types can be combined into more complex transition structures like in Fig. 1 and Fig. 3. However, there are various combinations which do not seem to make sense, e.g., in the SFC shown in Fig. 3. There we have the transition from s_4 to s_1 which jumps out of a parallel branch, the converging transition from s_2 to s_5, which jumps from one simultaneous branch to another, and the transition from s_5 and s_6 to s_7, which is a convergence of simultaneous sequences of two steps which are part of an alternative branching starting in step s_3.

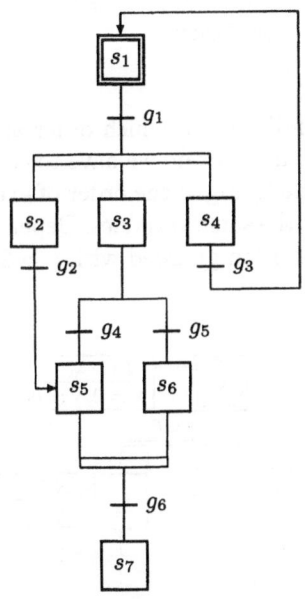

Fig. 3. Unsafe SFC

Although the standard forbids to use these kinds of "unsafe" or "unreachable" SFCs, it does not give a precise characterization of this phenomenon. For the time being we do not want to pose any explicit restrictions on the SFC syntax. Mainly because we want to allow as much freedom as possible and because there are commercial tools available which "support" SFCs with these kinds of transitions and do simulations on them. Hence, in the following we define a semantics for sequential function charts which can also cope with such ill-formed constructions.

2.2 Ambiguities

The standard defines rules for building an SFC from the aforementioned basic elements and describes how to execute SFCs by giving evolution rules similar to the firing rules of Petri nets. However, execution is only defined on an abstract level not taking into account concrete aspects of program execution. As SFC is a *programming language,* the exact semantics of execution is of interest and it is therefore important to consider the PLC-specific cyclic execution of SFCs. In every scan cycle first the current input from the environment (i.e., from the sensors of a plant such as pressure or temperature sensors) is read and stored. Then the PLC program is executed based on the stored input, i.e., the actions of the active steps are executed, which may change the output, and afterwards the transitions are taken. At the end of each cycle the output is sent to the environment, i.e., to the actuators of a plant such as valves or motors.

Although the semantics of SFCs on an abstract level seems to be quite simple, the exact semantics on an operational level is sometimes far from obvious. Let us have a close look at some key issues.

How to deal with parallelism? In which order are actions of parallel steps executed? Is there any order at all or do we have to cope with non-determinism? As illustrated by the example in Fig. 4 the order of execution makes a difference if the actions read or modify the same variables. Depending on whether executing a_1 before a_2 or not, the transition guarded with $y = 2$ is enabled or not.

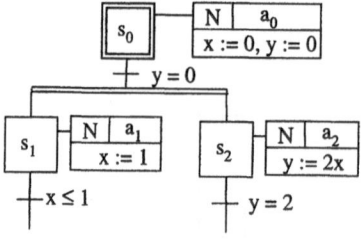

Fig. 4. In which order are the actions a_1 and a_2 executed?

The execution order is also not clear if we have more than one action associated to a step. Are they executed from top to bottom or according to a different rule?

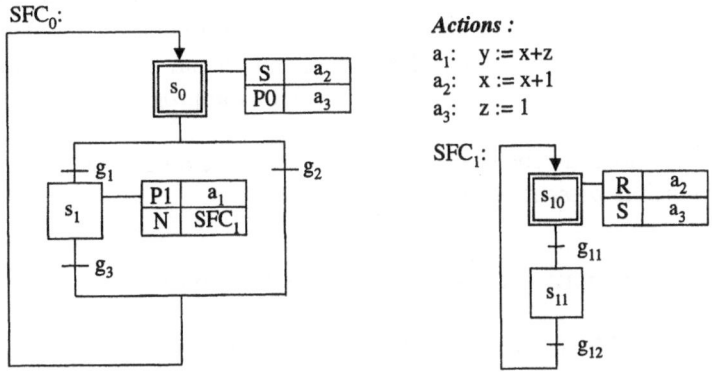

Fig. 5. How to deal with hierarchy?

How to deal with hierarchy of SFCs? Fig. 5 shows a top-level SFC SFC_0 with a second SFC nested in step s_1 (SFC_1). Has the top-level SFC higher priority, that is, are the actions of the top-level SFC executed prior to the actions of the nested SFC? If we enter s_1 in SFC_0, does the execution order of actions depend on the hierarchy, i.e., do we first execute a_1 and then the actions a_2 and a_3 of SFC_1? Can SFC_1 reset a_2 or has the top SFC priority and a_2 is executed? Which step of the nested SFC will be entered if it is called again? For instance, if we enter step s_1 again, do we always activate s_{10} or is there a notion of history, and the last active step of SFC_1 (which may also be s_{11}) therefore gets activated?

2.3   Possible Answers to Ambiguities

The standard does not provide any explicit answer to the questions posed above. For the execution order of actions a comparison of different SFC programming tools of some major PLC vendors [7] yields that there exist various orders on actions, e.g., for one tool actions are executed according to the alphabetic order of action names, for another one by user-defined orders, and so on. However, in no case there is non-determinism. This seems to be reasonable since PLCs are in general deterministic. The semantics defined in the following copes with these different semantics by introducing a parameter for the order of actions. Another parameter is introduced for the order of transitions to reflect priorities if several transitions of an alternative branching are enabled simultaneously.

For the questions concerning history one may deduce from the standard that actions exist globally within the SFC, that means we have a global execution order within the SFC and its nested SFCs. This also means that a reset of an action will also effect the action if it is called within a nested SFC.

Furthermore we define that an SFC action may either have or have no history, such that it is either possible to always re-enter in the last active step or always re-enter in the initial step.

Finally, there is the question whether it is possible to create algebraic loops, e.g., is it possible that a nested SFC calls the top-level SFC again with a different qualifier? In general this is not forbidden, but in our framework we assume systems without algebraic loops and leave it to the program designer to avoid these.

These decisions are the basis for a clear non-ambiguous syntax and semantics of SFCs which is presented next.

3   Formal Untimed Syntax and Semantics

3.1   Syntax of SFCs with Actions

SFCs (or PLC programs in general) have different types of variables, such as input variables, output variables, and local variables. The values of the variables may belong to different data types such as Boolean or integer. The valid variable and data types are regulated by the standard IEC 61131-3, already mentioned above. We abstract from these different variable and data types by simply saying that a PLC has a set of variables X which may have different values. To describe the values of all variables we use the notion of a *state:*

Definition 1 (State). *A state is a type-preserving function σ assigning a value to each variable in X. Let Σ be the set of all states.*

A state (i.e., the values of the variables) can be modified by *state transformations*. In the standard different types of programming languages are defined for such state transformations. We abstract from these languages by simply saying that a state transformation is a function that transforms a given state into another state. Here state transformations are deterministic; in non-deterministic languages a state is transformed into one of several possible successor states.

Definition 2 (State transformation). *A state transformation is a function $f : \Sigma \rightarrow \Sigma$. Let F be the set of all state transformations.*

Each step of an SFC is labeled with a (possibly empty) set of *action blocks*, which are pairs of action names and qualifiers. We associate either a unique state transformation or a call of a nested SFC with an action name. Moreover, we simply say *actions* when in fact referring to action names.

Definition 3 (Action name, action block). *An action name is an identifier for either a state transformation $f \in F$ or an SFC S (defined below). An action block is a pair (a, q) consisting of an action name a and an action qualifier q, where $q \in \{N, S, R, P0, P1\}$.*

Let B denote the set of all action blocks. For any action block $b \in B$ we denote by b_a the projection to the action name and by b_q the projection to the qualifier.

We define a *guard* as a Boolean expression reasoning about variables and step activities. Syntactically, the activity of step s_i is expressed by the term $s_i.X$.

Definition 4 (Guard). *A guard g is a Boolean expression over variables and step activities. We denote the set of all guards by G.*

Moreover, we need an order on actions as well as on transitions. These allow to determine in which order actions are executed and which transition will be taken if several are in conflict with each other. In conflict means that more than one alternative transition is enabled. Hence, the order on transitions rules out any non-determinism. Let *SFC* be the set of sequential function charts, which are defined next.

Definition 5 (SFC). *A sequential function chart (SFC) is a 9-tuple $S = (X, S, A, s_0, T, block, \sqsubseteq, \prec, h)$, where*

- *X is a finite set of variables,*
- *S is a finite set of steps,*
- *A is a finite set of actions, which might be SFCs,*
- *$s_0 \in S$ is the initial step,*
- *$T \subseteq (2^S \setminus \{\emptyset\}) \times G \times (2^S \setminus \{\emptyset\})$ is a finite set of transitions,*
- *$block : S \to 2^B$ is an action labeling function which assigns a set of action blocks to each step,*
- *$\sqsubseteq \subseteq A \times A$ is an total order on actions, used to define the order in which the active actions are to be executed,*
- *$\prec \subseteq T \times T$ is a partial order on transitions, to determine priorities on conflicting transitions, and*
- *$h \in \{0, 1\}$ is a parameter which determines whether the SFC is executed with history ($h = 1$) or without ($h = 0$).*

We uniquely represent a transition by its set of source steps, its guard and its set of target steps.

When putting a sequential function chart into formal syntax the main task is to determine the orders $\sqsubseteq$ and $\prec$. As mentioned in Sect. 2.1 these orders are in general implementation dependent and should be chosen in a meaningful way or according to the respective programming tool.

For any SFC S, we use $X_S, S_S, \ldots, h_S$ to denote the components of S.

3.2   Semantics of SFCs with Actions

In this section we provide an operational semantics for SFCs. Let $S = (X, S, A, s_0, T, block, \sqsubseteq, \prec, h)$ be an SFC, and let $S_i = (X_i, S_i, A_i, s_{0,i}, T_i, block_i, \sqsubseteq_i, \prec_i, h_i)$, $i = 1, \ldots, n$, be the SFCs nested recursively inside the steps of S. For a global, flat access to the nested structure we distinguish between elements which are defined globally within the SFC and its nested SFC actions (the set of variables, the non-SFC actions, and the order on actions $\sqsubset$; for a flat access we have, e.g., $\bar{A} = A = A_1 = \ldots = A_n$), and elements which are defined for each SFC differently (these are, e.g., the set of steps, the set of transitions, and the order on transitions). For a global access we define the global set of steps $\bar{S} = S \cup S_1 \cup \ldots \cup S_n$; in the same way we extend the other components which differ for each SFC.

In the following we assume that the SFCs are nested in such a way that there are no algebraic loops, e.g., there are no conflicting circular action qualifiers for action names.

There are several things we have to keep track of when observing executions of the SFC S. First, we need information about the current state of S, i.e., the values of its variables. Moreover, we have to know in which steps of S and its sub-SFCs $S_1, \ldots, S_n$ control resides and whose actions are to be performed in a cycle.

It is crucial to distinguish between *ready steps* and *active steps*. Active steps are the ones control resides in and their actions will be performed. On the other hand, there might be steps where control resides in, but their actions will not be performed. The reason is, these steps belong to a nested SFC S_i which is currently not activated, i.e., there is no action active which points to S_i. Control is "waiting" there to resume. We call all steps where control resides in *ready steps*. Hence, each active step is also a ready step, but the converse does of course not hold.

Moreover, *active actions* are actions which will potentially be executed in the current SFC cycle. This means, unless there is no matching reset action these actions will be performed. *Stored actions* are the ones which have been tagged with an S qualifier and potentially keep on being active outside their step of activation.

We store the information about the state and the other information of S in a *configuration*:

Definition 6 (Configuration). *A configuration c of S is a 5-tuple $(\sigma, readyS, activeS, activeA, storedA)$, where $\sigma \in \Sigma$ is the state of the variables, $readyS \subseteq \bar{S}$ is the set of ready steps, $activeS \subseteq \bar{S}$ is the set of active steps, $activeA \subseteq \bar{A}$ is the set of active actions, and $storedA \subseteq \bar{A}$ is the set of stored actions, i.e., the ones which might remain active outside the step they were called. Moreover, let C denote the set of all configurations.*

Such a configuration is modified in the *cycles* of a PLC. In a cycle the following sequence of tasks is performed:

1. Get new input from the environment and store the information into state σ.
2. Execute the set *activeA* of active actions and update σ accordingly.
3. Determine the set of next *readyS*, *activeS*, *activeA*, and *storedA*.
4. Send the outputs to the environment by extracting the required information from the new state σ.

We do not specify formally how to interact with the environment, but focus on items 2 and 3.

First, we define *executions* by means of configuration changes within a cycle. In order to do so, we associate a transition system to an SFC and use the following notations: For every transition (χ, g, χ') where χ and χ' are sets of steps let $source(\chi, g, \chi') = \chi$ denote the set of all source steps and $target(\chi, g, \chi') = \chi'$ the set of all target steps. We extend these notions to sets of transitions in a pointwise fashion.

A prerequisite for a program evaluation is an interpretation of the guards. We interpret a guard by the set of configurations it describes.

Definition 7 (Guard interpretation). *Given a guard $g \in G$ and a configuration $c \in C$, we say that "c satisfies g" or "g is valid in c", denoted by $c \models g$, if the expression g evaluates to true under c.*

The semantics of an SFC is based on the transition system describing its operational behavior:

Definition 8 (Transition System of an SFC). *With every SFC $S = (X, S, A, s_0, T, block, \sqsubset, \prec, h)$ we associate a transition system $\mathcal{E}(S) = (C, c_0, \longrightarrow)$, where C is the set of configurations, $c_0 \in C$ is the initial configuration, and $\longrightarrow \subseteq C \times C$ is the transition relation, which is defined by:* $(\sigma, readyS, activeS, activeA, storedA) \longrightarrow (\sigma', readyS', activeS', activeA', storedA')$ *if and only if*

1. $\sigma' = (a_m \circ \cdots \circ a_1)(\sigma)$, *where* $a_1 \sqsubset \cdots \sqsubset a_m$ *and* $\{a_1, \ldots, a_m\} = activeA \setminus SFC$,
2. $readyS' = (readyS \setminus source(taken)) \cup target(taken)$, *where*
   a) $enabled = \{(\chi, g, \chi') \in \bar{T} \mid \chi \subseteq activeS \wedge (\sigma', readyS, activeS, activeA, storedA) \models g\}$, *and*
   b) $taken = \{t = (\chi, g, \chi') \in enabled \mid \neg \exists t_1 = (\chi_1, g_1, \chi_1') \in enabled : \chi \cap \chi_1 \neq \emptyset \wedge t_1 \gtrless t\}$, *and*
3. $activeS'$, $activeA'$ *and* $storedA'$ *are computed by*

$$(\alpha_0, \beta_0) := \varphi(\alpha_{ini}, \emptyset, S)$$
$$(\alpha_1, \beta_1) := \varphi(\alpha_0, \beta_0, S_{i_1})$$
$$\vdots$$
$$(\alpha_k, \beta_k) := \varphi(\alpha_{k-1}, \beta_{k-1}, S_{i_k})$$

where φ is defined in Fig. 6, S is the top-level SFC, the set $\{S_{i_1}, \ldots, S_{i_k}\} = storedA \cap SFC$ contains the SFCs in storedA, and α_{ini} is the initial mapping of stored actions $a \in storedA \setminus SFC$ to $\{S\}$ and to $\emptyset$ for all other actions. Then, $activeS' = \beta_k$, $activeA' = \{a \in \bar{A} \mid \alpha_k(a) \cap \{N, PO, P1\} \neq \emptyset \wedge R \notin \alpha_k(a)\}$ and $storedA' = \{a \in \bar{A} \mid S \in \alpha_k(a) \wedge R \notin \alpha_k(a)\}$.

The initial configuration $c_0 = (\sigma_0, readyS_0, activeS_0, activeA_0, storedA_0)$ is given by: σ_0 is the predefined initial state of the variables (Booleans set to false, numerical variables to 0), $readyS_0 = \bar{s}_0$, and $activeS_0$, $activeA_0$, and $storedA_0$ are determined from (α_0, β_0) like the primed ones above.

function $\varphi(\alpha, \beta, \Gamma)$
(* (I) newsteps are the local ready steps, i.e., the active ones *)
  if $h_\Gamma = 1$
  then $newsteps := S_\Gamma \cap readyS'$
  else $newsteps := S_\Gamma \cap \bar{s}_0;$
  $\alpha' := \alpha;$
  $\beta' := \beta \cup newsteps;$
(* (II) collect the relevant actions *)
  for all $s \in S_\Gamma, b \in block(s):$

$$\alpha'(b_a) := \alpha'(b_a) \cup \begin{cases} \{\text{P0}\} & \text{if } b_q = \text{P0} \wedge s \in source(taken) \\ \{\text{P1}\} & \text{if } b_q = \text{P1} \wedge s \in target(taken) \\ \{b_q\} & \text{if } b_q \in \{\text{N}, \text{S}, \text{R}\} \wedge s \in newsteps \end{cases}$$

(* (III) go into recursion for every new SFC which is not reset *)
  for all $s \in newsteps, b \in block(s):$
    if $b_a \in SFC \wedge \text{R} \notin \alpha'(b_a) \wedge \alpha'(b_a) \neq \emptyset$
      then $(\alpha', \beta') := \varphi(\alpha', \beta', b_a);$
  return (α', β')

Fig. 6. Recursive action labeling collection

Let us take a detailed look at the definition above. One transition in the transition system above corresponds to one PLC cycle. First of all in step 1 of Definition 8 the current active actions are ordered and executed accordingly. If two active actions access a common variable (e.g., x in Fig. 4), the result may depend on the action ordering $\sqsubset$.

In step 2 we determine the new ready steps. These are the old ones plus the targets of the taken transitions, but without their source steps. We distinguish *taken* and *enabled* transitions as follows: A transition is enabled if it is an outgoing transition of an active step and its guard is satisfied by the current configuration. A transition t is taken if it additionally has the highest priority among its competing ones (transitions t_1 sharing at least one common source step with t), which is expressed by the $\prec$ relation.

In step 3 the new active steps, active actions and stored actions are computed recursively on the structure of the SFC by the auxiliary function φ. The function φ has the parameters α, β, and Γ, where α is a mapping from action names to sets of qualifiers and $\beta \subseteq \bar{S}$ is a set of steps. Calling φ for a specific SFC Γ with empty α and β results in the pair (α', β'), where α' contains for every active action all the "activated" qualifiers of the active actions in Γ and its recursively nested SFCs, and β' contains all active steps.

This is computed as follows: starting on with the top-level of Γ, we compute in (I) *newsteps*, which is the set of active steps on this level. The function α is copied to α' and β' is the old β conjoined with the new active steps. In (II), α' is extended by further qualifiers for specific actions. The inclusion of qualifiers depends on whether these qualifiers become relevant now or not. The pulse qualifiers are relevant when taking a transition. The other qualifiers are relevant when remaining in the active steps (i.e., *newsteps*). Finally, in (III) we go into recursion for every sub-SFC of the current one which has become active after computing the new active steps and implicitly the new active actions. These are the SFCs associated to the new steps which are not reset.

The recursion of φ is finite since we assumed that the nested SFC structure does not contain algebraic loops, see Sect. 2.2.

In step 3 of Definition 8 φ is called for the initial set of α, which is just the mapping of stored actions to the corresponding qualifier and the empty set for β. φ then needs to be called again for all k stored SFCs which are in $storedA$. The result of the application of φ is (α_k, β_k), where β_k corresponds to the new active steps, and $activeA'$ and $storedA'$ are the projections of α_k to the corresponding qualifiers taking into account any resets.

An execution sequence of an associated transition system is called *run*.

Definition 9 (Run of $\mathcal{E}$). *A run r over a transition system $\mathcal{E} = (C, c_0, \longrightarrow)$ is a finite or infinite sequence $\langle c_0, c_1, \ldots \rangle$ with $c_i \longrightarrow c_{i+1}$ for all i.*

The operational semantics $[\![S]\!]$ for an SFCs S is given by the set of runs of its associated transitions system $\mathcal{E}(S)$.

3.3   Example

For the SFC given in Fig. 5 we explain how the semantics works for crucial issues such as actions, where the execution order matters, and hierarchy of SFCs.

Assume the global order on actions is given by $a_1 \sqsubset a_2 \sqsubset a_3$, and the local order on transitions is given by $g_1 \prec g_2$. Let the initial configuration for the SFC be (we write functions as sets of pairs):

$$\sigma_0 = \{(x,0), (y,0), (z,0)\},$$
$$readyS_0 = \bar{s}_0 = \{s_0, s_{10}\},$$
$$activeS_0 = \{s_0\},$$
$$activeA_0 = \{a_2\}, \text{ and}$$
$$storedA_0 = \{a_2\}.$$

Furthermore we assume that the action SFC_1 has history, i.e., $h_1 = 1$. Top-level SFCs always have history ($h = 1$).

Assume, g_1 and g_2 are not true until we are in cycle number 14, but then both guards g_1 and g_2 evaluate to true. At this point

$$\sigma = \{(x,13), (y,0), (z,0)\},$$

the sets of active steps, ready steps etc. have not changed compared to the initial configuration. We compute according to step 1 of Definition 8:

$$\sigma' = a_2(\sigma) = \{(x,14), (y,0), (z,0)\},$$

and according to step 2 of the same definition:

$$readyS' = (\{s_0, s_{10}\} \setminus \{s_0\}) \cup \{s_1\} = \{s_1, s_{10}\}.$$

Moreover, $enabled = \{((\{s_0\}, g_1, \{s_1\}), (\{s_0\}, g_2, \{s_0\}))\}$, and since $((\{s_0\}, g_1,$ $\{s_1\}) \prec (\{s_0\}, g_2, \{s_0\}))$, we have $taken = \{((\{s_0\}, g_1, \{s_1\}))\}$. For the computation of the new active steps and actions we have to take the nested SFC_1 into account and recursively determine $activeS'$, $activeA'$ and $storedA'$ using the auxiliary function φ. Because $storedA \cap SFC = \emptyset$, i.e., there is no stored SFC, we only need to compute $\varphi(\alpha_{ini}, \emptyset, SFC_0)$ for the top-level SFC which is SFC_0. The initial mapping α_{ini} of stored actions is given by

$$\alpha_{ini}(a_1) = \emptyset,$$
$$\alpha_{ini}(a_2) = \{S\},$$
$$\alpha_{ini}(a_3) = \emptyset, \text{ and}$$
$$\alpha_{ini}(SFC_1) = \emptyset.$$

First, we determine the active steps of the top-level SFC by

$$newsteps = \{s_0, s_1\} \cap \{s_1, s_{10}\} = \{s_1\}.$$

We set $\alpha' = \alpha_{ini}$ and $\beta' = \{s_1\}$. To update α', all relevant action qualifiers are collected. This yields

- $\alpha'(a_3) = \{P0\}$, since $(a_3, P0)_q = P0$ and $s_0 \in source(taken)$,
- $\alpha'(a_1) = \{P1\}$, since $(a_1, P1)_q = P1$ and $s_1 \in target(taken)$, and
- $\alpha'(SFC_1) = \{N\}$, since $(SFC_1, N)_q \in \{N, S, R\}$ and $s_1 \in newsteps$.

Next, we go into recursion because there is a new SFC, which is not reset, i.e., $SFC_1 \in SFC$, $R \notin \alpha'(SFC_1)$ and $\alpha'(SFC_1) \neq \emptyset$. Therefore, we compute $(\alpha', \beta') := \varphi(\alpha', \beta', SFC_1)$. This results in

$$newsteps = S_1 \cap readyS' = \{s_{10}\}, \alpha' = \alpha, \text{ and } \beta' = \{s_1, s_{10}\}.$$

The update of α' by collecting the relevant actions for all steps of SFC_1 yields

- $\alpha'(a_2) = \{S, R\}$, since $(a_2, R)_q \in \{N, S, R\}$ and $s_{10} \in newsteps$ and
- $\alpha'(a_3) = \{P0, S\}$, since $(a_3, S)_q \in \{N, S, R\}$ and $s_{10} \in newsteps$.

Since there are no new SFCs, the function φ terminates and returns $\beta_0 = \beta'$ as given above and $\alpha_0 = \alpha'$ with

$$\alpha_0(a_1) = \{P1\},$$
$$\alpha_0(a_2) = \{S, R\},$$
$$\alpha_0(a_3) = \{P0, S\}, \text{ and}$$
$$\alpha_0(SFC_1) = \{N\}.$$

Hence, we obtain

$$activeS' = \beta_0 = \{s_1, s_{10}\}, activeA' = \{a_1, a_3, SFC_1\}, \text{ and } storedA' = \{a_3\}.$$

Note, if we continue to compute the configuration for the next cycle 15, the order on actions is important as more than one action is active:

$$\sigma' = (a_3 \circ a_1)(\sigma) = \{(x, 14), (y, 14), (z, 1)\}.$$

In this case a different order on a_1 and a_3 would lead to a different configuration where $\sigma'(y) = 15$. Furthermore, since we do not reset a_3 which is set in step s_{10} of SFC_1, the action a_3 will still be executed even if SFC_1 is no longer active.

4   Formal Extension to Timed SFCs

The SFCs presented earlier do not support any time or timing behavior. However, the standard defines the notion of time and timers which allows to test and reason about the amount of time a step has been active and to start actions after a delay or for some limited time only. In this section we give an introduction to timed SFCs. We explain the main features and how to extend the current SFC semantics to timed SFCs.

4.1   Timed Syntax

Guards are Boolean expressions over variables, where $s_i.X$ denotes that step s_i is active and $s_i.T$ is the time that s_i has been active since its last activation. In addition to the qualifiers presented in Sect. 2.1 there are a number of time related qualifiers:

qualifier	meaning
L t	Limited execution for time span t
D t	Delayed execution after time span t
SL t	Set Limited execution for time span t
SD t	Set Delayed execution after time span t
DS t	Delayed Set execution after time span t

All these qualifiers are followed by some duration and their meaning is as follows: The limited qualifier L behaves like the non-stored qualifier N with the only difference that the corresponding action becomes at latest inactive when the associated duration has elapsed. Moreover, it is possible to delay the activation of an action for a certain time after the step has become active using the D qualifier. The L and D qualifiers can be combined with S yielding DS, SD and SL. An action associated with DS will only be activated if the delay time is reached *before* the step is left, whereas an SD action always becomes active after the elapsed time, independent of the step activity. Similar, an SL action is (in contrast to L) *always* activated for t time units. We denote the action labeling function extended by the additional qualifiers by *block**.

Although the action qualifier concept is defined using well-understood function blocks, the definitions in the standard still are ambiguous. For example, assume an SFC which calls an SD action in one step and in the next step calls the action again with the SD qualifier but with a different delay time. Assume that the activity time of the first step has been shorter than the first delay time, i.e., the action is not yet activated when it is called in the next step with a different delay time. Which delay time now is relevant? These ambiguities clearly show that there is a need for an SFC semantics which gives answers to these open questions. Here, we assume that any call of a timed action resets the corresponding timer. This means delays or limited actions restart the moment they are called. However, other interpretations are possible.

To reason about timed SFCs we introduce the notions of *clocks* and *stopwatches*.

Definition 10 (Stopwatch, Clock). *A stopwatch θ_s is a real valued variable that has a dynamical behavior given by either $f(\theta_s) = \dot{\theta}_s = 1$ if the stopwatch is running, or $f(\theta_s) = \dot{\theta}_s = 0$ if it is stopped, whereas a clock θ_a cannot be stopped, i.e., the dynamical behavior is always $f(\theta_a) = \dot{\theta}_a = 1$. Both can be reset to zero.*

To describe the values of all stopwatches and clocks we use the notion of a *clock evaluation ν*, which is a function assigning a value to each stopwatch or clock.

Since guards may reason about the time a step is active or has been active before, each step needs a stopwatch which is reset to zero when the step is entered, runs when the step is active, and is stopped when the step is deactivated. Second, we need stopwatches because we define that hierarchically nested SFCs have history, i.e., after deactivation nested SFCs are activated in the step they have been last. The notion of history includes that the SFCs remember the values of their clocks at the point of deactivation if they are activated again.

Additionally we need a clock for those actions which are associated with an SD or SL qualifier, because these actions might be deactivated (SL) or activated (SD) independently from a step activity. Clocks are sufficient, because according to the standard, guards cannot access the time an action has been active, and, therefore, we do not need to memorize the activity time after the action has been deactivated.

We define a timed SFC as follows:

Definition 11 (Timed SFC). *A sequential function chart (SFC) $S = (X, \Theta, S, A, s_0, T, block^*, \sqsubset, \prec, h)$ consists of:*

- *X, S, A, s_0, T, $\sqsubset$, $\prec$ and h as defined for the untimed SFC (Definition 5),*
- *$block^*$, the extended action labeling function, and*
- *a finite set Θ of stopwatches and clocks.*

4.2   Timed Semantics

The global state of an SFC (including all its nested SFCs) is given by the values of all its variables, the evaluation of clocks and stopwatches, the sets of active and ready steps and the sets of active and stored actions. In addition to stored actions we also have to remember *stored delayed actions* associated to a step with an SD qualifier, which potentially need to be activated after the corresponding step has been deactivated, as well as *stored limited actions* indicated by the SL qualifier, which potentially have to be executed for a certain time after the activating step has been deactivated.

We describe the global state of an SFC S by a configuration, given by:

Definition 12 (Timed Configuration). *A configuration c of S is an 8-tuple $(\sigma, \nu, readyS, activeS, activeA, storedA, storedDA, storedLA)$, where*

- $\sigma, readyS, activeS, activeA, storedA$ are defined as for the untimed configuration (Definition 6) and
- ν is the evaluation of clocks and stopwatches,
- $storedDA \subseteq \bar{A}$ is the set of stored delayed actions, and
- $storedLA \subseteq \bar{A}$ is the set of stored limited actions.

The timed SFC program executions are again defined by means of configuration changes within a cycle. We define two different types of transitions, $c \xrightarrow{a}_t c'$ which describes the changes of the configuration due to the program execution (which is considered to take no time) and and $c \xrightarrow{\delta}_t c'$ which describes the change of the configuration due to the elapse of time, this means it describes the change of ν.

A transition $c \xrightarrow{a}_t c'$ in this transition system is computed by the following sequence:

1. Determine the new state σ' and $readyS'$ as for the untimed configuration.
2. Determine $activeS'$, $activeA'$, $storedA'$, $storedDA'$ and $storedLA'$. The new sets are computed recursively on the structure of the SFC using the auxiliary function φ as defined in Sect. 3.2 but augmented with the handling of the timed action qualifiers.
3. Stopwatches and clocks are reset to zero if one of the following conditions holds:
    - The stopwatch θ_s belongs to a step s which has been activated in this cycle, i.e., $s \in activeS' \setminus activeS$.
    - The clock θ_a belongs to an action a which has been activated "stored delayed" in this cycle, i.e., $a \in storedDA' \setminus storedDA$.
    - The clock θ_a belongs to an action a which has been activated "stored limited" in this cycle, i.e., $a \in storedLA' \setminus storedLA$.

A transition $c \xrightarrow{\delta}_t c'$ in this transition system changes ν as follows:

- $\nu'(\theta_s) = \nu(\theta_s) + \delta$ if and only if the stopwatch θ_s belongs to a step $s \in activeS$, i.e., a step which is active, and
- $\nu'(\theta_a) = \nu(\theta_a) + \delta$ for all clocks θ_a.

A timed execution sequence $\langle c_0 \xrightarrow{\delta_0}_t c_1 \xrightarrow{a}_t c'_1, \ldots \xrightarrow{\delta_i}_t c_{i+1} \xrightarrow{a}_t c'_{i+1} \cdots \rangle$ is called *timed run*. Note that the time which elapses between two program executions is δ_i, which is the cycle time of the PLC. In PLCs, the cycle time usually is not fixed; some PLCs allow to define a fixed cycle time or an upper time bound. The operational semantics of an SFC S is given by the set of runs of its associated transition system.

5   Adaption to Tool Semantics

As already mentioned, the crucial step for adapting the semantics to a specific tool semantics is the definition of the orders on actions $\sqsubseteq$ and the order on transitions $\prec$ as implemented in the tool.

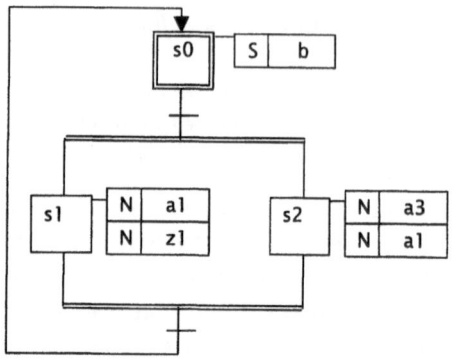

Fig. 7. Example for the ordering $\sqsubseteq$ on actions

For the example presented in Fig. 7 we show how the order can be adapted to different orders on actions which we found to be implemented in different SFC programming tools of some major PLC vendors, for details see [8]:

1. Alphabetical order:

$$a_1 \sqsubseteq a_3 \sqsubseteq b \sqsubseteq z_1.$$

2. Graphical order, from left to right and top to bottom:

$$b \sqsubseteq a_1 \sqsubseteq z_1 \sqsubseteq a_3 \sqsubseteq a_1'.$$

As implemented in the tool, the action a_1 is executed twice, which is not in accordance with the standard. It has to be considered also twice in the order on actions, which can be achieved by introducing two different action names a_1 and a_1'.

3. The order is defined by the user, for example:

$$z_1 \sqsubseteq a_1 \sqsubseteq a_3 \sqsubseteq b.$$

The adaption works similarly for the different transition orders which where found to be implemented in programming tools. Consider the examples presented in Fig. 8. The corresponding orders on transitions are (for the sake of readability, we use t_i as a placeholder for the transition guarded by g_i when describing the order $\prec$):

1. No explicit or implicit priorities, SFC (a) in Fig. 8:

$$\prec = \emptyset.$$

If there are no priorities at all, it is recommended to ensure that conflicting transitions are never enabled simultaneously, e.g., by selecting disjoint guards.

2. Priority from left to right, denoted by a *-notation (this is defined in the standard), SFC (b) in Fig. 8:

$$\prec = \{(t_1, t_{12}), (t_1, t_3), (t_{12}, t_3)\}.$$

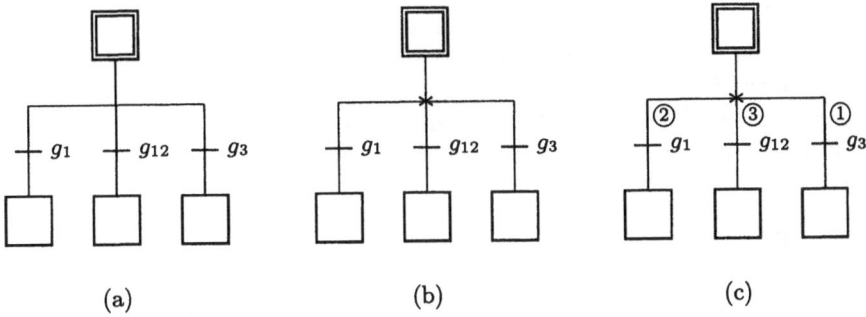

Fig. 8. Example for the ordering $\prec$ on transitions

3. Priorities explicitly given by the user, SFC (c) in Fig. 8

$$\prec = \{(t_3, t_1), (t_3, t_{12}), (t_1, t_{12})\}.$$

4. The leftmost transition always has priority if it is enabled. If it is not enabled, the priority is defined by a transition number which is automatically generated by the programming tool. For this example, assume the numbers to be as given for SFC (c) in Fig. 8 :

$$\prec = \{(t_1, t_{12}), (t_1, t_3), (t_3, t_{12})\}.$$

6   Conclusions

In this work we presented a number of ambiguities and incomplete definitions of the IEC 61131-3 standard for the PLC programming and structuring language Sequential Function Charts (SFC). Moreover, we pointed out that these shortcomings can lead to different implementations of the same SFC, which poses a potential safety hazard. A formal semantics is a first step to avoid such threats. We proposed a formal semantics for untimed SFCs and an extension of this semantics to timed SFCs. This semantics covers the particularities of SFCs such as parallelism, hierarchy, actions and activity manipulations. Moreover, the introduced parameters on actions and transitions gives the semantics the flexibility to adjust precisely to a number of existing interpretations found in PLC programming tools.

Future work is to develop a simple and "clean" semantics and propose it for a future edition of the standard to support the portability of SFC programs among users of different PLC development tools.

Acknowledgments. This work was supported by the German Research Council within the DFG Priority Programme "Integration of Software Specification Techniques for Applications in Engineering" under grants RO 1122/10-2 and EN 152/32-2.

National ICT Australia is funded through the Australian Government's *Backing Australia's Ability initiative,* in part through the Australian Research Council. Nanette Bauer contributed to this work during her time at the Process Control Group of Prof. Engell, University of Dortmund.

Finally, we thank the anonymous referees for their comments.

References

1. Jiang, J., Holding, D.: The formalisation and analysis of sequential function charts using a petri net approach. In: Proceedings of 13th World Congress of IFAC. (1996) 513–518
2. Anderson, S., Tourlas, K.: Design for proof: An approach to the design of domain-specific languages. Formal Aspects of Computing **10** (1998) 452–468
3. Bornot, S., Huuck, R., Lakhnech, Y., Lukoschus, B.: An abstract model for sequential function charts. In: Discrete Event Systems: Analysis and Control, Proceedings of WODES 2000: 5th Workshop on Discrete Event Systems, Ghent, Belgium, August 21–23, 2000. The Kluwer International Series in Engineering and Computer Science (2000) 255–264
4. International Electrotechnical Commission, Technical Committee No. 65: Programmable Controllers – Programming Languages, IEC 61131-3. second edn. (1998) Committee draft.
5. International Electrotechnical Commission, Technical Committee No. 848: IEC 60848, Preparation of function charts for control systems. (1992)
6. David, R., Alla, H.: Petri Nets & Grafcet. Prentice Hall (1992)
7. Bauer, N., Treseler, H.: Vergleich der Semantik der Ablaufsprache nach IEC 61131-3 in unterschiedlichen Programmierwerkzeugen. GMA Kongress, 2001, Baden-Baden, Germany (2001)
8. Bauer, N.: Formale Analyse von Sequential Function Charts. PhD thesis, Lehrstuhl für Anlagensteuerungstechnik, Universität Dortmund (2004) Shaker Verlag, Aachen.

Introduction to Subject Area "Verification"

Frank Ortmeier, Wolfgang Reif, and Gerhard Schellhorn

Lehrstuhl für Softwaretechnik und Programmiersprachen,
Universität Augsburg, D-86135 Augsburg
{ortmeier, reif, schellhorn}@informatik.uni-augsburg.de

Over the last two decades the use of software in technical applications has dramatically increased. Almost all real-world systems are now embedded systems consisting of hardware and software components. Just think of modern automobiles; every new car comes equipped with computers that have many tasks in almost all parts of the car: fuel injection rates of the engine, airbags, anti-blocking systems (ABS) for brakes or the anti-theft device are some examples.

With the use of software the complexity of such systems and therefore the risks associated with failures have increased too. Failure of the ABS can result in bad injuries or even fatalities. But cars are only the tip of the iceberg. There are far more critical embedded systems in our environment like air planes, high speed railways or nuclear power plants. Such systems must not fail.

To assure safety thorough analysis is required. This can be done by the integration of techniques of modern software specification with engineering techniques - the topic of this volume and the DFG focus area program 1064. In this part we will cover one such technique in particular: verification.

Verification allows to rigorously prove that a certain property holds for a formal system model. Application of verification on critical embedded systems is the strongest analysis techniques available to ensure safety. However the task of formally analyzing a complex embedded system requires some effort and specialized techniques. This task can be split in three parts:

1. Building a formal model of the system
2. Identifying the important safety properties
3. Verification of the properties for the given system

The first step towards applying any verification technique is to build a formal model of the system. There exists a wide variety of possible modeling languages. Generic languages are based on algebraic (e.g. CASL [1], CSP [2]), model-oriented (e.g. VDM [3], Z [4], B [5]) or state-based (e.g. Statecharts [6], SDL [7], TLA [8], ASM [9], hybrid automata [10]) approaches, and there is an abundance of problem-specific languages too. Which one is the best, depends on the characteristics of the problem at hand. Are the data structures more important or are dynamic sequences of actions and reactions the central part of the system? Is a continuous time model necessary or can all aspects be modeled in discrete time? Such questions help in choosing the most appropriate modeling language. Typically, a specification language provides adequate support and intuitive models

H. Ehrig et al. (Eds.): INT 2004, LNCS 3147, pp. 419–422, 2004.

only for a few of these aspects. But often industrial systems have many facets, so several models are required. Therefore one of the important research tasks in supporting formal system specification and verification is to provide approaches that correlate or integrate different views of systems. One, but not the only attempt at integration is to define a formal semantics for the different models of UML [11]. The invited paper [12] by *D. Bjorner, A. Haxthausen, C.W. George, C.K. Madsen, S. Holmslykke* and *M. Pěnička* discusses this and gives other approaches for the domain of railway systems: The RAISE specification language (RSL) and its integration with UML class diagrams, Petri Nets, Live Sequence Charts and State charts is considered.

Integrating specification formalisms is also the topic of the contribution [13] of *M. Kardos* and *F.-J. Rammig* of the *ISILEIT* group. Their approach is targeted towards software for distributed production control systems. SDL is used to model component structure and signal flow, while UML state machines describe the individual components. An integrated semantics of both specification languages is defined in terms of AsmL models. These also serve as the basis for model checking to verify system properties.

The second step is to determine and formalize the safety properties the system is expected to fulfill. Determining safety properties is not an easy task and safety analysis techniques like FTA [14], FMEA [15], Hazop [16] from engineering can help to find them. Combining safety analysis techniques from engineering with a systematic process of formal specification and verification is the aim of the *ForMoSA* project (*F. Ortmeier, G. Schellhorn, A. Thums* and *W. Reif*). Their approach [17] starts with failure-sensitive specification to detect hazards. Fault tree analysis (FTA) is then used to analyze the hazards. In combination with a formal model, FTA can be given a formal semantics that can be used to verify the completeness of FTA as well as to validate the formal model. FTA is used for qualitative as well as quantitative analysis of the model, and combined with safety optimization. The approach is evaluated using the industrial case study "height control in the Elbtunnel".

Describing safety relevant properties of specifications with the graphical formalism of live sequent charts is discussed in the paper of the *USE* group (*M. Brill, W. Damm, J. Klose* and *B. Westphal*). The contribution [18] shows how to integrate these into the development process of the widely used V-model, and how to provide effective verification support. The results are exemplified using the reference case study "Funkfahrbetrieb".

After accomplishing the first two steps, the third step is clear. Prove the properties of step two for the model obtained at step one. Two possibilities exist to prove a property: interactive verification with tools like Isabelle [19], PVS [20], ACL2 [21], KIV [22] and model checking, using tools such as SMV [23], Spin [24], Uppaal [25] or the verification environment of statemate [26]. Interactive verification is more powerful, but depends heavily on interaction with a human expert. The big advantage of model checking is that proofs are fully automatic. However the technique is limited to finite-state systems.

Development of efficient verification systems is a complex problem in itself. One solution is to use existing tools, and to use a translation of the domain-specific specification language to the language of the verification tool. This approach was used in the *SFC-Check* project by *N. Bauer, R. Huuck, S. Lohmann, B. Lukoschus, O. Stursberg* and *S. Engell.* Their contributrion [27] is concerned with the development of model checking support for programmable logic controllers (PLCs), which are in widespread industrial use. They present a systematic approach to develop PLC programs from specifications using sequential function charts (SFCs). At the core of their approach are translations of SFC models to automata as used in the model checking tools Cadence SMV and Uppaal that allow to prove safety properties of PLC programs formally.

Sometimes using existing tools is too inefficient. Therefore the group *J. Ruf, R. J. Weiss, T. Kropf* and *W. Rosenstiel* developed an efficient real-time model checker, called RAVEN, themselves. RAVEN's architecture, specification language and logic CCTL are described in the final contribution [28]. They use simulation techniques to reveal critical states which are then used in model checking. This enables them to analyse larger designs at the cost of reduced coverage. The reference case study of a holonic production system is used to demonstrate the approach.

Summarizing part "verification" of this volume we think that the papers of this part are an important contribution towards a better understanding of the task involved in formal specification and verification of embedded systems. Within the focus area program formalizations for several application domains have been developed. New techniques to state safety properties intuitively and to do safety analysis on a formal basis have been provided, as well as proof support has been implemented. This results in intuitive modeling techniques, better understandable formal analysis methods and easier proofs.

References

[1] CoFI (The Common Framework Initiative): CASL Reference Manual. LNCS 2960 (IFIP Series). Springer (2004)

[2] Hoare, C.A.R.: Communicating Sequential Processes. Prentice Hall (1985)

[3] Jones, C.B.: Systematic Software Development using VDM. 2nd edn. Prentice Hall (1990)

[4] Spivey, J.M.: The Z Notation: A Reference Manual. 2nd edn. Prentice Hall International Series in Computer Science (1992)

[5] Abrial, J.R.: The B-Book: Assigning Programs to Meanings. Cambridge University Press (1996)

[6] Harel, D.: Statecharts: A visual formalism for complex systems. Science of Computer Programming **8** (1987) 231–274

[7] International Telecommunications Union (ITU): ITU-T Recommendation Z.100, Specification and Description Language (SDL). (2002) available at HTTP://WWW.SDL-FORUM.ORG.

[8] Lamport, L.: The temporal logic of actions. ACM Transactions on Programming Languages and Systems **16** (1994)

[9] Gurevich, M.: Evolving algebras 1993: Lipari guide. In Börger, E., ed.: Specification and Validation Methods. Oxford University Press (1995) 9 - 36

[10] Henzinger, T.: The theory of hybrid automata. In: Proceedings of the 11th LICS, IEEE Comp. Soc. Press (1996) 278 - 292

[11] The Object Management Group (OMG): OMG Unified Modeling Language Specification Version 1.5. (2003) available at HTTP://WWW.OMG.ORG/TECHNOLOGY/DOCUMENTS/FORMAL/UML.HTM.

[12] Bjørner, D., George, C.W., Haxthausen, A.E., Madsen, C.K., Holmslykke, S., Pěnička, M.: "UML–ising" formal techniques. In: this volume. Springer LNCS (2004)

[13] Kardos, M., Rammig, F.J.: Model based verification of distributed production control systems. In: this volume. Springer LNCS (2004)

[14] Vesley, W., Dugan, J., Fragole, J., II, J.M., Railsback, J.: Fault Tree Handbook with Aerospace Applications. NASA Office of Safety and Mission Assurance, NASA Headquarters, Washington DC 20546. (2002)

[15] Reifer, D.: Software failure modes and effects analysis. IEEE Transactions on Reliability 28 (1979) 147 - 249

[16] Fenelon, P., McDermid, J., Nicholson, A., Pumfrey, D.: Experience with the application of HAZOP to computer-based systems. In: Proceedings of the 10th Annual Conference on Computer Assurance, Gaithersburg, MD, IEEE (1995)

[17] Ortmeier, F., Thums, A., Schellhorn, G., W.Reif: Combining formal methods and safety analysis - the for mossa approach. In: this volume. Springer LNCS (2004)

[18] Brill, M., Buschermöhle, R., Damm, W., Klose, J., Westphal, B., Wittke, H.: Formal verification of LSCs in the development process. In: this volume. Springer LNCS (2004)

[19] Paulson, L.C.: Isabelle: A Generic Theorem Prover. LNCS 828. Springer (1994)

[20] Owre, S., Rushby, J.M., Shankar, N.: PVS: A Prototype Verification System. In Kapur, D., ed.: Automated Deduction - CADE-11. Proceedings. LNAI 607, Berlin, Saratoga Springs, NY, USA, Springer (1992)

[21] Kaufmann, M., Moore, J.: An industrial strength theorem prover for a logic based on common lisp. IEEE Transactions on Software Engineering 23 (1997)

[22] Thums, A., Schellhorn, G., Ortmeier, F., W.Reif: Interactive verification of statecharts. In: this volume. Springer LNCS (2004)

[23] McMillan, K.L.: Symbolic Model Checking. Kluwer Academic Publishers (1990)

[24] Holzmann, G., Holzmann, G.: The Spin Model Checker: Primer and Reference Manual. Addison Wesley (2003)

[25] Amnell, T., Behrmann, G., Bengtsson, J., D'Argenio, P.R., David, A., Fehnker, A., Hune, T., Jeannet, B., Larsen, K.G., Möller, M.O., Pettersson, P., Weise, C., Yi, W.: UPPAAL - Now, Next, and Future. In Cassez, F., Jard, C., Rozoy, B., Ryan, M., eds.: Modelling and Verification of Parallel Processes. Number 2067 in Lecture Notes in Computer Science Tutorial, Springer–Verlag (2001) 100–125

[26] Bienmöller, T., Damm, W., Wittke, H.: The STATEMATE verification environment – making it real. In Emerson, E.A., Sistla, A.P., eds.: CAV'00: 12th international Conference on Computer Aided Verification. Number 1855 in LNCS, Chicago, IL, USA, Springer (2000) 561–567

[27] Bauer, N., Engell, S., Huuck, R., Lohmann, S., Lukoschus, B., Remelhe, M., Stursberg, O.: Verification of PLC programs given as sequential function charts. In: this volume. Springer LNCS (2004)

[28] Ruf, J., Weiss, R.J., Kropf, T., Rosenstiel, W.: Modeling and formal verification of production automation systems. In: this volume. Springer LNCS (2004)

"UML–ising" Formal Techniques

Dines Bjørner[1], Chris W. George[2], Anne E. Haxthausen[1],
Christian Krog Madsen[3], Steffen Holmslykke[1], and Martin Pěnička[4]

[1] Computer Science and Engineering Dept., Informatics and Mathematical Modelling
Inst., Technical University of Denmark, DK–2800 Kgs.Lyngby, Denmark,
{db,ah}@imm.dtu.dk, steffen@holmslykke.com
[2] Director ai., UNU/IIST, P.O.Box 3058, Macau SAR, China, cwg@iist.unu.edu
[3] Rovsing A/S, Dyregårdsvej 2, DK–2740 Skovlunde, Denmark,
christian@krog-madsen.dk
[4] Faculty of Transportation, Czech Technical University, Na Florenci 25, CZ-11000
Prague 1, The Czech Republic, penicka@fd.cvut.cz, martin@imm.dtu.dk.

Abstract. This invited paper presents a number of correlated specifications of example railway system problems. They use a variety of partially or fully integrated formal specification. The paper thus represents a mere repository of what we consider interesting case studies.

The existence of the Unified Modeling Language [10,67,36,20] has caused, for one reason or another, the research community to try formalise one or another facet of UML. In this paper we report on another way to achieve what UML attempts to achieve: Broadness of application, convenience of notation, and multiplicity of views. Whether these different UML views are unified, integrated, correlated or merely co–located is for others to dispute. We also seek to support multiple views, but are also in no doubt that there must be sound, well defined relations between such views.

We thus report on ways and means of integrating formal techniques such as RAISE (RSL) [58,59], Petri Nets [56,62,37,61,41], Message and Live Sequence Charts [42,43,44,64,13], Statecharts [23,24,26,27], RAISE with Timing (TRSL) [18,45,46], and TRSL with Duration Calculus [79,30]. In this way one achieves a firm foundation for combined uses of these formal development techniques, one that can be believably deployed for as wide a spectrum, or even a wider spectrum of software (and hardware) development, as, respectively than UML.

1 The Problem

1.1 The Issues

When we describe, in informal, yet reasonably precise natural (or at least domain specific professional) language the entities, the functions, the events and behaviours of an application domain, then we encounter, perhaps, little, if any problem. Our use of natural language is very flexible. Without hardly noticing it, we slip from one mode of description to another mode. (What these modes are will be apparent in the next paragraph.)

H. Ehrig et al. (Eds.): INT 2004, LNCS 3147, pp. 423–450, 2004.
© Springer-Verlag Berlin Heidelberg 2004

When, now, on the basis of the informal narrative, we wish to formalise this description, then we might very well encounter serious problems. We refer here to the current inability of any one formal specification language to cater for all kinds of modes: Functional, imperative (ie., with states being changed by assignments to variables), logical, temporal, and concurrency modes, the latter with events and behaviours. In particular we often slip, in natural language, from decribing such *qualitative* aspects of timing as concurrent behaviours and their synchronisation and communication, to such *quantitative* aspects of timing as absolute and relative time: *"12:05 am"* to *"after 5 minutes and 30 seconds"* — without hardly noticing it.

Put differently: Some formal specification languages may cater, as does RSL, the specification language of RAISE [58,59], for functional, imperative, logical, and parallel behaviours — but RSL does not cater, neither for "true" concurrency, nor for time. Also: The diagrammatic constructs of Petri Nets [56,62, 37,61], of Statecharts [23,24], and of Live Sequence Charts [13] cater for the qualitative facets of concurrency and timing (as does RSL), but they do so diagrammatically, and as such they are indeed oftentimes more appealing to casual readers than "flat" texts (ie., RSL). Similarly RSL's "flat text" module structuring (schemes, classes and objects) are, to some, inferior in communicability to UML's Class Diagrams [10,67,36].

This therefore is the problem: To combine, to integrate, uses of two or more formalisms in one specification — such that we can still retain (most of) the virtues of any of the formal notations: For example abstraction, reasoning, and refinement.

1.2   Integrating Formal Techniques

No one formal specification language can reasonably be expected to cover all modes of descriptions, all kinds of universes of discourse.

There is, therefore, an effort going on, world–wide, in integrating, in combining, different specification paradigms, such as mentioned above. Notable efforts can be referenced:

Combining Statecharts and Z for the design of safety-critical control systems [75] (1996), Integrated Formal Methods [17] (1996), A combination of Object–Z and CSP [14] (1997), Specifying embedded systems with Statecharts and Z [19] (1998), An Operational Semantics for Timed RAISE, TRSL [18] (1999), Linking DC together with TRSL [30] (2000), Study of graphical and temporal specification techniques [49] (2003), Integration of Specification Techniques [48] (2003).

An underlying theme here is that of Unifying Theories of Programming [32] (1998), Unifying Theories of Parallel Programming [77] (2002), and Semantic Integration of Heterogeneous Software Specifications (2003) [65].

Many other references could be given to papers that seeks to provide answers to integration issues: [75,17,14,32,19,11,60,77].

1.3   Structure of Paper

The paper is structured as follows: First (Sect. 2) we provide a setting, basically common to the whole paper, namely a specification, in RSL, of properties of the layout of railway nets. First we present it in a "flat" version of RSL, ie., without RSL's parameterised **scheme** and **class** facilities. Then we present "the same" specification with those modularising facilities (Sect. 3). From that, without much analysis, we present a UML Class Diagram (Sect. 4). Sect. 5 discuses relations between RSL and UML.

Then we "pick" another, albeit related, problem, one of timing, and show (Sect. 6.1) its specification in RSL extended with timing [18], and Timed RSL extended with durations [30], in the sense of the Duration Calculus [79] (Sect. 6.2).

Independently we show an example of combining a RSL specification with Petri Nets (Sect. 7), and finally a specification embodying Live Sequence Charts and Statecharts (Sect. 8)

1.4   Prerequisites

Professional software engineers today are expected to be sufficiently versant in either of the notational systems and intentions of VDM, Z, RAISE, or B [15,76, 59,1]. Enough to understand this paper's use of RSL [58]. They are likewise expected to be sufficiently versant in UML's usage of Petri Nets, Message Sequence Charts (MSCs) and Statecharts (SCs) to likewise follow the paper's use of those mechanisms, including Live Sequence Charts. As for TRSL (Timed RSL) and DC (Duration Calculus) we do not expect the same insight – so, please consider this paper a good reason for "catching up" by reading the referenced TRSL paper [18] or PhD Thesis [78], respectively DC book [79] (or original paper [80]). There will be ample references, later, to books on UML, Petri Nets, MSCs, SCs, etc.

2   "Flat" RAISE (DB)

Our "running" example is taken from the domain of railways. First informally, as a rough sketch supported by a "snapshot" layout diagram. Then formally.

We constrain ourselves to the modeling of just the static aspects of the topology of a railway net. That is: Of net, lines and stations. And of units of lines and station (and hence of nets). And of connectors of units. Examples of a net, of two lines and two stations, of both lines consisting each of three linear units. Of the stations consisting of tracks (ie., platform tracks and sidings), and of otherwise also consisting of simple switch, simple crossover, and of switchable crossover units.

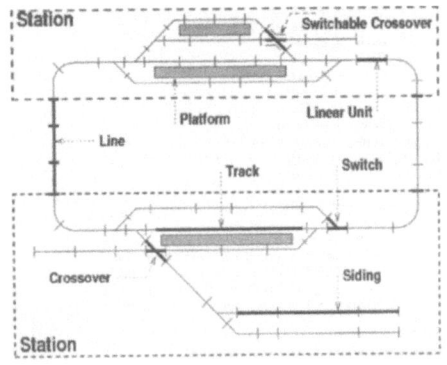

2.1 Informal Description

We narrate a precise, yet informal description:

We introduce the phenomena of railway nets, lines, stations, tracks, (rail) units, and connectors.

1. A railway net consists of one or more lines and two or more stations.
2. A railway net consists of rail units.
3. A line is a linear sequence of one or more linear rail units.
4. The rail units of a line must be rail units of the railway net of the line.
5. A station is a set of one or more rail units.
6. The rail units of a station must be rail units of the railway net of the station.
7. No two distinct lines and/or stations of a railway net share rail units.
8. A station consists of one or more tracks.
9. A track is a linear sequence of one or more linear rail units.
10. No two distinct tracks share rail units.

11. The rail units of a track must be rail units of the station (of that track).
12. A rail unit is either a linear, or is a switch, or a is simple crossover, or is a switchable crossover, etc., rail unit.
13. A rail unit has one or more connectors.
14. A linear rail unit has two distinct connectors, a switch rail unit has three distinct connectors, crossover rail units have four distinct connectors (whether simple or switchable), etc.
15. For every connector there are at most two rail units which have that connector in common.
16. Every line of a railway net is connected to exactly two, distinct stations of that railway net.
17. A linear sequence of (linear) rail units is a non-cyclic sequence of linear units such that neighbouring units share connectors.

The numbering of the text items is used as cross references in Sects. 2.2, 3 and 4.

2.2 Formal Description

And finally, in this introductory example, we formalise the previous informal narrative.

```
type
    N, L, S, Tr, U, C
value
1.  obs_Ls: N → L-set,
1.  obs_Ss: N → S-set,
2.  obs_Us: N → U-set,
3.  obs_Us: L → U-set,
5.  obs_Us: S → U-set,
8.  obs_Trs: S → Tr-set
12. is_Linear: U → Bool,
12. is_Switch: U → Bool
12. is_Simple_Crossover: U → Bool,
12. is_Switchable_Crossover: U → Bool
13. obs_Cs: U → C-set

17. lin_seq: U-set → Bool
    lin__seq(us) ≡
      ∀ u:U • u ∈ us ⇒ is_Linear(u) ∧
      ∃ q:U* • len q = card us ∧ elems q = us ∧
        ∀ i:Nat • {i,i+1} ⊆ inds q ⇒ ∃ c:C •
          obs_Cs(q(i)) ∩ obs_Cs(q(i+1)) = {c} ∧
      len q > 1 ⇒ obs_Cs(q(i)) ∩ obs_Cs(q(len q)) = {}
```

Some formal axioms are now given, not all !

axiom

```
1.  ∀ n:N • card obs_Ls(n) ≥ 1,
1.  ∀ n:N • card obs_Ss(n) ≥ 2,
3.  l:L • lin_seq(l)
4.  ∀ n:N, l:L • l ∈ obs_Ls(n) ⇒ obs_Us(l) ⊆ obs_Us(n)
5.  ∀ n:N, s:S • s ∈ obs_Ss(n) ⇒ card obs_Us(s) ≥ 1
6.  ∀ s:S • obs_Us(s) ⊆ obs_Us(n)
7.  ∀ n:N,l,l':L• {l,l'} ⊆ obs_Ls(n)∧l≠l' ⇒obs_Us(l)∩ obs_Us(l')={ }
7.  ∀ n:N,l:L,s:S•l ∈ obs_Ls(n)∧s ∈ obs_Ss(n)⇒
        obs_Us(l)∩ obs_Us(s)={ }
7.  ∀ n:N,s,s':S• {s,s'} ⊆obs_Ss(n)∧s≠s' ⇒obs_Us(s)∩ obs_Us(s')={ }
8.  ∀ s:S • card obs_Trs(s) ≥ 1

9.  ∀ n:N, s:S, t:T • s ∈ obs_Ss(n) ∧ t ∈ obs_Trs(s) ⇒ lin_seq(t)
10. ∀ n:N, s:S, t,t':T •
      s ∈ obs_Ss(n) ∧ {t,t'} ⊆ obs_Trs(s) ∧ t≠t'
        ⇒ obs_Us(t) ∩ obs_Us(t') = {}
15. ∀ n:N •
      c ∈ ∪ { obs_Cs(u) | u:U • u ∈ obs_Us(n) }
        ⇒ card{ u | u:U • u ∈ obs_Us(n) ∧ c ∈ obs_Cs(u) } ≤2
16. ∀ n:N,l:L • l ∈ obs_Ls(n) ⇒
      ∃ s,s':S • {s,s'} ⊆ obs_Ss(n), ∧ s≠s' ⇒
        let sus = obs_Us(s), sus' = obs_Us(s'), lus = obs_Us(l) in
        ∃ u:U•u ∈ sus,u':U•u' ∈ sus',u'',u''':U ∈ {u'',u'''}⊆lus•
        let scs = obs_Cs(u), scs' = obs_Cs(u'),
          lcs = obs_Cs(u''), lcs' = obs_Cs(u''') in
        ∃ l c,c':C • c ≠ c' ∧ scs ∩ lcs = {c} ∧ scs' ∩ lcs' = {c'}
end end
```

Elsewhere we have shown extensions of the above model into simple dynamics of unit switching [6], of principles of modeling such domains as railways [8], of possible relations between these kind of railway models and control theory [7], of using such models as that above for modeling train maintenance [57], train staff rostering [71], etc. Modeling the scheduling of trains, based on simpler models than the above, was shown in [9].

3   RAISE Model with Schemes (SH)

The previous specification was expressed in "flat" RSL. Next, and in preparation for the UML Class Diagram "rendition", we show a "structured" version of the above "flat" formulas. The structuring is afforded by RSL's **schema** and **class** mechanisms. Without much comments we present these schemes.[1] The model presented in this section is somehow "equivalent", we claim, to the model just presented in section 2.2. The difference is in the use of parameterized schemes. Using schemes we can break the model into smaller modules. Each sort from the flat model is placed in a separate scheme and the functions and axioms which are associated with the sort are included with it. This should give an intuitive division of the flat model which may be more easily comprehended.

```
scheme Connectors = class type C end

scheme Units(connectors : Connectors) =
class
    type U
    value
        12 is_Linear: U→Bool,
        12 is_Switch: U→Bool,
        12 is_SimpleCrossover: U→Bool,
        12 is_SwitchableCrossover: U→Bool,
        13 obs_Cs: U→connectors.C-set,
    17 lin_seq: U-set→Bool
    lin_seq(us) ≡
        (∀ u:U•u ∈ us ⇒ is_Linear(u)∧
        (∃ q:U*•len q = card us∧elems q=us∧
            (∀ i:Nat•{i,i+1}⊆inds q ⇒
            (∃ c:connectors.C•
                obs_Cs(q(i)) ∩ obs_Cs(q(i+1))={c}∧
                len q>1 ⇒
                    obs_Cs(q(i)) ∩ obs_Cs(q(len q))={ })))))
    end
```

We could single out each of the (so far mentioned) four disjoint kinds of *Units*, representing them as schemes. We show it only for the linear case:

```
scheme Linear(connectors : Connectors) =
extend Units(connectors) with
class
    type UL = U
    axiom
        ∀ l:UL•is_Linear(l)
            ∧∼is_Switch(l)
            ∧∼is_SimpleCrossover(l)
            ∧∼is_SwitchableCrossover(l),
        ∀ l:UL: card obs_Cs(l)=2
end
```

We go on:

```
scheme Sequence(
    connectors: Connectors,
    units: Units(connectors)) =
```

```
class
    type Seq
    value obs_Us: Seq→units.U-set
    axiom ∀ s: Seq•units.lin_seq(obs_Us(s))
end
```

```
scheme Lines(
    connectors: Connectors,
    units: Units(connectors)) =
extend Sequence(connectors,units) with
class
    type L
    value
        obs_Seq: L→Seq,
        obs_Us: L→units.U-set
        obs_Us(l) ≡ obs_Us(obs_Seq(l))
end
```

```
scheme Tracks(
    connectors: Connectors,
    units: Units(connectors)) =
extend Sequence(connectors,units) with
class
    type Tr
    value
        obs_Seq: Tr→Seq,
        obs_Us: Tr→units.U-set
        obs_Us(t) ≡ obs_Us(obs_Seq(t))
end
```

```
scheme Stations(
    connectors: Connectors,
    units: Units(connectors),
    tracks: Tracks(connectors,units)) =
class
    type S
    value
        5 obs_Us: S→units.U-set,
        8 obs_Trs: S→tracks.Tr-set
    axiom
        5 ∀ s:S•card obs_Us(s)≥1,
        8 ∀ s:S•card obs_Trs(s)≥1,
        7 ∀ s,s′:S•s≠s′
            ⇒ obs_Us(s) ∩ obs_Us(s′)={ }
end
```

---

[1] The item numbers of some of the formulas of this section derive from Sect. 2.1.

```
scheme Nets(
    connectors: Connectors,
    units: Units(connectors),
    lines: Lines(connectors,units),
    tracks: Tracks(connectors,units),
    stations: Stations(connectors,units,tracks)) =
class
    type N
    value
    1 obs_Ls: N→lines.L-set,
    1 obs_Ss: N→stations.S-set,
    2 obs_Us: N→units.U-set
```

```
axiom
1 ∀ n:N•card obs_Ls(n)≥1,
1 ∀ n:N•card obs_Ss(n)≥2,
4 ∀ n:N,l:lines.L•l ∈ obs_Ls(n)⇒
        lines.obs_Us(l)⊆obs_Us(n),
6 ∀ n:N,s:stations.S•s ∈ obs_Ss(n)⇒
        stations.obs_Us(s)⊆obs_Us(n),
7 ∀ n:N,l:lines.L,s:stations.S•
    l ∈ obs_Ls(n)∧s ∈ obs_Ss(n)
        ⇒lines.obs_Us(l) ∩ stations.obs_Us(s)={ }
end
```

4   The UML Model (SH)

The two formal models of Sect. 2.2 and Sect. 3 were based on the informal description of railway nets (Sect. 2.1). The model in this section is expressed in UML but reflects the parameterised scheme model (of Sect. 3). This should of course amount to a model that is "equivalent" to the formal models. It is however known that the language of Class Diagrams is not as powerful an expression tool as is, for example, RSL. Properties expressible in, for example RSL, cannot be expressed by the Object Constraint Language, OCL [73,74], of UML. Notwithstanding, it is still a good idea to try express certain of the properties of the formal models in class diagrams. Our model is presented in figure 1.

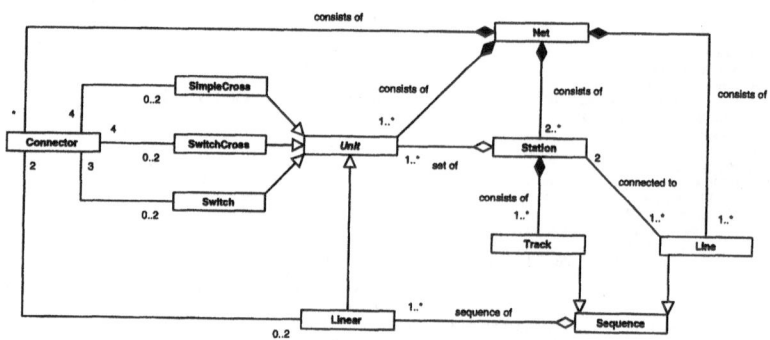

Fig. 1. UML Class Diagram for Rail Nets

In our class diagram for rail nets, the model has been divided into several "smaller" pieces which describe "smaller" parts. In this case the classes represent the phenomena introduced in the informal description and corresponding to the schemes of Sect. 3.

Items 1[2], 2, and 8 describe a *consist of* relationship between two phenomena. The latter item describes that a station consists of one or more tracks. This fits with the whole–part relationship that *composition* provides for in class diagrams.

---

[2] The item numbers of this section derive from Sect. 2.1.

Here the station is the whole and it is not complete unless it has tracks and the tracks cannot exist without a station. As an example, item 8 is depicted, in the class diagram, as a solid line between the *Station* and *Track* classes; the first is marked with a filled diamond at the end of the line — indicating that it is the *whole*.

Items 3, 9, and 5 use respectively a *sequence of* and a *set of* to describe a relationship. This is again a whole–part relationship. The parts are, however, already part of the net. So to be able to maintain a reference to an existing part a *shareable* aggregation is used as a relation. As an example, item 3 is depicted, in the class diagram, as a solid line between the *Station* and the *Unit* classes; the first is marked with an hollow diamond at the end of the line — indicating that it is the *whole*.

In item 12 a unit is described as being either a *Linear*, *Switch*, *SimpleCross*, or *SwitchCross*. In the class diagram this is expressed by a *generalization* relationship where the *Unit* is an *abstract class*. Its class name is written in italics — so it cannot be instantiated.

Both the informal description in item 12 and the corresponding way it is modeled in the class diagram suggests that another axiom should be added. In the formal model four boolean functions are used to determine which type a given unit is. Here an axiom could be added, one which ensures that a unit only can be of one type. This is achieved in the class diagram since an object only can instantiate one class. The axiom could be as follows:

$$\forall \ u{:}U \bullet is\_Linear(u) \Rightarrow$$
$$\sim(is\_Switch(u) \lor is\_SwitchableCrossover(u) \lor is\_SimpleCrossover(u))$$

Additional axioms should be added for each of the three other possible situations.

The two items 13 and 14 are overlapping. The latter expresses more properties. The latter explicitly describes the number of connectors which a given unit must have, while the former just states that a unit has at least one connector attached. If the latter is fulfilled then so is the former which makes it superfluous in this model. This was noticed while drawing the associations between the *Unit* class and its specializations. Here item 14 would in the class diagram amount to an *association* between each of the *specialized* classes of *Unit* and (and to) the *Connector* class. Item 13 would be an association between the abstract *Unit* class and (and to) the *Connector* class. If these were to be added to the class diagram, then it would mean that each of the specialisations, due to inheritance, also would have this relation (through generalisation), which is, however, not intended.

It is not possible to diagram items 4, 6, 7, 10, 11, 15, 16, and 17 in a class diagram, since they describe requirements to the instances of the static structure. As an example, item 4 is used and redisplayed for convenience: "The rail units of a line must be rail units of the railway net of the line." To be able to express this requirement we must be able to identify a particular unit and if it is part of a line then it must also be part of the net. This could, however, be achieved by using the Object Constraint Language [20, sec. 6]. We will not do so here.

5   Discussion: RSL and UML (SH)

During the creation of the RSL and the UML class diagram models, some observations have been made. These will be discussed in this section.

5.1   UML and RSL Relationship

While making the modular RSL model of Sect. 3, and the UML model of Sect. 4, it was intuitively decided which constructs to use in the languages. These choices are commented upon with regard to a more general relationship between the two languages.

Entity sets described in the informal description have in the RSL model been represented by sorts: Besides a few observer functions they are further unspecified. In the class diagram they are represented by classes which can be instantiated as objects. There is a resemblance here with RSL schemes since they also can be instantiated (as RSL objects). The style which have been chosen in the RSL model is applicative (ie., functional). There is perhaps a closer relationship between schemes and classes if an imperative modeling style had been used since the object in RSL would then contain a state.

One could argue that the models described are still in an initial phase and it is too early to determine what a state for a given phenomena should consist of. This is also apparent in the class diagram since none of the classes have any attributes nor operations which is also the reason for not including the compartments in the diagram.

The associations used in the class diagram are in the RSL specification described using observer functions on the sorts. Links, which in UML are instances of associations, are in UML models terms used to communicate messages; that is, invoke a method at the target object. As an alternative to the observer functions in RSL channels might be used as a representation.

The generalization relationship in UML and the **extend** construct in RSL seem quite similar since they both take respectively a class and a scheme and adds more information. A specialised class in UML can add attributes or operations to the ones already present in the generalised class. This is also possible with the **extend** construct of RSL. However before the generalisation versus extend relationship can be discussed it should be determined whether or not the UML class can be represented by schemes in RSL.

There are of course many more elements in UML but those used in the Fig. 1 are the most essential. Therefore this discussion will be constrained to those.

5.2   References

Although RSL has modules, it may be claimed not to be "a true" object oriented ("OO") language. This does not, however, mean that it is impossible to express object oriented models in RSL. The reason that RSL may be judged not to be "immediately" object oriented may be the claim that RSL does not provide for object references. But since objects of RSL can be grouped into **object arrays,** indexing can replace linking.

As an example the three schemes *Connectors*, *Units*, and *Lines* from section 3 can be used. The headers of the mentioned schemes are replicated below for convenience. The first scheme has no parameters since it does not use any sorts or functions from outside its own scheme. The *Units* scheme needs to know of the *Connectors* scheme since it uses its sort.

scheme Connectors = **class** ... **end,**
scheme Units(connectors:Connectors) = **class** ... **end**

The *Lines* scheme need only information from the *Units* scheme and not from the *Connectors* scheme. However to be able to instantiate the *Units* scheme an object instantiated from the *Connectors* scheme must be provided. It is not possible to pass an already instantiated object of units as the only parameter to the *Lines* scheme or formulated in another way it is not possible to pass an object by reference. This is a major difference between RSL and object oriented modeling. Thus it is necessary to give an object of type *Connectors* as parameter although it is not used by the *Lines* scheme.

scheme Lines(connectors:Connectors,units:Units(connectors)) = **class** ... **end**

It is, however, all a matter of how one approaches the modeling, the abstraction level and the refinement of models. Through a suitably chosen approach one may claim that RSL provides for all that "OO" provides.

5.3   Circularity

An association with composite aggregation in the class diagram which has the same class at each end introduces a recursive description. It is possible to define recursive structures in RSL using variants however it is not permitted to make a recursive type definition nor recursive modules. In this case a scheme is not a good choice for representing a UML class.

Recursive definitions have not been used in any of the RSL models nor in the UML models but was considered with respect to units and connectors. The question is whether a connector is an independent phenomena or a part of a unit. The latter seems to be best for describing railway nets. If a connector is part of a unit then aggregation should be used where a unit specialisation is the whole and the connector is the part. This would also mean that it is actually two connectors which is connected or, perhaps a better way to express it, is that when to units are connected then the connectors at the ends merge into one connector.

The actual recursive solution was considered in the case where there still would be two connectors when two units are connected. That is the connectors are connected to each other. This would mean that a connector is part of a unit which would be modelled with aggregation and it would be connected to another connector which would be modelled with a ordinary association from the *Connector* class to itself; Hence the recursive definition.

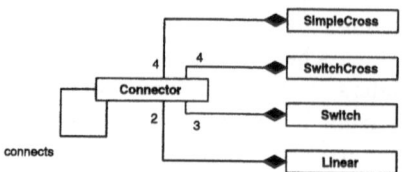

Fig. 2. Alternative model for connectors and specialized units.

5.4   Class Diagram Limitations

As mentioned in section 4 the class diagram could not contain all the information given in the (in)formal description(s) of railway nets. Particularly information that referred to the unique identity of an instance. Here it is necessary to use the Object Constraint Language.

It is possible to express some information in the diagram which in the RSL models are described using axioms. Examples are constraints on numbers, such as the minimum number of stations in a net. This is expressed in class diagrams using multiplicity.

· · ·

In [16] a formal model has been presented, in RSL, of UML's Class Diagram concept, together with a mechanism, a kind of "compiling algorithm" which translates UML Class Diagrams into RSL. Ongoing work at the first (DB) and second (CWG) co–authors' institutions, are carrying on this work of combining RSL with the graphics of UML's Class Diagrams. The fifth co–author (SH) is involved in this work.

6   RAISE and Temporality (CWH+AH)

6.1   Timing and RAISE: TRSL

'Timed RSL', TRSL, was first treated in [18].

RSL originally had no built–in way to model time. Time could of course be modeled using RSL, but this is not in general very satisfactory. Without a built–in notion of time it would be impossible, for example, to specify basic components of timed systems such as "time out".

The extension of RSL to Timed RSL (TRSL) is minimal syntactically: there are just two additions. First is the type **Time**, just a synonym for the non–negative subtype of the existing type **Real**. Second is the new expression "**wait** e", where e is an expression of type **Time**.

The semantic changes are, of course, more considerable, but still largely confined to the constructs intended to specify communication and concurrency. The semantics is based on Wang Yi's work on Timed ccs [78], adapted to support value passing communication. It assumes that only the wait expression, input and output can consume time, adopts the principle of maximal progress, and includes time dependence. Time dependence enables a parallel expansion rule, but also adds expressiveness.

Methodologically, the intention is to develop specifications initially without regard to time, following the normal RAISE method, reaching an imperative concurrent specification: essentially a collection of communicating processes. At this point time is introduced in terms of wait expressions, and possibly extra choices for detections of time outs or other time dependent behaviour. There is more on the method in section 6.2.

We give here a few illustrative fragments. First, **wait** may just indicate a delay. Execution of the expression:

sensor_state := high ; **wait** δ ; sensor_state := low

will set and keep *sensor_state* high for precisely time δ, and then make it low.

A time out can be modeled by an external choice involving a **wait**. Suppose we need to take some special (abnormal) actions if a signal *normal* does not occur within time t. The expression:

normal? ; ...

▯

wait t ; abnormal!()

will take the first choice provided an output on the channel *normal* occurs within time t. Otherwise, at time t, the wait terminates and the second choice becomes available. Provided there is some process waiting to handle the output *abnormal*, the principle of maximal progress will ensure the second choice occurs, and we would say the normal behaviour has timed out.

An example illustrating the use of time dependence will be given in section 6.2.

In [46,45] denotational semantics of Timed RSL are given using Duration Calculus, to the combination of which we now turn.

6.2   TRSL and Duration Calculus

The Duration Calculi are covered in the seminal [79].

While TRSL is well–suited for timed design specifications, DC is well–suited for timed requirement specifications. This suggests the following development method [30] (illustrated in Fig. 3) for real-time systems integrating TRSL and DC specifications:

1. The RAISE method [59] is used for developing a specification of the un–timed properties of the system, starting with an abstract, property–oriented RSL specification and ending with a concrete, implementation–oriented RSL specification.

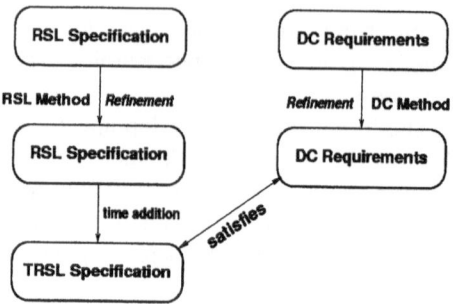

Fig. 3. A Development Method for Real-time Systems

2. In parallel with the RSL development of the un–timed system, a DC requirement specification of the real time properties of that system is developed.
State variables in the DC specification are variables defined (at least) in the
last RSL specification (and in the TRSL specification).
3. Timing information is added to the RSL specification achieving a TRSL specification of a real-time implementation.
4. It must be verified that the TRSL specification satisfies the DC specification.

Hence, there is no syntactic integration between the DC and TRSL specification,
but only a consistency requirement that state variables used in the DC specification are variables defined in the TRSL specification. The integration is made in
the form of a satisfaction (or refinement) relation. The approach for defining this
relation has been to make an abstract interpretation within the DC formalism of
TRSL process definitions. Technically this is done by extending the operational
semantics of TRSL [18] with behaviours which are DC formulas describing (parts
of) the history of the observables of the system. The satisfaction relation between sentences in the two languages is then defined in terms of behaviours. The
formal definition and proof rules can be found in [30].

Due to space limitations we just show a very simple example illustrating
steps 2-4.

Problem description: Our goal is to specify those components of a railway
control system that should perform train detection.

In the considered system sensors are used for train detection. When a train
starts passing a sensor, the sensor should immediately become "high" and after
a while it should fall back to "low". In order for the control system to be able
to detect the high state the sensor must stay in the "high" state for a certain
minimum of time, δ. Because of this requirement, trains should arrive at the
sensor at least δ time apart. It may be safe to just record this as an assumption,
because we know it is ensured by other parts of the system, or because δ (perhaps
a fraction of a second for electronic equipment) is orders of magnitude less than
an interval between trains could be. But sometimes such assumptions need to
be checked at runtime, and that is what we assume here, as it gives us an

opportunity to illustrate the use of time dependence. We assume that an error must be recorded if two trains arrive within δ of each other.

DC requirements: The requirement on the sensor is:

$$\Box((\lceil \text{sensor\_state=low} \rceil \bullet \lceil \text{sensor\_state=high} \rceil \bullet \lceil \text{sensor\_state=low} \rceil) \Rightarrow \ell \geq \delta)$$

This requirement says that any complete period with "high" state (i.e. one with a "low" state before and after) has a duration (ℓ) of at least δ.

TRSL Specification:

value δ : Time
type SensorState == low | high
channel detect_train, error, train_detected : **Unit**

value
    detect : **Unit** → **in** detect_train **out** train_detected, error **Unit**
    detect() ≡
      while true do
        let t = detect_train? **in**
          if t $\leq$ δ **then** error!()
          else train_detected!()
          end
        end
      end,

    sensor : **Unit** → **in** train_detected **write** sensor_state **Unit**
    sensor() ≡
      local variable sensor_state : SensorState:= low **in**
      while true do
        train_detected? ; sensor_state := high ; **wait** δ ; sensor_state := low
      end
    end

The channel *detect_train* represents the hardware train detection unit. We assume that every train enables an output on this channel.

The purpose of the process *detect* is to check that trains are at least time δ apart. Provided trains are sufficiently separated it signals their arrival to the *sensor* process; otherwise it signals an error. *detect*'s behaviour depends on the time t that it waits for input on the *detect_train* channel.[3] If t is too small an error is signaled. Otherwise the detection event is passed to the *sensor* process

---

[3] An input or output can optionally return the time that it waited for synchronisation: this supports time dependence, i.e. following behaviour can depend on the value of this time.

using another channel *train_detected*. If we had made the assumption that trains could not possibly arrive within time δ of each other, process *detect* and the channel *train_detected* would be unnecessary, and *sensor* could directly access the channel *detect_train*.

The process *sensor* controls the sensor state *sensor_state*: In each cycle, right after receiving a message (on *train_detected*) from the *detect* process that a train has arrived, *sensor_state* stays "high" for exactly δ time units and then becomes low. (Hence, it satisfies the DC requirement.)

Note that correct behaviour of *detect*, in the sense of only reporting actual errors (trains too close together), assumes that the value t is the same as the time since the last train, i.e. since the last communication on *detect_train*. This will only be true if there is no wait anywhere in the loop except for the communication on *detect_train*. This in particular means that the *sensor* process must always be ready to input on *train_detected* when *detect* is ready to do output on *train_detected*, i.e. *sensor* must have a cycle time of at most δ. This is clearly satisfied by *sensor*.

Satisfaction Relation: The following satisfaction relation expresses that the *sensor* process satisfies the previously stated DC requirement:

sensor() **satisfies**
$\Box((\lceil\text{sensor\_state=low}\rceil \bullet \lceil\text{sensor\_state=high}\rceil \bullet \lceil\text{sensor\_state=low}\rceil) \Rightarrow \ell \geq \delta)$

It can be proved using proof rules in [30] and DC proof rules.

7   Petri Nets and RAISE

We assume basic knowledge of Petri Nets: [56,62,37,61,38,41].

7.1   The RAISE Part (DB)

First we augment our model of railway nets with dynamics of these railway nets. We introduce defined concepts such as paths through rail units, state of rail units, rail unit state spaces, routes through a railway network, open and closed routes, trains on the railway net, and train movement on the railway net.

Informal description:

18. A path, $p : P$, is a pair of connectors, (c, c'),
19. which are distinct,
20. and of some unit.[4]

21. A state, $\sigma : \Sigma$, of a unit is the set of all open paths of that unit (at the time observed).[5]

---

[4] A path of a unit designate that a train may move across the unit in the direction from c to c'. We say that the unit is open in the direction of the path.

[5] The state may be empty: the unit is closed.

22. A unit may, over its operational life, attain any of a (possibly small) number of different states ω, Ω.
23. A route is a sequence of pairs of units and paths —
24. such that the path of a unit/path pair is a possible path of some state of the unit, and such that "neighbouring" connectors are identical.
25. An open route is a route such that all its paths are open.
26. A train is modelled as a route.
27. Train movement is modelled as a discrete function (ie., a map) from time to routes
28. such that for any two adjacent times the two corresponding routes differ by at most one of the following:
    a) a unit path pair has been deleted (removed) from one end of the route;
    b) a unit path pair has been deleted (removed) from the other end of the route;
    c) a unit path pair has been added (joined) from one end of the route;
    d) a unit path pair has been added (joined) from the other end of the route;
    e) a unit path pair has been added (joined) from one end of the route, and another unit path par has been deleted (removed) from the other end of the route;
    f) a unit path pair has been added (joined) from the other of the route, and another unit path par has been deleted (removed) from the one end of the route;
    g) or there has been no changes with respect to the route (yet the train may have moved);
29. and such that the new route is a well-formed route.

Formalisation:

```
type
18. P′ = C × Ç
19. P = {| (c,c′):P′ • c≠c′ |}
21. Σ = P-set
22. Ω = Σ-set
23. R′ = (U × P)*
24. R = {| r:R′ • wf_R(r) |}
26. Trn = R
27. Mov′ = T ⇸ Trn
28. Mov = {| m:Mov′ • wf_Mov(m) |}

value
21. obs_Σ: U → Σ
22. obs_Ω: U → Ω

axiom
  ∀ u:U •
    let ω = obs_Ω(u), σ = obs_Σ(u) in
      σ ∈ ω ∧ 20.
    let cs = obs_Cs(u) in
      ∀ (c,c′):P • (c,c′) ∈ ∪ ω ⇒ {c,c′} ⊆ obs_Cs(u)
    end end

24. wf_R: R′ → Bool
    wf_R(r) ≡
      len r > 0 ∧
      ∀ i:Nat • i ∈ inds r let (u,(c,c′)) = r(i) in
        (c,c′) ∈ ∪ obs_Ω(u) ∧ i+1 ∈ inds r ⇒
        let (_,(c″,_)) = r(i+1) in c′ = c″ end end
```

```
25. open_R: R → Bool
    open_R(r) ≡
      ∀ (u,p):U×P • (u,p) ∈ elems r ∧ p ∈ obs_Σ(u)

27. wf_Mov: Mov → Bool
    wf_Mov(m) ≡ card dom m ≥ 2 ∧
      ∀ t,t′:T • t,t′ ∈ dom m ∧ t < t′
      ∧ adjacent(t,t′) ⇒
        let (r,r′) = (m(t),m(t′))
                      (u,p):U×P • p ∈ ∪ obs_Ω(u) in
28a. (ld(r,r′,(u,p)) ∨ 28b.  rd(r,r′,(u,p)) ∨
28c. la(r,r′,(u,p)) ∨ 28d.  ra(r,r′,(u,p)) ∨
28e. ldra(r,r′,(u,p))∨ 28f. rdla(r,r′,(u,p))∨
28g. r=r′) ∧ wf_R(r′)
        end

adjacent: T × T → Bool
adjacent(t,t′) ≡ ~∃ t″:T • t″ ∈ dom m ∧ t < t″ < t′

ld,rd,la,ra,ldra,rdla: R × R × P → Bool

ld(r,r′,(u,p)) ≡ r′ = tl r   pre len r>1
rd(r,r′,(u,p)) ≡ r′ = fst(r)  pre len r>1
la(r,r′,(u,p)) ≡ r′ = ⟨(u,p)⟩  r
ra(r,r′,(u,p)) ≡ r′ = r  ⟨(u,p)⟩
ldra(r,r′,(u,p)) ≡ r′ = tl r  ⟨(u,p)⟩
rdla(r,r′,(u,p)) ≡ r′ = ⟨(u,p)⟩  fst(r)

fst: R ⥲ R′
fst(r) ≡ ⟨ r(i) | i in ⟨1..len r−1⟩ ⟩
```

So the above models that rail units change state. What makes rail units change state ? Well, firstly, external stimuli may change the state of a switch or a crossover switch; secondly signals, in stations and along lines imply the closing of sequences of units. Thirdly these signals and switches are according to certain rail line and station switch interlocking protocols. How the latter protocols are specified will be the subject of the next subsection, Sect. 7.2 and of Sect. 8.

7.2   The Petri Net Part (MP+CKM)

We shall, in this section, model one set of proper interlocking control requirements. We shal do so by means of Petri Nets. There are other ways of doing that: [52,53,54,55] uses ccs ([51]), [39,3] uses Z ([70,70,76]), [69] uses CSP ([33, 66,68]), and [47,28] uses RAISE, and so forth. Others have used Petri Nets: [4,5, 72]. What we shal show is another approach.

We shall be using *Place Transition Nets* for our example.

Route Descriptions: Since interlocking has to do with setting up proper routes from station approach ("line departure") signals to platform (ec.) tracks, and from these to the lines connecting to other stations, we shall focus on constructing, for all such "interesting" routes of a station a Petri Net that models a proper interlocking control scheme.

Routes are described in terms of Units, Switches and Signals. In the previous section (Sect. 7.1) formulas 23 and 24 defined routes as sequences of pairs of units and paths, such that the path of a unit/path pair is a possible path of some state of the unit, and such that "neighbouring" connectors are identical. There can be many such routes in a station. We are interested only in routes which start at an approach signal and ends either at the track or on the line. In the example station of Fig. 4 there are 16 such routes.

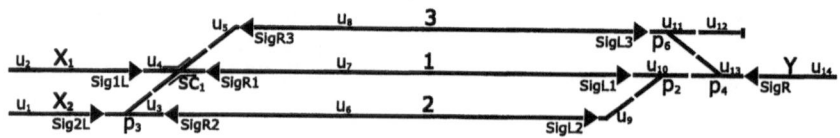

Fig. 4. Example Station

Interlocking Tables: Now, depending on the local, or national traditions and rules & regulations, there are such rules & regulations which stipulate how signals and switches are to be set (and reset) in order to facilitate the safe movement of trains within a station.

One can formalise such rules (see, for example, [39]). From a mechanisation of such a formalisation and from the specific topology of a station layout, for example that abstracted in Fig. 4, one can then construct an interlocking table, such as for example the one given Table 1. Each row in this table corresponds to a proper route. The table expresses for each interesting route the requirements for switches (points and switchable crossovers) and the requirements for signal states. The table also lists all units which compose the route. If there are no

Table 1. Interlocking Table for Routes through the Example Station

Requirements: Routes	Switches					Signals									Units
	sc_1	p_2	p_3	p_4	p_6	$1L$	$2L$	$L1$	$L2$	$L3$	R	$R1$	$R2$	$R3$	
1. $Sig_{1L} - 1$	S	–	S	–	–	G	–	–	–	–	–	R	–	R	u_2, u_4, u_7
2. $Sig_{1L} - 3$	T	–	S	–	–	G	–	–	–	–	–	R	–	R	u_2, u_4, u_5, u_8
3. $Sig_{2L} - 1$	T	–	T	–	–	R	G	–	–	–	–	R	R	R	u_1, u_3, u_4, u_7
4. $Sig_{2L} - 2$	–	–	S	–	–	–	G	–	–	–	–	–	R	–	u_1, u_3, u_6
5. $Sig_{2L} - 3$	S	–	T	–	–	R	G	–	–	–	–	R	R	R	u_1, u_3, u_4, u_5, u_8
6. $Sig_{L1} - Y$	–	S	–	S	S	–	–	G	R	R	R	–	–	–	u_{10}, u_{13}, u_{14}
7. $Sig_{L2} - Y$	–	T	–	S	S	–	–	R	G	R	R	–	–	–	$u_9, u_{10}, u_{13}, u_{14}$
8. $Sig_{L3} - Y$	–	–	–	T	T	–	–	R	R	G	R	–	–	–	u_{11}, u_{13}, u_{14}
9. $Sig_R - 1$	–	S	–	S	S	–	–	R	R	R	G	–	–	–	u_{13}, u_{10}, u_7
10. $Sig_R - 2$	–	T	–	S	S	–	–	R	R	R	G	–	–	–	u_{13}, u_{10}, u_9, u_6
11. $Sig_R - 3$	–	–	–	T	T	–	–	R	R	R	G	–	–	–	$u_{13}, u_{10}, u_{11}, u_8$
12. $Sig_{R1} - X_1$	S	–	S	–	–	R	–	–	–	–	–	G	–	R	u_4, u_2
13. $Sig_{R1} - X_2$	T	–	T	–	–	R	R	–	–	–	–	G	R	R	u_4, u_3, u_1
14. $Sig_{R2} - X_2$	–	–	S	–	–	–	R	–	–	–	–	–	G	–	u_3, u_1
15. $Sig_{R3} - X_1$	T	–	S	–	–	R	–	–	–	–	–	R	–	G	u_5, u_4, u_2
16. $Sig_{R3} - X_2$	S	–	T	–	–	R	R	–	–	–	–	R	R	G	u_5, u_4, u_3, u_1

requirements on the setting of switch or signal, it is marked with dash (–). In this paper, we do not show, how to formally construct such table, but we refer to [21,39,22,69].

We can now start to build up Petri Nets for a partial railway net from four subparts: Petri Net for a Unit, for a Switch (ie., Point or Switchable Crossover), for a Signal, and Petri Net for a Route. Pls. observe that all units have a basic Petri Net. Additionally Switches have additional basic Petri Nets — as we shall soon see. And, finally, although Routes are basically sequences of Units, also Routes have their separate basic Petri Nets. The Petri Net of a Route is then a composition of all its Unit, all its Switch, and all its Signal Petri Nets — where the composition is specified by the Interlocking Table.

Petri Net for Units: A Unit can be in two basic states. It is either free (a new route can be opened through the unit) or not (ie., blocked, there is an already opened route through the unit).

The Petri Net for Units is shown in Fig, 5(a). Two places represent the two states F̲ree and B̲locked. The initial marking consists of a token at the Free place.

One can notice, that Petri Net for a Unit in Fig. 5(a) will interminably circulate ("oscillate"). But this is not the final Petri Net for a route. It is just one component. Later on, extra arcs will be added. They will prevent "oscillations".

Petri Net for Switches: A Switch can be either a point or switchable-crossover. A typical switch has two states: S̲traight and T̲urn. A switch may be required to be set in certain state in two ways: as a direct part of a route, or because it must be set for side protection (to avoid trains touching each other). In the

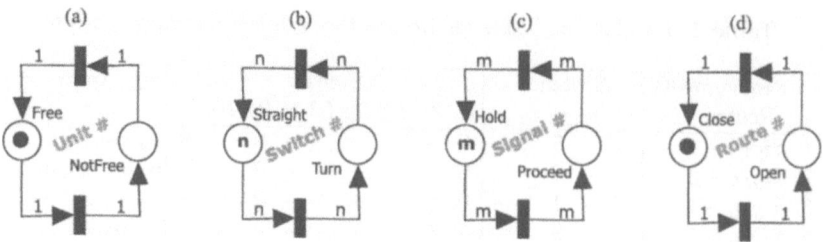

Fig. 5. Petri Nets for (a) Units, (b) Switches, (c) Signals, and (d) Routes

both cases, if there is a open route through switches, these switches must never change their states.

Thus the Petri Net for a switch has two places representing the two mentioned states $\underline{S}$traight and $\underline{T}$urn. The initial marking consists of n tokens at the Straight place, where n is the total number of routes which require settings of that switch. This number can be found from the Interlocking Table (here Table 1) as a count of required setting in the switch column. For the example station in Fig. 4, one finds that for switchable–crossover $sc1$, n is 8; for point $p2$, n is 4; etc.

The switch can change state if and only if all n tokens are available. Later on, when the whole Petri Net will be constructed, open routes though the switch cause decreases of switch token numbers. This will ensure that the switch can only change its state when no route — that requires the actual state — is active. But still the switch can be part of several routes, as long as these routes require the switch to be in the same state. These requirements are captured by the Petri Net in Fig. 5(b).

Petri Net for Signals: A signal has two states: $\underline{H}$old and $\underline{P}$roceed[6]. The Petri Net for a signal has two places representing the two settings $\underline{H}$old and $\underline{P}$roceed. The initial marking consists of m tokens at the Hold place, where m is the number of routes which require setting of that signal. With Table 1, for the example station in Fig. 4, one finds that for for signal Sig_{1L}, m is 8, for signal Sig_{2L}, n is 6, etc.

The signal can only change setting if all m tokens are available. This will ensure that the signal can only change its state when no route that requires the actual state is active; but still the signal can be part of several routes, as long as these routes require the signal to be in the same state. These requirements are captured by the Petri Net in Fig. 5(c).

Petri Net for Routes: In formula 25 of Sect. 7.1 you can find that routes can be open or close. A route can be open only when all its requirements on switch settings, signal settings and units occupancies are fulfilled.

The Petri Net for a route also has two places representing the two states: $\underline{O}$pen and $\underline{C}$losed. The initial marking consists of one token at the Closed place.

---

[6] This is a simplistic view – a real signal is able to indicate the speed with which it may be passed.

The basic Petri Net for a route is shown in Figure 5(d). This corresponds to the route that has no requirements on switches, signals or units.

Construction of Petri Net for Interlocking Tables: In this paragraph we will show, how to construct the Petri Net, for the interlocking table of a station, from the four components already described (unit, switch, signal and route). This Petri Net will be made by adding extra pairs of arcs for each requirement between these components.

The example station of Fig. 4 will be composed by these components: 16 Petri Nets for routes, 14 Petri Nets for units, 5 Petri Nets for switches and 9 Petri Nets for signals — the station shown has these numbers.

A route can be open, when all units, that the route is composed from, are free (not occupied by train or blocked by another route in the station). To satisfy this requirement, between each route Petri Net and all unit Petri Nets that make up the route, a pair of arcs needs to added. Fig. 6.A shows how.

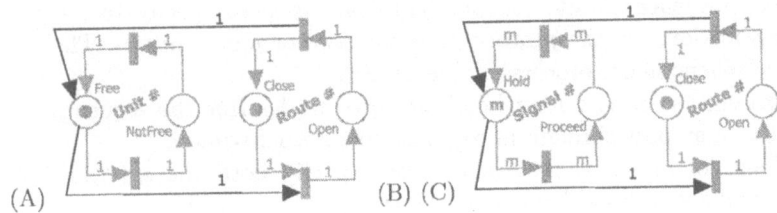

Fig. 6. Arc additions for Route (A) Units, (B) Switches and (C) Signals

For each switch requirement it must be ensured that the switch cannot change state while the route thought that switch is open. To satisfy this requirement, between each route Petri Net and all switch Petri Nets of that route, a pair of arcs have to be added. The particular insertion of arcs depend on the required state of the switch (as given in the Interlocking table). This insertion is captured in the Petri Net of Fig. 6.B. Note, that in the figure it is assumed the route requires the switch to be set to the Turn state. The case for Straight follows.

The signal can be in Proceed state only and only if the route that starts at the signal is open. How to add a pair of arcs for a signal is illustrated in Figure 6.C. This is clearly the pre–condition for opening the route, the same as the pre–condition for adding switches.

Summary: The full Petri net for the example railway station and interlocking table thus contains 16 Petri Nets for routes, 14 Petri Nets for units, 5 Petri Nets for switches, and 9 Petri Nets for signals. The interlocking table then dictates "zillions" of arcs to be inserted — so many that "readable" diagrams become impossible. Clearly, though, a case for tools. These tools can then create the complete control program, based on Petri Nets, for a station, and can check for liveness, deadlock, etc.

7.3 Integrating RAISE and Petri Nets

In [48][7] RSL models are given of the static and the dynamic semantics of Condition Event, Place Transition and Coloured Petri Nets. In ongoing work we are, amongst many other things, exploring the usefulness of translating Petri Nets to RSL for control purposes [2].

8 RAISE with Live Sequence Charts and Statecharts (CKM+MP)

Live Sequence Charts (LSCs) derive from Message Sequence Charts: [12,42,43, 50,44,64,63,34,35] and are first proposed in [13] and further studied in [40,31]. In [48,49][8] RSL, respectively process algebraic models are given of Message and of Live Sequence Charts and of their relation to RSL.

Statecharts were introduced by and in: [23,24,26,27,25].

In [48,49][9] models are given of Statecharts in, and of their relation to RSL.

Live Sequence Charts (on one hand) are used to specify the sequences of communication, i.e. the protocol, between two or more entities. These may be physical phenomena, processes, objects, etc.

Statecharts (on the other hand) are used to describe the sequences of states an entity may pass through in response to external stimuli.

When combined, these two methods specify both the external behaviour (LSC) and the internal behaviour (Statechart) of an entitiy.

8.1 Problem Description

The most important safety property of a railway line is that two trains are not allowed to move in opposite directions on that line. In order to ensure that the two stations at either end of the line agree on the direction trains are allowed to move at a given time. What is called a Line Direction Agreement System (LDAS) is thus introduced.

If a station wants to send a train along the line, it must first check with the LDAS if the line is open in the required direction. If so, the train may proceed along the line. If not, the opposite station must agree to changing the direction. This is only possible if there are currently no trains en–route.

8.2 External Communication: LSCs

The externally visible behaviour of the LDAS is illustrated using Live Sequence Charts. The three entities are Station A (SA), the Line Direction Agreement System (LDAS) and Station B (SB). In addition, the station managers are represented using the notation traditionally used for UML actors.

---

[7] See http://www.krog-madsen.dk/page.php?id=10

[8] See http://www.krog-madsen.dk/page.php?id=10

[9] See http://www.krog-madsen.dk/page.php?id=10

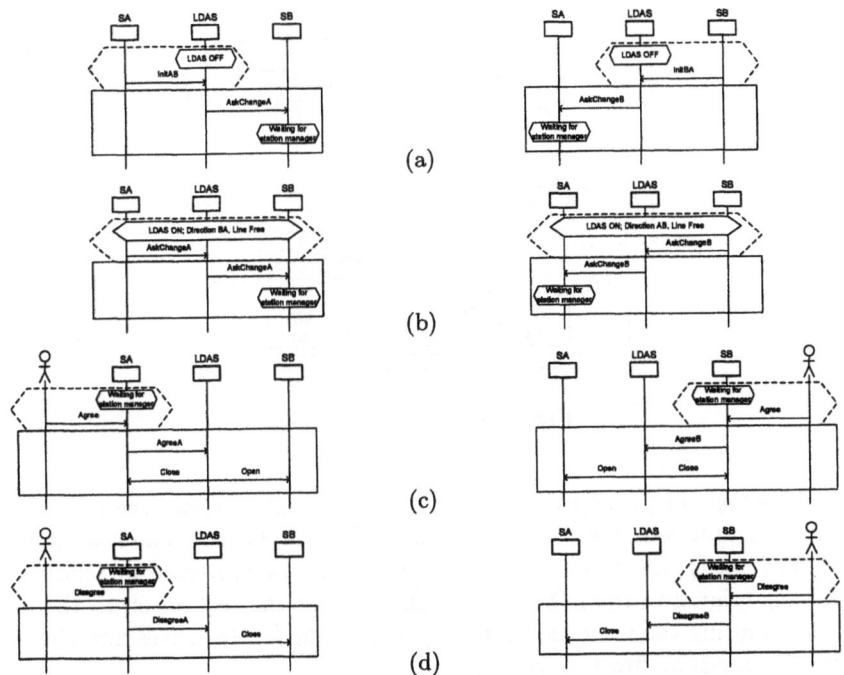

Fig. 7. (a) Initial LDAS, (b) Request Direction Reversal, (c) Request Approval (d) Request Rejection

The charts in Figure 7(a) illustrate the situation when the LDAS has been turned off. One of the stations asks the LDAS to open the line, and the LDAS passes the request on to the other station, awaiting a response. The process of reversing the direction of the line is similar, see Figure 7(b).

If the station manager approves the request to reverse the direction, the LDAS will instruct the stations to open, respectively, close their end of the line, thus effecting the direction reversal, see Figure 7(c).

If the station manager rejects the request to reverse the direction, the LDAS will notify the requesting station to keep its end of the line closed, see Figure 7(d).

8.3   Internal Behaviour: Statecharts

The internal behaviour of the LDAS is illustrated by a Statechart, see Figure 8. The LDAS has some initial state called DEAD, in which no direction along the line is open. This state can only occur when the LDAS is powered up after having been shutdown (due to a failure or emergency stop). The LDAS stays in the initial state until a request to open the line in either the A to B or B to A direction arrives in the form of the InitAB or InitBA signals. Next, the opposite station will send an Agree or Disagree signal to either approve or veto the opening of the line. If the opening is vetoed, the LDAS returns to the DEAD

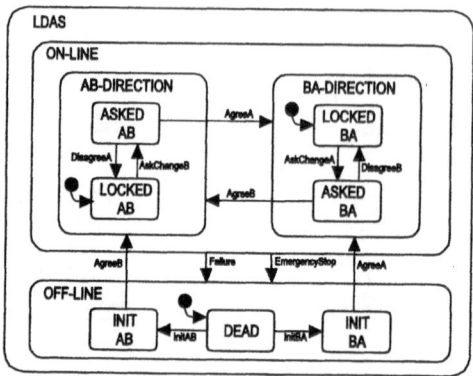

Fig. 8. Statechart for LDAS

state. If the opening is approved, the LDAS moves into a state where the line is open in one direction, represented by LockedAB or LockedBA. The station whose end of the line is closed may request the direction to be reversed by sending the AskChange signal to the LDAS. The LDAS passes the request on to the other station, awaiting the response. If it is approved, the LDAS moves into the state where the opposite direction is locked.

8.4   Relation to RSL Model, Satisfaction Relation

The LSC and the Statechart models prescribe requirements to an orderly protocol aiming at a secure change of line direction. That is: That protocol is not specified in terms of RSL, but as shown, by the diagrams. Still the RSL model "survives": The actions and the state changes implied by the diagrams and to be effected, can now be individually prescribed in RSL. These RSL prescriptions are rather directly concerned with the setting of states (ie., signals) as expressed in the dynamic model of the railway net states.

In [2], and based on the work of [48,49] we shall explore tools for translating Lice Sequence Charts (LSCs) and Statecharts (SCs) into RSL.

In [48] it is shown how to establish and verify a criterion of correctness, ie., a satisfaction relation, between LSC and SC specificatioms, on one hand, and RSL specifications on the other hand. To express and prove this satisfaction relation, as is noted in [48], clearly needs tool support.

9   Review and Future "Challenges"

9.1   Some Review Comments

The present paper has but shown a number of examples. We claim that several of these link two or more "formalisms". Yet not much, really, was said about it (except in Sect. 6.2). To properly "link–up" is a nice "challenge" — one which is next for several of us. [48] (based on ideas of [30,29]) provides several such "link–ups".

9.2   A Research Programme: Challenge # 1

In Sect. 1.2 we mentioned: [75,17,14,32,19,11,60,77,49,48,65] as indicative of the research in the "integration" area. We have mostly followed ideas of George and Haxthausen [29]. These, many other publications, and annual conferences, *IFMs: Integrating Formal Methods,* together amply cover the problem area touched upon in this paper. We see it as a Grand Challenge, as a *"Man on Mars"* project: To device, ie., to research and develop a complementary set of formal specification languages (SLs), with comprehensive, cross–SL proof systems, that "covers the ground". A 20+ year challenge !

9.3   A Software Engineering Programme: Challenge # 2

But all this, ie., the R&D hinted at in Sect. 9.2, is in vain if industry, the developers of software, do not take software (and, in general hardware + software) development seriously. So, commensurate with advances in our ability to actually develop provably correct, pleasing and effective computing systems, goes, hand–in–hand, the task, the pedagogic, didactive, educational, training and socio–economically based challenge of making sure that the software (etc.) engineering graduates that have been taught this ability, also actually deploy their skills, responsibly, when in industry. Another Grand Challenge, another *"Man on Mars"* project. Another, or the same 20 years, to turn our industry into a responsible one ?

Acknowledgements. The first author acknowledges, with thanks his co–authors with whom it is a joy to work. Thanks are also due the organisers of *INT 2004,* the Third International Workshop on *Integration of Specification Techniques for Applications in Engineering,* Barcelona, Spain, March 28, 2004, namely the partners in the German Research Council's Priority Programme of the *Integration* project alluded to above. In particular the first author's thanks goes to Prof. Wolfgang Reif of Augsburg for inviting him to write and present this paper. It's been a very worthwhile and "revealing" effort !

References

1. Jean-Raymond Abrial. *The B Book: Assigning Programs to Meanings.* Tracts in Theoretical Computer Science. Cambridge University Press, Cambridge, England, 1996.
2. Steffen Andersen and Steffen Holmslykke. "UML–ised" Formal Tools for the RAISE Tool Set. M.Sc. Thesis Project, Department of Computer Science and Engineering, Institute of Informatics and Mathematical Modelling, Technical University of Denmark, Building 322, Richard Petersens Plads, DK–2800 Kgs.Lyngby, Denmark, 2004–2005 2003. Pre–MSc Thesis project: Spring 2004 Lyngby; main M.Sc. Thesis Project Fall/Winter 2004/2005 UNU–IIST Macau / NUS Singapore.

3. Ales J. Anot. Using Z Specification for Railway Interlocking Safety. Periodica Polytechnica, Transport Engineering Series vol.28, no. 1–2, pp 39–53, Department of Information and Safety Systems Faculty of Electrical Engineering University of Zilina, Vel'ký diel, Zilina 010 26, Slovak Republic, 2000. .

4. Gérard Berthelot and Laure Petrucci. Specification and validation of a concurrent system: an educational project. *International Journal on Software Tools for Technology Transfer*, 3(4):372–381, September 2001. Special section on the practical use of high-level Petri Nets.

5. J. Billington and C. Janczura. Removing Deadlock from a Railway Network Specification. In *Australian Engineering Mathematics Conference (AEMC'96)*, pages 193–200, Sydney, Australia, July 1996. (Australian Engineering Mathematical Society ?).

6. Dines Bjørner. Formal Software Techniques in Railway Systems. In Eckehard Schnieder, editor, *9th IFAC Symposium on Control in Transportation Systems*, pages 1–12, Technical University, Braunschweig, Germany, 13–15 June 2000. VDI/VDE-Gesellschaft Mess– und Automatisieringstechnik, VDI-Gesellschaft für Fahrzeug– und Verkehrstechnik. Invited talk.

7. Dines Bjørner. Dynamics of Railway Nets: On an Interface between Automatic Control and Software Engineering. In *CTS2003: 10th IFAC Symposium on Control in Transportation Systems*, Oxford, UK, August 4-6 2003. Elsevier Science Ltd. Symposium held at Tokyo, Japan. Editors: S. Tsugawa and M. Aoki.

8. Dines Bjørner, Chris W. George, and Søren Prehn. Computing Systems for Railways — A Rôle for Domain Engineering. Relations to Requirements Engineering and Software for Control Applications. In *Integrated Design and Process Technology. Editors: Bernd Kraemer and John C. Petterson*, P.O.Box 1299, Grand View, Texas 76050-1299, USA, 24–28 June 2002. Society for Design and Process Science.

9. Dines Bjørner, C.W. George, and S. Prehn. *Scheduling and Rescheduling of Trains*, chapter 8, pages 157–184. *Industrial Strength Formal Methods in Practice*, Eds.: Michael G. Hinchey and Jonathan P. Bowen. FACIT, Springer–Verlag, London, England, 1999.

10. Grady Booch, Jim Rumbaugh, and Ivar Jacobson. *The Unified Modeling Language User Guide*. Addison-Wesley, 1998.

11. Robert Büssow, Robert Geisler, and Marcus Klar. Specifying safety-critical embedded systems with Statecharts and Z: A case study. In E. Astesiano, editor, *Fundamental Approaches to Software Engineering: First International Conference, FASE'98, Held as Part of the Joint European Conferences on Theory and Practice of Software, ETAPS'98, Lisbon, Portugal, March/April 1998*, volume 1382 of *Lecture Notes in Computer Science*, pages 71–87. Springer-Verlag, 1998.

12. CCITT. CCITT Recommendation Z.120: Message Sequence Chart (MSC), 1992.

13. Werner Damm and David Harel. LSCs: Breathing life into Message Sequence Charts. *Formal Methods in System Design*, 19:45–80, 2001. Early version appeared as Weizmann Institute Tech. Report CS98-09, April 1998. An abridged version appeared in *Proc. 3rd IFIP Int. Conf. on Formal Methods for Open Object-based Distributed Systems* (FMOODS'99), Kluwer, 1999, pp. 293–312.

14. Clemens Fischer. CSP-OZ: A combination of Object-Z and CSP. Technical Report TRCF-97-2, Universität Oldenburg, 1997.

15. John Fitzgerald and Peter Gorm Larsen. *Software System Design: Formal Methods into Practice*. Cambridge University Press, The Edinburgh Building, Cambridge CB2 2RU, UK, 1997. To appear.

16. Ana Funes and Chris W. George. Formal Foundations in RSL for UML Class Diagrams. Research Report 253, UNU/IIST, P.O. Box 3058, Macau, May 2002. Published as chapter VIII Formalizing UML Class Diagrams of UML and the Unified Process, Liliana Favre (ed.).

17. A. Galloway. *Integrated Formal Methods*. PhD thesis, University of Teeside, 1996.

18. Chris W. George and Yong Xia. An Operational Semantics for Timed RAISE. In Jeannette M. Wing, Jim Woodcock, and Jim Davies, editors, *FM'99 — Formal Methods*, pages 1008–1027. FME, Springer–Verlag, 1999.

19. W. Grieskamp, M. Heiseland, and H. Dörr. Specifying embedded systems with Statecharts and Z: An agenda for cyclic software components. In E. Astesiano, editor, *Fundamental Approaches to Software Engineering: First International Conference, FASE'98, Held as Part of the Joint European Conferences on Theory and Practice of Software, ETAPS'98, Lisbon, Portugal, March/April 1998*, volume 1382 of *Lecture Notes in Computer Science*, pages 88–106. Springer-Verlag, 1998.

20. Object Management Group. *OMG Unified Modelling Language Specification*. OMG/UML, http://www.omg.org/uml/, version 1.5 edition, March 2003. www.omg.org/cgi-bin/doc?formal/03-03-01.

21. Kirsten Mark Hansen. Validation of a railway interlocking model. In M. Bertran M. Naftalin, T. Denvir, editor, *FME'94: Industrial Benefit of Formal Methods*, pages 582–601. Springer-Verlag, October 1994.

22. K.M. Hansen. *Linking Safety Analysis to Safety Requirements*. PhD thesis, Department of Computer Science, Technical University of Denmark, Building 344, DK-2800 Lyngby, Denmark, August 1996.

23. David Harel. Statecharts: A visual formalism for complex systems. *Science of Computer Programming*, 8(3):231–274, 1987.

24. David Harel. On visual formalisms. *Communications of the ACM*, 33(5), 514–530 1988.

25. David Harel and Eran Gery. Executable object modeling with Statecharts. *IEEE Computer*, 30(7):31–42, 1997.

26. David Harel, Hagi Lachover, Amnon Naamad, Amir Pnueli, Michal Politi, Rivi Sherman, Aharon Shtull-Trauring, and Mark B. Trakhtenbrot. STATEMATE: A working environment for the development of complex reactive systems. *Software Engineering*, 16(4):403–414, 1990.

27. David Harel and Amnon Naamad. The STATEMATE semantics of Statecharts. *ACM Transactions on Software Engineering and Methodology (TOSEM)*, 5(4):293–333, 1996.

28. A. Haxthausen and T. Gjaldbæk. Modelling and Verification of Interlocking Systems for Railway Lines. In *10th IFAC Symposium on Control in Transportation Systems, Tokyo, Japan, August 4–6 2003*.

29. Anne Haxthausen. Some approaches for integration of specification techniques (invited extended abstract), 2000.

30. Anne Haxthausen and Yong Xia. Linking DC together with TRSL. In *Proceedings of 2nd International Conference on Integrated Formal Methods (IFM'2000), Schloss Dagstuhl, Germany, November 2000*, number 1945 in Lecture Notes in Computer Science, pages 25–44. Springer-Verlag, 2000.

31. Patrick Heymans and Yves Bontemps. Turning high-level Live Sequence Charts into automata. In Tarja Systa and Albert Zundorf, editors, *Proceedings of the First International Workshop on Scenarios and State Machines (SCESM), (ICSE'02 workshop)*, 2002.

32. C. A. R. Hoare and Jifeng He. *Unifying Theories of Programming*. Prentice-Hall, 1998.

33. C.A.R. Hoare. *Communicating Sequential Processes*. C.A.R. Hoare Series in Computer Science. Prentice-Hall International, 1985.

34. ITU-T. ITU-T Recommendation Z.120: Message Sequence Chart (MSC), 1996.

35. ITU-T. ITU-T Recommendation Z.120: Message Sequence Chart (MSC), 1999.

36. Ivar Jacobson, Grady Booch, and Jim Rumbaugh. *The Unified Software Development Process*. Addison-Wesley, 1999.

37. Kurt Jensen. *Coloured Petri Nets – Basic Concepts, Analysis Methods and Practical Use, Volume 1 Basic Concepts*. EATCS Monographs on Theoretical Computer Science. Springer-Verlag, 1992.

38. Ekkart Kindler, Wolfgang Reisig, Hagen Volzer, and Rolf Walter. Petri net based verification of distributed algorithms: An example. *Formal Aspects of Computing*, 9(4):409–424, 1997.

39. T. King. Formalising British Rail's Signalling Rules. In M. Bertran M. Naftalin, T. Denvir, editor, *FME'94: Industrial Benefit of Formal Methods*, pages 45–54. Springer-Verlag, October 1994.

40. Jochen Klose and Hartmut Wittke. An automata based interpretation of Live Sequence Charts. In T. Margaria and W. Yi, editors, *TACAS 2001*, LNCS 2031, pages 512–527. Springer-Verlag, 2001.

41. Lars M. Kristensen, Soren Christensen, and Kurt Jensen. The practitioner's guide to Coloured Petri Nets. *International Journal on Software Tools for Technology Transfer*, 2(2):98–132, 1998.

42. Peter B. Ladkin and Stefan Leue. Analysis of Message Sequence Charts. Technical Report IAM 92-013, Institute for Informatics and Applied Mathematics, University of Berne, Bern, Switzerland, 1992.

43. Peter B. Ladkin and Stefan Leue. What do Message Sequence Charts mean? In *FORTE*, pages 301–316, 1993.

44. Peter B. Ladkin and Stefan Leue. Interpreting Message Flow Graphs. *Formal Aspects of Computing*, 7(5):473–509, 1995.

45. L. Li and Jifeng He. A denotational semantics of Timed RSL using Duration Calculus. Research Report 168, UNU/IIST, P.O.Box 3058, Macau, 1999. Published in Proceedings of The Sixth International Conference on Real-Time Computing Systems and Applications (RTCSA'99), pp. 492-503, IEEE Computer Society Press.

46. L. Li and Jifeng He. Towards a denotational semantics of Timed RSL using Duration Calculus. Research Report 161, UNU/IIST, P.O.Box 3058, Macau, April 1999. Accepted for publication by Chinese Journal of Advanced Software Research.

47. Morten Peter Lindegaard, Peter Viuf, and Anne Haxthausen. Modelling Railway Interlocking Systems. In *Proceedings of the 9th IFAC Symposium on Control in Transportation Systems 2000, June 13-15, 2000, Braunschweig, Germany*, pages 211–217, 2000.

48. Christian Krog Madsen. Integration of Specification Techniques. M.Sc. Thesis Project, Department of Computer Science and Engineering, Institute of Informatics and Mathematical Modelling, Technical University of Denmark, Building 322, Richard Petersens Plads, DK–2800 Kgs.Lyngby, Denmark, 30 November 2003.

49. Christian Krog Madsen. Study of Graphical and Temporal Specification Techniques. Pre–Thesis Project, Department of Computer Science and Engineering, Institute of Informatics and Mathematical Modelling, Technical University of Denmark, Building 322, Richard Petersens Plads, DK–2800 Kgs.Lyngby, Denmark, June 2003.

50. S. Mauw and M. A. Reniers. An algebraic semantics of basic Message Sequence Charts. *The Computer Journal*, 37(4):269–277, 1994.

51. R. Milner. *Communication and Concurrency*. C.A.R. Hoare Series in Computer Science. Prentice Hall, 1989.
52. M.J. Morley. Modelling British Rail's Interlocking Logic: Geographic Data Correctness. Technical Report ECS-LFCS-91-186, University of Edinburgh, 1991.
53. M.J. Morley. Safety in railway signalling data: A behavioural analysis. In J. Joyce and C. Seger, editors, *Proc. 6th annual workshop on higher order logic and its applications, Vancouver, 4-6 August*, pages 465–474. Springer–Verlag Lecture Notes in Computer Science, Vol.780, 1993–4.
54. M.J. Morley. *Safety Assurance in Interlocking Design*. PhD thesis, University of Edinburgh, 1996.
55. M.J. Morley. Safety-level communication in railway interlockings. *Science of Computer Programming*, 29(1-2):147–170, July 1997.
56. Carl Adam Petri. *Kommunikation mit Automaten*. Bonn: Institut für Instrumentelle Mathematik, Schriften des IIM Nr. 2, 1962.
57. Martin Pěnička, Albena Kirilova Strupchanska, and Dines Bjørner. Train Maintenance Routing. In *FORMS'2003: Symposium on Formal Methods for Railway Operation and Control Systems*. L'Harmattan Hongrie, 15–16 May 2003. Conf. held at Techn.Univ. of Budapest, Hungary. Editors: G. Tarnai and E. Schnieder, Germany.
58. RAISE Language Group. *The RAISE Specification Language*. BCS Practitioner Series. Prentice Hall Int., 1992.
59. RAISE Method Group. *The RAISE Development Method*. BCS Practitioner Series. Prentice Hall Int., 1995.
60. G. Reggio and L. Repetto. Casl-Chart: A combination of Statecharts and of the algebraic specification language Casl. Technical Report DISI-TR-00-2, DISI, Università di Genova, 2000.
61. W. Reisig. *Elements of Distributed Algorithms: Modelling and Analysis with Petri Nets*. Springer Verlag, 1998.
62. Wolfgang Reisig. *A Primer in Petri Net Design*. Springer-Verlag, 1992.
63. M. Reniers. Static semantics of Message Sequence Charts, 1995.
64. M.A. Reniers. Syntax requirements of Message Sequence Charts. In R. Braek and A. Sarma, editors, *Proceedings of the 7th SDL Forum*, 1995.
65. Martin-Große Rhode. *Semantic Integration of Heterogeneous Software Specifications*. Monographs in Theoretical Computer Science. An EATCS Series. Springer–Verlag, Heidelberg and Berlin, Germany, 2004.
66. A.W. Roscoe. *Theory and Practice of Concurrency*. C.A.R. Hoare Series in Computer Science. Prentice–Hall, 1997.
67. Jim Rumbaugh, Ivar Jacobson, and Grady Booch. *The Unified Modeling Language Reference Manual*. Addison-Wesley, 1998.
68. Steve Schneider. *Concurrent and Real–time Systems — The CSP Approach*. Worldwide Series in Computer Science. John Wiley & Sons, Ltd., Baffins Lane, Chichester, West Sussex PO19 1UD, England, January 2000.
69. A.C. Simpson, J.C.P. Woodcock, and J.W. Davies. The mechanical verification of Solid State Interlocking geographic data. In L. Groves and S. Reeves, editors, *Proceedings of Formal Methods Pacific*, pages 223–242, Wellington, New Zealand, 9–11 July 1997. Springer–Verlag.
70. J. M. Spivey. *Understanding Z: A Specification Language and its Formal Semantics*, volume 3 of *Cambridge Tracts in Theoretical Computer Science*. Cambridge University Press, January 1988.

71. Albena Kirilova Strupchanska, Martin Pěnička, and Dines Bjørner. Railway Staff Rostering. In *FORMS2003: Symposium on Formal Methods for Railway Operation and Control Systems*. L'Harmattan Hongrie, 15–16 May 2003. Conf. held at Techn.Univ. of Budapest, Hungary. Editors: G. Tarnai and E. Schnieder, Germany.

72. W.M.P. van der Aalst and M.A. Odijk. Analysis of railway stations by means of interval timed colored Petri Nets. *Real-Time Systems*, 9(3):241–263, 1995. .

73. Jos Warmer and Anneke Kleppe. *The Object Constraint Language: Precise Modeling with UML*. Addison-Wesley Publ. Co., October 13 1998. 144 pages, ASIN: 0201379406, Paperback.

74. Jos Warmer and Anneke Kleppe. *The Object Constraint Language: Getting Your Models Ready for MDA*. Addison-Wesley Publ. Co., 2nd edition, August 29 2003. 240 pages, ISBN: 0321179366, Paperback.

75. M. Weber. Combining Statecharts and Z for the design of safety-critical control systems. In M. Gaudel and J. Woodcock, editors, *FME 96: Industrial Benefit and Advances in Formal Methods*, volume 1051 of *Lecture Notes in Computer Science*, pages 307–326. Springer-Verlag, 1996.

76. J. C. P. Woodcock and J. Davies. *Using Z: Specification, Proof and Refinement*. Prentice Hall International Series in Computer Science, 1996.

77. J. C. P. Woodcock and Arthur Hughes. Unifying theories of parallel programming. In Chris George and H. Miao, editors, *Formal Methods and Software Engineering: 4th International Conference on Formal Engineering Methods, ICFEM 2002 Shanghai, China*, volume 2495 of *Lecture Notes in Computer Science*, pages 24–37. Springer-Verlag, October 21–25 2002.

78. Wang Yi. *A Calculus of Real Time Systems*. PhD thesis, Department of Computer Sciences, Chalmers University of Technology, Göteborg, Sweden, 1991.

79. Chaochen Zhou and Michael R. Hansen. *Duration Calculus: A Formal Approach to Real–time Systems*. Monographs in Theoretical Computer Science. An EATCS Series. Springer–Verlag, 2004.

80. Chaochen Zhou, C.A.R. Hoare, and A.P. Ravn. A Calculus of Durations. *Information Proc. Letters*, 40(5), 1992.

Model Based Formal Verification of Distributed Production Control Systems

Martin Kardos and Franz-J. Rammig

Design of Parallel Systems
Heinz Nixdorf Institute
Fuerstenallee 11
D-33102 Paderborn
Germany
{kardos,franz}@uni-paderborn.de

Abstract. The design of software for distributed production control systems (DPCS) is an error prone task. Ensuring the correctness of the design at the earliest stage possible is a major challenge in any software development process. In this context, formal verification is a very appealing approach in addition to simulation and testing, since it implies an exhaustive exploration of all possible behaviours of a system. In this paper, we present an approach towards model based formal verification for DPCS by means of model checking. The presented work is a part of the ISILEIT project that aims at the development of a seamless methodology for the integrated design, analysis and validation of distributed production control systems.

A prerequisite for model based formal verification is the existence of a formal model of the designed system. According to the ISILEIT design methodology a system is specified and modelled using an integrative specification language that combines modeling concepts taken from two different specification languages, namely the UML and the SDL languages. However, supporting formal verification for such a heterogeneous language implies requirements on formal unification and semantic integration of the adopted modeling concepts. In our approach the Abstract State Machines (ASM) formalism represents the formal platform for the unification and semantic integration. We show how the ASMs, in particular the AsmL language, have been successfully applied for creating a rigorous unified semantic model that integrates the semantics of UML State Machines, SDL Block Diagrams and Story Diagrams which form the core of the integrative specification language used in ISILEIT.

Besides the integration purpose, the ASMs serve as a basis for the application of model checking techniques. Therefore, the rest of the paper presents the work on adoption of state-of-the-art model checking techniques in order to support model checking of the ASM (AsmL) models.

1 Introduction

Today's production control systems can be characterized as highly centralized software systems running on the dedicated hardware. With increasing complexity of production systems the centralized model of control can not meet newly arising requirements, such as easy re-configurability and adaptation to the changes of the production

H. Ehrig et al. (Eds.): INT 2004, LNCS 3147, pp. 451–473, 2004.

process, that significantly help to shorten the time-to-production factor. Therefore the inflexible centralized control models have to be replaced by more efficient distributed control models. Of course, such a crucial change in the design process requires new modeling approaches and software development techniques for production of correct, stable and flexible distributed software systems. Moreover, analysis and verification techniques that can handle the issues incidental to the distributed systems have to be provided as well.

The ISILEIT project [1] aims at the development of a seamless methodology for the integrated design, analysis and validation of distributed production control systems (DPCS). Its particular emphasis lies on (re-)using existing techniques, which are used by engineers in industry, and improving them with respect to formal analysis, simulation and automatic code generation. Since the definition of the methodology is out of scope of this paper we recommend the reader to [2] for further details. The work presented in this paper deals with formal verification of an integrative specification language upon which the design methodology in ISILEIT is built. This language combines several heterogeneous modeling languages, concretely the SDL, UML and Story Diagrams, into a unique graphical language that can capture all aspects of a distributed production system. The main objective of our work resides in providing a formal verification technique based on a solid formal background that can be integrated into the ISILEIT's design methodology.

The remainder of the paper is organized as follows. Section 2 describes the work on formalizing the semantics of the integrative specification language used in ISILEIT by means of the ASM-theory based specification language AsmL. In Section 3 the integration of a model checking based verification technique into the design process for DPCS is discussed. Section 4 presents a model checking approach towards formal verification of the AsmL specifications. In this section, the focus is put on the description of the proposed on-the-fly algorithm and its functional parts. In the Section 5 the related work is discussed. Finally, the paper is closed with conclusions and a brief outlook on the future work in Section 6.

2   Formalizing Semantics of the Integrative Specification Language

The main prerequisite for integration of formal verification techniques into the design process of DPCS is the presence of a rigorous formal semantics of the modeling paradigm, in our case represented by the integrative specification language combining UML [3], SDL [4] and Story Diagrams [5]. Therefore, choosing the right formal method was one of the crucial decisions to be taken, especially when the heterogeneity of the modeling languages and the intended "model checking" verification technique had to be considered. In our approach the *Abstract State Machines* (ASMs) [6] has been chosen as a suitable formalism for defining the formal semantics of used modeling paradigm. The ASMs have proven their strong modeling and specification abilities in various application domains [7]. In addition, the operational semantics of ASMs turned out to be highly suitable for the application of model checking techniques. Besides ASMs, we also adopted the AsmL language [8], an executable specification language built upon the theory of Abstract State Machines that comes with rich and precisely defined syntax and a dedicated set of tools. We used AsmL for constructing the semantic models of the languages contained in our modeling paradigm.

Of course, formalizing the complete semantics of all participating languages would be a tedious task, especially when the complexity and vastness of the whole UML and SDL is considered. Therefore, our aim was not to formalize the complete semantics of every participating language, but instead, we considered only those semantic parts that are used in the ISILEIT design methodology and that are supported by our design tool FUJABA [9]. Concretely we have formalized the operational semantics of *SDL Signal Flow Model*, *UML State Machine* and *Story Diagrams*.

The next three sections describe the formalization process using the AsmL as the description language. Due to the space limitations we focus only on substantial aspects omitting deeper technical details.

2.1   SDL Signal Flow Model

A distributed production system can be characterized as a system whose control is decentralized and distributed into the network of control nodes communicating and exchanging data with each other. Every node controls a dedicated hardware device such as a robot, storage, a switch, etc. The nodes run their control behaviour in parallel and communicate asynchronously by sending signals through the network.

For modeling the aspects of the control distribution and the asynchronous communication we adopted into our modeling language the SDL block diagrams and the SDL signal flow model(SFM) from the latest SDL 2000 standard [4][10], respectively. In Figure 1, an example of SDL block diagram depicting our case study, a simple Manufacturing Flow System, is shown.

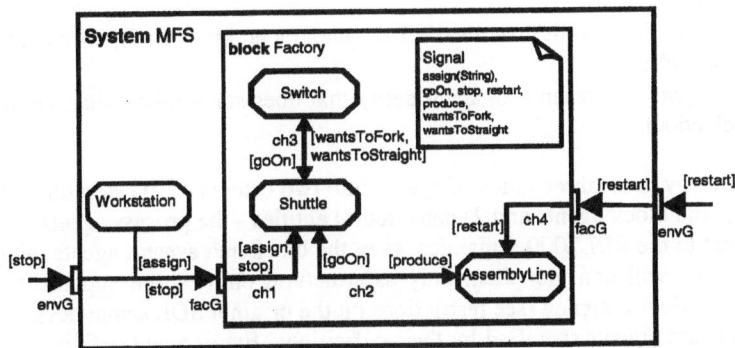

Fig. 1. SDL Block diagram of the Manufacturing Flow System

The system (the outermost block) consists of the *Workstation* process and the *Factory* block, which is further decomposed into several subprocesses. Gates are placed at the boundaries of the blocks acting as input/output ports for communicated signals, e.g. the *EnvG* gate acts as an input port for the signals *Stop* and *Restart* coming to the *MFS* system from the environment. The signals are communicated through the channels that interconnect processes and blocks. For example, the process *Shuttle* sends the signals *WantsToFork* or *WantsToStraight* to the process *Switch* via the channel *ch3*.

2.1.1 Restrictions on the Original SDL Semantics

As already mentioned, we have adopted only small part of the overall SDL semantics, concretely the Signal Flow Model (SFM) semantics. In addition we imposed following restrictions on the taken semantics:

- we support the concept of SDL agents recognizing the system, block and process agents
- we adopted the concept of agent types and their instances excluding the parameterization and specification facilities
- the body definition of the adopted agent types are restricted to only describe the structural decomposition and communication primitives; there are no other concepts like variables, procedures, SDL state machines, etc.
- the *system* and *block* agents are supposed to be pure structural entities, i.e. they have no behaviour (no state machine)
- *process* agents are the only entities that have behaviour expressed in form of a state machine
- the behaviour of a *process* agent is a UML state machine not an SDL one (the semantics of the process definition has not been taken from SDL)

2.1.2 SDL Agents

A common modeling entity in SDL is an agent. SDL recognizes three different kinds of agents:

- *system agent* - is the outermost agent entity that encapsulates the modelled system, i.e. its behaviour and structure definition, and that separates the system from its environment
- *block agent* - is an entity used to define system's architecture by means of system decomposition
- *process agent* - represents an agent entity that does some processing, i.e. it has its own behaviour

We can classify those three kinds of agents into two categories: 1) structural entities - the system and block agents and 2) behavioural entities - the process agents. Although with respect to the SDL2000 semantics, even the block and system agents might have behaviour, we will consider them only as structural entities and suppose that they have no behaviour assigned (see restrictions on the original SDL semantics).

SDL agents are always specified by their definitions. Every agent definition has corresponding agent type that can be defined explicitly or it can be implicitly derived from the agent definition. Agent definitions represent the basic modeling entities a system is build up from. Additionally, agent definitions or agent types are the only entities that can have gate and channel definitions. Figure 1 shows a block diagram where all entities represent particular agent definitions.

In AsmL we model the different agent kinds by the enumeration AgentKind.

enum AgentKind

  System

  Block

  Process

Before the execution or simulation of an SDL model, the agent definitions have to be instantiated. An instantiated agent definition can be understood as a set of agent instances that share particular communication entities defined by the agent definition such as gates, a set of communicated signals, etc. We model such an instantiated agent definition by the class AgentInstSet.

class AgentInstSet **extends** ASMAgent

  kind **as** AgentKind

  inGates **as** Set **of** Gate

  outGates **as** Set **of** Gate

override procedure program()

procedure outputSignal(sname **as** Identifier, sender **as** Identifier,

                      receiver **as** Identifier?, via **as** Seq **of**

                      Identifier, vals **as** Seq **of** SignalValue)

AgentInstSet introduces new attributes: kind - identifies the kind of an SDL agent, inGates - a set of input gates and outGates - a set of output gates. Every agent instance set has to take care of the distribution of signals coming to its input gates to the appropriate agent instances. This behaviour is represented by the program() method of the AgentInstSet class. In order to allow the agent instances to send signals the agent instance set provides a method outputSignal() that is shared by all its agent instances.

    The concrete agent instance is modelled by the AgentInst class.

class AgentInst **extends** ASMAgent **implements** IStateMachineOwner

  behavior **as** IStateMachine?

  inPort **as** Gate

  public procedure SendEvent(e **as** IEvent, receiver **as** Identifier)

  override procedure program()

The AgentInst class introduces two new attributes: behavior - contains a state machine that models agent's behaviour, inPort - a local input gate from which the state machine dispatches the signals. The program() method executes agent's behaviour in form of the state machine runs. Additionally, method SendEvent() is provided for the state machine to initiate the sending of an event (a signal).

2.1.3 Signals

Basic communication primitives for information exchange between the SDL agents are signals. A signal can be seen as a collection of data that 1) indicates the communicating entities, 2) transports communicated data, 3) stores routing information needed for successful transportation. We recognize three types of signals: `plain` signals - usual inter-agent communication, `timer` signals - triggered by the system timers, and `exception` signals - indicating exceptional situations. A signal is modelled by the class `Signal`.

```
enum SignalType

   Plain

   Timer

   Exception
```

```
class Signal implements IEvent

   name as Identifier

   stype as SignalType

   sender as Identifier

   receiver as Identifier?

   via as Seq of Identifier

   values as Seq of SignalValue

   var arrival as Time
```

2.1.4 Gates

The exchange of signals between SDL agents is modelled by means of gates. Gates serve as communication end-points the channels are connected to. A gate forms an interface for *serial* and *unidirectional* communication between two or more agents. In order to recognize input and output directions we defined the enumeration `GateDirection`.

```
enum GateDirection

   InDir

   OutDir
```

The gate itself is modelled by the class Gate that has identifier, direction and associated queue attributes.

class Gate

    ident **as** Identifier

    direction **as** GateDirection

    var queue **as** Seq **of** Signal = []

By definition, SDL allows to delay the communication by delaying the signals on the channels. Following the SDL semantics, the delay has been moved into the gates by associating a time-ordered signal queue with the gate. Thus, when a signal arrives to a gate it is inserted into the gate's queue according to its time stamp. When the queue already contains a signal with the same time stamp, the new signal is inserted after this signal but before the signal with the next time stamp value. Dispatching a signal from the gate means taking the first (head) element out of the queue. The methods isEmpty() and dispatchSignal() are provided to support signal dispatching. In addition, class Gate contains methods for inserting and removing signals to/from the queue.

class Gate

    function isEmpty() **as** Boolean

    procedure dispatchSignal() **as** Signal

    procedure insert(s **as** Signal, t **as** Time)

    procedure delete(s **as** Signal)

We also define a global variable Gates that represents the domain of all gates contained in the system.

var Gates **as** Set **of** Gate = {}

2.1.5 Channels
A channel represents an abstract communication medium transporting the signals from a source gate to a destination gate. A channel can be either *unidirectional* or *bidirectional*. Following the SDL semantics we model the channel by splitting it into the *unidirectional* links, in such a way that every link takes care of conveying signals in one direction. A link is modelled by the Link class that inherits from the ASMAgent class.

```
class Link extends ASMAgent

  source as Gate

  target as Gate

  accepted as Set of Identifier

  delayed as Boolean

  override procedure program()

  function delay(min as Time, max as Time ) as Time
```

The Link class introduces new attributes: source - the source gate, target - the destination gate, accepted - a list of the signals accepted by the link, delayed - a flag indicating whether the transportation is delayed. Because the Link extends the ASMAgent it has its own program running in parallel with other agents.

In order to model delayed communication, class Link provides the method delay() that either generates the delay values constrained by the given interval - for delaying channels or returns a zero delay - for non-delaying channels.

The path (a sequence of links) a signal can be conveyed through conforms to the routing mechanism that has to be defined. But we want our SFM model not to be bounded to one concrete routing strategy, so that we will have more freedom for further experimentation. Therefore we abstract the routing mechanism by the method compatible() that decides which link can convey the particular signal. Of course, for the simulation purposes an appropriate implementation of this method is needed.

```
function compatible(target as Gate, si as Signal) as Boolean

  return true
```

2.1.6 Time Concept and Timers
In SDL a notion of time is presented when dealing with delayed communication or timers. Therefore an appropriate time concept has to be defined in our semantic model as well. Following the proposed time concept for SDL semantics [10] we abstract the continuous time to a sequence of discrete time points at which a system is observed. The time points are modelled by the monotonic variable Now. The evolution of time is modelled by the method evolveTime().

```
var Now as Time = 0

procedure evolveTime()

  Now:= Now + 1
```

SDL supports timers to allow the modeling of time-triggered actions. Timers produce special timer signals that might trigger state transitions inside the agent state machines. Actually, a timer can be seen as a special signal that can be activated and de-activated. Thus, we model a timer by the class Timer that inherits the properties of the class Signal. It has additional attributes: duration - the duration time and owner - agent owning the timer, and methods: isActive() - indicates if the timer is active, setTimer() - sets the timer by inserting the timer signal into the agent's input port, and resetTimer() - resets the timer by removing the timer signal from the input port.

class Timer **extends** Signal

owner **as** AgentInst

duration **as** Time

function Active() **as** Boolean

procedure setTimer(val **as** Seq **of** SignalValue, t **as** Time)

procedure resetTimer()

2.1.7 Execution Semantics

The Signal Flow Model conforms to a distributed system with asynchronously and in parallel running agents that communicate between each other by sending signals over the channels. This distributed nature of the SFM requires appropriate modeling constructs that will allow specifying the SFM semantics in the distributed manner. Because of a lack of existence of any constructs in AsmL that would allow us to describe directly the control distribution we introduce own modeling constructs to achieve this support. We define the ASMAgent class representing the base class for all those agents that have their own programs and that run their programs in parallel. All such agents are stored in the Agents variable.

var Agents **as** Set **of** ASMAgent = {}

abstract class ASMAgent

ident **as** Identifier

owner **as** ASMAgent?

virtual procedure program()

Following the SDL semantics, all agents ought to run in parallel. Additionally, all signals communicated via non-delayed channels have to be conveyed and processed before the next observed time point will appear.

The parallel agent execution requirement is satisfied by calling the program() method for every ASM agent contained in the Agents set using the ASM rule **forall**. Besides the ASM agents representing the SDL agents, the Agents set contains also those ASM agents that run the behaviour of the links (signal transportation entities).

This in fact models the parallelism between the inter-agent communication and the control behaviour inside every process agent.

The second requirement on signal communication is achieved by guarded evolution of time. We allow the time to evolve only then when all signals designated for processing at the current time has been already processed.

```
procedure RunSFM()

  step while true

    forall a in Agents

      a.program()

    if CanEvolveTime() then

      evolveTime()
```

This precondition is checked by the CanEvolveTime() method that simply checks if there exist any gates having a signal ready for dispatching at the current time. Note that the function isEmpty() returns true if there are no signals to be dispatched at the current time, even though the queue of the gate might not be empty.

```
function CanEvolveTime() as Boolean

  return forall g in Gates holds g.isEmpty()
```

The execution of an AsmL specification always starts in the method called Main(). In our case the Main() method runs two sequential substeps. At first, the whole SFM specification is initialized with an instance of the concrete system. Afterwards the execution of the SFM itself is started by calling the method RunSFM().

```
procedure Main()

  step

    Initialize()

  step

    RunSFM()
```

2.2   UML State Machines

The Signal Flow Model, presented so far, is aimed to capture the architectural and communication aspects of a distributed production control system. In this section we focus on modeling the behaviour inside the control nodes of a DPCS. According to the ISILEIT methodology the control behaviour is modelled by means of the UML state machine. Therefore, this section introduces the semantic model of the UML state machine (currently the version 1.4 is supported).

The UML state machine is modelled by the UMLStateMachine class containing following attributes: owner - a reference to the owner of the state machine (an SDL process agent in our case), states - a set of all contained states, root - the uppermost state, upState - a relation describing the nesting hierarchy of the states, transitions - a set of all contained state transitions, and events - a set of all events recognized by the state machine. The current state configuration of the state machine is stored by the currentState variable. The state machine maintains two event queues the eventQueue and the completionEventQueue for storing the external and the internally generated completion events, respectively.

```
class UMLStateMachine implements IStateMachine

  owner as IStateMachineOwner? = null

  states as Set of State

  root as State

  upState as Map of State to State

  transitions as Set of Transition

  events as Set of IEvent

  var currentState as Set of State = {}

  var eventQueue as Seq of IEvent = []

  var completionEventQueue as Seq of IEvent = []
```

2.2.1 States

A state is a condition during the life of an object or an interaction during which it satisfies some condition, performs some action, or waits for some event. We define a base class State containing attributes common to all state kinds, such as the state name(name), the state kind (kind) and the completion event(compEvent) that is allowed to be undefined.

```
class State

  name as Identifier

  kind as StateKind

  compEvent as IEvent?
```

UML recognizes two basic kinds of states: a *simple* state and a *composite* state. A simple state is a state that does not have substates, i.e. it can not be further decomposed. A composite state, in contrary, is decomposed into two or more concurrent substates or into mutually exclusive disjoint substates. Additionally, UML introduces also so called *pseudostates*. We define the enumeration StateKind that defines all state kinds supported by our semantic model. We excluded some UML pseudostates that are not supported by our modeling tool such as *join, fork, choice* and *junction* pseudostates.

enum StateKind

   Simple, Sequential, Concurrent, Initial, History, Final

The simple state is modelled by the class SimpleState extending the State class and adding following attributes: entryAct - an action executed when the state is entered, exitAct - an action executed when the state is exited, doAct - an action representing state's internal activity and defer - a set of deferable events.

class SimpleState **extends** State

   entryAct **as** Action?

   exitAct **as** Action?

   doAct **as** Action?

   defer **as** Set **of** IEvent

The sequential composite state is modelled by the class SeqState extending the SimpleState class and introducing new attributes containing the initial pseudostate(init), the final state(final) and possibly the history state(history).

class SeqState **extends** SimpleState

   init **as** State

   final **as** State?

   history **as** HistoryState?

Analogously, the concurrent composite state is modelled by the class ConState introducing one new attribute concurrentComp that contains a sequence of sequential composite states corresponding to the individual regions of the concurrent state.

class ConState **extends** SimpleState

   concurrentComp **as** Seq **of** SeqState

Finally, we introduce the class HistoryState that models both types of the history states emerging in UML, i.e. the *deep* and the *shallow* history. The field config is supposed to store the current state configuration of the containing sequential state in case of firing an inter-level transition that exits the sequential state.

```
class HistoryState extends State

    isDeep as Boolean

    var config as Seq of State = []
```

2.2.2 Transitions

A simple transition is a relationship between two states indicating that an instance in the first state will enter the second state and perform specific actions when a specified event occurs provided that certain specified conditions are satisfied. We model a transition by the class Transition containing information such as transition source state (source), target state (target), triggering event (tr_event), assigned action (action) and guarding condition (guard). In addition, the transition owns a flag indicating whether it is an internal transition (isInternal) and an index (orderIndex) used by the collision resolution when several transitions with the same source are enabled at the same time.

```
class Transition

    source as State

    target as State

    tr_event as IEvent

    guard as Guard?

    action as Action?

    isInternal as Boolean

    orderIndex as Integer
```

2.2.3 Events

An event is a noteworthy occurrence that may be of several kinds according to its trigger. An event can be triggered when a designated condition becomes true, or by receipt of an explicit signal from one object (signal event), or by receipt of a call for an operation (call event), or by the passage of a designated period of time after a designated event or the occurrence of a given date/time (timer event).

We model an event by the class Event implementing the interface IEvent. The interface defines basic functionality the event (signal) implementation should provide.

```
class Event implements IEvent

  name as Identifier

  public property Name as Identifier

    get return name

  public function IsEqual(e as IEvent) as Boolean

    return name = e.Name
```

2.2.4 Actions and Guards

Inasmuch as the intention is to keep the semantic model of UML state machine working over the abstract states without considering any details about state contents, we introduce only simple base classes modeling actions and guards.

```
class Action

  name as Identifier



class Guard

  name as Identifier
```

2.2.5 Execution Semantics

The execution of a UML state machine comprises of a sequence of run-to-completion steps. A *run-to-completion step* represents the processing of a single event started in a stable state configuration, followed by firing of enabled transitions and execution of associated actions until the next stable state configuration is reached. In the UMLStateMachine class a run-to-completion step is modelled by the MakeStep() method.

```
class UMLStateMachine

  procedure MakeStep()

    var e as IEvent = selectEvent()

    step while e <> null

      step

        let ft = firableTrans(e)
```

```
step foreach t in ft

  fireTransition(t)
```

```
step

  updateEvents(e, [], getNewCompletionEvents())
```

```
step

  if completionEventQueue.Size > 0 then

    e := completionEventQueue.Head

  else

    e := null
```

At first, an external event for processing is dispatched by a call to the selectEvent() method. Afterwards, the set of all transitions enabled for firing is computed. Consequently, every transition is fired by calling the fireTransition() method. Then a set of possible completion events is computed and the state machine queues are updated (method updateEvents()). If there is some completion event in the completionEventQueue queue then it is selected and fired. The method finishes after all completion events has been fired, i.e. the machine has reached next stable state configuration.

2.3 Story Diagrams

The semantic model of UML state machines, presented above, abstracts the structure of a system state. It means that all elements using the state structure such as actions and guards are abstracted. However, the design process of DPCS must support also modeling actions and activities that work over concrete system state representation. For this purpose we adopted the Story Diagrams [5] that provide us a graphical language for modeling the action bodies. A story diagram is a combination of the UML activity and collaboration diagrams with the story patterns. Basically, the interpretation of a story diagram leads to a sequence of story patterns applied on an object graph representing a system. Due to space limitations we focus here only on the semantics of a story pattern.

A story pattern is the basic execution primitive in the story diagram. It executes over an *object oriented graph* representing the instance of a system. Therefore, the semantic model of Story Diagrams has to include information about the system object structure that is usually expressed in form of a class diagram. This implies the inclusion of the class diagram semantic in the semantic model of Story Diagram.

A class diagram is viewed as a graph and modelled by the class Scheme that contains following attributes: nodeLabels - a set of nodes (classes) in the scheme graph (class diagram), edgeLabels - a set of edge labels (association names), attributes - a set of all attributes collected from all classes, associations - a map of edges to their corresponding association information, isAs - a set of node pairs that have inheritance relationship.

class Scheme

  nodeLabels **as Set of** NodeLabel

  edgeLabels **as Set of** EdgeLabel

  attributes **as Set of** Attribut

  associations **as Map of** EdgeLabel **to** Association

  isAs **as Set of** (NodelLabel, NodelLabel)

An object oriented graph consists of a scheme defining the system structure and an extension graph containing a concrete graph instance conforming to the given scheme. It is modelled by the class ObjectGraph containing attributes: nodes - a set of nodes (objects), edges - a set of edges (links), nodeLabel - a map of a node to its corresponding label from the scheme, attrValues - a map yielding for every pair of node and attribute its assigned current value.

class ObjectGraph

  scheme **as** Scheme

  nodes **as Set of** Node

  edges **as Set of** Edge

  nodeLabel **as Map of** Node **to** NodeLabel

  attrValues **as Map of** (Node, Attribut) **to** AttributValue

Basically, a story pattern can be viewed as a graph rewrite rule. Generally, a graph rewrite rule consists of a pair of graphs, the left-hand side and the right-hand side. The graph of the left-hand side describes a „before" situation, i.e. a cut-out of the current object structure that is going to be modified. The right-hand side graph describes the „after" situation, i.e. how the cut-out of the current object structure should be changed by the rule. Usually, these two graphs are quite similar. For that reason, we model a story pattern using only one object graph with additionally annotated nodes, edges and attribute assignments. Nodes and edges can be marked for deletion or creation, while the attribute annotation only indicates whether its mapping to a value represents a value assignment. A story pattern is modelled by the class StoryPattern consisting of an object graph (objGraph) and marking maps (nodeMark, edgeMark and isValAssignment).

enum Mark

  Match, Match_Destroy, Create

```
class StoryPattern

  objGraph as ObjectGraph

  nodeMark as Map of Node to Mark

  edgeMark as Map of Edge to Mark

  isValAssignment as Map of (Node, Attribut) to Boolean
```

The execution semantics of a story pattern is modelled by the method Execute(). It first tries to find a subgraph matching the story pattern in the given host object graph. On success, the matching pairs are stored in the variables matchedNodes and matchedEdges. The execution continues by the deletion of nodes and edges marked for deletion (the deletion preserves graph well-formedness) followed by the creation of the new nodes and updating of the attribute values. On return the method indicates whether the execution was successful.

```
class StoryPattern

  var matchedNodes as Set of (Node, Node)

  var matchedEdges as Set of (Edge, Edge)



  procedure Execute(hostGraph as ObjectGraph) as Boolean

    if FindMatch(hostGraph) then

      step

        DoDelete(hostGraph)

      step

        DoCreate(hostGraph)

      step

        UpdateAttrValues()

      return true

    else

      return false
```

2.4   Composition of Semantic Models

Any of the semantic models presented in the previous sections captures a specific aspect of a DPCS system. Moreover, the models have been designed in a way to loosen their coupling to maximal possible level. This, on one hand, allows us to validate every model separately and, on the other hand, give us freedom in the way we compose them. For example, one can first focus only on the evaluation of individual state machines by taking only the semantic model of the UML state machine. Afterwards, the SDL Signal Flow Model can be added in order to evaluate the interactions between the individual state machines. Finally, the semantic model of Story Diagrams can be added allowing the evaluation of actions inside the state machines. In this way, it is possible to process the evaluation of particular aspects of the system at different abstraction levels [11]. This idea we further follow in the application of the model checking method for formal verification of designs of distributed production control systems.

3   Integrating Model Checking into the Design Process for DPCS

One of the main objectives of the ISILEIT project was the integration of model checking verification techniques supporting the design process with fully automated verification facilities. Our solution resides in the development of a model checking technique capable to work with AsmL models that can be integrated into the overall ISILEIT design process as shown in Figure 2 (the verification part).

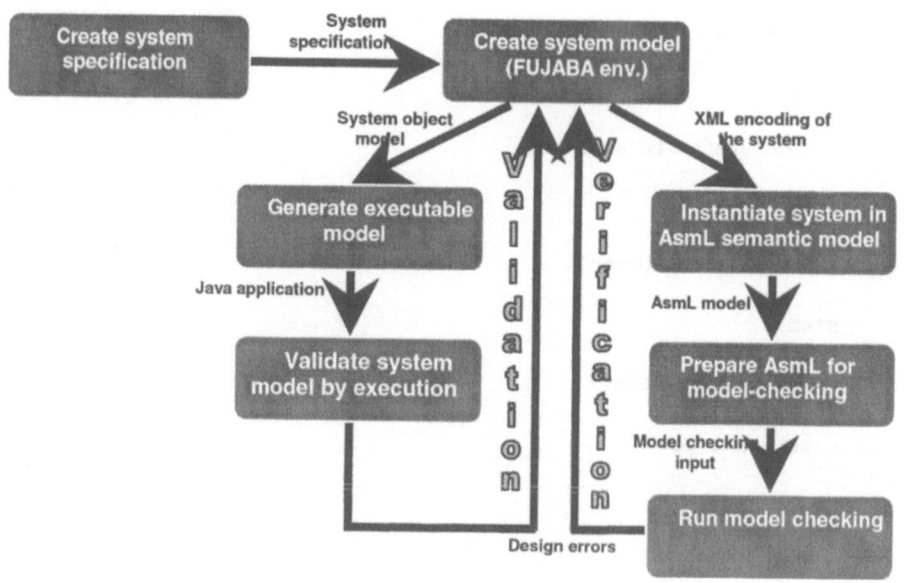

Fig. 2. Design process in ISILEIT

The integration is based on the existence of a formal semantic model of the modeling paradigm described in AsmL. We have presented this model in the Section 2. The integration itself resides in transforming the graphical diagrams describing the modelled system into the semantic model, i.e. into its individual submodels. This is done by exporting the system model from our modeling tool FUJABA into an XML file. Consequently, the file is imported and a corresponding instance of the system is created inside the semantic model. The semantic model initialized with a system instance serves as an input to the model checking method presented in the next section.

4   Model Checking Approach

4.1   Model Checking AsmL Models

One of the qualities of AsmL is the high expressivity and richness of the language that allows us to keep the semantic models in a readable and comprehensible form. This gives us flexibility in further maintenance of the semantic models and eases their modification and updating. However, in order to keep this advantage of AsmL we need to provide such a model checking approach that imposes the least restrictions on the AsmL specification. Concretely, an AsmL specification should be allowed to fully exploit the robust data type system built-in into AsmL, should allow dynamic object creation as well as usage of whole operational functionality provided by AsmL. The only constraint imposed on a specification is related to the size of its state space that has to be finite. The model checking approach presented in the next sections obeys all these requirements. It can be classified as an on-the-fly approach working over the explicit ASM state.

4.2   On-the-Fly Model Checking

The intended model checking approach is depicted in Figure 3. First of all, a particular AsmL specification and the property to be verified are provided as inputs. The property is specified in form of a temporal logic formula. In the first step, the temporal formula is transformed into a property automaton. As next, the AsmL specification is compiled and prepared for an on-the-fly exploration. When both steps are successfully finished, the verification algorithm is started. During this process the state space exploration of a given AsmL specification is driven by the verification algorithm in an on-demand manner. The verification process may terminate in one of the following states: 1) in the OK state, after the whole state space has been explored and no contradiction of the property has been detected, 2) in the contradiction state, if a state of the system is found that does not satisfy the property and a counter example is produced 3) in the exception state, when an exception inside the specification is thrown during the state space exploration, and 4) in the user termination state, if the verification process was forced by the user to terminate.

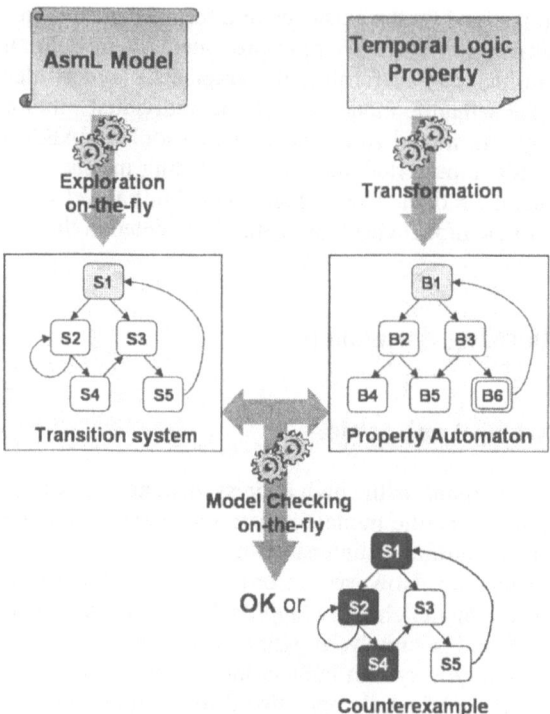

Fig. 3. On-the-fly model checking of AsmL

4.2.1 Property Specification and Transformation

During model checking a system is verified against a property describing the desired system behaviours. The property is expressed in form of a temporal logic formula. There exist several kinds of temporal logics, e.g. CTL, LTL, CTL* which usually differ in the set of expressible behaviours. In our approach we consider the CTL* logic that subsumes both CTL and LTL. The transformation of a CTL* formula into an automaton is done following the method introduced in [12]. This method uses a set of predefined goal-directed rules to derive the states of specialized tree automata called alternating Büchi tableau automata (ABTAs). An ABTA represents the property automaton showed in Figure 3.

4.2.2 Transition System Construction

A transition system (a state transition graph) derived from an AsmL specification represents all possible runs of the specification. Obviously, the construction of such a transition system is, with respect to the needed time and resources, the most costly part of the overall model checking process. Therefore, we propose an on-the-fly construction approach that exploits the exploration function built-in in the AsmL Toolkit. This function allows us to drive the exploration of a system state space according to the demands of the verification algorithm. Additionally, the configurability of the exploration process gives us the apparatus to control how the state space is going to be explored.

4.2.3 Verification Algorithm

The model checking algorithm adopted in our approach originates in the work presented in [12]. It works over a product automaton, constructed from the produced property automaton and the transition system. Since, in our case, the transition system is generated in an on-the-fly manner, the original algorithm had to be adapted accordingly. In addition, the algorithm was redesigned in order to achieve a certain generics with respect to the implementations of transition system and property automaton. This should give us more freedom for experiments towards achievement of optimal implementations. We also replaced the recursive algorithm by a non-recursive one in order to avoid problems with stack overflow when considering systems with very deep execution paths.

5   Related Work

Nowadays a plethora of design tools can be found supporting either UML or SDL language for the system modeling. The main problem with those tools is that they come with some built-in support for model validation that depends strictly on the semantics prescribed by the tool implementation that is not formalized and usually even not fully compatible with the semantics of the reference language. In contrary, our approach is built on a rigorous formal semantic model, with a clear structure and form, precisely describing supported semantic parts of the given language(s). In addition the semantic model is not strongly dependent on the tool implementation and used notation and can be easily adapted and maintained. Another crucial difference compared to the commercial tools resides in the form of supported verification methods. While the commercial tools concentrate on supporting the system validation by simulation and testing, in our approach the main focus is put on providing a fully automated formal verification method, concretely by adapting the model checking techniques, as supplement to the usual simulation approach.

Of course, there is a lot of ongoing work on model checking state-of-the-art modeling languages like UML [13,14,15,16,17]. The basic idea of all these methods is to transform the UML model to the input language of an existing model checking tool, such as SMV, SPIN or UPPAAL for example. In other words, the semantics of the UML model is reflected through the input language of some model checker. The expressiveness of model checker's input language usually limits the expressiveness of the checked UML model. Unlike these methods, our method presented in this paper uses the ASM-based executable specification language AsmL to define the semantics of the UML model. The expressive power of AsmL allows us to formalize the semantics of any complex UML model that implies no constraints on used UML diagrams at the user's side. In addition, the resulting AsmL specification can be executed or tested by the tools coming with AsmL.

Since AsmL is quite a new language, there are no published approaches aimed at model checking AsmL yet. However, a few papers can be found concerning the model checking of the Abstract State Machines [18,19,20]. Basically, we can identify two main approaches both based on the translation of the selected subsets of ASMs into the input language of an existing model checking tool. In the [18,19] an ASM model is first simplified by flattening the data structure and the corresponding ASM rules, and then translated (by direct mapping) to the SMV [21] input language. The approach introduced in [20] follows a similar strategy, but uses the SPIN [22] model checker and its PROMELA language. The main drawbacks of both approaches consist in the constraints imposed on the supported ASM models. On the other hand, imposing such constraints seemed to be an inevitable decision in order to bridge the gap between the different expressive power of ASMs and the model checker languages. Our method can avoid this problem by model checking AsmL specifications directly.

6   Conclusion and Future Work

In this paper we have presented an approach on integration of a formal verification technique, represented by the model checking technique, into the ISILEIT's design methodology for distributed production control systems. Although the approach has been designed focusing at the application domain of DPCS, it could be also reused in connection with different application domains and modeling languages as well.

The main ideas, presented in this paper, consist in using the AsmL specification language to acquire a formal semantic model of the integrated specification language used in ISILEIT and consequently applying the model checking technique directly on the resulting AsmL semantic model. In addition, we have introduced an on-the-fly model checking method developed for this purpose.

Currently we have finished the implementation of the proposed model checking algorithm and have started the validation phase. Consequently, the integration process into the design tool FUJABA will be completed and the whole methodology will be evaluated on our reference case study.

References

[1] Integrative Specification of Distributed Control Systems for the Flexible Automated Manufacturing (ISILEIT), German Research Foundation (DFG) program "integrative specification of engineering applications".: http://www.upb.de/cs/isileit/

[2] W. Schäfer, R. Wagner, J. Gausemeier, R. Eckes: An Engineer's Workstation to support Integrated Development of Flexible Production Control Systems, this volume

[3] Booch, G., Rumbaugh, J., Jacobson, I.: The Unified Modeling Language User Guide. Addison-Wesley, Reading, Massachusetts, 1999.

[4] ITU-T Recommendation Z.100, Specification and Description Language (SDL), International Telecommunication Union (ITU), Geneva, 1994 + Addendum 1996.

[5] T. Fischer, J. Niere, L. Torunski, A. Zündorf: Story Diagrams: A new Graph Rewrite Language based on the Unified Modelling Language and Java; in Proc. of the 6th International Workshop on Theory and Application of Graph Transformation (TAGT), Paderborn, November 1998, LNCS, Springer Verlag.

[6] Y. Gurevich: Evolving Algebras 1993: Lipari Guide; E. Börger (Eds.): Specification and Validation Methods; Oxford University Press, 1995.

[7] Abstract State Machines home page: http://www.eecs.umich.edu/gasm/

[8] Y. Gurevich,W. Schulte,C. Campbell,W. Grieskamp. AsmL: The Abstract State Machine Language Version 2.0. http://research.microsoft.com/foundations/AsmL/default.html

[9] FUJABA home page: http://www.uni-paderborn.de/cs/fujaba/

[10] R. Eschbach, U. Glässer, R. Gotzhein, M. von Löwis and A. Prinz: Formal Definition of SDL-2000 - Compiling and Running SDL Specifications as ASM Models. Journal of Universal Computer Science (J.UCS), October 2001.

[11] H. Giese, M. Kardos and U. Nickel: Integrating Verification in a Design Process for Distributed Production Control Systems. Second International Workshop on Integration of Specification Techniques for Applications in Engineering (INT 2002). Grenoble, France, April 2002.

[12] G. Bhat, R. Cleaveland, and A. Groce: Efficient model checking via Buchi tableau automata. Technical report, Department of Computer Science, SUNY, Stony Brook, 2000

[13] T. Schäfer, A. Knapp, and S. Merz. Model Checking UML State Machines and Collaborations. In Proc. Wsh. Software Model Checking, Volume 55(3) of Elect. Notes Theo. Comp. Sci., Paries, 2001.

[14] A. Knapp, S. Merz, and C. Rauh. Model Checking Timed UML State Machines and Collaborations. Proc. 7th Int. Symp. Formal Techniques in Real-Time and Fault Tolerant Systems, LNCS 2469, pages 395-416. ©Springer, Berlin, 2002

[15] K. Diethers, U. Goltz and M. Huhn. Model Checking UML Statecharts with Time. In Proc. of the Workshop on Critical Systems Development with UML, 2002.

[16] A. David, M.Möller, and W. Yi. Formal Verification of UML Statecharts with Real-Time Extensions. In Proc. of FASE 2002 (ETAPS 2002). LNCS 2306, p218-232, 2002.

[17] S. Gnesi and D. Latella. Model Checking UML Statechart Diagrams using JACK. In Proc. Fourth IEEE International Symposium on High Assuarance Systems Enginering, IEEE Press, 1999.

[18] G. del Castillo and K. Winter: Model checking support for the ASM high-level language. In S. Graf and M. Schwartzbach, editors, Proc. on 6th Int. Conf. TACAS 2000, volume 1785 of LNCS, pages 331-346, 2000.

[19] Kirsten Winter: Model Checking Abstract State Machines, Ph.D. thesis, Technical University of Berlin, Germany, 2001.

[20] A. Gargantini, E. Riccobene, S. Rinzivillo: Using Spin to Generate Tests from ASM Specifications, In E. Börger, A. Gargantini, E. Riccobene, editors, Proc. of 10th International Workshop on Abstract State Machines 2003, Taormina, Italy, March 3-7, 2003

[21] K. McMillan: Symbolic Model Checking, Kluwer Academic Publishers, Boston (1993).

[22] G. J. Holzmann: The model checker SPIN. IEEE Transactions on Software Engineering, May 1997.

Combining Formal Methods and Safety Analysis – The ForMoSA Approach

Frank Ortmeier, Andreas Thums, Gerhard Schellhorn, and Wolfgang Reif

Lehrstuhl für Softwaretechnik und Programmiersprachen,
Universität Augsburg, D-86135 Augsburg
{ortmeier, thums, schellhorn, reif}@informatik.uni-augsburg.de

Abstract. In the ForMoSA project [18] an integrated approach for safety analysis of critical, embedded systems has been developed. The approach brings together the best of engineering practice, formal methods and mathematics: traditional safety analysis, temporal logics and verification, and statistics and optimization.

These three orthogonal techniques cover three different aspects of safety: fault tolerance, functional correctness and quantitative analysis. The ForMoSA approach combines these techniques to answer the safety relevant questions in a structured and formal way. Furthermore, the tight combination of methods from different analysis domains yields results which can not be produced by any single technique.

The methodology was applied in form of case studies to different industrial domains. One of them is the height control of the Elbtunnel in Hamburg [17] from the domain of electronic traffic control, which we present as an illustrating example.

Keywords: fault tree analysis, dependability, optimization, safety analysis, embedded systems

1 Introduction

Safety is an important property of embedded systems. Their complexity and the role of software used in them constantly increases. This makes new techniques necessary, that can deal with complex hardware-software systems. Safety covers many different aspects like functional correctness, fault tolerance or risk minimization. Therefore, different techniques are necessary to deal with different aspects.

To achieve this we combine methods from three different domains: software engineering, engineering and mathematics. To assure a high level of confidence formal methods from software engineering have been used. Safety relevant properties may be analyzed by safety analysis techniques from engineering. Mathematical methods from statistics and optimization can yield good quantitative approximations for risk.

In section 2 we develop a new technique to find failure modes. Failure modes are an important input for many safety analysis techniques [14,21] like failure

H. Ehrig et al. (Eds.): INT 2004, LNCS 3147, pp. 474–493, 2004.

modes and effects analysis (FMEA) or fault tree analysis (FTA). The combination of FTA and formal methods results in formal FTA. Formal FTA, described in Sect. 3 integrates the rigorous proof concepts of formal methods into the reasoning process of FTA. Bringing statistical distributions into fault trees yields parameterized risk approximations. This allows to quickly evaluate the effects of different component configurations or changing working environments. This technique is demonstrated in Sect. 4. Mathematical safety optimization is presented in Sect. 5. It produces an optimal configuration for the free parameters of a system. This helps to reduce the time required for testing and fine tuning a system.

Our experience is, that no single technique can produce all the results of a combined approach. A suitable methodology, which tries to maximize the mutual benefits is presented in Sect. 6. An application of this methodology on a real-world case study - the electronic height control of the Elbtunnel - is shown in section 7. Section 8 concludes the paper.

2   Failure-Sensitive Specification

Failure modes are important for many safety analysis techniques. A failure mode is a specific way in which a component may fail. The leaves of all fault trees are failure modes. The starting column of FMEA also contains the failure mode to be examined. Normally failure modes are specified in an informal and manual way. Failure-sensitive specification [16] allows to find and characterize failure modes in a structured formal way. The basic idea is to use one formal specification of the system as description of the intended system behavior and to use a completely different formalism in parallel to describe failure modes. Completeness of the found list of failure modes can then be shown. As formal models for the intended system we use state charts with the semantics of [7].

For better understanding we will give an example of a simple switch in parallel with the formal definitions of failure-sensitive specification. Every system component reacts on a certain set of (boolean) input signals and produces some (boolean) output signals as answers to these inputs. Let Ω be the set of all possible combinations of signals - called the chaotic model.

Figure 1 shows this for the example of a simple switch. On the left a formal model of the switch is shown in state chart notation. The box in the middle shows the relevant input and output signals. For the example: The behavior of a switch depends on whether it was ON (=signal ON_{in}) or OFF (=signal OFF_{in}) and if it is pressed (=signal Press) or not. As reactions one may observe whether the switch is ON (=signal ON_{out}) or OFF (=signal OFF_{out}). Note, *Omega* does not contain any functional information thus it includes the correct behavior of a switch as well as possible failure scenarios.

The right column shows the chaotic model. It contains all possible combinations of inputs and outputs. Each row of the table is to be read as a scenario, where ON_{in}, OFF_{in} and Press are the input signals and ON_{out} and OFF_{out} are output signals, which are produced by the component in response to the in-

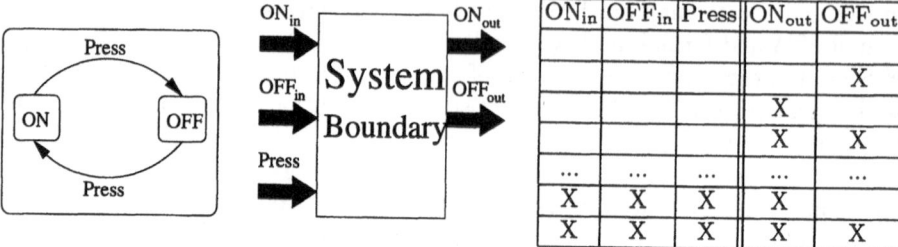

ON$_{in}$	OFF$_{in}$	Press	ON$_{out}$	OFF$_{out}$
				X
			X	
			X	X
...	...	...	...	...
X	X	X	X	
X	X	X	X	X

Fig. 1. Chaotic model of a switch

puts. An "X" means the signal is present and a blank means the signal is not present. So each IO-scenario $\Phi \in \Omega$ is represented by a pair (s,t) of sets of input and output signals. This (finite) set of scenarios is the starting point for a failure-sensitive specification. Formally, the chaotic model is defined as Cartesian product of input and output signals.

Definition 1 (Chaotic model). *Let the system boundaries $SIG := IN \cup OUT$ be described by a set of input signals IN (called input set) and a disjoint set of output signals OUT (called output set). The chaotic model of the system is the Cartesian product of the power sets of the set of input and output signals. $\Omega := \mathcal{P}(IN) \times \mathcal{P}(OUT)$. The elements of Ω are called scenarios.*

Specification information is now subsequently added by rules and the set Ω is restricted according to these requirements. Formally, the specification process is defined as follows:

Definition 2 (Specification Rules). *A specification rule SpecRule is defined to be a boolean expression over SIG. Each rule can be identified with a corresponding set $SPECRULE_i := \{\Phi \in \Omega | SpecRule_i(\Phi)\}$.*

Specification rules are often formulated as properties, which should hold for a component, e.g. "if the switch was off and pressed, then it must be on"(RULE1).

In the example, RULE1 removes all rows in which an "X" is present in the "OFF$_{in}$" and in the "Press", but not in the "ON$_{out}$" column. Note, that the complement of a rule - against Ω - is then a failure mode. This is because a definition of failure is "faulty behavior" or "behavior against the specification". For example the failure mode "fails to close" is the complement of RULE1. Finding a complete list of failure modes is thus equivalent to finding a complete list of SpecRules.

A specification is described as set intersection of the specification rules. The failure-sensitive specification FS for n SpecRules is

$$FS := \bigcap_{j=1}^{n} SPECRULE_j$$

In real problems boolean expressions are usually not sufficient. Therefore, we define projection operators $\pi : SIG \rightarrow PL(SC)$, where PL(SC) denotes the predicate logic formulas over the signature of the state chart SC. These operators associate the elements of the FS with a predicate logic formula over the state chart.

In the example these operators are simple identities. E.g. ON_{in} would be associated with the (boolean) state variable ON. In other applications these projections are not simple identities. For example in the radio-based level crossing [13] case study the signal "before critical point" is associated with "pos > CP".

Assume, that a state chart model of the intended behavior of the component is available. We can then define completeness of failure modes formally. The completeness criterion will be that, "the state chart shows exactly the behavioral patterns of the failure-sensitive model and vice versa". Or in other words: the IO-relation of the state-chart model is equal to the failure-sensitive model. To prove this equivalence we identify each scenario $\Phi = (s,t) \in FS$ with an formula $F(\Phi)$ of the logic ITL [6] over the state chart model:

$$F(s,t) = \bigwedge_{x \in s} \pi(x) \wedge \bigwedge_{x \in IN \setminus s} \neg\, \pi(x) \wedge \circ (\bigwedge_{x \in t} \pi(x) \wedge \bigwedge_{x \in OUT \setminus t} \neg\, \pi(x))$$

In this definition $\circ$ denotes the NEXT-operator. If in any trace σ of the state chart the formula $F(\Phi)$ is valid at a certain time t, then this means that the transition (σ_t, σ_{t+1}) shows the IO-behavior Φ. Now, behavioral equivalence of failure-sensitive specification FS and state chart SC is defined as follows:

Definition 3 (Behavioral equivalence). *A state chart SC and a failure-sensitive specification FS are behaviorally equivalent (SC $\cong$ FS) , if*

1. on all runs of SC, always $\bigvee_{\Phi \in FS} F(\Phi)$ holds.   *("SC $\leq$ FS")*

2. for every $\Phi \in FS$ exists a run of SC, for which at some time $F(\Phi)$ holds.   *("FS $\leq$ SC")*

So if SC is a model of the intended system and if $SC \cong FS$ then the list of specification rules is complete - and so is the list of failure modes. Note, that this list is not unique. It is, for example, always possible to combine two rules into one with logical conjunction. But the resulting failure mode is then also the combination (disjunction) of the two original failure modes. This allows us to find a complete list of failure-modes, which can then be used for formal safety analysis. The properties above may be expressed in CTL as well and can be verified automatically using for example the statemate model certifier. On the other hand ITL is integrated into the KIV interactive theorem prover (see [23] in this volume). So it is possible to do failure-sensitive specification for both finite and infinite state systems.

It is interesting, that behavioral inclusion ($FS \leq SC$) is enough to ensure a complete list of failure modes. The reason is, that if the failure-sensitive model can show less behavior, then it is has more or stricter specification rules than necessary. This means, the model has more or more general failure modes than necessary. A safety analysis done with this list of failure modes is already safe.

3   Formal FTA

A well-known safety analysis technique is fault tree analysis (FTA, [25], [26]). FTA was developed for technical systems to analyze if they permit a hazard (top event). The top event is noted at the root of the fault tree. Events which cause the hazard are given in the child nodes and analyzed recursively, resulting in a tree of events. Each analyzed event (main event) is connected to its causes (sub-events) by a gate in the fault tree (see Fig. 2). An AND-gate indicates that all sub-events are necessary to trigger the main event, for an OR-gate only one sub-event is necessary. An INHIBIT-gate states that in addition to the cause stated in the sub-event the condition (noted in the oval) has to be true to trigger the main event. The inhibit gate is more or less an AND-gate, where the condition does not have to be a fault. The leaves of the tree are the failure modes (basic events) for the top event, which have to occur in combination (corresponding to the gates in the tree) to trigger the top event. A combination of basic events

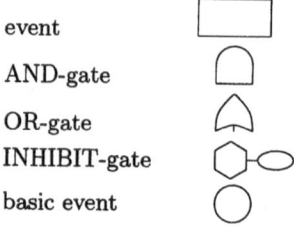

Fig. 2. Fault Tree Symbols

which leads to the hazard is called a *cut set*. A *minimal cut set* is a cut set which can not lead to the top level hazard, if only one event of the set is prevented. This information helps to identify failure events whose exclusion secures the system. If for example one event occurs in different minimal cut sets, the probability of the top level hazard will strongly decrease, if this event can be excluded.

Minimal cut sets can be computed from fault trees by combining the primary events with boolean operators as indicated by the gates. A minimal cut set then consists of the elements of one conjunction of the disjunctive normal form of the resulting formula.

Given a formal system model, we defined a formal semantics of this informal technique. Each gate is represented by an interval temporal logic (ITL) formula. Temporal formulas in ITL are built from first-order formulas using propositional connectives and the following temporal operators[1]: $\Box \; \varphi$ ("in all initial intervals φ"), $\boxdot \; \varphi$ ("in all subintervals φ"), $\Diamond \; \varphi$ ("in some initial interval φ"), $\diamondsuit \; \varphi$ ("in some subinterval φ"), and $\varphi \; ; \; \psi$ (read φ chop ψ: "the interval can be split, such that φ holds in the first part and ψ in the second").

---

[1] ITL also defines quantification and many other derived operators not needed here. More information may be found in [2][6]

The formalization of FTA showed, that defining the semantics of an OR-gate simply as a disjunction is insufficient, since it does not take into account that the sub-events (causes) usually happen *before* the main event (consequence), and that events may have duration. Therefore, we distinguish between decomposition gates (D-gates) and cause-consequence gates (C-gates). We get 7 types of gates. In figure 3 the FTA formulae for D-gates (left column) and C-gates (right column) are shown. D-OR- and D-AND-gates (D, D) can be defined canonically:

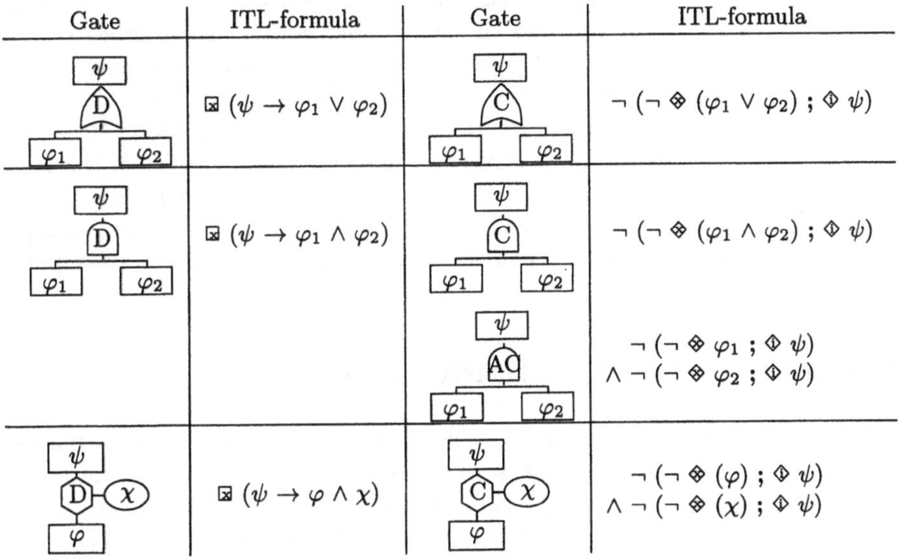

Gate	ITL-formula	Gate	ITL-formula
ψ / D / φ_1 φ_2	$\boxdot (\psi \rightarrow \varphi_1 \vee \varphi_2)$	ψ / C / φ_1 φ_2	$\neg (\neg \circledast (\varphi_1 \vee \varphi_2) \, ; \, \Diamond \, \psi)$
ψ / D / φ_1 φ_2	$\boxdot (\psi \rightarrow \varphi_1 \wedge \varphi_2)$	ψ / C / φ_1 φ_2	$\neg (\neg \circledast (\varphi_1 \wedge \varphi_2) \, ; \, \Diamond \, \psi)$
		ψ / AC / φ_1 φ_2	$\neg (\neg \circledast \varphi_1 \, ; \, \Diamond \, \psi)$ $\wedge \neg (\neg \circledast \varphi_2 \, ; \, \Diamond \, \psi)$
ψ / D—X / φ	$\boxdot (\psi \rightarrow \varphi \wedge \chi)$	ψ / C—X / φ	$\neg (\neg \circledast (\varphi) \, ; \, \Diamond \, \psi)$ $\wedge \neg (\neg \circledast (\chi) \, ; \, \Diamond \, \psi)$

Fig. 3. Formal semantics of fault trees

for example the D-AND-gate (D) states, that whenever the effect ψ happens, both causes φ_1 and φ_2 must happen as well. A C-OR-gates (C) states, that it must not be possible to split a run, such that none of the causes φ_1 and φ_2 ever happens in the first half, but the consequence ψ happens at the beginning of the second half. In other words: if the consequence happens, one of the causes must have happened before (*completely*, if it has duration, therefore the chop is necessary). Causes and consequences must not overlap. The asynchronous and synchronous C-AND-gates (C, AC) are similar, they require that both causes must have happened (at the same time) before the consequence. The conditions for D-INHIBIT- and C-INHIBIT-gates ($\text{D}\!-\!\bigcirc$, $\text{C}\!-\!\bigcirc$) are the same as for the D-AND-gate and AC-gate.

Hansen et al. [11] defines cause/consequence gates in Duration Calculus (DC, [27]), but their definition does not meet the requirement, that causes are completed before the consequence. A subsequent publication [10] is restricted to decomposition gates. Bruns and Andersen [5] also define a fault tree semantics using μ-calculus. They also distinguish between cause/consequence and decomposition gates. Only events without duration are considered. For this special case, our semantics is equivalent (see [24] for details).

For the semantics in Fig. 3, the following theorem was proven:

Theorem 1 (completeness theorem (minimal cut set theorem)). *If all conditions of a fault tree can be verified, and if for each minimal cut set at least one of its basic events is prevented from happening on each run, then the top-level event will never happen.*

For a complete fault tree it is sufficient to prevent only one primary event of each minimal cut set, to avoid the fault under consideration altogether. A complete fault tree is therefore a partial proof for the safety of the system. The completeness theorem gives a formal justification for the use of minimal cut sets in safety analysis, even for cases where timing conditions are relevant [19].

The theorem is proved using structural induction over the size of the fault tree. The basic fact underlying the proof is transitivity of the cause-consequence relation. The proof was done formally with the KIV system ([3]), using an algebraic specification of the syntax and semantics of continuous Interval Temporal Logic.

4   Parameterized, Quantitative FTA

In reality it is not only interesting which reason might cause system failure, but also how probable this failure is. In safety analysis, there exists a variety of techniques for assessing failure probabilities. One of them is quantitative FTA.

The idea of quantitative FTA is to take the fault tree and calculate the minimal cut sets. To approximate the risk, probabilities are assigned to each primary failure PF. Assuming statistical independence[2], the probability of a minimal cut set MCS can then be approximated by:

$$P(MCS) := \prod_{PF \in MCS} P(PF)$$

If second and higher order terms are neglected the probability of the hazard H may be approximated by the sum of all minimal cut sets of the fault tree:

$$P(H) := \sum_{MCS \in MCSS_H} P(MCS)$$

$MCSS_H$ denotes the set of all minimal cut sets of the fault tree for hazard H. Given a fault tree and the probabilities of all primary failures this allows to calculate the hazard probability. This technique is widely used in practice and more details may be found in [26].

---

[2] If statistical dependence is to be examined, then FTA is often not the method of choice, because calculating dependent probabilities can be very hard. In this case probabilistic model checking ([1]) can help, where the failure probabilities are already included into the system model.

The drawback is, that this is a static analysis, which has to be redone every time some parameter changes. This is unnecessary: if a system has free parameters like safety gaps, timeouts or maintenance intervals, then it is much more convenient to replace the static probabilities by probability distributions. Many random variables may be approximated by well-known standard distributions. For safety analysis the most important ones are exponential and normal distributions. More information on probability distributions may be found in [20].

To obtain a parameterized probability for the hazard, we use the same approach as standard quantified FTA but replace the static probabilities of the primary failures with parameterized probability distributions. So P(H) no longer is a fixed value but rather a function of the free parameters $X_1, \ldots, X_n$. Now it is very easy to examine the system in dependence of the free parameters.

$$P(H)(X_1, .., X_n) := \sum_{MCS \in MCSS_H} \prod_{PF \in MCS} P(PF)(X_1, .., X_n)$$

However, there are still possibilities to improve this approach for quantitative approximation. Often the events of a cut set lead to the hazard only, if some constraints (which are no faults) are satisfied, e.g. only if the system is in a certain operation mode. Constraints are typically derived from INHIBIT-gates, since the side-condition χ of an INHIBIT-gate is a a formal description of a necessary constraint. Constraint probabilities are multiplied with a cut sets probability. So the final formula to calculate a hazards probability is:

$$P(H)(X_1, .., X_n) := \sum_{MCS \in MCSS_H} P_{constraint}(MCS) \prod_{PF \in MCS} P(PF)(X_1, .., X_n)$$

Constraint probabilities result in a much more precise quantitative approximations for the hazards occurrence.

5   Safety Optimization

Safety optimization is the next step towards formal safety analysis. It deals with the problem of choosing free parameters. Many industrial projects start in a testing phase to find out the optimal working parameters. For safety analysis this is not a feasible approach, since probabilities are low by design, e.g. one hazard in 100 years. Therefore, to find an optimal configuration for some parameters would require to test the system several 100 years (at least 100 years per configuration).

The problem becomes more interesting and complicated if two or more competing hazards are investigated. Consider e.g. the pre-flight safety check of an airplane. The most critical hazard is, that an unsafe airplane passes the test. A competing hazard is, that a technically okay airplane fails the test. It is intuitively clear, that it is not possible to minimize both hazards at the same time. A fair balance must be found.

To find it, we set up a mathematical optimization problem, which combines the results of (formal) FTA with parameterized probabilities. A cost function is defined, which measures risk in estimated costs (costs are also used for calculations whether operation of the system is profitable). For many domains a good cost function is the weighted sum of all hazards probabilities:

$$f_{cost}(P(H_1), .., P(H_m)) := \Sigma_{i=1}^{m} Cost_{H_i} P(H_i)$$

The weight of each hazard represents the costs it usually causes. The given cost function describes the mean expected costs that all hazards together will cause. The hazards probabilities $P(H_i)$ are substituted with the parameterized probabilities of the previous section.

$$f_{cost}(X_1, .., X_n) := \Sigma_{i=1}^{m} Cost_{H_i} \sum_{MCS \in MCSS_{H_i}} P(MCS) \prod_{PF \in MCS} P(PF)(X_1, .., X_n)$$

The cost function now no longer depends on the hazards probabilities, but on the probabilities of the primary failures and constraints. More specifically, it depends on the choice of the free parameters of the system. In other words: Minimization of the cost function will result in an optimal set of free parameters. The minimization may be solved with any mathematical tool or optimization algorithm ([9], [15]). Newtons Method is often a good choice, as usually the function is twice continuously differentiable and an appropriate initial guess is easy to find.

6   Methodology

The previous section outlined formal safety analysis techniques. In this chapter we will describe how these techniques may be combined in an efficient way. Figure 4 shows the interaction of our techniques as a graph. Arrows represent dependencies, and the time line is from left to right.

The top trace - informal specification, formal functional model, functional correctness - represents the standard approach of formal software development in computer science. The bottom trace - informal specification, traditional FTA, quantitative FTA - is the methodology for traditional safety analysis with FTA.

The ForMoSA techniques are in between these two boundaries. They combine the tools of formal verification techniques with the matters of safety analysis. This yields a mutual benefit: the results of safety analysis techniques are now built on a solid formal foundation, and the formal model is validated by checking the proof obligations of FTA.

Typically, the connection arrows between the different techniques represent their interdependence. Method A yields new results for method B, which in turn results in a feedback to method A. An example for this process may be found in [17], where the methodology for tightly versus loosely coupled FTA is presented. We can not present all the details here, but we will try to describe the whole approach for formal safety analysis.

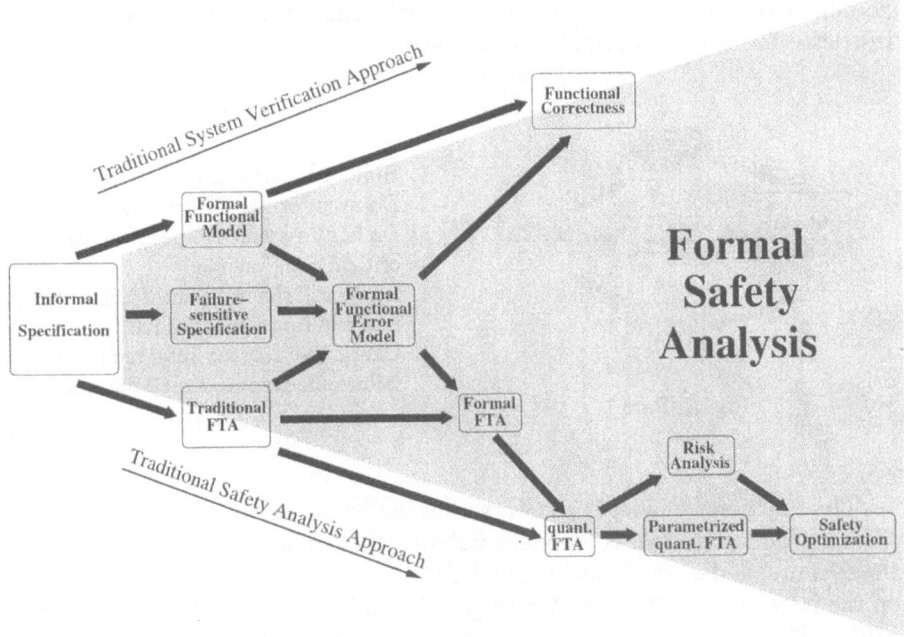

Fig. 4. Interaction of techniques

6.1 The ForMoSA Approach

The ForMoSA approach may be split into three different sections. The first deals with building a formal specification, which also models possible failures. We call this the functional error model. The second part deals with qualitative analysis. The goal in this part is to find the causal dependencies between component failures and system failure. The last step deals with quantitative approaches. Namely, the approximation of hazard probabilities and the optimization of the system. The parts are not completely disjoint. But it is also possible to skip various work packages within one block, if they seem not adequate or - more probable - if time is too short to do the full analysis process.

6.2 Building the Formal Model

This block subsumes the following steps: building the functional model, failure-sensitive specification, traditional FTA and building the functional error model. We suggest to stick to the methodology sketched in Fig. 5.

As a first step, we set up an informal (requirements) specification of the system to build, and describe the potential hazards informally. The description fixes domain specific notions.

Based on the informal description a formal model is specified, that describes the intended functional behavior, called the functional model. This model usually does not describe any component failures. We typically use state charts (or more restricted forms of automata) to describe it.

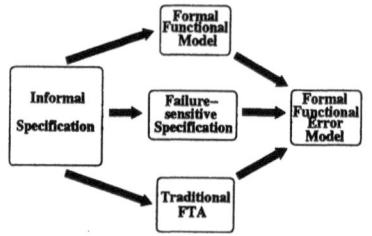

1. Build a functional system model.
2. Do an informal FTA of the system.
3. Do failure-sensitive specification for all critical components.
4. Integrate the relevant failure modes into the functional model.
5. Check for correct integration of the failure modes into functional model.

Fig. 5. Part 1

The functional model is of course not sufficient for formal safety analysis, since it will not contain component failures. To derive critical components and their failure modes, we do an informal FTA for the hazards of the system, based on the informal specification. We suggest to do FTA *independent* of the formal model. This has two advantages: first, an informal FTA can be done by an expert of the domain, without knowledge of formal specifications. Second, it avoids the danger that FTA finds hazards only, that are already suggested by the formalization. This methodology is different from the one proposed in [4], which suggests to generate fault trees from formal models.

If an informal FTA finds, that there are components with a large number of failure modes, we set up failure-sensitive specifications for these components. If these are proven to be equivalent to the functional model of the component, then a complete list of failure modes has been obtained. This comprehensive list gives a good idea of what can go wrong in each component.

Finally, we combine the results of all three techniques into the functional error model that adds component failures to the functional model. Not all component failures that were found by failure-sensitive specification have to be added, but at least those which appear as leaves in the fault trees are necessary. For others, a domain expert has to check whether they are relevant in practice.

Integration of failures is done in two steps. First for each failure mode, an additional chart with two states "OK" and "Error present" describing the occurrence of the failure is added. This chart describes when and how the failure mode takes place. Transitions between the two states indicate, whether the error occurs randomly, has conditions for occurrence (e.g. electric power must be present), and whether it can be repaired. In the second step the effects of the failure mode have to be integrated. In many cases this is done by changing the guard condition of a transition to a disjunct with "Error present". However, sometimes additional states or even changes in the design may be necessary.

In the last step the correct integration of the failure modes into the functional model can be verified. This is done by proving behavioral equivalence of the new functional error model and a failure-sensitive specification model, where the integrated failure modes have been dropped, see Sect. 2.

The functional error model, that is the final result of this work, does not only model the intended functionality but also possible component failures and errors.

6.3 Qualitative Analysis

This part integrates traditional FTA and formal methods as shown in Fig. 6. Both methods can be used to analyze possible causes for hazards. While the traditional verification task tries to show the absence of the hazard (if all components of the system working properly) and tries to find design flaws, traditional FTA accepts the hazard, but tries to find out the reasons. Formal verification is based on a solid formal foundation. Traditional FTA is not formal at all and its results largely depend on the skill of the engineer.

Formal FTA fills the gap between those to bounds. It has both a solid formal semantics ([19]) and allows to reason about failures as causes for hazards. Formal FTA is a significant improvement over verification or FTA, but it requires the effort to build a good functional error model, which is used as its foundation.

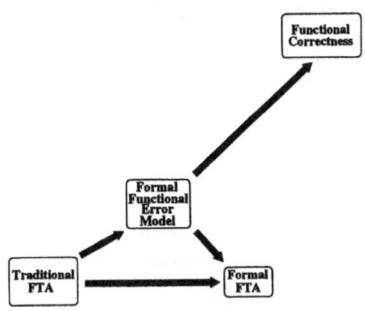

1. Verify functional correctness of the functional error model.
2. Do traditional FTA (if not already done before).
3. Do formal FTA.

Fig. 6. Part 2

The starting point for formal FTA is the fault tree of traditional FTA. As a first step, each event of the fault tree has to be defined as a formula over the system model. Events, for which this is difficult or impossible, usually indicate, that the functional error model is still not adequate and has to be changed. Such cases should be rare, since the informal fault tree has already been taken into account when the failure modes were chosen and integrated.

Formal FTA results in a set of temporal logics formulae which have to be proven correct for the functional error model. If all proof obligations are proven valid, then the fault tree is complete. This means no branches have been forgotten. More specifically it has been proven, that for a complete fault tree the prevention of one element of every minimal cut set results in the prevention of the hazard. This is the formal equivalent to the intuitive understanding of a fault tree in engineering.

In addition to formal FTA, formal verification may also be applied to ensure functional properties of the system. Typically, functional properties are proved under the condition that all components work properly.

Note that another use of formal methods — to prove the absence of hazards provided all components work properly — becomes conceptually obsolete using formal FTA. This is, because formal FTA even verifies which combination of components must fail to allow the hazard to occur. This is a much stronger property. Nevertheless we suggest to verify the absence of design flaws for the functional model before doing a safety analysis. First, proofs over the (smaller) functional model are often easier than proofs over the (more complex) functional error model. Second, they can be done before a (costly) safety analysis is attempted, that may turn out to be obsolete since the design was (irreparably) flawed.

The main result of this part is a precise description of the qualitative relationship between component failures and hazards. This relationship is essentially captured by the minimal cut sets.

6.4 Quantitative Approaches

The third part of our approach deals with quantitative analysis. It includes quantitative FTA, parameterized FTA and safety optimization. The idea is to use the results of part two for calculating probabilities. In a second step the free parameters are taken into account.

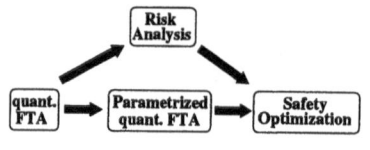

Fig. 7. Part 3

1. Do quantitative FTA.
2. Determine free parameters.
3. Do (quantitative) parameterized FTA.
4. Do a risk analysis to determine concurring hazards costs.
5. Do mathematical optimization.

We start by doing a quantitative FTA. This helps in two aspects. First, it gives a rough upper bound estimation of the hazards probabilities. This allows to decide at an early stage, whether the system has a high probability of working correctly or not. Second, quantitative FTA requires to approximate all primary failures probabilities. In this process it often becomes clear, that some of these approximations depend on parameters. These probabilities are good candidates for parameterized probabilities.

The next step is to determine the free parameters of the system (e.g. the runtime of a timer), specific to the system at hand, and to parameterize FTA.

For every primary failure it must be examined, in which way it depends on the free parameters. The probabilities are replaced by probability distributions. The correct choice of a matching distribution is a problem of statistics. For many problems - in particular for failure rates - exponential distribution is a good choice. If it is not clear, which distribution should be used, then it is necessary to do a standard statistical analysis (see e.g. [20]).

To make the hazards comparable, risk analysis [8] is the method of choice. For the final step of the analysis it is necessary to have a function describing the importance of the different hazards. A good choice is to use a cost function. This function is the sum of all hazards mean costs. The mean cost of a hazard are given by the product of the hazards probability and its costs. However, our approach does not depend on the exact type of function. The most adequate cost function may only be determined by domains experts.

The last step is optimization. In this step an optimal configuration for the free parameters may be found. If the probability distributions are twice continuously differentiable and the cost function as well, then Newtons Method is a good choice as optimization algorithm. For other problems there exists a variety of different optimization algorithm, but in practice most problems may be modeled with the standard set of probability distributions for which Newton is applicable.

The result of this step is an optimal configuration of the system with respect to the input data. Inputs are the used distributions and the hazards relationship of importance.

7   Applications

In this section we present an application of our approach on a real world case study. The examined problem is the new Elbtunnel in Hamburg. This is a road tunnel beneath the river Elbe in Hamburg. It connects the city with the harbor. Up to now the tunnel consists of 3 tubes (west, middle and east) with 2 lanes each. Now a new fourth tube has been built. The new tube is higher to allow over-high - more than 4 meters height - vehicles (OHVs) to pass. Therefore a new height control system becomes necessary, which significantly extends the old one.

The old system consisted of light barriers across all lanes, that triggered an emergency stop for vehicles higher than 4 meters. For the new tunnel, the existing height control had to be enhanced, such that it allows over-high vehicles to drive through the new, higher tube, but not through the old ones.

In the following, we will distinguish between *high vehicles* (HVs), which may drive through all tubes and *over-high vehicles* (OHVs), which can only drive through the new, fourth tube. Figure 8 sketches the layout of the tunnel. Only the northern entrance is shown, as we will only discuss the crossing from north to south.

The system uses two different types of sensors. Light barriers (LB) are scanning all lanes of one direction to detect, if an OHV passes. For technical reasons they cannot be installed in such a way, that they only supervise one lane. Therefore overhead detectors (OD) are necessary to detect, on which lane a HV passes. The ODs can distinguish vehicles (e.g. cars) from high vehicles (e.g.

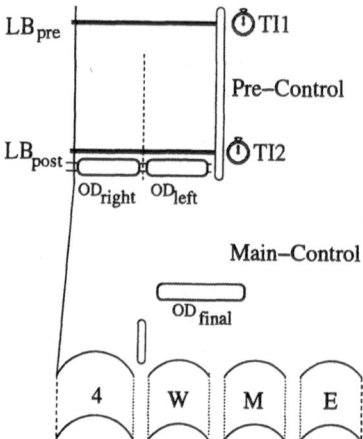

Fig. 8. Layout of the northern tunnel entrance

buses, trucks), but not HVs from OHVs (but light barriers can!). If the height control detects an OHV heading towards a different than the fourth tube, then an emergency stop is signaled, locking the tunnel entrance.

The idea of the height control is, that the detection starts, if an OHV drives through the light barrier LB_{pre}. To prevent unnecessary alarms through faulty triggering of LB_{post} (e.g. by a passing bird), the detection there will be switched off after expiration of a timer (30 minutes). Road traffic regulations require, that after LB_{pre} both HVs and OHVs have to drive on the right lane through tunnel 4. If nevertheless an OHV drives on the left lane towards the west-tube, detected trough the combination of LB_{post} and OD_{left}, an emergency stop is triggered. If the OHV drives on the right lane through LB_{post}, it is still possible for the driver to switch to the left lanes and drive to the west- or mid-tube. To detect this situation, the height control uses the OD_{final} detector. To minimize undesired alarms (remember, that normal HVs may also trigger the ODs), a second timer will switch off detection at OD_{final} after 30 minutes. For safe operation it is necessary, that after the location of OD_{final} it is impossible to switch lanes. Infrequently, more than one OHV drive on the route. Therefore the height control keeps track of several but at the most three OHVs.

In the following we will present the safety analysis of this system according to the presented approach. It is not possible to show the whole analysis in this paper. We will rather take some parts of the analysis as explanation of all steps. The example can be modeled as a finite state system, and model checking can be applied to verify properties. The ITL formalizations of failure-sensitive specification and formal FTA may be transfered into an equivalent CTL semantics, if the basic events have no duration (see [22]). The verification has been done with the SMV-tool.

7.1 Building the Formal Model

The formal model of the Elbtunnel consist of 10 parallel automata (three for modeling OHVs, three for modeling HVs, two timers, the pre-control and the post-control). Figure 9 shows the automaton for an OHV.

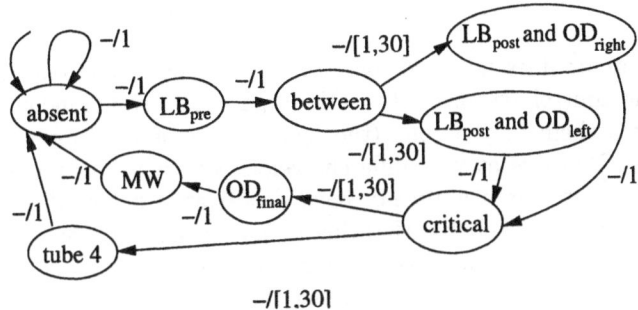

Fig. 9. Automaton modeling an OHV

For the sake of readability we extend the normal notation of finite automata with timing conditions $[t_1, t_2]$. This means the transition may be taken indeterministically between time t_1 and t_2. The translation into a standard automaton is fairly easy, by introducing intermediate states.

To obtain the failure modes we constructed a failure-sensitive specification for each component of the system. The most interesting component is the OHV. The failure-sensitive specification for an OHV consists of boolean signals abstracting the states of the OHV. These are used as input and output. In addition to the states of the automaton two input signals for the two timers TI1 and TI2 are necessary, since the informal specification requires different behavior of an OHV depending on the timeout signals of TI1 and TI2. Altogether we get 20 inputs and outputs. This results in 2^{20} different input-output scenarios. Failure-sensitive specification yielded 13 different failure modes for an OHV. Some of them can be ruled out by simple comparison with reality. For example it is not possible, that an OHV suddenly starts existing in one section without traveling through the others. Another failure mode "vehicle does not stop despite stop signals" has also been ignored, as system failure is obvious. But many other failure modes are important like "vehicle needs longer than runtime of timer 1 for section 1" or "vehicle passes through OD_{left} *and* OD_{right}".

Altogether failure-sensitive specification resulted in 30 proof obligations that were proven with SMV. In practice this helped us to find a lot of errors in the SMV specification. When proofs failed we discovered in some cases, that our formalization of the failure mode was not precise enough, in others we found that our system model was not consistent with our intuitive understanding.

7.2 Qualitative Analysis

The central safety property of the Elbtunnel is: Given no component fails, then it is always true, that whenever an OHV tries to enter another but the fourth tube, an alarm has been signaled. In CTL this formula has the following form:

$$AG((OHV_1 = MW \lor OHV_2 = MW \lor OHV_3 = MW) \to CO_{post} = stop)$$

This theorem[3] does not hold for our system. Why? The reason lies in the design of the control system. If two OHVs pass LB1 simultaneously, then the system counts them only as one (the light barrier is only interrupted once). If the two OHVs drive at very different velocities, then it is possible that the final overhead detector has already been deactivated before the second OHV reaches it. It is very improbable, that this scenario would have been discovered by simple testing of the system. This problem can be solved by installing additional overhead detectors at LB1 or by changing the control system, such that main-control is always active for the whole runtime of timer 1.

Traditional FTA for collision yields a fault tree, which has leaves only, where sensors failed in such a way, that they missed the detection of an vehicle (mis-detection). It seemed clear, that it would have no impact on safety, if the sensors detected to often (false detection). However, it turned out, that a false detection of LB_{post} is even a primary failure. This means if everything works correctly, but the second light barrier has a false detection (e.g. a passing bird), then a collision is possible. The scenario is easy to construct. An OHV passes LB_{pre}, immediately after this a bird triggers LB_{post}, when the OHV reaches LB_{post} it is deactivated, and when the OHV finally reaches OD_{final} this sensor is already deactivated again. This resulted in a forgotten branch in the fault tree. Because of this we could not prove the fault tree to be complete. And thus formal FTA led us to the forgotten branch in the fault tree.

7.3 Quantitative Analysis

For quantitative FTA there are a lot of probability approximations for failures and traffic conditions necessary. We will not go into detail, but only give the results. The overall probability for the hazard evaluates to 3^{-8} per minute or one hazard every 64 years. The false alarm rate is around 3^{-4} or one false alarm every two days. This is a very good result for the system and gives confidence.

We will now parameterize the probabilities. Obviously free parameters of the system are the runtimes of the timers. The probability for an OHV getting into a traffic jam for more than the runtime of a timer of course depends on this parameter. We call this failure mode overtime $OT_{1/2}$. A good model for the driving time of OHVs from LB_{pre} to LB_{post} and from LB_{post} to the tunnel is normal distribution [4]. $P_{OHV_{1/2}}(Time \leq T)$ denotes the probability for a driving

---

[3] The CTL-operator AG means "on all paths it is always true, that ...".

[4] truncated at zero; mean time $\mu = 4$ minutes; standard deviation $\sigma = 2$ minutes

time $\leq$ T. We can then calculate $P(OT_1)$ in dependence of the runtime T1 of timer 1:

$$P(OT_1)(T1) = 1 - P_{OHV_1}(Time \leq T1)$$
$$where\ P_{OHV_1}(Time \leq T) := \frac{1}{\int_0^\infty exp(-\frac{(x-\mu)^2}{2\sigma^2})dx} \int_0^T exp(-\frac{(x-\mu)^2}{2\sigma^2})dx$$

Timer 2 is treated analogously. The hazards probability is now a function of the runtimes of the timers. The runtimes of the timers have not only an influence on probabilities in the fault tree of the collision hazard, but also on the fault tree for false alarms. So both hazards probabilities are now formulated in terms of timer runtimes. The last thing we now need is a cost function. A rough approximation is that a collision costs 100000 times the money of a false alarm. Fig. 10 shows this cost function.

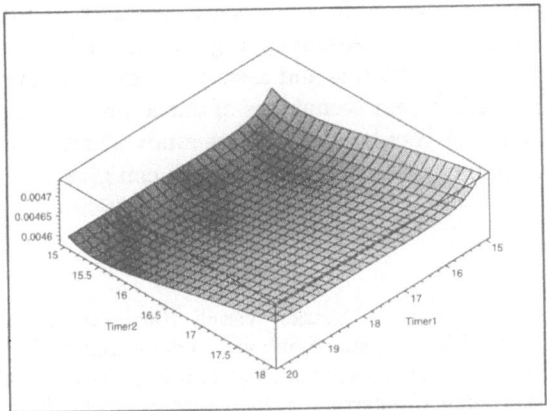

Fig. 10. The cost function around its minimum

It turns out, that the optimal configuration is 19 minutes for timer 1 and 15.6 minutes for timer 2. This is a big improvement compared to the initial values proposed - 30 minutes for both timers. However, the resulting failure probabilities do not improve as much for collision it stays at 3^{-8} and the false alarm rate drops by 10% to 2.7^{-4}. This is due to another design problem, which can also be found with parameterized probabilities. If the frequency of correctly driving OHVs is introduced as free parameter, then it turns out that over 80% of these vehicles trigger a false alarm. The reason lies in detector OD_{final}. This detector always stays activated for the runtime of timer 2 (and whenever an OHVs passes the tunnel, it will be activated). During the runtime of timer 2 it is almost sure (more than 80%), that a bus, minivan or normal truck will pass the sensor, but every detection at the sensor immediately triggers an alarm. If one takes into account, that this means the frequency of false alarm is roughly proportional to the frequency of OHVs, it becomes obvious that we have found a design flaw. The problem can be solved easily by introducing a third light barrier at OD$_{final}$. This reduces the false alarm rate by more than one order of magnitude and removes the dependence of the false alarm rate on the OHV rate.

8 Conclusion

Our experience is that it is important to combine different techniques for safety analysis. This is because different methods not only examine different aspects of the system, but also give contrary views [12]. Therefore an integrated approach is needed. The growing complexity of embedded systems makes a formal process necessary. Formal reasoning helps to better understand how unwanted and unintended events are propagated through the system and which effects they have.

The ForMoSA approach is an integrated formal methodology. It includes different techniques to cover different aspects on safety as well as a solid formal foundation for qualitative reasoning. Together this addresses many common problems of safety critical systems and assures a very high level of safety.

We illustrated the different techniques of our approach on a real world case study - the Elbtunnel in Hamburg. This case study shows, that no single technique can give all results the combined approach can give.

References

[1] Christel Baier, Edmund M. Clarke, Vassili Hartonas-Garmhausen, Marta Z. Kwiatkowska, and Mark Ryan. Symbolic model checking for probabilistic processes. In *Automata, Languages and Programming*, pages 430–440, 1997.

[2] M. Balser. *Verifying Concurrent System with Symbolic Execution – Temporal Reasoning is Symbolic Execution with a Little Induction*. PhD thesis, University of Augsburg, Augsburg, Gemany, 2004. (to appear).

[3] M. Balser, W. Reif, G. Schellhorn, K. Stenzel, and A. Thums. Formal system development with KIV. In T. Maibaum, editor, *Fundamental Approaches to Software Engineering*, number 1783 in LNCS, pages 363–366. Springer-Verlag, 2000.

[4] M. Bozzano, A. Cavallo, M. Cifaldi, L. Valacca, and A. Villafiorit. Improving safety assessment of complex systems: An industrial case study. In K. Araki, S. Gnesi, and D. Mandrioli, editors, *FM 2003: Formal Methods*, number 2805 in LNCS, pages 208–222. Springer, 2003.

[5] G. Bruns and S. Anderson. Validating safety models with fault trees. In J. Górski, editor, *SafeComp'93: 12th International Conference on Computer Safety, Reliability, and Security*, pages 21 – 30. Springer, 1993.

[6] A. Cau, B. Moszkowski, and H. Zedan. *ITL – Interval Temporal Logic*. Software Technology Research Laboratory, SERCentre, De Montfort University, The Gateway, Leicester LE1 9BH, UK, 2002. www.cms.dmu.ac.uk/~cau/itlhomepage.

[7] W. Damm, B. Josko, H. Hungar, and A. Pnueli. A compositional real-time semantics of STATEMATE designs. In W.-P. de Roever, H. Langmaack, and A. Pnueli, editors, *COMPOS' 97*, volume 1536 of *LNCS*, pages 186–238. Springer, 1998.

[8] ECSS. Dependability. In European Cooperation for Space Standardization, editor, *Space Product Assurance*. ESA Publications, 2001.

[9] A. H. G. Rinnooy Kan G. L. Nemhauser, editor. *Optimization*, volume Vol 1. Elsevier Science Publishers B.V, 1989.

[10] K. Hansen, A. Ravn, and V. Stavridou. From safety analysis to software requirements. *IEEE Transactions on Software Engineering*, 24(7):573 – 584, July 1998.

[11] K. M. Hansen, A. P. Ravn, and V. Stavridou. From safety analysis to formal specification. ProCoS II document [ID/DTH KMH 1/1], Technical University of Denmark, 1994.

[12] E.G. van den Blieck J.L. Rouvroye. Comparing safety analysis techniques. *Reliability Engineering & System Safety*, 2002.

[13] J. Klose and A. Thums. The STATEMATE reference model of the reference case study 'Verkehrsleittechnik'. Technical Report 2002-01, Universität Augsburg, 2002.

[14] N. Leveson. *Safeware: System Safety and Computers*. Addison Wesley, 1995.

[15] David G. Luenberger. *Linear and nonlinear programming*. Addison-Wesley Publishing Company, 1989.

[16] F. Ortmeier and W. Reif. Failure-sensitive specification: A formal method for finding failure modes. Technical Report 3, Institut für Informatik, Universität Augsburg, 2004.

[17] F. Ortmeier, W. Reif, G. Schellhorn, A. Thums, B. Hering, and H. Trappschuh. Safety analysis of the height control system for the Elbtunnel. *Reliability Engineering and System Safety*, 81(3):259–268, 2003.

[18] F. Ortmeier and A. Thums. Formale Methoden und Sicherheitsanalyse. Technical Report 15, Universität Augsburg, 2002. (in German).

[19] G. Schellhorn, A. Thums, and W. Reif. Formal fault tree semantics. In *Proceedings of The Sixth World Conference on Integrated Design & Process Technology*, Pasadena, CA, 2002.

[20] Klaus Schürger. *Wahrscheinlichkeitstheorie*. R. Oldenbourg Verlag, 1998.

[21] N. Storey. *Safety-Critical Computer Systems*. Addison-Wesley, 1996.

[22] A. Thums and G. Schellhorn. Model checking FTA. In K. Araki, S. Gnesi, and D. Mandrioli, editors, *FME 2003: Formal Methods*, LNCS 2805, pages 739–757. Springer-Verlag, 2003.

[23] A. Thums, G. Schellhorn, F. Ortmeier, and W.Reif. Interactive verification of statecharts. In *this volume*. Springer LNCS, 2004.

[24] A. Thums, G. Schellhorn, and W. Reif. Comparing fault tree semantics. In D. Haneberg, G. Schellhorn, and W. Reif, editors, *FM-TOOLS 2002*, Technical Report 2002-11, pages 25 – 32. Universität Augsburg, 2002.

[25] W. E. Vesely, F. F. Goldberg, N. H. Roberts, and D. F. Haasl. *Fault Tree Handbook*. Washington, D.C., 1981. NUREG-0492.

[26] W. Vesley, J. Dugan, J. Fragole, J. Minarik II, and J. Railsback. *Fault Tree Handbook with Aerospace Applications*. NASA Office of Safety and Mission Assurance, NASA Headquarters, Washington DC 20546, August 2002.

[27] Zhou Chaochen and M. R. Hansen. Duration calculus: Logical foundations. In *Formal Aspects of Computing*, pages 283–330, 1997.

Formal Verification of LSCs in the Development Process*

Matthias Brill[1], Ralf Buschermöhle[2], Werner Damm[1], Jochen Klose[3],
Bernd Westphal[1], and Hartmut Wittke[2]

[1] Carl von Ossietzky Universität Oldenburg
Department für Informatik, PO Box 2503, 26111 Oldenburg, Germany
{brill,damm,westphal}@informatik.uni-oldenburg.de
[2] OFFIS, Escherweg 2, 26121 Oldenburg, Germany,
{wittke,buschermoehle}@offis.de
[3] Bombardier Transportation
Wolfenbüttler Straße 86/Obergstraße 5, 38102 Braunschweig, Germany
jochen.klose@de.transport.bombardier.com

Abstract. This paper presents how a model-based development process can be enhanced by the combination of using Live Sequence Charts (LSC) as the formal language to describe interactions together with automatic formal verification techniques that decide whether communication sequences are exhibitable or adhered to by the system. We exemplify our approach on the V-model, a widely used development process, considering a (Statemate) statecharts design of the reference case study "Funkfahrbetrieb" (FFB) and discuss potential assets and drawbacks. We sketch a set of best practices on the use of LSC features and emphasise the possibilities for re-use of LSCs in the different activities of the development process. To give evidence for feasibility of automatic formal verification of LSCs, as well as its limitations, we present our approaches to the verification of possible and mandatory LSC requirements on Statemate models. We report experimental results we have obtained from formal verification of the FFB and briefly discuss the treatment of Statemate's different notions of time.

1 Introduction

In order to increase software quality and to be able to cope with ever increasing complexity of software under design, standardised *development processes* or *process models* have been devised. A development process typically comprises a number of *activities* with rules which activity to carry out when and promises that following these rules enhances software quality. The aim is to ensure that no important aspect of the system under design is overlooked. Well-known examples are the Rational Unified Process (RUP) [1], a highly customisable framework for

* This research was supported by the German Research Council (DFG) within the priority program Integration of Specification Techniques with Engineering Applications under grant DA 206/7 and by the German Department of Education and Research (BMBF), research project 'ViSEK', under grant 01ISA02G.

H. Ehrig et al. (Eds.): INT 2004, LNCS 3147, pp. 494–516, 2004.

various process models, or the class of so called *agile processes*, Extreme Programming [2] being a prominent representative. More elaborated process models like the V-model [3] distinguish activities and *products* (or *documents*). Each activity has a number of products of a certain type as prerequisite and a number of products of a certain type as outcome. Due to this focus on products and dependencies induced by activities, (high-level) activities remain manageable even when carried out non-sequentially.

In the following, we will concentrate our discussion on the V-model for its widespread use in the domain of safety critical systems and its combination of being at the same time very detailed and general. Instead of insisting on particular languages for products, the V-model in detail specifies *what* a product shall describe and *recommends* specific methods, i.e. languages or notations like flow-charts, or even gives general product templates to be used in particular situations. A template, for example, specifies that each *requirement analysis* must have a unique identification number. Given this freedom of choice in the V-model, products may in particular be *executable models* of the system under design on different levels of abstraction, for example using visual formalisms like the Statemate [4] statecharts, as in our running example, or the UML [5]. We call a development process *model-based* if it comprises formal, declarative requirements specifications complemented by the development of an executable formal model of the system under design that abstracts from platform characteristics, like concrete programming languages.

Using a model-based development process like the V-model provides for a number of advantages over development processes that "postpone" the necessary formalisations towards the implementation activities. Firstly, formal methods avoid ambiguous interpretation of documents and efforts spent in "disambiguating" natural language texts. This is a prime advantage that provides the possibility to exactly determine the meaning of a document some time after it has been written. This is in general impossible with natural language text and even more so if different developers are involved in the different activities or if the final implementation is carried out by a sub-contractor. Secondly, using formal methods *continuously*, i.e. taking the model and the specification as input of each activity in order to be re-used for refinement, principally allows to apply the following computer aided techniques on each stage of the development process to detect errors on the level of single components[1]:

- simulation,
- automatic checks for common minor design errors, for instance, write/write or read/write hazards, i.e. non-determinism, in concurrent parts,
- automatic formal verification to check whether the model satisfies the complementing declarative specification,[2] and
- automated test-generation and testing.

---

[1] We use the name *component* in an informal way only to denote any discriminable part of the system for which an *interface* can be identified.

[2] The contrast between a model closer to an implementation and a complementing declarative specification is not as clear cut as it might seem. For example, Harel's

Continuous use of formal methods in particular reliefs the designer from the necessity to each time translate the textual specifications to the input formalisms of the employed tools.

Thirdly, executable models allow for early, "virtual" integration to detect errors on the level of component integration. This integration of *models* can be subject of integration tests before the actual implementation starts in order to increase confidence in the system design. In case of errors, a continuous use of a formal methods makes the necessary *changes* trace- and manageable.

In the following, we will elaborate on the usage of Live Sequence Charts (LSCs) [7] as a rigorous formal specification language for the products concerned with so-called *interaction modelling* in a model-based use of the V-model in combination with (UML or, as in our running example, Statemate) statecharts for the executable model.

Recall that LSCs, as a derivative of the well-known Message Sequence Charts [8], express communications between components of a system or between an environment and the interface of a single component. LSCs can be used to denote positive and negative *scenarios*, i.e. communication sequences that the system under design should or should not be able to adhere to, to denote *requirements*, i.e. communication sequences that the system under design must adhere to under certain premises and assumptions, and finally to denote *test-vectors*, i.e. a set of input stimuli together with the expected reaction of the system. Furthermore we report on the development of automatic formal verification techniques for LSCs, namely an integration of LSC verification into the Statemate Verification Environment (STVE) [9]. The V-model is to a large extend representative for other process models hence the proposals of the following sections are anticipated to be analogously transferable to other (model-based) process models.

The remainder of the paper is structured as follows. In Sec. 2 we briefly present the sub-module *system development* of the V-model putting emphasis on those places where LSCs are beneficially used and those places where the V-model in general already requires *verification*, since these obligations can be discharged by automatic formal verification for LSCs. Section 2 already assumes a basic understanding of the expressiveness of LSCs although most mentioned features should at least become clear in Sec. 3. We recommend the reader unfamiliar with LSCs to consider turning to the companion article [10] first. Section 3 reports on a successful use of LSCs on a Statemate model of the case-study "Funkfahrbetrieb" and presents scenario and requirement LSCs together with general recommendations when to use which feature. Section 4 takes a closer look on automatic formal verification as applied to the LSCs from Sec. 3. Here we discuss the particular verification strategy for scenarios (existential LSCs), the different approaches to handle assumptions, and the different time models of Statemate. Section 5 concludes and names as further work to provide LSC verification as presented in the former sections also in the domain of UML models.

Play-In/Play-Out approach [6] synthesises a system's behaviour on-the-fly from a set of LSCs.

2   Development Process – LSCs in the V-Model

The V-model [3] is a process model that has found wide acceptance in the domain of safety critical systems, due to its rather detailed definition and at the same time generality by not targeting a specific design paradigm or language. It only names requirements on the content of documents and *recommends* the use of particular formalisms, e.g., flow charts, or product templates for particular activities. We exemplify the use of LSCs in model-based development processes using the V-model for these reasons and since it is in many respects representative for other development processes hence allows for easy transfer of its extensions to other process models.

The V-model comprises four sub-modules: project management, configuration management, quality assurance, and system development. In the following we concentrate on the sub-module system development (SD) since this is the place where products regarding the system structure, the functional and non-functional requirements, the implementation, and test results are used, i.e. those domains where LSCs find beneficial application.

Most notably, the V-model definition from 1997 already foresees the use of models, of formal specifications, and (formal) verification methods and techniques (cf. Fig. 1). But the intended approach is to explicitly formalise specific textual specifications and manually conduct correctness proofs, possibly aided by theorem-proving software. Due to the required effort for this approach, as of today the V-model is typically *tailored* in contracts between the customer and the supplier to explicitly exclude formal specifications and application of

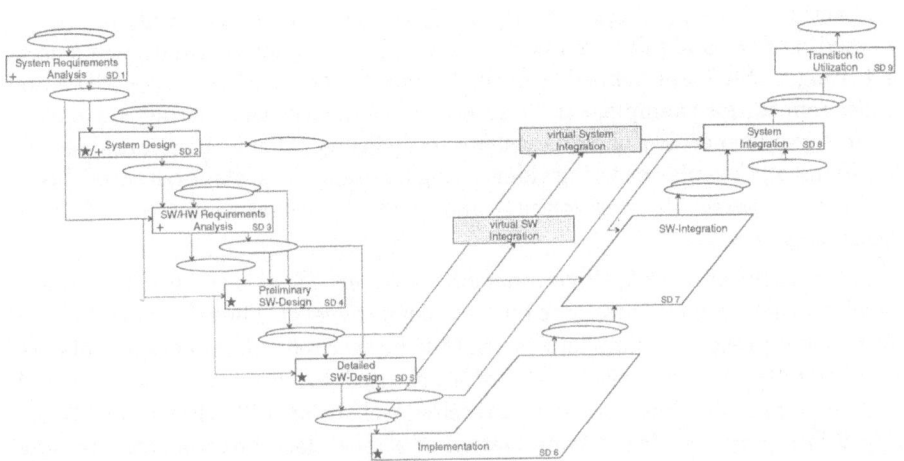

Fig. 1. Schema of sub-module *system development* (SD) of the V-Model. Polygons represent *activities* and ellipses represent *products*. Dashed arrows represent *dependencies*, i.e. which products are the result of an activity or required by it as inputs, respectively. Activities where formal verification is already recommended are marked by '★', activities where formal verification can additionally be applied when using the model-based approach presented in this paper are marked by '+'.

formal verification techniques. Continuous use of LSCs and the use of automatic formal verification as discussed in Sec. 4 are anticipated to significantly reduce this effort.

Sub-module SD comprises nine top-level activities that are further decomposed into sub-activities (cf. Fig. 1). Activity *System Requirements Analysis*, SD 1, develops *user requirements* from the *initial specification* that is typically natural language text describing the basic functionality or, when doing a redesign, so-called *legacy code*, i.e. the documentation and implementation of an existing system. This activity may already produce a model with the level of abstraction being the system, i.e. those parts visible to the customer. LSCs can be used as a formal language to describe basic functionality in terms of scenarios of inter-component communication on a high level of abstraction, possibly including non-functional requirements like response times. Known *protocol requirements*, i.e. behaviour that the system *must* adhere to in each situation where particular premises are met can be stated in terms of universal LSCs (cf. [10] and Sec. 3).

The purpose of activity *System Design*, SD 2, is to design the system architecture technically. This includes interfaces, assignment of user requirements to elements of the technical architecture, and specification of the system integration, an input of activity SD 8. The LSCs from SD 1 can be re-used and turned into more precise LSCs referring to the notions and interfaces developed in SD 2. Furthermore the LSCs from SD 1 already comprise hints for the system architecture since system components occur in an LSC in the form of instance lines and component interfaces occur in an LSC in form of the set of messages originating and ending at the instance line corresponding to the component.

In activity *SW/HW Requirements Analysis*, SD 3, the requirements produced by activities SD 1 and SD 2 are made more precise and quality requirements used for testing in SD 7 are defined. Hence the model and the LSCs from SD 2 are further refined, for example, earlier scenarios may leave the ordering of particular messages unspecified using *coregions* (cf. [10]). A refinement is obtained by identifying a particular ordering. Identifying overlapping parts, existential LSCs can be *decomposed* (or *modularised*) and *strengthened* into universal LSCs as discussed in Sec. 3.

The purpose of activity *Preliminary SW-Design*, SD 4, is to obtain products describing the system architecture on each hierarchy level. Thus in a model-based development process, the model from SD 3 is further refined, its components are recursively structured. Existential LSCs are used to capture the typical and required communications on each hierarchy level. In an LSC the system is addressed in a *gray-box view*, a combination of a true black-box view, where only the interfaces of a component are considered, and a true glass- (or white-) box view, where all internals of a component are always visible to its environment. In the gray-box view, components possibly belonging to different hierarchy levels may be considered at once but each of them is itself considered to be a black-box that is only referred to by its interface. Everything outside the considered components, their environment, can be used in a gray-box view LSC, represented by *environment instance lines*.

In a model-based process, the models produced by activity SD 4 should already be executable (or simulateable) to some amount[3] and hence can be subject to a first "virtual" system integration using the test-cases developed in SD 2. That is, it is not the implementation that is subject of the integration but only the model (cf. Fig. 1).

In activity *detailed design*, SD 5, the products from SD 4 are used to design the behaviour of components. In a model-based development process at last in SD 5 the structured components are equipped with a description of behaviour, for example Statemate statecharts or UML state-machines. All components with behavioural description are possibly subject to simulation, and *existential* or *universal* formal LSC verification that establishes for a given existential LSC that the model is able to show the given communication sequence or for a given universal LSC that the system *always* adheres to it when its prerequisites are met, respectively. Simulation and existential verification are aids for "debugging", i.e. to uncover deviations between the model and the user requirements from SD 1 or refined requirements from SD 2 to SD 3. In a model-based process, the products produced by activity SD 5 can be subject to module test and to a complete "virtual" system integration for which the testing sub-activities of SD 7 and SD 8 can already be started to detect problems in the interplay of components before starting the actual implementation (cf. Fig. 1).

Activity *Implementation*, SD 6, produces the actual, target platform dependent implementation using the products from SD 5. In a model-based process this ranges from using a code-generation facility if the behavioural model is complete, over manual completion of automatically generated code fragments, to complete manual implementation, possibly by an external supplier who is different from the designer.

Activities *Software* and *System Integration*, SD 7 and SD 8 deal with integration and testing of modules obtained from SD 6 on the component level or integrating, testing, and deploying components on the system level. For testing, some LSCs produced in activities before can be re-used as *test vectors*, i.e. to denote a combination of input stimuli and expected outcome. This is similar to existential verification where the goal is to obtain evidence for the model being able to follow a certain communication sequence (cf. Sec. 4), but here it is the *system implementation* that is required to adhere to a test scenario given in form of an LSC [11,12]. In a model-based process, a complete, formally verified model resulting from SD 5 can furthermore act as a "golden device" from which test-vectors are automatically derived to test the implementation if it is not obtained by code-generation from the model, for example, since the implementation is carried out by an external supplier.

Finally, within the products of activity *Transition to Utilisation* LSCs can be re-used to serve documentary purposes.

---

[3] Earlier activities may well produce executable models, too.

3   Case Study "Funkfahrbetrieb"

"Funkfahrbetrieb" (FFB) is a procedure for radio based control of level crossings (crossings for short) designed by the German rail company Deutsche Bahn to reduce costs for deployment and maintenance of trackside equipment. The idea is to let a train that approaches a crossing announce itself by radio and ask the crossing to secure itself, i.e. to switch on traffic lights and lower the barriers. A defined amount of time later the train asks whether the crossing is safe and drives on only if the crossing reports itself to be safe *and* if the crossing can be passed within a given amount of time depending on the current travelling speed. After the train has passed the crossing, as indicated by a trackside sensor, the crossing shall open the barriers and switch off the traffic lights. If the crossing does not report itself to be safe on the train's request, e.g. due to a failure of a traffic light, the train is supposed to stop before the crossing. The crossing may then for example be secured manually by the driver. In this case of hardware failures or if the train recognises and announces that it cannot pass the crossing within the given time-limit, the crossing is completely opened again. It is supposed that the train-side equipment ensures that a train never passes an unsecured crossing. For details of the case study the reader is referred to [13] that in particular reports on an implementation of a demonstrator that will be used to evaluate the model presented in the following.

For the model and LSCs discussed in the remainder of this section, i.e. the system structure, component behaviour description, scenarios, and the requirements, a summary [14] of the official documents served as the initial requirements (input to SD 1). Only later has the official document [15], an extensive natural language specification of user requirements (output of SD 1), become accessible and been considered.

The development of the model did not exactly follow the V-model but focused on the LSC specific methodology outlined in [16,17,18,19]. But a significant amount of products required by the V-model have been produced and the verification technology required in the activities marked in Fig. 1 have been developed and evaluated, hence the model and the accompanying LSCs exemplify the proposed use of LSCs in general and the language's features in particular in specific activities of sub-module SD. In the following, we will only present a representative part of the model and the LSC specification. For details of the model and more LSC specifications the reader is referred to [16,17].

3.1   System Structure

Figure 2 shows a Statemate *activity chart* of the complete system structure on the top-level.[4] In Statemate, the functional decomposition into components is modelled by activity charts. A functional unit is called *activity* (not to be confused with activities in the V-model). Activities are depicted using solid or

---

[4] For brevity, the representation is substituted, i.e. shows all levels of nested activities at once.

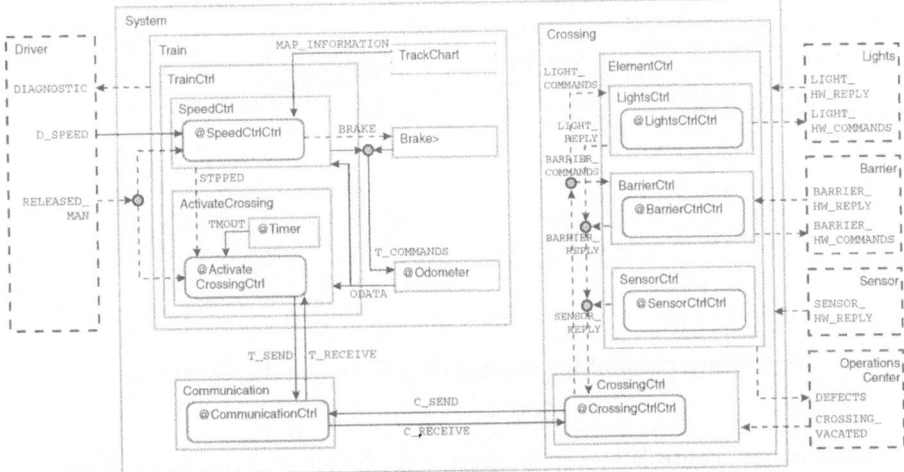

Fig. 2. Substituted Statemate model of the FFB: the *system* comprises a *train* and a *crossing* connected by a *communication* activity. Both, train and crossing, are further decomposed into sub-activities. Boxes with rounded corners expand into statecharts defining the behaviour. Dashed boxes, e.g. *driver*, constitute the system's *environment*.

dashed rectangles and can be structured into a hierarchy of other activities. The behaviour of an activity is typically described in form of a Statemate statechart [20]. In the activity chart, those activities equipped with behaviour are graphically depicted by containing a rectangle with rounded edges. Information exchange between activities, called *flow*, is depicted by arrows leading from sender to receiver, splits or joins of flows are shown using small circles. We call a communication following a flow *sending an event* and consider the set of flows originating or ending at an activity to be its interface. Note that the diagram shown in Fig. 2 is already the final outcome of activity SD 4. We don't show intermediate products for brevity.

Within the top-level activity 'System' there are three activities modelling a train ('Train'), a level crossing ('Crossing'), and in order to be able observe failure of the communication, an explicit communication component ('Communication'). The activity 'Train' interacts with a number of flows from the environment that are grouped in the *external activity* 'Driver' (graphically represented by dashed line rectangles), for example with the driving speed given by the driver or an event indicating that the driver has manually released the brake after an emergency halt. The train is further decomposed into sub-activities 'Brake', 'Odometer', and 'TrainCtrl' and a data-store 'TrackChart' containing the route atlas. The most interesting sub-activity is 'TrainCtrl' that is further decomposed into 'SpeedCtrl', an abstract, discretised implementation of the *braking curve* present in real trains. It controls acceleration and deceleration of the train according to the driver's command and it initiates an emergency halt if the train is approaching a crossing but can not reach it in time. Sub-activity 'Ac-

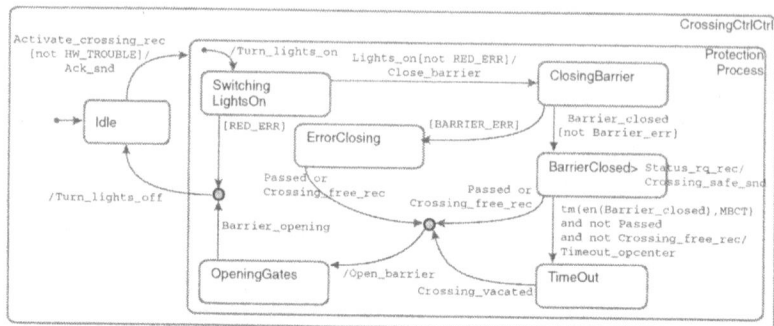

Fig. 3. Behaviour of the crossing controller in terms of a statechart.

tivateCrossing' controls communication with the crossing, i.e. it establishes the communication, requests the crossing to secure itself, and later asks whether the crossing is secure.

Analogously, activity 'Crossing' is further structured. The 'CrossingCtrl' is responsible for controlling the communication and the correct sequence of switching traffic lights and moving barriers. Actual control of enclosed elements is delegated to sub-activities of component 'ElementCtrl', e.g., 'LightsCtrl' for the traffic lights. They interact with the environment that is grouped into four external activities for traffic lights, barriers, the train sensor, and a central operation centre. For example, the crossing can command the barriers to close (grouped in flow 'BARRIER_HW_COMMANDS') and the barriers can indicate a failure to the crossing (grouped in flow 'BARRIER_HW_REPLY').

Figure 3 gives an example of the behavioural description of an activity in form of a statechart, namely that of the crossing controller 'CrossingCtrl' that handles the communication with the train and supervises the activities nested within activity 'ElementCtrl'. Initially, the crossing controller is 'Idle'. On receiving a request to secure itself (event 'Activate_crossing_rec'), e.g., from an approaching train, it switches to state 'ProtectionProcess' if all hardware is operational (no 'HW_TROUBLE'). First the lights are switched on (to 'SwitchingOnLights'), then the barriers are closed (to 'ClosingBarriers'), and then the crossing is considered to be safe (in 'BarrierClosed'). In this state a request asking whether the crossing is safe ('Status_rq_rec') is positively answered. If the trackside sensor detected a train passing by (event 'Passed' is received) or if the train announces that it will not reach the crossing in time (event 'Crossing_free_rec'), the barriers are opened up again and the lights switched off (back to 'Idle').

3.2   Scenarios at the Crossing

As soon as the structure of, for example, the crossing activity is established in SD 2, first positive and negative scenarios in form of existential LSCs can be written. These LSCs are desired (positive) or forbidden (negative) instances of communication sequences.

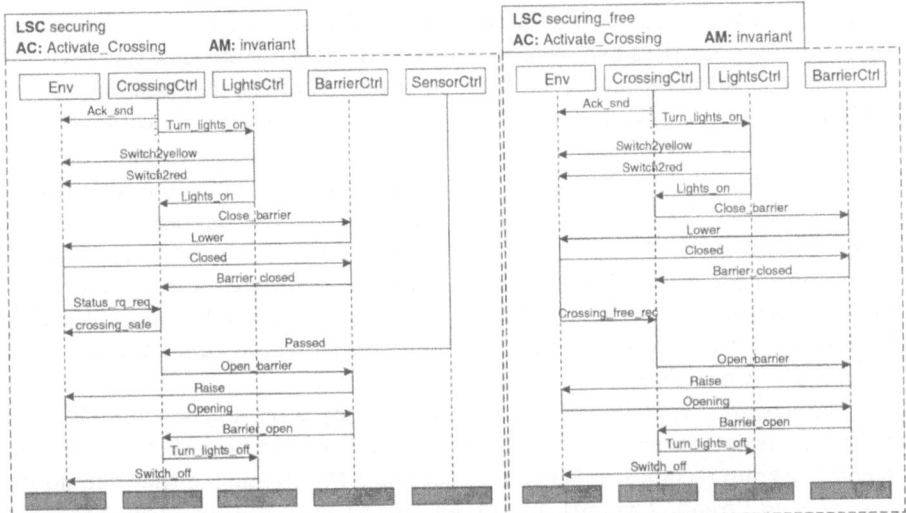

(a) Existential LSC showing the desired interaction at the crossing.

(b) Existential LSC for the crossing showing an error case.

Fig. 4. Existential LSCs for the Statemate model of the FFB.

Figure 4(a) shows the existential LSC (as indicated by the dashed border) '*securing*' that describes a scenario of the crossing being successfully secured, a train passing by, and the crossing being opened up again. It refers to 'CrossingCtrl' and the sub-activities 'LightsCtrl', 'BarrierCtrl', and 'SensorCtrl' of activity 'ElementCtrl' and to the environment under the name 'Env'. The environment instance line represents all activities from Fig. 2 external to the crossing controller since the LSC focuses on the crossing and abstracts from the structure of the environment. In the example, the component 'Communication' belongs to the environment since it lies outside the crossing controller.

The LSC is *activated*, as indicated by the *activation condition* (AC), when event 'Activate_crossing_rec' is received by 'CrossingCtrl'. The LSC has *activation mode* (AM) "invariant" that, in contrast to "initial", states that the scenario need not start at system start time but anytime during a *run* of the system, i.e. a sequence of system states. The scenario begins with the crossing controller acknowledging the request ('Ack_snd') and asking the lights controller to turn on the traffic lights ('Turn_lights_on'). The order of these two events is not important in the scenario, hence they are grouped inside a coregion as indicated by the dashed line in parallel to the instance line. The scenario then requires the lights controller to switch on first the yellow and then the red lights, and reporting success to the crossing controller ('Turn_lights_on'). Analogously the barrier controller lowers the barriers and reports success ('Barrier_closed'). The scenario continues by the crossing controller receiving the query for whether it is secure ('Status_rq_rec') that it answers positively ('Crossing_safe_snd'). When the train now passes the crossing, this is recognised by the sensor controller that sends a 'Passed' event to the crossing controller that in turn first supervises opening of the barriers and then turning off the lights. Note that the LSC comprises hot locations as indicated by solid segments of the instance lines as well as cold locations. Semantically, a hot (also called *mandatory*) location *requires* progress, i.e. the location must *finally* be left, the subsequent communications must be observed. In existential LSCs this is an over-specification wrt. existential verification that aims at obtaining example runs as discussed in Sec. 4.3. There the intention that an existential LSCs should completely be traversed is implemented, hence all locations are effectively considered to be hot. But it is good specification style to point out those points where liveness is required. This effort pays off when modularising and strengthening existential LSCs into universal LSCs as discussed in Sec. 3.3.

The scenario '*securing_free*' shown in Fig. 4(b) is to large amounts identical to the scenario '*securing*'. They differ in that the latter one shows a situation where the train recognises that it does not reach the crossing in time and notifies the crossing ('free'). The crossing is then opened since the train will stop before the crossing as discussed above. It is typical that a scenario showing the "good case" is complemented by a similar scenario showing the "bad case", that could be either a positive scenario showing how the system reacts to the bad case as in the example or a negative scenario that states that a bad case should not happen at all.[5]

3.3   Requirements on the Crossing

Recall that the semantics of an existential LSC is *not* that, *whenever* a crossing is secure but the train does not reach it in time, *then* the crossing is opened, but that the system should be able to show at least a single run where the crossing is opened up after receiving a 'Crossing_free_rec' event.

In order to specify *mandatory* requirements, also called *protocol specifications*, *universal* LSCs are used. They express that a requirement should always be fulfilled given particular circumstances. A universal LSC uses more features of the LSC language to be more precise wrt. to the protocol and to specify the "circumstances", i.e. the activation time is typically characterised by a pre-chart instead of only an activation condition as shown in the examples in Sec. 3.2. Furthermore the protocol LSC, called *commitment LSC*, is accompanied by a set of *assumptions* on the behaviour of the environment as discussed in Sec. 3.4. Practically, universal LSCs can often be obtained from previously written existential LSCs by *modularisation* and *strengthening*.

Consider for example the existential LSCs '*securing*' and '*securing_free*' from Sec. 3.2. They are mostly identical in the first parts that describe the communications to secure the crossing and in the last parts that describe the communications for an opening of the crossing. Hence they can be modularised into four LSCs describing the securing and opening of the crossing and the two different

---

[5] Technically, a negative scenario is specified by moving the whole communication to the pre-chart (cf. [10]) and beginning the main-chart with *condition* 'false'.

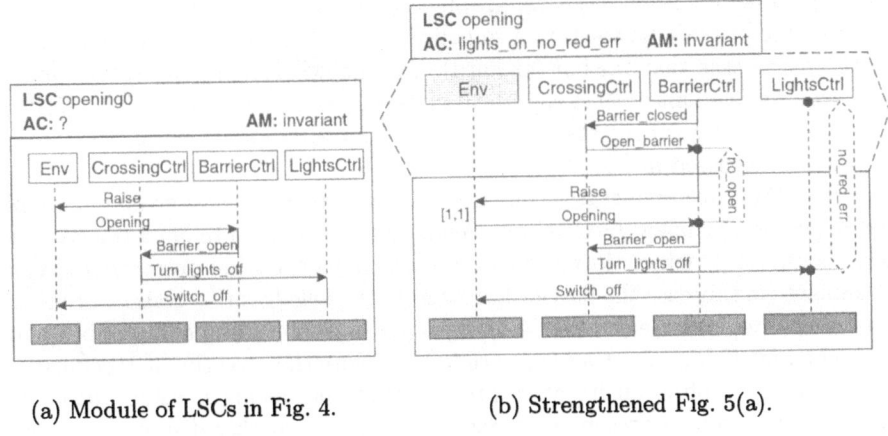

(a) Module of LSCs in Fig. 4.   (b) Strengthened Fig. 5(a).

Fig. 5. Development of a universal LSC for the opening of the crossing.

parts, namely a train passing through or a train not arriving in time. Figure 5(a) shows a straightforward modularisation of the LSCs from Fig. 4, where the border is now solid indicating a universal LSC. But in LSC '*opening0*' it is not clear what should be the activation condition. We want to express that this opening procedure should be taken only in case the crossing is secure and the crossing controller has issued the command to open ('Open_barrier').

Figure 5(b) shows the final, strengthened LSC. It has been equipped with a *pre-chart*, graphically indicated by a large dashed condition symbol enclosing the upper half of the instance lines, that semantically requires that any observation of the communications from the pre-chart within a run of the system implies that the run adheres to the behaviour shown in the *main chart* (or *body*) (cf. [10]). Thus in this case it is stated that the opening procedure should be observed whenever the barrier has successfully been closed ('Barrier_closed') and then the crossing controller orders to open the barrier ('Open_barrier').

Furthermore, the LSC has been extended by two *local invariants*, graphically indicated by vertical condition symbols, that state that a particular condition should hold during a span of time. In the example they are both *cold* (also called *possible*) as indicated by the dashed border. If a system run violates any of the two conditions 'no_open' (the barriers are not prematurely opened) or 'no_red_err' (the red traffic lights do not report failure), then the LSC is exited successfully. That is, the considered run need not adhere to the rest of the LSC. It is considered to satisfy the LSC up to the considered point in time (but it may well violate the LSC later if the LSC is activated again at a later point in time). The local invariant on premature opening is exclusive on the upper end, i.e. 'no_open' must hold only after the point in time where 'Open_barrier' has been observed, and inclusive on the lower end, i.e. 'no_open' should hold up to and *including* the point in time where the event 'Opening' is observed. Thirdly, the leftmost instance line has been designated to be an *environment instance* in contrast to the previous examples, where 'Env' is only a name. Identifying

'Env' to be an environment axis, graphically indicated by shading the head of the instance line, allows to state a so called *internal assumption* on the environment. In this case that the barrier hardware acknowledges the 'Raise' command after exactly one unit of time as indicated by the *timing interval* '[1,1]' (cf. [10]). Assumption/commitment style specification and appropriate verification techniques are discussed in Sec. 3.4.

Altogether '*opening*' states that the crossing adheres to the given communication protocol to open the crossing *whenever* the command to open the crossing is issued in a state where the crossing is secure, under the assumption that the environment (in this case the barrier hardware) acknowledges the 'Raise' command within one step of time (cf. Sec. 4.4), and unless premature opening happens or the red traffic lights report a hardware failure. Note that creating a specification like '*opening*' is often an iterative process of strengthening if using automatic formal verification as presented in Sec. 4: the model-checker disproves the first version and yields a counter-example, the specifier fixes either the specification or the model, tries again, is again disproved by the model-checker, etc.

3.4   Assumption/Commitment Style Verification

LSCs are in particular well suited for so called *assumption/commitment style*[21] specification and *compositional verification*, where a commitment specification is verified under a number of assumptions. An example is the LSC '*opening*' shown in Fig. 5(b): the system is required to adhere to the (commitment) specification under the assumption that the barrier hardware acknowledges the 'Raise' command in time. If the barrier hardware was explicitly modelled, then this assumption should be stated and proven separately. In combination with '*opening*' one could then conclude that the whole system always satisfies the overall requirement on opening the crossing. This kind of reasoning is called compositional verification.

LSCs provide two possibilities to state assumptions: integrated into the commitment LSC and external, as a completely separate LSC. Internal assumptions are written using a designated instance environment line. All communications originating at the environment instance line including their temporal relations to other communications is taken as an assumption. For example, when checking whether the system satisfies the LSC, the model-checker can be considered to *drive* these communications in contrast to all other communications that are only *observed*. In contrast, external assumptions are specified in completely separate LSCs that may have a pre-chart to express the assumption that a particular sequence of communications is always followed by a particular other sequence of communications. Hence a complete LSC protocol specification consists of a universal commitment LSC with possibly empty pre-chart, together with a possibly empty set of LSCs designated to be assumptions. From the point of view of writing specifications, internal assumptions are preferred since they show all relevant things in a *single* chart. External assumptions are more suitable when an assumption should be re-used in multiple protocol specifications or when the above mentioned implication of one sequence by another should be expressed. Of course whenever using assumptions, care has to be taken that the assumptions actually hold, i.e. the affected components satisfy them. Since a good reactive system design should cope with all possible inputs, assumptions on the system's environment should only be used to separate cases.

3.5   Usage of Features in Existential and Universal LSCs

The LSCs presented in the previous sections are quite representative for the typically different usage of LSC features in existential and universal LSCs. In the following we briefly name these characteristics as orientation for writers of LSC specifications. Existential LSCs for scenarios tend to be rather large showing long sequences of communications. They typically don't need a pre-chart since one is interested in *complete traversal* of the chart (cf. Sec. 4.3). Coregions, i.e. regions on an instance line that leave the exact ordering of events unspecified, are more often used in existential LSCs to provide possibility for refinement and strengthening. As mentioned in Sec. 3.2, existential LSCs need not but should contain hot locations where liveness is actually required. In contrast, universal LSCs typically are rather short focusing on a particular property. They usually have a pre-chart that exactly characterises the activation point, local invariants that express internal assumptions, precise timing requirements, and few coregions.

4   Automatic Formal Verification for LSCs

LSCs are a visual formalism with rigorous formal semantics and thus can directly be subject to automatic formal verification, provided the model is also equipped with a formal semantics. In the following sections we will elaborate on the techniques employed to verify the LSCs shown in Sec. 3, report on execution times, and in particular prove it to be feasible for models comparable in size to the "Funkfahrbetrieb" model. We begin in Sec. 4.1 with the discussion of verification of universal LSCs since this is a straightforward case of verifying that a model satisfies a specification and continue with a brief elaboration on the treatment of the different kinds of assumptions in Sec. 4.2. Verification of existential LSCs is special wrt. the expected answer. One is not interested in just getting the confirmation "yes, the system is able to follow the given scenario" but one wants to get hold of an example run, at best a maximal run traversing the LSC completely. How this example run is obtained is discussed in Sec. 4.3. Section 4.4 briefly discusses the impact of Statemate's specialty of two different notions of time on LSC verification for Statemate when the LSC comprises timing annotations.

4.1   Universal Verification

The formal semantics of an LSC is the language accepted by the *symbolic timed automaton* obtained by the *unwinding procedure* presented in [10]. By definition,

Table 1. Verification run times for universal LSC on 'Crossing'

Property	Figure	Semantics	Interpretation	Result	Time	Time (abstr.)
opening	5(b)	step	weak	true	25.0 s	–
			strict	true	58.7 s	–
opening2	in [17]	superst.	weak	true	119.3 s	12.1 s
			strict	true	144.2 s	13.7 s

the automaton accepts exactly those runs of the system that satisfy the LSC. The work [22] provides an algorithm to translate a symbolic (untimed) automaton to a Linear Time Logic (LTL) formula that together with the approach to interpret timing annotations (as discussed in Sec. 4.4) yields an LTL formula for each LSC. Hence given a *finite state machine* representation of the model, automatic formal verification of LSCs with assumptions is straightforwardly obtained by application of assumption/commitment style LTL model-checking.

Table 1 exemplarily gives the run-times for verification of two LSCs in both the weak and the strict interpretation (cf. [10,17]). The measured time considers only the pure processing time used by the model-checker, i.e. compilation times for model and LSC are not included. As shown in the first row, the LSC *opening* (cf. Fig. 5(b)) can directly, i.e. without applying any data abstraction [23], be verified in rather short time[6] when relating timing annotations to Statemate's *synchronous time model* as discussed in Sec. 4.4. The second row gives the results for an LSC from [17] that is an equivalent of *'opening'* with the timing annotation adopted to Statemate's *asynchronous time model* (cf. Sec. 4.4). For this example, run-time can significantly be improved when a data abstraction is manually applied that abstracts from a concrete computation of the (already rather coarsely discretised) braking curve.

According to [17], formal verification of universal LSCs for the train component or the whole system is in most cases feasible if the data abstraction is manually applied. If abstraction from the braking curve values is not possible, then the model-checking task does not terminate within a given bound of five hours. Data abstraction is, for example, not applicable to a property that states that, in case of any error, the train stops before reaching the crossing, since in this case the train's position and speed must be known accurately.

From the methodological point of view, each successful verification of a universal LSC with pre-chart should be accompanied by an existential verification of only the pre-chart due to the interpretation that the pre-chart implies the main-chart: if no witness exists for only the pre-chart, then the whole LSC is trivially satisfied.

---

[6] All results have been produced on a SUN Blade 1000 equipped with 750 MHz UltraSparc processors and 2.5 GB RAM running Solaris 8. The VIS [24] version used is 1.3.

4.2 Internal and External Assumptions

Recall from Sec. 3.4 that we distinguish external and internal assumptions. Concerning formal verification, external assumptions are treated just like the commitment LSC, i.e. translated to LTL, and passed to an assumption/commitment model-checker.

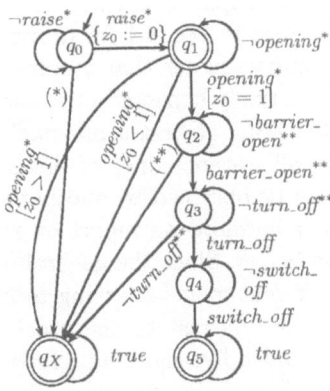

For internal assumption the situation is different. We have to distinguish the following two kinds of internal assumptions: those of the *true liveness* kind, i.e. there exists a hot location on an environment instance line that is not restricted by a timing constraint with finite upper bound, and those of the *bounded liveness* kind, i.e. each hot location on an environment instance line is accompanied by a timing constraint with finite upper bound. Internal assumptions of the bounded liveness kind can be treated by using a variant of the unwinding procedure from [10] that produces an automaton that simply *accepts* all those runs where the assumption is *violated.* Hence if a run is found that is not accepted by this automaton, then it violates the specification *and* satisfies the internal assumptions, otherwise it would have been accepted. Figure 6 shows the timed automaton obtained by the adopted unwinding algorithm for LSC 'opening'. The transitions from $q_0, \ldots, q_3$ to the exit state q_X are regularly generated by the unwinding algorithm for the local invariants. The clock constraints $[z_0 > 1]$ and $[z_0 < 1]$ are additionally introduced by the adopted unwinding

Fig. 6. Automaton for the body of *'opening'* (Fig. 5(b)) in the weak interpretation with integrated assumption. Transition labels marked with a single '*' conjointly refer to both invariants 'no_open' and 'no_red_err' and those marked with the double '**' conjointly refer to invariant 'no_red_err'.

procedure to accept those runs, where event 'opening' occurs too early or too late. State q_1 is made an additional accepting state by the adopted unwinding to accept those runs where the event 'opening' does not occur at all.

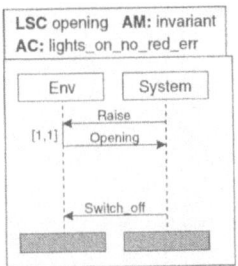

Fig. 7. External assumption extracted from the LSC in Fig. 5.

If there is an internal assumption of the true liveness kind then all internal assumptions are treated by automatic *assumption extraction* [17]. This procedure yields a new LSC that comprises only the environment instance lines of the original LSC and a single instance line into which all other instance lines are collapsed. The verification procedure is then identical to the one with manually written external assumptions. Figure 7 exemplarily shows the assumption LSC extracted from the commitment LSC 'opening'. Note that the environment line remains unchanged while all communications between the environment and the considered system components are represented by a single 'System' instance line. All locations of the 'System' instance line are cold since the assumption should not state any liveness assumptions over the system.

4.3 Existential Verification

In principal, existential LSCs can be verified using the same procedure as described in Sec. 4.1 for universal LSCs. Yet this would produce only the unsatisfactory answer that a scenario is indeed feasible for a system. In contrast, the intuitively expected outcome is a *witness*, i.e. a run of the system that satisfies the LSC, at best a maximal run. That is, a run that reaches all final locations of all instance lines of the LSC. In the following we'll discuss how this witness can be obtained by another variant of the unwinding procedure detailed in [10]. Furthermore we report on run-times measured for the existential LSCs shown in Sec. 3. Since the general approach is *falsification* (as explained below), three different model-checking techniques apply and have been evaluated.

In contrast to the procedure for treatment of internal assumptions of the bounded liveness kind (cf. Sec. 4.2) that changed the timed automaton to accept more runs, the procedure for witness generation generates an automaton where only the single state corresponding to complete traversal of the LSC is turned into an accepting one. The actually issued verification task is then to try to prove that the single accepting state is *not* reachable. If the model-checker is able to *disprove* this claim then it produces a counter-example that leads to the additional state, hence is just the witness we were looking for. Otherwise, there is at first no hint, *where* the traversal got stuck. A straightforward strategy to solve such issues is to manually shorten the LSC and to first try to obtain a witness for the first half etc.

For example consider the existential LSC shown in Fig. 8 together with the timed automaton giving its semantics. It describes a scenario on the top-level of components, between a train, the communication component, and the crossing. It shall be activated by the train sending to the communication component its status request that asks the crossing whether it is secure and it expects that the communication component forwards the request to the crossing, and that in case the crossing is secure, the reply from the crossing is issued and also forwarded

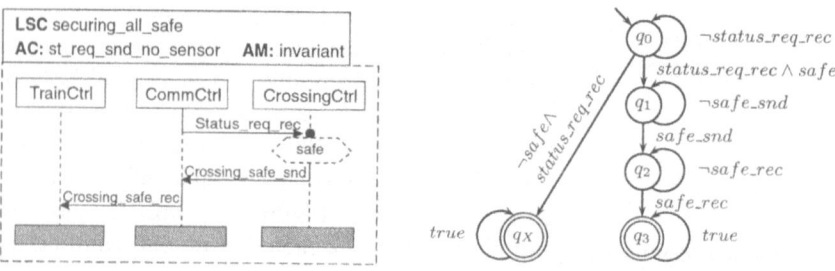

Fig. 8. Existential LSC for a positively answered status request and the automaton for its body in the weak interpretation.

Table 2. Verification run times for existential LSCs on 'Crossing'

Property	Figure	Semantics	Interpre-tation	VIS		Prover BMC	Trace length
				MC	ET		
securing	4(a)	step	weak	750.9 s	15.4 s	228.9 s	31
			strict	776.4 s	16.4 s	174.2 s	31
		superstep	weak	timeout	39.9 s	2539.2 s	45
			strict	timeout	54.9 s	1999.5 s	45
securing free	4(b)	step	weak	488.4 s	13.4 s	190.3 s	29
			strict	75.1 s	17.1 s	104.0 s	29
		superstep	weak	timeout	35.1 s	1238.3 s	41
			strict	timeout	35.5 s	1325.4 s	41

by the communication component to the train. Note that the timed automaton has two accepting states: first, q_X corresponding to the case that the crossing is *not* secure and hence need not reply and second, q_3 corresponding to complete traversal of the LSC. For this example, the variant of the unwinding algorithm would choose q_3 to be the only accepting state.

Concerning *negative* scenarios one should be aware that a witness clearly indicates presence of an error but the result that a witness could *not* be produced has to be interpreted with great care. Verifying that a system is not able to follow a given negative scenario does not imply that the system does never reach the *intended* error condition. There might exist a run that only *slightly* deviates from the negative scenario and hence does not qualify as an example run but that leads to the intended error condition. This risk is obviously the higher the more specialised and concrete the negative scenario LSC is.

Table 2 exemplarily gives the run-times[7] for verification of the two existential LSCs from Sec. 3 in both the weak and the strict interpretation (cf. [10]) and for both the step and the superstep semantics of the model (cf. Sec. 4.4). In this case, the same LSC can be used for both semantics since there are no timing intervals or timers present. The fifth to seventh column correspond to three different techniques used to solve the falsification task, where a missing time value in a field indicates that the corresponding model-checking technique did not produce a witness within five hours. Column VIS/MC gives results obtained using the standard model-checking procedure. The figures in column VIS/ET have been obtained using an algorithm provided by the underlying model-checker VIS [24] called *reachability-based model-checking with early termination* that can be applied to *state invariants*, i.e. temporal logic formulae of the form 'AG p' where p is a proposition. This method, instead of employing the standard backward-oriented fix-point iteration, performs a forward-oriented reachability analysis and terminates immediately as soon as p can be disproved. The results in column Prover/BMC have been obtained using *bounded model-checking* [25] with the Prover engine [26] as underlying SAT solver. The rightmost column gives the length of the resulting witness, i.e. the number of steps from the initial step to complete traversal of the LSC.

---

[7] Cf. footnote 6 on page 508.

For all three techniques an implementation of the timed automaton in the model-checker's system description language has been constructed [27] and parallel composed to the model instead of using the translation of the whole automaton to an LTL formula. This approach in particular enables the use of VIS/ET and bounded model-checking.

The LSC 'securing free' from Fig. 4(b) that describes the opening of the crossing due to receiving the 'Crossing_free_rec' message from the train is slightly simpler than the LSC 'securing' (Fig. 4(a)). Thus it requires only about two thirds of the time necessary to find a witness for 'securing'. The bounded model-checking approach performs rather poorly compared to the reachability-based technique. The key point for the behaviour of the bounded model-checking approach is the length of the witness: short witnesses are easily found by bounded model-checking, whereas long ones require an increased amount of time, since more iterations of formula generation and SAT-checker runs are necessary.[8] We report only qualitatively from [17] that witnesses for existential LSCs over the complete system or the train could only be obtained using bounded model-checking. Both other techniques did not terminate within a given limit of five hours due to significantly higher complexity of the train component that comprises, e.g., an abstract braking curve and rather large timeouts. But the witnesses found by bounded model-checking are relatively short compared to the trace lengths for most LSCs on the crossing only.

4.4   LSC Timer and the Statemate Time-Models

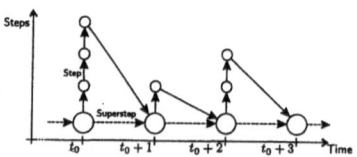

Fig. 9. Abstract representation of steps and supersteps: in the superstep semantics, a step is executed in zero-time, time only passes between supersteps.

The internal assumption in LSC 'opening' shown in Fig. 5(b) comprises the timing interval '[1,1]'. It results, according to the unwinding procedure presented in [10], in timers in the automaton that have to be interpreted when translating to temporal logic for model-checking. In the following we briefly discuss the explored options in the context of Statemate's two notions of time, since the work [22] only elaborates on the translation of untimed automata.

A specialty of the Statemate semantics of statecharts is support for two models of time [20], the *synchronous time model* (or *step semantics*) and the *asynchronous time model* (or *superstep semantics*). In both semantics, a single step basically consists of considering the inputs and, depending on the current state, possibly taking a transition (in each active concurrent state ("AND-state")),

---

[8] Although it has to be noted that the bounded model-checking way has been used in a very straightforward way, i.e. it has been tried to solve each single trace length – one can significantly improve on this by immediately trying to solve a trace of length, for example, 50, or by increasing the length in coarser steps.

thereby executing the transition's actions which may change local values and outputs. The difference lies in the decision when time advances and when the values of *external* inputs of a component, i.e. inputs which are not controlled by other components in the system, may change. In the step semantics, time advances one unit after each step (that itself is considered to take zero-time) and external input values may also change after each step. Hence the step semantics models that the system reacts on each vector of input stimuli by a single step. The superstep semantics models that the system reacts by a *sequence* of computations on each change of external inputs and time advances by one time unit only between supersteps, while single steps are still considered to execute in zero-time. A *superstep* is a sequence of steps s.t. the first step is a reaction on changed values of external inputs and the sequence ends with the first *stable state* in the sequence or is infinite and never reaches a stable state. A system state is called *stable* if the system can't execute further steps unless external inputs change since all internal events have been processed. *External* inputs are assumed to change value only at superstep boundaries (cf. Fig. 9).

In the synchronous time model, the interpretation of timing annotations in an LSC, i.e. of timing intervals and timers (cf. [10]), is canonical. A time unit corresponds to taking a step, that is, in the synchronous time model the LSC shown in Fig. 5 requires the communication '*opening*' exactly one step after 'Raise'.

For the asynchronous time model, we see three principally reasonable choices:

1. all timing annotations refer to supersteps and hence to time
2. all timing annotations refer to steps. Time (superstep) requirements are expressed by explicitly using an auxiliary output of the model that is set at every superstep boundary. Or, alternatively, an LSC is extended by an instance line explicitly representing a clock and special variables of domain "time" that are assigned the current clock value and can be queried within conditions. This approach is used in [28] using an unbounded counter, hence it is unsuitable for finite state model-checking
3. the expressivity of LSCs is extended by annotating each timing constraint with whether it refers to counting steps or to time

Approaches 1 and 2 turned out to be too restrictive [17]. There are occasions where the specifier needs to refer to both, single steps in the model and the model's notion of time, hence from a practical point of view, approach 3 is desirable. In the evaluation we report on [17], approach 2 has been used for simplicity. In the STVE, a step of the Statemate model is equal to a transition of the model's finite state machine representation in the model-checker. Hence timing intervals can be expanded into sequences of modal "next" operators. But it turned out that there are two major drawbacks rendering it impractical: firstly, an LSC referring to supersteps becomes unnecessarily large and complex. For example, an LSC requiring a duration of n supersteps comprises n combinations of local invariants and conditions referring to the auxiliary output. Thus the explicit encoding of supersteps easily outweighs the events representing relevant communications. Secondly, this approach can, in a single LSC, only express requirements concerning exact or minimal numbers of supersteps. That is, a maximal number of supersteps or a non-trivial timing interval can only be required by a combination of multiple LSCs, hence obscuring the relevant communications further.

For an implementation of tools supporting approach 3, there are two promising directions which are subject to further work. First, the temporal logic way can be extended by parallel composing auxiliary *observer automatons* to the model that observe reaching of superstep boundaries. In the formula, one can then refer to their states, that is, the interpretation of the above mentioned indicator for reaching a superstep is shifted from the LSC into an observer automaton. Alternatively, the observer automaton [27] for the whole LSC that is already used for witness generation as discussed in Sec. 4.3 can be extended to reset and increment a time counter as long as the commitment and all assumptions are *iterative*, i.e. external assumption LSCs that are not re-activated as long as they are active, since the LSC being iterative is a pre-requisite of the approach of [27]. Both directions imply that the LSC language is extended by means to annotate timing requirements, i.e. timer set/reset/timeout and timing intervals, by the time they refer to, i.e. whether they refer to steps or the model's notion of time.

5   Conclusion and Further Work

We have explicated how model-based development processes can be enhanced by the use of visual formalisms like LSCs in combination with automatic formal verification technology as presented in Sec. 4.

We exemplified our claims on the V-model that already requires activities to create formal specifications and conduct formal verification, but considers formalisation of requirements to be a separate sub-activity *in addition* to development of the informal requirements. Directly using LSCs to describe interaction sequences eliminates these sub-activities, provides the benefits of a precise formal specification, and has high potential for re-use. Abstract existential LSCs derived from initial requirements can later be refined along the increasing detailedness of the model. And they can be modularised and strengthened into universal LSCs that can be subject to automatic formal verification.

Further work consists of continuation of the work reported in [29], a transfer to the domain of UML models of the results obtained for Statemate models as presented in this paper. In [29] we give an interpretation of LSCs for the domain of UML models and provide an approach to treat a priori unbounded UML models with finite-state methods exploiting object symmetries to be able to employ query reduction [30,31] and an abstraction called data-type reduction [30]. The open questions concern the topic of abstraction refinement, i.e. a heuristically chosen initial abstraction may be too coarse yielding a false negative (or spurious counter-example). Then the abstraction should be refined and the verification task tried again for whether the specification is proven to hold, disproved by a true counter-example, or again resulting only in a false negative.

References

1. Jacobson, I., Booch, G., Rumbaugh, J.: The Unified Software Development Process. Addison Wesley (1999)
2. Beck, K.: Extreme Programming Explained. Addison Wesley (1999)
3. EStdIT, B.d.I.: V-Model, Development Standard for IT-Systems of the federal Republic of Germany (1997)
4. Harel, D., Lachover, H., Naamad, A., Pnueli, A., Politi, M., Sherman, R., Shtull-Trauring, A., Trakhtenbrot, M.: STATEMATE: A working environment for the development of complex reactive systems. IEEE Transactions on Software Engineering **16** (1990) 403 – 414
5. OMG: 1.4-uml-01-09-67 (2001)
6. Harel, D., Marelly, R.: Come, Let's Play: Scenario-Based Programming Using LSCs and the Play-Engine. Springer-Verlag (2003)
7. Damm, W., Harel, D.: LSCs: Breathing Life into Message Sequence Charts. Formal Methods in System Design **19** (2001) 121–141
8. ITU-T: ITU-T Recommendation Z.120: Message Sequence Chart (MSC). ITU-T, Geneva (1999)
9. Bienmüller, T., Damm, W., Wittke, H.: The statemate verification environment - making it real. In Emerson, E.A., Sistla, A.P., eds.: Proceedings CAV 2000. Number 1885 in LNCS, Springer-Verlag (2000) 561–567
10. Brill, M., Damm, W., Klose, J., Westphal, B., Wittke, H.: Live sequence charts. In: this volume. (2004)
11. Klose, J., Kropf, T., Ruf, J.: A Visual Approach to Validating System Level Designs. In: Proceedings ISSS 2002, ACM Press (2002) 186–191
12. Klose, J., Lettrari, M.: Scenario-based Monitoring and Testing of Real-time UML models. In Gogolla, M., Kobryn, C., eds.: UML 2001 - The Unified Modeling Language: Modeling Languages, Concepts, and Tools. Volume 2185 of LNCS., Springer Verlag (2001)
13. Hänsel, F., Poliak, J., Slovák, R., Schnieder, E.: Reference case study for comparison and validation of formal specifications using a model demonstrator. In: this volume. (2004)
14. Jansen, L.: Referenzfallstudie Verkehrsleittechnik (1997) ⟨http://www.iva.ing.tu-bs.de/institut/projekte/Referenzfallstudie_vklt/referenz.html⟩, 16.5.2004.
15. AG, D.B.: Betriebliches Lastenheft für FunkFahrBetrieb (1996) Minimalkonzept, Version 2.0.
16. Klose, J., Thums, A.: The Statemate Reference Model of the Reference Case Study 'Verkehrsleittechnik'. Technical report, University of Augsburg (2000) ⟨http://www.Informatik.Uni-Augsburg.DE/swt/formosa/RefVL/bericht.ps.gz⟩.
17. Klose, J.: Live Sequence Charts: A Graphical Formalism for the Specification of Communication Behavior. PhD thesis, Carl von Ossietzky Universität Oldenburg (2003)
18. Klose, J., Moik, A.: Modellierung der FORMS-Fallstudien mit Statemate. In Schnieder, E., ed.: Proceedings FORMS 2000. Number 441 in Fortschritt-Berichte VDI Reihe 12, VDI Verlag (2000)
19. Damm, W., Döhmen, G., Klose, J.: Secure Decentralized Control of Railway Crossings. In Gnesi, S., Latella, D., eds.: Fourth International ERCIM Workshop on Formal Methods in Industrial Critical Systems. (1999)
20. Harel, D., Naamad, A.: The statemate semantics of statecharts. ACM Trans. Softw. Eng. Methodol. **5** (1996) 293–333

21. Josko, B.: Modular specification and verification of reactive systems. Carl von Ossietzky Universität Oldenburg (1993) Habilitationsschrift.
22. Schlör, R.C.: Symbolic Timing Diagrams: A Visual Formalism for Model Verification. PhD thesis, Universität Oldenburg (2000)
23. Clarke, E.M., Grumberg, O., Peled, D.A.: Model Checking. The MIT Press, Cambridge, Massachusetts (1999)
24. The VIS Group: VIS : A System for Verification and Synthesis. In: Proceedings CAV 1996. Number 1102 in LNCS (1996)
25. Biere, A., Cimatti, A., Clarke, E., Zhu, Y.: Symbolic model checking without BDDs. In Cleaveland, W.R., ed.: Tools and Algorithms for the Construction and Analysis of Systems. Part of European Conferences on Theory and Practice of Software, ETAPS'99, Amsterdam. Volume 1579 of LNCS., Springer-Verlag (1999) 193–207
26. Sheeran, M., Stålmarck, G.: A tutorial on Stålmarck's proof procedure for propositional logic. In Gopalakrishnan, G., Windley, P.J., eds.: Proceedings FMCAD'98. Volume 1522 of LNCS. (1998) 82–99
27. Grégoire, B.: Automata oriented program verification. Master's thesis, Facultés Universitaires Notre-Dame de la Paix, Namur (2002)
28. Harel, D., Marelly, R.: Playing with Time: On the Specification and Execution of Time-Enriched LSCs. In: Proceedings MASCOTS 2002. (2002)
29. Damm, W., Westphal, B.: Live and let die: LSC-based verification of UML-models. In de Boer, F.S., Bonsangue, M.M., Graf, S., de Roever, W.P., eds.: Formal Methods for Components and Objects, First International Symposium, FMCO 2002, Leiden, The Netherlands, November 5-8, 2002, Revised Lectures. Number 2852 in LNCS, Springer-Verlag (2003)
30. McMillan, K.L.: A Methodology for Hardware Verification using Compositional Model Checking. Science of Computer Programming **37** (2000) 279–309
31. Xie, F., Browne, J.: Integrated State Space Reduction for Model Checking Executable Object-oriented Software System Designs. In Kutsche, R.D., Weber, H., eds.: Proceedings FASE 2002. Volume 2306 of LNCS., Springer-Verlag (2002)

Verification of PLC Programs Given as Sequential Function Charts

Nanette Bauer[1], Sebastian Engell[2], Ralf Huuck[3], Sven Lohmann[2],
Ben Lukoschus[4], Manuel Remelhe[2], and Olaf Stursberg[2]

[1] BASF AG, 67056 Ludwigshafen, Germany
nanette.bauer@basf-ag.de
[2] Process Control Laboratory (BCI-AST)
University of Dortmund, 44221 Dortmund, Germany
{s.engell|s.lohmann|m.remelhe|o.stursberg}@bci.uni-dortmund.de
[3] National ICT Australia Ltd (NICTA),
The University of New South Wales, Sydney, Australia
rhuuck@cse.unsw.edu.au
[4] Institute of Computer Science and Applied Mathematics
University of Kiel, 24098 Kiel, Germany
bls@informatik.uni-kiel.de

Abstract. Programmable Logic Controllers (PLC) are widespread in the manufacturing and processing industries to realize sequential procedures and to avoid safety-critical states. For the specification and the implementation of PLC programs, the graphical and hierarchical language Sequential Function Charts (SFC) is increasingly used in industry. To investigate the correctness of SFC programs with respect to a given set of requirements, this contribution advocates the use of formal verification. We present two different approaches to convert SFC programs algorithmically into automata models that are amenable to model checking. While the first approach translates untimed SFC into the input language of the tool Cadence SMV, the second converts timed SFC into timed automata which can be analyzed by the tool UPPAAL. For different processing system examples, we illustrate the complete verification procedure consisting of controller specification, model transformation, integration of dynamic plant models, and identifying errors in the control program by model checking.

Keywords. Analysis, Automata, Model Checking, Logic Control.

1 Introduction

A large part of the control software of processing and manufacturing systems performs logic and supervisory control. Logic control is characterized by the reaction of the controller to events generated by the plant (e.g., a relevant quantity exceeds a threshold), and the controller selects one out of finitely many control actions. The two major objectives of such controllers are (a) the realization of sequential procedures, as for example to establish a given sequence of production

H. Ehrig et al. (Eds.): INT 2004, LNCS 3147, pp. 517–540, 2004.

steps, and (b) to ensure a safe operation of the plant. The latter may involve to initiate an emergency routine if a malfunction or a deviation from the desired operation is detected. While many industrial logic controllers are still implemented in the languages *instruction list, ladder diagram,* or *continuous function charts* [1], the so-called *Sequential Function Charts* (SFC) become increasingly important and accepted. By using SFC, which are standardized according to [2], the control logic can be specified in an intuitive way. Sequential, parallel, and nested procedures are represented graphically, and subfunctions given in any of the other languages listed above can be embedded. Irrespectively of the language chosen to model the controller, the correctness with respect to the intended behavior of the controlled system is, of course, crucial. This is most apparent for safety specifications, i.e., the objective of the logic controller is to prevent that the plant runs into a state which is harmful for the personnel, the equipment, or the environment of the plant. While it is industrial practice to rely on extensive testing to check that the controller is correct, academia has intensively studied the technique of formal verification for this purpose. It performs a manual or algorithmic proof that a logic controller complies with a set of formal requirements and has been investigated in, e.g., [3,4,5,6]. From the various known verification techniques [7], we focus on *model checking* [8] which (partially) computes the reachable set of a state-transition model and evaluates if a formal requirement expressed in temporal logic holds for this set.

In order to apply model checking to controllers given as SFC, the latter first have to be translated into a state-transition model. The approach in [9] uses Petri-Nets as the target format while the methods in [10,11] transform the SFC into automata and apply model checking afterwards. This contribution follows the latter approach and describes three important extensions:

(a) We explicitly account for the cyclic operation mode of the hardware on which logic controllers are usually executed, i.e. of Programmable Logic Controllers (PLC). Each cycle of this mode consists of a scanning step (in which the inputs from the plant are read), the step of executing possible transitions of the SFC, and finally writing the outputs to the plant.

(b) We present transformation schemes to convert SFC into the input language of two different tools for model checking. The first scheme is applicable to SFC without real-time quantifiers. Such charts are transformed into the input format of the tool Cadence-SMV [12] which is known to be efficient for large finite-state automata [13]. The second approach considers real-time specifications of the control program by transforming the SFC into timed automata using a procedure based on graph grammars. To verify timed automata, the tool UPPAAL is applied [14].

(c) For processing and manufacturing systems, many requirements are usually formulated for the controlled plant, i.e., it is not sufficient to consider only a model of the controller for verification, but one has also to consider the plant behavior. For the two approaches listed above, we describe how an appropriate model of the plant behavior (specified either as a finite state automaton or a timed automaton) can be used to verify whether the controlled plant shows the intended behavior.

2   Verification Objectives and Modeling Alternatives

Figure 1 summarizes our overall design procedure for logic controllers: The controller is constructed as an SFC in a manual design procedure in which a specification of the control goals and the expected plant behavior are taken into consideration. This step involves to formulate a sequence of control actions that realize the goals given an intuitive understanding of how the plant reacts to these actions. Depending on whether the controller includes timed actions, the SFC is translated into a finite state automaton (FSA) or a timed automaton (TA). The analysis tool (optionally) composes the controller with a formal model of the plant and checks the validity of a formalized representation of the requirements. The plant model is also represented as FSA or TA, depending on whether quantitative time is relevant for the analysis task. If the analysis reveals that the requirements are met, the SFC can be transferred to the PLC. A violation of the requirements may either be due to a wrong controller design (i.e., the SFC has to be modified) or to an insufficiently detailed plant model (i.e., a less conservative one has to be employed). In order to illustrate the choice of a plant model and a typical set of requirements, we consider the simple processing system shown in Fig. 2: The plant consists of two tanks *T1* and *T2* with heating devices *H1* and *H2*, a condenser *C1*, a pump *P1*, four on-off valves *V1* to *V4*, and sensors for monitoring if thresholds for the liquid levels (*LI*), the temperature (*TI*), the concentration (*QI*), and the flow (*FI*) are exceeded. The nominal operation of this system (and thus a control goal) is as follows: *T1* is first filled through *V1* with a liquid that contains a dissolved substance. The liquid is heated up in *T1* by the heater *H1* until the boiling point is reached. By further supplying heat, a certain amount of solvent is evaporated until the concentration of the liquid has reached a desired concentration. During the evaporation, vapor is condensed in *C1* which is cooled by a cooling agent that is supplied through *V4*. When the evaporation is finished, the liquid is transferred from *T1* into *T2* through *V2*. This procedure is repeated twice until *T2* is filled with three batches from

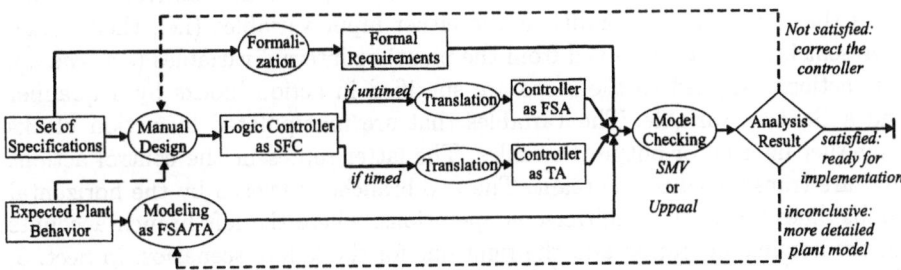

Fig. 1. The controller design procedure with: TA - timed automaton, FSA - finite state automaton, SFC - sequential function charts.

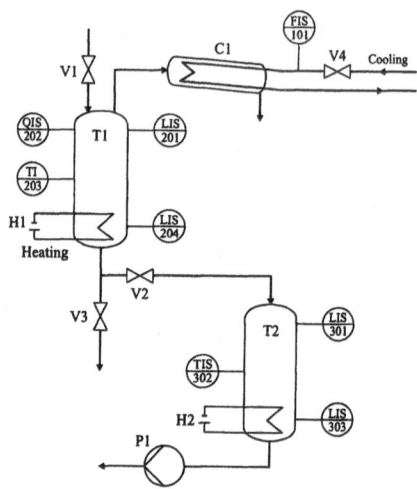

Fig. 2. Flowchart of an evaporator system.

T1. The content of *T2* (the product) is then pumped out of *T2* through *P1*, and afterwards the complete operation can start again. In addition, two disturbance scenarios are considered, an appropriate handling of which constitutes two further control objectives: (a) In the event of a cooling failure (detected by *FIS101*) the evaporation is stopped after a short period of time (to avoid overpressure) and, if the concentration goal is not reached by then, the content of *T1* is disposed through *V3*. (b) In the event of a heating failure, *T1* is also emptied immediately through *V3*, since the process control goal cannot be achieved in any case. In both cases the nominal operation should be resumed when the faulty devices have been repaired or replaced.

A possible SFC controller as a result of manual design is shown in Fig. 3. Each step is denoted by a rectangle and a step identifier (*S0* is the initial step). The transition between two consecutive steps (marked by a bold horizontal line) carries a condition given as a Boolean expression. If the latter evaluates to *true*, the transition can be taken and the following step becomes active. The variables that occur in the conditions are either input variables (i.e., their values represent information received from the plant) or internal variables (e.g. *count*). The actions assigned to the steps are specified in action blocks by a qualifier and a Boolean variable. The variables that are manipulated by action blocks are either internal or output variables. The latter represent the control actions that are transmitted to the plant. The two branches enclosed by the horizontal double lines represent simultaneous operations, where the left branch accounts for the nominal operation and the right one for the failure scenarios. In Sect. 3, the syntax and semantics of SFCs is described in more detail, and Sect. 5 contains a description of how the SFC in Fig. 3 realizes the desired operation of the evaporator.

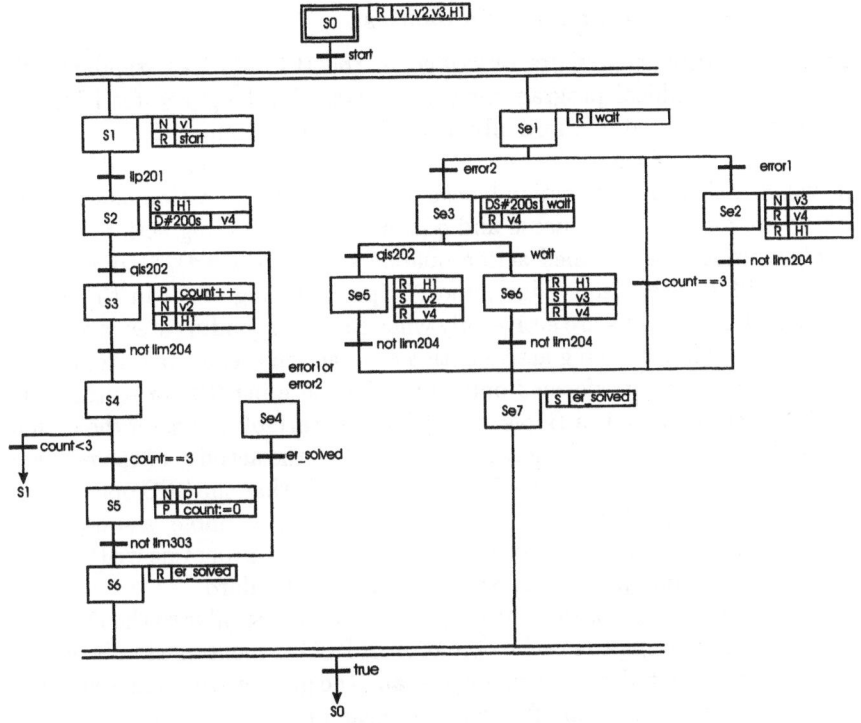

Fig. 3. SFC-controller for the evaporation system.

For systems like the controlled evaporator, the verification usually aims at checking requirements that are of the following type: (a) it has to be checked whether the controller indeed realizes the desired production sequence; (b) safety guidelines imply that unsafe states (as a maximum or minimum temperature in *T1*) are never reached, and (c) the SFC must never be deadlocked. The first two requirements can obviously only be checked if a plant model is employed that represents the behavior of quantities like levels, temperatures, and concentrations. The last requirement should be checked for arbitrary values of the input variables, i.e., a plant model is not required for (c). Section 5 describes the verification of the first two requirements for the evaporator system, while Sect. 3 deals with the structural analysis of SFC.

3   Analysis of Untimed SFC Programs

This section describes the algorithmic verification of SFC programs without time quantifiers using the model checker Cadence SMV (CaSMV). While the method proposed in Sect. 4 is, of course, also applicable to untimed SFC, we deem it preferable to use CaSMV in this case due to the known efficiency of symbolic model checking for untimed models.

3.1   The SFC Language and Semantics

Sequential function charts are described in the IEC 61131-3 standard [2] as elements of a graphical programming and structuring language for PLCs, and the syntax and semantic is formally defined in [15]. For an SFC S, this syntax introduces the symbol S for its sets of steps with an initial step s_0 and a function *block* which assigns a set of action blocks to each $s_i \in S$. An action block is a pair (a, q), where a is an action name and q is one of the following action qualifiers. We only consider the untimed action qualifiers N (non-stored), R (reset), S (set or stored), P1 (pulse, rising edge), and P0 (pulse, falling edge) in this section. While non-stored actions are active only when its corresponding step is activated, stored actions continue being active until a reset action is executed. Actions with the pulse qualifier are performed only once when entering (P1) or exiting (P0) a step. If the action name is a Boolean variable, the variable is *true* if the action is active and *false* otherwise. Action qualifiers control the activity of the respective action depending on the activity of steps. We assume that the SFC operates only on Boolean variables. Action names refer to a Boolean variable, a subordinated SFC (thus enabling nested or hierarchical structures) or programs written in one of the other programming languages defined in the standard.

The execution of SFC is described by evolution rules similar to the firing rules of Petri nets considering the cyclic operation of PLC as mentioned in Sect. 1, i.e. the actions are executed first in each cycle, and the guards are evaluated and the enabled transitions are taken afterwards. In general, the actions are executed in a fixed order given either explicitly or implicitly. Whenever a nested SFC gets deactivated, its enabled transitions are still taken in that cycle, but then the nested SFC becomes inactive and its current location is marked as a *history step* from which the executions resumes if this SFC is activated again. All steps that are "active" in a cycle (meaning that their actions are executed) are called *active steps*. The union of history steps and active steps is called *ready steps*. The actions which are potentially executed in a cycle are called *active actions* and the ones which have been activated by an S-qualifier and which have not yet been reset are called *stored actions*.

The formal operational semantics for SFC according to [15] is based on *configurations* describing a system state as follows:

Definition 1 (Configuration). *A* configuration *of an SFC and its sub-SFC is a 5-tuple* $(\sigma, readyS, activeS, activeA, storedA)$, *where σ is the state (i.e., a function assigning a value to each variable), and readyS denotes the set of ready steps, activeS the set of active steps, activeA the set of active actions, and storedA the set of stored actions.*

Such a configuration is modified within a PLC cycle as follows: (1) get new input from the environment and store the information in σ; (2) execute the set *activeA* of active actions and update σ accordingly; (3) determine *readyS*, *activeS*, *activeA*, and *storedA*; (4) send the outputs to the environment by extracting the required information from the new state σ.

For each cycle the new active steps are the old ones plus the targets of the taken transitions, but without their source steps. Moreover, the new active steps, active actions, and stored actions are computed recursively on the structure of the SFC [15]. The semantics of an SFC is given by its possible set of configuration sequences. A configuration sequence consists of a possibly infinite number of transformations of configurations, where each PLC cycle corresponds to one transformation.

3.2 Translation to CaSMV

CaSMV [12] is a symbolic model-checker [16,17,8] which supports the algorithmic verification of temporal logic properties of Kripke structures. The transition relation of a Kripke structure is expressed in CaSMV by evaluation rules depending on the current and the next state of each system variable q (q and next(q) in CaSMV notation). In order to translate an SFC to CaSMV, we mimic the transition relation on a configuration of the SFC semantics. We initially assume that each action changes an output variable—in this case, an explicit ordering of the actions is not necessary since actions do not share output variables. We also start without an explicit order of transitions which allows us to additionally check for conflicting transitions automatically. Later we show how to extend this framework by embedding orders on transitions and actions resulting in a deterministic execution model. This enables us to deal with more complex actions and situations where a variable is modified by more than one action.

Data Structure of the CaSMV Module. A system modeled in CaSMV can be composed from components called *modules*. One module describes the SFC and its actions, and further modules may describe the environment or parts thereof. The translation from a system of SFC into a CaSMV module requires the following Boolean variables:

- ready_si for each step s_i, i.e., one variable for each step of the top level SFC and the subordinated ones. These variables model whether the respective step is ready, i.e. the step is active or control resides in it and waits to resume.
- guard$i$ for each guard g_i. This variable represents the transition condition and is in general a Boolean expression formulated over program variables and *input variables* input$i$ (e.g., process variables from the plant to be controlled) and the *activity of steps* step.Xi, where, e.g., step.X1 evaluates to *true* whenever step s_1 is active.
- active_ai for each action a_i. This variable is introduced to code whether an action is active or not. This action can be an SFC itself.
- stored_ai for each action a_i, which indicates if an action is currently stored, i.e., it has been activated in the current or a previous step by an S qualifier.

A CaSMV module has *input parameters* for each Boolean input variable of the SFC program. The behavior of the input variables is a-priori chaotic, i.e., they might take any possible value, unless not otherwise specified. This allows to check the SFC program as an open system. Any restrictions on the behavior of input variables can be modeled in an additional CaSMV module representing the environment.

Evolution of State Variables. Next we define how to code the transition relation on the variables defined above. This is of special interest for the activity of actions, which are tagged by qualifiers. Therefore, we explicitly define the next-state of all variables, except for guards and input variables, since inputs are provided by the environment and the truth values of guards are determined by the evaluation of the Boolean expressions which they represent.

Ready steps. The ready variable $\texttt{ready\_s}i$ of a step s_i is *true* if and only if there is a transition taken into s_i or it is already *true* and there is no transition taken leaving s_i. Inside a nested SFC, transitions can only be taken if the nested SFC itself is active. In detail, for a nested SFC given by an action a_k, the variable $\texttt{ready\_s}i$ for each step s_i of a_k can only be changed if $\texttt{active\_a}k$ holds.

Active actions. The value of $\texttt{active\_a}k$ for the activity of an action a_k depends on the activity of the steps s_j with $(a_k, q) \in block(s_j)$, and the qualifier q tagged to a_k. The expression for determining $\texttt{next}(\texttt{active\_a}k)$ is defined by $(\texttt{act\_N\_steps} \vee \texttt{act\_S\_steps} \vee \texttt{act\_P1\_steps} \vee \texttt{act\_P0\_steps} \vee \texttt{stored\_a}k) \wedge \neg\texttt{act\_R\_steps}$ where

- $\texttt{act\_N\_steps} = \bigvee_{\{s_j \mid (a_k,N) \in block(s_j)\}} (\texttt{next}(\texttt{ready\_s}j) \wedge \texttt{next}(\texttt{active\_a}l))$,
- $\texttt{act\_S\_steps} = \bigvee_{\{s_j \mid (a_k,S) \in block(s_j)\}} (\texttt{next}(\texttt{ready\_s}j) \wedge \texttt{next}(\texttt{active\_a}l))$,
- $\texttt{act\_P1\_steps} = \bigvee_{\{s_j \mid (a_k,P1) \in block(s_j)\}} (\neg\texttt{ready\_s}j \wedge \texttt{next}(\texttt{ready\_s}j))$,
- $\texttt{act\_P0\_steps} = \bigvee_{\{s_j \mid (a_k,P0) \in block(s_j)\}} (\texttt{ready\_s}j \wedge \texttt{next}(\neg\texttt{ready\_s}j))$, and
- $\texttt{act\_R\_steps} = \bigvee_{\{s_j \mid (a_k,R) \in block(s_j)\}} (\texttt{next}(\texttt{ready\_s}j) \wedge \texttt{next}(\texttt{active\_a}l))$.

(In the definitions above, a_l denotes the SFC to which s_j belongs.)

Thus, an action will become active if one of the following conditions hold: the step with which the action is associated becomes active and the action itself is tagged with the qualifier N or S; a step the action belongs to will be entered in the next cycle and the action is tagged with the qualifier P1; the step the action belongs to is active and will be inactive in the next cycle and the action is tagged with the qualifier P0, or the action is a stored one (see below). Resetting an action always has higher priority and, thus, will in any case deactivate a_k.

Stored actions. The value $\texttt{stored\_a}k$ is set to *true* if one or more steps where a_k is associated to are active and a_k is tagged with an S qualifier and there is no matching reset. It is set to *false*, whenever a matching reset action is called. Thus the next value of $\texttt{stored\_a}k$ is defined by $\texttt{next}(\texttt{stored\_a}k) = (\texttt{act\_S\_steps} \vee \texttt{stored\_a}k) \wedge \neg\texttt{act\_R\_steps}$.

Initialization. The *initial ready step* s_0 of the top-level SFC is initialized to *true*, denoting that this step is active at the beginning. All other steps are initially set to *false*. For reasons of simplicity, we assume that the initial step of the top level SFC contains no nested SFC. This does not limit the set of SFC that can be translated, because each SFC can be transformed into one that meets this constraint. Furthermore, all variables encoding that an action is active or stored are initially *false*.

Extension to Orders on Actions and Transitions. The translation presented above does not consider orders on actions and on transitions. Furthermore, it only works for actions which map their activity to an output variable. However, this approach can be extended to consider orders on transitions and actions. To take the order on transitions into account we modify the guards of the transitions such that there are no more conflicts. This can be done statically by adding constraints such that a transition is enabled if and only if its guard holds and no other higher-priority transition which shares at least one common source step is enabled.

To consider more complex actions which make it necessary to deal with the order on actions we introduce a new CaSMV variable output$i$ for each output variable which is modified by more than one action. Each of these new variables is modified in a *micro-cycle* by all actions which access this output variable, while using the correct action ordering. Furthermore, we need a *global cycle* for the synchronization of all micro-cycles and for the execution of the remaining actions as described above.

3.3   Example: Application to a Chemical Plant

The presented approach is applied to a batch laboratory plant in which two products are simultaneously produced from three raw materials in three reactors [18]. We focus here only on the production of one product in one of the reactors.

Process and Control Program. Figure 4 shows the reactor T_3 used to form the product C from two raw materials, referred to as A and B. The tanks T_1 and T_2 are used as buffers for A and B, and they are filled through the valves V_1 and V_2. The production procedures starts by filling A into T_3 through V_3, and afterwards the contents of T_2 are filled into T_3 through V_4. B immediately reacts with A to C, and the product C can be withdrawn through V_5 for further processing. The vessels are equipped with sensors LIS+ and LIS− for detecting that upper and lower threshold for the liquid levels are crossed. T_3 is additionally equipped with a stirrer M.

Figure 5 contains a control program consisting of a top-level SFC which triggers the following three parallel processes: (a) *filling* T_1 *with* A given by action a_1 in step s_2, (b) *filling* T_2 *with* B given by action a_2 in step s_5, and (c) *reaction in* T_3 *and emptying* T_3 given in step s_7 as action a_3. The action a_3 is given as a separate SFC. Due to conflicting processes, such as "empty contents

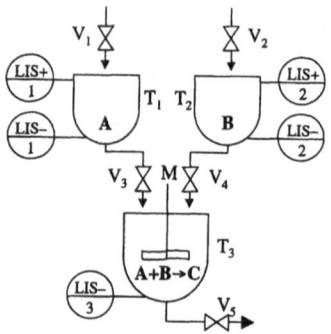

Fig. 4. A part of the multi-product batch plant

of T_1 into T_3" (a sub-step of a_3) and "fill T_1 with A", the waiting steps s_1, s_4 and s_{10} are included to ensure that certain conditions (given as guards) hold before the processes start. Apart from a_3, the actions are very simple since the activity simply determines the value of an output variable, e.g., V_1 is open as long as a_1 is active.

Translation to CaSMV. The translation of the control program into CaSMV code follows directly from the definitions in Sect. 3.2. Figure 6 shows two examples for defining the transition relation on state variables, where the CaSMV code contains the symbols '&', '|', (and '!') denoting the logical 'and', 'or' (and 'not'). The step s_{12} of the nested SFC will become ready if the preceding step s_{11} is currently ready, the SFC it is nested in is active, and the guard "LIS− 1" of the transition connecting these two steps will evaluate to *true*. On the other hand, step s_{12} will become inactive, if it is currently ready, its SFC is active and the outgoing transition condition will hold. In any other case, s_{12} keeps its current value. The action a_5 will become active if either s_{11} is active (i.e., s_{11} is

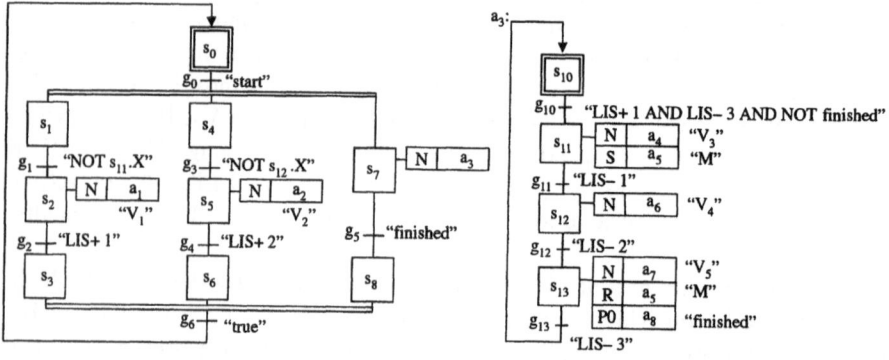

Fig. 5. Control SFC for the production in reactor T_3

```
default next(readyS_s12) := readyS_s12; in case{
   (readyS_s11 & next(LISminus1) & activeA_a3) : next(readyS_s12) := 1;
   (readyS_s12 & next(LISminus2) & activeA_a3) : next(readyS_s12) := 0;}


default next(activeA_a5) := 0;
in case{
   next(readyS_s13) & next(activeA_a3) : next(activeA_a5) := 0;
   (next(readyS_s11) & next(activeA_a3)) | next(storedA_a5) :
     next(activeA_a5) := 1;}


default next(storedA_a5) := storedA_a5;
in case{
   next(readyS_s13) & next(activeA_a3) : next(storedA_a5) := 0;
   next(readyS_s11) & next(activeA_a3) : next(storedA_a5) := 1;}
```

Fig. 6. CaSMV code fragments for the SFC a_3

ready and a_3 active) or a_5 is stored and s_{13} is not active. In any other case, a_5 will be inactive. Furthermore, a_5 is stored if s_{11} is active, and a_5 is not stored if it is reset in s_{13}.

Specification of Verification Tasks. The translated SFC is checked for the following properties: (a) reachability of each step to ensure that the SFC does not contain unused code; in CaSMV the corresponding CTL specification is for a step s_i: SPEC EF si, i.e., there exists an execution path by which s_i is eventually reached; (b) the absence of deadlocks by checking that each run by which s_i is reached can be extended such that s_i is reached once more: SPEC AG (AF si); and (c) plant specific requirements: For batch plants, the conflicting allocation of equipment by different production steps is often important; e.g. the steps "emptying contents of T_1 into T_3" and "filling T_1 with A" are in conflict since they compete for tank T_1. Therefore, it has to be verified that each piece of equipment is exclusively used by one process at a time. As an example, we check for tank T_1 that the valves V_1 and V_3 are never open at the same time, specified by: SPEC AG !(V1 & V3).

The verification tasks presented here are independent of a specific environment, they reason about the control software only. In order to verify, e.g., that there is no overflow in a tank, parts of the plant and the environment have to be included into the model and have to be checked in combination with the controller.

Verification Results. All verification tasks presented above are checked within a fraction of a second on a Sun UltraSPARC 1. This is not surprising, since the model is still of small size and for illustration purpose only. It is verified that every step is reachable and there are no deadlocks. We also verified that the tanks T_1 and T_3 are never filled and emptied at the same time. However, tank T_2 does not fulfill this requirement. The counter trace produced by CaSMV shows that both valves V_2 and V_4 may be open simultaneously. This happens because when entering step s_5 it is only required that step s_{12} is not active (NOT $s_{12}.X$), i.e., that filling T_2 does not start if it is already in the emptying phase. However, when entering s_{12} there is no condition that checks if the tank is still in the filling phase. Hence, the verification detected a flaw in the control program which is not obvious to see, and the counter trace helps to see why it happened and how to prevent it.

4   Model Checking of Timed SFC

In timed SFC, time specifications in the transition conditions and actions have to be considered. Timed action qualifiers can be recognized by the letter D for delayed actions and L for time-limited actions. Both can be combined with the "set" qualifier S. [2] defines five timed qualifiers: L, D, LS, SD, and DS. Timed transition conditions contain inequality expressions that compare a timer variable with a real-valued expression. In most cases, timer variables reference step timers which store the time elapsed since the corresponding step was activated the last time. Step timers are denoted by the step name extended with the suffix ".T". Finally, the PLC cycle itself affects the timed behavior of an SFC.

4.1   Timed Automata and Uppaal

In order to check the timing properties of a given SFC, it has to be transformed into a formalism that enables appropriate timed analysis based on automatic verification software. The timed automaton (TA) formalism satisfies this requirement and is used here. The graphical representation of TA consists of nodes that are called locations, and directed arcs that represent the discrete transitions [19]. The current state of a timed automaton is given by the current location together with the valuation of integer and clock variables. The valuations of all clock variables grow with the same rate corresponding to the progress of time; the only way to influence a clock variable is to reset it to zero by a transition assignment. Informally, the semantics of a TA can be understood such that (i) the TA can stay at most as long in the current location as an *invariant* (a condition for the clock values) is satisfied, (ii) a transition can be taken when a condition for the clock values called *guard* is fulfilled, and (iii) a transition can reset clocks.

We refer to the specific form of TA used within the verification tool UPPAAL [20,21]. In the UPPAAL language, a model consists of a collection of timed automata that can communicate via shared variables and channels. Channels are used to synchronize the processes, i.e., certain transitions of different automata can be forced to be taken synchronously. The channels have to be declared globally and are referenced in the synchronization labels of those transitions that are synchronized. In the synchronization label the name of the channel has to be followed either by an exclamation mark or by a question mark, indicating a sending or receiving role of the transition. Only two transitions can synchronize at a time using a binary channel. For this, one transition has to be sender and the other has to be receiver on the same channel. Non-deterministic situations occur when several senders and receivers may use a channel at the same time. Other elements specific to UPPAAL such as broadcast channels, urgent locations and committed locations will be explained in the context of the representation of SFC. For a formal definition of the UPPAAL language we refer to [19,22].

4.2   Representation of SFC in Uppaal

The UPPAAL tool includes a graphical user interface for modelling TA and for an interactive animation of the behavior. To make use of these features in verifying SFC programs, it is necessary to convey the structure of the SFC as far as possible to the TA domain, thus to enable the user to identify certain SFC components in the TA model. In the case of an SFC without parallel branches, as shown in Fig. 7(a), the complete structure of steps and transitions can be reproduced by the locations and the transitions of a single automaton. This even applies to complex SFC including nested loops and alternative branches. However, parallel branches as shown in Fig. 7(b) cannot be represented in one automaton such that the structure is preserved. Therefore, a connected group of parallel sequences is represented by one location in the embedding automaton, and additional automata represent the parallel branches. This will be explained in detail below. Note that the locations mentioned above do not represent the activity of steps but determine which steps are ready, i.e. they represent the union of history steps and active steps. To mark the set of active steps, additional Boolean variables are used with names which are composed of the step name and the suffix "_X".

The set of active actions is also represented by Boolean variables with names formed of the action name and the suffix "_Q". In the standard, a logic diagram including flip-flops, timers, and logical operations, defines how the value of an action variable has to be computed. The circuit can be divided into sections that independently model the dynamic behavior of the qualifiers P0, P1, S, L, D, LS, SD, and DS, and a section that describes the superposition of the results together with the qualifiers N and R. For each qualifier, a Boolean input denotes whether the qualifier is in use by the currently active steps or not. We use integer variables for modeling this. The name of such a variable is the concatenation of the action name and the qualifier symbol. The value of the variable determines the number of currently active steps that use the given combination of action and qualifier. The qualifier sections and the superposition section of the logic diagram are modelled by individual timed automata. Hence, for each action at least one and at most nine automata have to be instantiated depending one the qualifiers used in the SFC program.

Finally, we have to consider the PLC cycle semantics. This is achieved by an automaton that forces the other automata of the SFC program to execute their transitions in a fixed order. This *coordinator* also advances time in an appropriate way. To illustrate the interplay of all automata, consider the SFC given in Fig. 7(a) and the automatically generated timed automata in Fig. 8. The SFC program consists of one simple SFC without simultaneous sequences so

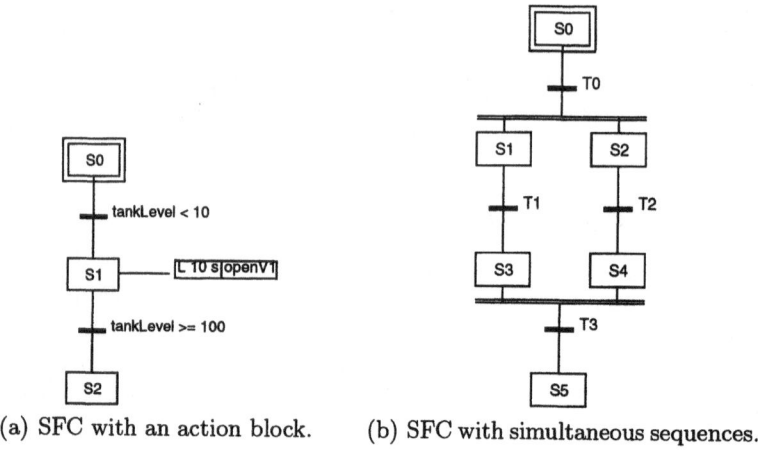

(a) SFC with an action block.   (b) SFC with simultaneous sequences.

Fig. 7. Two simple examples of SFC.

that only one automaton is needed to model the sequence of steps and transitions (Fig. 8(b)). The action block attached to the step S1 evokes the action openV1 with the qualifier L for a time-limited activity with a duration of 10 sec. For the action openV1 two automata are needed: one for the dynamic behavior of the L qualifier of openV1 (Fig. 8(c)) and one to compute the action activity variable openV1_Q (Fig. 8(d)). The automaton shown in Fig. 8(a) coordinates the other three automata in order to emulate the PLC cycle.

Coordinator. The coordinator forces the other components to perform their transitions in a fixed order by the use of binary synchronization channels with the prefix "call_". So-called committed locations, denoted by a "c", are used here to avoid any (non-deterministic) advance of time during the computations. Only in the location of the coordinator that is not marked as committed, the time progresses in order to model the delay between the PLC cycles. The maximum time delay of this location is given by the invariant on the clock variable c_tick that is reset when the location is entered. The minimum delay is given by the guard of the outgoing transition. Thus the delay is deterministic if both are equal.

Simple Step Sequence. Each step and each transition of the SFC has its counterpart in the step sequence automaton, i.e., whenever a transition is taken in the SFC, the corresponding transition in the TA is also taken. Note that the transitions of the automaton can only be taken if the corresponding step activity variables are true; this is important for subordinated SFC. An additional committed location is used to initialize the automaton of the top level SFC graph. Transitions with identical source and target location (self-loops) are necessary in order to prevent deadlocks since the coordinator has to synchronize with

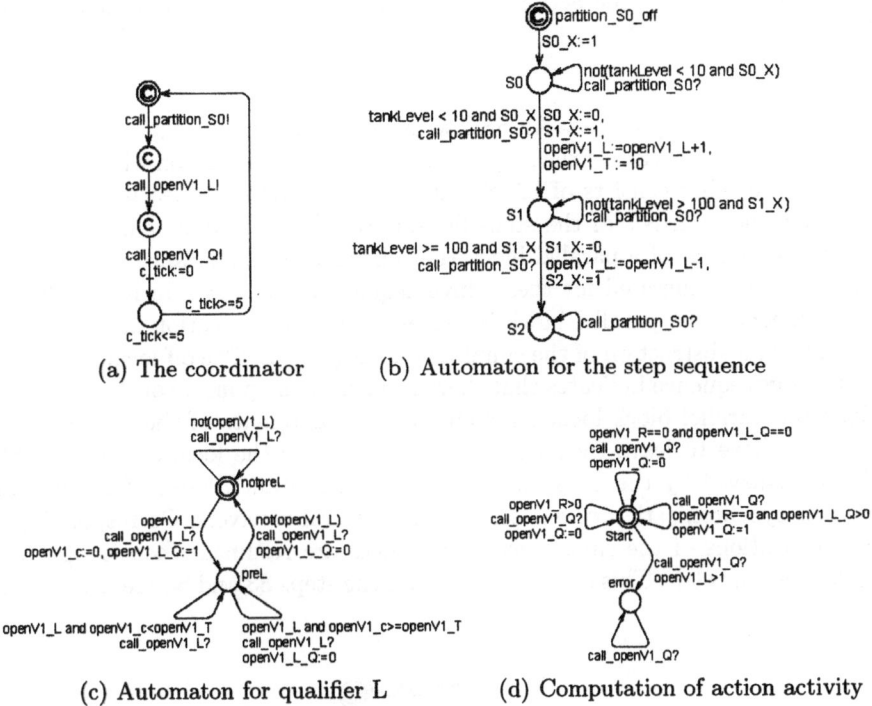

(a) The coordinator

(b) Automaton for the step sequence

(c) Automaton for qualifier L

(d) Computation of action activity

Fig. 8. Automata resulting from the SFC shown in Fig. 7(a).

every other automaton (even if the latter does not change its location). The step activity variables S0_X, S1_X, and S2_X are updated only when the current location changes. The action input variable openV1_L is incremented when the location S1 is entered, and decremented when it is left. An additional variable openV1_T conveys the duration parameter to the action automata.

Action Automata. Fig. 8(c) shows the automaton for the behavior of the L qualifier of the action openV1. openV1_c is the clock variable used for the time limiting function. When the integer variable openV1_L becomes greater than zero, the initial location is left, the clock is set to zero, and the output variable openV1_L_Q is set to true. The automaton returns to the initial location only when openV1_L becomes zero again. The output variable openV1_L_Q is set to false when the clock reaches the time limit or when openV1_L becomes zero before the time limit is reached. Fig. 8(d) shows the output automaton for the case that only the qualifier L appears in the SFC. The qualifiers R (reset) and N (not stored) are always included. Note that the reset qualifier has the highest priority. The automaton contains an error location in order to detect forbidden situations defined in the standard, e.g., it is not allowed that steps which reference the same action with a timed qualifier are active at the same time.

Simultaneous Sequences. An SFC with two simultaneous sequences is shown in Fig. 7(b): one consists of the steps S1 and S3 and the transition with the guard T1, and the other consists of S2, S4, and the transition labelled with T2. The main sequence consists of the steps S0 and S5, the transitions guarded by T0 and T3, as well as of a parallel block that encloses the simultaneous sequences. The automata generated for these three sequences are shown in Fig. 9. In the main sequence, the parallel block is represented by one location only, i.e., this location is an abstraction of the simultaneous sequences. The off location of a simultaneous sequence indicates that there is no ready step inside of the sequence. When the parallel block location is entered, the automata of the simultaneous sequences have to leave their off locations and enter the locations S1 and S2. This is achieved by the broadcast channel enter_ParallelBlock_S1S2 which allows the synchronization of one sender with several receivers. Correspondingly, the off locations of the simultaneous sequences are resumed when the parallel block location is left. This can only happen if the steps S3 and S4 are active. The

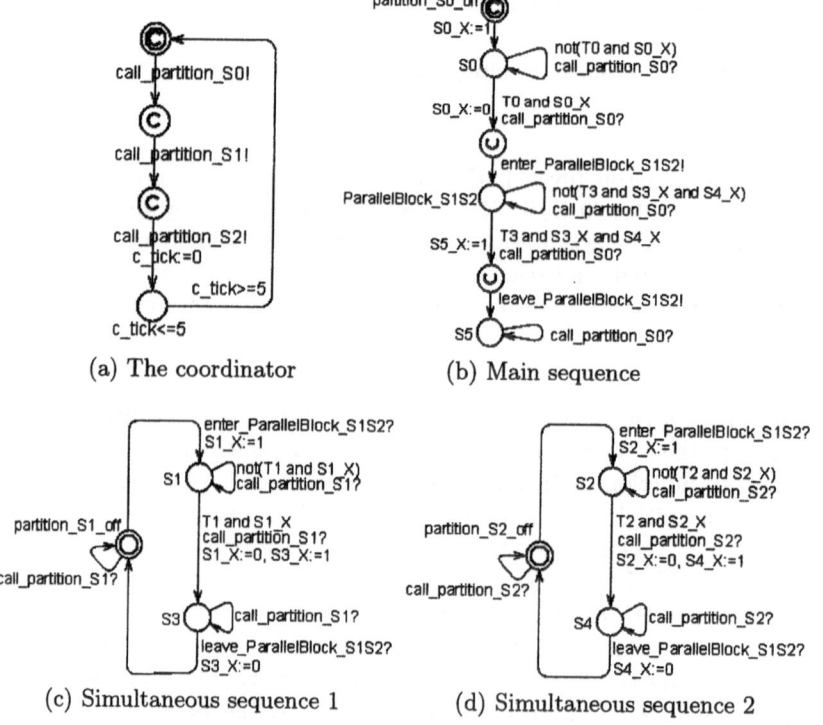

(a) The coordinator   (b) Main sequence

(c) Simultaneous sequence 1   (d) Simultaneous sequence 2

Fig. 9. Automata resulting from the SFC shown in Fig. 7(b).

urgent locations (denoted by an "u") before and after the parallel block location are necessary for the synchronization, since UPPAAL does not support multiple synchronization labels on one transition. Urgent locations have a lower priority than committed locations but are also left instantly.

Hierarchical SFC with History. Subordinated SFC are executed as long as the action they are associated with is active. Hence, it is necessary to deactivate and to activate a subordinated SFC depending on an action activity variable. This is achieved by additional self-loops. Assume that the simple SFC shown in Fig. 10 depends on the action activity variable SFC2_Q. At the beginning, the current location is S1, but the step activity variable S1_X is zero, which means that the step S1 is ready, but not active. The self-loops on the right hand side of the locations model the activation of the corresponding step by setting the step activity variable to one (and incrementing possible action reference variables). The self-loops on the left hand side of the automaton model the deactivation of the SFC by setting the step activity variable to zero (and decrementing possible action request variables). This implementation corresponds to hierarchy with history since the SFC resumes the last step that was activated before. For an implementation without history, all deactivation transitions must lead to the initial location.

4.3   Translation Procedure

We now describe the automatic generation of the UPPAAL model from the SFC.

Translation of Actions. First, all combinations of action names and qualifier symbols that appear in the action blocks of the steps have to be retrieved from the given SFC. For each combination, a corresponding qualifier automaton has to be instantiated (except for the qualifiers N and R), and an action reference variable is declared. In addition, an action control automaton is created for each action.

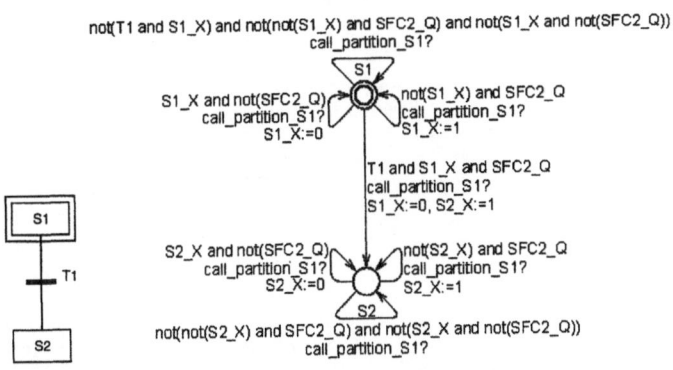

Fig. 10. The SFC associated to the action "SFC2" and the corresponding automaton.

Translation of Charts. The most difficult task in the translation of an SFC program is to identify the simultaneous sequences and to reject malformed charts. A possibility to achieve this in a reliable way even for complex charts containing nested simultaneous sequences (as shown in Fig. 11(a)), entwined loops, and alternative branches is the use of graph grammars [23]. The graph grammar shown in Tab. 1 consists of a set of transformation rules that are applied iteratively to the given chart in order to reduce the graph. The left hand side pattern of a rule defines the situation in which the rule can be applied, and the right hand side gives the result of the transformation. For example, applying the first rule requires an initial step of the chart, and applying the rule replaces the initial by a partition node. In our implementation of the corresponding SFC parser, a rule is always applied to all matching patterns of the graph, before applying another rule. The rules are applied from the first to the sixth, before the procedure continues again with the first one until no further rule can be applied anymore. If the final graph contains only one partition node, the parsing was successful, if not the SFC contains a syntactical error (as, e.g., that two simultaneous sequences lead into a single step).

For illustration, consider the example shown in Fig. 11, and the following sequence of rules:

- rule 1: replace S0 by partition node P0
- rule 2: replace S1 by P1, replace S2 by P2, replace S3 by P3 ($\rightarrow$ Fig. 11(b))
- rule 3: P1 takes T1 and S4, P2 takes T2-S5, P3 takes T3-S6 ($\rightarrow$ Fig. 11(c))
- rule 6: replace P1 and P2 by PB-Step1 ($\rightarrow$ Fig. 11(d))
- rule 2: replace PB-Step1 by partition node P4

Table 1. Parse grammar for SFC graphs.

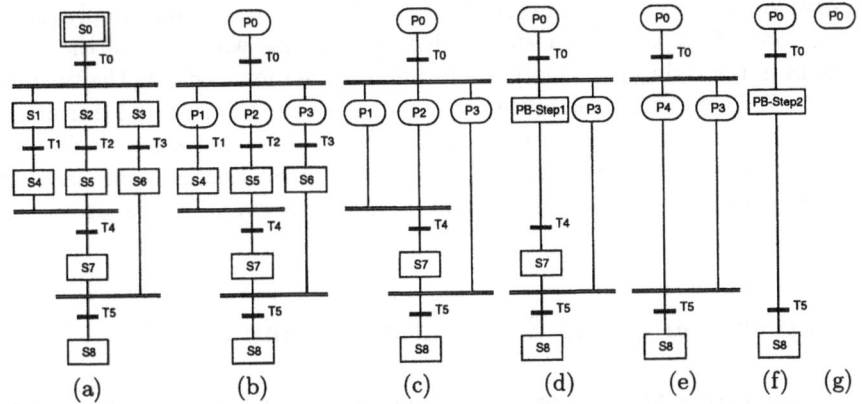

Fig. 11. Successive reduction of a complex SFC graph.

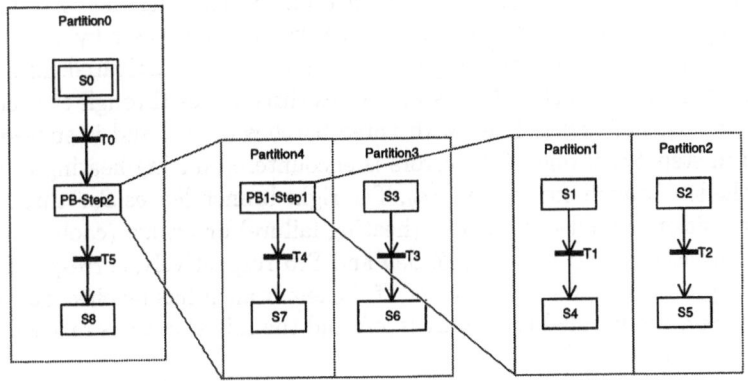

Fig. 12. The identified partitions of the given SFC.

- rule 3: P4 takes T4 and S7 ($\rightarrow$ Fig. 11(e))
- rule 5: replace P4 and P3 by PB-Step2 ($\rightarrow$ Fig. 11(f))
- rule 3: P0 takes T0 and PB-Step2, P0 takes T5 and S8 ($\rightarrow$ Fig. 11(g)).

The partition nodes represent the (nested) simultaneous sequences and the main sequence of the graph. The steps and transitions that belong to a partition are those which are removed by the corresponding transformation step. In the case of a successful transformation, the identified partitions (Fig. 12) are used for the generation of the timed automata: for each partition, a separate automaton is introduced such that the steps and SFC transitions contained in the partition are mapped directly into locations and transitions of the automaton. Depending on whether the SFC graph belongs to the top level or a lower level, and whether the partition contains the initial step or not, different elements such as self-loops, additional locations, etc., are added to the graphs similar to the automata shown in Fig. 9 and Fig. 10.

Generation of the Coordinator. The coordinating automaton simply establishes a loop of steps and transitions that synchronize with each of the other automata in the right order. Only one location is used for modeling the time delay of the PLC cycle. The algorithm that generates all locations and transitions considers the fact that the qualifier automata have to be executed before the corresponding action control automaton. The order of executing the partition automata does not influence the resulting state of the overall model at the end of a cycle.

5   Application to the Evaporation Example

The method described in the previous section is now applied to the evaporation example introduced in Sect. 2. The SFC shown in Fig. 3 realizes the desired operation in the following sense: In the initial step *S0*, the valves *V1*, *V2*, and *V3* are closed and the heater *H1* is switched off by resetting the corresponding Boolean variables. *S0* is left when an input variable *start* is set by an operator, and two parallel branches (starting with *S1* and *Se1*) are activated. In nominal operation (the left branch), the system cycles three times through the sequence from *S1* to *S4*, i.e., *T2* is filled with three batches of *T1*, and is subsequently emptied in step *S5*. If one of the errors is encountered during heating or evaporation, the left branch enters step *Se4*. The right branch leaves *Se1* through one of the transitions labelled by *error1* (heating failure) or *error2* (cooling failure). The actions assigned to *Se2*, or *Se3*, *Se5* and *Se6* respectively, correspond to the exception procedures described above. If the left branch has reached *S6* and the right one *Se7*, the parallel branching is left and the initial state is reached again.

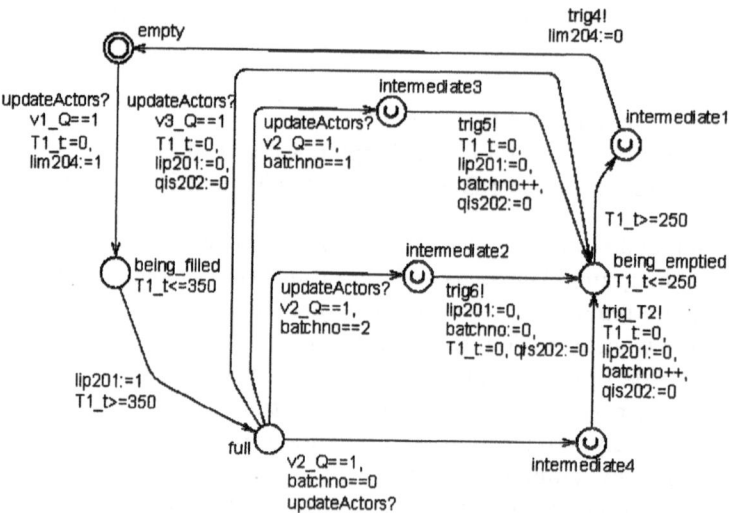

Fig. 13. TA model of the level in tank *T1*.

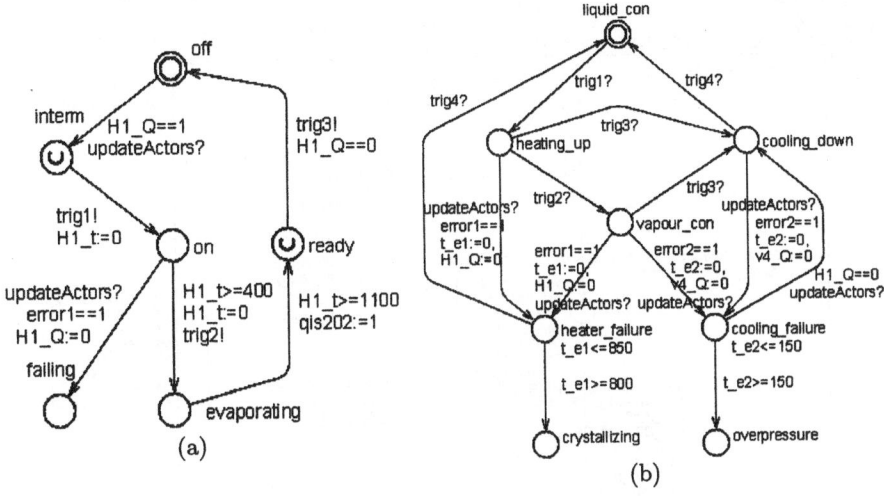

Fig. 14. TA models for the heater *H1* (a) and the state of aggregation of the fluid in *T1* (b).

As mentioned in Sect. 2, the objective of verifying that the temperature in *T1* does never exceed a maximum or minimum value (leading to overpressure or to crystallization in *T1*), requires to consider the plant behavior. We employ a model consisting of one TA each to represent the fluid level of tank *T1*, the level of tank *T2*, the heating effect of the heater *H1*, the state of aggregation of the fluid in *T1*, the mode of operation of the condenser, and an additional automaton that models the occurrence of a failure of the heater or of the condenser. Three of these automata are exemplarily shown in Fig. 13 and 14.

In all cases, the transition times between two events are determined based on measurements for the corresponding laboratory plant, e.g. *T1* is filled in 350 sec (compare to the invariant of the location *being_filled* in Fig. 13). The communication among the plant automata and with the controller automata is realized by synchronization labels and integer variables used in the guard conditions of transitions. The automaton in Fig. 14(b) contains two unsafe plant states, *crystallizing* and *overpressure*, the reachability of which is checked in the verification. It is assumed that the liquid in *T1* crystallizes between 800 and 850 sec after a failure of *H1* occurs, and that the pressure in the evaporator exceeds a critical limit 150 seconds after a cooling failure if heating is continued.

The plant model is composed with the automata generated by the automatic transformation procedure described in Sect. 4. The transformation of the SFC program shown in Fig. 3 yielded 22 automata overall. Three of these correspond to the partitions obtained from applying the rules of the graph grammar. The partition that corresponds to the error handling (the right branch in Fig. 3) is shown in Fig. 15. Another 18 automata represent the action qualifiers, and the model is completed by the coordinator automaton. The relatively large number

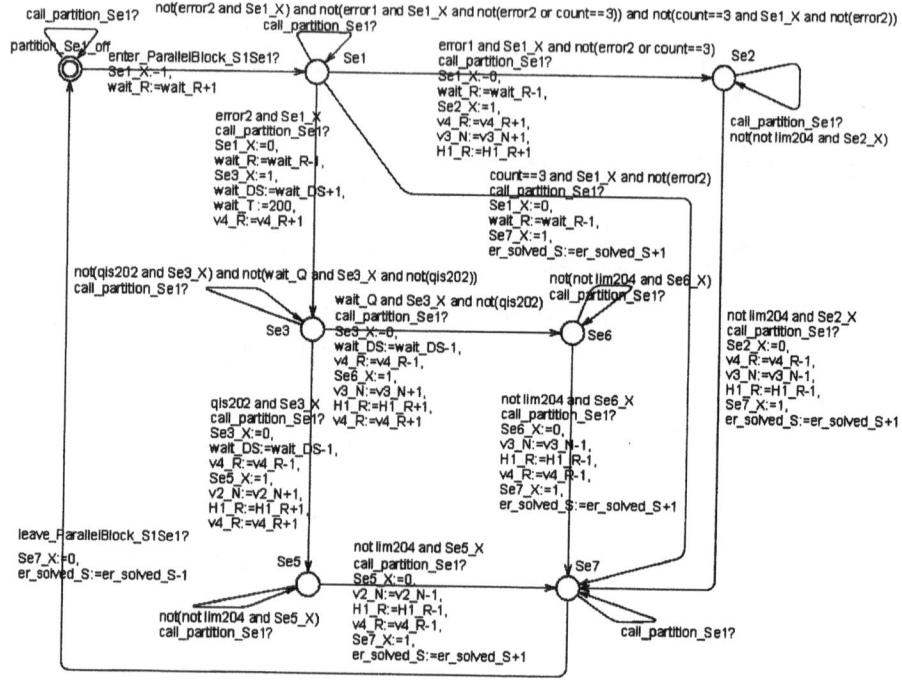

Fig. 15. TA-model of the controller branch for error handling.

of automata is a result of the precise emulation of the PLC behavior. However, the overall number of locations is rather small (111), the number of clocks is moderate (10), and the controller part of the model is completely deterministic.

We first verify the safety requirement that the system must never reach the states *crystallizing* and *overpressure* (according to requirement (b) in Sect. 2). On a PC with a 1000 MHz-Duron processor, the analysis with UPPAAL (version 3.4) terminates after less than 10 seconds with the result that both states are not reachable, i.e. the controller is designed correctly with respect to the safety requirement. To verify that the controller realizes the desired production cycle (requirement (a)), we analyze for the plant automaton of the tank *T2* whether the state *emptied* is reachable after the tank was filled. For illustration, a relatively large PLC cycle time of 50 sec was chosen for these experiments. This analysis terminates after approx. 15 minutes with the result that the state is reachable. The difference in computation time for both experiments is due to the different length of the traces that lead to the final states for the two requirements.

6   Conclusions

The benefits of the approach presented here are (i) it starts from a controller representation that is a de-facto standard for specifying PLC programs in industry, and (ii) the procedure is completely algorithmic once the SFC controller, the formal requirements, and the plant model are available. The steps of designing the SFC controller, obtaining the plant model, and correcting the design in case of a negative verification result, can obviously not be accomplished completely algorithmically. Our current aim is, however, to develop a scheme to derive the SFC program systematically from the set of specifications (usually given in natural language). When applying the approach described here, an important issue is to employ a plant model of sufficient accuracy. At least for chemical processing systems, we have experienced that FSA models are often not sufficient to verify the exclusion of safety-relevant plant states. The use of TA models is appropriate if the transition times between certain events can be estimated (or measured) accurately and conservatively. If this is not possible, one can start from hybrid dynamical models and derive TA algorithmically, e.g., by the procedures described in [24].

The choice of the plant model but also the level of detail of the controller model determines the complexity of the verification task. A system of the size of the example in Sect. 5 can be verified in a few minutes. It should be mentioned, however, that the main complexity here arises from the fact that the PLC cycle is mapped into the TA model. To reduce this source of complexity we currently investigate how to separate the verification of requirements for which the cyclic operation is relevant from the analysis of those for which it is not.

Acknowledgments. This work was financially supported by the German Research Council (DFG) within the priority program *Integration of Software Specification Techniques for Applications in Engineering* under the grants EN 152/32-2 and RO 1122/10-2. Nanette Bauer contributed to this work during her time at the Process Control Lab, University of Dortmund. National ICT Australia is funded through the Australian Government's *Backing Australia's Ability initiative,* in part through the Australian Research Council.

References

1. Lewis, R.: Programming industrial control systems using IEC 61131-3. IEE (1998)
2. International Electrotechnical Commission, Technical Committee No. 65: Programmable Controllers – Programming Languages, IEC 61131-3. (2003) Ed. 2.0.
3. Moon, I., Powers, G.J., Burch, J.R., Clarke, E.M.: Automatic verification of sequential control systems using temporal logic. AIChE Journal **38** (1992) 67–75
4. Kowalewski, S., Engell, S., Preussig, J., Stursberg, O.: Verification of logic controllers for continuous plants using timed condition/event system models. Automatica **35** (1999) 505–518
5. Lampérière, S., Lesage, J.J.: Formal verification of the sequential part of PLC programs. In Boel, R., Stremersch, G., eds.: Discrete Event Systems, Kluwer Academic Publishers (2000) 247–254
6. Bauer, N., Huuck, R.: Towards automatic verification of embedded control software. In: Proc. 2nd Asia-Pacific Conf. on Quality Software. (2001) 561–567

7. Clarke, E., Wing, J.: Formal methods: State of the art and future directions. ACM Computing Surveys **28** (1996) 626–643
8. Clarke, E., Grumberg, O., Peled, D.: Model Checking. MIT Press (1999)
9. Fujino, K., Imafuku, K., Yamashita, Y., Nishitani, H.: Design and verification of the SFC program for sequential control. Comp. Chem. Eng. **24** (2000) 303 – 308
10. L'Her, P., Scharbarg, J., Le Parc, P., Marce, L.: Proving sequential function chart programs using automata. LNCS **1660** (1998) 149 – 163
11. Bornot, S., Huuck, R., Lakhnech, Y., Lukoschus, B.: Verification of sequential function charts using SMV. In: Proc. Int. Conf. on Parallel and Distributed Processing Techniques and Applications. (2000) 2987–2993
12. McMillan, K.: The SMV Language. Cadence Berkeley Labs. (1999) http://www-cad.eecs.berkeley.edu/kenmcmil/language.ps.
13. Burch, J.R., Clarke, E.M., McMillan, K.L., Dill, D.L., Hwang, L.: Symbolic model checking: 10^{20} states and beyond. Information and Comp. **98** (1992) 142–170
14. Havelund, K., Larsen, K., Skou, A.: Formal verification of a power controller using the real-time model checker UPPAAL2K. In: Proc. 5th AMAST Workshop, ARTS'99. (1999) 277–298
15. Bauer, N., Huuck, R., Lukoschus, B., Engell, S.: A unifying semantics for sequential function charts. In: This volume. (2004)
16. Clarke, E., Emerson, E.: Synthesis of synchronisation skeletons for branching time temporal logic. In Kozen, D., ed.: Workshop on Logic of Programs. Volume 131 of LNCS., Springer-Verlag (1982) 52–71
17. Queille, J., Sifakis, J.: Specification and verification of concurrent systems in CE-SAR. In: 5th Int. Symp. on Progr. Volume 137 of LNCS., Springer-Verlag (1982) 337–350
18. Bauer, N., Kowalewski, S., Sand, G., Löhl, T.: A case study: Multi product batch plant for the demonstration of control and scheduling problems. In: Proc. Analysis and Design of Mixed Processes. (2000) 383–388
19. Larsen, K.G., Pettersson, P., Yi, W.: Compositional and Symbolic Model-Checking of Real-Time Systems. In: Proc. of the 16th IEEE Real-Time Systems Symposium, IEEE Computer Society Press (1995) 76–87
20. Behrmann, G., David, A., Larsen, K.G., M ller, O., Pettersson, P., Yi, W.: UPPAAL – present and future. In: Proc. of 40th IEEE Conference on Decision and Control, IEEE Computer Society Press (2001)
21. Larsen, K.G., Pettersson, P., Yi, W.: UPPAAL in a Nutshell. Int. Journal on Software Tools for Technology Transfer **1** (1997) 134–152
22. Aceto, L., Bergueno, A., Larsen, K.G.: Model Checking via Reachability Testing for Timed Automata. In: Proc. 4th Int. Workshop on Tools and Algo. for the Constr. and Analysis of Systems. Volume 1384 of LNCS., Springer-Verlag (1995) 263–280
23. Ehrig, H., Engels, G., Kreowski, H.J., Rozenberg, G.: Handbook of graph grammars and computing by graph transformation: vol. 2: applications, languages, and tools. World Scientific Publishing Co., Inc. (1999)
24. Stursberg, O.: Analysis of switched continuous systems based on discretization. In: Proc. 4th Int. Conf. on Automation of Mixed Processes. (2000) 73–78

Modeling and Formal Verification
of Production Automation Systems[*]

Jürgen Ruf, Roland J. Weiss, Thomas Kropf, and Wolfgang Rosenstiel

Wilhelm-Schickard-Institut für Informatik, Universität Tübingen
Sand 13, 72076 Tübingen, Germany
{ruf,weissr,kropf,rosenstiel}@informatik.uni-tuebingen.de

Abstract. This paper presents the real-time model checker RAVEN and
related theoretical background. RAVEN augments the efficiency of traditional symbolic model checking with possibilities to describe real-time
systems. These extensions rely on multi-terminal binary decision diagrams to represent time delays and time intervals. The temporal logic
CCTL is used to specify properties with time constraints. Another noteworthy feature of our model checker is its ability to compose a system
description out of communicating modules, so called I/O-interval structures. This modular approach to system description alleviates the om-
nipresent state explosion problem common to all model checking tools.
The case study of a holonic[1] material transport system demonstrates how
such a production automation system can be modeled in our system. We
devise a detailed model of all components present in the described system. This model serves as basis for checking real-time properties of the
system as well as for computing key properties like system latencies and
minimal response times. A translation of the original model also allows
application of another time bounded property checker for verification of
the holonic production system. Finally, we present an approach combining simulation and formal verification that operates on the same system
model. It enables verification of larger designs at the cost of reduced
coverage. Only critical states detected during simulation runs are further subjected to exhaustive model checking. We contrast the runtimes
and results of our different approaches.

1 Introduction

Real-time systems pervade almost every aspect of our daily life. Accelerating
a contemporary vehicle initiates a plethora of processes involving micro controllers: fuel injection should be optimized for economical fuel usage and for
smooth engine operation, wheelspinning should be avoided based on data provided by special sensors, and so on. The same applies to aerospace industry,

---

[*] The results described in this article have been achieved in the course of the DFG
project GRASP within the DFG Priority Programme 1064.

[1] A holon is an autonomous and cooperative unit of a manufacturing system for transforming, transporting, storing and/or validating information and physical objects.

H. Ehrig et al. (Eds.): INT 2004, LNCS 3147, pp. 541–566, 2004.
© Springer-Verlag Berlin Heidelberg 2004

medical systems, home entertainment, telecommunication, large-scale industrial manufacturing, and of course the classical computer industry. Even in outdoor activities we rely on integrated circuits in equipment like avalanche transceivers and GPS receivers.

Establishing the correctness of these systems poses an increasingly difficult and time-consuming challenge in the design process. Two aspects primarily motivate the significance of the verification process:

Safety-critical systems. These systems mandate error-free operation because malfunctioning could endanger human life or the environment. Obviously, an erroneous circuit in a car controller unit constitutes a major threat for passengers and road users.

Economic risks. It is of primary importance to detect design errors in early stages of the development process. Once a hardware chip is shipped, it becomes extremely expensive to fix an overlooked fault. The Pentium floating point bug has cost Intel millions of dollars because of an insufficient verification process.

The ever increasing system complexity and shorter development cycles make verification the bottleneck in the design process. Nowadays, verification consumes up to 80% of the development time.

Simulation of the design under verification is the predominating validation technique. A testbench provides an executable model with stimuli and monitors the resulting outputs. However, for large systems simulation cannot provide a complete coverage of the system. Simulation time is becoming a prohibiting factor.

This has ignited interest in formal methods that can provide better coverage and run more efficiently in certain scenarios. Equivalence checking has become state of the art in verifying evolutionary changes in designs even for very large hardware circuits.

However, if no *golden design* exists, this technique is not applicable. Formal property checking is bridging this gap. Property checking tools try to automatically prove properties extracted from the design description against a system model, or to generate a counter example trace if the property is violated.

In this paper we present a toolset that offers the verification engineer various options for verifying real-time systems. Special emphasis is put on realizing solutions that deal with the timing aspect of these systems. We exemplify our approaches with a holonic material transport system, because production automation systems make up an important application area for real-time systems.

The rest of this paper is structured as follows. Next we present our formal model of timed systems, followed by an introduction to temporal logics for specifying real-time properties and algorithms for model checking such properties. Thereafter, the outline of our toolchain is sketched and we explain our tools in more detail. Afterward, we describe the model of a material transportation system and how our tools can help to gain confidence in the system model. We give some experimental results and conclude.

2   Formal Model of Timed Systems

A crucial property of production automation systems is the ability to express time constraints. Furthermore, it is desirable to compose a system's model out of multiple components. Our formal model of timed systems is an extension of traditional Kripke structures, which are commonly used to describe reactive systems [1].

2.1   Interval Structures

Interval structures are based on Kripke structures. We use the notion of clocks to represent time. Every structure of our system contains exactly one clock representing time from a discrete domain. A clock is reset if a transition fires.

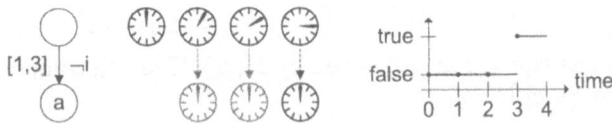

Fig. 1. Example interval structure. Delay times δ_i on timed tranisitions are required to be positive integers, i.e. $\delta_i > 0$. Arrows at clocks indicate possible transitions, and the black arrow indicates the nondeterministically chosen one. The timing diagram reflects this behavior.

Fig. 1 shows a simple interval structure on the left-hand side. Clocks depict the progress of time for this interval structure, and where applicable the clocks are associated with possible state transitions symbolized by arrows. Finally, the figure contains the timing diagram for atomic proposition a when the last transition out of three possible transitions is taken.

Definition 1. An interval structure $\Im$ is a tuple $\Im = (P, S, S_0, T, L, I)$ with a set of atomic propositions P, a set of states S, a set of initial states S_0, a transition relation between the states $T \subseteq S \times S$ such that every state in S has a successor state, a state labeling function $L : S \mapsto \wp(P)$ and a transition labeling function $I : T \mapsto \wp(\mathbb{N})$.

The only difference to Kripke structures are the transitions which are labeled with delay times (not restricted to intervals). Every state of the interval structure must be left at the latest after the *maximal state time*.

Definition 2. The maximal state time of a state s is the maximal delay time $maxTime : S \mapsto \mathbb{N}$ of all outgoing transitions of s, i.e.

$$maxTime(s) := \max \{t \mid \exists s'.(s, s') \in T \wedge t = \max(I(s, s'))\}. \tag{1}$$

We also have to consider the elapsed time to determine the transition behavior of the system. Hence, the actual configuration of a system is given by pairs consisting of a state s and the actual clock value v.

Definition 3. A configuration $g = (s, v)$ is a state s associated with a clock value v. The set of all configurations of an interval structure $\Im = (P, S, S_0, T, L, I)$ is given by:

$$G = \{(s, v) \mid s \in S \wedge 0 \leq v < maxTime(s)\} \tag{2}$$

The semantics of interval structures is given by runs which are the counterparts of paths in Kripke structures.

Definition 4. Given the interval structure $\Im = (P, S, S_0, T, L, I)$ and a starting configuration $g_0 \in G$. A run is a sequence of configurations $r = (g_0, g_1, ...)$. For all $g_j = (s_j, v_j) \in G$ it holds that either

- $g_{j+1} = (s_j, v_j + 1)$ with $v_j + 1 < maxTime(s_j)$ or
- $g_{j+1} = (s_{j+1}, 0)$ with $(s_j, s_{j+1}) \in T \wedge v_j + 1 \in I(s_j, s_{j+1})$.

The set of all runs starting in g_0 is given by $\Pi(g_0)$. The i-th component of a run can be accessed by $g[i] := g_i$.

The semantics of an interval structure can also be given in terms of Kripke structures. The Kripke structure corresponding to an interval structure is obtained with a stutter state expansion operation transforming an interval structure into a Kripke structure. For every timed transition, this operation introduces new stutter states and connects them in a chain like fashion. These chains are connected with the original states of the interval structure. In the Kripke structure we call these states main states (in contrast to stutter states). Stutter state exapansion is visualized in Fig. 2.

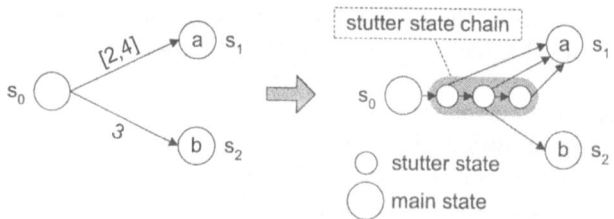

Fig. 2. Expansion of interval structure to Kripke structure.

The symbolic representation of interval structures is realized by extended characteristic functions. We group together all configurations containing the same interval structure state and map this state to the set of the corresponding clock values. All other states are mapped to $\emptyset$. For the symbolic representation of the transition relation, we map pairs of states to the set of corresponding delay times.

2.2 I/O-Interval Structures

Interval structures are well suited for modeling single real-time processes, but less for systems consisting of several components. Interval structures have no explicit input variables, i.e., if different interval structures communicate with each other, they have to share state variables. I/O-interval structures are better suited for modeling communicating processes. However, the result of composing I/O-interval structures is again one interval structure, the latter being better suited for model checking.

I/O-interval structures have a set of dedicated input variables P_{in}. Transitions are labeled with Boolean conditions with regard to these inputs. Input conditions have to hold during the corresponding transition times, i.e., input insensitive edges carry the formula *true*.

We formalize Boolean formulas using sets of allowed values for the input variables. An element of the set $Inp := \wp(P_{in})$ defines exactly one value for each input variable: the propositions contained in the set are *true*, all others are *false*. Hence, an element of the set $\wp(P_{in})$ defines all possible combinations of input values for one edge. For example, given the inputs a and b, the set $\{\{a\}, \{a, b\}\}$ is represented by the Boolean function $(a \wedge \neg b) \vee (a \wedge b) = a$. This example shows that the variable b does not affect the formula, i.e., the transition labeled with the formula a may be taken independently from input b.

Definition 5. An I/O-interval structure $\Im_{I/O}$ is defined by a tuple $\Im_{I/O} = (P, P_{in}, S, S_0, T, L, I, L_{in})$. The components P, S, S_0, L and I are defined analogously to interval structures, P_{in} is a finite set of atomic input propositions, the transition relation $T \subseteq S \times S$ connects pairs of states, and $L_{in} : T \mapsto \wp(Inp)$ is a transition input labeling function.

To access the first (second) state of a transition $t \in S \times S$ we write $t[1]$ ($t[2]$). This access operator is defined for all elements consisting of multiple components. We assume the following restriction on the input labeling:

$$\forall t_1, t_2 \in T. \left(\begin{array}{c} (t_1[1] = t_2[1] \wedge t_1 \neq t_2) \rightarrow \\ (L_{in}(t_1) = L_{in}(t_2) \vee L_{in}(t_1) \cap L_{in}(t_2) = \emptyset) \end{array} \right) \qquad (3)$$

Formula (3) ensures that if there exist several edges starting in the same state, then their input restrictions are either equal or disjoint. Thus, input valuations on timed edges build clusters, i.e., disjoint sets of input values. All clusters of one state are disjoint, i.e., each valuation of input variables is a representative of its cluster. This condition is important to ensure an efficient translation of I/O-interval structures into Kripke structures for composition. For every cluster we have to introduce a separate chain of stutter states.

Definition 6. The cluster function $C : S \times Inp \mapsto \wp(Inp)$ computes all input valuations of a cluster represented by an arbitrary member (input valuation) of the cluster

$$C(s, i) := \begin{cases} L_{in}(s, s') & \text{if } \exists s' \in S.(s, s') \in T \wedge i \in L_{in}(s, s') \\ \emptyset & \text{otherwise} \end{cases} . \qquad (4)$$

Now we describe the semantics of the I/O-interval structures by defining runs. We first need the maximal state time.

Definition 7. The maximal state time $maxTime : S \times Inp \mapsto \mathbb{N}$ is the maximal delay time of all outgoing transitions with respect to the input cluster.

$$maxTime(s, i) := \\ \max \{v \mid \exists s' \in S.(s, s') \in T \wedge i \in L_{in}(s, s') \wedge v \in \max(I(s, s'))\} \quad (5)$$

Configurations in I/O-interval structures consist of the actual state, the elapsed time, and the actual input values.

Definition 8. A configuration $g = (s, i, v)$ of an I/O-interval structure is a state s associated with an input valuation $i \in Inp$ and a clock value v. The set of all configurations of an I/O-interval structure is given by:

$$G = \{(s, i, v) \mid s \in S \wedge i \in C(s) \wedge v < maxTime(s, i)\} \quad (6)$$

Definition 9. Let $\Im_{I/O} = (P, P_{in}, S, S_0, T, L, I, L_{in})$ be an I/O-interval structure. A run is a sequence of configurations $r = (g_0, g_1, ...)$ with $g_j = (s_j, i_j, v_j) \in G$ and for all j it holds that either

- $g_{j+1} = (s_j, i_{j+1}, v_j + 1)$ with $v_j + 1 < maxTime(s_j, i_j) \wedge i_{j+1} \in C(s_j, i_j)$ or
- $g_{j+1} = (s_{j+1}, i_{j+1}, 0)$ with $t = (s_j, s_{j+1}) \in T \wedge v_j + 1 \in I(t) \wedge i_{j+1} \in P_{in}$.

We assume that for every configuration and for every input valuation there exists a successor configuration. Hence, for edges with delay times greater than one there has to be a fail state which is visited if the actual input does not fulfill the current input restriction and the delay time is not reached. This implies that transitions either have no input restriction or, if a transition with delay time δ has an input restriction $f(a_1, ..., a_n)$, there must exist a transition with interval $[1, \delta - 1]$ and input condition $\neg f(a_1, ..., a_n)$ which connects the starting state with the fail state. For unit-delay edges we have to ensure that for all input evaluations there exists a successor state.

We use a graphical notation for I/O-interval structure as shown in Fig. 3. Variables a_i represent the inputs of the modeled sub-system, and f denotes a function $f : P_{in}^n \mapsto \mathbb{B}$. We omit the delay time if $\delta_1 = \delta_2 = 1$.

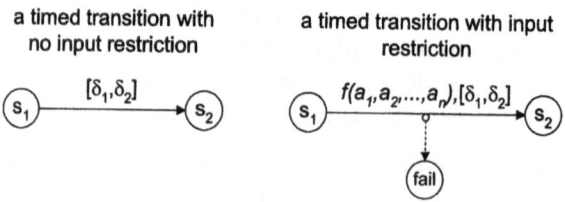

Fig. 3. Graphical notation for I/O-interval structures.

3   Property Specification with Real-Time Temporal Logics

In the previous section we have detailed our formalism called I/O-interval structures for describing timed system models. On these models, we want to check or prove real-time properties.

We are mainly dealing with reactive systems, and temporal logic is a formalism for describing transition sequences in such systems. A temporal logic provides *path quantifiers* A (all) and E (exists), and *temporal operators* X (next), F (eventually/in the future), G (globally), and U (until) additional to the typical boolean connectives.

The most widely used temporal logics in model checking and related formal verification techniques are *Computation Tree Logic* (CTL) and *Linear Temporal Logic* (LTL). Both describe overlapping subsets of CTL*, i.e. CTL* is expressive enough to state all formulas from LTL and CTL, but there exist formulas in LTL that are not expressible in CTL and vice versa. For a more detailed discussion on these fundamental temporal logics refer to chapter 3 in [1].

A major characteristic of temporal languages is the underlying model of time. In branching temporal logics, a moment in time can branch into various futures. Thus, infinite computation trees describe the systems that are subject to property checking. CTL is one such temporal logic, and it is well suited for algorithmic verification. Checking a transition system against a property given in CTL takes time linear in the length of the property specification. However, in linear temporal logics like LTL each moment in time has only one possible future. Therefore, formulas in linear temporal logics are interpreted over linear sequences that describe one computation of a system. Model checking takes time exponential in the length of a LTL specification. However, LTL is commonly regarded as more intuitive. Furthermore, dynamic validation is inherently linear as computation sequences are generated. This allows linear temporal logic specifications to be used in contexts ranging from dynamic validation to full formal verification. A thorough discussion on the trade-offs between branching and linear temporal logics is presented in [2].

All these logics have in common that they express time only implicitly, e.g. a property specifies that a state is eventually or never reached. However, real-time systems such as production automation systems often require conformance to strict time bounds. Time constraints are very important to maximize throughput times and to minimize wait times of workpieces. But furthermore, timing constraints also have a safety aspect, since the movements in such a production automation system consume time, they have to be scheduled such that no accident occurs.

In order to make time constraints explicit in property specifications we have introduced a variant of CTL called *Clocked CTL* (CCTL), and a variant of LTL called *Finite Linear Time Temporal Logic* (FLTL). We will briefly describe these two temporal logics in this section.

3.1   CCTL

CCTL [3] is a temporal logic extending CTL with quantitative bounded temporal operators. In contrast to CTL its semantics is defined over interval structures and it contains two new operators which make the specification of timed properties easier. It is a variant of RTCTL [4] adapted to our needs. The syntax of CCTL is the following:

Definition 10. Let P be a set of atomic propositions, $m \in \mathbb{N}$, and $n \in \mathbb{N} \cup \{\infty\}$. The set of all syntactically correct CCTL formulas is the smallest set satisfying the following properties:

- $P \subseteq \mathcal{F}_{CCTL}$
- if $\phi, \psi \in \mathcal{F}_{CCTL}$, then also $\neg\phi, \phi \wedge \psi, \phi \vee \psi, \phi \rightarrow \psi, \phi \leftrightarrow \psi \in \mathcal{F}_{CCTL}$
- if $\phi, \psi \in \mathcal{F}_{CCTL}$, then also
  $\mathsf{AX}_{[m]}\phi, \mathsf{AG}_{[m,n]}\phi, \mathsf{AF}_{[m,n]}\phi, \mathsf{A}(\phi\mathsf{U}_{[m,n]}\psi), \mathsf{A}(\phi\mathsf{C}_{[m]}\psi), \mathsf{A}(\phi\mathsf{S}_{[m]}\psi) \in \mathcal{F}_{CCTL}$
- if $\phi, \psi \in \mathcal{F}_{CCTL}$, then also
  $\mathsf{EX}_{[m]}\phi, \mathsf{EG}_{[m,n]}\phi, \mathsf{EF}_{[m,n]}\phi, \mathsf{E}(\phi\mathsf{U}_{[m,n]}\psi), \mathsf{E}(\phi\mathsf{C}_{[m]}\psi), \mathsf{E}(\phi\mathsf{S}_{[m]}\psi) \in \mathcal{F}_{CCTL}$

We also support the temporal operators C (conditional) and S (successor). Operator C requires formula ψ to hold if ϕ was true in the previous $m-1$ steps, and operator S is a special case of operator U with $m = n$.

All interval operators can also be used with a single time-bound. In this case the lower bound is set to zero by default. If no interval is specified, the lower bound is implicitly set to zero and the upper bound is set to infinity. If the EX-operator has no time bound, it is implicitly set to one. A definition of the formal semantics of CCTL is given in [5].

Example: Signals a and b will become true simultaneously in the next 30 time steps: $\mathsf{EF}_{[30]}a \wedge b$.

3.2   FLTL

FLTL extends LTL with bounded temporal operators. The main difference however lies in the definition of the formal semantics. LTL is defined over infinite sequences, whereas FLTL is defined over finite sequences. The reason for defining FLTL over finite state sequences comes from its application in simulation for validating formal properties. A simulation run always generates only a finite trace of the system's behavior. If the simulation terminates one does still like to argue about the specification's state, i.e. if the formula holds or not. Because this predication is not always decidable with finite sequences, the definition of the formal semantics of FLTL applies a third state: *pending*. For a detailed discussion and definition of the semantics of FLTL refer to [6].

Definition 11. Let P be a set of atomic propositions, $m \in \mathbb{N}$, and $n \in \mathbb{N} \cup \{\infty\}$. The set of all syntactically correct FLTL formulas is the smallest set satisfying the following properties:

- $P \subseteq \mathcal{F}_{FLTL}$
- if $\phi, \psi \in \mathcal{F}_{FLTL}$, then also $\neg\phi, \phi \wedge \psi, \phi \vee \psi, \phi \rightarrow \psi, \phi \leftrightarrow \psi \in \mathcal{F}_{FLTL}$
- if $\phi, \psi \in \mathcal{F}_{FLTL}$, then also $\mathsf{X}_{[m]}\phi, \mathsf{G}_{[m,n]}\phi, \mathsf{F}_{[m,n]}\phi, \phi\mathsf{U}_{[m,n]}\psi \in \mathcal{F}_{FLTL}$.

Example: Signal a will become active for the first time at time step 300: $\neg a U_{[300]} a$.

3.3 Higher Level Property Specification

Formulating property specifications in temporal logics has turned out to be difficult even for engineers with a mathematical background. Therefore, efforts were taken to provide means of specifying properties at a higher abstraction level such that they are easier to grasp for the human reader. We integrated two approaches into our toolchain:

1. Graphical notations of properties with Live Sequence Charts (LSC).
2. Natural language property specification based on specification patterns.

The brief discussion on higher level property specification in this section will focus on these two techniques.

Live Sequence Charts. Live Sequence Charts [7] were introduced to overcome the major shortcomings of Message Sequence Charts (MSC) and Sequence Diagrams (SD) from UML [8]. The criticism of MSCs and SDs concentrates on these points:

– Only an existential view of the system is supported.
– The point of activation of the chart is unclear.
– No means to specify the necessity to reach certain points in the chart.
– There is no formal semantics for SDs.

In [9], an algorithm is detailed that allows extraction of an automaton from a LSC. This automaton is then checked against a system model. Thus, LSCs are used as graphical notation for property specifications.

Natural language property specification. Another idea to facilitate property specifications is to use natural language expressions and convert them into temporal logic formulas. The idea originated in the context of specification patterns [10]. These patterns classify common property specifications into categories for later reuse. In [11], a predefined grammar consisting of structured English sentences is introduced with which the user can specify properties. These will be translated into CCTL formulas thereby fixing the semantics of the structured sentences.

RT-OCL. Industrial modeling mostly relies on UML. In accompanying work [12], a state-oriented real-time OCL extension (RT-OCL) was developed that allows modelers to specify state-oriented real-time constraints over UML models. The semantics of RT-OCL is described by mapping temporal OCL expressions to CCTL formulas. Thus, we have a transition path from UML to our lower level formalisms.

4   Model Checking CCTL Formulas

After presenting real-time property specifications and I/O-interval structures to describe modular timed systems, we will now explain how classical CTL model checking algorithms can be extended to cope with such systems and CCTL specifications.

4.1   Composition

Typical model checking algorithms work on one structure. The link between modular system descriptions and a monolithic structure necessary for model checking is the definition of structure *composition*. Composition defines the product structure of the original module structures. It also takes into account communication between structures. The outline of the algorithm for interval structure composition looks as follows:

1. Expand all modules and substitute their input variables by the connected outputs.
2. Compose the expanded structures.
3. Reduce the composed Kripke structure.

Composition of Kripke structures is established model checking technology. Therefore, we define the composition of interval structures by means of Kripke structures. First, we convert interval structures to equivalent Kripke structures by expansion (see figure 2). Thereafter, a reduction operation *reduce*() on Kripke structures replaces adjacent stutter states by timed edges.

The composition of I/O-interval structures where every free input is bound to an output of another module results in an interval structure, i.e., no free inputs remain. If we restrict ourselves to closed systems, then this definition can also be applied to I/O-interval structures.

4.2   Model Checking

After composition our approach allows the direct transfer of symbolic CTL model checking techniques to real-time model checking. As a consequence, the basic approach is similar to CTL model checking: building the syntax graph, computing sets of configurations (extension sets) representing subformulas of the checked property, and checking if the set of initial states is in the extension set of the complete specification.

Definition 12. Let $\Im = (P, S, S_0, T, L, I)$ be an interval structure and let ϕ be a CCTL formula. The extension set of ϕ is defined through:

$$[\phi] := \{g \in G \mid g \models \phi\} \tag{7}$$

CTL model checking algorithms can be directly used to check CCTL specifications. However, adaptations have to be made if operators carry time bounds. In this case, the fixpoint iteration is aborted if the time bound is reached. If the time bound of the operator is infinity, then the recursion has to be performed until a fixpoint is reached.

The main operation carried out during extension set computation for CCTL operators is determining predecessor configurations. This is done by taking the union of local and global predecessor computations. Local predecessor computation is restricted to configurations with non-zero clock values, whereas global predecessor computation is confined to configurations with zero clock values. The latter requires taking into account the whole transition relation.

Recursive definitions for all operators and algorithms for optimized extension set computation are given in [3]. The real-time model checking algorithms implemented in RAVEN have been formally verified in [13].

4.3 Implementation

In symbolic CTL model checking, state sets and transition relations are represented by characteristic functions which in turn are represented by reduced ordered binary decision diagrams (ROBDDs, [14]). For timed model checking state sets and relations are – due to the additional timing information – represented by extended characteristic functions which can in turn be represented by multi terminal BDDs (MTBDDs, [15]).

5 The Overall Picture

In the preceding sections we have established the necessary theoretical and technological background underlying our verification techniques. In this section we give a general overview of the tools and how they relate to each other.

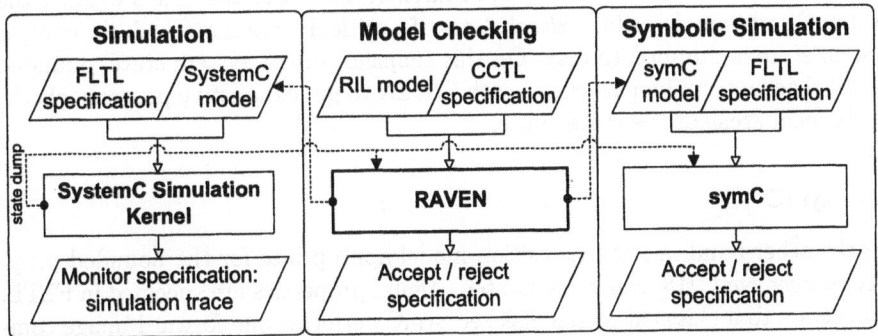

Fig. 4. Outline of the toolchain. Solid arrows show the typical flow of one tool, whereas dashed arrows represent transformations such that input for another verification technique is generated.

Fig. 4 shows the top-level outline of our toolchain. At its heart lies RAVEN (Real-Time Analysis and Verification Environment), a MTBDD- based model checker that supports CCTL property specifications. RAVEN's major invention is to allow checking discrete timing properties of the modeled system. In addition to these property checking facilities, RAVEN features algorithms to analyze system latencies and response times.

5.1 RAVEN

The system model for RAVEN is given in RIL (RAVEN Input Language, a notation for I/O-interval structures), which will be discussed in more detail in Section 6. This model description can be translated into other formats by RAVEN, i.e. the RIL model is the reference description for our other tools. We therefore provide a consistent integration of all tools with respect to one system model.

The main tasks of RAVEN after parsing the input file are the construction of the MTBDDs for each process, and composition and synthesis of the MTBDD for the system transition relation. The resulting MTBDDs are then used for checking specifications and for answering timing queries.

After composition, RAVEN can be switched to an interactive mode allowing the user to manipulate his specifications and queries and to add new ones. RAVEN supports a command line interface as well as a graphical user interface.

5.2 SystemC

On the one hand, the RIL model can be translated into a SystemC [16] model. This model can be compiled into an executable system model which is run with the SystemC simulation kernel and its associated semantics [17]. In Section 7.2, a short overview of SystemC is given.

SystemC supports traditional trace generation in various waveform formats, but in [6] a checker for FLTL formulas was presented that can be linked against SystemC code. Thus, functional verification is augmented by formal methods.

This approach can be carried even further. The formulas linked against the SystemC code can describe *critical states*. If a critical state is reached, the current system state is dumped to disk. On this snapshot of the system state, bounded model checking can be performed with RAVEN to get exhaustive property checking in local areas of the state space.

5.3 symC

On the other hand, a state transition model appropriate for the bounded property checker symC [18] can be generated. Again, properties are specified in FLTL. In contrast to a classical model checker, symC performs one forward image computation at a time, i.e. the current set of states is replaced by the set of states reachable with one transition. This results in an efficient verification for properties with large time bounds by avoiding fixpoint iterations and reachable state set computations.

However, both the SystemC checker and the bounded property checker symC can be used as standalone tools. In this case, the outcome of the design phase is a SystemC model or a symC model, respectively.

6   The Input Format RIL

We now give an informal introduction to the contents and structure of a RIL file. RIL is a simple format for specifying I/O-interval structures, property specifications as temporal logic formulas, and analysis queries. A more detailed description is available in [19], along with a complete grammar for RIL.

6.1   I/O-Interval Structures

Each RIL module contains one I/O-interval structure. The structures are defined as state transition graphs. The transitions are labeled with time intervals and input restrictions. Inputs are functionally connected to output variables of other modules. A RIL description of the I/O-interval structure depicted in Fig. 1 looks as follows:

```
MODULE structure
   SIGNAL  a : BOOL
   INPUT   i := m.output   // connect to output of module m
   DEFINE  s0 := !a
   INIT    s0
   TRANS   |- s0 -- !i : [1,3] --> a := true
END
```

An I/O-interval structure is introduced by the keyword MODULE followed by the module's name. The following sections define a module's behavior:

Signals. The definition of signals is a white space separated list of single signal definitions, which consist of a signal identifier and its associated type. Each module has to have at least one signal.

Input signals. An input definition is a Boolean formula over the signals and definitions of other modules. This is the only interface of a module to other modules, i.e. the remaining module description may only access local identifiers.

Definitions. A definition is an abbreviation of a Boolean equation by an identifier. These definitions have the same syntax as input definitions with the exception that only local identifiers may be used in the formula. Identifiers used for signals, inputs, and definitions have to be unique in a module, but different modules may use identifiers with the same name.

Initial states. These definitions are given as Boolean formulas. In the example, it is s0, i.e. $a = false$. There exists a CHOOSE-operator to select nondeterministically an initial value out of a set of values.

State transitions. Transitions[2] are specified with statements conforming to the following syntax:

```
|- start-state-equation -- input-condition : time-restriction
   --> signal-assignments !-> alternative-signal-assignments
```

The start state and input restrictions are both described with a Boolean formula. The formulas may use all local signals, input signals, and definitions. Time restrictions are comma separated lists of intervals or single expressions over natural numbers. All specified values are interpreted as possible delay times. There also exists the possibility to use global time constants. Operator `!->` describes alternative states if the input condition fails during the delay time. RAVEN allows mixing timed modules with fully synchronous modules. Their transition relation is defined by a conjunctively connected sequence of Boolean formulas with no timing information.

6.2   Global Definitions

Time definitions. RAVEN can only work with constant time values, but for an easier parameterization of modules with different times there exists the possibility to define global time constants which may be used in the delay time specification of the modules.

Boolean functions. Each global function is associated with an identifier. These functions can be interpreted as modules without signals and therefore without a transition relation and without states.

Property specifications. RAVEN checks each CCTL formula present in section SPEC of the RIL input file. A CCTL formula is specified in this way:

identifier := *cctl-formula*

The formulas are built upon the signals, definitions, and inputs of modules as well as the global definition names. For identifying local signal names, they are preceded by the module name and separated by a dot.

Property analysis. Property analysis allows a designer to extract characteristic time bounds from a system description. Typical problems are minimal and maximal delay times between events, e.g., how long does it take to process a workpiece in a production system. The current version of RAVEN supports three different algorithms[3]:

MIN. Requires two sets of configurations (see Definition 8): the start and the destination configurations. Then this algorithm computes the minimal delay time which is necessary to reach a configuration of the destination set starting in a configuration of the start set.

MAX. Computes the maximal delay time which may appear between a configuration of the destination set starting in a configuration of the start set.

---

[2] RAVEN supports a more intuitive state transition notation since version 2.

[3] The algorithms are directly derived from ideas of Campos and Clarke which used similar algorithms based on a ROBDD representations [20].

STABLE. Requires one set of configurations and computes the length of the longest path which does not leave the given set.

A set of configurations is specified via CCTL formulas. For example, the following query computes the time a machine may stay idle:

machine_idle := STABLE(¬machine.processing)

7 Verification Approaches Augmenting Model Checking

We have explained the major features of RAVEN in Section 5.1. Once we have a RIL model, we can verify it not only with RAVEN itself, but also with the other available techniques and software artifacts from our toolset as outlined in Fig. 4. Key to this procedure are RAVEN's built-in model translators. In this section we describe our verification approaches augmenting model checking.

7.1 Time Bounded Property Checking with symC

In [18] we proposed a formal verification technique for time bounded property checking of I/O-interval structures. The technique performs forward image computation for state traversal, a characteristic shared by forward model checking [21][4]. Properties are specified with FLTL formulas, therefore a tight integration with other property checking tools is provided. The temporal logic formulas are converted to special finite state machines, so-called AR-automata [6], which can then be used in the symbolic execution phase.

For system description, symC uses its own input language that captures finite state machines. Such symC models can either be written by hand, or they can be generated from Verilog netlists or RIL models. The automatic transformation from RAVEN to symC input files allows us to check one model description with both verification tools. Fig. 5 shows the general operation of symC, the tool based on this approach.

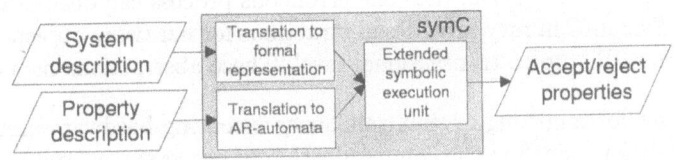

Fig. 5. Overview of symC operation.

The current implementation of symC uses a BDD-based approach, where one symbolic execution step corresponds to one forward image computation of the given state set. In contrast to standard state space traversal techniques, in this

---

[4] However, our property checking algorithms are quite different.

method we forget already visited states. The symbolic execution is stopped if a given time bound k is reached, or the property can either be proven correct or incorrect in the current state. The time bound k is either predefined by the user or determined by the formula if no infinite operators are used.

Both, the system description and the AR-automata, are translated to BDDs. In order to avoid the construction of the complete transition relation we use a set of transition relation partitions together forming the whole relation T.

The main iteration of our checking algorithm works in two steps. In the first step we compute the successor states of the AR-automata and we check whether a formula is accepted or rejected. In the second step of each iteration we perform one symbolic execution step on the system under inspection. During image computation we build the conjunction of all partitions on-the-fly to obtain the successor state set.

We do not build the complete state space, a feature shared with bounded model checking [22]. Rather, from a given start set we visit states reachable within a given time bound. The choice of the start set allows tuning a symC execution either towards complete coverage or towards smaller memory footprint and faster runtime. Experimental results [18] show that this approach outperforms other property checking methods for certain classes of systems and properties. This technique is well suited for properties with large time bounds.

7.2   Simulation with SystemC

Simulation and modeling with SystemC. SystemC [16] is a C++ library developed to support modeling at the system level, but also at other levels of abstraction, such as register transfer level (RTL). The modeled systems may be composed both of hardware and software components. The whole library is written in ISO/ANSI compliant C++ [23] and therefore runs on all standard compliant C++ compilers. It constitutes a domain specific language embodied in the library's data types and methods.

The SystemC core language is built around an event-driven simulation kernel which allows efficient simulation of compiled SystemC models. Processes in SystemC are nonpreemptive, thus one erroneous process can deadlock the simulator. The SystemC library provides abstractions for hardware objects that allow modeling from RT up to transactional level. These abstractions include:

- Processes for modeling of simultaneously executing hardware units.
- Channels for modeling the communication of processes, as well as ports and interfaces for flexible interchangeability of channels.
- Events for modeling the interaction between processes and channels.
- Modules for modeling the structural and hierarchical composition of the described system models.
- Hardware specific data types like signals, bitvectors, and floating point numbers of fixed and variable width.
- A notion of time is supported with clock objects. Clocks generate timing signals such that events can be ordered in time.

The SystemC library and reference implementation of the simulation kernel are available for free [24] in source code. Companies are encouraged to provide Intellectual Property (IP) cores in this standardized description language.

Verification extensions for SystemC. Despite the fact that we are able to handle models with symC where RAVEN is running out of memory, we still run into problems for very large designs. Here, we try to take advantage of classical simulation, but enrich it with formal methods.

The first step was to extend SystemC models with assertions expressed as temporal logic formulas [6]. Depending on the translation scheme, these assertions are either compiled into a library that is linked against the SystemC executable, or they can be added dynamically during execution. A special intermediate language [25] supports these different translation schemes. With this technique, checking executable system models against formal properties can start at the highest abstraction levels.

The methodology just mentioned is instrumental in another approach that combines functional and formal verification. Once the system model has been converted into a RIL model it can be model checked with RAVEN. However, for large designs we run into the state explosion problem. In order to still be able to perform limited checking, we support the following technique.

The RIL model is translated into an executable SystemC model and a temporal formula is checked against this model during simulation using our checker library. The formula has to conform to this structure:

$$AG(critical\_state \rightarrow required\_temporal\_behavior) \tag{8}$$

Whenever the formula *critical_state* is true during simulation, the current *critical* system state is dumped to a state file.

After simulation, we use RAVEN to check the *required_temporal_behavior* against the RIL model. The dumped state files are used to set up the initial state for the model checker. The checked formula is restricted to a finite time bound t_{max}, thus we avoid the construction of the complete state space. Of course, we can now only argue about the system behavior in this time bounded state space.

Summarizing, the user guides the verification process by pointing out critical states from which local state space traversal is performed within a limited time scope. Fig. 6 shows the overall flow of this combined approach.

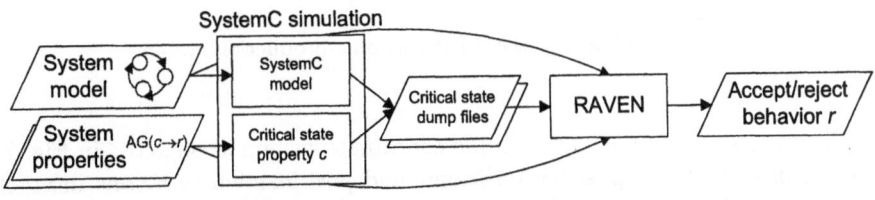

Fig. 6. Combined approach using SystemC and RAVEN.

8   Modeling Production Automation Systems in RIL

We now describe how production automation systems can be modeled with I/O-interval structures. For this purpose, a holonic production system is taken as an example.

8.1   The Holonic Production System

The holonic material transport system consists of an input station, three machines, an output station and three automatic transport vehicles, the so-called *holons*. Two of the three machines are for workpiece processing, one is for cleaning. All holons are identical. The task of the holons is to move workpieces to the two processing units. After processing, the workpieces have to be moved to the cleaning machine. From this station the workpieces have to be transported to the output station. Effectively, a workpiece travels from the input station to the output station, and visits all machines on the way in order. Transportation of the same workpiece can be accomplished by different holons, because a holon's task is renegotiated after it has dropped a workpiece at a unit.

8.2   RIL-Model of the Holonic Production System

We started the modeling process of the system at a high abstraction level with a MFERT [26] description. MFERT is a language for the description of production automation systems. After analyzing this MFERT document, we have split the physical units into one or more processes. Each process is modeled by an I/O-interval structure, i.e. a RIL module. We obtained the following units: three holons, one input station, one output station, two processing machines, and one cleaning machine. From now on, we will no longer differentiate between the machines.

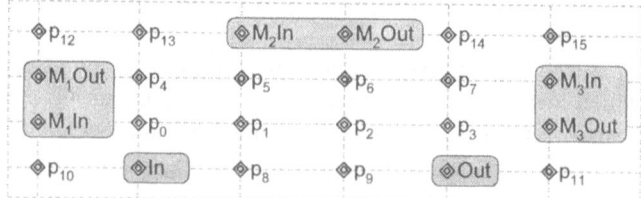

Fig. 7. Coordinate system of the holonic production system.

The units are positioned in a simple coordinate system as depicted in Fig. 7. Holons can move to all possible positions, and positions where holons interact with the machines are marked with rounded rectangles. Each machine has an associated position for receiving workpieces from holons (M_1In - M_3In), as well as for dumping them (M_1Out - M_3Out). The input and output stations have just one position for dumping (In) and receiving (Out) workpieces, respectively.

We will now describe the behavior and structure of the identified units and how they are composed from RIL modules. All modules communicate through a common broadcast channel. A starburst in the graphical notation depicts signals broadcasted to this channel. All mentioned time delays are local to the module, and given in clock ticks of the modeled system.

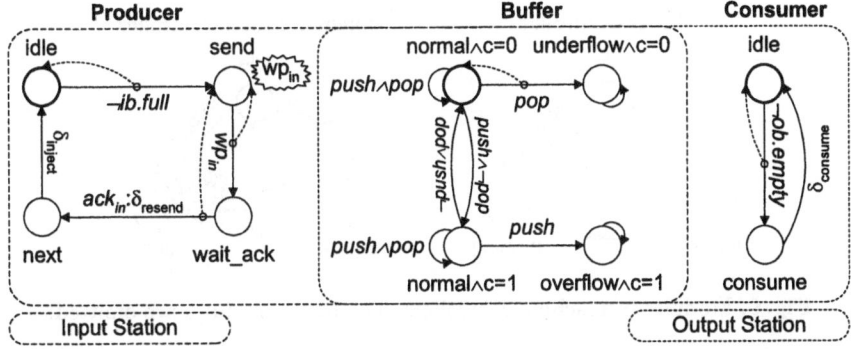

Fig. 8. Modules for input and output stations. The input station consists of producer and buffer, whereas the output station is made up of buffer and consumer.

Input station. We model the input station such that it never runs out of workpieces. It consists of two modules: a producer and a buffer.

The producer generates a raw workpiece if the buffer is not full. It then broadcasts signal wp_{in} and waits for the signal to appear on the broadcast channel. Then the producer sends the workpiece to the station's buffer whenever a holon acknowledges interest in retrieval with signal ack_{in}. If the acknowledgment is not given within δ_{resend} clock ticks, the sending procedure is repeated. Otherwise, the producer waits δ_{inject} ticks and the cycle starts anew. The producer's I/O-interval structure is given in Fig. 8.

Items are pushed from the producer to the buffer and from there they are retrieved by holons. Similar buffers will be used in other modules, the only difference is the direction of the push and pop operations. Pushing adds and popping removes one item from the buffer. The buffer can be in state *normal*, *underflow*, or *overflow*. Counter c holds the number of workpieces stored, with a fixed capacity of buf_{size} items. In Fig. 8, a buffer capable of holding one workpiece is illustrated.

Output station. The output station is modeled very similarly to the input station. However, the producer module is replaced by a consumer module. The consumer removes finished workpieces from the output buffer if the buffer is not empty. After a delay of $\delta_{consume}$ ticks the consumer is ready to retrieve another workpiece. The output buffer works exactly as the input buffer described above, with the exception that workpieces are pushed to the buffer by holons and popped from it by the consumer. The consumer is depicted in Fig. 8.

Machines. Machines are composed of five modules. Each machine has an associated input (ib) and output buffer (ob) where holons can drop or pick up workpieces. They also have an internal buffer (mb) for holding workpieces. Finally, two modules control the machines communication behavior and the transportation of workpieces between the buffers (see Fig. 9).

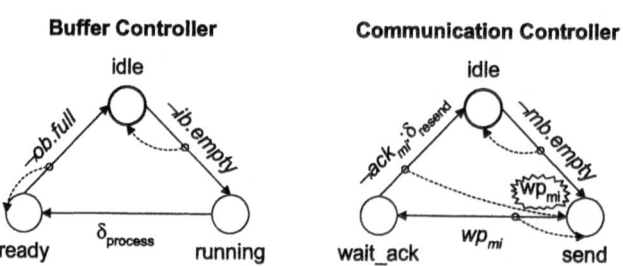

Fig. 9. Modules of machine controllers. The buffer modules are omitted.

The buffer controller first checks for a workpiece in input buffer ib and changes to state *running* if ib is not empty. After a delay of $\delta_{process}$ ticks it transitions to state *ready*. If output buffer ob is not full the controller can finally become *idle* again.

The communication controller first polls for a nonempty machine buffer mb and then goes to state *send*. There it broadcasts signal wp_{mi} to request a holon. If this signal appears on the broadcast channel, the controller waits for a holon to acknowledge the request within δ_{resend} clock ticks.

A workpiece moves through a machine's buffers in this order: First, a holon has to drop a workpiece at the machine's input buffer from where it has to be transported to the machine's internal buffer. After processing, it is finally stored in the output buffer where a holon has to pick it up. The buffers follow the same scheme as shown in Fig. 8.

Holons. A holon's state is encoded with the following variables:

- The task currently assigned to the holon (s).
- Its position (pos, see Fig. 7) and orientation (dir: left, right, up, down).
- Flags denoting if the holon is currently *moving* or *finishing* a rotation[5].

The large amount of states (82) prohibits the module's complete graphical presentation. Therefore, we explain the module's main characteristics informally. A holon basically behaves as follows:

A holon starts by waiting for orders. Now, one of the machines or the input station can request retrieval of a workpiece at its output buffer by broadcasting

---

[5] Holons can move forward one step at a time, and they can be rotated by 90°.

to the communication channel (wp_x). All holons waiting for orders answer by sending their distance to the requesting unit. The signal of the nearest holon prevails[6], and this holon acknowledges the request (ack_x). It follows a predetermined path to the unit and retrieves the workpiece. The holon's task is updated to transporting the item to the input buffer of the next unit, e.g. after retrieving a workpiece from the last machine, the item is transported to the output station. If the buffer is full, the holon waits for an empty slot. Then, it is free to wait for new orders.

The bulk of a holon's module consists of the path finding algorithm. Basically, whenever a holon is assigned the task to move to some machine and pick up or put down a workpiece there, the same procedure is applied. Depending on the current position and orientation, a holon either turns into the right direction, or, if the direction is correct, it moves one step forward after the specified move delay time. If a holon finds its way blocked – a holon checks if another holon occupies the position one step ahead and one step ahead to the right – it rotates and tries an alternative path to its destination. This procedure is repeated until the holon arrives at the destination and performs the requested operation. Thus, for every coordinate, a path to all machines is encoded in these transitions. The path finding algorithm provides basic collision protection, but no special means are taken to prevent deadlocks.

9 Experimental Results

The model of the holonic production system described in Section 8 is the basis for the results reported here. We have created three variants of the model for our experiments. They differ only in the number of holons present in the system. Currently, we have models with one (M_1), two (M_2) and three holons (M_3).

9.1 Checked Properties

We perform two measurements with the applicable tools and report the resulting runtimes. The first property P_1 is intended to give a general idea of how the tools compare to each other, whereas the second property P_2 tests a real life requirement of the model.

P_1. This property simply checks if the output station Out will eventually consume a workpiece, i.e. a workpiece was processed by all machines and the holons provided the necessary transportation between the stations. We check for the occurrence of this event within n time steps, both existentially and universally:

$$\text{EF}[n](\text{OutConsumer.s} == \text{OutConsumer.consume}) \qquad (9)$$

$$\text{AF}[n](\text{OutConsumer.s} == \text{OutConsumer.consume}) \qquad (10)$$

---

[6] Distances are given in chessboard metric.

P_2. The holonic production system does not contain explicit collision freeness by design. Therefore, it is crucial to check the system model for this property, i.e. the model checker has to prove that the system's behavior implicitly models collision free operation. We check that whenever a holon is blocked, in the next time step after the move delay time (mt) holons do not occupy the same position:

$$AG(\ (\text{h1.blocked} \vee \text{h2.blocked} \vee \text{h3.blocked}) \rightarrow AG[mt+1]($$
$$(\text{h1.pos} \ != \text{h2.pos}) \wedge (\text{h1.pos} \ != \text{h3.pos}) \wedge (\text{h2.pos} \ != \text{h3.pos}) \ )) \qquad (11)$$

9.2 Measurements

All measurements were conducted on a Linux PC with a 2.8 GHz Pentium 4 processor and 1 GB of RAM installed.

We used this configuration for the experiments: $\delta_{move} = 4$, $\delta_{rotate} = 1$, $c = 1$ for the input and output station's buffer, $c = 2$ for the machines' input and output buffers, $\delta_{inject} = 4$, $\delta_{resend} = 2$, $\delta_{process} = 3$, and $\delta_{consume} = 1$.

P_1. Checking property P_1 only makes sense with RAVEN and symC because Formulas (9) and (10) do not conform to the structure required by the SystemC approach (see Formula (8)). We report the result for models M_1, M_2, and M_3 with different time bounds n in Table 1.

We see that RAVEN is unable to check properties for models with more than one holon in the system. RAVEN runs out of memory in the reduction phase of I/O-interval structure composition (see Section 4.1), because the model becomes too large. On the other hand, once all preparations for model composition have finished, the actual model checking does not vary significantly depending on time bound n.

Global definitions in the RIL model allow configuring buffer capacities and time delays of the system. Some of these configurations may produce systems

Table 1. Results for checking P_1 using RAVEN and symC with different time bounds. Times are given in seconds, followed by an indicator if P_1 is true (t) or false (f).

time bound	10	50	100	200	500	∞
			RAVEN			
M_1, existentially	57.44 (f)	57.85 (f)	58.31 (f)	58.89 (t)	59.03 (t)	62.31 (t)
M_1, universally	57.92 (f)	58.07 (f)	58.37 (f)	59.0 (f)	59.22 (f)	62.1 (f)
M_2			measurement terminated after one hour ($mtaoh$)			
M_3			$mtaoh$			
			symC			
M_1, existentially	0.03 (f)	0.39 (f)	2.16 (f)	3.36 (t)	3.45 (t)	n/a
M_1, universally	0.03 (f)	0.38 (f)	2.14 (f)	22.55 (f)	296.12 (f)	n/a
M_2, existentially	0.07 (f)	0.76 (f)	7.32 (f)	150.86 (t)	151.1 (t)	n/a
M_2, universally	0.08 (f)	0.77 (f)	7.31 (f)	1540.78 (f)	$mtaoh$ (f)	n/a
M_3, existentially	0.25 (f)	1.29 (f)	17.23 (f)	979.36 (t)	972.12 (t)	n/a
M_3, universally	0.26 (f)	1.22 (f)	16.77 (f)	$mtaoh$ (f)	$mtaoh$ (f)	n/a

Table 2. Results for checking P_2 using SystemC (model running for 10000 cycles) and RAVEN.

	simulation time	nr. of critical states	model checking
M_2	4.6 sec.	161	7.24 sec. (t)
M_3	83.3 sec.	9685	16.45 sec. (t)

Table 3. Results for checking P_2 using symC for different time bounds.

	1000	2500	5000	10000
M_2, universally	1.33 sec. (t)	3.11 sec. (t)	9.02 sec. (t)	32.76 sec. (t)
M_3, universally	7.88 sec. (t)	9.85 sec. (t)	15.43 sec. (t)	39.47 sec. (t)

that contain paths which do not consume workpieces. The configuration used in the experiments produces such an unreliable system. This can be observed in the results for checking P_1 universally.

We are able to check properties with symC against all three models within given time bounds. In most cases, symC outperforms RAVEN. However, once symC has to traverse a huge state space for formulas that are still pending RAVEN may overtake again, e.g. universal quantification with a time bound of 500 steps.

P_2. For property P_2, we restricted the tests to symC and the combined SystemC/RAVEN approach. RAVEN was unable to check models with more than one holon, but for collision detection in P_2 we need at least two holons in the system.

Checking P_2 with SystemC is performed in the three-step procedure described in Section 7.2. First, the RIL model is translated into SystemC model. The model is simulated and our checker library checks the critical state condition. If the condition evaluates to *true*, the current system state is dumped. Finally, RAVEN performs a time bounded check of the required system behavior with all dumped states used as initial states. In our experiment, the local state space traversal is limited to 7 steps, because we are only interested in collisions directly after the blocking of at least one holon. In Table 2, we report the time for simulating 10000 time steps of the SystemC model, the number of critical states collected, and the time for model checking the local state space, both for M_2 and M_3.

To check P_2 with symC, we universally test for the required temporal behavior from the initial state. Thus, the comparison with the SystemC approach does not completely match. As we see in Table 3, we can also check the property with symC, however we get complete coverage within this range. For model M_3, symC even beats the combined SystemC and RAVEN approach.

The results for checking P_2 are always true with both verification approaches, which means that for the observed simulation runs we can guarantee collision freeness.

The experiments show that depending on the checked properties and the requirements on the checks, different verification tools excel in different areas. Model checking gives the user complete coverage of the model, however it suffers from the state explosion problem. Here, the other approaches can help to validate properties. An important task of the verification engineer is to select the appropriate tool to handle a specific verification problem.

9.3   Comparison with Other Tools

Both RAVEN and symC were compared with other tools. However, a fair assessment is very difficult to achieve. Each tool has its strengths and weaknesses, its own semantics of the time model, its own execution model and communication scheme. In addition, the tools have specification languages with differing expressiveness.

In [3] various model checkers with support for explicit time representation were benchmarked with simple but scalable examples. The measurements showed that RAVEN is slower for smaller models, but can beat all other tools when the model's size reaches a certain threshold. Among the competing model checkers were UPPAAL [27], KRONOS [28] and Verus [29].

10   Conclusions and Future Work

We have presented a toolbox for modeling and verifying real-time systems with a special focus on production automation systems. For this purpose, we devised a formal model of timed systems. The model is represented by an interval structure, which can be composed of multiple components, the I/O-interval structures. We also introduced the time bounded temporal logics CCTL and FLTL. They allow property specifications based on linear or branching time, respectively. The detailed model of a holonic material transportation system was presented in order to show how the different software assets available in our toolchain can be applied.

Central to our various verification approaches is RAVEN, a real-time model checker. A RIL model can be translated into other models with RAVEN such that the other tools can be applied where RAVEN meets its limitations. These tools are:

- The bounded property checker symC. Time bounded properties specified in FLTL are verified against a system model encoded as a finite state machine. An exhaustive state space traversal is avoided.
- A checker library for checking FLTL formulas against executable SystemC models.
- Localized property checking with RAVEN. A critical state detection mechanism based on our checker library dumps critical state files from simulated SystemC models. These files initialize the state for model checking with RAVEN with a fixed time bound.

The experiments performed on the model of the holonic material transportation system stress the fact that not one verification technique alone suffices to meet the demands of an efficient and complete system validation process. Critical system components require a fully formal proof of correctness, whereas in other areas a semi-formal approach combining both formal and functional verification is the only way to handle large designs.

Currently, we are working on enhancing symC. The dynamic nature of symC allows guiding of the symbolic execution process, which might help in finding error states or proofs more efficiently, i.e. parts of the state space will not be traversed at all.

Furthermore, we are investigating possibilities to provide an integrated verification environment that handles all parts of our toolbox and helps the verification engineer to coordinate his efforts.

References

1. Clarke, E.M., Grumberg, O., Peled, D.E.: Model Checking. The MIT Press (1999)
2. Vardi, M.Y.: Branching vs. linear time: Final showdown. In: European Joint Conferences on Theory and Practice of Software (ETAPS 2001). (2001) Invited paper.
3. Ruf, J., Kropf, T.: Symbolic verification and analysis of discrete timed systems. Journal on Formal Methods in System Design **23(1)** (2003) 67–108
4. Emerson, E.A., Mok, A.K., Sistla, A.P., Srinivasan, J.: Quantitative temporal reasoning. In Clarke, E.M., Kurshan, R.P., eds.: Computer Aided Verification, 2nd International Workshop. Volume 531 of Lecture Notes in Computer Science., Springer (1991) 136–145
5. Ruf, J., Kropf, T.: Modeling and checking networks of communicating real-time process. In Pierre, L., Kropf, T., eds.: Correct Hardware Design and Verification Methods. Volume 1703 of Lecture Notes in Computer Science., Springer (1999) 256–279
6. Ruf, J., Hoffmann, D.W., Kropf, T., Rosenstiel, W.: Simulation-guided property checking based on a multi-valued AR-automata. [30] 742–748
7. Damm, W., Harel, D.: LSCs: Breathing life into message sequence charts. Journal on Formal Methods in System Design **19(1)** (2001) 45–80
8. Object Management Group (OMG): Unified Modeling Language (UML), Version 1.5. www.omg.org (2003) Document formal/03-03-01.
9. Klose, J., Kropf, T., Ruf, J.: A visual approach to validating system level designs. In: 15th International Symposium on Systems Synthesis, ACM Press (2002) 186–191
10. Dwyer, M.B., Avrunin, G.S., Corbett, J.C.: Patterns in property specifications for finite-state verification. In: 21. International Conference on Software Engineering, ACM Press (1999) 411–420
11. Flake, S., Müller, W., Ruf, J.: Structured english for model checking specification. In: Methoden und Beschreibungssprachen zur Modellierung und Verifikation von Schaltungen und Systemen. 3. GI/ITG/GMM Workshop, VDE Verlag (2002) 99–108
12. Flake, S., Müller, W., Ruf, J.: A UML/OCL extension for state-oriented temporal properties with applications for manufacturing systems. (2004) This volume.

13. Reif, W., Schellhorn, G., Vollmer, T., Ruf, J.: Correctness of efficient real-time model checking. Journal of Universal Computer Science, Special Issue on Tools for System Design and Verification **7(2)** (2001) 194–209
14. Bryant, R.E.: Symbolic boolean manipulation with ordered binary-decision diagrams. ACM Computing Surveys **24(3)** (1992) 293–318
15. Bahar, R.I., Frohm, E.A., Gaona, C.M., Hachtel, G.D., Macii, E., Pardo, A., Somenzi, F.: Algebraic decision diagrams and their applications. In: Proceedings of the 1993 IEEE/ACM International Conference on CAD, IEEE Computer Society Press (1993) 188–191
16. Grötker, T., Liao, S., Martin, G., Swan, S.: System Design with SystemC. Kluwer Academic Publishers (2002)
17. Müller, W., Ruf, J., Hoffmann, D.W., Gerlach, J., Kropf, T., Rosenstiel, W.: The simulation semantics of SystemC. [30] 64–70
18. Ruf, J., Peranandam, P.M., Kropf, T., Rosenstiel, W.: Bounded property checking with symbolic simulation. In: Forum on Specification and Design Languages. (2003)
19. Ruf, J.: RAVEN: Real-time analyzing and verification. Technical Report WSI 2000-3, University of Tübingen (2000)
20. Campos, S.V., Clarke, E.M.: Real-time symbolic model checking for discrete time models. In Rus, T., Rattray, C., eds.: Theories and Experiences for Real-Time System Development. Volume 2 of Amast Series In Computing. World Scientific Publishing Corporation, Inc., River Edge, NJ, USA (1994) 129–145
21. Iwashita, H., Nakata, T.: Forward model checking techniques oriented to buggy designs. In: Proceedings of the 1997 IEEE/ACM International Conference on CAD, ACM and IEEE Computer Society Press (1997) 400–4004
22. Biere, A., Cimatti, A., Clarke, E.M., Strichman, O., Zhu, Y.: Bounded model checking. In Zelkowitz, M., ed.: Highly Dependable Software. Volume 58 of Advances in Computers. Academic Press (2003)
23. ISO/IEC: Programming Languages – C++. 2. edn. Number 14882:2003 in JTC1/SC22 – Programming languages, their environment and system software interfaces. International Organization for Standardization (2003)
24. VA Software Corporation, Open SystemC Initiative: Open SystemC Initiative. www.systemc.org (2004)
25. Krebs, A., Ruf, J.: Optimized temporal logic compilation. Journal of Universal Computer Science, Special Issue on Tools for System Design and Verification **9(2)** (2003) 120–137
26. Flake, S., Müller, W.: A UML profile for MFERT. Technical Report 4, C-LAB Paderborn (2002)
27. Bengtsson, J., Larsen, K.G., Larsson, F., Pettersson, P., Yi, W.: UPPAAL - a tool suite for automatic verification of real-time systems. In Alur, R., Henzinger, T.A., Sontag, E.D., eds.: Hybrid Systems III: Verification and Control, Springer (1996) 232–243
28. Yovine, S.: KRONOS: A verification tool for real-time systems. International Journal on Software Tools for Technology Transfer (STTT) **1 (1-2)** (1997) 123–133
29. Campos, S.V.A., Clarke, E.M., Minea, M.: The Verus tool: A quantitative approach to the formal verification of real-time systems. In Grumberg, O., ed.: Computer Aided Verification, 9th International Conference. Volume 1254 of Lecture Notes in Computer Science., Springer (1997) 452–455
30. Nebel, W., Jerraya, A., eds.: Design, Automation and Test in Europe, DATE 2001. In Nebel, W., Jerraya, A., eds.: Design, Automation and Test in Europe, DATE 2001, IEEE Press (2001)

On Model Integration and Integration Modelling
Introduction to the Subject Area Integration Modelling

Martin Große-Rhode

Fraunhofer ISST Berlin, Germany
Martin.Grosse-Rhode@isst.fraunhofer.de

Abstract. Integration is a necessary activity in each software development process. Within a model-based approach also the models that are used must be integrated. Model integration has two dimensions: On the one hand, the model components that result from the decomposition of the system under consideration have to be put together. On the other hand, different views onto the system are distinguished and modelled separately in order to decrease the complexity of the development process; the according models also must be brought together again.
Integration models are meta-level definitions of model integration methods. Ideally they can be instantiated with arbitrary kinds of models and modelling languages, which then yields an integration method for these models. In this introduction integration modelling is put into perspective; integration models are presented in the following contributions.

1 Model-Based Software Development and Viewpoints

Model-based and model-driven software development processes focus on models as the adequate representations of analysis results and design decisions. Models shall replace programming language texts as the primary artefacts and become the essential documents produced by and visible to the stakeholders of the software system. In a *model-based* process all activities of the development, the maintenance, and the evolution of a software system shall be based on models and result in models. The aim of *model-driven* software development is even to reduce the creative part completely to the model level, and have all code and further artefacts generated automatically from the models.

Due to this shift of focus modelling languages become ever more important, and ever more languages appear on the market. Although the introduction of the Unified Modeling Language (UML) might lead to the assumption that there is now one common, universal modelling language, a closer look at model-based software development processes shows that we must face the same phenomenon as in the domain of programming languages: there is no universal modelling language, new languages are continuously produced, and new languages are continuously needed.

This multitude of languages does not only concern the domain of software engineering in its entirety. Rather, within each single software development project different modelling languages are used, and each individual participant of the

H. Ehrig et al. (Eds.): INT 2004, LNCS 3147, pp. 567–581, 2004.

project is confronted with and has to use different languages. This is essentially a consequence of the separation-of-concerns principle applied to model-based software development. The process of building models is decomposed according to different aspects or viewpoints, and for each viewpoint a modelling language is chosen that is adequate for representing those properties and design decisions that are addressed by this viewpoint. Thus, instead of looking for the universal modelling language, the viewpoint model from the very beginning has favoured the usage of multiple, tailor-made languages.

A consequence of the viewpoint approach is that there are different, heterogeneous models that have to be integrated. Model-based software engineering thus requires model integration, which means that appropriate means have to be provided that allow us to use the collection of viewpoint models virtually as one global specification of the system under construction. All research projects in the Focus Area Program have worked on such model integrations, where the kind of models, notations, and languages that are used and the way in which they interplay were induced by the specific needs and approaches. The reference case studies and the investigations of the integrations on different kinds of *charts* (state charts, message sequence charts, life sequence charts, etc.) documented in this volume show instances of model integrations for specific applications.

For the meta-level discussion on model integration in general, i.e. independently of a set of concrete specification languages or a specific application, the subject area *Integration Modelling* had been founded within the Focus Area Program. Comparing the approaches that were developed in the different projects the general issues of model integration were discussed: What exactly are the subject and the purpose of model integration? What are the tasks and activities of the model integration within a software development process? Which integration means are required and how can or should they be used to achieve an integrated, continuous model-based software development process? An *integration model* gives answers to these questions and provides generic means for the *model integration.* In this way it supports the flexible design of software development processes that are based on integrated viewpoint models and employ adequate, integrated notations.

Two integration models are presented in this volume, both of which are based on formalisations of specification languages and semantics. In [SBK04] a formal model of object-oriented systems is given and viewpoints as parts or projections of the structure and behaviour of a system according to the formal model are defined. In this way integration of viewpoint specifications of object-oriented systems is given at the semantic level. Using a general framework for specification techniques (analogous to the institution approach [GB92]) integration can then be captured at the abstract language level. The approach presented in [OP04] addresses the orthogonal issue of the integration of specification modules that are given in different notations. That means, heterogeneity at the presentation level is addressed, which usually also induces semantic heterogeneity. In the formal framework of institutions heterogeneous modular specifications are defined abstractly, which makes precise and supports the issues of consistency checking and formal reasoning within heterogeneous specifications.

In the remainder of this introduction the general topic of integration modelling is discussed a bit further. First the subject and problem scope of integration is discussed in that the main sources of heterogeneity of models are reviewed. Then the solution space is addressed by looking at different possible levels of integration.

2   Sources of Heterogeneity and the Need for Integration

Although the use of viewpoint models in software development processes has become a de facto standard, the problem of having to deal with heterogeneous models and the need for explicit integration at the model level that are implied by this approach have not yet been fully resolved.

At the system level it is well accepted and understood that within the development of a reasonably complex software system an explicit integration activity is required. Its components and the systems it interacts with are developed at different sites and under different circumstances. Some components are bought, some are taken over from other systems, and some are newly developed. This results in a certain—unavoidable—heterogeneity of the components of the system as well as its interfaces to other systems. The components are implemented with different languages, they are usually configurable such that they can (and must) be adapted to the infrastructure of the overall system, they might be based on implicit technical or architectural assumptions, etc. Such heterogeneous components have to be brought together in order to obtain a well-functioning system at the end, and it is obvious that system integration is necessary as an explicit part of the development process.

A model-based development process is also a good precondition for a planned system integration. It provides the overall system plan as well as the contracts the components have to fulfill. Modelling all relevant aspects of such contracts in a system specification yields much more reliable descriptions than the traditional interfaces that essentially give information on static structures. Moreover, the models of the components allow us to check whether they satisfy their contracts and fit into the system plan.

However, as mentioned above, an integration task analogous to the system integration task occurs at the model level. Both the system and each component are represented by sets of heterogeneous viewpoint models, different modelling languages are used, perhaps even different decompositions into viewpoints have been chosen, etc.

To better understand the kind of heterogeneity and demand for integration that arises at the level of models and modelling languages a closer look at the sources of model heterogeneity is helpful. One of the most prominent sources of—and at the same time a recommendation for—the use of heterogeneous modeling languages is the Reference Model of Open Distributed Processing RM-ODP [ODP]. In its architectural framework for the structuring of the specification of systems, *viewpoints* are introduced as a decomposition of the development process according to some particular concern. Five viewpoints are defined,

- the *enterprise viewpoint*, which is concerned with the purpose, scope, and policies governing the activities of the specified system within the organisation of which it is a part;
- the *information viewpoint*, wich is concerned with the kinds of information handled by the system and constraints on the use and interpretation of that information;
- the *computational viewpoint*, which is concerned with the functional decomposition of the system into a set of objects that interact at interfaces – enabling system distribution;
- the *engineering viewpoint*, which is concernded with the infrastructure required to support system distribution;
- the *technology viewpoint*, which is concerned with the choice of technology to support system distribution.

These viewpoints may refer to any part of a system, subsystem or component. Thus the decomposition of the design process into viewpoints is orthogonal to the decomposition of the system into parts. The ODP-standard emphasises, moreover, that for each viewpoint a specifc, adequate specification language should be used. That means, instead of looking for the one universal language heterogeneous modelling is prefered.

Also the UML introduces model heterogeneity. Its languages support the specification of different aspects of a system, that may be grouped for instance as follows.

- The *structure* of the system is modelled by class diagrams on the type level, object diagrams on the instance level, and package diagrams for the namespace organisation and model management.
- The *behaviour* of the system is modelled by use case diagrams for the initial requirements capturing, interaction diagrams for the interaction and communication between system elements (like agents, objects, or components), and state machine diagrams for the behaviour of individual elements. Activity diagrams are moreover used to model not fully localised behaviour at arbitrary abstraction levels.
- The *implementation* and *deployment* of the system are modelled by component and deployment diagrams.

The classification[1] here thus refers to formal aspects—structure, behaviour, implementation / deployment—rather than to the contents or purpose as in the classification introduced by the RM-ODP. Nevertheless, it results in a system model that consists of a collection of diagrams given in different notations that address different aspects of one system.

---

[1] The number of diagram types changes with the different UML versions, as well as their names and aims. Note that the classification given above is not part of the UML standard, but given here for comparison.

Language or modelling frameworks like ODP and UML introduce heterogeneity explicitly. Beyond that there is the more traditional source of heterogeneity given by notations, languages, and tools that have been used in an organisation for a longer period and are meanwhile established. The investments into these modelling environements, both in terms of the financial investment and the organisational and educational overhead, cannot be neglected, which usually means that these modelling languages and tools must be incorporated into further developments. Moreover, tools like the Matlab/Simulink tool-suite [Bis97, MW] or notations like the IEC 61131-3 languages for the programming of control systems [SFC93] are well established and offer good support for systems developments in engineering applications. These are to be combined with the notations that are used by software engineers, as for instance the UML. Finally, even within a framework like the UML, there are different versions (UML 1.x, UML 2.0) and tool-dependent variants, as for instance the different variants of state charts both in UML-tools and non-UML-tools.

Viewpoint models are partial and incomplete. Two conclusions can be drawn of these observations. First, according to the viewpoint approach, models of software systems are always partial and incomplete. A single model even of a relatively small part of a system never specifies this part completely, but always only addresses some specific aspect. A class diagram specifies the static structure of a system, and each system that conforms to the class diagram must show this structure. Its behaviour, however, is not at all constrained by the class diagram. Thus there are (infinitely) many systems that conform to the class diagram, but show significantly different behaviours. A state chart specifies the behaviour of an object, but its structure is not shown and not specified by the state chart. Formally, any implementation of its actions and guards is admissible since there is no information on the effects of the actions on the values of the object's attributes and no information on the definition of the guards given in the state chart, beyond their names. Thus, there are again (inifnitely) many objects that conform to the state chart. In this sense, each model considered in isolation, is partial and incomplete.

Note that in this discussion a rather fine grained notion of model has been used. Models are considered as the documents that are produced and used within the system's development. In the UML context one often finds another definition, where these documents are called diagrams which are considered as views onto the entire model.[2] In this case, one would have to speak of diagram integration rather than model integration, and the integrated diagrams would become the overall model. The problems, however, remain the same ones.

Viewpoint models are heterogeneous. The second conclusion is that models are heterogeneous and this heterogeneity cannot be avoided. Thereby heterogeneity appears at different levels. At the lowest level different aspects of the system

---

[2] It is not entirely clear then what the model is, unless it is just the sum of the views, in which case the idea of views becomes void.

are specified, i.e., we have heterogeneity w.r.t. the *contents* of the models. Usually views are not orthogonal, which means that for each pair or collection of viewpoint models there are system elements or properties that are addressed by several of the models. Thus there is always the potential of conflicts in the sense that the information given in some viewpoint model on one system element or property might contradict the information given in another viewpoint model on the same element or property. A viewpoint model may *overlap* (in its contents) with another one, as for instance a collaboration diagram and a state chart. The former specifies the inter-object behaviour, the latter specifies the intra-object behaviour. If the object specified by the state charts takes part in the collaboration it has to conform to both models, which constrain its behaviour from different points of view. A viewpoint model may also be a *supplement* to another one. A state chart supplements a class diagram with behaviour information, a sequence diagram supplements a use case with more precise interaction scenarios. In both cases model integration must provide the possibility to check (at least theoretically or manually) whether the models are consistent with each other, i.e., whether they are free of contradictions.

If the same aspect of a system is concerned by several viewpoint models, heterogeneity may occur at the second level in that there are different underlying *modelling concepts* or paradigms according to which the models are constructed. The behaviour of the system might be specified for instance in terms of the causal relationships of state transformations or the temporal ordering of atomic uninterpreted actions. States may be data states given for instance by the values of object attributes, or abstract atomic control states. Communication may be modeled as message exchange or via the usage of some shared structure, etc. Analogously, there are different concepts of component composition. There are for instance closed and open semantics of component specifications. Given a closed semantics only those actions of a component are represented that the component is able to perform actively as a stand alone component. The behaviour of a Petri net, for example, is usually conceived in this way. Composition with other components then adds further action possibilities to this behaviour in that inputs to the component are provided. If other Petri nets put tokens on some interface places of a given Petri net more of its transitions are enabled and may fire. In the open semantics the behaviour of a component is conceived as the maximal set of activities it might perform in some environment. Processes in CCS and other process calculi for instance contain input actions which are actions that the process may engage in provided the environment initiates them. In this case the actual behaviour of a component in an environment is a subset of its "stand-alone-behaviour" and composition is defined as the restriction of the "stand-alone-behaviour" to the behaviour in this environment. That means that composition subtracts some possible actions.

At the third level, even when using the same concepts these may be expressed in different notations, analogous to the use of different programming languages for the implementation of one abstract algorithm. Thus there is (obviously) also heterogeneity at the syntactic level.

3   Levels of Integration

Corresponding to the different sources and levels of heterogeneity also model integration can be addressed at different levels.

Syntactic Integration. Syntactic integration addresses syntactic heterogeneity. That means that viewpoint models are given in different languages, but the semantic relationships of the models or the languages are clear. In this case concrete translations of the languages or transformations of the models are required that realise the semantic correspondences.

Syntactic integration may support any integration task. It says *how* to perform this task, based on the knowledge *what* has to be done. In fact, it is the desired final form of an integration task since it provides the means to express what has to be done in a concrete syntax, which is a necessary precondition for automation and tool support. The results of the project ISILEIT presented in [BGN+03, GKN02] for example address concrete syntactic realisations of model integrations. In the project USE Life Sequence Charts [DH01] have been integrated also on the syntactical level into a UML-based process (see [KL01,BDK+02]), which supports in particular the relative verification of the specifications.

Translations of notations that express identical (or closely related) semantic concepts are one kind of integration tasks. Syntactic integration defines how such translations are represented. For the exchange of models among different UML tools for example XMI yields a syntactic integration in this sense. It supports the tranlsation between the internal languages of the tools.

Another kind of tasks concerns the comparison of semantically overlapping viewpoint models and the check of their consistency. To compare collaboration diagrams and state charts, for example, a projection of the behaviour of the set of objects specified by the collaboration to the behaviour of the object specified by the state chart is needed. This projection also has to adjust the different granularities of the behaviour specifications. In a state chart the consumption of an event (the arrival of a message) and the execution of an action (sending a message) are represented as one step, whereas in a collaboration diagram these are two distinct steps. A syntactic integration would provide a syntactic definition of this projection that allows the comparison and consistency check for these types of models. Similar transformations and consistency checks are required for models that supplement other ones. In these cases essentially given refinement relationships have to be checked.

Syntactic integration addresses languages rather than individual models, since the idea is to have model transformations that can be defined uniformly as translations of the languages. A common approach is to define metamodels for the definition of the languages (see e.g. [GKM00]) or refer to the given metamodels as in the case of UML models and define transformations and translations by referring to the terms of these metamodels.

Beyond these translations and model transformations another dimension of syntactic integration is the construction of new modelling languages by the integration of languages that address different modelling aspects. Some prominent

examples are the integration of the process calculus CCS and the algebraic specification language ACT ONE (or the functional programming language ML) to
LOTOS [Bri89] (ELOTOS [ELO01]), algebraic high level nets as the integration of Petri nets and algebraic data type specifications [RV87,Rei91], μ-SZ as
the integration of state charts and the model based specification language Z
[BDG+96,BGK98], and CSP-OZ as the integration of the process caluclus CSP
with ObjectZ, the object oriented extension of Z [Fis97].

As mentioned above, any syntactic integration is based on semantic relationships. Each model and each language has a meaning, be it precisely defined or
not, and any syntactic definition of a translation, a transformation, a comparison, or a consistency check is just the syntactic representation of a semantic
concept. A tranlsation maps syntactic expressions of one language to syntactic expressions of another language *such that* the meaning of the expressions
is preserved. This is not an additional property of *good* translations, but the
very definition of a translation. Analogously, transformations and comparisons
are syntactic representations of semantic concepts: projections, refinements, adjustments, or whatsoever. A consistency check tells us whether models are free
of contradictions, which obviously refers to their meaning. Sometimes this underlying semantic concept is defined explicitly in a further language and the
correctness of the syntactic representation is shown, sometimes only the syntactic definition is given and the semantic concept is defined implicitly as the
one that is realised by the syntactic representation. But also in the latter case
usually an informal explanation of the semantic concept is given, together with
a correspondingly informal justification of the syntactic representation.

Methodologic Integration. A more pragmatic approach is realised with methodologic integrations. They address the development process and are based on the
observation that consistency is the desired state of the models, but does not
hold at every point of time during the modelling process. Distributed modelling
implies that intermediate results are produced by different persons or teams that
do not have the possibility to coordinate their activities permanently. Instead
a process has to be defined that clarifies at which points local results have to
be synchronised. Methodologic integration defines such processes by specifying
the roles that are involved in the development process, the activities that are
to be performed, and the artefacts that are to be produced as results of the activities. These are interconnected by specifying the assignment of the activities
to the roles and the interdependencies of activities and artefacts. As an integration method it has to specify in particular when artefacts have to be integrated.
That means that it has to provide means to compare models, state correspondences between models, check their consistency, and suggest corrective activities
if models turn out not to be consistent.

Methodologic integration embeds syntactic integration into a development
process. It admits inconsistent states of development within certain local
activities and enforces synchronisation at defined points of time. It requires
syntactic integration means: comparisons, correspondence declarations, consis-

tency checks, and corrective activities must be provided to be incorporated into the process.

The ViewPoint-Framework introduced by Finkelstein and Kramer [FKN+92] offers a template for dealing with heterogeneous models in such an integrative development process. A model is accompanied by further documents that embed the model respectively its actual state into the development process. A template has five slots:

- In the *style slot* the notation is defined, i.e., a reference to the language definition, its version, etc. is given.
- In the *domain slot* the area of concern is given, specifying which application domain is addressed and which viewpoint is taken.
- The *specification slot* contains the specification (the model) in its current state.
- The *work plan slot* contains information on the construction and maintenance of the specification: activities that can be performed to construct and manipulate models, triggers that initiate certain activities, for instance corrections after the detection of inconsistencies, and dependencies and schedules of the activities.
- The *work record slot* contains the development history of the specification and may serve as a version management.

In the formalisation of the ViewPoint-Framework developed in the project INTAS [GEMT00,EGH+00] intra-viewpoint check actions and inter-viewpoint check actions have been defined based on distributed graph transformations. The former define how consistency checks can be executed within one language, the latter deal with heterogeneous models given in different languages.

The above mentioned approaches state how model integration can be incorporated into a development process and how the necessary activities can be represented and implemented. The semantic foundation of the activities, i.e., the justification of the transformations, comparisons, consistency checks, corrective actions, etc., is only implicitly addressed. Semantic integration approaches are complementary in that they address the question for the contents of these activities. That is, they investigate *what* has to be done, rather than *how* and *when* it can be done. Thus syntactic and methodologic integrations have an interface to semantic integrations that are their logical preconditions.

Semantic integrations can be based on different kinds of semantics. Ontological approaches refer to the meaning of the terms that are used in the models, as understood by the human actors. This is sometimes called the *contents* of the models. Formal semantic approaches, on the other hand, refer to mathematical interpretations of the modelling concepts.

Ontologic Integration. Model integration can be understood in analogy to system integration, as mentioned in the introduction. Current investigations on large information systems, in particular web-based information systems, suggest ontologies as a means to achieve an integration of heterogeneous information sources. The Semantic Web [W3C], to mention just the most prominent example, provides a common framework, based on the Resource Description Format RDF [RDF], that allows data to be shared and reused across application, enterprise, and community boundaries (see [HTM02]).

Looking at model-based development processes as social activities, where people are working together on a common project and models are used to convey the information between the project members, an ontological approach can be used also to support the desired model integration at the contents level. An ontology is a formal (machine readable) explicit representation of the objects, concepts, and other entities and the relationships that hold among them, that is not private to some individual, but accepted by a group [Gru93]. The aspect of machine readability addresses the desired tool support for the integration; having a representation means to have an explicit specification of the concepts and their relationships. The most important part concerning the integration, however, is given by the last part of the definition: the specification of the concepts must be shared by all participants of the development process, i.e., there must be an explicit and binding agreement on a specific ontology. The ontology thereby has to cover all relevant aspects of the modelling process. This comprises the application domain and the realisation or implementation domain, as well as the modelling concepts that are used. In the project KNOSSOS corresponding activities towards the definition of an ontology for the model-based development of embedded control systems in the railways domain have been undertaken [FJS96,JS00,SJ01].

Formal Semantic Integration. Semantic integration addresses the fundamental questions for the relationships that exist between the models. If formal modelling languages are used, i.e., languages that have formal semantics, then the contents of the integration tasks can be defined directly with reference to these semantics. The basisc question w.r.t. integration, wether models specify overlapping parts of a system and whether they do this consistently, is a semantic question, and formal semantics offer the possibility to investigate this question with mathematical rigor.

Beyond that, the findings of such investigations can be carried over also to less formal modelling languages in that the principles that have been found are rephrased at the level of the considered modelling languages.

Semantic integrations can be achieved in two ways. First, mutual correlations between languages can be investigated. That means that for each pair of languages their relationship is clarified by defining the mappings or relations between their semantic domains. These results are then specific for the considered languages and do not directly yield an integration model that can be carried over to other languages.

Second, a common semantic domain can be constructed where all models and languages can be interpreted. This semantic domain must provide an adequate structure to support

- the interpretation of all kinds of models,
- composition operations to reflect the composition of models at the semantic level,
- refinement relations or more general development relations that express the semantic relationships that may exist among models,
- compositionality results that state under which conditions composition operations are compatible with the development relations.

Concerning the first point, the interpretation of models will—in general—yield a set of admissible interpretations for each model, due to the fact that models are partial and incomplete. Since the elements of the common semantic domain must cover all system aspects and a single model only constrains some of them, there are usually (infinitely) many semantic interpretations of one model. The semantic development relations are the building blocks for the comparisons that shall be made. The composition operations support incremental integrations in that first model components are compared and integrated by establishing one of the relations among them, and then the considered components are composed. Taking into account the compositionality conditions these relations then carry over to the composed models. A formal semantic domain of this kind has been worked out in the project IOSIP [Gro04]. A plain mathematical definition of systems is given there, with categorical composition operations and development relations. In the project ISILEIT abstract state machines (formerly called evolving algebras [Gur91,Gur94]) are used as the semantic domain, which yields in particular an immediate tool support for integration (see [GKN02,NK03]).

Conceptually this kind of formal semantic integration works for collections of viewpoint models. The sets of admissible interpretations for all models are defined as subsets of the semantic domain, they are transformed according to the semantic relationships that are postulated, and finally their intersection is checked as to whether there is a common interpretation for all models, which would prove their consistency. As a method, however, one would like to have a more uniform approach, where at least the interpretations need not be defined individually, but the semantics of the languages are reconstructed in terms of the semantic domain. One must keep in mind, however, that languages in general are not as unique as to support this aim strictly. Very often languages can be used in many different ways or styles, and then a single global semantics definition does not suffice for a general integration method.

If the semantics of a language is reconstructed, however, then it must be made sure that the reconstruction is faithful, i.e., the semantic reconstruction coincides with the original definitions or explanantions of the semantics. Furhtermore, the structure of the language, i.e., the composition operations and refinement relations it provides, must be faithfully reconstructed in the semantic domain, too. Thus the structure of the semantic domain is not only used to support the integration tasks as discussed above, but to reflect the structure of the languages and make them comparable.

Semantic integrations alone do not provide integration methods. As discussed above, their results have to be reflected at the syntactic level of the languages that are used or in a specific integration language to become usable for the engineers who are concerned with the model integration. Furthermore a method has to be provided that explaines which steps have to be performed in which order, and how the different integration tasks can be accomplished.

4   Conclusion

Model integration is a constituent of every continuous model-based software systems development process. Integration models define how models can be integrated, independently of specific notations, languages, methods, or specification paradigms. They define what the integration tasks are, what their semantic contents are, how the integration tasks can be expressed syntactically, and how they are integrated into the overall development process. These different aspects of integration models, discussed above under the headings of syntactic, methodologic, ontologic, and formal semantic integration, are usually not separated in the sense that an integration model for only one of the aspects is defined. As mentioned above there are interfaces between these aspects, and a complete integration model has to cover them all. The integration of viewpoint specifications presented in [BSBD99,BBDS99,BBD+00] for example defines an integration model with emphasis on semantic concepts and syntactic representations in the languages Z and CSP. This is induced by the context of the RM-ODP that these contributions refer to, which also defines the methodologic background. Also the model integration presented in [Egy99,EM00] incorporates semantic, syntactic, and methodologic aspects, with an emphasis on applicability in the context of UML-based development processes and integration of UML models with architectur descriptions.

On the other hand, also explicit integration models have different scopes. Some are bound to more or less specific assumptions on the modelling languages or methods. For example, choosing UML as the modelling framework is a pragmatic assumption that is justified because of the broad acceptance of the UML, but excludes for instance more formal specification languages, and thus also excludes more precise integrations. Other integration methods, however, strive to be as independent of languages and methods as possible. Thus, there is a continuous spectrum ranging from the implicit integration models of well-defined model integrations to the explicit generic integration models, rather than a pure dichotomy.

References

[BBD+00]   E.A. Boiten, H. Bowman, J. Derrick, P.F. Linington, and Steen M.W.A. Viewpoint consistency in ODP. *Computer Networks*, 34(3):503–537, 2000.

[BBDS99]   H. Bowman, E. A. Boiten, J. Derrick, and M. W. A. Steen. Strategies for consistency checking based on unification. *Science of Computer Programming*, 33:261–298, 1999.

[BDG+96]   Robert Büssow, Heiko Dörr, Robert Geisler, Wolfgang Grieskamp, and Marcus Klar. *μSZ* – Ein Ansatz zur systematischen Verbindung von Z und Statecharts. Technical Report 96-32, Technische Universität Berlin, February 1996.

[BDK+02]   J. Bohn, W. Damm, J. Klose, A. Moik, and H. Wittke. Modeling and validating train system applications using statemate and live sequence charts. In *Proc. Int. Conf. Integrated Design and Process Technology (IDPT2002)*, 2002.

[BGK98]   R. Büssow, R. Geisler, and M. Klar. Specifying safety-critical embedded systems with statecharts and Z: a case study. In E. Astesiano, editor, *Proc. 1st Int. Conf. on Fundemantal Approaches to SoftwareEngineering (FASE'98)*, pages 71–87. Springer LNCS 1382, 1998.

[BGN+03]   S. Burmester, H. Giese, J. Niere, M. Tichy, J.P. Wadsack, L. Wagner, R. Wendehals, and A. Zündorf. Tool integration at the meta-model level within the FUJABA tool suite. In *Proc. Workshop on Tool-Integration in System Development (TIS) at ESEC/FSE 2003*, pages 51–56, 2003.

[Bis97]   R.H. Bishop. *Modern Control Systems Analysis and Design Using MATLAB and Simulink*. Addison Wesley, 1997.

[Bri89]   Brinksma, E. (ed.). Information processing systems – Open Systems Interconnection – LOTOS – A formal description technique based on the temporal ordering of observational behaviour. ISO 8807, 1989. International Standard.

[BSBD99]   H. Bowman, M.W.A. Steen, E.A. Boiten, and J. Derrick. A formal framework for viewpoint consistency. Computing Laboratory Technical Report 22-99, University of Kent at Canterbury, December 1999. URL http://www.cs.ukc.ac.uk/people/staff/jd1/pubs.html.

[DH01]   W. Damm and D. Harel. Lscs: Breathing life into message sequence charts. *Formal Methods in System Design*, 19(1):45–80, 2001.

[EGH+00]   B.E. Enders, M. Goedicke, T. Heverhagen, R. Tracht, and P. Tröpfner. Towards an integration of different specification methods by using the viewpoint framework. In M.M. Tanik and A. Ertas, editors, *Proc. 5th World Conference on Integrated Design and Process Technology (IDPT 2000)*. Society for Design and Process Science, 2000.

[Egy99]   A. Egyed. *Heterogeneous View Integration and its Automation*. PhD thesis, University of Southern California, Los Angeles, April 1999.

[ELO01]   ISO/IEC 15437, Information Technology - Enhancements to LOTOS, 2001.

[EM00]   A. Egyed and N. Medvidovic. A formal approach to heterogeneous software modeling. In T. Maibaum, editor, *Fundamental Approaches to Software Engineering (FASE 2000)*, pages 178–192. Springer LNCS 1783, 2000.

[Fis97]   C. Fischer. CSP–OZ: A combination of Object–Z and CSP. In H. Bowman and J. Derrick, editors, *Formal Methods for Open Object–Based Distributed Systems (FMOODS'97)*, volume 2, pages 423–438. Chapman & Hall, 1997.

[FJS96]   A. Fay, L. Jansen, and E. Schnieder. Towards a knowledge-based decision support system for high speed train traffic control. In *Proceedings of the World Congress on Railway Research (WCRR '96)*. Association of American Railroads., 1996.

[FKN+92]   A. Finkelstein, J. Kramer, B. Nuseibeh, M. Goedicke, and L. Finkelstein. Viewpoints: A framework for integrating multiple perspectives in system development. *International Journal of Software Engineering and Knowledge Engineering*, 2(1):31–58, March 1992.

[GB92]   J. Goguen and R.M. Burstall. Institutions: Abstract model theory for specification and programming. *Journal of the ACM*, 39(1):95–146, 1992.

[GEMT00]   M. Goedicke, B. Enders, T. Meyer, and G. Taentzer. Viewpoint–oriented software development: Tool support for integrating multiple perspectives by distributed graph transformations. In S. Graf and M. Schwartzbach, editors, *Proc. Tools and Algorithms for the Construction and Analysis of Systems (TACAS 2000), at ETAPS 2000*, volume 1785 of *Springer LNCS*, pages 43–47, 2000.

[GKM00]   R. Geisler, M. Klar, and S. Mann. Precise semantics of integrated modeling languages by formal metamodeling. In M.M. Tanik and A. Ertas, editors, *Proc. 5th World Conference on Integrated Design and Process Technology*. Society for Design and Process Science, 2000.

[GKN02]   H. Giese, M. Kardos, and U.A. Nickel. Towards design verification and validation at multiple levels of abstraction. In *Proc. IFIP World Computer Congress, Stream 7 on Distributed and Parallel Embedded Systems (DIPES2002), Montreal, Canada, August 2002*, 2002.

[Gro04]   M. Große–Rhode. *Semantic Integration of Heterogeneous Software Specifications*. EATCS Monographs in Theoretical Computer Science. Springer Verlag, Berlin Heidelberg New–York, 2004.

[Gru93]   T.R. Gruber. A translation approach to portable ontologies. *Knowledge Acquisition*, 5(2):199–220, 1993.

[Gur91]   Y. Gurevich. Evolving algebras, a tutorial introduction. In *Bulletin of the EATCS 43*, pages 264 – 284. Springer Verlag, 1991.

[Gur94]   Y. Gurevich. Evolving algebra 1993. In E. Börger, editor, *Specification and Validation Methods*. Oxford University Press, 1994.

[HTM02]   J. Hendler, Berners-Lee T., , and E. Miller. Integrating applications on the semantic web. *Journal of the Institute of Electrical Engineers of Japan*, 122(10):676–680, 2002.

[JS00]   L. Jansen and E. Schnieder. Traffic control systems case study: Problem description and a note on domain-based software specification. In H. Ehrig, M. Große-Rhode, and F. Orejas, editors, *Proc. International Workshop on Integration of Specification Techniques with Applications in Engineering (INT 2000)*, pages 41–47, 2000.

[KL01]   J. Klose and M. Lettrari. Scenario-based monitoring and testing of real-time uml models. In *Proc. UML 2001*, 2001.

[MW]   The MathsWorks. URL http://www.mathworks.com/.

[NK03]   U.A. Nickel and M. Kardos. ASMs as integration platform towards integration of distributed production control systems at multiple levels of abstraction. In *Proc. 10th International Workshop on Abstract State Machines*, 2003.

[ODP]   ISO/IEC International Standard 10746, ITU–T recommendation X.901–X.904: Reference model of open distributed processing – Parts 1–4.

[OP04]   F. Orejas and E. Pino. On the integration of heterogeneous modular specifications. In this volume, 2004.

[RDF]   World Wide Web Consortium. Resource Description Format. URL http://www.w3.org/RDF/.

[Rei91]   W. Reisig. Petri Nets and Algebraic Specifications. In Rozenberg/Jensen, editor, *High Level Petri Nets*, 1991.

[RV87]   W. Reisig and J. Vautherin. An algebraic approach to high level Petri nets. In *Proceedings of the 8th European Workshop on Petri Nets, Zaragoza*, 1987.

[SBK04]   G. Schröter, B. Braatz, and M. Klein. Semantical integration of object-oriented viewpoint specification techniques. In this volume, 2004.

[SFC93]   International Electrotechnical Commission. International Standard 61131, Programmable Controllers. Part 3: Programming Languages. IEC, 1993.

[SJ01]   E. Schnieder and L. Jansen. Begriffsmodelle der Automatisierungstechnik – Basis effizienten Engineerings. In E. Schnieder, editor, *Engineering komplexer Automatisierungssysteme (EKA 2001)*, pages 1–27, 2001.

[W3C]   World Wide Web Consortium. Semantic Web. URL http://www.w3.org/2001/sw/.

On the Integration of Modular Heterogeneous Specifications

Fernando Orejas and Elvira Pino

Departament LSI
Universitat Politècnica de Catalunya,
Campus Nord, Mòdul C5, Jordi Girona 1-3, 08034 Barcelona, Spain
orejas@lsi.upc.es

Abstract. The specification and modelling of reasonably large software systems is usually a complex task that involves the description of several aspects or dimensions that are not easily described by means of a single specification technique or formalism. However, an obvious problem in this context is to know how can we be sure that these specifications are consistent and really model the system that we want to design. A second problem is how to verify or prove properties about these systems. In this paper, we will provide a formal framework that will allow us to reason about heterogeneous specifications and we will present some results concerning these two problems.

1   Introduction

The specification and modelling of reasonably large software systems is usually a complex task that involves the description of several aspects or dimensions that are not easily described by means of a single specification technique or formalism. For instance, we may have to describe how a given system is decomposed in different components or subsystems and, for each of these components (or for the system as a whole), we have to describe its functionality and its dynamic behavior. Also, we may want to describe how components interact or communicate and, perhaps, how components move among different locations.

Moreover, when describing some specific aspect, depending on the level of refinement, we may like to use different formalisms. Typically, one would use logical formalisms at the early phases and more operational ones at later stages. For instance, the functionality of a component may be described at some early phase using equational or first-order logic, and using graph-transformation at a later stage. Similarly, its behavior may be described using a temporal logic, at an early stage, and using a process algebra at a later phase.

The definition of a wide-spectrum formalism that could cover the description of all aspects and views of a given system does not seem a reasonable solution. The intended wide applicability of the formalism would probably result in a complexity that would make difficult its use and hinder the construction of deductive or verification tools. Nevertheless, at some point, some specification languages were defined that would put together, in an integrated way, some of these different dimensions. For instance the

H. Ehrig et al. (Eds.): INT 2004, LNCS 3147, pp. 582–601, 2004.

most common case was the integration of functional and process specifications and the usual solution was the definition of a language that would mix in an appropriate way these two aspects considered. The best known example of this approach is, probably, the language LOTOS that integrated the algebraic specification language ACT ONE with the process algebra ccs [15]. Instead, the most accepted current approach consists in facing the specification and modelling of a complex system by dealing separately, using different formalisms, with the various aspects and views of the system. The UML [4] is a well-known example of this approach. Then, each formalism may be reasonably simple and, as a consequence, it may have equipped with some good verification tools.

However, the obvious problem is to know how can we be sure that these specifications are consistent and really model the system that we want to design. A second problem is whether we can use the tools associated to each formalism for the verification of the complete system.

A second kind of heterogeneity that is worth to study can be found in the modelling of component-based systems where different components are described using different formalisms (this does not exclude the case where each component is itself heterogeneous in the former sense). At the implementation level, this is a standard practice in software architectures such as CORBA or COM+. In this paper, we will also consider this second kind of heterogeneous specifications, based on some ideas that can be found in [22,18].

In this paper, after discussing, at a general level, the main issues concerning heterogeneous specifications, we will provide a formal framework that will allow us to reason about these specifications and we will present some results concerning the problems mentioned above. In particular, on one hand, we will provide some reasonable sufficient conditions for the consistency of heterogeneous component-based systems. On the other hand, we will present a deduction rule, which is sound in our formal framework, that allow us to prove properties of a heterogeneous specification using the deductive tools or methods associated to the formalisms involved.

The paper is organized as follows: in the rest of this introduction we will review some of the main ideas used for dealing with heterogeneous specifications. In the second section we introduce some notation and basic definitions. In section 3, we present our concept of heterogeneous system. In the following section, we present our results about consistency. Finally, in section 5, we briefly discuss how to reason about about heterogeneous specifications.

Many of the ideas presented in this paper, in a preliminary form and restricted to the case of heterogeneous component-based systems, were presented at IDPT 2002 [22].

1.1 Semantic Integration of Heterogeneous Specifications

The most obvious way of ensuring that a specification is consistent is to provide a model for it. If we are dealing with a heterogeneous specification, where different views are described using different specification formalisms, this means finding some kind of structure that could be a model of all these formalisms. This is the underlying idea of defining a basic semantic framework for defining the semantics of heterogeneous specifications.

This approach has been studied in detail by Martin Grosse-Rhode in his habilitation thesis [13] (see also his recent book [14]) and within the project IOSIP (see e.g. [3]) in the subject area "General Framework for Integration Modellin" in the DFG focus area program on "Continuous Software Engineering". The approach is based on considering that a model of a system is defined at two levels. At the first level we have a state transition diagram that represents, in principle, all the possible states and all the state changes of the given system. In order to be general enough, states are assumed to be algebras and transitions are algebra transformations. At the second level a second state transition diagram represents the actual behavior of the system. A graph morphism establishes the relation between these two diagrams.

Let us see a simple example. Let us suppose that our system is a traffic light. In this case, the states will be algebras having just a constant operation, called *colour*, whose values may be *red*, *yellow* and *green*. This means that we have three possible states. Then the possible state transformations include all the possible assignments to the constant in order to change the color of the light. This would be the first level of the model. Now, at the second level we have the actual behavior that the traffic light will have, where not all the possible color changes are possible. For instance, we may think that our traffic light will have four different states: R, Y_1, Y_2 and G and transitions $R \rightarrow Y_1$, $Y_1 \rightarrow G$, $G \rightarrow Y_2$ and $Y_2 \rightarrow R$. The associated graph morphism would map the states R and G to the states where the value of *color* is *red* and *green*, respectively. On the other hand, the morphism would also map the states Y_1 and Y_2 to the state where the value of *color* is *yellow*. In the figure below, the upper part represents the diagram including the three data states and all the possible state transformations. Similarly the diagram in the lower part represents a state transition diagram where the states implicitly contain information about the expected behavior of the traffic lights. For instance, we may consider that the state Y_1 implicitly tells us that this state occurs after a red light and before a green light. Similarly, the state Y_2 implicitly tells us that this state occurs after a green light and before a red light. However, in both cases the *color* is *yellow*. Finally, the morphism relating the two diagrams (for instance, mapping Y_1 and Y_2 to *yellow*) is represented by the dashed arrows.

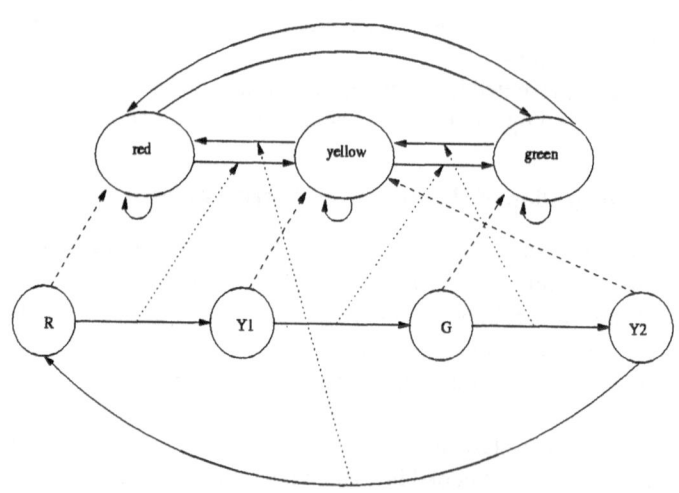

In [8], we presented an integration paradigm based on a very similar kind of models. The main difference was that we used another level below these two for defining data types and a fourth layer for architectural constructions.

In his work, Grosse-Rhode, in addition, studied several operations for putting together models and for refining them. On the other hand, in [12], he showed how this kind of models could be used for giving semantics to UML.

Now, the idea of how to use this kind of semantic frameworks is quite simple. If we want to give semantics to specifications including different units involving several formalisms, first we have to provide a semantic definition for each of the formalisms involved, in terms of the given semantic framework. Then, we can build the semantics of a given specification defining a structure which is, simultaneously a model of all the formalisms or (perhaps equivalently) by putting together the semantics of each unit. The specification will be inconsistent if we are unable to find such a structure or to put together the semantics of the units in a proper way.

Reasonably, the new semantics of each formalism (defined in terms of the semantic framework) should be more concrete than its "standard" semantics. The reason is that, in some sense, the new semantics should include information about other views of a given system. In this sense, if we call $SemFrame$ the class of models associated to the semantic framework, $Mod_{\mathcal{F}}$ the class of models associated to the standard semantics of a formalism $\mathcal{F}$ and $Spec_{\mathcal{F}}$ the class of specifications associated to $\mathcal{F}$, then there should exist some mapping (or functor if the classes above are categories) $Abs : SemFrame \rightarrow Mod_{\mathcal{F}}$ such that $Abs(\mathcal{M})$ should be a model of a specification $SP \in Spec_{\mathcal{F}}$ according to the standard semantics if (and perhaps only if) $\mathcal{M} \in SemFrame$ is a model of SP according to the new semantic framework.

Now, the second problem is whether we can use deductive tools associated to the formalisms used in the specification of a given system to verify some kind of properties of the system. In particular, let us suppose that we are interested in using a logic $\mathcal{L}$ for expressing properties about our systems. This means that we should have defined a proper notion of satisfaction for the class of models of our semantic framework, $\models \subseteq SemFrame \times Formula(\mathcal{L})$. Let us suppose that we have a deductive tool for the formalism $\mathcal{F}$ for verifying the properties expressed in $\mathcal{L}$, i.e. we are able to prove whether $SP \models_{\mathcal{F}} \alpha$, where SP is a specification written using the formalism $\mathcal{F}$ and $\alpha \in Formula(\mathcal{L})$. In this context, if we are able to prove that for every $\mathcal{M} \in SemFrame$ we have that $Abs(\mathcal{M}) \models_{\mathcal{F}} \alpha$ implies that $\mathcal{M} \models \alpha$, then we can use this tool to verify that a heterogeneous specification specification involving a unit using $\mathcal{F}$ satisfies α. In particular, proving that this unit satisfies α would mean that the whole system satisfies α. However, if we prove that this unit does not satisfy α then this could be a false negative, i.e. it may be possible that the whole system does satisfy α.

1.2 Homogeneous Translation of Heterogeneous Specifications

A variation of the previous approach for dealing with specifications involving several formalisms is based on finding an adequate translation of all these formalisms into a single one. This is the approach considered when using Rewriting Logic or HOL [17,24] to "represent" heterogeneous specifications. The idea is that this formalism should be sufficiently "low level" so the we are able to "code" adequately any specification formalism into it. In this context, a heterogeneous specification would become homogeneous by translating all its specification units into that single formalism.

Obviously, these translations should be adequate so that the semantics of specifications should be preserved in the sense discussed in the previous subsection. This means that this kind of coding should not only be defined at the syntactic level but also at the semantic level. For instance, similarly to what we required in the previous section, we may ask that if $\mathcal{F}$ is an arbitrary specification formalism, $\mathcal{BF}$ is the basic formalism used in the integration and $\tau : Spec(\mathcal{F}) \rightarrow Spec(\mathcal{BF})$ is a translation from specifications over $\mathcal{F}$ into specifications over $\mathcal{BF}$, then there should be an associated semantic transformation Abs_τ mapping models of translated specifications into models of these specifications, i.e. if $SP \in Spec(\mathcal{F})$ then for every $\mathcal{M} \in Mod(\tau(SP))$ we should have that $Abs_\tau(\mathcal{M}) \in Mod(SP)$.

In this context, the consistency problem of heterogeneous specifications is reduced to checking the consistency of the translated specification in the basic formalism. Moreover, if this formalism is equipped with prototyping tools for the execution of specifications then these tools may also be used for prototyping the heterogeneous specifications. It is enough to execute their associated translations.

Using the deduction tools associated to the basic formalism for verifying a heterogeneous specification is slightly more involved. In principle, these tools would allow us to prove properties within the formalism. However the verification problem is often presented as showing that a system described using a given formalism satisfies some properties expressed in a different formalism. For instance, a system may be described using a process algebra like ccs and the properties may be expressed using a temporal logic. However, the solution is not difficult. If we want to show that the given system satisfies some properties expressed in this new formalism then we may also translate that formalism and use the deduction tools associated to the basic formalism.

1.3   Heterogeneous Component Systems

In the previous subsections we have considered heterogeneous systems where different formalisms are assumed to describe different aspects or viewpoints of a given system or component. In this section we consider a simpler kind of situation. In particular, we consider component-based or modular systems where different components or modules may be described or implemented using different formalisms. The situation is simpler because typically modules and components are loosely connected, which means that the interactions between them (and, as a consequence, between the associated formalisms) may be limited to the interfaces. Nevertheless, this may obviously depend on the kind of component systems that we consider.

In this case, the semantics of these systems may be seen, informally, as the class of all the models that can be built putting together the semantics of the components. In this context, one can expect to prove that if all the modules in the system are consistent and we compose them in an adequate way then the system is also consistent. However, as we will see in this paper, things are not so easy. On the other hand, one can also expect that we can reason about the global system by reasoning "locally" about the specifications in the modules, using deductive tools associated to each formalism. As we will also see, this is true. However, with respect to the this problem, dealing with this kind of specifications is not simpler than dealing with the general case.

2 Algebraic Preliminaries

In this section we briefly present basic notions and notation that we will use along the paper.

Our specifications will be built over arbitrary *institutions* [11] of the form

$$\mathcal{I} = (\underline{\mathsf{Sig}}, \mathsf{Sen}, \mathsf{Mod}, \models)$$

where as usual,

- $\underline{\mathsf{Sig}}$ denotes the category of signatures of $\mathcal{I}$;
- $\mathsf{Sen} : \underline{\mathsf{Sig}} \to \underline{\mathsf{Set}}$ denotes the functor that maps every signature Σ into the set of all Σ-sentences and every signature morphism into the mapping that translates sentences from one signature into sentences of the other;
- $\mathsf{Mod} : \underline{\mathsf{Sig}} \to \underline{\mathsf{Cat}}^{op}$ denotes the functor mapping every signature Σ into the category of all Σ-structures and every signature morphism h into its associated forgetful functor U_h;
- finally, $\models$ denotes the satisfaction relation of the given institution.

Moreover, we assume that institutions are equipped with some notion of signature inclusion (see, e.g., [6]).

We say that $\mathcal{I}$ is an *exact* institution iff $\underline{\mathsf{Sig}}$ has finite colimits and, in addition, Mod transforms finite colimits in $\underline{\mathsf{Sig}}$ into limits in $\underline{\mathsf{Cat}}$. In what follows, we will assume that all institutions are exact.

To fix notation, in what follows, we will write $b \cup_{a,f,g} c$ to denote the pushout of objects b and c with respect to an object a and morphisms $f : a \to b$ and $g : a \to c$. Similarly, we may write $b \cap_{a,f,g} c$ to denote the pullback of b and c with respect to an object a and morphisms $f : b \to a$ and $g : c \to a$. Moreover, we may write $b \cup_a c$, respectively, $b \cap_a c$, if f and g are clear from the context.

Given an institution $\mathcal{I}$, we consider that a specification over $\mathcal{I}$ is a pair consisting of a signature and a set of axioms $SP = (\Sigma, Ax)$. Given a specification SP, we will assume that Σ_{SP} denotes the signature of the specification SP and Ax_{SP} the set of its axioms, i.e. if $SP = (\Sigma, Ax)$ then $\Sigma_{SP} = \Sigma$ and $Ax_{SP} = Ax$. Given a specification $SP = (\Sigma, Ax)$ we define its class of models $\mathsf{Mod}(SP)$ in the standard way, i.e. as the class of all models in $\mathsf{Mod}(\Sigma)$ satisfying all axioms in Ax.

Specifications in an institution $\mathcal{I}$ form the category $\underline{\mathsf{Spec}}_{\mathcal{I}}$ (or just $\underline{\mathsf{Spec}}$ if $\mathcal{I}$ is clear from the context) whose objects are all pairs (Σ, Ax), where Σ is a signature in $\underline{\mathsf{Sig}}$ and Ax is a set of Σ-sentences, i.e. $Ax \subseteq \mathsf{Sen}(\Sigma)$, and whose morphisms $h : (\Sigma, \overline{Ax}) \to (\Sigma', Ax')$ are signature morphisms $h : \Sigma \to \Sigma'$ satisfying $\mathsf{Sen}(h)(Ax) \subseteq Ax'$.

2.1 Arrows Between Institutions

In this subsection we recall the notions of *institution representation* [28] (also called *plain map of institutions* by Meseguer [16]), and of institution *semi-representation* defined by Tarlecki in [29], which will be needed in the paper.

The notion of an institution representation represents the idea that an institution is encoded in terms of another one. In the case of semi-representations this encoding is only at the level of signatures and models.

Definition 1. *Given institutions $\mathcal{I}$ and $\mathcal{I}'$, an institution representation (or plain map) between $\mathcal{I}$ and $\mathcal{I}'$ is a 3-tuple $r = (S, m, a) : \mathcal{I}' \to \mathcal{I}$ consisting of:*

1. *a functor $S : \underline{Sig'} \to \underline{Sig}$, and*
2. *a natural transformation $m : Mod \circ S^{op} \to Mod'$, that is a collection of functors $\{m(\Sigma) : Mod(S(\Sigma)) \to Mod'(\Sigma)\}_{\Sigma \in \underline{Sig'}}$.*
3. *a natural transformation $a : Sen' \to Sen \circ S$, that is a collection of functors $a(\Sigma) : Sen'(\Sigma) \to Sen(S(\Sigma))$ for every $\Sigma \in \underline{Sig'}$,*

satisfying the plain *or* representation *condition:*

$$\forall \Sigma \in \underline{Sig'}, \forall A \in Mod(S(\Sigma)), \forall \varphi \in Sen'(\Sigma) :$$

$$m(\Sigma)(A) \models'_{\Sigma} \varphi \Leftrightarrow A \models_{S(\Sigma)} a(\Sigma)(\varphi)$$

The pair $r = (S, m) : \mathcal{I}' \to \mathcal{I}$ is called a semi-representation.

Being concrete, the intuition of an institution representation is that each signature $\Sigma \in \underline{Sig'}$ is translated into a signature $S(\Sigma) \in \underline{Sig}$, the sentences over Σ in $\mathcal{I}'$ are translated into sentences over $S(\Sigma)$ in $\mathcal{I}$ and, dually, the models over $S(\Sigma)$ in $\mathcal{I}$ are translated into models over Σ in $\mathcal{I}'$. We could have used a more general notion of institution (semi-) representation. For instance, the notion of simple map of institutions ([16]), where signatures in the institution $\mathcal{I}'$ are encoded in terms of theories in the institution $\mathcal{I}$. We have not done this for simplicity, although we think that this would have not posed any significant technical problems.

3 Heterogeneous Systems Modular over Institutional Frameworks

In this section we introduce the syntactic and semantic definition of the notions of specification module and heterogeneous system considered.

The notion of module that we consider is inspired in the one defined in [10] and is quite close to the notion studied in [7] (also used in [20]) and to other module notions (e.g. [27]). However, here we do not assume that a module describes an independent part of a system. On the contrary, in general we will assume that a module describes a view of (part of) a given system. Technically, this means, on one hand, that our modules will have a loose semantics. The reason is that we must consider that all models sharing the view described by the module could be considered models of the module. On the other hand we must lift the usual restriction that modules should be persistent (e.g., see [7]) which has been substituted by a weaker notion of conservativeness. The intuition behind our concept is the following one: a module MOD is some kind of specification unit that not only consists of a specification BOD of the "objects" (partly) described in the unit, but also includes two additional interface specifications: the first one, the import specification IMP, specifies the part of BOD that "is needed to know" about the rest of the system; the second one, the export specification EXP, specifies what the module "offers", that is, EXP is the visible part of BOD. In addition, BOD may contain an internal (non-visible) part specifying some auxiliary components.

Definition 2. *A module specification in a given institution* $\mathcal{I}$ *is a 5-tuple*

$$MOD = (IMP, EXP, BOD, s : IMP \to BOD, v : EXP \to BOD)$$

where EXP is the export interface specification, IMP is the import interface specification, BOD is the body specification and, s and v are specification inclusions representing the relations among these specifications in $\underline{\mathsf{Spec}}_{\mathcal{I}}$.

Following the intuitions discussed above, we consider that the semantics of a module MOD is just the class $U_v(\mathsf{Mod}(BOD))$. This may be considered too simple, but it is actually a generalization of the most standard semantics. Often modules are seen as some kind of functions that, given some kind of realization of the import specification yield a realization of the export specification. In our case, in general, we can not see our modules as functions. If we consider that a model of MOD, $A = U_v(A')$ with $A' \in \mathsf{Mod}(BOD)$, represents the result of "applying" MOD to $A_0 = U_s(\mathsf{Mod}(A))$, then one cannot ensure that, for a given $A_0 \in \mathsf{Mod}(IMP)$, there will be a unique $A' \in \mathsf{Mod}(BOD)$ such that $A_0 = U_s(\mathsf{Mod}(A))$. Actually, there may be no such A', or there may be many. On the other hand, a module is conservative if every model of the import specification can be extended to a model of the body. Formally, MOD is *conservative* if the existence of such A' is guaranteed, i.e., $U_s(\mathsf{Mod}(BOD)) = \mathsf{Mod}(IMP)$.

It may look surprising that the import interface of a module apparently plays no significant role in its semantics, but just in the notion of conservativeness. Actually, this can be considered quite reasonable. Interfaces are important when putting together several modules to build a modular system. In this sense, one may see the role of the import interface in the semantics of modular systems (see def. 5) and in the definition of complete modular systems (see def. 7).

A modular system, where all the modules are defined over the same institution, is seen as a collection of modules together with some global description of the system, e.g. the facilities or operations offered by the system. In our case, as said in the introduction, we regard this description just as a signature, although we could also consider that it includes some axioms describing global properties of the system. The modules are bound to this global signature by means of fitting (signature) morphisms, matching the services or operations imported and exported by a module with the global operations offered by the system. In this context, these signature morphisms play the role of (implicitly) interconnecting the modules of a given system. However, if each module is defined over a different institution and the system itself (i.e. its global signature) is also defined over a different institution then there should be a well-defined relation between all these institutions allowing to relate the signatures of the modules with the signature of the system and the semantics of the modules with the semantics of the system.

A heterogeneous institutional framework consists of a collection of institutions $\{\mathcal{I}_j\}_{1 \leq j \leq n}$ used for writing the modules together with an institution $\mathcal{I}$ which represents the logic language used for describing the "services" that are specified by the global system. Then, the institutions $\{\mathcal{I}_j\}_{1 \leq j \leq n}$ are mapped into $\mathcal{I}$.

Definition 3. *We say that $\mathcal{IF} = (\mathcal{I}, \{\mathcal{I}_j, r_j\}_{1 \leq j \leq n})$ is an institutional framework if,*

1. *$\mathcal{I} = (\underline{\mathsf{Sig}}, \mathsf{Mod}, \mathsf{Sen}, \models)$ and $\mathcal{I}_j = (\underline{\mathsf{Sig}}_j, \mathsf{Mod}_j, \mathsf{Sen}_j, \models^j)$ for every j, $1 \leq j \leq n$, are exact institutions having pullbacks of signatures with respect to monomorphisms.*
2. *For every j, $1 \leq j \leq n$, $r_j = (S_j, m_j, a) : \mathcal{I}_j \to \mathcal{I}$ is a semi-representation of institutions.*

If, for each j, r_j is a representation, then $(\mathcal{I}, \{\mathcal{I}_j, r_j\}_{1 \leq j \leq n})$ is called a strong institutional framework.

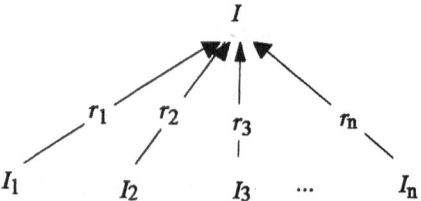

Now, we can define the notion of modular system over a heterogeneous institutional framework. Every module of such kind of system is written in an institution of the collection $\{\mathcal{I}_j, r_j\}_{1 \leq j \leq n}$. The additional institution $\mathcal{I}$ describes the operations exported by the system. More specifically, a heterogeneous modular system consists of a global signature of the global institution $\mathcal{I}$ and a collection of modules defined over the non-global institutions. The signatures of the export and import interfaces are mapped to the global signature such that common elements are mapped to the same elements:

Definition 4. *A heterogeneous modular system over a global signature Σ_G and an institutional framework $(\mathcal{I}, \{\mathcal{I}_j, r_j\}_{1 \leq j \leq n})$, is a pair*

$$\mathcal{SM} = (\Sigma_G, \{(MOD_j, i_j, e_j)\}_{1 \leq j \leq n})$$

where Σ_G is a signature in $\underline{\mathsf{Sig}}$ of $\mathcal{I}$, and for each j, $1 \leq j \leq n$,

- *$MOD_j = (IMP_j, EXP_j, BODj, s_j, v_j)$ is a module in the institution $\mathcal{I}_j$, and*
- *$i_j : S_j(\Sigma_{IMP_j}) \to \Sigma_G$ and $e_j : S_j(\Sigma_{EXP_j}) \to \Sigma_G$ are two signature monomorphisms in $\underline{\mathsf{Sig}}$ such that if $\Sigma_{COM_j} = \Sigma_{IMP_j} \cap_{\Sigma_{BOD_j}, s_j, v_j} \Sigma_{EXP_j}$ is a pullback in $\underline{\mathsf{Sig}}_j$:*

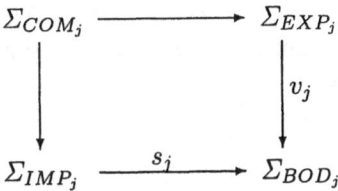

then the diagram below is also a pullback in **Sig**:

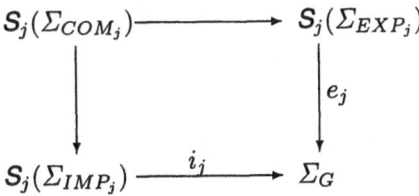

Remarks 1

1. Since the specifications COM_j include the common elements of IMP_j and EXP_j, then the above pullback for $S_j(\Sigma_{COM_j})$ states that these common elements must be bound to the same elements of the global signature Σ_G through i_j and e_j. Moreover, the mappings i_j and e_j are defined to be monomorphisms. The reason is that we consider that a given operation offered by a system cannot be internally defined in terms of two different operations within the same module.

2. It may be noted that a modular system of this kind may be "incomplete" in the sense that there may be "elements" in the global signature which are not exported or not "defined" by any module of the system. It may also happen that an element in the global system may be defined by several modules which may provide different views on that element.

3. In contrast with other approaches (e.g. [7]), our modules are not composed directly, by defining a connection (e.g. a morphism) between the import specification of one module and the export specification of another module, but indirectly, through a binding of these specifications to the global signature. In particular, given the modules MOD_1 and MOD_2, if we want to connect IMP_1 with EXP_2 we would need to define the morphisms $i_1 : S_1(\Sigma_{IMP_1}) \to \Sigma_G$ and $e_2 : S_2(\Sigma_{EXP_2}) \to \Sigma_G$ such that $i_1(S_1(\Sigma_{IMP_1}))$ is a subsignature of $e_2(S_2(\Sigma_{EXP_2}))$. A study of the relation of this kind of indirect composition with a number of operations for composing modules (e.g. [7]) in the homogeneous case can be found in [25]. In particular, our modular system may include circular definitions, in the sense that a module $MOD1$ may import a definition exported by $MOD2$, which itself imports another definition exported by $MOD1$. We just have to connect the corresponding signatures by means of common bindings to Σ_G.

The following very simple example presents a modular system defining the semantics of a simple imperative language $\mathcal{L}$.

Example 1. Let $\mathcal{SM_L} = (\Sigma_G, \{(MOD_j, i_j, e_j)\}_{j=1,2})$ in $\mathcal{IF} = (\mathcal{I}, \{\mathcal{I}_j, r_j\}_{j=1,2})$ be the following heterogeneous modular system defined to simulate executions of programs in the following language $\mathcal{L}$:

```
c::= id:= E | c;c | if E then c else c | while E do c
E::= id | E*E | E = E | ¬ E | E∧ E| E∨E
```

Then, assuming the usual semantics for imperative languages:

Table 1. Global signature of example 1

```
Signature ΣG:
  Sorts ident, value, state, exp, com
  Functions
    empty: ⟶ state
    ass: state, ident, value ⟶ state
    val: state, ident ⟶ value
    id: ident ⟶ exp
    -*-: exp, exp ⟶ exp
    etc,...
    e: exp, state ⟶ value
    _ := _ : ident, exp ⟶ com
    _ ; _ : com, com⟶ com
    if _ then _ else: exp, com, com ⟶ com
    while _ do _ : exp, com ⟶ com
    c: com, state ⟶ state
```

- States are functions s: ident → value
- Expressions are functions E: states → value
- Commands are functions c: states → states

In particular, $\mathcal{IF}$ and $\mathcal{SM_L}$ consist of:

- The global institution $\mathcal{I}$ is the institution of first-order logic with equality and the global signature Σ_G defining the language $\mathcal{L}$ can be found in table 1.
- The first module MOD_1, presented in table 2, defines the operational semantics of $\mathcal{L}$. In particular, BOD_1 is a logic program that simulates the execution of programs in the language $\mathcal{L}$, that is, it implements the usual semantics of imperative languages such as $\mathcal{L}$. We may consider that its associated institution $\mathcal{I}_1$ is Horn clause logic or, better, the institution $\mathcal{DLP}$ defined in [23]. IMP_1 and EXP_1 are just signatures defining the interfaces of MOD_1.
- $\mathcal{I}_2$ is the institution of equational logic and MOD_2 presented in table 3, is the module specifying the symbol table required for executions.
- The semi-representation binding $\mathcal{I}_1$ to $\mathcal{I}$, at the signature level, transforms predicate symbols $p : s_1 \ldots s_{n-1} s_n$ into the function symbol $p : s_1 \ldots s_{n-1} \longrightarrow s_n$. At the model level, the semi-representation is defined in the obvious way.
- The (semi)-representation binding $\mathcal{I}_2$ to $\mathcal{I}$ is just the obvious embedding.

Table 2. MOD_1 of example 1

```
Signature IMP₁:
  Sorts ident, value, state
  Functions
    empty: ⟶ state
    ass: state, ident, value ⟶ state
    val: state, ident ⟶ value
Signature EXP₁:
  Sorts exp, com
  Functions
    id: ident ⟶ exp
    -*-: exp, exp ⟶ exp
    etc,...
    _ := _ : ident, exp ⟶ com
    _ ; _ : com, com⟶ com
    if _ then _ else: exp, com, com ⟶ com
    while _ do _ : exp, com ⟶ com
  Predicates
    e: exp, state, value
    c: com, state, state
Program BOD₁:
  ΣBOD₁ = IMP₁ ∪ EXP₁
  Clauses
    e(x, s, val(s,x)).
    e(E₁ * E₂, s, v₁ * v₂) :− e(E₁,s,v₁), e(E₂,s,v₂)
    e(E₁ = E₂, s, v₁ = v₂) :−          "
    e(E₁ < E₂, s, v₁ < v₂) :−          "
    e(E₁ ∧ E₂, s, v₁ ∧ v₂) :−          "
    e(E₁ ∨ E₂, s, v₁ ∨ v₂) :−          "
    e(¬E, s, v) :− e(E, s, ¬v)
    c(x := E, s, ass(s,x,v)) :− e(E,s,v)
    c(C₁;C₂,s₁,s₂) :− c(C₁,s₁,s'), c(C₂,s',s₂)
    etc,...
```

- The morphisms s_j, v_j are just the obvious inclusions.
- The morphisms e_j, i_j binding (the translation of) the import and export signatures into the global signature are, again, the obvious inclusions (modulo the signature translation in the case of MOD_1. It may be noted that these morphisms implicitly describe the composition of MOD_1 with MOD_2 connecting (through Σ_G) the import of MOD_1 with the export of MOD_2.
- The semantics of this system would, obviously, depend on the semantics of the specifications included in the modules. For instance, we may consider that the semantics of these modules is defined by means of a free generating constraint in the corresponding formalisms (Horn logic and equational logic), more or less in the spirit of the semantics of the modules in [7]. In this case, and if we assume that the basic types (booleans, values, etc) are defined by means of a single structure, the semantics of the system will consist of a single model (up to isomorphism), where

Table 3. MOD_2 of example 1

```
Specification IMP₂:
  Sorts ident, value, bool
  Functions
    _ = _ : ident, ident ⟶ bool
    _ * _ : value, value ⟶ value
    true ⟶ value
    false ⟶ value
    etc ...
  Equations
    {Those defining value and ident}
Signature EXP₂:
  Sorts ident, value, table
  Functions
    ε_t: ⟶ table
    mod_t: table, ident, value ⟶ table
    val_t: table, ident ⟶ table
Specification BOD₂:
  Σ_BOD₂ = Σ_IMP₂ ∪ Σ_EXP₂
  Equations = Ax_IMP₂ ∪
∀x₁, x₂, x : ident, v₁, v₂, v : value, t : table
  ass_t(mod_t(t, x, v₁), x, v₂) =_eq mod_t(t, x, v₂)
  val_t(mod_t(t, x, v₁), x) =_eq v₁
  x₁ ≠ x₂ ⟹ mod_t(mod_t(t, x₁, v₁), x₂, v₂) =_eq
      mod_t(mod_t(t, x₂, v₂), x₁, v₁)
  x₁ ≠ x₂ ⟹ val_t(mod_t(t, x₁, v₁), x₂) =_eq
      val_t(t, x₂)
  val_t(ε_t, x) =_eq ?
```

the basic state model is described by the symbol table module (MOD_2) and the rest of the semantics is described by MOD_1.

We define the semantics of a heterogeneous modular system as the class of all models (of the global signature) which can be seen as models of each module:

Definition 5. Let $\mathcal{SM} = (\Sigma_G, \{(MOD_j, i_j, e_j)\}_{1 \leq j \leq n})$ be a heterogeneous modular system over a global signature Σ_G and an institutional framework $(\mathcal{I}, \{\mathcal{I}_j, r_j\}_{1 \leq j \leq n})$, the semantics of $\mathcal{SM}$, denoted $[\![\mathcal{SM}]\!]$, is defined as:

$$[\![\mathcal{SM}]\!] = \{A \in Mod(\Sigma_G) | \forall (MOD_j, i_j, e_j), A \models_{\langle i_j, e_j \rangle} MOD_j\},$$

where $A \models_{\langle i_j, e_j \rangle} MOD_j$, $A \in Mod(\Sigma_G)$ satisfies MOD_j with respect to i_j and e_j, if there exist an $A_j \in Mod_j(BOD_j)$ such that:

1. $m_j(\Sigma_{IMP_j})(U_{i_j}(A)) = U_{s_j}(A_j)$ and
2. $m_j(\Sigma_{EXP_j})(U_{e_j}(A)) = U_{v_j}(A_j)$

Where the diagram below shows the functionality of the functors involved:

$$Mod(\Sigma_G) \xrightarrow{\quad U_{e_j} \quad} Mod(S_j(\Sigma_{EXP_j})) \xrightarrow{\quad m_j(\Sigma_{EXP_j}) \quad} Mod_j(\Sigma_{EXP_j})$$

with vertical arrows U_{i_j} from $Mod(\Sigma_G)$ to $Mod(S_j(\Sigma_{IMP_j}))$, $m_j(\Sigma_{IMP_j})$ from $Mod(S_j(\Sigma_{IMP_j}))$ to $Mod_j(\Sigma_{IMP_j})$, U_{v_j} from $Mod_j(\Sigma_{BOD_j})$ to $Mod_j(\Sigma_{EXP_j})$, and U_{s_j} from $Mod_j(\Sigma_{IMP_j})$ to $Mod_j(\Sigma_{BOD_j})$.

As usual, we say that $\mathcal{SM}$ is consistent if it has some models, i.e. if $[\![\mathcal{SM}]\!] \neq \emptyset$

4 Consistency of Heterogeneous Modular Systems

In the previous section, we have introduced our notion of heterogeneous modular system, now we will see some general sufficient conditions that can ensure the consistency of these systems. It should be obvious that,in the case where modules describe different views of a system, we may always have inconsistent specifications caused by two modules describing contradictory or incompatible views. For this reason, in this section we will concentrate in the special case of heterogeneous modular systems where each module is assumed to completely describe part of the given system.

A heterogeneous modular system may be inconsistent for several reasons. For instance, if a module is inconsistent then the overall specification will obviously be inconsistent too. But the situation is actually worse, a system including just one consistent and conservative module may still be inconsistent. The reason is that some models in the institution of the module (which may happen to include the models of the module) may be not the representation of any model in the global institution. This may be the case, for example, in the case of the semi-representation, defined in example 1, binding the institutions $\mathcal{I}_1$ and $\mathcal{I}$. In particular, the models in $\mathcal{I}_1$ that include non-functional predicates (i.e., predicates p, where there exist a, b and c such that $p(a, b)$ and $p(a, c)$ hold and $b \neq c$) are not the representation of any model in $\mathcal{I}$. This means that if the module MOD_1 would include the specification of a non-functional predicate then, most probably, the global system including MOD_1 would be inconsistent. This is not the case if the given (semi-)representation (S, m, a) *admits model expansion*, i.e. if m is pointwise surjective on objects, which means that for each signature Σ, $m(\Sigma)$ is surjective. If this is not the case, if the given (semi-)representations do not admit model expansion, the consistency of a module, when "translated" by the representation would need to be proved in the global institution. In this case, we may also want to consider an alternative definition of conservativeness, instead of the one presented in Section 3.

Definition 6. *Let $r = (S, m) : \mathcal{I}' \to \mathcal{I}$ be an institution semi-representation and let $MOD = (IMP, EXP, BOD, s : IMP \to BOD, v : EXP \to BOD)$ be a module over $\mathcal{I}'$, we say that MOD is conservative with respect to r if for every*

$A_1 \in Mod(S(\Sigma_{IMP}))$ such that $m(\Sigma_{IMP})(A_1) \in Mod(IMP)$ there exist $A_2 \in Mod(BOD)$ and $A_3 \in Mod(S(\Sigma_{EXP}))$ such that:

- $U_v(A_2) = m(\Sigma_{EXP})(A_3)$
- $U_s(A_2) = m(\Sigma_{IMP})(A_1)$

In what follows, we will provide a definition that characterizes, on one hand, that all the elements of the global signature are defined adequately in some module, on the other hand, that every element is defined just in one module and, finally, that the import specification of each module is not contradictory with the what is specified in the rest of the modules. We will call these specifications *complete*. In addition, we will show that complete specifications are consistent under adequate assumptions of module correctness.

Definition 7. *Let $SM = (\Sigma_G, \{(MOD_j, i_j, e_j)\}_{1 \leq j \leq n})$ be a heterogeneous modular system over a global signature Σ_G and an institutional framework $(\mathcal{I}, \{\mathcal{I}_j, r_j\}_{1 \leq j \leq n})$, we say that SM is (Σ_0, Σ_G)-complete if we can define a sequence of pushouts of signatures, as in the diagram below, for some family of morphisms f_j, $j = 1, \ldots, n$*

$$S_1(\Sigma_{IMP_1}) \longrightarrow S_1(\Sigma_{EXP_1'}) \quad S_2(\Sigma_{IMP_2}) \longrightarrow S_2(\Sigma_{EXP_2'}) \qquad\qquad S_n(\Sigma_{EXP_n'})$$

$$\downarrow f_1 \qquad\qquad\qquad\qquad \downarrow f_2 \qquad\qquad\qquad\qquad \cdots$$

$$\Sigma_0 \longrightarrow \Sigma_1 \longrightarrow \Sigma_2 \qquad\qquad \Sigma_n$$

such that:

1. $\Sigma_n = \Sigma_G$
2. for every $j = 0, \ldots, n-1$, the set

$$\{A \in Mod(\Sigma_j) / \forall k(k < j) A \models_{\langle i_k, e_k \rangle} MOD_k$$

$$\wedge m_j(\Sigma_{IMP_{j+1}})(U_{f_{j+1}}(A)) \in Mod_j(IMP_{j+1})\}$$

is not empty.
3. for every $j = 1, \ldots, n$, $\Sigma_{EXP_j'}$ is the result of the following pushout:

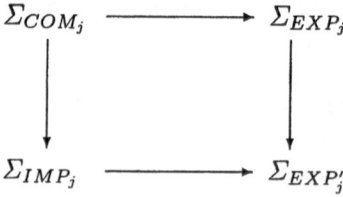

Essentially, the above definition says that the given system may be described by a hierarchical composition of the given modules. The signature Σ_0 is supposed to describe the elements which are assumed to be predefined (built-in) in the system. In many cases, we could consider Σ_0 to be the empty signature. Conditions 1) and 3) of the definition ensure that every element in Σ_G (except those in Σ_0) are defined exactly in one module. The second condition guarantees that the import of each module is consistent with what has been defined by the previous modules in the hierarchy. One may notice that this condition is weaker than the standard condition used for module composition (see e.g. [7]). In particular, in [7] we can compose two modules MOD_1 and MOD_2 if we can define a fitting morphism $h : IMP_2 \rightarrow EXP_1$. This is, more or less equivalent (it depends on the notion of specification morphism considered) to say that $h : \Sigma_{IMP_2} \rightarrow \Sigma_{EXP_1}$ such that $U_h(\text{Mod}(EXP_1)) \subseteq \text{Mod}(IMP_2)$. However, in our context we would just ask that $U_h(\text{Mod}(EXP_1)) \cap \text{Mod}(IMP_2) \neq \emptyset$

Now, we can see that a (Σ_0, Σ_G)-complete modular system consisting of internally correct modules is consistent provided there exist some Σ_0-models when dealing with representations that admit model expansion:

Theorem 1. *Let* $SM = (\Sigma_G, \{(MOD_j, i_j, e_j)\}_{1 \leq j \leq n})$ *be a* (Σ_0, Σ_G)-*complete modular system over a global signature* Σ_G *and an institutional framework* $(\mathcal{I}, \{\mathcal{I}_j, r_j\}_{1 \leq j \leq n})$, *such that, for every* j, MOD_j *is conservative and every* r_j *admits model expansion. Then if* $\text{Mod}(\Sigma_0)$ *is not empty then* SM *is consistent.*

Proof. We proceed by induction on the number of modules. If there are 0 modules then the proof is trivial. For the induction case, from condition 2) and the induction hypothesis we know that there is at least a model A_j of Σ_j that satisfies all modules MOD_i, for i smaller than j and that $\text{m}_{j+1}(\Sigma_{IMP_{j+1}})(U_{f_{j+1}}(A_j)) \in \text{Mod}_{j+1}(IMP_{j+1})$. Let $B_j = \text{m}_{j+1}(\Sigma_{IMP_{j+1}})(U_{f_{j+1}}(A))$. Now, since MOD_{j+1} is assumed to be conservative there should be a $B_{j+1} \in \text{Mod}_{j+1}(BOD_{j+1})$ such that $U_{s_{j+1}}(B_{j+1}) = B_j$. Let $C_{j+1} = U_{v_{j+1}}(B_{j+1}) \in \text{Mod}_{j+1}(EXP_{j+1})$ and let $D_{j+1} = C_{j+1}|_{COM_{j+1}} = B_{j+1}|_{COM_{j+1}}$. Now, since all institutions are assumed to be exact, we can build the amalgamation $B_{j+1} +_{D_{j+1}} C_{j+1}$ and since r_{j+1} admits model expansion there should be a $C'_{j+1} \in S_{j+1}(\Sigma_{EXP'_{j+1}})$ such that $C_{j+1} = \text{m}_{j+1}(\Sigma_{EXP'_{j+1}})(C'_{j+1})$. Again, since the global institution is also assumed to be exact, we can also build the amalgamation $A_j +_{B_j} C'_{j+1}$. Let $A_{j+1} = A_j +_{B_j} C'_{j+1}$. By construction $A_{j+1} \models_{\langle i_k, e_k \rangle} MOD_k$ for every $k \leq j+1$.

The same result can be obtained if the semi-representations in the institutional framework do not admit model expansion, but each module MOD_j is internally correct with respect to r_j:

Theorem 2. *Let* $SM = (\Sigma_G, \{(MOD_j, i_j, e_j)\}_{1 \leq j \leq n})$ *be a* (Σ_0, Σ_G)-*complete modular system over a global signature* Σ_G *and an institutional framework* $(\mathcal{I}, \{\mathcal{I}_j, r_j\}_{1 \leq j \leq n})$, *such that, for every* j, MOD_j *is internally correct with respect to* r_j. *Then if* $\text{Mod}(\Sigma_0)$ *is not empty then* SM *is consistent.*

Proof. The proof is very similar. If there are 0 modules then the proof is again trivial. For the induction case, given a model A of Σ_j that satisfies all modules MOD_i, for i smaller than j, it is not difficult to build a model Σ_{j+1} extending A and satisfying MOD_j, using correctness of MOD_j with respect to r_j and the exactness of the global institution.

5   Reasoning About Heterogeneous Modular Systems

In the previous section, we have discussed how can we ensure the consistency of a heterogeneous modular system. In this section, we will briefly discuss how one can prove properties about this kind of systems. In particular, we may want to prove consistency, if the conditions that ensure them can not be met, or we may want to prove that some global properties are satisfied by the given system.

Now to build proofs in a heterogeneous framework means, in some sense, combining axioms and formulas from the different institutions involved in the framework. The simplest way, in our case, consists in assuming that the given heterogeneous framework is strong, i.e. it involves institution representations and not only semi-representations. This means that we are now able to translate formulas from the institutions associated to the given modules into formulas from the global institution. In this context, we may provide an obvious solution for the problem of reasoning about such kind of system: it is enough to flatten the system just putting together the translated specifications from all the modules involved and, then, use standard deduction techniques in the global institution.

This solution, however, has two main drawbacks. The first one is that, in this flattening we would need to extend the global specification with all the bodies of the modules involved yielding a larger and more complex specification, which will be more difficult to reason about. The second and most important problem is that it may be unrealistic to think that all the formulas in the modules' institutions can be translated into the global institution. For instance, a module specification may include a free generating constraint, so that its semantics is a class of free models or in order to ensure some fixed interpretation to a certain sub-specification.

Instead, we think that a better solution is to try to build structured proofs generalizing the approached surveyed in [2] to the heterogeneous case. In particular, this means that, when we try to prove a property about the whole system, we build a proof including subproofs (in the associated institutions) for lemmas that are consequence of the modules' specifications. Moreover, these subproofs will be typically obtained using deduction tools associated to the modules' institutions. It should be clear that the soundness of this approach is a consequence of the plain representation condition of institution representations and of the satisfaction condition of institutions:

Proposition 1. *Let* $SM = (\Sigma_G, \{(MOD_j, i_j, e_j)\}_{1 \leq j \leq n})$ *be a heterogeneous modular system over a global signature* Σ_G *and an institutional framework* $(\mathcal{I}, \{\mathcal{I}_j, r_j\}_{1 \leq j \leq n})$, *such that* $r_j = (S_j, m_j, a_j)$ *for all* $1 \leq j \leq n$ *are institution representations. Then the following deduction rule is sound:*

$$\frac{MOD_j \models_{\mathcal{I}_j} \varphi}{SM \vdash e_j^{\#} \circ a_j(\Sigma_{EXP_j})(\varphi)} \quad \varphi \in \mathsf{Sen}_j(\Sigma_{EXP_j}) \quad \textbf{(lift)}$$

Proof. Let $\varphi \in \mathsf{Sen}_j(\Sigma_{EXP_j})$ be a consequence of MOD_j in $\mathcal{I}_j$. If A is a model of SM this means that $\mathsf{m}_j(U_{e_j}(A)$ is a model of MOD_j, i.e. $\mathsf{m}_j(U_{e_j}(A) \models_{\mathcal{I}_j} \varphi$. This means that $U_{e_j}(A) \models_{\mathcal{I}} a_j(\Sigma_{EXP_j})(\varphi)$, because of the plain representations condition. But this means that $A \models_{\mathcal{I}} e_j^{\#} \circ a_j(\Sigma_{EXP_j})(\varphi)$.

Remarks 2

1. *This rule is also sound if the representations r_j are only partial, in the sense that not all the sentences from the institutions $\mathcal{I}_j$ can be translated into the institution $\mathcal{I}$.*
2. *Even if the deduction systems associated to all the institutions involved are complete, then these lifting rules (together with the other deduction rules associated to the given institutions) are not complete. In particular, if the given representations do not admit model expansion then these proof systems will, in general, not be complete. For more details about this issue one may consult [5].*

To end, let us see a very simple example of a heterogeneous proof for the modular system $\mathcal{SM_L}$ of example 1:

Example 2 (A proof in $\mathcal{SM_L}$).
We want to prove the property that says that the value of the variable x after executing the assignment $x:=E$ in a state s is exactly the value of the expression E in s, i.e.:

$$\mathcal{SM_L} \models_{\Sigma_G} \texttt{val}(\texttt{c}(x:=E,s),x) =_{eq} e(E,s)$$

Now, in the body of MOD_1 the following condition holds (actually it is an axiom):

(1) $MOD_1 \vdash_{\mathcal{I}_1} \texttt{c}(x:=E,s, \texttt{ass}(s,x,v)) :- e(E,s,v)$

This axiom can be translated and lifted to the global system:

(2) $\mathcal{SM_L} \vdash_{\mathcal{I}} e(E,s)=_{eq} v \rightarrow \texttt{c}(x:=E,s) =_{eq} \texttt{ass}(s,x,v)$ *(lift)*

Using standard deduction in first-order logic, we have:

(3) $\mathcal{SM_L} \vdash_{\mathcal{I}} \texttt{c}(x:=E,s) =_{eq} \texttt{ass}(s,x,e(s,E))$

Now, in the body of MOD_2 the following condition holds (it is again an axiom):

(4) $MOD_2 \vdash_{\mathcal{I}_2} \texttt{val\_t}(\texttt{mod\_t}(s,x,v),x) =_{eq} v$

Again, we can lift this axiom:

(5) $\mathcal{SM_L} \vdash_{\mathcal{I}} \texttt{val}(\texttt{ass}(s,x,v),x) =_{eq} v$ *(lift)*

Finally, using again standard deduction in first-order logic, we end the proof in three more steps:

(6) $\mathcal{SM_L} \vdash_{\mathcal{I}} \texttt{c}(x:=E,s) =_{eq} \texttt{ass}(s,x,e(E,s))$

(7) $\mathcal{SM_L} \vdash_{\mathcal{I}} \texttt{val}(\texttt{ass}(s,x,v),x) =_{eq} v$

(8) $\mathcal{SM_L} \vdash_{\mathcal{I}} \texttt{val}(\texttt{c}(x:=E,s),x) =_{eq} e(E,s)$

Acknowledgements. This work has been strongly influenced by our cooperation on integration topics with the group of Hartmut Ehrig at TU Berlin. In particular, we would like to mention our participation in the three workshops on integration INT 2000, INT 2002 and INT 2004. This work is partially supported by the Spanish project MAVERISH (TIC2001-2476-C03-01), by the CIRIT Grup de Recerca Consolidat 2001SGR 00254 and by the RTN Segravis (RTN2-2001-00346).

References

1. E. Astesiano, H-J. Kreoski, and B. Krieg Brueckner (editors). *Algebraic Foundations for System Specification*. IFIP State-of-the-art Reports, Springer-Verlag, 1999.
2. M. Bidoit, M.V. Cengarle, and R. Hennicker. Chapter 11: Proof Systems for Structured Specification and Their Refinement. In [1], 1999.
3. B. Braatz, M. Klein, G. Schroeter, Semantical Integration of Object-Oriented Viewpoint Specification Methods. To appear in this volume.
4. Grady Booch, Jim Rumbaugh, Ivar Jacobson: *The Unified Modeling Language User Guide*, Addison-Wesley, 1998.
5. M. Cerioli and J. Meseguer. May I borrow your logic?. *Theoretical Computer Science*, 173:311–347, 1997.
6. R. Diaconescu, J. A. Goguen, P. Stefaneas. Logical support for modularisation. Report Prog. Res. Group, Oxford University, 1991
7. H. Ehrig, B. Mahr. *Fundamentals of Algebraic Specification 2: Module Specifications and Constraints*, vol. 21 of *EATCS Monographs on Theor. Comp. Science*. Springer Verlag, Berlin (1990).
8. Hartmut Ehrig, Fernando Orejas: Integration Paradigm for Data Type and Process Specification Techniques. *Bulletin of the EATCS* 65: 90-97 (1998)
9. H. Ehrig, F. Orejas, B. Braatz, M. Klein, M. Piirainen. A Generic Component Framework for System Modeling. In *Proc. FASE 2002*, Springer LNCS 2306 (2002), pp. 33–48.
10. H. Gaifman and E. Shapiro. Fully abstract compositional semantics for logics programs. In *Proc. Sixteenth Annual ACM Symp. on Principles of Programming Languages*, pages 134–142, 1989.
11. J.A. Goguen and R.M. Burstall. Institutions: Abstract model theory for specification and programming. *Journal of the ACM*, 39(1):95–146, 1992.
12. M. Große-Rhode. Integrating Semantics for Object-Oriented System Models. In *Proceedings ICALP 2001*, Fernando Orejas, Paul G. Spirakis, Jan van Leeuwen (eds.) Springer LNCS 2076 (2001), pp. 238–255.
13. M. Große-Rhode. *Semantic integration of heterogeneous formal specifications via transformation systems*. Habilitation Thesis. TU Berlin (2001).
14. M. Große-Rhode. *Semantic integration of heterogeneous software specifications*. Springer 2004.
15. Information processing systems - Open Systems Interconnection - LOTOS - A formal description technique based on the temporal ordering of observational behaviour. International Standard ISO 8807, ISO, 1989
16. J. Meseguer. General logic. In *Logic Colloq.'87*, pages 279–329. H.-D. Ebbinghaus et al. eds., North Holland 1998.
17. J. Meseguer: Conditioned Rewriting Logic as a United Model of Concurrency. Theor. Comput. Sci. 96(1): 73-155 (1992)
18. Till Mossakowski: Heterogeneous Development Graphs and Heterogeneous Borrowing. Proc. *FoSSaCS 2002*, Springer Lecture Notes in Computer Science 2303 (2002),326-341.
19. M. Navarro, F. Orejas, and A. Sanchez. On the correctness of modular systems. *Theoretical Computer Science*, 140:139–177, 1995.
20. F. Orejas. *Chapter 6: Structuring and Modularity*. In [1], 1999.
21. F. Orejas, E. Pino. A general algebraic framework for studying modular systems. in Proc. 14th International Workshop on Algebraic Development Techniques (WADT'99, Château de Bonas, France), Springer Lecture Notes in Computer Science 1827: 271–290, 2000.
22. Fernando Orejas, Elvira Pino: Heterogeneous Modular Systems, Proc. IDPT 2002, Pasadena.

23. F. Orejas, E. Pino, and H. Ehrig. Institutions for logic programming. *Theoretical Computer Science*, 173:485–511, 1997.
24. Lawrence C. Paulson: Mechanizing UNITY in Isabelle. ACM Trans. Comput. Log., 1(1): 3-32 (2000).
25. E. Pino. *An Algebraic Study of Modularity in Logic Programming*. PhD thesis, Dept. de Llenguatges i Sistemes Informàtics. Universitat Politècnica de Catalunya, 1999. http//www.upc.lsi.es/~pino.
26. H. Reichel. Initiallity restricting algebraic theories. In *Proc. Mathematical Foundations of Computer Science 80*, pages 504–514. Springer LNCS 88, 1980.
27. D.T. Sannella and A. Tarlecki. Toward formal development of ml programs: Foundations and methodology. In *Proc. TAPSOFT'89*, pages 375–389. Springer LNCS 352, Barcelona 1989.
28. A. Tarlecki. Moving between logical systems. In *Recent Trends in Algebraic Development Techniques*, pages 478–502. Springer LNCS 1130, 1996.
29. A. Tarlecki. Towards heterogeneous specifications. In *Proc. Workshop on Frontiers of Combining Systems FroCoS'98*. Applied Logic Series, Kluwer Academic Publishers, 1998.

Semantical Integration of Object-Oriented Viewpoint Specification Techniques

Benjamin Braatz, Markus Klein, and Gunnar Schröter

Technische Universität Berlin, Germany
{bbraatz,klein,schroetg}@cs.tu-berlin.de

Abstract. Complex systems have many heterogeneous aspects, which can be specified comprehensibly and adequately by viewpoint specification techniques dealing only with a suitable subset of these aspects. A methodology for the formal integration of collections of such viewpoint specification techniques is introduced and applied to object-oriented systems. As a main result, it is shown, how the semantical consistency of viewpoint specification techniques can be checked in this framework.

1 Introduction

Viewpoints as in [1] and [2] were introduced with the aim to ease the specification of complex systems. The main idea of these approaches is reduce the accessible aspects of the specification such that the developers only have to deal with those aspects of the system, that are important for the current task. The rest of the system is hidden and not considered in the viewpoint. This allows to keep the viewpoint specifications small and comprehensible. Since the single viewpoints are not assumed to be disjoint in these approaches, it is possible to specify the same aspect of a system in different viewpoints. Thus, the developers are enabled to create redundant specifications in the overlapping parts of the viewpoints, which is a means to ensure that two viewpoints have been specified with a common interpretation of the overlapping properties. But at the same time, the viewpoint based approaches allow the specification of inconsistent systems, this means to use a contradictory specification of the same property in different viewpoints. Thus, the application of a viewpoint guided software engineering process should contain a check of consistency.

This work, as part of the national priority program on "Integration of Software Specifications for Applications in Engineering" (see [3]), is concerned with such consistency checks. In [4] a first idea of a consistency check by the construction of a selected semantic model was presented by an example. This paper is meant to give a formal and more detailed explaination of the constructions needed for the intended semantic integration.

Semantic integration in this sense needs a common semantic domain for the used specification techniques. We decided to use an object-oriented instantiation of the transformation systems of Große-Rhode (see [5]) for this purpose. It has been shown in a number of small case studies (see e. g. [5,6,7]), that transformation systems are powerful enough to model the semantics of a large variety

H. Ehrig et al. (Eds.): INT 2004, LNCS 3147, pp. 602–626, 2004.
© Springer-Verlag Berlin Heidelberg 2004

of specification techniques, e. g. UML class diagrams (see [8]), the process calculus CCS (see [9]), Petri nets (see e. g. [10]), graph grammars (see e. g. [11]), the integrated process technique LOTOS (see [12]) and the parallel programming language UNITY (see [13]). Hence, transformation systems are suitably complex to serve as a concrete semantic domain for the integration of viewpoint specifications from many heterogeneous techniques, specifying all the different aspects of the intended systems.

Since we want to model object-oriented systems, it is senseful to restrict the semantic domain to a specific object-oriented instantiation of tranformation systems, because such a restriction reduces the possibilities of different interpretations into the common semantic domain, and thus eases the semantic integration. In [5] such an instantiation was presented that took special care of the expressible properties of a selection of UML diagrams (see [14]). We will use a condensed and simplified instantiation in this paper.

The paper is organized as follows. In Sect. 2 we will present a formal and abstract framework for viewpoint specification techniques. In doing so we introduce the relevant notions for viewpoint specifications that are used in the rest of the paper. Section 3 introduces the above mentioned instantiation of transformation systems, called object-oriented transformation systems. Afterwards, we define a set of viewpoints for object-oriented transformation systems. In Sect. 5 we show, how the consistency of the viewpoints defined before can be checked constructively.

2   Abstract Framework for Viewpoint Specification Techniques

In this section a formal concept for viewpoint specification techniques is introduced, which will be applied to specifications of object-oriented systems in the subsequent sections. This concept is formal in the sense that we assume a specification technique to be equipped with a model-theoretic semantics, i. e. a specification has an assigned class of mathematical models satisfying the specification. This notion of formal specification technique has close relations to institutions (see [15]) and specification frames (see [16]).

Definition 1 (Specification Technique). *A specification technique is given by a class* **Mod** *of models and a class* **Spec** *of specifications with a semantic funtion Mod:* **Spec** $\rightarrow$ $\mathcal{P}(\textbf{Mod})$ *assigning a class of satisfying models to each specification. (See Fig. 1.)*

A viewpoint specification technique is a special kind of specification technique, which models specific properties of complex system models and abstracts from the other aspects of the system. This is formalized by an intermediate semantics, which should be related to the commonly used semantics for the corresponding specification technique, e. g. algebra or structure classes for equational or first order logics or labeled transition systems for process algebras, statecharts and the like. This intermediate semantics is related to the universe

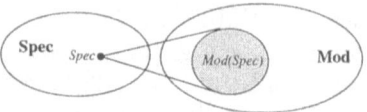

Fig. 1. Specification technique

of complex models by a view, which is a function abstracting from the properties not described by the specification technique. A concrete model is then a model of a viewpoint specification if its view is contained in the semantics of the specification.

Definition 2 (Viewpoint Specification Technique). *A viewpoint specification technique regarding a class* **Mod** *of concrete models is given by a class* **VSpec** *of viewpoint specifications, a class* **Sem** *of abstract models, a semantic function Sem:* **VSpec** $\to \mathcal{P}($**Sem**$)$, *and a view View:* **Mod** $\to$ **Sem**.
It becomes a specification technique w. r. t. **Mod** *in the sense of Def. 1 by the definition of a concrete semantic function Mod:* **VSpec** $\to \mathcal{P}($**Mod**$)$ *induced by*

$$Mod(VSpec) := \{M \in \mathbf{Mod} \mid View(M) \in Sem(VSpec)\}$$

for all VSpec $\in$ **VSpec**. *(See Fig. 2.)*

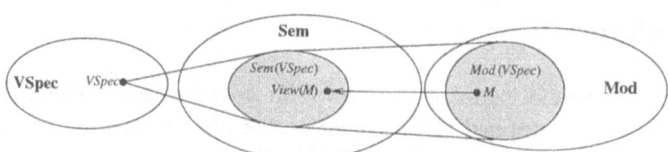

Fig. 2. Viewpoint specification technique

Note, that the abstract semantics is considered to be a loose class of models. If a tight semantics is needed, for example for the final specification of the static data types, it can be achieved by assigning a one-element class (or a class of isomorphic models) to the specifications.

Now, a system specification technique is again a special kind of specification technique, which is supposed to provide the means to specify entire systems. For this purpose it allows specifications, which can contain viewpoint specifications from a family of viewpoint specification techniques w. r. t. the same concrete model class. The semantics of such a system specification is defined to be the intersection of the semantics of the contained viewpoint specifications.

Definition 3 (System Specification Technique). *Given an I-indexed family* (**VSpec**$_i$, **Sem**$_i$, *Sem$_i$*, *View$_i$*)$_{i \in I}$ *of viewpoint specification techniques as in*

Def. 2 w. r. t. the same model class **Mod**, *a system specification technique is a specification technique in the sense of Def. 1 given by the class*

$$\mathbf{SSpec} := \mathcal{P}(\{ VSpec_i \mid i \in I, VSpec_i \in \mathbf{VSpec}_i\}),$$

of system specifications and the model function $Mod: \mathbf{SSpec} \to \mathcal{P}(\mathbf{Mod})$ *defined by*

$$Mod(SSpec) := \{M \in \mathbf{Mod} \mid \forall VSpec_i \in SSpec: View_i(M) \in Sem_i(VSpec_i)\}$$

for all $SSpec \in \mathbf{SSpec}$. *(See Fig. 3.)*

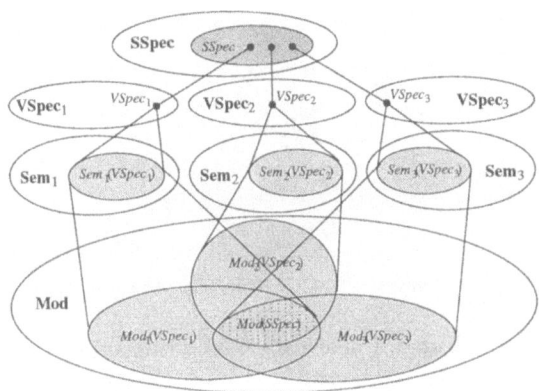

Fig. 3. System specification technique

The notion of system specifications over a family of viewpoint specification techniques is related to the notion of heterogeneous modular systems over an institutional framework in [17] in this volume, where the single abstract semantics, as well as the global concrete semantics are given by institutions and the views are given by institution representations.

Now, that we have a model-theoretic semantics for system and viewpoint specifications, we can define the important notion of consistency to be just the existence of a model for the specification.

Definition 4 (Consistency of Specifications). *Given a specification technique* (**Spec**, *Mod*) *as in Def. 1, a specification Spec* $\in$ **Spec** *is consistent, if and only if* $Mod(Spec) \neq \emptyset$.

We want to prove the consistency of specifications by the contruction of a canonical model $Can(Spec) \in Mod(Spec)$ for each specification $Spec$, if such a contruction is possible, leading to a partial function $Can: \mathbf{Spec} \to \mathbf{Mod}$. If we can give sufficient criteria for the definedness and soundness of this construction, i. e. if the constructed model really is a model of the specification, these are also sufficient criteria for the specification to be consistent.

Lemma 1 (Canonical Model Construction). *Given a specification technique* (**Spec**, *Mod*) *as in Def. 1 and a (partial) function Can:* **Spec** $\rightarrow$ **Mod**, *a specification Spec* $\in$ **Spec** *is consistent, if Can(Spec) is defined and Can(Spec)* $\in$ *Mod(Spec).*

Proof. The lemma follows immediately from Def. 4, because the existence of $Can(Spec) \in Mod(Spec)$ implies $Mod(Spec) \neq \emptyset$. $\qquad\qquad\qquad\square$

The construction of canonical models for system specification techniques will be approached by first constructing canonical models $Can_i(VSpec_i)$ for the single viewpoint specifications $VSpec_i$, which should be composed step by step (if possible) to yield a model for the system specification (see Fig. 4).

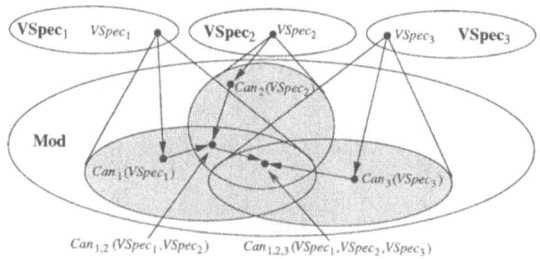

Fig. 4. Canonical model construction

In later stages of our work we want to derive syntactical consistency criteria for a system specification $SSpec$ stating under which conditions a canonical model for $SSpec$ can be constructed, i. e. $Can(SSpec)$ is defined and an element of the shared model class $\bigcap_{i \in I} Mod_i(VSpec_i)$. Of course, the formulation of such criteria needs a formal syntax. These two aspects are only sketched in the present paper.

In the next section we will define a concrete semantic domain for object-oriented systems, for which viewpoint specification techniques will be given in Sect. 4 and consistency will be examined in Sect. 5.

3   Object-Oriented Transformation Systems

In this section we will present an object-oriented instantiation of the transformation systems of Große-Rhode (see [5]). Various instantiations of transformation systems for object-oriented systems have already been given in [5,6,7], where objects were formalized as algebras and systems as configurations of several algebras. We use a simpler version in this contribution, where entire object configurations are modeled as single algebras.

Transformation systems integrate data aspects into a transition system by labeling not only the transitions with actions, but also the control states with data states. For the formalization of this labeling, homomorphims of so called transition graphs are used, which are directed graphs, whose nodes are called states and whose edges are called transitions. Transition graphs have a dedicated state, which is the source of all initializations and target of all finalizations of the system. Moreover, there is an idle transition for each state.

Definition 5 (Transition Graph). *A transition graph* $TG = (CS, T, in, id)$ *consists of a class CS of (control) states, a family $T = (T(c, d))_{c,d \in CS}$ of transition sets for all pairs of states, an initialization and finalization state $in \in CS$ and an idle transition $id(c) \in T(c, c)$ for each state $c \in CS$.*
The class of transition graphs is denoted by **TG**.

Morphisms of transistion graphs are graph morphisms that have to preserve the initialization/finalization state *in* and the mapping of the idle transistions *id*.

Definition 6 (Transition Graph Morhpism). *Given two transition graphs* $TG = (CS, T, in, id)$ *and* $TG' = (CS', T', in', id')$, *a transition graph morhpism* $h = (h_{CS}, h_T) : TG \to TG'$ *consists of a mapping* $h_{CS} : CS \to CS'$ *and a family of mappings* $h_T = (h_{T(c,d)})_{c,d \in CS}$ *with* $h_{T(c,d)} : T(c, d) \to T'(h_{CS}(c), h_{CS}(d))$, *such that* $h_{CS}(in) = in'$ *and* $h_{T(c,c)}(id(c)) = id(h_{CS}(c))$ *for all* $c \in CS$.

The labels used in a transformation system are provided by a data space framework, which defines a class of data space signatures and assigns a data space to each of these signatures. These data spaces are transition graphs consisting of data states, used to label the control states, and actions, used to label the transitions between control states.

Definition 7 (Data Space Framework). *A data space framework* $(\mathbf{DSig}, \mathbf{D}_-)$ *is given by a class* **DSig** *of data space signatures and a function* $\mathbf{D}_- : \mathbf{DSig} \to$ **TG**, *which assigns a data space*

$$\mathbf{D}_{DSig} = (CS_{DSig}, T_{DSig}, in_{DSig}, id_{DSig}) \in \mathbf{TG}$$

to each $DSig \in \mathbf{DSig}$, *where the states in* CS_{DSig} *are called data states and the transitions in* T_{DSig} *are called actions.*

In [5] data space frameworks defined by concrete institutions and actions parameterized from the data states are examined, where the case of partial algebras as states is treated in more detail.

Since we want to model object-oriented systems, we define a data space framework, where typical entities of object-oriented systems, such as object sorts, attributes, methods and constructors are modeled. In order to integrate some basic data types, which consist of values rather than objects, we also consider data sorts and data functions.

Attributes are unary functions from an object sort into some other sort, so that objects can be attributed by other objects and basic values. Methods and constructors define the dynamic behavior of a system. They are called with input parameters, where methods have a special input parameter, which is the object, on which the method is called, and they return with a return parameter, which is supposed to be the created object for constructors.

Enhancements like inheritance, multiplicities and associations are not treated in this paper due to lack of space, but they could easily be integrated in a more sophisticated data space framework. Partially these aspects are already considered in [5,6,7].

Definition 8 (Object-Oriented Data Space Signature). *An object-oriented data space signature $DSig = (DS, Fun, OS, Attr, Meth, Constr)$ consists of*

- *a set DS of data sort symbols,*
- *a family $(Fun_{w \to s})_{w \in DS^*, s \in DS}$ of data function symbols $f: w \to s \in Fun$,*
- *a set OS of object sort symbols, where $S = DS \uplus OS$ denotes the set of all sort symbols,*
- *a family $(Attr_{c \to s})_{c \in OS, s \in S}$ of attribute symbols $c.att: s \in Attr$,*
- *a family $(Meth_{c,w \to s})_{c \in OS, w \in S^*, s \in S}$ of method symbols $c.meth(w): s \in Meth$, and*
- *a family $(Constr_{w \to c})_{w \in S^*, c \in OS}$ of constructor symbols $con(w): c \in Constr$,*

*The class of object-oriented data space signatures is denoted by **OODSig**.*

The data states of object-oriented transformation systems are defined by carrier sets for data and object sorts, (partial) data functions for function symbols and (partial) attribution functions for attribute symbols. The possible actions are call and return actions for methods and constructors, assignment actions for attributes, and internal actions τ.

Definition 9 (Object-Oriented Data Space). *The data space $\mathbf{D}_{DSig}$ of an object-oriented data space signature $DSig \in \mathbf{OODSig}$ is given by the following contents:*
The class CS_{DSig} of data states is given by the class of all

$$A = ((A_s)_{s \in S}, (f_A)_{f \in Fun}, (att_A)_{att \in Attr})$$

with a carrier set A_s for each sort $s \in S$, a partial data function $f_A: A_w \to A_s$ for each function symbol $f: w \to s \in Fun$ and a partial attribution function $att_A: A_c \to A_s$ for each attribute symbol $c.att : s \in Attr$.
The initialization state in_{DSig} is given by the empty carrier set $in_{DSig,s} := \emptyset$ for each sort $s \in S$ and undefined data and attribution functions $f_{in_{DSig}} := \emptyset$ for each function symbol $f \in Fun$ and $att_{in_{DSig}} := \emptyset$ for each attribute symbol $att \in Attr$.
The sets $T_{DSig}(A, B)$ of actions are given by

$$
\begin{aligned}
T_{DSig}(A,B) := {} &\{\mathrm{call}_{meth}(p_0, p_1, \ldots, p_n) \mid c.meth(s_1 \ldots s_n) : s \in Meth, \\
&\quad p_0 \in A_c, p_1 \in A_{s_1}, \ldots, p_n \in A_{s_n}\} \cup \\
&\{\mathrm{ret}_{meth}(ret) \mid c.meth(s_1 \ldots s_n) : s \in Meth, ret \in B_s\} \cup \\
&\{\mathrm{call}_{con}(p_1, \ldots, p_n) \mid con(s_1 \ldots s_n) : c \in Constr, \\
&\quad p_1 \in A_{s_1}, \ldots, p_n \in A_{s_n}\} \cup \\
&\{\mathrm{ret}_{con}(ret) \mid con(s_1 \ldots s_n) : c \in Constr, ret \in B_c\} \cup \\
&\{\mathrm{ass}_{att}(obj, val) \mid c.att : s \in Attr, obj \in A_c, val \in A_s\} \cup \\
&\{\tau\}
\end{aligned}
$$

*with call and return actions for methods and constructors, assignment actions
for attributes, and an internal action τ.
The idle transition $id_{DSig}(A) := \tau$ is given by the internal action for all $A \in
States_{DSig}$.*

Object-oriented transformation systems consist of an object-oriented data
space signature and a control graph with labels in the object-oriented data space.
Moreover, we require a static part containing data sorts and data functions,
which are fixed for all data states of the system.

Definition 10 (Object-Oriented Transformation System). *An object-oriented transformation system $TS = (DSig, St, CG, m)$ consists of an object-
oriented data space signature $DSig = (DS, Fun, OS, Attr, Meth, Constr)$, a static
part $St = ((St_s)_{s \in DS}, (f_{St})_{f \in Fun})$ with carrier sets St_s and partial data functions
f_{St}, a control transition graph $CG = (CS, T, in, id)$ and a transition graph mor-
phism $m: CG \to \mathbf{D}_{DSig}$, such that $St \subseteq m(cs)|_{DS,Fun}$ for all $cs \in CS \setminus \{in\}$.
The class of all object-oriented transformation systems is denoted by* **OOTS**.
(See Fig. 5 for an example.)

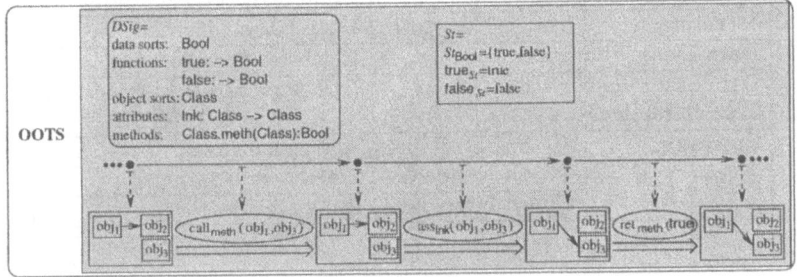

Fig. 5. Object-oriented transformation system

The object-oriented transformation systems according to this definition differ
from the object-oriented instantiations of transformation systems in [5] mainly
in three regards: A static part is not explicitly considered in [5], object configurations are modeled as families of algebras instead of single algebras, and
associations are modeled explicitly to allow the handling of multiplicities and
visibilities.

Now, that we have a formal notion of models of object-oriented systems, we
will define some viewpoint specification techniques in the sense of Def. 2 for these
models in the next section.

4   Viewpoints on Object-Oriented Transformation Systems

In this section we want to define viewpoint specification techniques for object-oriented systems, where we will mainly consider techniques with relation to the UML (see [8]). According to the formal framework presented in Sect. 2 and especially Def. 2, we will consider the object-oriented transfomation systems as the common model class (i.e. **Mod = OOTS**) and for each viewpoint specification technique *VP* we will define an abstract model class **Sem**$_{VP}$ and a view *View*$_{VP}$: **OOTS** → **Sem**$_{VP}$, which abstracts object-oriented transformation systems into this class.

The viewpoints can be organized according to the layers of the integration paradigm for data type and process modeling techniques of Ehrig and Orejas, presented in [18] and equipped with a formal model in [19], where we add a layer for the system structure, which is only implicitly considered by signatures in [19]. An overview of the layers of the integration paradigm, the viewpoints and corresponding viewpoint specification techniques is given in Table 1.

Table 1. Layers of the integration paradigm and corresponding viewpoints

Layer	Viewpoint	Specification Technique
Structure	System Structure	UML Class Diagrams
Data Types	Static Data Types	Algebraic Specifications
Data States and Transformations	Method Effects	OCL Pre- and Post-Conditions
Processes	Method Structures	Action Language
	Object Protocols	Statechart Diagrams
	Object Interaction	Sequence Diagrams

In the following subsections we will examine the viewpoints "System Structure", "Static Data Types", "Method Effects" and "Method Structures". The specification of object protocols by statechart diagrams and their consistency with the viewpoints treated here has been sketched on a conceptual level in [4]. The relations between statechart and sequence diagrams were investigated in [5], based on a transformation system semantics for both techniques.

We will not define the formal syntax for each of the viewpoint specification techniques. The alignment of this work with meta-modeling using typed graphs for the formal definition of visual languages as presented e.g. in [20], however, seems to be a valuable line of future research.

4.1   System Structure

In this viewpoint we want to model the system structure, where we choose to demand the whole structure to be given in one viewpoint specification, i.e. there

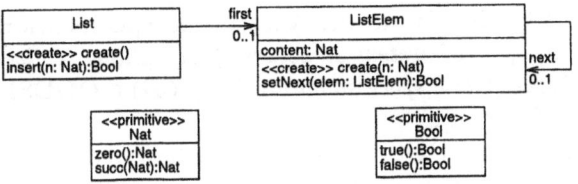

Fig. 6. Specification by class diagram

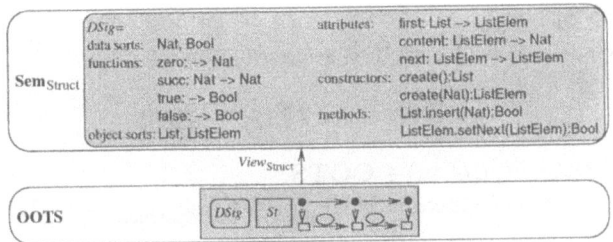

Fig. 7. System structure of the example

has to be a complete class diagram for the entire system. This is a methodological decision to ensure syntactical consistency. If all the viewpoints could add entities to the system, inconsistencies due to different namings in different viewpoints could arise. By demanding a single specification of the whole structure, these inconsistencies can be detected by checks against this specification.

As a running example we will consider classes of linked lists and list elements. The structure of this example is specified by the class diagram in Fig. 6. Lists contain a reference to the first element of the list, while each list element has a reference to the next one and carries a natural number as date, which is why we need natural numbers as static data type. Additionally, there is a static data type for Boolean values, which are used as return values for some of the methods. Data types are marked by the UML stereotype << primitive >>, which is used for data types without object identities in [8]. We only consider those methods needed in the following occurences of the example, i. e. constructors for both classes, a method insert to insert natural numbers into the list and a method setNext to manipulate the reference next of list elements.

The semantics of a class diagram can be given by a data space signature, which contains all entities declared in the diagram. We can abstract from everything except the structure by simply projecting the signature out of an object-oriented transformation system. The structure of the running example is given by the view in Fig. 7.

The following definition summarizes, how class diagrams can be used as a viewpoint specification technique in the sense of Def. 2, where we also give the induced model function according to Def. 2.

Definition 11 (System Structure Viewpoint Specification Technique).
The class $\mathbf{VSpec}_{\text{Struct}}$ *of system structure specifications is given by class diagrams with an induced data space signature* $DSig(CD) \in \mathbf{OODSig}$ *for each class diagram* $CD \in \mathbf{VSpec}_{\text{Struct}}$.
The class $\mathrm{Sem}_{\text{Struct}} := \mathbf{OODSig}$ *of system structure models is given by the class of all object-oriented data space signatures.*
The semantic function $\mathrm{Sem}_{\text{Struct}}\colon \mathbf{VSpec}_{\text{Struct}} \to \mathcal{P}(\mathbf{Sem}_{\text{Struct}})$ *is given by the one-element set*

$$\mathrm{Sem}_{\text{Struct}}(CD) := \{DSig(CD)\}$$

for all $CD \in \mathbf{VSpec}_{\text{Struct}}$.
The view $View_{\text{Struct}}\colon \mathbf{OOTS} \to \mathbf{Sem}_{\text{Struct}}$ *is given by*

$$View_{\text{Struct}}(TS) := DSig$$

for all $TS = (DSig, St, CG, m) \in \mathbf{OOTS}$.
This leads to the model function $Mod_{\text{Struct}}\colon \mathbf{VSpec}_{\text{Struct}} \to \mathcal{P}(\mathbf{OOTS})$ *given by*

$$Mod_{\text{Struct}}(CD) := \{(DSig, St, CG, m) \mid DSig = DSig(CD)\}$$

for all $CD \in \mathbf{VSpec}_{\text{Struct}}$.

4.2   Static Data Types

This viewpoint is concerned with the data sorts and functions, which are static for all states of the system. To realize the seperation of concerns, all other viewpoints should be defined loosely w. r. t. the data types.

Since the UML does not provide means to specify static data types, we use algebraic specifications as viewpoint specification technique. We only need equational specifications (see [21]) for our example, but more sophisticated logics could also be used.

In our running example, we want the static data types to be Boolean values and natural numbers. We use an ad-hoc notation based on the OCL for algebraic specifications as shown in Fig. 8. Since there are no equalities, which have to hold in these small examples, we just use initial constraints to forbid unspecified equalities and unreachable data elements in the algebras. For larger applications of the framework the integration of some mature algebraic specification framework like CASL (see [22]) or the set-theoretic notation Z (see [23]) would be useful extensions.

The semantics of such a specification are all pairs of signatures and algebras, where the signature includes the signature of the algebraic specification and the reduct of the algebra satisfies the specification. For equations as in our example this means, that for all assignments of the variables in the equations both sides of the equations are evaluated to the same elements.

Since all object-oriented transformation systems are required to have a static part, we can use a projection of the data type part of the signature and this

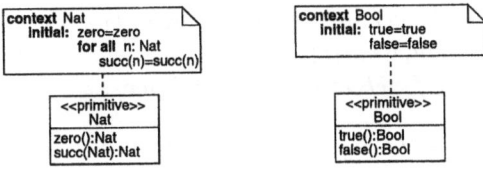

Fig. 8. Specification by algebraic specification

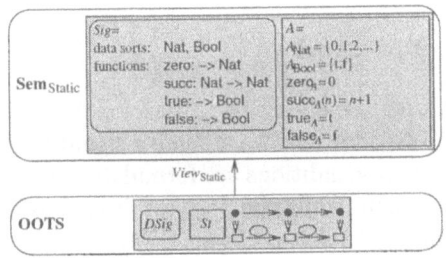

Fig. 9. Static data types of the example

static part as view of the system. The static data type view of our example can be seen in the view in Fig. 9.

We use the following notions for algebraic specifications. Let **AlgSig** be the class of all algebraic signatures and let **AlgSpec** be the class of all algebraic specifications, i.e. signatures with corresponding equations. The class $Alg(Sig)$ contains all algebras for the signature Sig.

Algebraic specifications as viewpoint specification technique in the sense of Def. 2 are given by the following definition.

Definition 12 (Static Data Type Viewpoint Specification Technique).
The class **VSpec**$_{Static}$ *of static data type specifications is given by algebraic specifications with data type signature $Sig(AS) \in$* **AlgSig** *for each algebraic specification $AS \in$* **VSpec**$_{Static} =$ **AlgSpec**.
The class

$$\mathbf{Sem}_{Static} := \{(Sig, A) \mid Sig \in \mathbf{AlgSig}, A \in Alg(Sig)\}$$

of static data type models is given by the class of pairs of algebraic signatures and corresponding algebras.
The semantic function $Sem_{Static}:$ **VSpec**$_{Static} \to \mathcal{P}(\mathbf{Sem}_{Static})$ *is given by the set*

$$Sem_{Static}(AS) := \{(Sig, A) \mid Sig(AS) \subseteq Sig, A|_{Sig(AS)} \models AS\}$$

for all $AS \in$ **VSpec**$_{Static}$.
The view $View_{Static}:$ **OOTS** $\to$ **Sem**$_{Static}$ *is given by*

$$View_{Static}(TS) := ((DS, Fun), St)$$

for all TS = (DSig, St, CG, m) ∈ **OOTS** *with data space signature DSig =*
(DS, Fun, OS, Attr, Meth, Constr).
This leads to the model function Mod$_{Static}$*:* **VSpec**$_{Static}$ *→ P(***OOTS***) given by*

$$Mod_{Static}(AS) := \{(DSig, St, CG, m) \in \mathbf{OOTS} \mid Sig(AS) \subseteq DSig,$$
$$St|_{Sig(AS)} \models AS\}$$

for all AS ∈ **VSpec**$_{Static}$.

4.3 Data Effects of Methods

This viewpoint deals with the effects the execution of methods has on the data
states. For pre- and post-conditions we assume a signature of the entities used in
the conditions and that pre-conditions are formulated over the input variables of
the corresponding operation, while the post-conditions use the output variables.

The effects of the method **insert** are specified by the OCL constraint in Fig. 10.
Namely, a list element with the given natural number should be inserted as the
new first element of the list, and the former first element should follow the new
element.

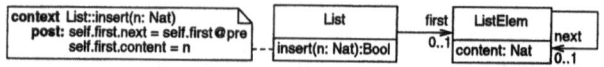

Fig. 10. Specification by OCL constraint

We formalize this by relations between input data states with input parameters and output data states with output parameters. Figure 11 shows the
abstraction of one execution of the method **insert**, where the signature and the
static part are omitted for readability reasons. Such an abstraction is included
in the effect relation for each execution of **insert** in the model.

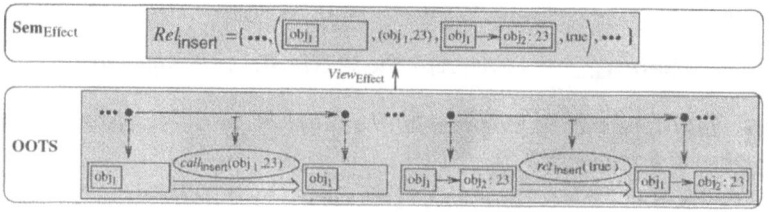

Fig. 11. Data effects of method **insert**

The formalization of OCL pre- and post-conditions as viewpoint specification
technique for method effects can be found in the following definition.

Definition 13 (Method Effect Viewpoint Specification Technique).
The class $\mathbf{VSpec_{Effect}}$ *of method effect specifications is given by OCL pre- and post-conditions with an induced data space signature $DSig(OCL) \in \mathbf{OODSig}$ for each OCL specification $OCL \in \mathbf{VSpec_{Effect}}$, pre-constraints $Pre(OCL, op)$ and post-constraints $Post(OCL, op)$ for each OCL specification $OCL \in \mathbf{VSpec_{Effect}}$ and each operation $op \in Meth \cup Constr$.*
The class

$$
\begin{aligned}
\mathbf{Sem_{Effect}} := \{ \ &(DSig, Rel) \mid DSig \in \mathbf{OODSig}, Rel = (Rel_{op})_{op \in Meth \cup Constr}, \\
&Rel_{op} \subseteq \{(A, in, B, out) \mid A, B \in CS_{DSig}, in \in A_w, out \in B_s\} \\
&\text{for } op \in Meth_{w \to s} \text{ or } op \in Constr_{w \to s} \}
\end{aligned}
$$

of method effect models is given by the class of pairs of data space signatures and families of effect relations.
The semantic function $Sem_{Effect}: \mathbf{VSpec_{Effect}} \to \mathcal{P}(\mathbf{Sem_{Effect}})$ is given by the set

$$
\begin{aligned}
Sem_{Effect}(OCL) := \{ \ &(DSig, Rel) \mid DSig(OCL) \subseteq DSig, \\
&\forall(A, in, B, out) \in Rel_{op}: (A, in) \models Pre(OCL, op) \\
&\Rightarrow (B, out) \models Post(OCL, op) \}
\end{aligned}
$$

for all $OCL \in \mathbf{VSpec_{Effect}}$.
The view $View_{Effect}: \mathbf{OOTS} \to \mathbf{Sem_{Effect}}$ is given by

$$
View_{Effect}(TS) := (DSig, Rel)
$$

for all $TS = (DSig, St, CG, m) \in \mathbf{OOTS}$, where the effect relations in Rel are generated by taking from each execution of an operation op in TS the data state and the input parameters of the call action and the data state and the return parameter of the corresponding return action.
This leads to the model function $Mod_{Effect}: \mathbf{VSpec_{Effect}} \to \mathcal{P}(\mathbf{OOTS})$ which assigns a set of transformation systems $TS = (DSig, St, CG, m)$ to each OCL specification $OCL \in \mathbf{VSpec_{Effect}}$, where this set contains all transformation systems of the following kind. The signature DSig has to be a subsignature of the signature of the OCL specification $DSig(OCL)$. For each occurence of an operation $op \in Meth \cup Constr$ in the models TS the state before the call has to satisfy $Pre(OCL, op)$ and the state after the return has to satisfy $Post(OCL, op)$.

4.4   Structure of Methods

While the last viewpoint abstracts from the concrete means, by which a method realizes its effects, this viewpoint, vice versa, abstracts from the effects and extracts the structure of methods.

Since this view is very close to programming and code generation, an abstract imperative language, such as the action languages of the UML, is appropriate to specify this viewpoint. The structure of the method insert is specified in Fig. 12, where we use a simple ad-hoc notation as action language. An exact treatment

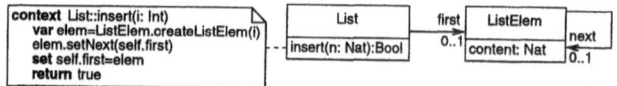

Fig. 12. Specification by action language

of the action language concept given in the UML should be given in a future refinement of the framework.

The semantics of such an action language expression is given by all labeled transition systems, whose complete traces (traces ending with a final state) are also complete traces of the bevaviour specified by the expression. This means, that a method may only deadlock, if the deadlock is also allowed in the labeled transition system of the action language expression.

The abstract models contain labeled transition systems for each method, which are derived from the transformation systems by forgetting the state labels and hiding the structure of called methods. Due to limited space, we cannot give the slightly complicated fully formal treatment of this construction here.

In Fig. 13 a part of the structural view of the method insert is shown, where all executions of the methods are merged into a single trace in the abstract view, because the actions are the same and the differences are only visible in the data states, which are forgotten by the view.

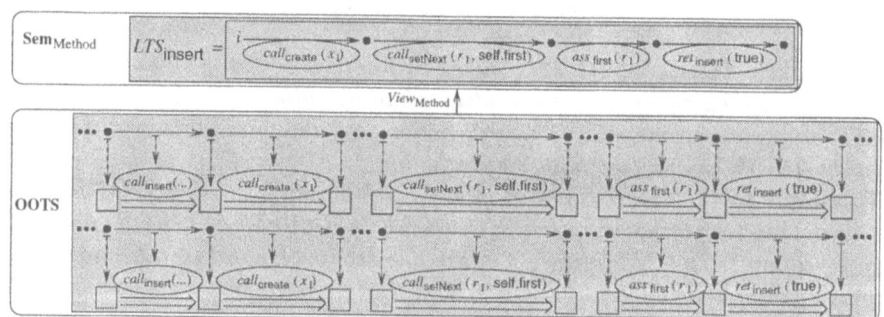

Fig. 13. Structure of method insert

Next, we show how the idea of an action language can be formalized in the framework of object-oriented transformation systems.

Definition 14 (Method Structure Viewpoint Specification Technique).
The class **VSpec**$_{Method}$ *of method structure specifications is given by action language expressions with an induced data space signature* $DSig(AL) \in$ **OODSig** *for each action language specification* $AL \in$ **VSpec**$_{Method}$. *Moreover, we assume that each action language expresion for an operation op induces a labeled transition system* $LTS(AL, op)$.

The class
$$\mathbf{Sem}_{\mathrm{Method}} := \{ \ (DSig, LTS) \mid DSig \in \mathbf{OODSig},$$
$$LTS = (LTS_{op})_{op \in Meth \cup Constr},$$
$$LTS_{op} = (S, Act_{DSig}, \rightarrow, i),$$
$$\rightarrow \subseteq S \times Act_{DSig} \times S, i \in S \ \}$$

of method structure models is given by the class of pairs of data space signatures and labeled transition systems for each method with initial states i corresponding to the beginnings of the methods, i. e. the states before the call actions. States that have no further states to be accessed by the $\rightarrow$ relation can only be reached by relation entries mapped with ret_{op}.
The semantic function $Sem_{\mathrm{Method}} \colon \mathbf{VSpec}_{\mathrm{Method}} \to \mathcal{P}(\mathbf{Sem}_{\mathrm{Method}})$ is given by the set

$$Sem_{\mathrm{Method}}(OCL) := \{(DSig, LTS) \mid DSig(AL) \subseteq DSig, LTS_{op} \subseteq LTS(AL, op)\}$$

for each $AL \in \mathbf{VSpec}_{\mathrm{Method}}$, where the second condition means that all traces for an operation op in the models have to be part of the labeled transition system induced by the specification $LTS(AL, op)$ and the traces in the model are only allowed to deadlock if this deadlock is also specified $LTS(AL, op)$.
The view $View_{\mathrm{Method}} \colon \mathbf{OOTS} \to \mathbf{Sem}_{\mathrm{Method}}$ is given by

$$View_{\mathrm{Method}}(TS) := (DSig, LTS)$$

for all $TS = (DSig, St, CG, m) \in \mathbf{OOTS}$, where $LTS = (LTS_{op})_{op \in Meth \cup Constr}$ is calculated by collecting all occurences of op in TS and gluing the corresponding traces in LTS_{op}. The data states are omitted in this construction.
This leads to the model function $Mod_{\mathrm{Method}} \colon \mathbf{VSpec}_{\mathrm{Method}} \to \mathcal{P}(\mathbf{OOTS})$

which assigns sets of transition systems $TS = (DSig, St, CG, m)$ to all specifications $AL \in \mathbf{VSpec}_{\mathrm{Method}}$, where we require that $DSig(AL) \subseteq DSig$ holds and for each occurence of an operation $op \in DSig(AL)$ the trace between the starting state and the final state of the operation has to be part of $LTS(AL, op)$ and the execution of the method may only stop, if we have a corresponding deadlock in $LTS(AL, op)$.

5   Consistency of Object-Oriented Transformation System Specifications

In this section we show how the consistency of a system specification, consisting of viewpoint specifications can be checked. We will present the explicit constructions needed for the consistency check for the viewpoint specification techniques presented in the previous section. Further viewpoints could be added and integrated in a similar way. The check is done by step-wise composition of the canonical models for the viewpoint specifications, where this process either yields a canonical model for the whole system specification or fails due to some inconsistencies, which can be characterized by the exact reason, why one of the compositions was not possible. Moreover, we give some syntactical conditions, when a canonical composition is possible, which could then be checked by development tools.

5.1   Construction of Canonical Models for Viewpoint Specifications

In this section we define the construction of canonical models for the four view-point specification techniques introduced in the last section. We will use these constructions to develop a corresponding construction of a cannonical model for system specifications using these four viewpoints. We can also understand this construction as an intra viewpoint consistency check, since the construction is only defined and sound w. r. t. the specification, if the corresponding viewpoint specification is free of contradictions. In the case of the sample four viewpoints we do not have such inconsistent specifications, and thus the canonical construc-tions become total mappings from the viewpoint specifications to the common domain of object-oriented transformation systems and the result is always a model of the specification.

In the case of the structure viewpoint the canonical model for a given class diagram CD is given by the following object oriented transformation system

$$Can_{\text{Struct}}(CD) = (DSig(CD), St_{CD}, CG_{CD}, m_{CD}),$$

where $DSig(CD)$ is the data space signature induced by the class diagram ac-cording to Def. 11. The static part St_{CD} is the empty algebra $\emptyset$. The control graph CG_{CD} is given by the data space induced by the data space signature, $\mathbf{D}_{DSig(CD)}$, according to Def. 9 and m_{CD} is an identical morphism in the cat-egory of transition graphs. This means control graph and data space are equal in this case. Since this model uses the data space signature $DSig(CD)$, Def. 11 implies $Can_{\text{Struct}}(CD) \in Mod_{\text{Struct}}(CD)$ for all $CD \in \mathbf{VSpec}_{\text{Struct}}$.

The canonical model for a given algebraic specification AS is given by

$$Can_{\text{Static}}(AS) = (DSig(AS), T_{AS}, CG_{AS}, \{* \mapsto in\})$$

with $CG_{AS} = (\{*\}, \{id(*)\}, *, id)$. The data space signature $DSig(AS)$ of the model is the induced signature $Sig(AS)$ given by the specification according to Def. 12. The static part of the transformation system is given by the quotient term algebra T_{AS} of the given specification AS. The control graph CG_{AS} con-tains a single state, which is mapped by m_{AS} to the initialization state of the data space in. This canonical model construction has a trivial dynamic part, i. e. the control graph is discrete, and thus, not controls any behaviour. The inter-esting part of the model is limited to T_{AS}. Since this model uses the signature induced by AS and the static part T_{AS} fulfills AS by construction, we have by Def. 12 that $Can_{\text{Static}}(AS) \in Mod_{\text{Static}}(AS)$ holds for all $AS \in \mathbf{VSpec}_{\text{Static}}$.

In the method effect viewpoint we construct the canonical model for a given specification OCL as follows

$$Can_{\text{Effect}}(OCL) = (DSig(OCL), \emptyset, CG_{OCL}, m_{OCL}),$$

where $DSig(OCL)$ is the data space signature induced by the specification OCL according to Def. 13. The control graph CG_{OCL} is a restriction of the induced data space $\mathbf{D}_{DSig(OCL)}$ of $DSig(OCL)$. This restricted graph only contains re-turn transitions that are compatible with the relation $Rel(OCL, op)$ for each

$op \in DSig(OCL)$. Thus, it is ensured that all runs of op in the model fulfill the specified post-conditions if the pre-conditions were valid in the state the operation was called at. The morphism $m_{OCL} : CG_{OCL} \rightarrow \mathbf{D}_{DSig(OCL)}$ is the obvious inclusion. Since this model uses the data space signaure $DSig(OCL)$ and all operation runs fulfill the pre- and post-conditions, we can conclude by Def. 13 that $Can_{\text{Effect}}(OCL) \in Mod_{\text{Effect}}(OCL)$ for all $OCL \in \mathbf{VSpec}_{\text{Effect}}$.

The canonical model for a given action language specification AL is given below

$$Can_{\text{Method}}(AL) = (DSig(AL), \emptyset, CG_{AL}, m_{AL}),$$

where $DSig(AL)$ is the data space signature of the action language specification according to Def. 14. The control graph CG_{AL} is a gluing of the labeled transition systems of the action language specification $LTS(AL, op)$ for all operations $op \in DSig(AL)$. The final states of completed traces of these labeled transition systems are again connected with the labeled transition sytems $LTS(AL, op)$ for all operations $op \in DSig(AL)$. The morphism m_{AL} maps complete traces into the data space, such that the labels of the transitions in the control graph are the same as the names of the actions they are mapped to. The model uses the data space signature $DSig(AL)$ and the single method runs satisfy $LTS(AL, op)$ for all operations $op \in DSig(AL)$ by construction of CG_{AL}. Thus, we have by Def. 14 that $Can_{\text{Method}}(AL) \in Mod_{\text{Method}}(AL)$ is valid for all $AL \in \mathbf{VSpec}_{\text{Method}}$.

5.2 Structural Consistency

Structural consistency, sometimes also called syntactical consistency, ensures, that all viewpoint specifications exclusively use entities, which are already declared in the structural viewpoint.

This is checked by composing each of the other canonical models with the canonical model of the class diagram, so that the resulting models all have the same data space signature, namely the signature induced by the class diagram. These constructions fail, if there are entities in the specifications of data effects or method structures, respectively, which are not declared in the structure specification. Thus, we obtain the general consistency condition

$$DSig(VSpec) \subseteq DSig(CD)$$

for all viewpoint specifications $VSpec$ for the viewpoints method effect and method structure. The static data type is examined in the next section. Assuming this condition we are able to lift the other viewpoint specifications to the larger data space signature of the system structure specification which is a further step in the construction of a canonical model for a system specification. We will realize this lifting by pullbacks in the category of transition graphs.

Given a viewpoint VP and the canonical model for a viewpoint specification $VSpec$ as constructed in Sect. 5.1,

$$Can_{\text{VP}}(VSpec) = (DSig(VSpec), \emptyset, CG_{VSpec}, m_{VSpec}).$$

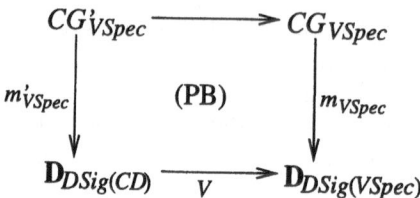

Fig. 14. Structural consistency

In Fig. 14 we see the control graph CG_{VSpec} and the data space $\mathbf{D}_{DSig(VSpec)}$ of such a given viewpoint specification $VSpec$, connected by the morphism m_{VSpec}. Since we assumed $DSig(VSpec) \subseteq DSig(CD)$ we can define a morphism V between the data space of the structure viewpoint specification and the data space $\mathbf{D}_{DSig(VSpec)}$ by $V_{CS}(A) = A|_{DSig(VSpec)}$ for all $A \in CS_{\mathbf{D}_{DSig(CD)}}$ and $V_T(t) = t \in T_{\mathbf{D}_{DSig(VSpec)}}(V(A), V(B))$, if $t \in DSig(VSpec)$, and τ, else. Now we can construct the pullback CG'_{VSpec} for $VP = Effect, Method$. On an intuitive level, this means that CG'_{VSpec} collects and identifies those states and transitions of $\mathbf{D}_{DSig(CD)}$ and CG_{VSpec} which have a common image in $\mathbf{D}_{DSig(VSpec)}$.

We can use the result of the pullback to define composed transition systems for specification techniques that do not affect the static part.

$$Can_{\text{Struct},\text{VP}}(CD, VSpec) = (DSig(CD), \emptyset, CG'_{VSpec}, m'_{VSpec}),$$

where CG'_{VSpec} is the result of the pullback construction. This definition directly implies that the composed models are a model for both, the class diagram and the other viewpoint specification technique, if the viewpoint specifcation technique does not affect the static part and if it allows its models to use a larger signature. Since this is the case for the viewpoints method effect and method structure, we can formulate the following lemma.

Lemma 2 (Syntactic Integration). *Given a class diagram CD and a viewpoint specification $VSpec$ for another viewpoint $VP \in \{Effect, Method\}$ we have*

$$Can_{\text{Struct}}(CD) \in Mod_{\text{Struct}}(CD) \wedge Can_{\text{VP}}(VSpec) \in Mod_{\text{VP}}(VSpec)$$
$$\Rightarrow Can_{\text{Struct},\text{VP}}(CD, VSpec) \in Mod_{\text{Struct}}(CD) \cap Mod_{\text{VP}}(VSpec).$$

Proof. The constructed model $Can_{\text{Struct},\text{VP}}(CD, VSpec)$ uses the data space signature $DSig(CD)$, and thus, we can conclude by Def. 11 for all class diagrams $CD \in \mathbf{VSpec}_{\text{Struct}}$ and all $VSpec \in \mathbf{VSpec}_{\text{VP}}$ that the constructed model is a model for the class diagram, i. e. $Can_{\text{Struct},\text{VP}}(CD, VSpec) \in Mod_{\text{Struct}}(CD)$. Since the pullback construction does not add any new states or transitions to CG_{VSpec} in CG'_{VSpec}, nor removes any, we can conclude that the composed model still fulfills $VSpec$. $\qquad\square$

5.3   Restriction According to the Static Part

In the next step of our construction we will constrain the control graph of the canonical model for the system structure viewpoint constructed before, such that only data states that fulfill the static part specification are accessed. For the canonical model $Can_{\text{Struct}}(CD) = (DSig(CD), \emptyset, CG_{CD}, m_{CD})$ we define the restriction as follows:

$$Res_{AS}(Can_{\text{Struct}}(CD)) = (DSig(CD), St, CG'_{AS}, m'_{AS}),$$

where the new control graph CG'_{AS} is given by

$$CS_{CG'_{AS}} = CS_{CG_{CD}} \setminus \{c \mid m_{CD_{CS}}(c) \not\models AS\} \text{ and}$$
$$T_{CG'_{AS}} = T_{CG_{CD}} \setminus \{T(c,d) \mid m_{CD_{CS}}(c) \not\models AS \vee m_{CD_{CS}}(d) \not\models AS\}$$

and m'_{AS} is the obvious restriction of m_{CD}, which was the identic morphism. Intuitively, we remove all states and the corresponding transitions from the control graph that are mapped to algebras in the data space that do not fulfill the static part St. Note that this construction is defined only if the signature of the static part specification $DSig(AS)$ is also contained in the signature of the structural specification $DSig(CD)$. If this is the case, the construction above ensures that the result is a model of both specifications.

Lemma 3 (Static Part Restriction). *Given an algebraic specification $AS \in$ $\mathbf{VSpec}_{\text{Struct}}$ and a class diagram $CD \in \mathbf{VSpec}_{\text{Struct}}$. If $DSig(AS) \subseteq DSig(CD)$ holds, then we have $Res_{AS}(Can_{\text{Struct}}(CD)) \in \text{Mod}_{\text{Struct}}(CD) \cap \text{Mod}_{\text{Static}}(AS)$.*

Proof. The constructed model uses the data space signature $DSig(CD)$, it is a model of the class diagram CD. Moreover, the model has the static part SP, and thus, is a model of the algebraic specification AS.   □

5.4   Integration of Method Effect and Structure

In this section we want to integrate the results of the previous constructions. Again, we will use pullbacks in the category of transition graphs. Given a canonical model for a class diagram CD after the restriction of the control graph with respect to a given algebraic specification AS, according to Sect. 5.3,

$$Res_{AS}(Can_{\text{Struct}}(CD)) = (DSig(CD), St, CG'_{AS}, m'_{AS}),$$

and given a canonical model for a method effect specification OCL which has been lifted to the signature of the class diagram CD, according to Sect. 5.2,

$$Can_{\text{Struct},\text{Effect}}(CD, OCL) = (DSig(CD), \emptyset, CG'_{OCL}, m'_{OCL}).$$

Figure 15 shows the control graph of the lifted canonical model for the method effect viewpoint (CG'_{OCL}) and the control graph of the restricted canonical model for the structure specification (CG'_{AS}). The construction of the canonical models ensures that both control graphs are mapped to the same data space, namely the data space induced by the data space signature of the class diagram, $\mathbf{D}_{DsigCD}$. Thus, we can construct the resulting control graph as the pullback $CG_{AS,OCL}$

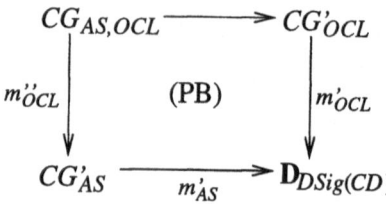

Fig. 15. Integration of Static Part and Method effect

of the given control graphs. This construction removes all states and connected transitions from the control graph of the lifted method effect model that are mapped to data states that do not fulfill the static data type specification AS. We can use the resulting control graph to define an integrated transformation system.

$$Can_{\text{Struct,Static,Effect}}(CD, AS, OCL) = (DSig(CD), St, CG_{AS,OCL}, m_{AS,OCL}),$$

where $m_{AS,OCL}$ is defined as $m'_{AS} \circ m''_{OCL}$. If we remove states and transitions from the control graph of the canonical method effect model, it might happen that we loose a state which was needed to fulfill the method effect specification, i. e. a state which was reached by a return action of an operation $op \in DSig(OCL)$ and which satisfied $Post(OCL, op)$. If this deleted state was the only state with these two properties reachable from the state where the operation was called and this starting state satisfies $Post(OCL, op)$, then this state should violate the static part specification as well, because otherwise, the resulting model would violate the method effect specification.

Lemma 4 (Integration of the Method Effect). *Given a class diagram* $CD \in \mathbf{VSpec}_{\text{Struct}}$, *an algebraic specification* $AS \in \mathbf{VSpec}_{\text{Static}}$, *and a method effect specification* $OCL \in \mathbf{VSpec}_{\text{Effect}}$. *Now we have*

$$Can_{\text{Struct,Static,Effect}}(CD, AS, OCL) \in$$
$$Mod_{\text{Struct}}(CD) \cap Mod_{\text{Static}}(AS) \cap Mod_{\text{Effect}}(OCL),$$

if the method effect specification OCL *ensures that a final state of an operation run satisfies* $Pre(OCL, op) \wedge SP$ *if* $Post(OCL, op) \wedge SP$ *was valid at the starting state.*

Proof. Since the model uses the data space signature induced by CD and the static part specified in AS, it satisfies CD and AS by construction. Moreover, the construction above ensures, that only complete traces of operation runs are removed and that the remaining ones satisfy the effect specification OCL.   □

In the next step we integrate the signature lifted canonical model into the last constructed model. Given an integrated canonical model of a class diagram, an algebraic specification and a method effect specification as defined above

$$Can_{\text{Struct,Static,Effect}}(CD, AS, OCL) = (DSig(CD), St, CG_{AS,OCL}, m_{AS,OCL})$$

and given a signature lifted model of a method structure specification

$$Can_{Struct,Method}(CD, AL) = (DSig(CD), \emptyset, CG'_{AL}, m'_{AL}).$$

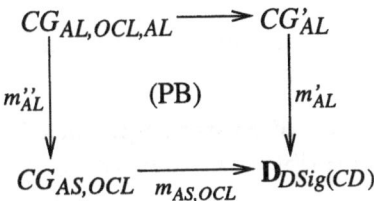

Fig. 16. Integration of Method Effect and Mehtod Structure

Again, the control graphs of the two models ($CG_{AS,OCL}$, CG'_{AL}) are mapped to the same data space $\mathbf{D}_{Dsig(CD)}$ by construction. This situation is depicted in Fig. 16. Thus, we are able to construct the pullback $CG_{AS,OCL,AL}$. This construction deletes all states and the corresponding transitions of the control graph of the lifted canonical model for the method structure specification which are mapped to data states that either do not satisfy the static part specification or that do not satisfy the method effect specification. We can now define the integrated canonical model for the four used viewpoint specification techniques.

$$Can_{Struct,Static,Effect,Method}(CD, AS, OCL, AL) =$$
$$(DSig(CD), St, CG_{AS,OCL,AL}, m_{AS,OCL,AL}),$$

where $m_{AS,OCL,AL} = m_{AS,OCL} \circ m''_{AL}$. In order to decide, whether this transformation system is a model of the method structure specification AL we have to check, whether we removed transitions from the control graph that were needed to finish an operation run. Moreover, $Post(OCL, op)$ has to be ensured in all operation runs that fulfilled $Pre(OCL, op)$ when they were called. More general, if we remove unique return transitions of an operation $op \in DSig(AL)$ then also the corresponding call transition should origin in a state not satisfying St or OCL which then would be removed by the restriction as well.

Lemma 5 (Integration of Method Structure Specifications). *Given a system specification* $(CD, AS, OCL, AL) \in \mathbf{SSpec}$. *Now we have*

$$Can_{Struct,Static,Effect}(CD, AS, OCL) \in$$
$$Mod_{Struct}(CD) \cap Mod_{Static}(AS) \cap Mod_{Effect}(OCL),$$
$$\Rightarrow Can_{Struct,Static,Effect,Method}(CD, AS, OCL, AL) \in$$
$$Mod_{Struct}(CD) \cap Mod_{Static}(AS) \cap Mod_{Effect}(OCL) \cap Mod_{Method}(AL),$$

if the operation runs specified by AL *preserve the static part* SP *and realize the effect specification* OCL.

Proof. The model $Can_{\text{Struct,Static,Effect,Method}}(CD, AS, OCL, AL)$ is in the model class $Mod_{\text{Struct}}(CD) \cap Mod_{\text{Static}}(AS) \cap Mod_{\text{Effect}}(OCL)$ by the assumption of the lemma and by the fact that the construction above only removes complete operation run traces, and thus, does not affect the validity of CD, AS, and OCL. Moreover, the model fulfills the specification AL, since all method runs with a structure different from the specified one are removed.   □

If we now combine the conditions for the the nested model classes, we can fomulate the following theorem.

Theorem 1 (Consistency of System Specifications). *A system specification* $(CD, AS, OCL, AL) \in \textbf{SSpec}$ *is consistent, if the following conditions are satisfied:*

1. *All entities used in AS, OCL and AL are declared in CD,*
2. *OCL preserves the static part specified by AS.*
3. *AL only uses attributes and data functions, which are ensured to be defined in the corresponding data states,*
4. *the method specifications in AL realize the pre- and post-conditions in OCL and preserve the static part.*

In this case a canonical system model can be constructed by step-wise composition of the canonical viewpoint models.

Proof. We start with the canonical models given in Sect. 5.1 which turned out to be in the model class of the corresponding specification. Using this, we can apply Lem. 2 for the integration of the cannonical models for CD, OCL, and AL. Thus, we obtain two signature lifted models that are in the corresponding shared model class. Lemma 3 is applicable because of condition 1 from above and yields an integrated model of CD and AS which satisfies both specifications. Using assumption 2 and Lem. 4, we obtain a model which satisfies CD, AS, and OCL. Finally, assumptions 3 and 4 together with Lem. 5 imply the stated consistency.   □

6   Conclusion

This paper presents a constructive consistency check for object-oriented specifications. In contrast to [4], where we introduced the idea of a constructive consistency check in an informal and example-oriented manner, we give a formal definition of the single construction steps in this paper. This is done by the definiton of a common semantic domain, object-oriented transformation systems. Based on this domain we define formal views for the semantic domain equipped with suiting specification techniques.

In order to be able to build larger software specifications, we want to develop structuring means for our semantic domain and the different specification techniques in the near future. Such compostion operations should preserve the consistency of the parts that are connected. An analogous procedure is planned for development and refinement relations, which are inter alia applied in [24] in this volume, where a concept for specification components is introduced. Such refinements should preserve the consistency of the system specifications.

Acknowledgements. This work is partially supported by the German DFG (German Research Council) project IOSIP (Integration of object-oriented software specification techniques and their application-specific extension for industrial production systems on the example of automobile industry) within the DFG Priority Programme "Integration of Software Specification Techniques for Applications in Engineering". We would like to thank Hartmut Ehrig and Martin Große-Rhode and the referees for their valuable comments on previous versions of the paper.

References

1. Finkelstein, A., Kramer, J., Nuseibeh, B., Finkelstein, L., Goedicke, M.: Viewpoints: A Framework for Integrating Multiple Perspectives in System Development. International Journal of Software Engineering and Knowledge Engineering **2** (1992) 31–58
2. International Organization for Standardization: ISO 10746:1998 – Information Technology – Open Distributed Processing – Reference Model. (1998)
3. Ehrig, H., Große-Rhode, M.: Integration von Techniken der Softwarespezifikation für ingenieurwissenschaftliche Anwendungen. Informatik Forschung und Entwicklung **16** (2001) 110–117
4. Schröter, G., Braatz, B., Ehrig, H., Klein, M., Bengel, M.: Semantische Konsistenz viewpoint-orientierter Modellierungstechniken am Beispiel der Produktionsautomatisierung. atp – Automatisierungstechnische Praxis (2004) To appear.
5. Große-Rhode, M.: Semantic Integration of Heterogeneous Software Specifications. Monographs in Theoretical Computer Science. Springer (2004)
6. Tenzer, J.: A Formal Semantics of UML Class Diagrams based on Transformation Systems. Forschungsbericht 2001/09, Fachbereich Informatik, TU Berlin (2001)
7. Parnitzke, D.: On Formal Semantics of Object Systems with Data and Object Attributes. Forschungsbericht 2001/05, Fachbereich Informatik, TU Berlin (2001)
8. Object Management Group: Unified Modeling Language – Version 2.0 (UML 2.0). (2004) Available from http://www.omg.org/.
9. Milner, R.: Communication and Concurrency. International Series in Computer Science. Prentice Hall (1989)
10. Reisig, W.: Petri Nets. Volume 4 of Monographs on Theoretical Computer Science. Springer (1985)
11. Rozenberg, G., ed.: Handbook of Graph Grammars and Computing by Graph Transformations, Volume 1: Foundations. World Scientific (1997)
12. International Organization for Standardization: ISO 8807:1989 – Information Processing Systems – Open Systems Interconnection – LOTOS – A Formal Description Technique Based on the Temporal Ordering of Observational Behaviour. (1989)
13. Chandy, K.M., Misra, J.: Parallel Program Design – A Foundation. Addison-Wesley (1988)
14. Object Management Group: Unified Modeling Language – Version 1.5 (UML 1.5). (2003) Available from http://www.omg.org/.

15. Goguen, J.A., Burstall, R.M.: Institutions: Abstract Model Theory for Specification and Programming. Journal of the Association for Computing Machinery **39** (1992) 95–146
16. Ehrig, H., Große-Rhode, M.: Functorial Theory of Parameterized Specifications in a General Specification Framework. Theoretical Computer Science **135** (1994) 221–266
17. Orejas, F., Pino, E.: On the Integration of Heterogeneous Specifications. In Ehrig, H., Damm, W., Desel, J., Große-Rhode, M., Reif, W., Schnieder, E., Westkämper, E., eds.: Integration of Software Specification Techniques for Applications in Engineering. Number 3147 in Lecture Notes in Computer Science. Springer (2004)
18. Ehrig, H., Orejas, F.: Integration Paradigm for Data Type and Process Specification Techniques. Bull. EATCS (1998) 90–97
19. Ehrig, H., Orejas, F.: A Conceptual and Formal Framework for the Integration of Data Type and Process Modeling Techniques. In: Graph Transformation and Visual Modeling Techniques (GT-VMT 2001). Number 50,3 in Electronic Notes in Theoretical Computer Science, Elsevier (2001)
20. Bardohl, R., Ehrig, H., de Lara, J., Taentzer, G.: Integrating Meta-Modelling Aspects with Graph Transformation for Efficient Visual Language Definition and Model Manipulation. In Wermelinger, M., Margaria-Steffen, T., eds.: Fundamental Approaches to Software Engineering (FASE 2004). Number 2984 in Lecture Notes in Computer Science, Springer (2004) 214–228
21. Ehrig, H., Mahr, B.: Fundamentals of Algebraic Specification 1 – Equations and Initial Semantics. Volume 6 of Monographs on Theoretical Computer Science. Springer (1985)
22. Mosses, P.D., ed.: CASL Reference Manual. Number 2960 in Lecture Notes in Computer Science. Springer (2004)
23. Spivey, J.M.: The Z Notation: A Reference Manual. Prentice Hall (1992)
24. Braatz, B., Klein, M., Schröter, G., Bengel, M.: A Formal Component Concept for the Specification of Industrial Control Systems. In Ehrig, H., Damm, W., Desel, J., Große-Rhode, M., Reif, W., Schnieder, E., Westkämper, E., eds.: Integration of Software Specification Techniques for Applications in Engineering. Number 3147 in Lecture Notes in Computer Science. Springer (2004)

Author Index

Lecture Notes in Computer Science

For information about Vols. 1–3126

please contact your bookseller or Springer

Vol. 3181: Y. Kambayashi, M. Mohania, W. Wöß (Eds.), Data Warehousing and Knowledge Discovery. XIV, 412 pages. 2004.

Vol. 3180: F. Galindo, M. Takizawa, R. Traunmüller (Eds.), Database and Expert Systems Applications. XXI, 972 pages. 2004.

Vol. 3179: F.J. Perales, B.A. Draper (Eds.), Articulated Motion and Deformable Objects. XI, 270 pages. 2004.

Vol. 3178: W. Jonker, M. Petkovic (Eds.), Secure Data Management. VIII, 219 pages. 2004.

Vol. 3177: Z.R. Yang, H. Yin, R. Everson (Eds.), Intelligent Data Engineering and Automated Learning – IDEAL 2004. XVIII, 852 pages. 2004.

Vol. 3176: O. Bousquet, U. von Luxburg, G. Rätsch (Eds.), Advanced Lectures on Machine Learning. IX, 241 pages. 2004. (Subseries LNAI).

Vol. 3175: C.E. Rasmussen, H.H. Bülthoff, B. Schölkopf, M.A. Giese (Eds.), Pattern Recognition. XVIII, 581 pages. 2004.

Vol. 3174: F. Yin, J. Wang, C. Guo (Eds.), Advances in Neural Networks - ISNN 2004. XXXV, 1021 pages. 2004.

Vol. 3173: F. Yin, J. Wang, C. Guo (Eds.), Advances in Neural Networks - ISNN 2004. XXXV, 1041 pages. 2004.

Vol. 3172: M. Dorigo, M. Birattari, C. Blum, L. M. Gambardella, F. Mondada, T. Stützle (Eds.), Ant Colony, Optimization and Swarm Intelligence. XII, 434 pages. 2004.

Vol. 3170: P. Gardner, N. Yoshida (Eds.), CONCUR 2004 - Concurrency Theory. XIII, 529 pages. 2004.

Vol. 3166: M. Rauterberg (Ed.), Entertainment Computing – ICEC 2004. XXIII, 617 pages. 2004.

Vol. 3163: S. Marinai, A. Dengel (Eds.), Document Analysis Systems VI. XI, 564 pages. 2004.

Vol. 3162: R. Downey, M. Fellows, F. Dehne (Eds.), Parameterized and Exact Computation. X, 293 pages. 2004.

Vol. 3160: S. Brewster, M. Dunlop (Eds.), Mobile Human-Computer Interaction – MobileHCI 2004. XVII, 541 pages. 2004.

Vol. 3159: U. Visser, Intelligent Information Integration for the Semantic Web. XIV, 150 pages. 2004. (Subseries LNAI).

Vol. 3158: I. Nikolaidis, M. Barbeau, E. Kranakis (Eds.), Ad-Hoc, Mobile, and Wireless Networks. IX, 344 pages. 2004.

Vol. 3157: C. Zhang, H. W. Guesgen, W.K. Yeap (Eds.), PRICAI 2004: Trends in Artificial Intelligence. XX, 1023 pages. 2004. (Subseries LNAI).

Vol. 3156: M. Joye, J.-J. Quisquater (Eds.), Cryptographic Hardware and Embedded Systems - CHES 2004. XIII, 455 pages. 2004.

Vol. 3155: P. Funk, P.A. González Calero (Eds.), Advances in Case-Based Reasoning. XIII, 822 pages. 2004. (Subseries LNAI).

Vol. 3154: R.L. Nord (Ed.), Software Product Lines. XIV, 334 pages. 2004.

Vol. 3153: J. Fiala, V. Koubek, J. Kratochvíl (Eds.), Mathematical Foundations of Computer Science 2004. XIV, 902 pages. 2004.

Vol. 3152: M. Franklin (Ed.), Advances in Cryptology – CRYPTO 2004. XI, 579 pages. 2004.

Vol. 3150: G.-Z. Yang, T. Jiang (Eds.), Medical Imaging and Augmented Reality. XII, 378 pages. 2004.

Vol. 3149: M. Danelutto, M. Vanneschi, D. Laforenza (Eds.), Euro-Par 2004 Parallel Processing. XXXIV, 1081 pages. 2004.

Vol. 3148: R. Giacobazzi (Ed.), Static Analysis. XI, 393 pages. 2004.

Vol. 3147: H. Ehrig, W. Damm, J. Desel, M. Große-Rhode, W. Reif, E. Schnieder, E. Westkämper (Eds.), Integration of Software Specification Techniques for Applications in Engineering. X, 628 pages. 2004.

Vol. 3146: P. Érdi, A. Esposito, M. Marinaro, S. Scarpetta (Eds.), Computational Neuroscience: Cortical Dynamics. XI, 161 pages. 2004.

Vol. 3144: M. Papatriantafilou, P. Hunel (Eds.), Principles of Distributed Systems. XI, 246 pages. 2004.

Vol. 3143: W. Liu, Y. Shi, Q. Li (Eds.), Advances in Web-Based Learning – ICWL 2004. XIV, 459 pages. 2004.

Vol. 3142: J. Diaz, J. Karhumäki, A. Lepistö, D. Sannella (Eds.), Automata, Languages and Programming. XIX, 1253 pages. 2004.

Vol. 3140: N. Koch, P. Fraternali, M. Wirsing (Eds.), Web Engineering. XXI, 623 pages. 2004.

Vol. 3139: F. Iida, R. Pfeifer, L. Steels, Y. Kuniyoshi (Eds.), Embodied Artificial Intelligence. IX, 331 pages. 2004. (Subseries LNAI).

Vol. 3138: A. Fred, T. Caelli, R.P.W. Duin, A. Campilho, D.d. Ridder (Eds.), Structural, Syntactic, and Statistical Pattern Recognition. XXII, 1168 pages. 2004.

Vol. 3137: P. De Bra, W. Nejdl (Eds.), Adaptive Hypermedia and Adaptive Web-Based Systems. XIV, 442 pages. 2004.

Vol. 3136: F. Meziane, E. Métais (Eds.), Natural Language Processing and Information Systems. XII, 436 pages. 2004.

Vol. 3134: C. Zannier, H. Erdogmus, L. Lindstrom (Eds.), Extreme Programming and Agile Methods - XP/Agile Universe 2004. XIV, 233 pages. 2004.

Vol. 3133: A.D. Pimentel, S. Vassiliadis (Eds.), Computer Systems: Architectures, Modeling, and Simulation. XIII, 562 pages. 2004.

Vol. 3132: B. Demoen, V. Lifschitz (Eds.), Logic Programming. XII, 480 pages. 2004.

Vol. 3131: V. Torra, Y. Narukawa (Eds.), Modeling Decisions for Artificial Intelligence. XI, 327 pages. 2004. (Subseries LNAI).

Vol. 3130: A. Syropoulos, K. Berry, Y. Haralambous, B. Hughes, S. Peter, J. Plaice (Eds.), TeX, XML, and Digital Typography. VIII, 265 pages. 2004.

Vol. 3129: Q. Li, G. Wang, L. Feng (Eds.), Advances in Web-Age Information Management. XVII, 753 pages. 2004.

Vol. 3128: D. Asonov (Ed.), Querying Databases Privately. IX, 115 pages. 2004.

Vol. 3127: K.E. Wolff, H.D. Pfeiffer, H.S. Delugach (Eds.), Conceptual Structures at Work. XI, 403 pages. 2004. (Subseries LNAI).